THE

# JOHN CHAPPELL
# NATURAL PHILOSOPHY

## SOCIETY

Papers by the members of the John Chappell Natural Philosophy Society
presented at their annual conference

College Park Maryland, United States, 2016

Edited by

DAVID DE HILSTER
ROBERT DE HILSTER
NICK PERCIVAL

*Caldeon, Michigan*

 **John Chappell**
Natural Philosophy Society
THE PUBLISHER

2016

Copyright (c) 2016 by the John Chappell Natural Philosophy Society All rights reserved.

Published by the John Chappell Natural Philosophy Society, Caledonia, Michigan.

No part of this publication may be reproduced, stored in a retrieval system, or transmitted in any form or by any means, electronic, mechanical, photocopying, recording, scanning, or otherwise, except as permitted under Section 107 or 108 of the 1976 United States Copyright Act, without either the prior written permission of the Publisher, or authorization through payment of the appropriate per-copy fee to the Copyright Clearance Center, Inc., 222 Rosewood Drive, Danvers, MA 01923, (978) 750-8400, fax (978) 646-8600, or on the web at www.copyright.com. Requests to the Publisher for permission should be addressed to the Permissions Department, John Chappell Natural Philosophy Society, 22936 Ironwedge Drive, Boca Raton, FL 33433, (310) 991-5744.

Limit of Liability/Disclaimer of Warranty: While the publisher and author have used their best efforts in preparing this book, they make no representations or warranties with respect to the accuracy or completeness of the contents of this book and specifically disclaim any implied warranties of merchantability or fitness for a particular purpose. No warranty may be created or extended by sales representatives or written sales materials. The advice and strategies contained herein may not be suitable for your situation. You should consult with a professional where appropriate. Neither the publisher nor author shall be liable for any loss of profit or any other commercial damages, including but not limited to special, incidental, consequential, or other damages.

Library of Congress Cataloging-in-Publication Data:

CNPS 2016 Annual Proceedings / David de Hilster, Robert de Hilster . . . [et al.].
p. cm.-(CNPS series in science annuals)

"CNPS-Publications."
Includes bibliographical references and index.
ISBN 978-1-365-21761-6 (pbk.)
Printed in the United States of America.

10 9 8 7 6 5 4 3 2 1

AT THE TIME OF PUBLISHING, THE DIRECTORS FOR THE JOHN CHAPPELL NATURAL PHILOSOPHY SOCIETY (CNPS) ARE AS FOLLOWS:

JULY 20, 2016

DR. CYNTHIA KOLB WHITNEY, CHIEF SCIENCE OFFICER
DAVID DE HILSTER, PRESIDENT
GREG VOLK, VICE-PRESIDENT
NICK PERCIVAL, SECRETARY
ROBERT DE HILSTER, TREASURER
RON HATCH, DIRECTOR
GLEN BORCHARDT, DIRECTOR
JEFF BAUGHER, DIRECTOR

*Caldeon, Michigan*

# Table of Contents

# Aberration of Electric Field and Velocity of Transmission of an Electrical Force

## Musa D. Abdullahi

*12 Bujumbura Street, Wuse 2, Abuja, Nigeria*
*e-mail: musadab@outlook.com*

An electron of mass m and charge $-e$ moving at angle $\theta$ to the accelerating force due to an electric field of intensity E, is subject to aberration of electric field as a result of relativity of velocity $(c-v)$ between the electrical force, transmitted with velocity of light c and the electron moving with velocity v at time t. The accelerating force $m(dv/dt)$ is less than the electrostatic force $eE$, the difference being the radiation reaction force. Motion of the electron with constant mass and its radiation power are treated under acceleration with $\theta = 0$ or deceleration with $\theta = \pi$ radians or at constant speed v, in a circle of radius r, with $\theta = \pi/2$ radians. It is shown that circular revolution of an electron round a central force of attraction is without radiation and stable, contrary to classical and relativistic electrodynamics.

**Keywords:** Aberration angle, acceleration, electric field, charge, mass, special relativity, velocity

## 1. Introduction

Aberration of electric field is a phenomenon similar to aberration of light discovered by English astronomer, James Bradley, in 1725 [1]. This discovery, which provided the first direct confirmation of motion of the Earth round the Sun, and gave a measure of the speed of light, is one of the most precise and significant findings in science. Aberration of light is a clear demonstration of the relativity of speed of light with respect to a moving object, contrary to the theory of special relativity [2] [2]. Aberration of light is now relegated to the background in favour of special relativity. It is hardly mentioned in modern physics because it is a contradiction of the principle of constancy of the speed of light according to the theory of special relativity. Aberration of light is considered as more of a subject in remote astronomy rather than a course in mundane physics.

Electromagnetic radiation, as well as electric force, is transmitted in space with the velocity of light. In the aberration of electric field there is relativity of velocity $(c-v)$ between an electrical force propagated with velocity of light c and an electron moving with velocity v. As such, the electrical force cannot catch up and impact on an electron also moving with velocity of light c. The velocity of light thus becomes the ultimate limit to which an electric field can accelerate an electron with emission of radiation and mass remaining constant.

As a result of aberration of electric field, for an electron of mass m and charge $e$ moving at time t with velocity v and acceleration $dv/dt$ in an electric field of intensity E, the accelerating force $m(dv/dt)$ is less than the impressed force or the electrostatic force $eE$, the difference is the radiation reaction force [4]. The radiation reaction force in rectilinear motion is $eEv/c$ and radiation power is $eEv2/c$. In circular revolution perpendicular to the electric field, the radiation power is zero. This makes revolution of an elec-

tron, round a positively charged nucleus, as in the Rutherford model of the hydrogen atom [5] without radiation and stable outside Bohrs quantum mechanics [6].

## 2. Aberration Angle

Figure 1 depicts an electron of mass m and charge $e$ moving at a point P with velocity v at an angle to the force of attraction due to an electric field of intensity E from a stationary source charge $+Q$ at a point O.

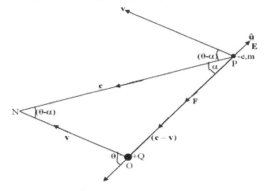

**Figure 1.** An electron of mass m and charge âĂŞe at a point P moving in an electric field of intensity E due to a stationary source charge +Q at O

The electron is subjected to aberration of electric field whereby the direction of propagation of the force of attraction, given by velocity vector c, is displaced from the instantaneous line PO through angle of aberration $\alpha$, such that:

$$sin(\alpha) = \frac{v}{c}sin(\theta) \qquad (1)$$

The astronomer James Bradley [1] first derived equation 1, as given by the sine rule with respect to the triangle PON in Fig. 1.

## 3. Velocity of Transmission of Electrical Force

In Fig. 1, the vector z = (v - c) is the relative velocity of trans-mission between the electrical force propagated with velocity of light c and the electron moving with velocity v, thus:

$$\mathbf{z} = (\mathbf{c} - \mathbf{v}) = -\sqrt{(c^2 + v^2 - 2cv\cos(\theta - \alpha)}\hat{\mathbf{u}} \quad (2)$$

where $(\theta - \alpha)$ is the angle between the vectors c and v and $\tilde{A}\dot{z}$ is a unit vector in the positive direction of the field E. The electron can move with $\theta = 0$, $\pi$, or $\pi/2$ radians.

With $\theta = 0$ there is motion in a straight line with acceleration and equations 1 and 2 give the relative speed of transmission of the electrical force as:

$$z = c - v \quad (3)$$

If $\theta = \pi$ radians, motion is in a straight line with deceleration and equations 1 and 2 give the relative speed of transmission as:

$$z = c + v \quad (4)$$

If $\theta = \pi/2$ radians and noting that $\sin\alpha = v/c$, there is circular motion with constant speed v, giving the speed of transmission of the force as:

$$z = \sqrt{(c^2 - v^2)} \quad (5)$$

Equations 3, 4, and 5 demonstrate the relativity of speed of light with respect to a charged particle moving with speed v.

## 4. Accelerating Force

The accelerating force F at time t, in an electric field of magnitude E, is put as:

$$\mathbf{F} = \frac{eE}{c}(\mathbf{c} - \mathbf{v}) = \quad (6)$$

$$= -\frac{eE}{c}\sqrt{(c^2 + v^2 - 2cv\cos(\theta - \alpha)}\hat{\mathbf{u}} = m\frac{d\mathbf{v}}{dt}$$

where $\hat{\mathbf{u}}$ is a unit vector in the positive direction of the electric field E. For motion in a straight line under acceleration, with $\theta = 0$ equations 1 and 2 give the vector equation:

$$\mathbf{F} = -eE(1 - \frac{v}{c})\hat{\mathbf{u}} = -m\frac{dv}{dt}\hat{\mathbf{u}} \quad (7)$$

The scalar first order differential equation, of motion for an accelerated electron, is:

$$eE(1 - \frac{v}{c}) = m\frac{dv}{dt} \quad (8)$$

For motion in a straight line under deceleration, with $\theta = \pi$ radians, equations 1 and 2 give the vector equation:

$$\mathbf{F} = -eE(1 + \frac{v}{c})\hat{\mathbf{u}} = m\frac{dv}{dt}\hat{\mathbf{u}} \quad (9)$$

The scalar first order differential equation, for a decelerated electron, is:

$$eE(1 + \frac{v}{c}) = -m\frac{dv}{dt} \quad (10)$$

Equations 9 and 11 are easily solved [? ] for a uniform electric field, of constant magnitude E, to give the speed v as a function of time t. Solutions of the first order differential equations, with constant coefficients, show that the speed of light c is the maximum attainable by the electron.

Where $\theta = \pi/2$ radians there is motion in a circle of radius r with constant speed v and centripetal acceleration v2/r. Noting that $\sin\alpha = v/c$, equation 1 and 2 give the vector:

$$\mathbf{F} = -eE\sqrt{(1 - \frac{v^2}{c^2})}\hat{\mathbf{u}} = -m\frac{v^2}{r}\hat{\mathbf{u}} \quad (11)$$

The scalar equation is:

$$eE\sqrt{(1 - \frac{v^2}{c^2})} = m\frac{v^2}{r} = m_o\frac{v^2}{r} \quad (12)$$

where mass m is a constant equal to the rest mass $m_o$. This is in contrast to the theory of special relativity where m is dependent on speed of the electron. Equation 13 can be written as:

$$\frac{eEv}{v^2} = \zeta = \frac{m_o}{\sqrt{(1 - \frac{v^2}{c^2})}} \quad (13)$$

The theory of special relativity made a mistake in identifying $\zeta$ (zeta) in equation 14, with mass m of the moving electron. Making $\zeta$ the same as physical mass m is a very expensive case of mistaken identity. Equation 14 is applicable only in circular motion and $\zeta$ is not a physical quantity but the ratio of electro-static force $(-eE)$ to centripetal acceleration $(-v2/r)$ in circular motion. This ratio can become infinitely large, without any problem, for motion in a circle of infinite radius, a straight line. The mass-velocity formula of special relativity is definitely wrong, more so by applying it to rectilinear motion..

## 5. Radiation Power

The difference between the accelerating force F, as given by equation 6, and the electrostatic force or impressed force $eE$, is the radiation reaction force, a vector $R_f$ given by:

$$\mathbf{R}_f = \frac{eE}{c}(\mathbf{c} - \mathbf{v}) + e\mathbf{E} \quad (14)$$

The radiation power $R_p$ is the scalar product $v.R_f$, thus:

$$\mathbf{R}_p = -\mathbf{v}.\mathbf{R}_f = -\frac{eE}{c}(\mathbf{c} - \mathbf{v}).\mathbf{v} + e\mathbf{E}.\mathbf{v} \quad (15)$$

With reference to Figure 1, radiation power $R_p$ is expressed in terms of the angles $\theta$ and $\alpha$, as:

$$R_p = \frac{eEv^2}{c} - eEvcos(\theta - \alpha) + eEvcos(\theta) \qquad (16)$$

Equation 17 shows that the radiation power is $eEv2/c$ under acceleration with $\theta = 0$ or under deceleration with $\theta = \pi$ radians. For there is circular revolution, round a central force of attraction, with zero radiation power.

## 6. Conclusion

Equations 3, 4 and 5 show that the speed of light, relative to an observer, can be subtracted from or added to, contrary to the relativistic principle of constancy of the speed of light for all observers, stationary or moving. So, a cardinal principle of the theory of special relativity is being debunked once more. Indeed, if the speed of light were independent of motion of the observer, it would have been impossible to measure the speed.

In equation 14 the relativistic mass-velocity formula is rationalized. Here, $\zeta$ (zeta) is not a physical mass but the the ratio of electrostatic force $(eE)$ to centripetal acceleration $(v2/r)$ in circular revolution. This ratio becomes infinitely large for rectilinear motion, without any problem of infinite masses. In a straight line, the arc of a circle of infinite radius, the centripetal acceleration is zero. Doing away with infinite masses at the speed of light, should bring great relief to physicists all over the world. An important result of this paper is contained in equation 17. Here, if $\theta = pi/2$ radians, there is circular revolution, round a central force of attraction, with zero radiation power. This makes Rutherfords nuclear model of the hydrogen atom inherently stable. Revolution in a circle is at constant radius with constant speed, without any change in potential or kinetic energy. Radiation takes place only where the electron is somehow dislodged from a circular orbit. It then revolves in an unclosed elliptic orbit with radial displacement and change in potential and kinetic energy and emission of radiation at the frequency of revolution, before reverting back to the stable circular orbit.

## REFERENCES

1. Various, *James Bradley.*, https://en.wikipedia.org/wiki/James_Bradley, 2016.
2. Albert Einstein, *On the Electrodynamics of Moving Bodies.*, Ann. PhysPhysical Review D, Vol 17, 891, 1905.
3. Einstein and Lorentz, *The Principles of Relativity.*, Matheun, London, 1923.
4. M. Abdullahi, *An Alternative Electrodynamics to the Theory of Special Relativity.*, 20th NPA Conference, 2013.
5. E. Rutherford, *The Scattering of alpha and beta Particles by Matter and the Structure of the Atom.*, Phil. Mag., 21, 669, 1911.
6. N. Bohr, *On the Constitution of Atoms and Molecules.*, Phil. Mag, 1913.

# An Explanation for the Cause of Force of Gravity outside General Relativity

## Musa D. Abdullahi

*12 Bujumbura Street, Wuse 2, Abuja, Nigeria*
*e-mail: musadab@outlook.com*

An electric charge, in the form of a spherical shell with uniform surface charge density, has constant potential and zero electric field inside the shell. The radial field, pulling the surface charge outwards, is balanced by inward surface tension, due to curvature of the shell, to form a stable particle. It is shown that the mass of the particle is proportional to the volume enclosed by the shell. Force of gravity is ascribed to the electric field of one charged particle being deflected by the presence of another charged particle such that force of repulsion is slightly reduced and force of attraction similarly increased. For bodies composed of equal amounts of positive and negative charges, the electrical fields exist in space with the electrical forces of repulsion and attraction, on a body, everywhere balancing out while gravitational forces of attraction add up. A Body moving under gravity, without any electrical force, should not emit any radiation.

**Keywords:** Coulombs law, electric charge, field, gravity, Newtons law, general relativity, radiation, space

## 1. Introduction

Since Sir Isaac Newton enunciated the universal law of gravity around 1687 [1], the cause of gravitation had defied explanation until Professor Albert Einstein came up with the theory of general relativity in 1915 [2]. General relativity, it was believed, explained gravitation in the context of curvature or warping of four-dimensional space-time continuum. Curved space, it was thought, pushes (accelerates) objects, like the Earth, to follow a particular path in the universe. The path of least resistance is a straight line in four-dimensional space-time but a curved orbit in three-dimensional space. The idea of time being a fourth dimension of space was a brilliant and revolutionary theory. A multidimensional space has stretched the modern physicists dimensions of imagination too far, but so far, without any physical or experimental verification.

Neutral matter is composed of equal numbers or equal amounts of positive and negative electric charges. In this paper free space is conceived as crisscrossed by electric fields emanating from point charges in matter and vanishing at infinite distances from the respective sources, in accordance with Coulombs inverse square law. The electric fields exist in space but balance out exactly everywhere, except in regions with isolated charges. So, bodies move in space under gravitational force but with zero electrical force.

A clear physical explanation for the cause of force of gravity has long been felt. Gravity, an all-pervasive force that affects everything in the universe, should have a simple and tenable explanation. The explanation given in this paper is based on Coulombs law of electrostatic force and an electric charge of magnitude $Q$ being a particle in the form of a spherical shell of radius $a$. It is shown [3] that such a charged particle is associated with constant poten-

tial $U$, intrinsic energy $W$, mass $m$ and volume $V$ enclosed by the shell.

Force of gravity between two particles is explained by considering the electric field of one charged particle of volume $V_1$ as being affected by the presence of another charged particle of volume $V_2$. This field effect may be by way of deflection or obstruction whereby the incident field on a charged particle is made to open out or close in, such that force of repulsion is slightly reduced and force of attraction similarly increased. The result is gravitational force of attraction in accordance with Newtons law. For two neutral bodies, separated in space, the electrostatic forces of repulsion and attraction balance out exactly everywhere while the gravitational forces of attraction add up.

### 1.1. Coulombs Law of Electrostatic Force

Coulombs law gives the force $f_E$ of repulsion or attraction between two electric charges of magnitudes $Q$ and $K$ separated by a distance $Z$ in space, as:

$$\mathbf{f}_E = \pm \frac{QK}{4\pi\varepsilon_o Z^2}\hat{\mathbf{u}} = K\mathbf{E} \tag{1}$$

$$\mathbf{E} = \pm \frac{Q}{4\pi\varepsilon_o Z^2}\hat{\mathbf{u}} \tag{2}$$

where $\varepsilon_o$ is a universal constant, the permittivity of free space, $\hat{\mathbf{u}}$ is a unit vector in the direction of force of repulsion and vector $E$ is the electric field intensity due to charge $Q$ acting at the location of charge $K$. Force of repulsion is regarded as positive and force of attraction as negative. Equation (1), one of the most important principles in physics, gives the force $f_E$ of repulsion or attraction between two electric charges as proportional to the product of their magnitudes and inversely proportional to square of the distance between them.

## 1.2. Newtons Universal Law of Gravity

Newtons law of gravity gives the force of attraction $f_G$ be-tween two particles (bodies or objects) of masses $m_1$ and $m_2$ separated by a distance $Z$ in space, as:

$$\mathbf{f}_G = -\gamma \frac{m_1 m_2}{Z^2}\hat{\mathbf{u}} = m_2 \mathbf{G} \qquad (3)$$

where $\gamma$ is the gravitational constant and vector $G$ is the gravitational field intensity due to particle of mass $m_1$ acting at the location of particle of mass $m_2$.

$$\mathbf{G} = -\gamma \frac{m_1}{Z^2}\hat{\mathbf{u}} \qquad (4)$$

## 1.3. Mass and Volume of an Electric Charge

This paper tries to find the cause of field of gravity and to answer the question why the force of gravity in Newtons law is always attractive in contrast to Coulombs law (equation 1) where the force is repulsive or attractive. This is done first by deriving an expression [3] for the mass $m_1$ of an electric charge of magnitude $Q$, in the form of a spherical shell of radius $a$, as $m_1 = \mu_o Q^2/4\pi a$ and for another charge of magnitude $K$ with radius $b$ as $m_2 = \mu_o K^2/4\pi b$. Substituting for the masses $m_1$ and $m_2$ in equation 3 gives the force of gravity $f_G$, between two electric charges, proportional to the product of squares of the two charges. as:

$$\mathbf{f}_G = -\frac{\gamma}{Z^2}\frac{\mu_o Q^2}{4\pi a}\frac{\mu K^2}{4\pi b}\hat{\mathbf{u}} = \frac{\mu_o K^2}{4\pi b}\mathbf{G} \qquad (5)$$

The gravitational field $G$, of charge $Q$ acting at the location of charge $K$, is given by:

$$\mathbf{G} = -\gamma \frac{\mu_o Q^2}{4\pi a Z^2}\hat{\mathbf{u}} \qquad (6)$$

The need now is to give a physical explanation for equations (5) and (6), This is done in the light of an assumption that an electric charge of magnitude $Q$ exists as a particle in the form of a spherical shell of radius $a$ with uniform surface charge density $\sigma$ per unit area, as shown in Fig. 1. For an electric charge of surface area $A_1 = 4\pi a^2$ and volume $V_1 = 4\pi a^3/3$, equation 6 becomes:

$$\mathbf{G} = -\gamma \frac{\mu_o (4\pi a^2 \sigma)^2}{4\pi a Z^2}\hat{\mathbf{u}} = -\gamma \frac{\mu_o 4\pi a^3 \sigma^2}{Z^2}\hat{\mathbf{u}} \qquad (7)$$

$$= -\gamma \frac{3V_1 \mu_o \sigma)^2}{Z^2}\hat{\mathbf{u}} = -\gamma v \frac{V_1}{Z^2}\hat{\mathbf{u}} \qquad (8)$$

where $\mu_o$ is the permeability of a vacuum and $v = 3\mu_o \sigma^2$ is regarded as a constant.

In equation (7) it is as if the gravitational field $G$ is caused by a spherical volume $V_1$ enclosed by the shell. This volume is of constant potential $U_1$ and zero electric field inside. Another way of expressing the situation, in the parlance of general relativity, is to say that the shell with uniform surface charge $\sigma$, constitutes a singularity from which an electric field emanates. The enclosed volume $V_1$

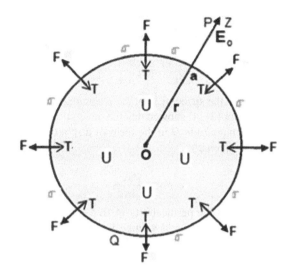

**Figure 1.** An electric charge of magnitude $Q$ in the form of a spherical shell of radius $r = a$, with uniform surface charge $\sigma$, constant electrostatic potential $U$ and zero electrostatic field inside the shell. There is an electrostatic field of intensity $\mathbf{E}_o$ and potential $\phi$ at a point $P$ distance $Z$ outside the shell. The radial force $\mathbf{F}$ exerted by the field is balanced by the surface $\mathbf{T}$ to form a stable particle

is a curvature or distortion of space which gives rise to a gravitational field in accordance with Newtons law.

## 2. Configuration of an Electric Charge

If a stationary particle of electric charge $Q$ is to assume any configuration, it is most likely be a spherical shell of radius $a$ as shown in Fig.1 for a positive or negative charge. Such a figure has zero electric field and constant potential $U$ inside the sphere. There is surface charge $\sigma$ per unit area, an electrostatic field of intensity $E_o$ and potential $\phi$ at a point $P$ distance Z from the center of the charge, outside the shell.

The electric field at the outer surface of the shell, in Fig. 1, pulls the shell outwards with force $\mathbf{F}$ per unit area while the tension due to the curvature of the spherical surface, pushes the shell inwards with force $\mathbf{T}$ per unit area. Equilibrium is reached at a certain formation where the action $\mathbf{F}$ is equal to the reaction $\mathbf{T}$ and a stable particle is obtained.

## 3. Energy, Mass and Volume of an Electric Charge

The intrinsic potential $U_1$ and energy $W_1$ of an electric charge of magnitude $Q$, in the form of a spherical shell of radius $a$, is given by the well-known classical formulas:

$$U_1 = \frac{Q}{4\pi \varepsilon a}; W_1 = \frac{Q^2}{8\pi \varepsilon a} \qquad (9)$$

where $\varepsilon_o$ is the permittivity of free space. $W_1$ is the work done in creating the charge from 0 to $Q$. If $\sigma$ is the charge per unit area of the spherical shell and with $v = 3\mu_o \sigma^2$, intrinsic energy $W_1$ (equation 9), for a sphere of surface area $A_1 = 4\pi a^2$ and spherical volume $V_1 = 4\pi a^3/3$ enclosed by the shell, becomes:

$$W_1 = \frac{3\sigma^2 V_1}{2\varepsilon_o} = \frac{v V_1}{2\mu_o \varepsilon_o} = \frac{v V_1 c^2}{2} \qquad (10)$$

where $c$ is the speed of light in a vacuum.

The author [3] [4] showed that the mass $m_1$ of an electric charge of magnitude $Q$ in the form of a spherical shell of radius $a$ is given by:

$$m_1 = \frac{\mu_o Q^2}{4\pi a} \qquad (11)$$

where $\mu_o$ is the permeability of free space. In terms of a sphere of radius $a$ and volume $V_1$ and uniform surface charge $\sigma$:

$$m_1 = 3\mu_o \sigma^2 V_1 = v V_1 \qquad (12)$$

where $v$ (upsilon) $= 3\mu_o \sigma^2$. The spherical volume $V_1$ is associated with intrinsic energy $W_1$ (equation 10) and mass $m_1$ (equation 12).

Substituting for the masses $m_1$ and $m_2$ from equation (12) into equation (3), gives Newtons law in terms of volumes $V_1$ and $V_2$ of electric charges $Q$ and $K$ respectively as:

$$\mathbf{f}_G = -\gamma v^2 \frac{V_1 V_2}{Z^2} \hat{\mathbf{u}} = v V_2 \mathbf{G} \qquad (13)$$

where the gravitational field intensity $G$, (equation 4), is:

$$\mathbf{G} = -\gamma v^2 \frac{V_1}{Z^2} \hat{\mathbf{u}} \qquad (14)$$

It is as if a gravitational field exists between two potential volumes $V_1$ and $V_2$.

## 4. Electrostatic and Gravitational Forces between Charges

Fig. 2 shows two isolated (positive or negative) electric charges of magnitudes $Q$ and $K$ in the form of spherical shells of radii $a$ and $b$ and masses $m_1$ and $m_2$. The separation between the charges, a distance $OP = Z$ in space is very much larger than the radius $a$ or $b$. The force $\mathbf{f}$ between the stationary charges, a combination of electrostatic force of repulsion or attraction (Coulombs law) and gravitational force of attraction (Newtons law), is put as:

$$\mathbf{f} = \pm \frac{QK}{4\pi\varepsilon_o Z^2} \hat{\mathbf{u}} - \gamma \frac{m_1 m_2}{Z^2} \hat{\mathbf{u}} \qquad (15)$$

where $\hat{\mathbf{u}}$ is a unit vector in the direction of force of repulsion and $\gamma$ is the gravitational constant. The first term on the right-hand side of equation (15) is the electrostatic force of repulsion or attraction between two isolated charges of magnitudes $Q$ and $K$, in accordance with Coulombs law of electrostatics. The second term of the equation is the gravitational force of attraction $\mathbf{f}_G$ between masses $m_1$ and $m_2$, as given by Newtons universal law of

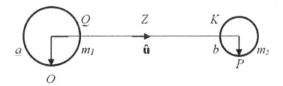

**Figure 2.** Electrostatic and gravitational forces between two isolated electric charges $Q$ and $K$ separated by a distance $Z$ in space.

gravity in equation (3). In terms of the electric charges $Q$ and $K$, $\mathbf{f}_G$ is given by:

$$\mathbf{f}_G = \frac{-\gamma}{Z^2} m_1 m_2 \hat{\mathbf{u}} = \frac{-\gamma}{Z^2} \left( \frac{\mu_o Q^2}{4\pi a} \right) \left( \frac{\mu_o K^2}{4\pi b} \right) \hat{\mathbf{u}} \qquad (16)$$

$$= \frac{-\gamma X^2}{Z^2} Q^2 K^2 \hat{\mathbf{u}}$$

$$\mathbf{X} = \frac{1}{ab} \left( \frac{\mu_o}{4\pi} \right)^2 \qquad (17)$$

where $\chi$ (chi) is a constant. In terms of the volumes of space $V_1$ and $V_2$ occupied by the respective charges equation (12), equation (16) becomes:

$$\mathbf{f}_G = \frac{-\gamma}{Z^2} m_1 m_2 \hat{\mathbf{u}} = \frac{-\gamma v^2}{Z^2} V_1 V_2 \hat{\mathbf{u}} \qquad (18)$$

Equations (15) and (16), with reference to Fig. 2, give the electrostatic and gravitational force between two charges $Q$ and $K$ as:

$$\mathbf{f} = \pm \frac{QK}{4\pi\varepsilon_o Z^2} \hat{\mathbf{u}} - \frac{\gamma \chi}{Z^2} Q^2 K^2 \hat{\mathbf{u}} \qquad (19)$$

The interpretation of equation (19) is that the electric field $E_1$ due to an electric charge $Q$, acting at the location of another electric charge $K$, is affected by the presence of the charge $K$, thus:

$$\mathbf{E}_1 = \pm \frac{Q}{4\pi\varepsilon_o Z^2} \hat{\mathbf{u}} - \frac{\gamma \chi}{Z^2} Q^2 K \hat{\mathbf{u}} \qquad (20)$$

Similarly, the electric field $E_2$ due to a charge $K$, acting at the location of another charge $Q$, is affected by the charge $Q$, thus:

$$\mathbf{E}_2 = \pm \frac{K}{4\pi\varepsilon_o Z^2} \hat{\mathbf{u}} - \frac{\gamma \chi}{Z^2} K^2 Q \hat{\mathbf{u}} \qquad (21)$$

While $E_1$ may not be equal to $E_2$, the product $E_1 K = E_2 Q$. The force on charge $Q$ is equal and opposite to the force on charge $K$. Equations (20) and (21) explain the cause of force of gravity, For two electric charges, as in Fig. 2, force of repulsion is slightly reduced while force of attraction is similarly increased due to the presence of one charge affecting the field of another. For a neutral body consisting of equal numbers or equal amounts of positive and negative electric charges, the electrostatic forces of repulsion and attraction, in accordance with Coulombs law, balance out exactly everywhere in space, while the gravitational forces of attraction, in accordance with Newtons law, add up.

## 5. Electric Field due to a Neutral Body

In Fig.2, let us replace the charge $Q$ at $O$ by a neutral body (with centre of gravity at $O$) composed of $N/2$ positive and $N/2$ negative electric charges, each of magnitude $Q_n$. Force on charge $K$ at $P$ is the sum of the forces given by equation (15), thus:

$$\mathbf{F} = \frac{K}{4\pi\varepsilon_o Z^2}\sum_{n=1}^{N}(-1)^n Q_n\hat{\mathbf{u}} - \frac{-\gamma\chi K^2}{Z^2}\sum_{n=1}^{N}(-1)^{2n}Q_n^2\hat{\mathbf{u}}$$

(22)

where $n$ is an integer: $1, 2, 3....N$. The first term, in the right-hand side of equation (22), the electrostatic force of repulsion and attraction, comes to:

$$\mathbf{F}_E = \frac{K}{4\pi\varepsilon_o Z^2}\sum_{n=1}^{N}(-1)^n Q_n\hat{\mathbf{u}} = K\mathbf{E} = 0 \qquad (23)$$

The charges $Q_n$ need not be of the same magnitude $Q$, so long as corresponding positive and negative charges balance out. It is stating the obvious that the electrostatic field at a point, due to a body composed of a very large number $N$ of equal positive and negative charges, is zero. The second term in equation (22) is the gravitational force of attraction, thus:

$$\mathbf{F}_G = -\frac{\gamma\chi K^2}{Z^2}\sum_{n=1}^{N}(-1)^{2n}Q_n^2\hat{\mathbf{u}} = -\frac{\gamma\chi K^2}{Z^2}\sum_{n=1}^{N}Q_n^2\hat{\mathbf{u}} \quad (24)$$

## 6. Gravitational Force of Attraction between Neutral Bodies

For a neutral body containing equal numbers or equal amounts of positive and negative electric charges, the electrostatic forces of repulsion and attraction cancel out exactly at every point in space, but the gravitational forces of attraction add up. From equation (16), the gravitational force of attraction $F_G$ between two bodies of masses $M_1$ and $M_2$ one containing $N_1$ identical charges each of magnitude $Q$ and the other containing $N_2$ identical charges each of magnitude $K$, is obtained as:

$$\mathbf{F}_G = -\gamma\frac{M_1 M_2}{Z^2}\hat{\mathbf{u}} = -\frac{\gamma\chi}{Z^2}\sum_{n=1}^{N}K^2\sum_{n=1}^{N}Q_n^2\hat{\mathbf{u}} \qquad (25)$$

$$= -\frac{\gamma\chi}{Z^2}N_1 N_2 Q^2 K^2\hat{\mathbf{u}}$$

The numbers $N_1$ and $N_2$ may, of course, be infinitely large. In terms of volumes $V_1$ and $V_2$ of the respective charges $Q$ and $K$, equations (12) and (18) give:

$$\mathbf{F}_G = -\frac{\gamma\upsilon^2}{Z^2}N_1 N_2 V_1 V_2\hat{\mathbf{u}} \qquad (26)$$

## 7. Conclusion

The following conclusions can be drawn:
1. Free space, as a vacuum, has no property.
2. Space is occupied by regions of matter with gravitational forces of attraction between them.
3. Space-time continuum of the theory of general relativity is not required to explain the force of gravity.
4. Particles, objects or bodies, composed of electric charges, give rise to electric fields in space in accordance with Coulombs inverse square law.
5. Electric fields, emanating from matter, crisscross space and balance out exactly everywhere, exerting no electrical force on charged particles or neutral bodies.
6. Force of gravity is the result of an electric field from one charged particle being affected by the presence of another charged particle such that force of repulsion is slightly reduced and force of attraction similarly increased.
7. For matter, composed of equal amounts of positive and negative electric charges, electrical forces of repulsion and attraction cancel out while gravitational forces of attraction add up.
8. Force of Gravity is a pulling force, a pull of one particle on another particle by virtue of its occupation of a volume of space enclosed by a spherical shell with uniform surface charge density The shell, as a surface charge, constitutes a singularity, which gives rise to an electric field and the enclosed volume, as a curvature or distortion of space, is supposed to be the source of a gravitational field.
9. Mass of a body is a quantity that can be expressed in terms of the numbers or quantities of electric charges constituting the body. Newtons universal law of gravity can be expressed in terms of electrical quantities. As such, gravitation is electrical in nature and its manifestation should be transmitted at the speed of light.
10. The electric fields in space exert no force on charged particles or neutral bodies. A body moves in space under a gravitational force without any radiation of energy, so that change in potential energy is equal to change in kinetic energy. There fore a gravitational wave should not be expected.

**Acknowledgement**

I am grateful to Mr. Bob de Hilster for putting this paper in a more readable form.

# REFERENCES

1. Isaac Newton, *Mathematical Principles of Natural Philosophy.*, University of California Press, 1905, translated 1964.
2. Einstein and Lorentz, *The Principles of Relativity.*, Matheun, London, 1923.
3. M. Abdullahi, *On the Energy and Mass of Electric Charges in a Body.*, http://www.musada.net/Papers/ Paper6.pdf, 2013.
4. M. Abdullahi, *An Alternative Electrodynamics to the Theory of Special Relativity.*, 20th NPA Conference, 2013.

# One Reality of Cosmos, Calendar, Clock, Compass, GPS and Much More

## Pal Asija

*One Reality Research Academy Shelton, CT. 06484 USA, palasija@gmail.com*

This paper is based on the premise that there is but one reality - a symphony of sciences and spirituality - stars and scriptures singing in unison - universal three dimensional dance(s) of and around barycenter(s). All knowledge domains (KDs) including sciences, spirituality and scriptures are infested with errors due to human limitations. Author makes the case that one reality is knowable by purging errors from all relevant KDs. More specifically the one reality (1-R) premise is illustrated by corrections to calendar, clock, compass and GPS. Cosmos Ipsa Loquitur (The Universe speaks for itself). This paper relates the limited 1-R delineated here to the larger picture of its relationship to the other entities and KDs. Finally it makes some recommendations for continued future research and confirmation by non-trivial experiments, in spite of the fact that much of it is self-evident. Included are a dozen appendices A-L.

**Keywords:** time, clocks, GPS, cosmos

## 1. Introduction

### 1.1. Background

I have a Vocation - Our Pal LLC for creation, protection and cashing of intellectual property including patents, trademarks, trade secrets, copyrights, licensing, technology transfer and much more. I have been serving the creative community with vision, wisdom, integrity, experience, skill, zeal, humility and attitude of gratitude for over four decades.

I also have an Avocation - One Reality Research, which is a symphony of sciences and Spirituality- singing of stars and scriptures in unison, universal dance of and around barycenter(s) - harmonization of all KDs thru purging of errors. On a credenza behind my desk are over 50 volumes of 2"wide 3-Ring Binders full of my handwritten notes, only ten percent of which is in digital form. It is work in progress that combines (liberal) arts and sciences.

Between my vocation and avocation I have no time for Vacation. But wait there is more. The money I make from my vocation is invested into my avocation. So I am broke all the time just the same. Sadly even after five decades I am still the only one in the world engaged in one reality research. CAVEAT: High Priests of most KDs think of me as 'Heretic'.

### 1.2. Designing the Cosmos

Man has never designed anything like the nature's designs from a simple blade of grass to human body which keeps on working in spite of all the abuse. Man will also never be able to design let alone prototype something as large as the universe spanning 80 orders of magnitude from top and bottom quark pairs to quasars and largest clusters of galaxies. In fact we can't even launch something like the mass and volume of the Eiffel Tower or the Freedom Tower with sufficient velocity eight km/sec to orbit the earth let alone escape velocity of 11.18 km/sec. Most creationists are convinced that (7 15 4) [English alphabet in base 10] did all that in the universe, with up to 10121 entities, in just one week. An epitome of naivetÃl'.

The ultimate system is our universe. The ultimate challenge is the design of our Bounded Universe (BU). It is within an Unbounded Universe (UU) which includes past, present and potential of the universe including its design, size, gravity, light, time, space, mass, motion, entropy and other key variables and unique features. It includes a systems approach to the universe which by definition is one (Universe = All that there is). In particular it relates a systems view of 1-R of the BU (FTPRDNFBU - Finite Temporal Physical Relative Discrete eNtropic Firmament Bound Universe) within UU (IEVACXFFU - Infinite Eternal Virtual Absolute Continuous eXtropic Firmament Free Universe)1 delineating its size, structure, soul and our special status on our precious privileged planet and how it all might relate to spirituality.

### 1.3. One Reality Research

In 1-R research we must think BIG and nothing finite is big enough. Paradoxically we must also concurrently learn to think SMALL and nothing finite is small enough; and we thought nanotechnology is too small to measure or dark/zero-point/free energy is too cheap to meter. This section illustrates the challenges of size and complexity of our BU. Science if purged from errors can act as a catalyst in pace of human progress, living in felicity and includes engineering, development of comfort gadgets and helping mankind sooner rather than later. Science can also open new avenues to new ideas, discoveries, inventions and technologies. Fortunately errors in sciences have not effected inventing, engineering, technologies, at least not so far, because even if and when the science is wrong, the engineers make things work by trial and error, ignoring the sciences and even doing just the opposite of what theoretical science dictates. A good example of it is GPS2 discussed later here in section four. The de facto role of KDs is to resist and postpone paradigm shift and peer review is a good way to accomplish it, as many have observed it and some have experienced it also. The current generation has a vested interest in preserving the status quo, but if we take the pro-active altruistic approach, there is light at the end of the tunnel (hopefully not light of an approaching high speed magnetic levitation train).

### 1.4. Systems in cosmos

System wide challenges deserve system wide solutions. No system or sub-system is an island. All sub-systems need to be updated and coordinated harmoniously, concurrently and in synchrony with cooperation and attitude of gratitude among all the key players. Piecemeal solutions not only do not work, they are counterproductive. All variables and parameters in a system need to be adjusted and updated concurrently with due diligence and due haste without waste.

Just as we cannot solve our problems in isolation except by cooperatively solving problems of those around us, so can we not solve problems and challenges in STEM (Science, Technology, Engineering and Mathematics) without first helping guardians of other knowledge domains (KDs) solve their problems, because no KD is an island. Ultimately all knowledge is 'one truth - one reality'.

We all originated from one, are all inseparably connected 'one to all and all to one' and interdependent 'one on all and all on one' and eventually we may all merge into unity in purpose if not logistically as well.

We are one much the same way our body is one comprising and cooperating among all its subsystems including nervous, respiratory, endocrine, blood circulation, muscular, digestive, skeletal, reproductive, urinary and the skin sub-system(s).

No part of the human body, no matter how insignificant in size or functionality, can say to another (part) "I have no need of thee". We cannot hope to purge errors in sciences without purging errors in other KDs.

## 2. One Reality Premise

1-R ignores man made boundaries of KDs or credentials of the originator of a particular perception of one reality. Any contradictions are purged from one reality of BU (space and time bounded universe) by employing familiar mathematical techniques such as LCM (Lowest Common Multiple) and HCF (Highest Common Factor) amongst others as applied to concepts instead of numbers. Since no problem is an island, no solution is an island either until all solutions merge into 1-R when this distinction vanishes.

The cartoon of Figure 1 illustrates the difference between reality and perception of reality. Reality is one, the perceptions of reality exceed seven billion. Below is the dialog between my pal dog and me (Our PalÂő). My Pal Dog: Who the (6 15 3 B)* do you think you are that your perception of one reality is better than mine. (*Alphabet in Hexadecimal) Our PAL Asija: It's not my pal, cause I 'm

**Figure 1.** One Reality of Our Pal's PAL

nobody. It's just for your consideration and the electronic trail for your posterity.

### 2.1. Basic Foundation

The challenges and errors in science(s) cannot be resolved without resolving those of spirituality and vice versa. No problem can be solved in isolation. No solution can be implemented in isolation. The author supports his position by examples from a wide range and variety of concepts from science(s) and spirituality.

The only hope for solving the '1-R' jigsaw puzzle is by sharing the pieces of the puzzle from all sources in all KDs of our 'But One Universe'. Unfortunately limited by Q0 we ignore 75

The universe by definition is one. Fact is stranger than fiction but 1-R is far more bizarre than even quantum physics, particle zoo, epi-epigenetics, and misnamed 'Near Death Experiences', sleep and dream research and neuroscience of parasites.

In the final analysis 'One Reality' speaks for itself (Cosmos Ipsa Loquitur - Universe Itself Speaks). Reality needs no scientists, high priests or lawyers for defense, prosecution. Plaintiffs who strictly conform their life to 1-R are immune and/or exempt.

### 2.2. Human Errors in All Knowledge Domains

All humans are limited in their perception and brain power. Humans are involved in all KDs. Therefore all KDs are infested with human errors. All knowledge is one truth one reality and yet there are differences and similarities between any two KDs, no matter how similar or different respectively.

In fact all KDs have a great variety of similarities and differences. No KD is an island. No KD is perfect. Due to inherent (by design) human limitations all KDs (from sciences to spirituality and everything in between) are infested with errors.

Generally anomalies (Pioneer 10 & 11), paradoxes (twin), conundrums (causes of red and blue shift) enigmas (wave particle duality) and all other contradictions and conflicts are symptoms of error infested knowledge (EIK).

Furthermore there is the possibility that even precession

of celestial bodies; introduction of fudge factors and constants of nature and multiplicity of theories (to explain the cause of gravity) may be hinting that none of them is right and none of us may be right.

All of these errors can be traced back to human limitations inter alia asinine assumptions, defective draconian definitions, and wrong, even absurd, world-views. In due course and with due diligence, it is entirely possible that these indices of errors can be made more specific and concrete such that they have general application to all KDs. EIK cannot be avoided except by concerted proactive effort jointly by all responsible citizens of the world now, here, ASAP.

### 2.3. Tiny Errors Mega Impact

We, even as credentialed experts, can be wrong even about simple things. For example the year in which Who/What Ever Creator (WEC) 7 17 4B8 [alphabet in octal] designed it. (See App. E - WEC by any other name). The solar system (SS) testifies the year as 364 days or 13 months of 28 days each or 52 weeks of 7 days each. It harmonizes with lunar calendar, obviates leap year corrections, sidereal time/day and the precession of equinoxes and solstices.

Likewise a day has 26 hours each of 56' and each minute of 56". In other words it simplifies life (even for prediction of tides and menstrual cycles of women) more so than switching to decimal currency did for billions of people in countries which had the vision and political will (chutzpah) to do it. Tiny errors with mega consequences are not limited to sciences but 'sneak-in' in other KDs also. Math is no exception as any banker who has inadvertently added or omitted a zero before issuing and/or cashing a check can testify.

## 3. Inspiration for Corrections

Corrections to any KD can be inspired by within or without the infested KD. Any KD (from Archaeology to Zoology) can provide inspiration for corrections, but this section is limited to corrections inspired by the solar system. Accordingly corrections inspired by scriptures and other KDs are beyond the scope of this epistle.

In view of Res Ipsa Loquitur - the Universe Speaks for Itself, 'if it is to be it is up to you and me' to change our calendar, clock, clock-face, compass and globe's latitude(s) and longitude(s) (lat/long) as it is naivetÃl' if not stupidity as well to expect the universe to change itself to conform to our erroneous calendar, clocks, compasses and lat/long etc.

### 3.1. Corrections to Calendar

The motivation for conforming to reality of 364 days can be derived from its many benefits inter alia (i) Solar calendar will conform to lunar calendar. (ii) The ease of 'Date-Day' concordance of any day in history or future when such correction is obviated by replacing LIC (Leap Infested Calendar) by LLC (Leap Less Calendar) with our without the intermediate step of LCC (Leap Corrected Calendar. (iii) Every date falls on the same day of the week

every month. (iv) Kindergarten kids (future savants) won't need to use nursery rhymes or count knuckles on the back of their fisted hands to determine if a particular month has 28, 29, 30 or 31 days. (v) Farmer's almanac(s) will be greatly simplified. (vi) Solstices and equinoxes will obviate adjustments. (vii) Even ladies menstrual cycle prediction will become more accurate and reliable. Fortunately by design of WEC, cycles of moon are dependent upon and are in synch with earth orbit around barycenter of earth and sun in 364 days. (viii) Sidereal v/s solar day differential vanishes when underlying errors from its foundational knowledge are purged, as our star (synodic day) is just as valid. For additional related corrections to calendar please refer to following appendices:

F - Flood; G - Timeline; H - A-Y (not A-Z) Days; I - Important dates in LLC (Leap Less Calendar); J - Seasons, equinoxes and solstices; K - Multifaceted synchronicity in 2015; and L - Leap in history of leap with graphic.

### 3.2. Corrections to Clock and Clock-face

The days in leap less calendar are 364, down from leap infested calendar of 365.2563(R2). The correction in the clock-face is upwards from 12 to 13 hours or ratio of $13/12 = 1.083(R)$ because a day has 26 hours and the clock face is only 12 hours. Accordingly each quarter must be changed from 90 to 91 degrees. Furthermore each hour has 56' and each minute 56" to result in 81,536 seconds or $X364 = 29,679,104 sec/year$ compared to our current leap infested calendar (LIC) and somewhat erroneous $365.256363X24X60X60 = 31,558,149 sec/yr$. This means that leap less seconds are fewer but longer or the seconds of leap infested year are more but of shorter duration.

The reason for using the 60 v/s the reality of 56 is grounded in tradition, history and precedent. The Samarians and Babylonians in Mesopotamians did not use decimal or hexadecimal but sexagesimal system of base 60 which started from counting on 12 phalanges of 4 fingers 3 each (distal, intermediate and proximal) of one hand X 5 fingers of the other hand = 60 and therefore we still use 3600 (60X60) secs/hour. For the same reason early calendars used 360 days/yr. Likewise the ratio of minutes and seconds of both time and direction(s) is LLC = .93(R) LIC.

Furthermore the sunrise and sunset (start/end of crescent to full gibbous) according to our current clocks is 2' and 48 sec = 168" or 3 minutes of 56X3 = 168 or 2.8' as 2.8 X 60 also equals 168 in LCC (Leap Corrected Clocks). However in Leap Less Clocks (LLC) the same sunrise/set duration = 3'X60= 180" or 3.25' as 3.25X56 = 182 seconds. It is not a mere coincidence that 24X7 = 168 and 26X7 = 182 as the ratio between LLC/LCC never changes 182/180 or 91/90 or 1.01(R)

These errors and their correctional benefits go far deeper than the benefits some nations realized when they changed to decimal currency. In a nutshell in addition to the calendar the benefits extend to all clocks, compasses, lat/long in many different KDs from archaeology to zoology.

### 3.3. Corrections to Compass and Lat/Long

Like the clock and the clock-face the compass also needs to be adjusted upwards from 360 to 364, a ratio of 91:90 or 1.01(R). Since our globe's lat/long are also based on 360 degrees they also should be adjusted upwards by the same ratio to make life easier for all of us and our posterity much more so than switching to decimal currency or metric system did. The exact tilt of the earth in leap less compass (LLC) degrees is 23.717421o (23.456789o LIC)

## 4. Global Positioning System (GPS)

The Global Positioning System is the prime example of errors in sciences. It's nexus to Einstein's (SRT or GRT)2 is debatable, but it is vicariously related to URL (Universal Relationship Law). The GPS is related to gravitational time dilation (-7.27 micro-sec/day) radially as well as to atmospheric time contraction (45.678 micro-sec/day) circumferentially.

$$Circumference = 2\pi r = \tau r \qquad (1)$$

$$\pi = 3.14159265 \, or \, \tau(2\pi) = 6.2831852 \qquad (2)$$

Initial correction of satellite clocks

$$45.678901 = 6.2831852 X 7.2700228 \qquad (3)$$

$$45.678901 - 7.2700228 = 38.408879 \qquad (4)$$

$$(2r - r) = r(2\pi - 1) = 7.27X(6.2831852 - 1) \qquad (5)$$

$$= 7.27X5.2831852 = 38.4 Micro - sec/day \, Q.E.D. \qquad (6)$$

I feel justified in using Quad Erat Demonstrandum because something man made (GPS) and something made by the nature have one to one relationship with each other with respect to radius and circumference. GPS is a measure of time radially and circumferentially while earth radius and circumference are metrics of distance(s), which allows us to reliably convert time to distance except for the annoyance of clock recalibrations due to atmospheric variations at earth level GPS clocks and instruments but not so much at the satellite 20,000 km (12,428 miles) in stratosphere.

Noteworthy and helpful to understanding are four observations. (i) By convention minus (-) is time dilation and plus (+) is time contraction. (ii) The radial component is gravitational. Due to lower gravity at the satellite level (12,500 miles or 20X106 m) the time dilates or the clock ticks slower as ticks are stretched further apart. (iii) Circumferential correction component is due to time contraction (not dilation) because of atmospheric differential between earth clocks in troposphere and satellite clocks in stratosphere as engineers slowdown satellite bound clock rates by 38.4 micros seconds per day to synchronize with ground based clocks. (iv) While the initial clock rate correction is in microsecond/day, periodic corrections due to local weather changes are merely in nanosecond/correction. Engineers made GPS work by trial and error by doing just the opposite of what Einsteinian SRT directed.

## 5. Design of the Universe

My 'Mission Impossible' here is to illuminate this topic of mega-complexity by taking systems approach to planning, design and execution of our universe as the ultimate system design challenge. My secondary objective is to justify that truth-in-teaching laws are necessary and doable at par with truth in advertising, lending, or any other regulated human endeavor or behavior. The 'Truth-in-Teaching' laws can be envisioned, if not achieved as well, by purging errors from all KDs. A tertiary objective is to give a few examples of errors in our most popular KDs from sciences, spirituality and scriptures.

You and I can optimize the design of any task at hand, within the parameters of the job-description, but WEC's job description has no such limitations and therefore the only one with abilities to optimize the design of the BU. It cannot do it all merely by snapping its fingers. The completed design can be unveiled in a couple of weeks, as anyone who has experienced overnight success, authored simulation software, attended a theatrical play, performed as cheer leader, produced a motion picture, launched a new product or won an election can testify.

Age of the Universe ascertained from the Big Bang (BB) alone is like the tip of the iceberg. It recognizes only 1/9th or 11% (13.7/123 billion years) as the history of the universe, but Torah recognizes even less (7180/137,174,210,013)X100% = 0.0000052342% or 5.23422 X 10-6%. This is a shocker for young earth creationists who are sure WEC created it all in one week 6000 years ago, just as Richard Dawkins and Christopher Hitchens are/were sure there is no-god or no good respectively.

### 5.1. Size and Complexity of the Universe

The size of the universe extends from 10-40 to 1040 meter radii. I also know that 1040 m radius is the largest entity in our universe (the boundary of the universe) and the smallest is its reciprocal 10-40 meter radius somewhat smaller than the Plank constant. Info about enormity, complexity and eight automatic (like automatic gear-shift X-mission of a motor vehicle) light speed zones and their speeds is in App. B.

Geometric center of the universe is nearly the same as our algebraic but the earth is at the center of the radius of the universe. So in this sense the earth is at the center of the universe after all, except it is at the center of the radius (not diameter) of the universe. WEC used geometric center which is 10-40 X 1040 = 100 = 1 whereas the algebraic center is (1040)/2 = 5 X 1039 which in our limited perception is middle of the radius (not diameter). Earth is also stationary with respect to centers of radii,

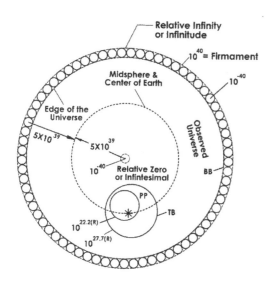

**Figure 2.** Gravity Globe in the Supra Universe not at geometric center at $100^0$ m but at algebraic center at $5X10^39m$. (All four graphics in this section five courtesy of Frank Melanson).

much like the ambulatory congenital twins in motion are stationary with respect to each other. Likewise the earth is also ambulatory around the sun, as long as the relative relationship between the earth and the sun is maintained by orbit of each around barycenter of solar system. The asterisk (*) in the gravity globe of Figure 2 represents the center of gravity/mass of the earth anchored to and yet gliding freely on the imaginary mid-sphere formed by mid points of the radii of the firmament of radius 1040 m at 5 X 1039 m. The following metaphor, legend will aid in the comprehension of the scope, scale and size of the BU as shown in Figure 2.

(a) PP (Ping Pong) Ball which represents and houses the solar system (SS) of 1011.1(R) m as well as the Milky Way (MW) extending to 1016.6(R) m.

(b) TB (Tennis Ball) includes all of the PP contents as well as the entire Virgo local (VL) cluster to 1022.2(R) m and Virgo super (VS) cluster to 1033.3(R). In the graphic 27.7(R) is intermediate (geometric mean) between 22.2(R) and 33.3(R) as contrasted from the arithmetic mean 5X1032.3(R)

(c) BB (Basket Ball) occupies all the contents of PP and TB and the rest of the observed (Laniakea Super Cluster) and yet to be observed star stuff to the edge of the universe. Its range extends to 1038.8(R) m. Unlike the PP and TB, its rotation is with respect the center of the diameter at 100=1m (aka the great attractor or the ultimate anchor). BB radius and diameter are almost the same as that of the firmament (limit of the universe).

Figure 2 shows not only the size of the universe but also location of our precious planet earth (*) in it. The total number of known particles in the universe may be up to10121. (My calculation is a few orders of magnitude

greater than that of Sir Roger Penrose as I use the metric of 1 atom/m3 and include a zoo of sub-atomic particles, three levels of quarks (up/down + charm/strange + top/bottom) and a great variety of escort particle(s) of ESR (Emerge Submerge Re-emerge) cycles.

An essential aspect of our universe is uniform gravity4 which is created by combined effect of three motions in 3D Euclidian absolute space having planes (three axis and three planes of 23.45o tilted orientation but perpendicular to each other) in three orthogonal frames of reference which are fed all the way back to earth via LSC (Laniakea Super Cluster or Immeasurable Heaven), VC (Virgo Cluster), MW (Milky Way) and the SS (Solar System) each in three different orthogonal planes.

To begin with earth and celestial axes are vertical, parallel and in synch. The celestial axis passes through the great attractor at the center of the universe, whereas earth axis passes through center of radius at 5X1039 m.

i Orbit of the earth (vertical axis) around the Sun in the ecliptic plane tilted 23.45o in the first frame of reference.

ii SS around MWBH anchor in the plane of the MW which is perpendicular to the plane of SS in the second orthogonal frame of reference (vertical plane around horizontal axis)

iii Orbit of the MW and VC around the Black hole as anchor of the VSC in the third frame of reference (lateral vertical plane around lateral horizontal axis) which is orthogonal to both the previous planes SS (tilted ecliptic plane) and the orthogonal MW Plane.

iv All the rest of the intra & intergalactic star stuff including gases filaments and walls, entire in the BU including LSC then rotates around the ultimate anchor, the great attractor located at the geometric center of radius at 10-40 X 1040 = 100 = 1, or algebraic center of the diameter of the firmament of radius of 1040.

Thus uniform gravity on both hemi-spheres of the earth towards the center is achieved by combined effect of three motions in 3D Euclidian absolute space having three planes and three axes of arbitrary orientation but perpendicular to each other in three orthogonal frames of reference which are fed all the way back to earth via LSC, VC, MW and SS. Three tilts of 23.45o each make (i) and (iv) make it vertical axis in horizontal equatorial planes of earth and the celestial sphere. This is why and how we in USA and our colleagues down under in Australia both feel upright gravity concurrently notwithstanding our respective heads and feet are opposite each other. Finally if the sun as the anchor were to suddenly disappear it will take 8 minutes for the planet to get dark but the gravity will vanish instantaneously and earth will fly off on a tangent until it falls within the Equilibrium Sphere (ES) of some other appropriate celestial body and orbits it. On the way it may acquire several smaller satellites.

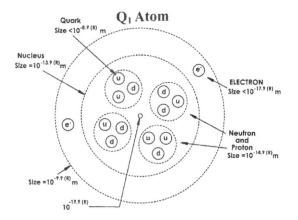

**Figure 3.** Sub-meter Femto-atomic Infrastructure with up/down quarks.

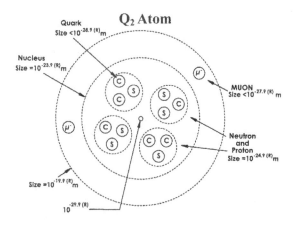

**Figure 4.** Yocto Scale Subatomic Infrastructure with Charm/Strange Quarks.

## 5.2. Sub-atomic Science(s) and spirituality

There can be harmony, even symphony between sciences and spirituality and one to one (1:1) relationship between them. Figure 3, 4 & 5 show sub-meter scale tri-level atomic infrastructure, which correlates quark structure Q1, Q2, Q3 to durable, soulical and spirit bodies respectively. The soul (charm/strange quark atoms) and spirit (top/bottom quark atoms) of the universe and the man and 4E in BU (Everything, Everybody, Everywhere, Every-time) is latent in the substructure of the atom. There are three levels below the Nano-substructure of the atom, which are shown in Figures 3, 4 & 5 excluding the quark-less body of Q0 which we discard at death. For the sake of completeness all four levels are listed below in descending (deepening) order of depth and size.

a) Q0 Nano-scale temporary body and brain we discard at death. Its range is 100 to 10-9.9(R) m. aka quark-less or Q-0 (Q-Zero). Each level of sex and eight gender orientations (12.5% each) is determined by Q1, Q2, Q3 (000-111). Each level contributes one bit of three bit binary code resulting in eight varieties of sex/gender

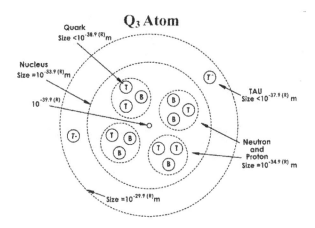

**Figure 5.** Nano-yocto scale Sub-atomic Infrastructure with top/bottom quarks.

of individuals (SXP/Iso-Cross phenomenon). As pairs 44.4(R) % are heteroes and gays, lesbians 27.7(R) % each resulting in total of 44.4(R) + 55.5(R) = 99.9(R) = 100% as pairs, partners or couples.

b) Q1 (Figure 3) has femto-scale Sub-atomic -range of (10-10 to 10-19.9(R) m), the durable body and brain (consciousness) that survives death, which includes up/down quarks or Q1 (Q-One). The Levels Q0 and Q1 are always in synch barring some trans-sexual surgery, mutations or medical intervention at Q0 level to correct it. Qo body is always left behind at death. Q1 durable body and brain continue. With Q2 and Q3 the triplet constitute body, soul and spirit of 4E in BU. Thus there are 8 basic types of each atom, mammal etc.

c) Q2 - Yoctoscale (scale (10-20 to 10-29.9(R) m) comprising mind and soul that accompanies level-Q1 metaphysical durable body at death. It includes charm/strange quarks or Q-2 (Q-Two), the infrastructure of which is in Figure 4.

d) Q3 - Nano-yocto scale (10-30 to 1039.9(R) m) comprising ethereal body and intelligence that accompanies levels Q1 and Q2. It includes top/bottom (aka truth/beauty) quarks or Q-3 as shown in Figure 5.

Why and how does WEC know more about us than we do or can ever know about ourselves? It is because WEC understands, directs, manages and controls the role of Q1, Q2 & Q3 via UVLM which then interacts with Q0 of BU via Q1, Q2 & Q3. The atoms of up/down quarks (Figure 3), charm/strange quarks (Figure 4) and top/bottom quarks (Figure 5) each ten orders of magnitude smaller than the preceding, starting with quark-less Q0 to Q3 with top/bottom quarks up to 10-38.9(R) meters.

WEC knows its creation(s) just as we know our designs. After all, WEC designed it with great purpose over 150.89 Ga extrapolated back from BB time, a deep time an order of magnitude deeper than the BB signature in nature.

What particle physicists observe in accelerators as three levels of quarks (up/down, charm/strange and top/bottom) spiritualist perceive as durable, soulical and spirit bodies respectively. In order to act in our enlightened best interest it is necessary to acknowledge and honor contributions of icons of science(s) and spirituality including those of Newton, Einstein, Darwin and NASA as their contributions far exceed any errors which of necessity are unavoidable due to 3P8S (3P = Perception, Processing and Presentation skills and 8S = 5 physical senses and 6th, 7th, & 8th three additional senses inspired by Q1, Q2 and Q3 respectively) limitations. At any rate their shortcomings are much shorter than our shortcomings. We should therefore make the corrections, purge the errors and move forward with an attitude of gratitude. Fixing the paradigm of KDs5 is long overdue.

Just as science is not only about facts, so engineering is also not only about comfort gadgets but instead serving man (mankind) or more broadly to facilitate (or at least not interfere) with WEC's anthropocentric mission for man on earth. Theoretical science is subjective. Engineering is objective. Technology is hybrid (subjective and objective concurrently). Some use math to obfuscate clear meaning. Math in the hands of an expert can more readily be used for deception more so than any natural language.

## 6. Gravity in Retrospect

Every orbit is in equilibrium. All motions are in equilibrium or seeking equilibrium until blocked by some obstacle creating the appearance of 'at rest'. In theory the apple and the earth both attract each other, in practice only the earth attracts the apple because the earth is already in equilibrium and it is the apple that is still desperately seeking the equilibrium. In theory there is no difference between theory and practice. In practice there is no similarity between theory and practice.

The sphere of equilibrium is defined by the masses of the orbiter and the anchor, with respect to a particular anchor. Each smaller body's (planet, galaxy etc.,) sphere of influence is different. Smaller the body smaller the RES/VES (Radius /Volume of Equilibrium Sphere). In case of comparably massive binary star pair, each acts as anchor for the other and the R/VES by definition is proportionally equal with opposite orientation.

It is time to correct our understanding of not only UGL (with heartfelt thanks to Sir Isaac Newton) but also many other misperceptions of '1-R' by purging one error at a time from each KD, one by one. UGL is misleading because it (UGL) is applicable only within the boundary of the equilibrium sphere. More specifically UGL is misleading because it fails to make any distinction between inside and outside of the equilibrium sphere. It does not even mention the concept of equilibrium sphere, let alone clarifying that application of UGL is limited to equilibrium sphere and has no applicability beyond its sphere of influence. The gravitational mutual attraction within equilibrium sphere is product of the masses divided by the prod-

uct of the distances as g = mM/Dd. It is preferable to use g = mM/Dd over mM/dD as a reminder and memorandum to ourselves as to which distance belongs with which mass. The upper and lower case of either mass or distance are transposed but not both.

M = mass of the anchor or orbited body; m = mass of the satellite or the orbiting body; d = distance between the CG of the m and barycenter D = distance between the CG of the M and the barycenter.

Small d is generally quite large compared to D whereas m is generally quite small relative to the anchor mass M. In case of binary star pair both masses are comparable and both distances from CG of each to barycenter are also comparable simplifying the attraction within the equilibrium sphere to g = M2/D2 or (m/d)2 since m=M and d=D. Gravitational constant is no longer needed.

Sir Isaac Newton was aware of mutuality of barycentric orbits but was also fascinated by mutuality of attraction in his UGL, coupled with the fact that he was enthusiastically enamored by application of 3rd law of motion to it.

Unfortunately Newton did not realize that the mutuality of attraction is applicable only within the sphere of equilibrium e.g. apple falling to the earth. There is no gravitational attraction and/or repulsion beyond the sphere of equilibrium, the radius at which an apple of a particular mass, density, shape and volume will orbit the earth when launched with escape velocity of 11.18 km/sec or greater or the moment the apple reaches equilibrium orbit around the earth.

Somehow we still pretend it to be true and valid concept and therefore keep struggling with Pioneer (10 & 11) anomalies and some of us even keep inventing dark matter (and even dark energy) to mask our ignorance in our erroneous understanding and perception of 1-R disregarding "There is But One Reality - A symphony of Science(s) and spirituality" here, there and everywhere.

Extending the application of Newton's 3rd law of equal and opposite action and reaction from mutuality of gravitational attraction within the equilibrium sphere (ES) to beyond, is both commendable and regrettable. It misled Newton to apply UGL to celestial bodies beyond ES, so as to extend the UGL to universal application, when in fact it is applicable only within the ESI (equilibrium sphere of influence).

Apple is either in equilibrium as satellite of the earth or not and even within the ES the apple is either at apparent rest due to an obstruction (attached to the tree or stopped at the surface of the earth) or not. In all cases the apple regardless of within or without ES is impotent to attract much larger body towards itself in spite of theoretical or philosophical mutuality of attraction as postulated, imagined or philosophized and used in UGL by Sir Isaac Newton himself.

Sun and the earth both orbit the barycenter (common center of mass) of sun and the earth. Earth in 364 days and the sun in 13 earth years or 13X364 = 4732 earth days, or 28 degrees of eccentric German Wankel engine style rotary piston like operation per earth year. Sun also has a similar unique barycentric relationship with other planets, but that's beyond the scope of this monograph. But for the pull and tug of other planets each orbit is circular if observed alone. Likewise moon also rotates as it orbits the earth 13 degrees per day (one diurnal rotation of the earth) which explains why the same near side (as contrasted from the far/dark side) of the moon faces the earth all the time as the moon orbits the earth. Thus moon, earth and sun are in synch with each other, each 13 X 28 = 364 (not 365.256363) days.

## 7. Summary

There is a happy ending to this story also. WEC is also in-charge of it all (good, bad, ugly evil and neutral) including your, Pope's and my (7 6 6 7 on phone pad or 20 17 17 20 alphabet in octal). WEC's mission for man on earth is on target, on track, and on time. It is continuously (26/7) involved in the creation (4E in BU) at all levels supra and infra by panthroptimality principle and opposition equilibria. WEC is anxious to have us understand its creation and has provided a plurality of means to do it. He/she/it is not in it for ego or self-aggrandizement, even though I confess I do not know what's in it for WEC. After all by definition absolute infinity is infinity regardless how much we add, subtract, divide or multiply it with.

Just like sometimes we wonder how we managed our home and office without paper-clip, rubber band or Post-It-NotesÂő (A registered federal trademark of 3M Corporation) let alone smart-phones and GPS, our posterity will wonder why we kept imposing erroneous KDs for so many centuries. We as responsible citizens of the world and trustees of the earth should teach intelligent (not always literal) interpretation of every KD. We will be blessed for purging the errors from our text books before giving them to students. This is still work in progress. It is a good start. Much has been done but even more remains to be done. Experiments need to be designed to confirm or falsify elements presented in this monograph about '1-R', all of which I entrust to savants. In fact the scope of 1-R research is so encompassing that it would take many such professional papers to do justice to it.

(i) One Reality of One Reality (1-R of 1-R)

(ii) Epi-genetics (and even epi-epigenetics) as applied to hetoros, homos you, me, LGBTQ and even the twelve ordinary men and the twelve extraordinary women of almost two millennia ago.

(iii) The true & real science & engineering of GPS.

(iv) 18 sleep and dream cycles, stages and phases.

(v) The uniform gravity on opposite hemispheres of the earth, with everyone feeling upright even our kissing cousins down under.

(vi) Nature and limitations of the WEC.

(vii) Design of the universe, with its enormity and complexity of mission, size, life and misnamed non-life.

(viii) Tri-level Quarks - Spirituality Interface(s) and the role of UVLM in them.

(ix) Seeing red white and blue (shift) due to Doppler or spectrograms of the media contents.

(x) Reversals in sciences and spirituality including neuroscience, genetics, intelligence of viruses and monotheistic religions.

(xi) Comparison and contrast between math of man and math in nature.

(xii) Universal Relationship Law (Here URL refers not to www.1-R.INFO but to a law comparable in scope to Newton's Universal Gravitation Law).

(xiii) Intra and interfaces among light, space, gravity and time as well as mass, motion, momentum and energy in addition to 3D space and objects, and 3T (Time, Temperature and eNtropy)

(xiv) The foundations for practically real time astronomy and cosmology.

(xv) Separating facts & fables in gravitational lensing

(xvi) Harmonization of permittivity, permeability, light speed and the characteristic impedance of space.

(xvii) Corrections to KDs in poetry, Q & A (Questions and Answers), NSTA (No Such Thing As) and TPM (This Probably Means) in addition to Sound Bytes NOW (App - C) and Insights NOW (Nuggets of Wisdom) App - D.

(xviii) How to Fix5 the Paradigm(s) of KDs.

(xix) 1-R of sciences, spirituality and societies.

(xx) WEC's captivating commercials and limitations.

## 8. Acknowledgment

I thankfully acknowledge funding by One Reality (1-R) Research Academy for research over the past five decades including preparation and publication of this paper with an attitude of gratitude.

## 9. Appendix A - 3 Questions for your amusement

1. What is the difference between a duck and an astrophysicist? (Hint: First find a similarity between astrophysicists and the ducks that does not apply to other professionals and mammals, then find the difference in that similarity.)

2. What's the 1st and still the best method of learning and teaching? (Hint: First determine what's common among all learning methods including scientific & faith methods.)

3. Where and under what circumstances zero, one, infinity and their reciprocals are prime numbers and equal each other? There are many other equally interesting and challenging questions pertaining to correct interpretation of sacred KDs, but advisedly are not included here as they do not belong in a professional scientific paper, notwithstanding my commitment to one reality (1-R) does not give me that option.

## 10. Appendix B: Eight Light Speed Zones of the Cosmos

Akin to automatic transmission shift of a motor vehicle.

| Sn/Qn | Speed | Space | Shell/Core | Content |
|---|---|---|---|---|
| S4 | $3X10^{38}$ | $10^{30} - 10^{39.9}$ | Outer | Cosmos |
| S3 | $3X10^{28}$ | $10^{20} - 10^{29.9}$ | Middle | Virgo Clusters |
| S2 | $3X10^{18}$ | $10^{10} - 10^{19.9}$ | Middle | Milky-Way |
| S1 | $3X10^{8}$ | $10^{0} - 10^{9.9}$ | Inner | Solar System |
| Q0 | $3.3X10^{-9}$ | $10^{0} - 10^{-9.9}$ | Outer | Quark-less |
| Q1 | $3.3X10^{-19}$ | $10^{-10} - 10^{-19.9}$ | Middle | up/down |
| Q2 | $3.3X10^{-29}$ | $10^{-20} - 10^{-29.9}$ | Middle | charm/strange |
| Q3 | $3.3X10^{-39}$ | $10^{-30} - 10^{-39.9}$ | Inner | top/bottom |

## 11. Appendix C - SOUND BYTES NOW (NUGGETS OF WISDOM)

- Nothing travels at speed of light, not even light.
- Before our FTPRDN-FBU, IEVACX-FFU was.
- Quasars are far out. Quarks are far in.
- Both WEC and No-WEC are equally ineffable.
- There are no oxymoron(s) in WEC's domain.
- Cause and Effect and past present and potential are concurrent in FFU.
- Cosmos Ipsa Loquitur - The Universe itself speaks.
- For man WEC is bizarre; for WEC man is bizarre.
- AA + BC or AA - AD = 5159 & Anniv. = BC+AD.
- We as students of Q0 ignore 75
- Carl Sagan was right. We are star stuff âĂę. and soul stuff and spirit stuff too.
- Law of infinitude of similarities and differences adds awe inspiring elegance to our universe.
- Thinking small is harder than thinking BIG even though quarks are as far-in as quasars far-out.
- Leap Less Calendar of SS is 364 days of 26 hours each of 56 minutes and each minute of 56 seconds.
- Celestial bodies spin, rotate, orbit in circular orbits around barycenter(s), distorting appearances.
- Reality is far more bizarre than man's wildest imagination.
- The unexpressed gene determines and controls which gene (allele) is expressed.
- Deep time is not deep enough because it is limited to BB.
- Diurnal day - 26 hours at 40o NE lat/long. present day Erzincan, Turkey time (GMT+2). (Gen. 1:5)
- Light destroys darkness. Ignorance masks 1-R. Special dark light reveals 1-R.
- Time dilation/contraction is not only about clocks but more importantly about time itself.
- It is not so much about SRT/GRT, nor about UGL but URL and the GPS6.
- From man's perspective modus operandi of WEC appears absolutely absurd and vice versa man's logic is foolishness to WEC.

- Richard Dawkins is right. We are all born with a god shaped hole in our heads, but it was placed there by WEC as a 'homing device'.
- Atmosphere (temperature, pressure, humidity etc.) effect both time and clocks proportionately to keep correct time.
- The WEC has limitations but only within space and time bounded universe for first time creation of BU and even then none compared to us.
- The leap less revolutions of the earth around the barycenter of the sun and earth are 364 and 13 earth years of the earth and sun respectively.
- Nothing is random, not even random number generator. Heisenberg's uncertainty principle itself is uncertain. Why he didn't apply it to his own law of uncertainty is beyond me.
- 4E in BU is 3D or no D including any force, one axially and another in a plane encompassing 2 axis which makes 3 orthogonal axis or components, just like 3M (Mass, Motion & Momentum) or no M and 3T (Time Temperature & nTropy).
- BB did not happen literally, but WEC deployed the BU and initiated time is 13,717,428,182 years ago as of Feb 15, 2015 (Jan 1, 2022 LLC).
- An angular organ (14 5 12 9 17)B12 or (G 5 E 9 J)B26 [English alphabet in base 12 and base 26 respectively] between the legs does not a man make nor its absence a woman (Gen. 2:21-22)
- Diurnal day (24/26 Hrs) begins and ends with sunset in the west and moonrise in the east concurrently, after 4 corrections (solar, lunar, axis and 11 days skipped in 1752 from Wed Sep 2 to next day Th 9/14 which is inherently inconsistent also.
- Weather the earth is gliding or the imaginary midsphere is gliding is relative, both are equally true. Either way both are inseparably related.

## 12. Appendix D - Insights NOW (Nuggets of Wisdom)

Unlike digital sound bytes (not analog sound bites) 'Insights NOW' require more than a phrase or single sentence, generally a paragraph to explain 1-R concepts.

1. - Those who think WEC created the cosmos in one week or the BB or evolution in 13.7 billion years, utterly hopelessly and miserably fail to guesstimate, appreciate let alone assimilate the complexity and the enormity of the universe and the WEC's mission for man on earth in the BU and how WEC, the BB or the evolution keeps it on track, on target and on time without compromising the mission or the freedom to choose. WEC invested 150.89 Ga based on extrapolated time back from the BB rate.

2. - The solar system created only one LLC (Leap-Less Calendar) of 364 days. It is not for the cosmos to correct itself to conform to our clocks, calendars

and compasses. We are obliged to conform to the calendar, clock and compass of the cosmos. Like the year of 364 days the compass is also of 364 degrees or 4 quadrants, as well as seasons of 91 days each. This in turn requires slight increase to lat/long from 360 degrees to 364 degrees again each of 56 minutes and 56 seconds, which simplifies life by many orders of magnitude than did the switch to decimal currency.

3. - (i) Unlike relative infinitesimal and infinitude, nihility and infinity are absolute and synonyms; (ii) nihility & infinity morph into 1-R in IEVACX-FFU (UU); (iii) Finite(s) can comprehend neither infinity, nor nihility; (iv) Nothing is more natural than WEC (v) Nothing affects nihility or infinity of IEVACX-FFU or (UU); (vi) Nihility, One and Infinity and their reciprocals are synonyms and prime numbers.

4. - 4E in BU (i) is alive; (ii) takes the path of least resistance; (iii) is ultimately made of virtual particle(s); regardless of size and duration; (iv) 4E in BU has signature of WEC who's been there, done that and knows every particle in BU (up to 10121); (v) is physical; (vi) Q1, Q2, Q3 are physical too; (vii) Metaphysical is physical also (vii) WEC is insult and praise proof and immune from all evil, is sensitive to BU's needs.

5. - Speed of light is a limit. It is not constant. It decreases with (increasing) density of medium, just the opposite of sound which speeds up with (increasing) density of medium. Sound cannot travel without a medium and light has no need to travel in the absence of a medium.

6. Similarities between man and WEC include
   i Planning (A century of planning saves an entire millennia in execution); (ii) Design by trial and error including trade-offs - typical engineers' modus operandi;
   ii Prototyping before manufacturing; and
   iii Beta testing before presentation to citizenry.

7. - Solar (Synodic) (as contrasted from sidereal day) and lunar calendars are harmonious. The primary cosmic LLC metric is 365.24R2, which gives conversion factor of 1.00341325(R6), when divided by 364. Lunar conversion factor is 29.46428571R6 [28+ (28/28o or 364/364o) +13/28] to 30.4368R2/(13/12). Furthermore 30.4368R2/1.083R=28.095571R6 and which when divided by solar correction factor = 28. For verification & confirmation 30.4368R2/29.46428571R6 = 1.03300887664524 which when divided thy the solar correction factor of 1.00341325R6= 1.0294R2, just as lunar monthly ratio 364/12= 30.3R divided by 29.46428571R6 also = 1.0294R2. Q.E.D.
Due to difference between solar and lunar correction factors, it is necessary to add back (reinsert) 11 days that were skipped in 1752 from Wed Sep.2 to next day Th. 9/14, when transitioning from corrected LIC to LLC on Feb 15, 2015 which is LLC new year 1/1/2022.

## 13. Appendix E - WEC by any other name

Both 'WEC and no-WEC' are equally ineffable. There are many names of WEC, but under the concept of 1-R there can be but one WEC. If you do not buy into this basic concept, then I am afraid we are wasting each other's time. If your religion dictates that BB (or X-Y-Z) is the sole WEC and evolution (or A-B-C) is the sole sustainer, or singularity, energy, nature and force then 'May the force be with you!' So be it, but please do not hold it against others who may believe differently. Temporarily we should agree to disagree. Since there can be only one WEC, we are all product of the same WEC regardless of the name we use.

## REFERENCES

1. P. Asija, *"Universe within Universe"* Proceedings of the NPA, v2, n1, pp. 8-11 (2005)
2. P. Asija, *"SRT v/s SRT"* Proceedings of the NPA, v6, n1, pp. 17-19 (2009).
3. P. Asija, *"A Systems View of the Universe as One Reality"* NPA v8, n1, pp.28-35 (2011)
4. P. Asija, *"Instant Gravity and Real Time Astronomy in a Real Time Universe"* Proceedings of the NPA, v7, n1, pp. 27-30 (2010).
5. P. Asija, *"How to Fix the Paradigm of Science"* Proceedings of the NPA, v7, n1, pp. 23-26 (2010)
6. P. Asija, *"GPS and SRT"* Infinite Energy, issue 95 Jan/Feb. 2011, p.

# Physical Explanation for Greater Earth Expansion in the Southern Hemisphere

Robert Berger* and David de Hilster[†]

*7653 NW 60th Lane, Parkland, FL 33067, robert@artfrombrazil.com
[†]22936 Ironwedge Dr., Boca Raton, Florida 33433, david@dehilster.com

Using the Particle Model as proposed by de Hilster and de Hilster [1] [2], a physical explanation for the greater expansion of the earth in the southern hemisphere as opposed to the north is given. This explanation requires assumption that earth expansion and mass increase are real.

**Keywords:** expansion tectonics, mass increase, particle model

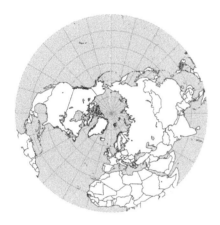

**Figure 1.** Northern hemisphere above the equator

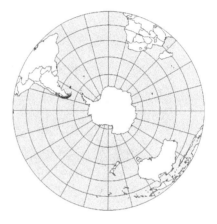

**Figure 2.** Southern hemisphere below the equator

## 1. Introduction

It is very obvious that when looking at a globe, that the majority of land mass is found in the northern hemisphere, and not the southern (see figure 5 and 6). There has never been a real explanation for this. Mainstream science that subscribes to plate tectonics would call it a random happen-stance caused by convection currents below the mantle.

Yet sea-floor expansion completely encompasses Antarctica as seen in figure 4 [2]. This is problematic for regular plate tectonics which says that the earth's radius is staying the same and does so by subduction or all the seafloor that is being created, must dive beneath the earth at some point.

## 2. Magnetic Fields

Dr. James Maxlow [4] has suggested that mass increase happens at the poles and where the solar wind of particles enters the earth. With the Particle Model as described by de Hilster and de Hilster, the magnetic field actually has a direction. In mainstream science, magnetic lines show arrows entering the north pole (see figure 5) but mainstream science has no physical model for what a magnetic field truly is. The Particle model has as physical model and says that magnetic fields are flows of G1 particles. And because of the right-hand rule as described by the Particle model, the actual flow of particles is the opposite of mainstream science and that G1 particles are entering the South Pole and exiting the North as seen in figure 6.

## 3. Mass Increase

The de Hilster describe mass increase as the combining of inflowing G1 particles with nucleons that are being spewed out by countless suns. Suns spew out G1 particles and nucleons and they enter the earth with more of them entering the south pole. Once inside, nucleons capture G1 particles and form new atoms eventually creating water, methane, and oil (see figure 8).

## 4. Conclusion

For the first time in expansion tectonics we have a possible explanation as to the reason why the earth is expanding more in the southern hemisphere than in the north. Using the de Hilster Particle Model not only gives us a theoretical explanation, but a physical model of one.

## MASS INCREASE

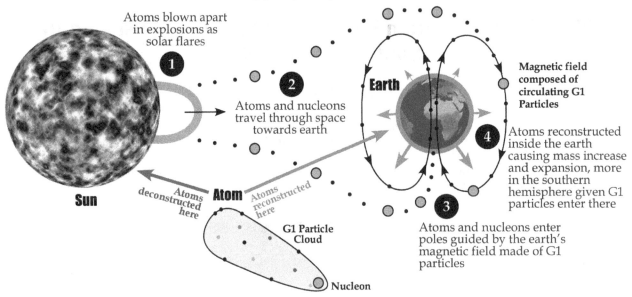

**Figure 3.** Mass increase as described by the Particle Model [1]

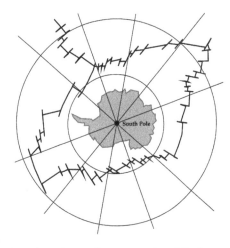

**Figure 4.** There is sea-floor expansion 360 degrees around Antartica

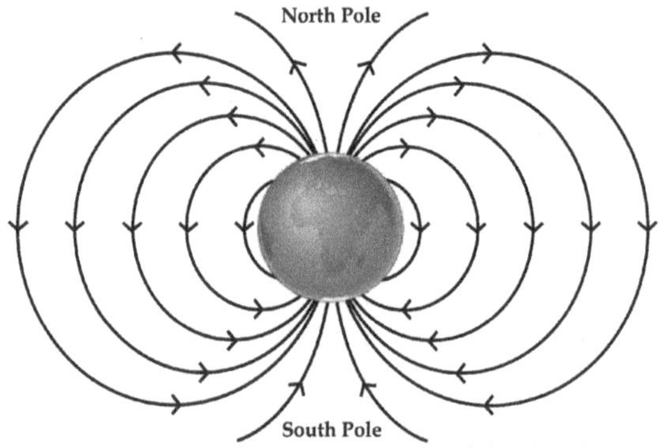

## REFERENCES

1. Robert de Hilster, David de Hilster, *A No-Math Physical Model of the Entire Universe*, John Chappell Natural Philosophy Society, 2016.
2. Robert de Hilster, *Gravity is Not for Free*, Self-Published 2015.
3. Samuel Carey *Theories of the Earth and Universe: A History of Dogma in the Earth Sciences.*, textttwww.RelativityOfLight.com, Stanford University Press; 1 edition (March 1, 1988)
4. James Maxlow *Terra non Firma Earth: Plate Tectonics is a Myth.*, Terrella Press; 1 edition (March 6, 2015) 2009-2011.

**Figure 5.** The traditional direction lines of magnetic fields are from south to north and are opposite of G1 particle flows as described in the Particle Model [1]

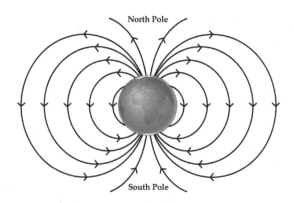

**Figure 6.** The direction of the magnetic field as descibed be the de Hilsters are moving out of the north pole, around the earth, and into the south pole

# The Solution to the Ice Age Extinctions

## Forrest Bishop

*POB 30121, Seattle, WA, 98113, forrestb@ix.netcom.com*

Hundreds of animal species famously died out during the last Ice Age. The reasons behind the Ice Age, Pleistocene, or Quaternary, megafaunal extinctions have been puzzled over for more than a century without any clear resolution. The problem has been called the 'Fermat's Last Theorem of paleobiology'. These extinctions took place over thousands of years and around the world, but there was a strange specificity about which animals could stay and which had to go. There are two major theories about what caused this, the human-hunting theory and the climate-change theory. Both, yet in curious ways, are wrong. The true cause has to do with particular strengths and weaknesses of biological processes, and it unfolded over almost the entire history of life on Earth.

This is a science story about a murder mystery. The title is a double entendre and this is the most important story ever told.

**Keywords:** Pleistocene, Quaternary, megafauna, extinction, Ice Age, climate change

## 1. Introduction

Science is a collection of stories we like to tell each other about how the world works. This one is a detective story, with some unwitting suspects, their multiple victims, and quiet heroes. The tale has been told before, with us, the human race, as the prime murder suspect. We, the usual suspects, are framed as the Scapegoat in those legends. Other accounts retell the coming of the Sky Monsters, different kinds of beings that go by different names. "Comet" is one of those names.

In a durable science story all the known pieces fit and work together. No part conflicts with any other part; no actor acts out of character. Nothing should have to be cut from whole cloth and entered into evidence without proof. This has been the problem with the account of the Ice Age deaths of the megafauna. [1] All of these wonderful animals had sailed through the previous Ice Ages unscathed. What was different this time? If human hunters killed off this one species then why didn't they kill off that other one, too? How could they possibly have exterminated any of them for that matter? Why did a colder climate kill animals that were better adapted for it than other animals that weren't as well adapted, yet survived? The biggest animals should have had the best chance of surviving the cold, not the worst. If the sabertooth cat got sabertooth-cat disease, then why didn't the lion get lion disease? If the gardener crept in through the window, why didn't the dog bark?

There were patterns to the murders in time and place as well as in the kinds of victims chosen. These patterns give us clues as to the modus operandi of the perpetrators, who were clearly very selective, very discriminating.

Certain tropes recur throughout natural history, most of which I'll have to leave out for brevity. One of course is inter-species warfare, another mass extinction. Another is a recurring theme in colonization: first the new life spreads out across the surface, there to ascend vertically into the space above. But patterns are made and patterns can be broken and this pattern was broken in the instant case.

One standard of proof for murder is 'beyond a reasonable doubt'. These cases generally involve events taking place a few weeks or months in the past, with the police detective acting as an historian and a scientist of sorts. They often enough result in false convictions, just as have the megafaunal extinctions. For events taking place thousands or millions of years ago, long before we arrived on the scene with the proper forensic tools, we have to look at as many suspects as possible, no matter how innocent they might appear to be. Maybe the butler did it. We'll have to investigate him of course, it's de rigueur for the genre, but we mustn't spoil the read by jumping to conclusions. Even if he had done it, he must have had accomplices for a job the size of this one.

In order to positively identify the suspects, as well as the heroes, we will need to reach back a long, long way in time. As with any crime, we try to come to an understanding of the criminal's means, their motive, and their opportunity in a given setting. We have to set the scene of the crime, look at the furniture around it, find out who the players are. For these particular suspects, their case history spans almost the entire record of life on Earth.

## 2. The Spring of Life

Like a camera lens, the further we try to look back in time the fainter the picture becomes, a hazy, distant mountain. As we look closer to our time, the story comes into better focus. The camera we have to use is the record in the stone. The lower the layer sits in the stratigraphic record, the older it should be.

None of the ancient dates are reliable; they all rely on untestable hypotheses- assumptions outside the purview of our science. No one can know if radioactive decay rates have been steady for billions of years past, or even if the Earth's history stretches back many billions of years. There is plenty of evidence that the decay rates aren't even steady today. No one has a calibrated "molecular clock" that can date genetic changes far into the past. No one was watching when the sedimentary rocks were laid down, tracking the actual rates of sedimentation, or even seeing quite *how* they were laid down.

For present purposes these dating details are not important. For ease of reference, I'll hew to the various published, though often in dispute, timelines as closely as possible. It is the sequence, the order of events, which matters, not the precise dating of each development. These developments follow in a logical order, the order found in the layers of rock, one more or less on top of the next, that seal the fossil remains. One thing led to the next, the next could not have happened otherwise, and some of it was written in stone, in a broken and cryptic language we have partially learned to read.

Four billion peer-reviewed years ago, the stones tell us that Earth's primordial atmosphere was made up mostly of nitrogen, carbon dioxide, and a few other gasses. There was no oxygen in the air at all, no life in the water, and the land was as desolate as the surface of Mars. Sometime after that life came in to being in the water, somehow. We do not know how or why this happened, nor have we been able to reproduce it in the lab. That mystery remains beyond the limits of our scientific knowledge, but, fortunately enough, won't spoil this tale.

These first carbon-based life forms were simple by the standards of today, single-celled, tiny bags of complex chemicals. They were like microscopic "plants" of sorts, lifeforms that could make more like themselves from the energy and chemicals in the world around them. Some of them became able to use the power of the Sun for their energy and got their carbon from carbon dioxide dissolved in the water. This was the first invention of photosynthesis, though it did not involve oxygen in any way. They were anaerobic organisms using other chemicals, perhaps dissolved iron and hydrogen sulphide. [2]

Three more complicated forms of life were invented along the way. One was the cell with a nucleus, which serves as an inner motte to keep and protect the DNA from invaders. Another was the rise of the multiple-cell form, a story easy enough to tell by imagining a division of a cell into two, which then stayed with each other, as embryonic cells do. The third kind is recognized as a type of invasion. One kind of cell entered into another of a different kind, whether by invitation or not, there to take up residence in a symbiotic relationship. The photosynthetic chloroplast and the animal mitochondria share this story, as the invaders that settled in. All higher forms of life- including us- are composites, chimeras, or mosaics, of all three of these processes.

Sometime after the invention of anaerobic photosynthesis a new kind of photosynthesis appeared, again we know not how. [3] These new microscopic creatures also used the power of the Sun and took in carbon dioxide, but they gave off highly-reactive, toxic oxygen in their waste. Over the next billion or two years, the two types of primitive "plant" life forms (no one is really sure what to call them) were in a struggle to the death. Each was the poison of the other. This may have been the first existential war on Earth, a war which only one of them could win. [4]

The microscopic anaerobic armies had already occupied all of the contested territory, the waters of the world. They had that advantage. But the younger aerobic organisms had a terrific weapon in the oxygen they gave off. Some of that went into the air and slowly oxidised the rocks on the land. It burned down the iron in the seawater too, oxidizing it. The rusted iron fell to the bottom of the sea, there to become our iron ore deposits. This was a long slow process until finally a tipping point was reached perhaps 850 million years ago, when the oxygen level rose to something like what it is today. The old anaerobic forms retreated to a few tiny strongholds and green, oxygenic photosynthesis became the way of life from then on. In this long global battle, Life had remodeled the air and the water of an entire planet, but there was an accumulating cost, a debit on account, to be paid for dearly come the future.

## 3. The Summer of Life

The Cambrian Explosion took place in two major phases. After a pre-Cambrian prelude, all kinds of new animals came into being to spread over the floor of the shallow sea, growing out of it, crawling across it, and burrowing into the sediment. Most of these models were entirely new- new body plans, new features like eyes and legs, new arrangements of parts. Then, after a long delay, more new kinds of life were invented that could float and swim, ascending into the waters above like the second stage of a rocket.

The trilobites are the most famous of these Cambrian critters. Darwin called their sudden appearance with no ancestors "undoubtedly of the gravest nature" for the fitness and survival of his theory. Since his time all sorts of other exotic Cambrian critters, some with fundamental design ideas, have been discovered: none of them have known ancestors either. Most of these fundamental types have disappeared without further trace, never to reappear, a lost mystery of not-convergent evolution.

We've seen two of the several kinds of creation of new life forms. For Invention of the First Kind, the new organisms appear in the fossil record as if from out of nowhere. Science may be able to explain how that works and reproduce it in the lab someday; today is not that day. In Invention of the Second Kind, two existing parent organisms create a child organism, like in the story about the chloroplasts. This second process is recognized in many ways in addition to sexual reproduction- hybridization, horizontal gene transfer, symbiosis, metamorphosis, mitochondria, and so on. Genetic engineering is an artificial form of the second kind. Neither of these two processes are Darwinian- there is no identifiable common ancestor; the new organism arises immediately. The creation of a new lifeform by the joining together of two older forms in one step is Darwin's Tree of Life turned exactly upside down. It is the opposite of descent by gradual modification. In the far distant future, a page or two from now, we will encounter a third kind of invention, almost as mysterious as the first, as if from ideas in the air.

The records and the stories are obscure here as to how and when the next epic expansion happened. In one story, an algae teamed up with a fungus, got up out of the water and called itself lichen, a land plant. These and other kinds of composite plant-things first stormed the beaches, then pushed upward and forward into the interior, breathing in carbon dioxide, exhaling oxygen. These original land plants were only a few centimeters tall at best, spreading out across the surface of the continents. Then new kinds of plants rose above the old ones as little stems. The stems didn't have much area to gather sunlight and $CO_2$, so a leaf came along. The stems with their leaves could now make the ascent into the space above as before, calling themselves ferns and trees, creating whole forests. The forests spread out to cover all of the continents, even Antarctica. There were new kinds of animals that could eat these new kinds of plants.

The first microscopic lifeforms left us their messages in ancient rock like mudstones, shales, and limestones, written in letters so tiny they cannot be seen by the unaided eye. Later on many fossils became large enough to see, then large enough to require trucks to haul their bones to the museum. The largest fossils of them all are those stones they left behind, not too tiny to see but too big to see. Some of these fossils are limestone reefs so gigantic they've become member states in the UN, like Tuvalu and Bermuda. Other marine fossils were given names like the Cliffs of Dover, or the Alps. The forests that once covered the continents have new names too, like Powder River Basin and Coal Measures Group. These are the fossils that tell us just how massive life use to be. By comparison, our world is a battered remnant of what once was.

In the warm and glorious salad days of the Summer of Life the Earth was alive all across the continents and from pole to pole. In a lighter gravity, giant dinosaurs arrived and giant dinosaurs departed. Some were so tall they could eat the giant leaves from the tops of the giant trees. They served even brontosaurus steaks at the drive-in restaurants in those high-flying days. This was a time when scholarly tripwires were invented. Giant flying things flew through the air; giant swimming things swum through the sea. Some days were warmer, others were cooler, some more humid, others more arid, but never was there ice at the poles. Mountains were raised up and mountains worn down; the continents split apart; the oceans opened up, rising onto the land only to fall back to the shelves; volcanoes erupted then were stilled. Flowers were invented towards the end of the dinosaur's reign, then grass, that uncanny flowering plant.

In all the ages before there had been no grass.

## 4. The Autumn of Life

Around the time the dinosaurs left us, or maybe sometime after, the Earth began to get colder. [5] There was a brief Indian Summer of an Eocene High, followed by the Azolla Event perhaps 50 million years ago. In that event, a floating super-plant either covered the beaches around the Arctic Ocean, or even covered the entire ocean itself, for thousands of years. As the Azolla plants died, they sank to the bottom. The meters-thick, carbon-rich sediments that they left spread across the floor of the Arctic Ocean are thought to be the last of the great carbon deposits on Earth.

The Azolla died off in the Arctic, never to return. As the Earth continued to cool, ice began to appear in Antarctica, the first frost of the approaching Winter. During and after the Azolla Event, the $CO_2$ concentration in the air dropped, as if the Arctic super-plants were using it up. But the $CO_2$ didn't recover the previous level after the plants were gone. Instead, the lower level persisted, with plenty of oscillations, and with the caveat again that our reading of the ancient records is spotty and prone to error. [6]

### 4.1. The Descent

In the earlier stories, new life spread out across the surface, then ascended into the space above. This pattern was broken in this case. Forests that once spanned continents and reached for the sky were destroyed, burned down and replaced by grasslands and deserts. [7] There had always been forest fires for as long as trees had existed, but this time there was something different. Before, when the trees burned down new tress would grow back up. This time the trees never returned.

The destruction took place in stages over millions of years. It started as a patchwork, or mosaic, of forest and grassland, then the grassy areas expanded and the forested land decreased. Eventually, and not that long ago, some regions became entirely grass and scrub lands- the Great Plains, the Savannah, the Steppes, the Outback. [8]

Sometime in this period, after the dinosaurs but before the Ice Ages, two new kinds of green photosynthesis came around somehow, a story you've heard before. Up until a few million years ago, all green, oxygenic plants were of a single kind, called "C3 photosynthesis", the kind that was invented back in the 'Spring of Life'. Two new types

are introduced in the 'Autumn of Life', called "CAM" and "C4" photosynthesis. These are both more adept at conserving water in arid conditions and at vacuuming up aerial $CO_2$. [9] CAM plays a lesser role in the world, found in succulents like pineapple and in desert plants.

C4-style photosynthesis becomes a popular choice for the grasses and sedges in the new grass lands, but not all at once. As before, there was a long period of 'gestation', as it were. Then, something like five million years ago, this type of grass became more prevalent. [10] As before, C4 photosynthesis did not arise in a single common ancestor and radiate out in a "Tree of Life", Darwinian fashion anymore than chloroplasts, mitochondria, eyes, or legs did. Instead, it appeared independently and nearly simultaneously in a wide variety of plants, as if the idea were plucked from the air. [11]

### 4.2. Sizing up a Hungry Herbivore

Naturally enough, along with the new grasslands came the animals that like to eat the grass and the animals that like to eat the animals that like to eat the grass.

There are limits to how big an animal can be, whether predator or prey. The most famous of these is the square-cube law, a static relation which limits the size of an animal in a gravitational field, for one important example. But there are dynamic limits as well. The bigger the animal, the more food it needs every day. The more food it needs, the further it has to travel from one food source to the next. The Blue Whale might be the epitome of this process; it has to sweep up huge volumes of water to filter out the krill. But it has an advantage over land animals- at low speeds it can move through the water very efficiently, almost without friction.

An herbivore has to walk across a two-dimensional terrain from one plant to the next, which costs a lot of energy. It usually has to eat a bit from many different plants and leave enough so the plant can grow back. The distance it has to travel depends on the size of the plant it is eating, the amount of vegetation per unit area. The size the plant can grow to depends on how fast it can grow between feedings. This adds up to a general rule: for a given rate of plant growth, the bigger the animal gets, the farther it has to walk for food.

A reduction in plant growth rates, for whatever reason, will affect the bigger animal much sooner because it can't walk too far for its food. With all else equal in a simplified example, if a 100 kg herbivore needs to move 10 km per day to get from one plant to the next, then a 1000 kg herbivore would need to move ten times as far, or 100 km per day. It also has to transport ten times as much mass over the extra distance, which takes ten times as much force. With energy as force times distance, the bigger animal would need 100 times as much food-energy to do that, not just ten times as much. So, just from this simple physics, the bigger animal has to eat more of the vegetation in a given area. It will exceed the carrying capacity of the land sooner than the smaller animal will.

## 4.3. The Biological Carbon Cycle

Our field detectives, the ones who specialize in cold cases, have dug up some tantalizing leads. Back in the early days of the oxygen wars, the original atmosphere of the Earth was mostly nitrogen and carbon dioxide. It turns out that the $CO_2$ content was something over ten percent of the total (>100,000 ppm), or at least 250 times as much as today's 400 ppm. Yet the global temperatures weren't that much different in the 'Spring of Life'; there were even several extended Ice Ages back then that don't bear on this story.

From that ancient time, through the Summer of Life, and on to the Azolla Event, the atmospheric $CO_2$ concentration had been falling on average, though with plenty of fluctuations. This reduction can't account for the size of those mountains of limestone and the rest because the amount of carbon in the air, even at 100 percent, is too little. What it does tell us is that the average replacement rate of carbon dioxide, spanning millions of years, has been just a bit lower than the consumption rate. Life had been just a bit too exuberant, too wasteful, starting from the very first carbon-bearing deposits laid down by the original anaerobic plant-things, through the spectacular Summer of Life, and on to the present day.

These $CO_2$ sources, which may be mostly volcanoes and seeps, are intermittent and fluctuating. No one actually knows where it all comes from. Perhaps some of the mass extinctions of the distant past (the 'Summer of Life') might have been caused or exacerbated by $CO_2$ starvation if the replacement rate temporarily dropped below the consumption rate.

The vegetation of the world, both on land and in the sea, acts like a tremendous, planetary-scale vacuum cleaner, sifting the carbon dioxide right out of the air. Each summer in the northern hemisphere where most of the plants live, the global atmospheric $CO_2$ level drops noticeably, by several ppm. It rises again in the winter, when the plants aren't growing as fast, and some are decomposing. We can make a lot of hay from this fantastic fact:

1. The vacuum nozzle effect. In order for the global $CO_2$ level to drop, the local $CO_2$ level has to drop a lot more, just as a vacuum cleaner is most powerful right at the nozzle. The air around a growing plant is going to be $CO_2$ starved (and oxygen enriched). *This is one of the major keys to the mystery of the Ice Age extinctions.*

2. The annual drop, in total tonnage, not ppm, must have been very much larger in the past, in the Summer of Life when the Earth was warmer and luxurious vegetation spanned the planet. Therefore the $CO_2$ concentration must have been much higher back then, otherwise the plants would have starved in late summer. This of course is supported by many other lines of inquiry.

3. A higher rate of photosynthesis would drop today's $CO_2$ summertime level down further than what we see. The faster the $CO_2$ is dropping out of the system, the faster it has to be replaced somehow. In the Summer of Life that replacement rate had to have been far higher than it is today because the total rate of photosynthesis (land and sea) was far higher. Most of the replacement $CO_2$ comes from volcanoes and fissures on land and under the sea, so these must be much less active today than yesterday.

4. The more tonnage of $CO_2$ in the annual cycle, the more of it that is precipitating out of the system and turning to stone.

As the carbon dioxide level falls below the maximum concentration that the plants can use, the rate of growth of the plants will slow down. All of the herbivores will have to to expend more energy to go from one now-smaller plant to the next. All of the predators have to expend more energy to track down their prey.

**\*\*\*\*\*\*\*\*\*\***

We've identified a rather large and insidious gang of suspects- photosynthetic plants, that is- for the impending mass murders, but we mustn't be too harsh in our judgment. After all, they were just doing their job and they had families to feed too- not to mention all those lovely and innocent animals they so selflessly supported. With these mitigating circumstances in mind, we'll need to investigate a little further before passing judgment. We'll also have to consider the sentencing so as not to inflict undue punishment. Ideally, the punishment should fit the crime, and this was a most uncanny crime.

## 5. The Winter of Life

The debate about the causes behind the Quaternary Extinction Event has gone on for a long time without resolution. The pattern of extinctions doesn't seem to make sense. Things don't add up. Into this vacuum other theories- stories- about exotic diseases, comets, and black swan events, have been put forth. I made up a new story awhile ago too, about Earth's gravity increasing just a tiny bit, just enough to make today's elephant and giraffe the biggest and the tallest possible animals, and the condor or albatross the biggest possible birds. Any of these things- comets, gravity, disease, hunting, black swans, the Ice Age [15], [5], and the climate, [13]- may well be a part of the truest story, but none of them can stand on their own. There are too many specific cases that don't fit: the Ice Age megafauna extinctions were so very selective. Very discriminating.

Many of the extinct animals were quite large, the biggest ever of their kind- beavers the size of bears, armadillos as big as cars, giant kangaroos, the largest mammals of all time, the largest marsupials of all time. All the horses and camels in the Americas died out along with giant eagles and terror birds, an even bigger cousin of the huge Komodo dragon, giant turtles, all kinds of different elephant-like animals in Africa, and so many more. Yet not very many plants went extinct, another curiosity, another clue. The sizing problem of a herbivore explains a great deal of the problem but is still too general.

**Figure 7.** Man, possibly with some of the Pleistocene giants

The human-hunting idea has what amounts to a military problem. Our ancient parents were as bands of Hobbits surrounded by armies of giant Orcs numbering in the hundreds of millions between their different kinds. A field marshal, reviewing his rag tag tribe of midgets armed with sticks and arrows, would have to weigh those facts against his enemy's tooth and claw, tusk, armor, size, and troop strength. He would have to retire from the field, discretion being the better part of valor.

We saw this dynamic play out in North America in historical times. The Great Plains Indians could not subdue the immense herds of bison that ranged across the prairie lands. Even after the gifts of the horse and the gun, there were still too many buffalo and not enough Indians. They couldn't build cities because cities need farms, and farms would be plundered by the Million Bison Army. So they had to move their teepees around, always being careful not to pick a place that was too lush, too open, too attractive. They lived on the fringes of Bison Kingdom.

As CO2 levels fell, C4 plants became more prevalent. This was when the ruminant grazing animals, such as cattle, were invented, animals with multiple-chamber stomachs and specialized, symbiotic bacteria that can ferment and digest the less-nutritious C4 plants. Bison, for example, graze on C4 plants. After the mass extinctions their predators were mostly gone along with their grazing competitors. The bison were alone on the range, free to take it over in vast numbers.

As C4 plants became more prevalent, other animals that were C3 grazers tried to make the switch with varying levels of success. [12] Some of them became hindgut ruminants, a sort of halfway measure. Other ate both kinds of plants. Towards the end, some of these different herbivores were competing with each other by eating from the same dwindling food supply.

There were hundreds of species that went extinct, thousands that survived, and each one has a story to tell. I haven't been able to investigate every case in this first story but so far the confirm rate is well in the majority. There are big C3 browsing animals that survived as well as small grazers that went extinct, so the match is good, but not perfect. The giraffe is a big browser but it has the distinguished advantage of being able to eat from the tops of C3 trees, where no other animal can reach. And so on.

## 5.1. World War C4

During this most recent Ice Age, the *average* atmospheric CO2 concentration dropped to about 180 ppm, the lowest level in the history of the Earth. As the ice sheets built up, the ocean level dropped, reducing the evaporation surface area that produces rain, so the global climate was also drier as well as colder.

The lower CO2 level can't explain by itself why only certain animals went extinct and others did not. Climate change- the Ice Age, the cold, the drier air, less rainfall- explains a great part of it, but it runs into the specificity problem. That should have affected many more plants and animals, not just certain ones. Like climate change, a lower CO2 level is too indiscriminate. But there is another diabolical piece to this puzzle, one I have not found put in its proper place before.

At low CO2 levels, C3 plants are competing, with major disadvantages, against C4 plants. [16] C4 plants have other advantages over C3 plants- they are more efficient with water use and better adapted to drier conditions. [17] They have a disadvantage of needing more energy to run their kind of photosynthesis but that can't help the C3 plant compete if the CO2 level is too low.

All year round a C3 plant in a field of C4 grasses is going to be relatively starved of CO2 because of the local "vacuum-cleaner nozzle" effect. That effect becomes more pronounced at lower concentration levels and in still or slowly-moving air near the ground. Imagine a huge expanse of C4 grassland with one C3 plant in the middle of it, with CO2 at 180 ppm. As air slowly moves across the plain, the C4 grass is vacuuming the CO2 out of it, even down to 20 ppm locally. As long as that air isn't mixing too much with the air overhead, the CO2 concentration will fall with the reach, the distance the air travels. Once it falls from 180 to about 120 ppm locally, C3 plants will stop growing altogether. If an animal eats that plant, the plant will not be able to grow back.

At the same time, the animals that eat the C3 plants, which also includes ruminant grazers that can eat both kinds, are preferentially removing the C3 varieties, which cannot grow back as fast as C4 plants. This opens up more growing area for the C4 grasses, shrubs, and what we call weeds for good reason.

As CO2 levels drop in summer, the relative C4 growing advantage increases. If the average in the record is 180 ppm, it might have been dropping to 170 ppm in late summer just from this cause. A summertime drop to 170 ppm globally implies an even greater drop locally, amplifying the already tremendous advantage that the C4 plants have. This is when many animals are eating the most to store up for winter. If the animal doesn't get enough food during this crucial time, it will die before the following spring. Most, but not all, of the herbivores that died were either C3 browsers, C3 grazers, or giant C4 grazers. The mystery of the Ice Age extinctions is mostly solved by this, with caveats and exceptions.

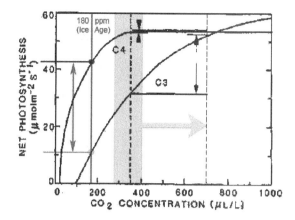

**Figure 8.** Generalized growth rates of C3 and C4 plants. Red double arrow is the C3-C4 growth-rate difference during the last Ice Age, at 180 ppm CO2. C3 plants stop growing (i.e. die) at 100 ppm; C4 plants stop at 20 ppm. Green band is the increase due to artificial CO2 emissions, from 280 ppm ca. 1900 to 400 ppm in 2016. When the CO2 concentration reaches over 800 ppm, C3 plants have the advantage (green arrow).

We see a potential repeat of the ancient, existential wars which gave us our oxygen atmosphere. At low CO2, C4 plants are the mortal enemies of C3 plants. The terrible CO2-vacuum weapon of C4 photosynthesis would assure their globalist victory and the annihilation of C3 plants and all that depend on them. If the unknown geological carbon sources were to shut off completely, the remaining C4 land plants would then be at war with each other, struggling over the last available atoms of carbon.

**********

There is more to C4 photosynthesis than simply a different chemical or metabolic pathway. It has certain architectural features about it, in the way the cells are arranged in rings, or wreaths, and in the layout of the core C4 photosynthetic process itself. With the older C3 process, both CO2 and O2 molecules are presented to the metabolic engines, which only need the CO2. The O2 then has to be sorted out and turned away after it has already gummed up the works, a sloppy process. The great advance of C4 was to solve this problem with the addition of a kind of airlock, a parlour if you will, where the CO2 is first introduced and the O2 is turned away at the door. The carbon is then ushered to the portal of the inner chamber where the fixation process will be done. You may think of it as the same function performed by the butler receiving visitors to the great house.

Very selective. Very discriminating.

## 6. Epilogue

**Figure 9.** Net change in regional biomass from satellite data, 1982-2011; darkest green represents >10 per cent increase [18]

Before the last Ice Age began, a new kind of creature, the one we call Man, came into the world somehow. We don't know quite how, scientifically, but there he is. He was small and weak compared to the giants that walked the Earth in those days, a bit like the mammals at the feet of the dinosaurs.

With the passing of the glorious beasts during the last and worst Ice Age, the way was made clear around the world for Man to come occupy the land. We did not take their world from them; they had to leave it. [19] We learned how to eat the grasses too: not by ruminating, by cooking them with fire. This was probably first tried out of desperation, when the game was gone and the famines began. The C3 and C4 grasses that had replaced the ancient forests became the basis of the Agricultural Revolution and the rise of our uncanny civilizations. Farms and towns were invented even as the last ice sheets were retreating to the North.

Then, a few lifetimes ago, our quiet heroes showed us how to rip the coal from the ground and turn it into the power of the Industrial Revolution, paving the way for the human population to increase many times over. In that process, the carbon in the fossil fuel was burned to CO2, enriching Earth's atmosphere once again.

The Earth is getting greener now, across the globe. [18] Our ascended satellites watch it growing, each decade more lush than the one before. [20] With the ongoing CO2 enrichment, food for over seven billion people is now grown on less land than it took to feed three billion just half a century ago. [21] More land is becoming available for wildlife. [22] The climate change people are also aware of these matters- the subject of this story- it is in their massive reports, filed under "Carbon Sink, Land". [23]

Compared to the permanent devastation that the very next drop in atmospheric CO2 could cause, an all-out nuclear war, or even an asteroid strike like in one of the dinosaur-extinction stories, are mere blips on the radar screen. A severe enough drop in aerial carbon dioxide would mean the extinction of all higher life on land, great and small. [24] Without this CO2 the Earth would revert to conditions worse than they were a billion years ago.

Life trapped in the oceans would go on for some time after that, freewheeling off the last remains of available carbon, but no matter how advanced the sea creatures become they would never be able to build a fire or reach for the stars. After the oceanic creatures pass away, no complex life would exist anywhere in the Universe that we know of.

In order to continue to exist and to prosper, life on Earth needs one more trick, the one thing that not one of the marvelous inventions of all the eons past had ever been able to accomplish. There has to be some way, somehow, to wrench the locked carbon up out of the earth, to throw it back into the air.

We are that way. We make the keys that unlock the carbon from the stone and return it to the world. We are the solution to the impending extinction of life and this is the most important story ever heard.

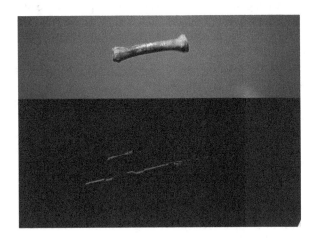

## REFERENCES

1.  Brook, Barry W. and David M. J. S. Bowman, *Explaining the Pleistocene megafaunal extinctions: Models, chronologies, and assumptions*, PNAS, 99, 2002, http://www.pnas.org/content/99/23/14624.full

2.  Cardona,Tanai, James Murray, and William Rutherford, *Origin and Evolution of Water Oxidation before the Last Common Ancestor of the Cyanobacteria*, Molecular Biology and Evolution, 32, 2015, http://mbe.oxfordjournals.org/content/32/5/1310

3.  Tomitani, Akiko, and Andrew H. Knoll, *The evolutionary diversification of cyanobacteria: Molecular-phylogenetic and paleontological perspectives*, PNAS, 103, 2006, http://www.pnas.org/content/103/14/5442.full

4.  Georgiades, Kalliopi and Didier Raoult, *The rhizome of Reclinomonas americana, Homo sapiens, Pediculus humanus and Saccharomyces cerevisiae mitochondri*, Biology Direct, 10, 2011, http://biologydirect.biomedcentral.com/articles/10.1186/1745-6150-6-55

5.  McCarroll, D., âĂŸStudy the past, if you would divine the futureâĂŹ: a retrospective on measuring and understanding Quaternary climate change, Journal of Quaternary Science, 30, 2015

6.  Pagani, Mark et al, *Marked Decline in Atmospheric Carbon Dioxide Concentrations During the Paleogene*, Science, 309, 5734, 2005

7. Osborne, Colin P., *Atmosphere, ecology and evolution: what drove the Miocene expansion of C4 grasslands?*, Journal of Ecology, 96, 2007, http://onlinelibrary.wiley.com/doi/10.1111/j.1365-2745.2007.01323.x/full

8. Norris, J. and J. L. Betancourt, *Inferences about winter temperatures and summer rains from the late Quaternary record of C4 perennial grasses and C3 desert shrubs in the northern Chihuahuan Desert*, Journal of Quaternary Science, 22, 2006, http://onlinelibrary.wiley.com/doi/10.1002/jqs.1023/abstract

9. Pascal-Antoine, Christin, et al, *Oligocene CO2 Decline Promoted C4 Photosynthesis in Grasses*, Current Biology, 18, 2008, http://www.cell.com/current-biology/fulltext/S0960-9822(07)02344-5

10. Osborne, Colin P and David J Beerling, *Nature's green revolution: the remarkable evolutionary rise of C4 plants*, PHILOSOPHICAL TRANSACTIONS OF THE ROYAL SOCIETY B,

11. Edwards, Erika J. and Stephen A. Smith, *Phylogenetic analyses reveal the shady history of C4 grasses*, PNAS, 107, 2010, https://www.ncbi.nlm.nih.gov/pmc/articles/PMC2823882/

12. Uno, Kevin T. et al, *Late Miocene to Pliocene carbon isotope record of differential diet change among East African herbivores*, PNAS, 108, 2011, http://www.pnas.org/content/108/16/6509.full

13. Bush, M. B. and M. R. Silman, *Observations on Late Pleistocene cooling and precipitation in the lowland Neotropics*, Journal of Quaternary Science, 19, 2004

14. Edwards, Erika J. et al, *The Origins of C4 Grasslands: Integrating Evolutionary and Ecosystem Science*, Science, 328, 5978, 2010

15. Tripati, Aradhna K et al, *Coupling of CO2 and Ice Sheet Stability Over Major Climate Transitions of the Last 20 Million Years*, Science, 326, 5958, 2009

16. Wand, S.J.E. et al, *Responses of wild C4 and C3 grass (Poaceae) species to elevated atmospheric CO2 concentration: a meta-analytic test of current theories and perceptions*, Global Change Biology, 5, 1999, http://www.co2science.org/articles/V2/N21/B3.php

17. L.H. Ziska and Bunce, J.A., *Effect of elevated carbon dioxide concentration at night on the growth and gas exchange of selected C4 species*, Australian Journal of Plant Physiology, 26, 1999, http://www.co2science.org/articles/V3/N10/B4.php

18. Zhu, Zaichun, et al, *Greening of the Earth and its drivers*, Nature Climate Change, 2016, http://www.nature.com/nclimate/journal/vaop/ncurrent/full/nclimate3004.html

19. Joseph, Rhawn, *Extinction, Metamorphosis, Evolutionary Apoptosis, and Genetically Programmed Species Mass Death*, Journal of Cosmology pp235-255, 2, 1, 2009

20. Ramsayer, Kate, *NASA studies details of a greening Arctic*, 2016, http://climate.nasa.gov/news/2447/

21. Rutan, Burt, *An Engineer's Critique of Global Warming 'Science'*, 2011, http://burtrutan.com/downloads/EngrCritiqueCAGW-v4o3.pdf

22. Unknown, *Photosynthesis and CO2 Enrichment*, 2009, https://buythetruth.wordpress.com/2009/06/13/photosynthesis-and-co2-enrichment/

23. *IPCC Fourth Assessment Report: Climate Change 2007 (AR4)*, 2007, http://www.ipcc.ch/report/ar4/

24. Moore, Patrick, *Should We Celebrate CO2?*, 2015, http://www.thegwpf.com/28155/

# The Forbidden Equation: $i = qc$

## Forrest Bishop

*POB 30121, Seattle, WA, 98113, forrestb@ix.netcom.com*

*Mr. Bishop's label "the forbidden equation" is actually quite appropriate. But, it is not just because he has found no one else who mentions or uses it; rather, it is because it should be forbidden from physics, not admired as a new discovery about physics. - Prof. William A. Gardner, Electrical Engineering, UC Davis*

There is any number of equations used to describe electric current. But there is one simple equation that is seldom to be found in any Academic textbook or Peer-reviewed journal article. Yet what I've named "The Forbidden Equation", $i = qc$, is nothing more or less than the defining equation of electric current, with $i$ the electric current, $q$ the net line charge per unit length, and $c$ the speed of light. It is apparent why this equation is buried so deeply as to be unheard of- it destroys the idea of electric current, and all that descends from that idea, by its very definition. There have been a few recent sightings of The Forbidden Equation, all curiously enough in papers addressing The Catt Question.

$i = qc$ is a mainstream equation, inseparably contained within their other electromagnetic equations and easily derived from them using elementary algebra. It is Gardner's Equation, Maxwell's Equation, and Einstein's Equation as well. Behold the abyss.

**Keywords:** Catt question, electric current, Maxwell Equations, transmission line, electric charge

## 1. $i = qc$: Introduction

There is any number, depending on whom you talk to, of equations used to describe electric current, but there is one simple equation gone missing. A years-long search has not turned it up in any of hundreds of relevant textbooks and papers. (late update- found it in one book, see Addendum) Yet $i = qc$ is nothing more or less than the defining equation of electric current, the continuity equation for electric charge in an electric circuit or a transmission line... or would be.

I stumbled across this little equation myself in 2008 while manipulating some of the other lesser-known equations of electric current, the ones they don't quite teach you in Physics, or Aerospace, or Electrical Engineering. At the time it seemed interesting but I did not work through its many ramifications until sometime later. [1] It is apparent why this equation is not to be mentioned- it destroys the idea of electric current by its very definition, as your messenger will show you. [2]

$i = qc$ is an old, though implicit, mainstream equation. It is not at all "Mr. Bishop's... new discovery about physics" as William A. Gardner thought. It is inseparably contained within the other conventional equations. It is Maxwell's Equation. It is Gardner's Equation, who is quite correct in that it should not be admired as a new discovery. [3] Yet even with coaching he was unable to provide a derivation, and apparently did not think such a derivation was possible. The promoters of Maxwell's Equations and the rest have clearly not thought through the math in their own theory(s).

In August of 2012, after my publication the preceding May [1], came the first Academic sighting of "The For-bidden Equation", from The Clarendon at Oxford, no less. [4] It came in an email, over the e-transom from a secondary source. We (Catt, myself, and other interested parties) were told that the author was a physics teacher or a physicist at The Clarendon who wished to remain anonymous. His friend at Oxford, Dr. John Roche*, said that "Anonymous of Clarendon", as we came to call him, had taken ill or something. To distinguish this work, we began to call his six-page, handwritten treatise "The Clarendon Letter", even though Anonymous had titled it "The Catt Question". [5] Anonymous surfaced later on and turned out to be Dr. C.W.P. Palmer, and the story we were told proved to be true.

*It turns out that Roche had earlier played a pivotal, historic role in the unfolding story of **The Forbidden Arrow**, the arrow that must not be noticed, drawn, or discussed, a tale for another day.

Poor Prof. C.W.P. Palmer of The Clarendon did not realize, at least not consciously, that he had committed a grave heresy. He did take the precaution of anonymously publishing The Forbidden Equation, and did lay low for some time, but I know for a fact, a provable fact, that he had not thought through the ramifications of this blasphemy. How could he? You see, The Forbidden Equation is so toxic, so devastating to Modern Physics that most of them have probably never even heard of it let alone thought about it.

My next sighting of The Forbidden Equation was in 2013, and again in a published response to The Catt Question. [6] This time the equation was a bit more disguised, broken into pieces. The Italian electrical engineering professors, like Palmer, attempted to join it up with their version of an equation for electron drift current. They left this derivation out of their IEEE article, opting instead to include it in a "physics education" magazine. This attempt at "joining two speeds together" fails for several reasons, not the least of which is that the particles in a current can only move at one speed at a time. Attempts by several people [7] to correct the sundry libels and errors of the Italians by publishing letters in these same journals were rebuked, though this may change.

In re: The Clarendon Letter; On 12/18/2012 1:36 PM, Ivor Catt wrote: [2]

Dear Forrest,

IC: *You point to the equation having been written by someone in the Establishment. Note that I have never written it...*

IC: *It is extraordinary that I have trouble progressing to the "obvious" conclusion...*

IC: *...Do you, Forrest, think that the mere statement* i = qc *refutes classical theory, showing us that since charge gained mass in around 1900, classical theory was no longer fit for purpose?*

FB: *Yes,* i = qc *means that q has to be massless because c is the only speed at which this equation can hold... The Clarendon man makes a valiant attempt to save classical theory... but his argument fails for several reasons.*

IC: *It is interesting to think of the possibility that when reasoning is taking one to see a fallacy in the classical paradigm, common sense ceases to operate, even in me...*

FB: *...we are all imprinted (or infected, choose your poison) with certain patterns of thought at a very early age that become such second nature that we don't even realize they are there. I don't think there was a vast conspiracy to squelch* i = qc*... rather it mostly\* happens as a natural progression in the transmission of culture.*

FB: *\*I'm thinking here of higher-ups that do occasionally see the problems but don't talk when there is a duty to speak...*

Behold the abyss:

## 2.  $i = qc$: Deriving The Forbidden Equation

There are a myriad of ways to derive $i = qc$ depending on which variables one begins with. With caveats, you may begin from Maxwell's Equations for example. You may also construct $i = qc$ by reconstituting the expression $i = Q/t$ (with $Q$ the charge passing through a plane), a truncated equation that can be found in many places. You may start from the equations found in Halliday and Resnick's *Physics (Vol II)*, in David Griffith's *Introduction to Electrodynamics* [8], in *The Feynman Lectures* [9], in JD Jackson's *Classical Electrodynamics* [4], or, most easily, from equations in Catt's *Electromagnetism I*. [11] All of the cases below are for perfect conductors in vacuum, the same conditions that the basic Maxwell's Equations are

derived under, with the speed of light $c \equiv c_o$ and wire resistance per unit length $R_L = 0$. This is called the "lossless" condition in electrical engineering, a topic discussed in the remarkable $i = qc$: **The Gardner Equation** section below.

### 2.1.  $i = qc$: Derivation from Observing a Voltage Step

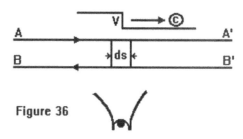

**Figure 1.**   Watching a step TEM wave pass by

Ivor Catt almost derives The Forbidden Equation in his unique fashion using differentials (Figure 1.). Excerpted from his *Electromagnetics I* [11], with $q$ the net electric charge per unit length that forms the electric current:

*"In order to discover how we characterise a transmission line we shall consider an observer watching a step passing him along a two-wire line (Fig.36).*

*"The observer knows... that electric charge is conserved... "In a time $\delta t$ the step will advance a distance $\delta s$ such that*

$$\frac{\delta s}{\delta t} = C \qquad (1)$$

[i.e. the step advances at the speed of light, $c$, his $C$ -FB]

*"Now we consider the conservation of charge. In a capacitor in general, $q = cv$. In our case, the charge $i\delta t$ entering the line in time $\delta t$ equals the charge trapped in charging up the next segment $\delta s$ of the line, $c\delta sv$, where c is the capacitance per unit length between the pair of wires, and $c\delta s$ is the capacitance of our section.*

$$i\delta t = vc\delta s \qquad (2)$$

*"which means that*

$$i = vcC \qquad (3)$$

End of excerpt. I recently spoke at great length with Ivor Catt about this derivation and about The Forbidden Equation. It was originally in his historic 1967 paper, *Crosstalk* [12] along with more analysis. He was one step removed from deriving $i = qC$ (using his notation), which can be found by substituting $q = cv$ back into Equ (3) to receive

**The Forbidden Equation**

$$i = vcC = qC \qquad (4)$$

Catt was using Equ (3) as an intermediate step in his mathematical proof of the existence of two modes of wave propagation in a four-conductor line, and so did not pursue this equation further. At eighty years old, he said that he had never seen The Forbidden Equation before (aside from my pointing it out). William A. Gardner and Harry H. Ricker III also stated that they have never seen it anywhere before. Ricker took the trouble to search his library and was only able to come up with one similar equation, $i = qv$, in an old book on transmission line theory.

### 2.2. $i = qc$: Derivation from $C_L = 1/cZ$: Another Forbidden Equation

Below I use a Forbidden Equation of Line Capacitance, $C_L = 1/cZ$, in one of my several derivations of $i = qc$. This derivation relies on another unfamiliar equation, but it is most compact and direct. I also 'discovered', or stumbled across, $C_L = 1/cZ$ in 2008, but I think I remember seeing it later in one old book on transmission lines. There are apparently different levels of Forbidden. It comes directly from generalizing the expression of permittivity in terms of $c_o$ and $Z_o$, Equ (1), and by multiplying it by the dimensionless, geometric form-factor $f$ for the two conductors of an electric circuit in the plane of their impedance, described in some few textbooks. [11]

In all of the below, $Z_o$ is the vacuum wave impedance, $Z$ is the characteristic, aka surge, aka line impedance, so that $Z = fZ_o$ and $c = c_o$. This is also vacuum-valued for all of the instant cases; material dielectric adds some irrelevant complexity to the argument. The $L$ subscript is used to set off quantities per unit length, $C_L$ is the capacitance per unit length (farad/m), $L_L$ is the inductance per unit length (henry/m), and $q_L \equiv q$ from above. Begin from the two published equations that are not to be found together on the same page [ units in square brackets ],

$$Z_o = \sqrt{\frac{\mu_o}{\varepsilon_o}} \quad \text{and} \quad c_o = 1/\sqrt{\mu_o \varepsilon_o} \qquad (5)$$

With the above two equations in front of you on the same page you may easily deduce the electric permittivity/constant and magnetic permeability/constant equations, in wave impedance, $Z_o$, and $c \equiv c_o$:

**A Couple More Forbidden Equations**

$$\varepsilon_o = \frac{1}{Z_o c_o} \quad \text{[ farad/m ]} \qquad (6)$$

and

$$\mu_o = \frac{Z_o}{c_o} \quad \text{[ henry/m ]} \qquad (7)$$

The line capacitance is the capacitance per unit length of the electric circuit, $C_L$ (Catt's $c$ above). It is found by multiplying the permittivity by the dimensionless geometric factor, $f$, where $f$ is calculated from the cross section of the two wires in the plane of impedance. [11]

$$C_L = \frac{\varepsilon_o}{f} \quad \text{[ farad/m ]} \qquad (8)$$

Substitute Equ (6) into Equ (8) to receive

**Another Forbidden Equation**

$$C_L = \frac{\varepsilon_o}{f} = \frac{1}{fcZ_o} = \frac{1}{cZ} \quad \text{[ farad/m ]} \qquad (9)$$

where $c \equiv c_o$ is the speed of light in vacuum, and $Z = fZ_o$ is the characteristic impedance of the electric transmission circuit line in vacuum.

With $V$ the voltage between the two wires of an electric circuit as measured in the plane of impedance,

$$C_L = \frac{q_L}{V} = \frac{1}{cZ} \quad \text{[ farad/m = (coul/m)(volt) ]} \qquad (10)$$

which can be rearranged to express the line charge (charge per unit length) as

$$q_L = \frac{V}{cZ} \quad \text{[ coul/m = (volt)/(m/s)/(ohm) ]} \qquad (11)$$

The general equation for the line impedance is

$$Z = \frac{V}{i} \quad \text{[ ohm = volt/amp ]} \qquad (12)$$

Solve Equ (12) for $V$ and substitute into Equ (11):

$$q_L = \frac{V}{cZ} = \frac{iZ}{cZ} \qquad (13)$$

Cancel $Z$ and rearrange to discover

**The Forbidden Equation**

$$i = q_L c \quad \text{[ amp = (coul/m)(m/s) ]} \qquad (14)$$

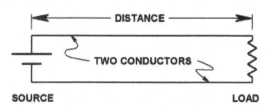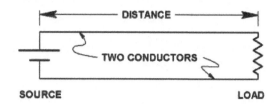

**Figure 2.** One phenomenon, two concepts. "Electric circuit line", "Electric transmission circuit line", "Electric transmission circuit", "Electric circuit", "Electric line", "transmission circuit line", "transmission circuit", "transmission line", etc. are used interchangeably. They are all different names for the same thing.

### 2.3. $i = qc$: Derivation from the Fusion of Two Common Line Equations

This derivation begins from the very well known equations for line capacitance and line inductance. I use an algebraic operation (which might have another name) which I call the "Fusion of Equations". The generic idea is to set *any* two equations each equal to a dimensionless 1, then to equate them with each other. This technique is explored in more depth in another pending paper of mine called **Maxwell's Algebra**.

Two different Forbidden Equations will emerge from the instant derivation, one is the title of this paper and the other is its "companion" equation for voltage in terms of the speed of light.

Rearrange the well-known equation for capacitance per unit length,

$$C_L = \frac{q_L}{V} \quad [\text{ farad/m = coul/volt }] \quad (15)$$

as

$$\frac{C_L V}{q_L} = 1 \quad [\text{ dimensionless }] \quad (16)$$

With $\phi_L$ the magnetic flux per unit length, rearrange the well-known equation for inductance per unit length,

$$L_L = \frac{\phi_L}{i} \quad [\text{ farad/m = (V-s)(amp-m) }] \quad (17)$$

as

$$\frac{L_L i}{\phi_L} = 1 \quad [\text{ dimensionless }] \quad (18)$$

Notice that both of the equations, when set equal to 1, are dimensionless. Any equation set to a dimensionless 1 can be equated with its inverse, which, as can be seen on rearrangement, is algebraically equivalent to squaring it. This is a special case of the general rule that any equation set to 1 can be equated with any other equation set to 1, *or its inverse*, as long as the 1 in both is dimensionless. I

will use this mathematical fact to find both The Forbidden Equation in $i$ and then its companion in $V$ from the same starting equations:

Equate the dimensionless line capacitance, Equ (16), with the inverse of the dimensionless line inductance, Equ (18):

$$\frac{C_L V}{q_L} = \frac{\phi_L}{L_L i} \quad [\text{ dimensionless }] \quad (19)$$

Set this equation to 1:

$$L_L C_L \frac{i}{q_L} \frac{V}{\phi_L} = 1 \quad [\text{ dimensionless }] \quad (20)$$

Since it is well known that

$$L_L C_L = \frac{1}{c^2} \quad [\text{ henry-farad}/m^2 = s^2/m^2 \text{ ]} \quad (21)$$

we can see immediately that

$$\frac{i}{q_L} \frac{V}{\phi_L} = c^2 \quad (22)$$

Again equate the dimensionless line capacitance, Equ (16), with the dimensionless line inductance, Equ (18), this time without inverting the latter:

$$\frac{C_L V}{q_L} = \frac{L_L i}{\phi_L} \quad [\text{ dimensionless }] \quad (23)$$

Set this equation to 1:

$$\frac{V}{i} \frac{\phi_L}{q_L} \frac{C_L}{L_L} = 1 \quad [\text{ dimensionless }] \quad (24)$$

Since it is well known that the electric transmission circuit line impedance can be expressed as

$$Z = \frac{V}{i} = \sqrt{\frac{L_L}{C_L}} \quad [\text{ohm}] \qquad (25)$$

or, after squaring and inverting as

$$\frac{1}{Z^2} = \frac{C_L}{L_L} \qquad (26)$$

we can see from substituting these two expressions for impedance into Equ (24) that

$$Z = \frac{\phi_L}{q_L} \qquad (27)$$

which may be another Forbidden Equation. Equate Equ (27) with Equ (25) as

$$Z = \frac{V}{i} = \frac{\phi_L}{q_L} \qquad (28)$$

and solve for $V$:

$$V = \frac{i\phi_L}{q_L} \qquad (29)$$

Substitute Equ (29) for $V$ into Equ (22):

$$\frac{i}{q_L}\frac{V}{\phi_L} = \frac{i}{q_L}\frac{1}{\phi_L}\frac{i\phi_L}{q_L} = c^2 \qquad (30)$$

Collect or cancel like terms:

$$\frac{i^2}{q_L^2} = c^2 \qquad (31)$$

Take the square root of Equ (31) and rearrange to yield

**The Forbidden Equation**

$$i = cq_L \equiv cq \qquad (32)$$

To find the companion to The Forbidden Equation, solve Equ (28) for $i$:

$$i = V\frac{q_L}{\phi_L} \qquad (33)$$

As before with Equ (30), substitute Equ (33) for $i$ into Equ (22):

$$c^2 = \frac{i}{q_L}\frac{V}{\phi_L} = V\frac{q_L}{\phi_L}\frac{1}{q_L}\frac{V}{\phi_L} = \frac{V^2}{\phi_L^2} = c^2 \qquad (34)$$

Take the square root of Equ (34) and rearrange to discover

**The Companion Forbidden Equation**

$$V = \phi_L c \qquad (35)$$

This equation can be interpreted as saying that whatever it is that is associated with the 'voltage' concept moves at the speed of light just as $i = q_L c$ does for electric current. The quantity $\phi_L$, the magnetic flux per unit length, is not usually used. Dimensionally it lies halfway between the magnetic flux and the magnetic-flux-areal-density. The objection could be raised that this is not a physical quantity, which I would agree with and extend to include $i$ and most of the rest. The speed of light, $c$, and the geometric form factor, $f$, come the closest to describing reality, the rest are at least one more step removed. Electric current itself, $i$, cannot exist as a circulating fluid. It fails to satisfy continuity among several other problems.

## 3. $i = qc$: A Continuity Equation

The continuity equation is a staple of physics and engineering. It mathematically expresses the idea that all of the material in a given flow- a "current"- has to be accounted for at all times and places along that flow. Material cannot simply appear and disappear without any accounting.

This equation applies to the water in a river, to the fluid flow in a pipe, to the stream-tubes in aeronautics, and of course to electric current in a wire. Kirchhoff's 1st law as used by electricians, "what goes in must come out", is a special case of the continuity equation applied to junctions for an incompressible flow and without sources or sinks.

A continuity equation can have only one velocity at any given point in the flow. This follows from the idea that a particle can only be moving in one direction at a time, and can only move at one speed at a time. In the general continuity equation,

**current = $\rho u A$**

where $\rho$ is the fluid density, $u$ is the speed of the fluid through the area, and $A$ is the area of the transverse cross-section that the fluid is flowing through. For electric current, $A$ would presumably be the cross-sectional area of the wire that is said to carry it and contain it within, like a pipe. For the usual case of the wires in a two-wire electric circuit the cross-sectional area, $A$, of the wires is constant.

There are three major types of density, often confused or not made clear in the literature: the linear-density, the areal-density, and the volume-density (line, area, volume). All three are used in various expositions on continuity. The equations above only use the linear-density of charge. $q_L$. "Current density", $J$, is actually an areal density: so many charges passing through an area per unit time. $\rho$ as used in the generic continuity equation is a volume density.

One common definition of electric current, in words, is "electric charges moving past a point along a wire". This is a reduced form of the continuity equation, as density

$\rho$ and area $A$ are missing. It's written in differential form, with $i$ the electric current, $Q$ an arbitrary amount of electric charge, and $t$ is time, as

$$i = \frac{\delta Q}{\delta t} \quad [ \text{ ampere } ] \tag{36}$$

which Miles Mathis [13] has shown does not add any more information than is already present in the algebraic form as

$$i = \frac{Q}{t} \tag{37}$$

This equation, $i = Q/t$, is behind the definition of the ampere, or, in MKSA dimensions, solving it for $Q$ forms the definition of electric charge in coulombs. Notice there is no sign of a velocity or an area in this equation. It's as if an aircraft designer had to design a wing knowing only how many air molecules pass by it each second.

There are two more "hidden" dimensions in $i = Q/t$ for the speed ratio- [ length/time ] or [ m/s ]. Written out in full, the dimensions are [ (coul/m)*(m/s) = (coul-m)/(m-s) ]. The two lengths look like they cancel, but they don't, not really. One refers to the length of the charged object and the other is tied up as part of the speed the object is moving at. For the "moving $i$", with the linear-charge-density $q_L$ or $Q/L$,

$$i = \frac{Q}{t} = \frac{Q}{L}\frac{L}{t} = q_L * \frac{L}{t} = q_L u \tag{38}$$

With this in mind we can unpack $q_L$ and write out an explicit continuity equation for electric current, $i = \rho_Q u A$, with $\rho_Q$ the volume-density of electric charge, $u$ the speed of the charged particles, and $A$ the cross section area of the wire.

The volume, $Vol$, is area * length, or $Vol = AL$. The volume density, $\rho_Q$, is

$$\rho_Q = \frac{Q}{Vol} = \frac{Q}{AL} \tag{39}$$

Rearrange this as

$$q_L = \frac{Q}{L} = \rho_Q A \tag{40}$$

Then to the full continuity equation:

$$i = \frac{Q}{t} = \frac{Q}{L}\frac{L}{t} = q_L(\frac{L}{t}) = q_L u = \rho_Q u A \tag{41}$$

The Forbidden Equation is a continuity equation with $c$ for the speed of the current. **A current can only have one speed.** Either

$$i = q_L c \quad \text{or} \quad i = Q_{Drift} u \tag{42}$$

with $Q_{Drift} > q_L$ and $u < c$, but not both at the same time, anymore than the water in a pipe can run at two different speeds with two different densities all at the same time and place.

The definition of the coulomb in terms of the ampere also has this hidden-variable problem. From Equ (38), with $t = 1$ second [ s ], $Q =$ one coulomb [ coul ], and $i =$ one ampere [ A ],

$$Q = it = A - s = \frac{A(D)}{c} \quad \text{with} \quad D = ct \tag{43}$$

The linear-density $q_L$, $Q/L$, or charge per length, is a slippery variable. There is no way to tell if it means a positive charge or a negative charge just by looking at it by itself, or even when it is in an equation. As the electron-current goes around the circuit, $Q$ has to change signs. Actually, this has to happen within the LOAD in Figure 2. But it can't change sign without running into the problems highlighted by the Palmer Equations.

## 4. $i = qc$: The Palmer Equations

To distinguish this paper from others of a similar title, and not knowing the author's name nor realizing that CWPP are his initials, we began to call his six-page, hand-written treatise "The Clarendon Letter" [4], even though the author had titled it "The Catt Question". It begins in a grand fashion:

*"Dear Mr Catt*

*"I'm concerned- indeed appalled- that your question has waited for so long for an answer, and apparently caused so much controversy. It seems to me a very straight-forward question which can be answered with reference to equations whose validity is unquestioned, and thus in a way which should command universal assent".*

The first three pages are devoted to debunking the "Southerner" theory of where the electrons come from in The Catt Question setup, that they rise up from within the wire. This had been promoted by Sir Michael Pepper of The Cavendish (Cambridge) and is of no further technical interest here.

There are two instances of The Forbidden Equation in The Clarendon Letter, one for each of the two wires. Palmer constructs these equations as part of a model, rather than derive them from basic mainstream equations as I did above. With $q$ and $q'$ the net line charges on the upper (signal) and lower (return) wires respectively, $e$ the electron charge, and $a$ the atomic spacing between the stationary charges (assuming one free electron per atom in a regular, 1D lattice, like a row of dots), Palmer states:

*"where $v$ and $v'$ are the drift velocities on the two lines. Similarly the net current on the two lines (from this particular line of charges) is*

$$i = 0 + \frac{(-e)(-v)}{a(1+\frac{v}{c})} = \frac{ev}{a(1+\frac{v}{c})} = cq \qquad (44)$$

*"for the signal line and*

$$i = 0 + \frac{(-e)(v')}{a(1-\frac{v'}{c})} = \frac{-ev'}{a(1-\frac{v'}{c})} = cq' \qquad (45)$$

*"on the return line. The drift velocity must be such that at each point on the surface of each conductor the surface current has the correct value determined by the equations above..."*

Palmer does not explain where the $cq$ terms come from; he did not respond to my asking. Since $i = i$ and $c = c$, we can see at once that $q = q'$. Changing the sign of $q'$ in the second equation won't solve the problem, either. As shown by considerations of continuity and voltage across the two wires, $q$ has to simultaneously be of both signs, which is physically impossible. $q'$ has to equal $-q$ in order to satisfy the requirement of net-negative charge on the lower wire and net-positive charge on the upper wire, while at the same time $q'$ has to equal $+q$ to satisfy continuity. The moving charges are thinned out on the upper wire, $q < \frac{e}{a}$, and they are bunched up on the lower wire, $q' > \frac{e}{a}$. Mathematically,

$$\frac{e}{a} > -q' = q = q' > \frac{e}{a} \qquad (46)$$

This equation has no solution. That suffices to falsify the model.

There is some confusion on the point of which directions the $v$'s are having the current going. The confusion stems from the ambiguity of the negative sign for $v$. If this $v$, and also the $v'$, are speeds, they both have to be non-negative numbers. Actually, both have to equal zero to satisfy the Palmer Equations. Either an object is moving or it is sitting still; it can't 'move negatively' for the same reason there is no such thing as negative degrees Kelvin. This negative-speed error is commonly made in areas outside of kinetic theory. The Drude/Fermi electron-gas model comes from kinetic theory, and the model that Palmer and the other Westerners are using is a simplified version of it.

Many times the confusion between speed and velocity works out in the end- the errors cancel- but here is an example of what can go wrong. There is already another quantity, electric charge, that is using negative numbers-

but a negative charge cannot cancel a negative speed anymore than a negative orange can cancel a negative apple to produce a positive orange-apple.

If $v$ is a velocity it would have to be in something like vector notation so as not to conflate its direction in space with the sign of the charges it is assigned to, which occurs as a result of treating it as a scalar. In his diagram we can clearly see that the electrons on the upper wire are moving to the left (Westward) in a standard coordinate system, and the one on the lower wire move to the right (Eastward), but that directionality doesn't carry over to a scalar speed, $v$. Pieraccini & Selleri [6] below make the same speed-is-not-velocity mistake as Palmer.

Since $i = i$ we can equate the terms of these two equations in $v$ and $v'$:

$$\frac{v}{(1+\frac{v}{c})} = \frac{-v'}{(1-\frac{v'}{c})} \qquad (47)$$

with $v'$ some speed less than the speed of light. Let $v' = Sc$, where $0 \le S \le 1$. Then

$$\frac{v}{(1+\frac{v}{c})} = \frac{-Sc}{(1-S)} \qquad (48)$$

which can be rearranged as

$$v - Sv = -Sc - Sv \qquad (49)$$

cancelling, we find that

$$v = -Sc = -v' \qquad (50)$$

This shows that the two different Palmer Equations are in fact the same equation written twice, with $v = -v'$ and $q = q'$. When applied all around the circuit, this equation has only one consistent solution: $v = 0$, $q = 0$, and $i = cq = 0$.

There is an implication in these equations for the drift speeds $v$ and $v'$, and indeed in all of the mainstream theory of electric current, that a line of negative charges moving Westward is physically the same as a line of positive charges moving Eastward. It's even worse, because the positive charges aren't moving at all; they are the protons of the fixed atoms. At least the old two-fluids idea (one invisible positive humor, one negative humor, each moving opposite directions) might have saved that part of the theory of electric current.

### 4.1. Electric Disconnection

In all of the many published responses to The Catt Question [14], not one of them has addressed the problems that arise when the charge carriers move from the lower wire, run through the load, and begin the trip back to the source on the upper wire. They have to thin out somehow, either by speeding up as they pass though the load, switching their signs, or something. The electrons would have to accelerate as they pass through, and presumably deliver power to, the load.

The compressed electrons on the ground wire would have to keep moving Eastwards even after a switch on it was opened back up; compressed air would not do that. After a switch is opened on the signal wire, the speedier, yet rarefied electrons that were moving Westward would have to stop and pile up, starting at the open switch and propagating as a density wave Eastward. The number of problems that people have been noticing with the electric-current picture has been increasing exponentially over the past few years, too many to keep track of.

No one has shown any mechanism by which the Eastward-moving TEM wave can generated a Westward force on the returning charge carriers either.

No one has shown how the electric field lines of the TEM wave, moving at the speed of light, are supposed to disconnect from one stationary or slowly-drifting charge carrier and reconnect to another one further down the line. This would violate Gauss' Law ($\nabla \cdot E = \rho$) in the process as the disconnected electric field lines momentarily dangle around somehow in space. The fallacy is quite like the problem of Magnetic Reconnection, in which it is claimed that magnetic field lines can disconnect and reconnect. That would create temporary magnetic monopoles, violating $\nabla \cdot B = 0$.

How are the speed-of-light field-lines handed off from one slowly-drifting electron to the next? How can the other side of the speed-of-light electric field hop from one stationary positive proton to the next?

## 5. $i = qc$: The Pieraccini-Selleri Equations

The next Academic sighting of The Forbidden Equation was in 2013, and again in a published response to The Catt Question. [6] This time the equation was a bit more disguised, broken into pieces. The Italian electrical engineers, like Palmer, attempted to join $i = qc$ up with their version of an equation for electron drift current, committing several grave errors in the process.

Many times when someone attempts to answer The Catt Question they end up (re)inventing a new model, or even a new theory. This is such a case as is both Palmer and Gardner. They have to make things up as they go because *there is no literature*, anymore than there is for The Forbidden Equation.

Pieraccini and his co-author Selleri had previously published yet another version of a response to The Catt Question in an IEEE magazine but did not publish The Forbidden Equation in it. That article was a MEMO, invited by an IEEE Associate Editor:

*I read a novel, L'anomalia [16]... authored by a colleague of mine, Massimiliano Pieraccini (University of Florence). The book... deals with a [scientist's] murder... Shortly before, he had declared that he was dealing with the Catt's electromagnetic "anomaly."..."*

*Since the "anomaly" deals with fundamental electromagnetics, and since Catt is that kind of unconventional researcher, moving outside of academia and structured research, which was indeed quite common in the past- especially in the 18th and 19th centuries ..." [15]*

In the IEEE article [17], the Italian's unconventional version of electromagnetic "Theory N+H" would have-

*"Moving charges do generate a field that interacts with charges down the transmission line at a speed c, even if the charges them selves move much slower. It is not a matter of moving charges generating a TEM wave, or a TEM wave moving the charges. Instead, it is a continuous back and forth, from moving charges to TEM wave to new moving charges, and again to TEM wave, and so on. [17]*

This is reminiscent of Feynman's "Dancing, Swishing Wave" [1], [9]-

*"a varying E field gives rise to a varying B field, which in turn gives rise to a varying E field, and so on. In this way the electric and magnetic fields of the wave sustain one another through empty space... by a perpetual interplay- by the swishing back and forth from one field to the other- they must go on forever... They maintain themselves in a kind of dance- one making the other, the second making the first- propagating onward through space..."*

Feynman does admit later, *"I'll tell you what I see. I see some kind of vague, shadowy, wiggling lines- When I talk about the fields swishing through space,* **I have a terrible confusion** *between the symbols I use to describe the objects and the objects themselves..."*

Combining Feynman's *"...and so on. In this way the electric and magnetic fields of the wave sustain one another... by... swishing back and forth from one field to the other... in a kind of dance"* with Pieraccini & Selleri's *"continuous back and forth, from moving charges to TEM wave to new moving charges, and again to TEM wave, and so on...* does not reduce the terrible confusion or address electric disconnection. Which swishes first, and so on?

In both the IEEE and the IOP articles they say that *"A possible analogy is the start of a marathon: the referee shoots the starting gun, the sound of the bang propagates in air, and each athlete begins to run when they hear it.",* which contradicts the "continuous back and forth" idea. If each of the runners heard the starting gun, began to accelerate up to running speed, and shouted out to the next runner down the line *as they were accelerating*, the analogy would be more accurate. This of course would introduce a time delay from one electron/runner to the next, dropping the TEM wave speed far below $c$. But the starting gun was already an independent, propagating TEM wave, so why would it even need to be heard by the runners in the first instance? What are the runners adding to the picture besides just getting in the way?

In the *IOP Physics Education* article [6], the authors introduce a figure with "...*two thin wires of radius a are sketched and the [TEM] wave is shown as it travels through a sampling cylindrical volume of [length]* $\Delta x$.

*The [TEM] wave travels at the speed of light, c, from point x to point* $x + \Delta x$ *in the time interval* $\Delta t = \Delta x/c$. *During this time a current I flows in the sampling volume from its left side at x, equalling*

$$I = \pi a^2 v e N \qquad (51)$$

"*where v is the drift velocity of the charges (in practice electrons, and the speed is much lower than the speed of light), [e is the elementary charge] charge* $(1.602 * 10^{-19} C)$ *and N is the concentration of free electrons in the metal (for copper it is* $8.4830 \times 10^{28} m^{-3}$"

This is their first equation, their Equ (1), a continuity equation. (I changed their elementary electron charge $q$ to the more commonly used $e$. $N$, the "concentration", is the particle volume-density. $eN = \rho_q$ of continuity Equ (41) above.)

With this equation, the authors would have the entire mass of free electrons in a volume, $\pi a^2 \Delta x$, squeeze over into a new volume of the same size in $\Delta t$ and beginning at $x + \Delta x$. The new mass of electrons is riding in right on top of the same mass and density of free electrons that is already present in the wire, ahead of the TEM wave. This results in a free-electron density of $2N$, an extraordinary claim. The new volume already has the same neutral,"at rest" density, so this process would double its free electron density in a compression process that would probably produce energy densities comparable to a nuclear bomb core. The existing electrons in the new volume can't get out of the way by moving forward, either.

They would like to have $v$ be the drift "velocity" (speed, actually, as Crothers [18] also points out) by their simple declaration, but this mass of electrons cannot satisfy that desire without moving at the speed of light for at least some portion of the journey- in jumping over to collide with the next electron, for example. That would also require either an infinite acceleration and deceleration of an ensemble of massive objects, or at least a speed in excess of superluminal for at least part of that journey. In either case, the mass of each electron would go to infinity in this microscopic version of The Catt Question.

By their equation below together with my equations above, this "unbalanced" (their word) mass and charge of electrons, $\pi a^2 \Delta x e N$, is emanating an electric field that is many orders of magnitude too strong to account for the voltage between the two wires. On the upper wire, the charged-particle density would have to be an equal and opposite $N$, which can only be accomplished by *removing all of the free electrons from the copper wire*. Continuing with this,

"*This incoming current lasts for a time interval* $\Delta t$ *and produces in the wire length* $\Delta x$ *an imbalance of charge* $\Delta Q$ *given by*

$$\Delta Q = I \Delta t = I \frac{\Delta x}{c} \qquad (52)$$

This "imbalance of charge" is presumably the same net linear line charge per unit length , my $q$ or $q_L$, described above. Dividing their second equation through by $\Delta x$ yields

$$\frac{\Delta Q}{\Delta x} = I \frac{\Delta t}{\Delta x} = I \frac{1}{c} \qquad (53)$$

Rearrange, with $q \equiv q_L \equiv \Delta Q/\Delta x$, and behold

**The Forbidden Equation**

$$I = \frac{\Delta Q}{\Delta x} c = q_L c \qquad (54)$$

Their $eN$ is the volume density of charge, $\rho_Q$ in Equ (40) above, $eN = \rho_Q$. Their $\pi a^2$ is the area $A$ of the wire cross section introduced in Equ (39) above. With those substitutions, and using my Equ (41) and their Equ (2), their Equ (1) reads

$$I = \pi a^2 v e N = A v \rho_Q = q_L v = q_L c \qquad (55)$$

or $v = c$. The drift velocity is the speed of light.

They then go on to construct a third equation and to discuss the electric field associated with $q_l$, conflating a longitudinal field with the transverse electric field, by using an un-sub-scripted, un-bolded letter "$E$" to ambiguously refer to both in two different equations, as Crothers also points out. [18] By this sleight-of-variables the speed $v = c$ from their first two equations is transformed into a much slowed drift speed, orders of magnitude lower. The same $v$ becomes two wildly-different speeds.

Crothers also notes a basic algebra error in their skin-effect derivation- the addition of a superfluous "2" as well as a confusion between velocity and speed, similar to Palmer's. In this same *IOP Physics Education* article, both their Figure 1. and Figure 2., showing the setup for The Catt Question, have the Gaussian analytic volume on the upper wire while in their text they claim to educate the reader as to conditions on the lower wire.

This construction fails for several reasons, not the least of which is that each of the particles in a current can only move at one speed at a time. Attempts by Catt, Ricker, Crothers, myself, and others to correct the sundry libels and errors made by the Italians by publishing letters in these same journals were rebuked, though this may change. [7]

## 6. $i = qc$: The Gardner Equation

Gardner states [3] that The Forbidden Equation is "Mr. Bishop's... new discovery about physics". He is quite mistaken- this is a mainstream equation, not "Mr. Bishop's", nor is it a new discovery. It is Maxwell's Equation. It is inseparably contained within the other mainstream equations. It is William A. Gardner's Equation.

An astonishing and historic set of email exchanges between Gardner and myself took place in late 2015, in what became a scientific case study. Not only are some of the alleged authorities unfamiliar with a fundamental equation ($i = qc$) in their own field, they can't even derive it after being given many clues. That last point is absolutely new to me, and can be used in future applications. Along with his sundry libels against me, Gardner was responding to my initial questions, in particular:

- Have you ever seen the equation $i = qc$?
- Can you derive $i = qc$?

A few of the many findings. William A. Gardner (WG):

- Stated that he had never seen i = qc before;
- Consistently failed to state that this is a mainstream equation;
- Failed to note that the lossless condition is a prerequisite for deriving Maxwell's Equations;
- Was not able to derive $i = qc$ even after coaching;
- Once he was shown a derivation of $i = qc$, he still could not understand its significance;
- Did not reprint or critique the actual derivation of $i = qc$, but only mentions it as "a few lines of algebra";
- Thought I was the author of The Clarendon Letter and critiqued that, though missed the analysis shown above;
- Created a novel, though easily falsified, theory of electromagnetism in the process of responding to The Catt Question (this is common);
- Brought up "frequency" several times in regards to The Catt Question and The Forbidden Equation (this is a common diversion from the DC setup, Pieraccini also does it in [6]);
- Padded out both the exchange and the essay with repetitive and irrelevant material, i.e noise (this is common);
- implied that vacuum and zero-resistance conductors are "non-physical", "lossless" situations (both are well-known experimental facts);
- Stated that lumped elements can be used but $i = qc$ can not ("lumps" are unreal, non-physical entities of no dimension)

The last two items listed are a remarkable inversion of the physical and the non-physical. Gardner uses the word "lossless" 13 times in his 7000 word essay, apparently without ever realizing that the lossless condition is used to develop all of Maxwell's Equations, along with the Lorentz force law. This can be seen by simple inspection: there are no resistivity terms, no $R$ or $G$ for resistance, or anything of the sort in any of those equations, nor in any of the standard equations used here to derive $i = qc$. This of course is standard practice in deriving or constructing any physical equation, to treat the ideal case first.

The "lumped element", on the other hand, is a purely mathematical fabrication, used for rule-of-thumb engineering work. It has no basis in reality. How big is a lump? Bigger than a breadbox? What is the coefficient of lumposity? This "Lumped Element Gambit" is also common, J. D. Jackson uses it as well. [4]

*"It should be clear that the Catt question about the fundamentals of electromagnetism in connection with transmission lines..." -WG*

A transmission line is physically the same thing as an electric circuit. What applies to the one applies to the other, without exception. There is no mention of transmission lines in The Catt Question. [5]

*"[The Catt Question] should not be addressed using non-physical models such as a lossless transmission line or a vacuous propagation medium..." -WG*

Maxwell's Equations are written for perfect conductors in a "vacuous propagation medium", i.e. a vacuum. They are "lossless" equations. If no Forbidden Equation then no Maxwell's Equations.

*"the so-called "forbidden equation" $i = qc$ introduced by a follower of Catt, Mr. Forrest Bishop, should actually be forbidden from use in any scientific studies of the fundamentals of electromagnetism because it is valid only for models of transmission lines that are non-physical (lossless) or, more generally, lines in which the drift speed of free electrons in the conductors equals or exceeds the propagation speed of the EM wave in the dielectric..." - WG*

*"In contrast, $i = qc$ is unlikely to ever be a useful approximation because there is unlikely to be any physically viable conditions under which the drift speed S in a physical conductor is almost as fast as the propagation speed c in a physical dielectric surrounding that conductor..." - WG*

The alleged drift speed is irrelevant. $i = qc$ refers to properties of the external TEM wave and the dielectric it is travelling through. This is easily seen by looking at what all of the equations above are in reference to. The Forbidden Equation, and the other equations it is related to, make no reference at all to the material properties of the wires, how many free electrons are available, the resistivity, or the purported drift speed, only to the cross-section geometry. $i = qc$ directly links the purported electric current with the dielectric material, not the wire material.

Gardner inadvertently highlighted an interesting point about the wire resistance. Adding resistance in to The Catt

Question makes the problem worse, not better. As the TEM step moves Eastward, the transverse voltage decreases due to resistive loss. The top of the step slopes down to the East, instead of being horizontal, so the very front of the wave has a lower height, a lower voltage, the further East it goes. The line charge, $q_L$, that comprises the electric drift current and terminates the transverse voltage, would have to diminish, from the original density launched from the source, to a lesser value, $q_L - q_{loss}$. **Where do these now-excessive $q_{loss}$ electrons go?**

*"this brief investigation of the Catt question is the necessity of understanding how to bring physics and mathematical models of physics (and their analysis) together in a meaningful way that does not allow mathematics to dictate non-physical "physics". Mathematics is an essential tool in science, but one that can easily be and is commonly misused- presumably unconsciously." -WG*

Presumably, and charitably, Gardner is unconsciously in error in his mis-characterization of how Maxwell's Equations and the equations used above were developed.

*"When he finally revealed his derivation (a few lines of algebra), it became clear that it is valid for only the non-physical uniform lossless transmission line with speed of propagation c. This mathematical result based on a non-physical model, is actually of no physical significance (and has no bearing on the Catt question)..." -WG*

Gardner did not address the "few lines of algebra" nor demonstrate any understanding of it. $i = qc$ is not about The Catt Question in the first place, nor did I ever state that it was. If Mr. Gardner's Forbidden Equation is of no physical significance then so are all of the other equations that rely on it. A lossy electric circuit does not alter the fact that $i = cq$, with $c$ understood as the propagation speed in the dielectric medium, vacuum or not. $R$ and $G$ attenuate the TEM wave, but they ideally do not alter its speed, and certainly not in the lossless Maxwell's Equations.

## 7. $i = qc$: A Gallery of Forbidden Equations

These are also Forbidden Equations of various degrees, with few, if any, sightings in the relevant mainstream literature. Some are very rarely seen but not quite as Forbidden, others are never found together on the same page. The geometric factor, $f$, is found in at least one old engineering book as well as in Catt; it may or may not be more common in newer books. The photon equations are my own discovery.

Most physics books use $Z_o$ for the vacuum wave impedance and $Z$ for characteristic and other impedances as used herein, the reverse of electrical engineering practice. $\lambda$, instead of $q$ or $q_L$, is usually used for the line charge density in physics books, but only in the Electrostatics section. It disappears from the Maxwell's Equations section, then sometimes reappears in Relativity.

Wave impedance of the vacuum, AND the speed of light, never put together on the same page in a physics book, both in permittivity and permeability:

$$Z_o = \sqrt{\frac{\mu_o}{\varepsilon_o}} \quad \textbf{WITH} \quad c_o = 1/\sqrt{\mu_o \varepsilon_o} \qquad (56)$$

With the above two equations in front of you on the same page you may deduce that:

Electric permittivity constant of the vacuum, in wave impedance, $Z_o$, and $c$ [farad/meter]:

$$\varepsilon_o = \frac{1}{Z_o c_o} \qquad (57)$$

Magnetic permeability constant of the vacuum, in wave impedance and $c$ [henry/meter]

$$\mu_o = \frac{Z_o}{c_o} \qquad (58)$$

Characteristic (surge) impedance of electric transmission line in magnetic flux/length and line charge [ohm]:

$$Z = f\sqrt{\frac{\mu_o}{\varepsilon_o}} = \frac{\phi_L}{q_L} \qquad (59)$$

Geometric factor in the plane of impedance of an electric circuit line [dimensionless]

$$f = f(a,b,r,) \qquad (60)$$

Vacuum capacitance per unit length of transmission circuit line, in $Z_o$, and $c$ [farad/meter]:

$$C_L = \frac{\varepsilon_o}{f} = \frac{1}{Z c_o} \qquad (61)$$

Vacuum inductance per unit length of electric transmission circuit, in $Z_o$, and $c$ [henry/meter]:

$$L_L = f\mu_o = \frac{Z}{c_o} \qquad (62)$$

Voltage in magnetic flux/length and $c$ [volt]:

$$V = \phi_L c_o \qquad (63)$$

Electric current in charge/length and $c$ [ampere]:

$$i = qc_o \qquad (64)$$

## 8. $i = qc$: THE MEMO

The Catt Question has been around for about 35 years, still in circulation, still not widely known, still diagnosing. The 'newer' Forbidden Equation is not a question, but an irrefutable assertion about conventional theory. It cannot be denied or waffled around. A child can stump a Noble Laureate with it, who will not have heard of it or received the memo. Therefore, it can be used over and over again in many venues:

- Have you ever seen the equation $i = qc$?
- Can you derive $i = qc$?

There are many different theories of electricity & magnetism both within and without academia. These can be grouped, after Catt, into three broad categories:

**Theory N**(ormal): Electric current creates electric and magnetic fields.

**Theory H**(eaviside): "We reverse this": electromagnetic fields create electric current.

**Theory C**(att): When a battery lights a lamp, electric current is not involved.

The mainstream Theory N comes in many different flavors and has several different schisms within it, not the least of which is the division between *electric circuit* and *transmission line*, a division that runs so deep it is reflected in the very layout of university campus architecture.

**Theory N, Version 1**, Dept. of Electrical Engineering: The lines are charged. (Westerners) This is needed to explain transmission line theory as well as the voltage between the wires of an electric circuit, a topic gone missing from Griffiths [8], Jackson [4], and others of that genre.

**Theory N, Version 2**, Dept of Physics: The lines are neutral. (Southerners) This is needed in order to derive Maxwell's Equations, Ampere's laws in particular. Griffiths [8] explains, p196, 202, 226.

Palmer, the Italians, and after awhile even Gardner, are what I call "Second Wave" responders to the Catt Question. They are using Theory H without acknowledging it, perhaps without even realizing it. The First Wave responders (Pepper, Josephson, etc.) were all attempting to answer it using two different versions of Theory N (conventional theory).

Over the past 35 years, The Catt Question itself has helped move the "Overton Window" of physics, i.e. the permissible range of discourse. Theory H had been suppressed over the past century. But the Question already

builds in, or "frames", the problem in terms of either Theory H or Theory N, V1, by using the TEM wave and negative charge on the line in its setup. The First Wave responders, especially the Southerners, were attempting to dodge that; the Second Wave Responders have accepted it and even use the "TEM wave" terminology, which had also disappeared from the literature.

Conspiracy Theory. The Second Wave responders did not "receive the memo" instructing them to avoid admitting to the existence of Catt and his Question. THERE WAS NO WAY TO SEND THE MEMO. If a memo had been sent out overtly to all Depts., posted in the halls, etc. it would have drawn attention to Catt, not suppressed him. Instead, they are looking at the First Wave responses and re-framing in terms of Theory H. As there is no literature on this, the very first question about electricity, they have to individually make up a new theory each time. This is why Palmer has to open his treatise with:

*"I'm concerned- indeed appalled- that your question has waited for so long for an answer, and apparently caused so much controversy. It seems to me a very straightforward question..."*

Pieraccini had come up with a different way of getting THE MEMO out with his 2011 murder mystery, *L'Anomalia* [16], published two years before the paper cited above. He spent five years writing this book, but then ended up publishing The Forbidden Equation after all. A revealing excerpt-

*'So what are you working on now?' Massimo asked Alexander [Kaposka]...*
*'On the Catt anomaly' replied Alexander seriously.*
*'Are you kidding?' 'Nobody with an ounce of common sense would risk their career and scientific reputation to study the Catt anomaly* [an earlier name for The Catt Question.] *Massimo thought, 'and even if they were spending time on this, they wouldn't be telling people about it'.*

The characters were attending a scientific conference. Later on, in the hotel room right next to Massimo's (this character is an obvious projection of the author), Massimo Redi (Francesco Redi, Arezzo) and his sidekick Fabio Moebius (the same/other side of the author) discover the lifeless body of Alexander Kaposka. But Kaposka wasn't killed by Massimo Redi: Massimiliano of Arezzo did it. Mystery solved, with a projected Mobius twist:

*"The teacher can begin the lesson by capturing the attention of the students with the 'dramatic' story of the conflict between an unconventional man (Catt) and academia. Afterwards, the teacher presents an intriguing (apparent) paradox. Finally, the teacher gives the solution as a sort of twist. This 'narrative structure' could be a valuable way to maintain high attention and interest of students during class."* -M. Pieraccini, [2013], *IOP Physics Education* [6]

*"Just the idea of twisting a scientific fact for narrative purposes makes me shudder. After all, my reputation would be at stake. And academia does not take these matters*

*lightly. I am absolutely not going to end up like Catt... or like Kaposka!"*- Massimiliano Pieraccini blog, May 24, 2011 [19] (translated from Italian.)

## 9.  $i = qc$: Requiem

The Forbidden Equation reveals another deep problem within The Narrative of academic physics, one which reaches back at least two centuries. It isn't just a falsification of the electric current hypothesis; there is also an insurmountable problem with the definition of electric charge and capacity. In all of the above I and the others used or implied the equation of capacitance, $C = Q/V$.

But the $Q$ in $C = Q/V$ has to be two different things at the same time: now it is the charge on one of the plates, and now it is the opposite charge on the other plate. This is merely one of the many problems with the notion that "math is the language of science".

One single variable, $Q$, is used to refer to two different quantities, with two different meanings, two faces. That duplicity flows throughout all of the current theories of electricity, only to circle back around and mathematically wreck the theory of electric current itself. That is the purpose of this exposition. In order to build a new house with new pieces, the old one must be razed.

The academic men described above do not have very many of the replacement pieces, but the discernible shift toward Theory H over the past ten years has given them a few. The ones with an unshakable belief in the Medieval poltergeist called electric current will remain embalmed in the 18th and 19th centuries, in the ivory-towered mausoleums where Pelosi's "unconventional researcher[s] moving outside of academia" interred them. They are not to be disturbed.

Industry bypassed academia a long time ago. Catt-like ideas are already being used in proprietary technology, here and there, in fits and starts. A lot more people know of these things- and of Catt- than are letting on: they have a different kind of problem with the memos. No one yet has all the pieces- we can tell by looking at what they produce and also, tellingly, what they do not produce. A qualitatively different kind of electric technology is slowly emerging, driven by these new ideas, almost indistinguishable from magic.

## 10.  $i = qc$: Addendum

An astonishing find was provided by Christopher Spargo in [20], pp 272-3. Morgenthaler has both a variant of The Forbidden Equation and the "Southerner" reply to The Catt Question together in the same section. He writes $J = \rho c$, and calls this the 'relativistic, convective current density'. Dividing through by the wire area, $A$, yields The Forbidden Equation.

Morgenthaler states that "*Mobile negative charge which is neutralized by the fixed positive charge of the lattice simply moves very slightly toward or away from the surface of the conductor as the electric field of the TEM pulse moves by. This creates the surface charges that are needed in order to originate and terminate the electric field.*"

In rebuttal, if the negative charges are already neutralizing the positive charges, then they are not available to terminate external TEM-pulse field lines. Shifting them around a bit doesn't change that. This is a very basic violation of Gauss' Law.

Secondly, the electrons have mass and so there would be a delay time as these particles accelerate and decelerate to shift into different positions. They can't have information available about the approaching transverse electric force of the TEM pulse because it is moving at the speed of light. It would already be upon them before they could move.

## REFERENCES

1.  Bishop, Forrest, *Reforming Electromagnetic Units, Equations, and Concepts: An Extension of Ivor Catt's Theory*, http://www.naturalphilosophy.org/pdf/abstracts/abstracts 6554.pdf, 2012.
2.  Catt, Ivor and Forrest Bishop, *Why the Obvious must not be Obvious*, http://www.ivorcatt.co.uk/x2cm.htm, 2012.
3.  Gardner, William A., *An Answer to the Catt Question And Related Issues in EM Theory*, http://www.ivorcatt.co.uk/x63m.htm, 2015.
4.  Palmer, Chris W.P., *The Clarendon Letter, titled The Catt Question*, http://www.ivorcatt.co.uk/x2beCattQuestion.pdf, 2012.
5.  Catt, Ivor, *The Catt Question*, http://www.electromagnetism.demon.co.uk /cattq.htm, 1982.
6.  Pieraccini, Massimiliano and Stefano Selleri, *An apparent paradox: Catt's anomaly*, http://iopscience.iop.org/article /10.1088/0031-9120/48/6/718, PHYSICS EDUCATION 54 2013.
7.  Ricker, Harry H., *Catt Question Letter*, John Chappell Natural Philsophy Alliance, http://www.naturalphilosophy.org/site/ harryricker/2015/11/21/catt-question-letter, 2015.
8.  Griffiths, David J., *Introduction to Electrodynamics (2nd ed)*, Prentice Hall, ISBN 0-13-481367-71989.
9.  Feynman, Richard and Matthew Sands, *The Feynman Lectures on Physics, (Commemorative Issue)*, Allan M. Wylde, 2 0-201-51004-9 (v.2)1989.
10. Jackson, John D., *Classical Electrodynamics (2nd ed)*, Wiley, ISBN 0-471-43132-X1975.
11. Catt, Ivor, *Electromagnetism 1.*, http://www.ivorcatt.com/em.htm, 2002.
12. Catt, Ivor, *Crosstalk (Noise) in Digital Systems*, https://archive.org/details/Crosstalk, 1967.
13. Mathis, Miles, *Calculus Simplified*, http://milesmathis.com/calcsimp.html, ca 2009.
14. multiple, *Tweaker's Asylum catt anomaly*, http://www.electromagnetism.demon.co.uk /Tweaker.htm, 2001.
15. Pelosi, Giuseppe, *IEEE Historical Corner, Foreword from the Associate Editor*, texthttp://ieeexplore.ieee.org/stamp/stamp.jsp? reload=true&arnumber=6387834, IEEE Antennas and Propagation Magazine 54 2012.
16. Pieraccini, Massimiliano, *L'Anomalia*, Rizzoli, 2011.
17. Pieraccini, Massimiliano and Stefano Selleri, *Cattâ ĂŹs Anomaly*, http://ieeexplore.ieee.org/xpl/articleDetails.jsp?

reload=true&arnumber=6387835, IEEE Antennas and
Propagation Magazine 54 2012.

18. Crothers, Steven J., *On an Apparent Resolution of the Catt
Question*, PROGRESS IN PHYSICS, http://www.ptep-
online.com/index_files/2016/PP-44-13.PDF, 2016.

19. Pieraccini, Massimiliano, *Massimiliano Pieraccini L'Anomalia Il Blog*, http://anomalia-
blog.rizzoli.eu/2011/05/24/il-mondo-reale, 2011.

20. Morgenthaler, Frederic R., *The Power
and Beauty of Electromagnetic Fields*,
http://eu.wiley.com/WileyCDA/WileyTitle/productCd-
1118057570.html, 2011.

# Proposal for Wavelength Meter in Motion to Test the Invariance of c

## Phil Bouchard

*20 Poirier Gatineau, Quebec J8V 1A6 Canada, pbouchard8@gmail.com*

A wavelength meter in motion is proposed to test directly the invariance of c as postulated by the Special Relativity, which is the first time this experiment is attempted [3]. Until now it was assumed aether, if it was found, was a static substance having a unique reference frame from which entities were traveling through and therefore must not be present if tests proved otherwise.

If we replace aether with graviton fields overlapping each other then we will have a reference frame that follows the rotation of the Earth. Thus to detect its presence, we will have to physically move against that rotating frame in order to detect a change in speed of light.

This is done by sending a laser beam in the same direction of the velocity vector of the moving apparatus, capturing the difference in wavelength as we will later see.

**Keywords:** light, relativity

## 1. Introduction

In Einstein's 1905 paper on Special Relativity, two postulates form the basis of the theory [1]:

1. First postulate (principle of relativity)
   The laws of physics are the same in all inertial frames of reference.
2. Second postulate (invariance of c)
   The speed of light in free space has the same value c in all inertial frames of reference.

It was assumed that the latter was already tested because of the Michelson-Morley experiment [2] and other replications favored the null hypothesis.

The aim of this experiment is to search for evidence of a variable speed of light. According to a recent study, it might be possible to predict all phenomena of the universe based on the fact that gravity is a particle. In contrast with the previously assumed static aether from which the bodies are moving through the graviton field will have the same spin of the emitting source. Therefore the failure to detect any movement by the Michelson-Morley experiment can be explained by the fact the reference frame simply had the same spin of the Earth. The reference frame simply follows the source of the strongest gravitational acceleration. This reference frame is the Earth for all low orbit experiments that tested Special Relativity, the Sun for solar system wide probes, and so on.

By sending the laser emitter and wavelength meter at a sufficiently large velocity compared to the inertial frame of Earth we hypothesize that a detectable variance in the speed of light will be seen, only now possible with recent advancements in high-precision metrology [5].

## 2. Variance of c and Wavelength in a Graviton Field

Although gravitons haven't been directly detected and might not even be possible [4], we hypothesize to detect its presence indirectly by observing a variance in both c and the wavelength of a photon from the graviton field it is traveling through. We reevaluate the absoluteness of the reference frames, henceforth to be referenced to as Finite Theory.

Since gravity obeys the principle of superposition, we will have to isolate which reference frame defines the absoluteness of the kinetic time dilation amplitude via the gravitational acceleration strength:

$$a_E = \frac{-Gm}{(x-i)^2} \tag{1}$$

$$a_S = \frac{-Gn}{(x-j)^2} \tag{2}$$

Where:
- m = $5.9736 \times 10^{24}$ kg (mass of the Earth)
- n = $1.98892 \times 10^{30}$ kg (mass of the Sun)
- i = $-6371000$ m (position of center of the Earth)
- j = $1.49597870691 \times 10^{11}$ m (position of the Sun)

Thus the reference frame for altitudes lower than the following is defined by the Earth:

$$x = \frac{(j-i)\sqrt{m \times n} + i \times n - j \times m}{n-m} \tag{3}$$

$$x = 2.5245 \times 10^8 m \tag{4}$$

By sending the experiment at a speed in the vicinity of the speed of sound, it should be sufficient to detect a

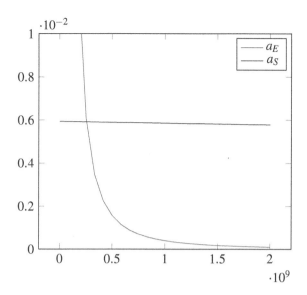

**Figure 1.** Gravitational Acceleration of the Earth and the Sun $(-m/s^2)$ vs. Altitude $(m)$

## REFERENCES

1. Albert Einstein, *Zur Elektrodynamik bewegter Körper. (German) [On the electrodynamics of moving bodies]"*, http://dx.doi.org/10.1002/andp.19053221004, Annalen der Physik 10 Vol. 322 pgs. 891-921 1905.
2. Michelson, Albert Abraham & Morley, Edward Williams, *On the Relative Motion of the Earth and the Luminiferous Ether.*, American Journal of Science Vol. 34 pgs. 333-345 1887.
3. Daniel Y. Gezari, *Experimental Basis for Special Relativity in the Photon Sector.*, arXiv:0912.3934 2009.
4. Tony Rothman, Stephen Boughn, *Can Gravitons Be Detected?.*, arXiv:gr-qc/0601043 2006.
5. *Luna, PHOENIX 1200 Tunable Laser Module & Wavemeter.*, http://lunainc.com/wp-content/uploads/2012/11/PHOENIX_1200_Data-Sheet_Rev06.pdf, 2013.

change wavelength directly proportionally while energy is conserved:

$$E = \frac{h(c - v_1)}{\lambda_1} \qquad (5)$$

$$E = \frac{h(c - v_2)}{\lambda_2} \qquad (6)$$

$$\lambda_2 = \frac{(c - v_2) \times \lambda_1}{(c - v_1)} \qquad (7)$$

$$\lambda_2 = 6.49987 \times 10^{-7} m \qquad (8)$$

Where:

- $c = 3 \times 10^8 m/s$
- $v_1 = 0 m/s$
- $\lambda_1 = 6.5 \times 10^{-7} m$
- $v_2 = 6125.22 m/s$

For a wavelength meter having an accuracy of $\pm 1.5 pm$ we should be able to confirm whether the change in wavelength occurs for the experiment in motion. The predicted difference of $1.3 \times 10^{-11} m$ $(\lambda_1 - \lambda_2)$ is large enough to be detected.

## 3. Acknowledgment

Thanks to Evan Adams for helping editing it and for reviewing related experiments.

# Special Relativity is Not Needed

## Robert de Hilster

*23344 Carolwood Ln, Boca Raton, FL 33428*
*robert@dehilster.com*

Many people have proved to themselves that Special Relativity is wrong. They know about the paradoxes, they know about the bad assumptions, they know about the mathematical errors. And yet it is still hard to provide absolute proof that it is wrong. After all, there are many others that are proving it right. This paper describes two things that proved to me that Special Relativity is wrong. The model is wrong and the interpretation of what each observer sees is wrong. My conclusion is that the transformation of length, time, and mass are not needed.

**Keywords:** relativity, light

## 1. Johnston's Model

There is a very good explanation of the development of the Special Relativity (SR) equation given in the reference [1]. Figures 1 and 2 show the models that are used by Robert Johnston. Quoting Johnston:

*"Imagine a spacecraft passing the Earth with velocity v. On the spacecraft is an observer and an apparatus that will flash a beam of light across the spacecraft (perpendicular to the spacecraft's motion). On the Earth is another observer."*

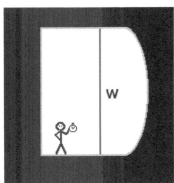

**Figure 1.**   Observer A

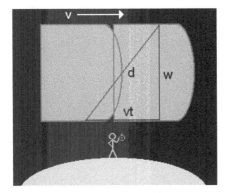

**Figure 2.**   Observer B

*"According to the observer on the spacecraft, the light beam travels a distance w, where w is the width of the spacecraft. However, the observer on Earth will see the light beam cover a greater distance, due to the motion of the spacecraft while the light beam is en route."*

## 2. The Wrong Model

Observer A is moving with the space craft and the model shows that he sees the light moving straight up. Observer B is on the earth and observes the light moving to the right at a 45 degree angle. Since they each see a different image, a transformation is needed. But wait! The two images are wrong.

### 2.1. Observer A

In Figure 1, observer A sees the laser beam moving straight up and is not aware that he is moving. There is no arrow showing the velocity v. He is not smart enough to look out the window and see the earth moving by. Even so, if the light beam is actually moving straight up he should know that the spacecraft is not moving relative to the laser beam that he sees, even though he sees the earth moving.

The laser is pointing straight up from the floor of the spacecraft. Each photon of the light beam should move in a straight up at speed c until it reaches the ceiling. The spacecraft, the observer, the laser source, and the air in the spacecraft are all moving to the right at speed v. Observer A should see each photon move backward because he an the spacecraft are moving forward.

### 2.2. Observer B

Observer B sees the spacecraft moving forward a velocity v and the laser beam moving up at speed c. The question is: "What causes the beam to move faster than the space ship?" Robert Johnston states: *"...the light beam covers a greater distance due to the motion of the spacecraft."* It is the motion of the spacecraft that pushes the light forward. I don't know of any force that does that!

## 3. Light

It could help if we had a better understanding of how we see the light beam. So here is a simple experiment.

Shine a red laser light on the wall. Do you see the red spot? Yes, but do you see the red beam going from the laser pointer to the wall? No? It's true, you can't see a photon moving in space unless it reflects off of something and then the reflection must hit your eye.

My wife suggested I spray hair spray in the room and then shine the laser light on the wall. Great! Now I can see the beam of light. Well, no, I am not seeing the beam of light. I see hair spray particles that are painted red by the laser light.

### 3.1. Image of the Red Dot

It turns out that when the laser light hits the wall, there are images of the red dot scattered in all directions. If there are twenty people in the room and they are all looking at the red dot on the wall, there must be twenty images of that red dot scattered from the wall. In fact there are millions of these images scattered around the room. And no matter where you are you see the red dot. They are not identical images. Each of us has a different view of the red dot. But we all call it a red dot.

### 3.2. Image of the Red Hair Spray Particles

In a very short interval of time the laser light (photons) will hit many hair spray particles. These photons will scatter in all directions sending similar images in all directions. One of the images reaches observer A and he sees the streams of red hair spray particles. If Observer A sees the the stream of particles shown in Figure 1, then observer B will see the same image.

## 4. What Really Happens

So what should each observer see?

### 4.1. Observer A

Figure 3 shows what observer A could see if the space craft is moving at a high speed.

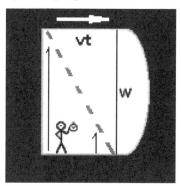

**Figure 3.** Observer A Actual Image

The spacecraft is shown when the first photon burst has reached the ceiling. The last one emitted is just above the floor. If observer A sees the dotted image in Figure 3, observer B will see a similar image.

## 5. No Translation Needed

There is one event. The red laser photons scattering from the hairspray particles. It will send nearly identical images of the particles to observer A and B. If observer A and

B see the same image, then there is no translation needed. The speed of an object does not change the scattered image of the object. Special relativity equations solve a problem that does not exist. It does not cause time dilation, nor length contraction, nor mass increase.

## REFERENCES

1. Wm Robert Johnston, *Some equations of special relativity.*, 26 July 2005.

# Earth Expansion Major Objections Solved

## David de Hilster

*22936 Ironwedge Dr, Boca Raton, FL 33433, david@dehilster.com*

The two main objections to Expansion Tectonics by those in the scientific community are lack of a mechanism for expansion and mass increase, and the presence of subduction. This paper will show that these are now solved.

**Keywords:** expansion tectonics, atomic structure

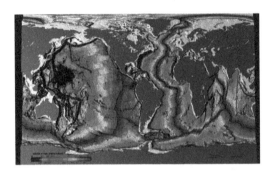

**Figure 1.** The map that changed everything: The NOSC mapping of seafloor bed ages in bands of 10s of millions of years.

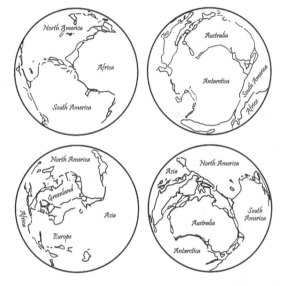

**Figure 2.** Four sides of the earth as shown once all the seafloor bed has been removed. You can see that the continents fit together in recognizable shapes without a lot of modification.

## 1. Introduction

In this author's mind, the evidence for and expanding and growing earth is overwhelming. The most compelling evidence being that when the seafloor bed (see figure 1) is removed by youngest to oldest, all the continents on the earth fit together with almost no modification (see figure 2). The chances of that happening are described by Stephen Hurrell, author of "Dinasaurs and the Expanding Earth" [1]:

"My original estimate for the Expanding Earth forming by chance alone was massively conservative. It isn't less than one chance in a million, or billion, or even a trillion. It's less than one chance in an octillion: a number so large I needed to look up its name. Now consider that the real Earth has multiple coastlines which all need to fit together. The probability of this happening by chance is so small it is virtually impossible." [3]

## 2. Subduction

One of the arguments we hear about why expansion tectonics is not the correct theory is that there is proof of subduction, and if the earth has been expanding, there could be no subduction. Subduction is where one tectonic plate does underneath another plate. Plate tectonics states that the radius of the earth stays the same, and that there is a conveyor belt that creates and destroys the seabed as see in figure 3.

In the "excitement" of a new wave of supporters who are discovering expansion tectonics, many proponents of

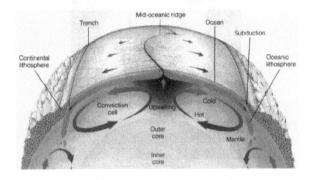

**Figure 3.** Subduction is where tectonic plates dive underneath another plate.

expansion tectonics wrongfully claim that subduction does not exist. It in fact does exist. Here are the confirmed subduction areas on the globe 4.

Expansion tectonics has some places where subduction will occur, although not like the plate tectonics would describe. The earth is not equally expanding. In fact, the

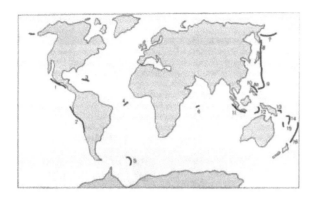

**Figure 4.** The known subduction zones are not enough to keep the earth at a constant radius. This is a problem for mainstream plate tectonics [2]

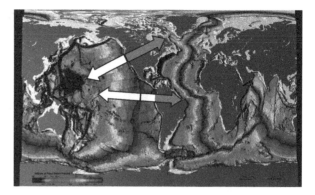

**Figure 7.** The arrows represent expansion with the read arrows representing where subduction should be occurring. This is only two of many examples.

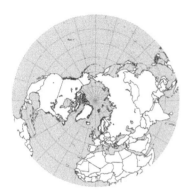

**Figure 5.** Northern hemisphere above the equator

bottom of the earth is expanding much more than the top, thus the reason for more land in the northern hemisphere (figure 5) than the southern (figure 6).

In figure 7, you can see where the earth is expanding starting on the west coast of Canada and the United States and works it way down the west coast of the Americas. The arrows represent the extent of the expansion with with being non-subducted expansion, and red arrows being subducted expansion. You can see that the expansion in

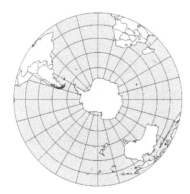

**Figure 6.** Southern hemisphere below the equator

north america to the east is going to have to subduct.

Without exhaustively looking at all the scenarios, it is easy to see that earth's expansion is not uniform and subduction not only can be a part of the expansion model, it can help predict those subductions perhaps even better than the plate tectonics model.

## 3. Mechanisms for Expansion

It is important to remember that although the term "Expansion Tectonics" in words only describes "size", the phrase itself is meant to include mass increase. Dr. James Maxlow, considered by many as the top expansion geologist in the world, coined the phrase but also includes mass increase as a part of that term as well. Maxlow has found geological evidence of mass increase. This is very important. It is not simply expansion.

There have been many mechanism that have been proposed for expansion including prime matter particles.

### 3.1. New Solution to Mass Increase

The author of this paper and his father, have come up with a solution to how mass increase happens [4]. The Particle Model of the Universe describes the universe as particles and the G1 or gravitron particle level 1 being the particle for light, gravity, the electron cloud, and electricity. Atomic structure is made up of nucleons (protons and neutrons), and G1 particles that are smaller and more numerous than the electron. Electrons don't exist in this model. Magnetic fields and charge are actually the results of clouds of moving G1 particles.

Mass increase happens when suns blow atoms apart and spew G1 particles and nucleons in all directions. The magnetic field of the earth are G1 particles that are circulating around the earth through the poles which then capture other G1 particles and nucleons that recreate atoms inside the earth.

## 4. Conclusion

The two major objections to expansion tectonics is the presence of known subduction and no mechanism for mass increase of the expansion. Given the fact that the earth does not expand uniformly, and with the new Particle Model of

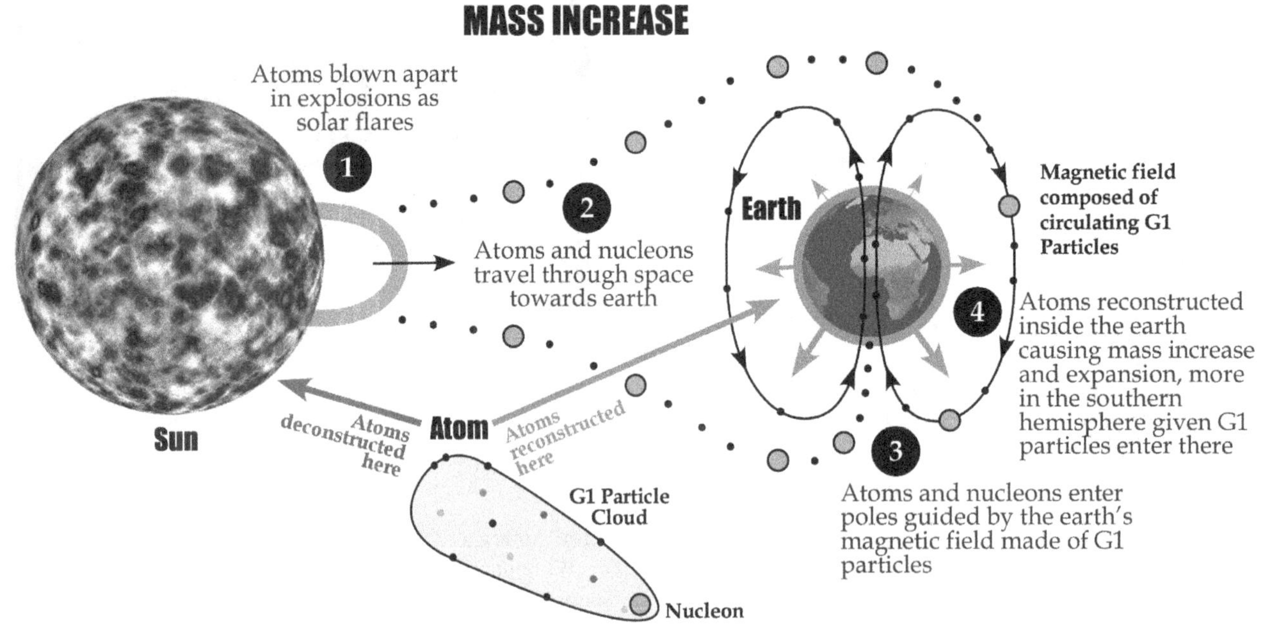

## MASS INCREASE

**Figure 8.**    Atoms are blown apart in the sun and all suns into G1 particles and nucleons which are reconstructed inside the earth

the universe able to explain mass increase, both of those objections have been answered.

## REFERENCES

1.  Stephen Hurrell, *Dinosaurs and the Expanding Earth.* , Third Edition9780952 260372011.
2.  Samuel Carey *Theories of the Earth and Universe: A History of Dogma in the Earth Sciences.*, textttwww.RelativityOfLight.com, Stanford University Press; 1 edition (March 1, 1988)
3.  Stephen Hurrell, *Probablity Analysis: Expanding Earth Theory is True.* texttthttp://www.dinox.org/propee.html , 2013.
4.  Robert de Hilster, David de Hilster, *Universe Hack 3.0 - A Particle Model of the Entire Universe.* The John Chappell Natural Philosophy Society , 2016.

# Microwaves from Extra Galactic Radio Sources found to Deflect only at Minimum Impact Parameter Corresponding to the Solar Plasma Limb

## E. H. Dowdye Jr.

*Founder Pure Classical Physics Research, Greenbelt Maryland 20770, USA,*
*e-mail: gravityfindings@gmail.com*

Findings show that the gravitational deflection of electromagnetic waves in the microwave frequency spectrum are severely impact parameter dependent at the plasma limb of the sun. By definition the impact parameter $\varepsilon$ is the nearest point of approach of a given ray of light or a ray of microwaves to the center of the gravitating mass M that is enclosed in an analytical Gaussian sphere of radius R. The light bending rule of General Relativity predicts that impact parameters of $\varepsilon \approx R$ for gravitationally bent rays of light and microwaves should occur in empty vacuum space as well as in the plasma limb of the sun, where $R$ is the radius of the analytical Gaussian sphere that encloses the gravitating mass $M$ of the sun. The past century of astrophysical observations show that the bulk of gravitational light bending effects has been observed primarily at the plasma limb of the sun, namely, at impact parameters of $\varepsilon \approx R$. With current technical means in Astrophysics, the gravitational light bending effect should be an easily observable effect for impact parameters corresponding to several solar radii above the plasma limb of the sun, namely, at $\varepsilon = 2R$, $\varepsilon = 3R$, $\varepsilon = 4R$, etc., etc., at $\varepsilon = nR$, for analytical Gaussian spheres of several solar radii R. The corresponding effects of gravitational deflection should be 1/2, 1/3, 1/4, ..., 1/n times 1.752 arcsec observed at the solar plasma limb. Of course, this assumes the light bending rule of General Relativity applies to all empty vacuum space above the surface of the sun as well as in the plasma limb. Findings show that the plasma atmosphere of the sun represents an *indirect interaction* between the gravitational gradient field of the sun and the microwaves from the extra galactic radio pulsar sources. A minimum energy path calculation, supporting this argument, leads to a derivation of the very same light bending equation obtained from the assumptions of General Relativity. This result was confirmed by a measurement on the gravitational deflection of microwaves at the Solar plasma limb by [6]. (1995), who used a very-long-baseline-interferometer (VLBI) technique. The researchers used extra galactic radio pulsar sources to determine the gravitational deflection of the microwaves from these sources at the solar plasma limb, obtaining a results to within 0.9998 +/- 0.0008 times 1.752 arcsec. PACS: 95.30Sf, 04.25.dg, 52/25/Qt. 52.40.Db

**Keywords:** light, relativity, stellar aberration, pulsar, de Sitter

## 1. Introduction

We shall examine the evidence for gravitational lensing in our region of space near to us, starting with the nearest star to us, our sun. The light bending rule of General Relativity predicts that a *direct interaction* takes place between the gravitational field of the lensing mass and the rays of light from the stars. The past century of the observed solar light bending effects were observed primarily at the thin plasma limb of the sun, namely, at impact parameters of $\xi \approx R$. The observations are consistent with an *indirect interaction* between the solar plasma limb exposed to the gravitational gradient field of the sun and the solar gravity itself. This argument is strongly supported by a calculation which led to a derivation of the very same light bending equation obtained by General Relativity. *Dowdye (2011)* [15] The derivation assumes a minimum energy path of waves propagating in the solar plasma atmosphere exposed to the gravitational gradient field of the sun. The researchers [6] made VLBI observations on extra galactic radio sources to determine the gravitational deflection of microwaves observed to deflect only at the plasma limb

of the sun. The researchers reported a gravitational deflection of 0.9998 +/- 0.0008 times 1.752 arcsec which confirms the minimum energy calculation for the gravitational deflection of microwaves propagating in the solar plasma reported in this work [15] *Dowdye (2011)*. Appendix A gives a detail calculation for the gravitational deflection of electromagnetic waves, also from the Reference [15] *Dowdye (2011)*.

Examining the lower boundary of the solar atmosphere and the plasma-free vacuum space several solar radii above the limb of the sun, the solar light bending effect acting on the rays of starlight appear to deviate from the predicted $1/R$ effect of the light bending rule of General Relativity. A close study of the stars in our own region of space, less than hundreds of light-years away, appear to exhibit the very same gravitational light bending effects as that of our nearest star, the sun. There are many cases whereby likely gravitational lenses and light sources are just by chance co-linearly aligned with earth based observers, presenting vast opportunities for the observation of Einstein rings as is predicted by the light bending rule of General Relativity. Thus, the images of the Einstein rings should be ever present in the star-filled skies. It should be no surprise, however, that the Einstein rings are **not** observed in the star-filled night skies as the required impact parameters would have to be such that the rays of starlight propagate well above the plasma limb of the potential stars. Any rays of starlight responsible for conveying the images of the Einstein rings to our telescope must propagate at astronomical distances in plasma-free space well above the stellar atmospheres of potential lensing stars. Any potential for a gravitational deflection must occur in the plasma-free space significantly above the plasma atmosphere of the lensing star. A gravitational deflection in that case would require a *direct interaction* between gravity and electromagnetism as is predicted by the light bending rule of General Relativity. Given the mean astronomical distances between the stars in our space, in the order of **light-years**, the failed observation of Einstein rings in our star-filled skies are primarily due to the **very short plasma limb focal length** of the potential lensing stars, in the order of **astronomical units (AU,s)**. Note: Our sun is but a typical lensing star and has a **plasma limb focal length** of **565 AU's.**

The observations convincingly show that an *indirectly interacting* medium containing gravitating matter such as plasma does not exist in the vacuum space at the site of Sagittarius A*, believed to be the site of a **Black Hole.** Such gravitating matter would be quickly gobbled up and consumed by the **Black Hole.** This is confirmed by the history of intense observations of the time resolved images collected from Sagittarius A* since 1992. Intense observations of collected images reveals to this date a clear lack of evidence for gravitational lensing or distortions due to lensing as can be seen in the recorded images of the **sun-like stars** orbiting about the super massive object at the site of Sagittarius A*. This topic will be covered in detail in Subsection 3.2.

## 2. The Important Fundamentals

An application of Gauss's law, applied to gravitation as well as to electromagnetism along with the principle of optical reciprocity clearly show that a co-linear alignment of the observer, the lens and the source is unnecessary for an observation of a gravitational light bending effect, as predicted by the light bending rule of General Relativity. The gravitational effect at the surface of an analytical Gaussian sphere due to the presence of a point-like gravitating mass that is enclosed inside of the sphere depends only on the quantity of mass enclosed. The size or density of the enclosed mass particle is not important. [14] The Gauss' law of gravity (see, e.g., Arfken 1995, Jackson 1998) is a Mathematical Physics tool that encloses a gravitating mass particle inside of an analytical Gaussian sphere of radius $R$. The gravitational field at the surface of this sphere depends solely on the mass $M$ that is enclosed. An analogy to this principle encloses an electrically charged particle inside of a Gaussian surface in application to the electric field of

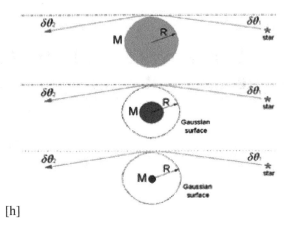

[h]

**Figure 1.** Gauss' Law is applied to Equal Gravitating Masses of Different Radii of Mass-Spheres enclosed within Spherical Gaussian Surfaces of the same radius $R$. This important principle graphically demonstrates that the gravitational deflection is dependent on the mass $M$ but is independent of the density of the enclosed mass.

the charged particle in the discipline of Electromagnetism (Jackson 1998). The principle of optical reciprocity (Born 1975, Potton 2004) simply states that the light must take the very same minimum energy path or least time path, in either direction between the source and the observer. This fundamental principle is an essential tool for the understanding of complex lensing systems in Astronomy and Astrophysics (Carrol et al. 1996).

### 2.1. Gauss Law applied to a Point-Like Gravitating Mass

Any gravitational effect acting on a light ray due to the presence of a gravitating point like mass at the impact parameter of $\xi = R$ theoretically depends on the amount of Mass $M$ that is enclosed within the analytical Gaussian sphere of radius $R$ as illustrated in Figure 1. Any gravitational effect that would be noted at the surface of the analytical Gaussian sphere should in principle be totally independent of the radius of the mass particle or the density of the mass that is enclosed within the Gaussian sphere of radius $R$. From Gauss's Law (Equation 2) equal masses of different radii will theoretically have equal gravitational effects at the surface of the Gaussian sphere. The light bending rule

$$\delta\theta = \frac{4GM}{Rc^2} \qquad (1)$$

of General Relativity is essentially a localized $\frac{1}{R}$ effect. We are dealing with astronomical distances. Thus, the bulk of the gravitational effect on the path of particles of light would takes place along a segment of the light ray that encloses the impact parameter $\xi$. This segment may be only several orders of magnitude greater than the radius $R$ of the Gaussian sphere that encloses the gravitating mass $M$. The predominant effect of the gravitational field on the bending of the light ray would occur along this short segment of the light path, maximizing at the point where the light ray is tangent to our analytical Gaussian sphere, namely, at the impact parameter $\xi = R$.

A Mathematical Physics tool known as Gauss' law (Arfken 1995),(Jackson 1998),

$$\int_S \vec{g} \cdot d\vec{A} = -4\pi GM \qquad (2)$$

is applied directly to the gravitating masses where the gravitational field $\vec{g}$ is a function only of the mass $M$ enclosed by the spherical Gaussian surface $S$. The gravitational flux at the surface of the analytical Gaussian sphere is totally independent of the radius $R$ of the sphere. (Born 1975) The idea here is that the gravitational field at this analytical Gaussian surface is only a function of the mass that it encloses. (Arfken 1995, Jackson 1998) Any mass $M$, regardless of the radius of the mass particle that is enclosed inside of the Gaussian spherical surface of radius R will contribute exactly the same gravitational potential at the Gaussian surface. In Figure 1, the gravitational field points inward towards the center of the mass. Its magnitude is $g = \frac{GM}{R^2}$. In order to calculate the flux of the gravitational field out of the sphere of area $A = 4\pi R^2$, a minus sign is introduced. We then have the flux $\Phi_g = -gA = -(\frac{GM}{R^2})(4\pi R^2) = -4\pi GM$. Again, we note that the flux does not depend on the size of the sphere. It is straightforwardly seen that a direct application of Gauss's law to the light bending rule, 1, coupled with the essential principle of *optical reciprocity* (Potton 2004), removes any requirement for a co-linear alignment of the light source, the point-like gravitating mass particle (the lens) and the observer for observation of a gravitational lensing effect as suggested by General Relativity. [14]

From Equation 2, the flux of the gravitational potential at the surface of the Gaussian spheres, as illustrated in Figure 1, is the same for all enclosed mass particles of the same mass $M$, regardless of the size of the mass particle. As a result, each mass particle will produce the very same gravitational light bending effect $\delta\theta = \delta\theta_1 + \delta\theta_2$, where $\delta\theta_1$ and $\delta\theta_2$ are the bending effects on the ray of light on approach and on receding the lens, respectively. This of course assumes the validity of Figure 1. This symmetry requirement suggests that $\delta\theta_1 = \delta\theta_2$. From Equations 1 and 3 it follows that $\delta\theta = 2\delta\theta_1 = \frac{4GM}{Rc^2}$ and $\delta\theta_1 = \delta\theta_2 = \frac{2GM}{Rc^2}$. This says that the total contribution of the light bending effect due to the gravitating point-like mass particle on any given infinitely long light ray is theoretically divided equally at the impact parameter $\xi \approx R$, separating the approaching segment and the receding segment of the optical path. A confirmation of this will be clearly seen later with application of the *principle of reciprocity* and a demonstration of a simple derivation of the equation of the Einstein ring, illustrating the *symmetry requirement* of General Relativity.

## 2.2. Optical Reciprocity applied to the Lensed Light Ray

In any space, the *principle of reciprocity* (Born 1975),(Potton 2004), a very fundamental principle of

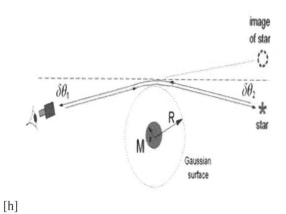

[h]

**Figure 2.** The Fundamental Principle of Optical Reciprocity Illustrated on a hypothetically Gravitationally Lensed Light Ray shows that the path of a Gravitationally Lensed Light Ray will be the same in both directions, from the source to the observer and from the observer back to the source.

optics, must hold as illustrated in Figure 2. The principle simply states that any photon or wave of light moving on a **preferred optical path**, from the source to the observer, must take the very same optical path from a hypothetical laser gun of the observer back to the source. As a consequence of this fundamental principle, any additional sources placed along the same preferred optical path will all appear to the observer to be located at the very same image position of the most distant source. As a consequence of this principle, all light emitting sources on a single preferred optical path will appear to the observer to be co-located at the very same point, appearing as a single light emitting source. This scarcely mentioned fundamental *principle of optics* is directly applicable to the Astrophysics at the galactic center. The total gravitational light bending effect acting on the light ray upon approach and upon receding a point-like gravitating mass is give by

$$\delta\theta = \delta\theta_1|_{\substack{approaching \\ the\ lens}} + \delta\theta_2|_{\substack{receding \\ the\ lens}} = \frac{4GM}{Rc^2} \qquad (3)$$

In this example the gravitating mass $M$ is chosen to be positioned at the midpoint on the line joining the observer and the light source for the simplified special case $D_L : D_{SL} : D_S = 1 : 1 : 2$. (Blandford et al. 1992) This simplified special case is illustrated in Figure 3.

The astronomical distance $D_L$ is the distance from the observer to the lens, $D_{SL}$ is the distance from the lens to the source and $D_S$ is the distance from the observer to the source. Also again, we note that this case is a simplified special case, where $D_L = D_{SL}$, presented in most academic textbooks. There is no requirement at all that the lens be positioned exactly at the midpoint for an observation of a theoretical Einstein ring. See Appendix B for the general case ($D_L \neq D_{SL}$). The vast astronomical distances between the stars most assuredly would present much larger impact parameters of $\xi$ much greater than the radius of the lensing stars under observation, on a much grander scale to any

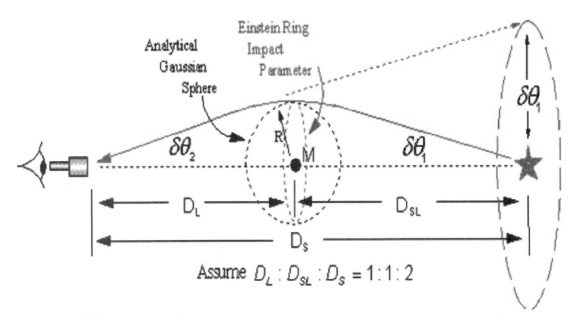

[t!]

**Figure 3.** A Symmetry Requirement for the assumption of the accumulative lensing effect using predictions according to the Light Bending Rule of General Relativity. A gravitation mass $M$ is chosen to be located at the midpoint on a line between the light source and the observer. $D_L$ is distance between the observer and the lens. $D_{SL}$ is distance between the lens and the source. $D_S$ is distance between the observer and the source. This is the simplified special case $D_L = D_{SL}$ presented in most academic textbooks.

bent light ray passing by the lensing stars. An *indirect interaction* between light rays and the gravitational field of the more distant stars could not occur in the plasma-free vacuum space. The mean astronomical distances in the celestial skies and consequently the much larger impact parameters $\xi$, much greater than the radius of the lensing star where gravitational bending of electromagnetic waves occur by means of an *indirect interaction* at the slellar plasma limb of the star, may be the most fundamental reason for the failed observation of Einstein rings in the star-filled skies.

### 2.3. Einstein Ring Equation derived from Symmetry Requirements Assumption

From symmetry we have

$$\delta\theta_1 = \delta\theta_2 = \frac{2GM}{Rc^2} \tag{4}$$

Again, the astronomical distance $D_L$ is the distance from the observer to the lens. Since we are dealing with very small angles, from Figure 3 the deflection of the light ray due to the gravitational effect on approach to the gravitating mass is just simply $\delta\theta_1 = \frac{R}{D_L} = \frac{2GM}{Rc^2}$ wherefrom $\frac{R^2}{D_L} = \frac{2GM}{c^2}$ and $\frac{R^2}{D_L^2} = \frac{2GM}{D_Lc^2} = \delta\theta_1^{\,2}$. Solving this for the radius of the impact parameter of the light ray and thus the radius of the Einstein Ring expressed in units of radians we have

$$\delta\theta_1 = \sqrt{\frac{2GM}{D_Lc^2}} \tag{5}$$

which is the radius of the Einstein ring in units of radians for a lens place exactly midway between the source and the observer. This is a special case, where $D_L = D_{SL}$. (See Appendix B for the general case $(D_L \neq D_{SL})$) Note that the gravitational bending effect on the light ray for the approach segment alone is exactly equal to the radius of the solved Einstein ring expressed in radians and is given as

$$\delta\theta_1 = \frac{2GM}{Rc^2} \tag{6}$$

This effect is exactly one half of the total accumulative gravitational effect acting on the light ray for the approach and receding segments. [14] This principle, an essential Mathematical Physics principle on lensing, is often totally missed by researchers attempting to deal with this topic. From symmetry requirement, the integral gravitational effect on a light ray upon approach to a gravitating mass positioned exactly at the midpoint of a line joining the source and the observer, must equal that of the integral gravitational effect on the light ray upon receding the gravitating mass

$$\delta\theta_1\big|_{\substack{approaching\\the\ lens}} = \delta\theta_2\big|_{\substack{receding\\the\ lens}} \tag{7}$$

as suggested by Equation 4 and the laws of conservation of energy and of momentum. [14] This is a rarely covered fundamental on gravitational lensing in the textbooks. The accumulative gravitational effect along the light ray must sum the total effects of gravity acting on the light ray for both the approach and receding segments of any ray of light passing by a point-like gravitating mass. [14] The total light bending effect is therefore

$$\delta\theta = \frac{4GM}{Rc^2} \qquad (8)$$

In all cases, the fundamental principle of optical reciprocity must hold. This is a given. The principle of optical reciprocity simply states that any light ray or a photon of light must take the very same path, along the same minimum energy path, in either direction between the source and the observer as depicted in Figure 2.

Using the light bending rule of General Relativity, it is straightforwardly and theoretically demonstrated that all observers of varying distances from a gravitating mass or lens should see an Einstein ring. Only a mid-field observer, one who is placed such that the lens is exactly mid way between the source and the observer, will derive Equation 6. This equation gives exactly the same numerical value as that given by Equation 5 for a simplified special case, where $D_L = D_{SL}$. This simple case is presented in most academic textbooks. Appendix B gives the general case where $D_L$ is **not** necessarily equal to $D_{SL}$. In the general case, the lens **may not** be placed exactly midway between the light source and the observer. The near-field observer, one who is near to the lens, and the far-field observer, one who is far from the lens, both will derive Einstein ring equations with coefficients corresponding to their unique geometries. Each observer has distinct sets of lensed light rays, each lensed light rays with their corresponding axis of symmetry. A light ray that is gravitationally bent by a point-like gravitating mass, as predicted by General Relativity, will always have an axis of symmetry associated with it. The axis of symmetry will be perpendicular to the line joining the source and the observer only when the lens is positioned exactly at the midpoint on the line joining the observer and the source. Theoretically, all observers should see, according to the light bending rule of General Relativity, an Einstein ring. [14] This essential key point is missed in all too many lectures on this subject matter.

## 2.4. Condition for Observing of an Einstein Ring using a Lens of 1 Solar Mass and 1 Solar Radius

Using the collected astrophysical data and the astrophysical constants from 1, we find that a stellar system that has 1 solar mass and 1 solar radius, Equation (8) yields a light bending angles of $8.4952 \cdot 10^{-6}$ radians. This angle is 0.0004867 degrees or 1.752 arcsec. The diameter of the solar disk is observed to be 0.55 degrees, a radius of 0.275 degrees. If the radius of the solar disk were compared with the angle of solar light bending of the plasma limb (in degrees), we would have a factor of $\frac{R(deg)}{\delta\theta(deg)} = 565.0$. This means that in order to observe an Einstein ring of a distant

**TABLE 1.** Astrophysical Data of the Sun

| | | |
|---|---|---|
| Solar Mass | M | $1.99 \cdot 10^{30} Kg$ |
| Solar Radius | R | $6.96 \cdot 10^{8} m$ |
| G Constant | G | $6.67 \cdot 10^{-11} m^3 s^2/Kg$ |
| Velocity of Light | c | $2.99792458 \cdot 10^{8} ms^{-1}$ |
| $\delta\theta$ (rad) | $\frac{4GM}{Rc^2}$ | $8.4952 \cdot 10^{-6}$ rad |
| $\delta\theta$ (deg) | $\frac{4GM}{Rc^2}$ | 0.0004867 deg |
| $\delta\theta$ (arcsec) | $\frac{4GM}{Rc^2}$ | 1.752 arcsec |
| Radius of Sun | R(deg) | 0.275 deg |
| Focal Length | $\frac{R(deg)}{\delta\theta(deg)}$ | 565.0 AU |

stellar light source due solely to the plasma limb of the sun, the observer would have to back away from the sun for at least 565 mean Earth orbital radii or astronomical units(AU's). This is the **focal length of the plasma limb lensing system** of the sun. It is that distance required for the parallel rays of starlight to converge to a point after being deflected by the solar plasma limb. If the observer were to back off to a distance greater than 565 AU's, then the chance of gravitationally bent light rays interacting solely with the plasma limb of a lensing star **would highly unlikely** produce images of Einstein rings at the site of observers beyond the plasma focal length of the lens. At astronomical distances, such light rays would be deflected completely away from all observers who are positioned beyond the plasma focal length of sun-like stars and would not be detected by these observers at all.

Because of the vast astronomical distances between the stars in our night skies, any gravitationally bent light ray would require much larger **impact parameters**, corresponding to distances clearly above the plasma limb of the lensing stars into empty vacuum space where there is virtually **no** chance for gravitational lensing effects directly caused by the stellar plasma limbs. If the light bending rule of Generally Relativity applied to the empty plasma-free vacuum space as well as the stellar plasma limbs, our night skies would be completely filled with images of Einstein rings and arcs. Thus, as a consequence of the extremely large impact parameters $\xi$, the bulk of the rays of starlight must propagate in the empty plasma-free vacuum space void of *indirectly interacting media* at the stellar plasma of the stars, as is confirmed by the observational evidence, i.e., **no** observations of Einstein Rings in the star-filled skies. This observation is consistent with the lack of observation of gravitational deflection of microwaves above the solar plasma limb, i.e., at the impact parameters $\xi > R$.

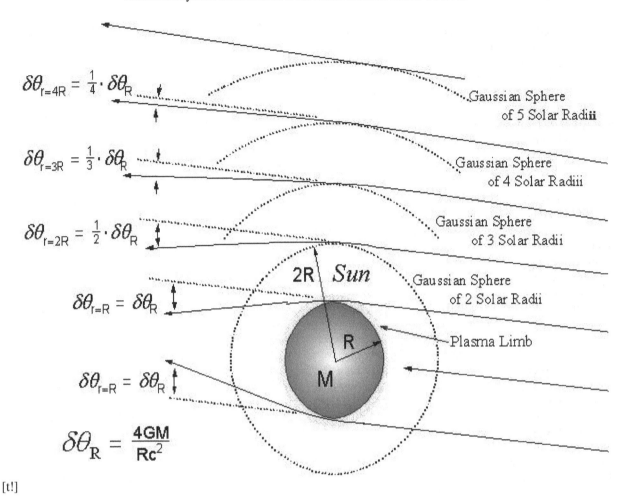

**Figure 4.** Gravitational Light Bending as function of various Gaussian Surface radii Impact Parameters as predicted by the light bending rule of General Relativity

## 3. The Important Fundamentals Correctly Applied

### 3.1. The Fundamentals applied to the Thin Plasma Rim of the Sun

Historically, the effect of light bending has been noted only at the solar limb. The thin plasma of the sun's atmosphere appears to be due to an *indirect interaction* between the rays of starlight and the gravitational field of the sun. Figure 4 illustrates the theoretical light bending effect of the sun at various radii of analytical Gaussian surfaces, concentric to the center of the sun as suggested by General Relativity. We note in Figure 4 that the bulk of the solar lensing effect is essentially a $1/R$ effect which is predominant along a segment of the light path that encloses the impact parameter, $R$, where the indicated light ray is tangent to the spherical Gaussian surfaces. Since the astronomical distances are extremely large, for all practical purposes, the total integrated $1/R$ effect of the light bending occurs along a segment of the light ray that is extremely short compared to astronomical distances. Theoretically, the light bending along the segment due to the gravity of a point-like mass on approach and on receding are virtu-

ally equal and divided at the impact parameter $R$ where the relation $\delta\theta_1|_{\substack{approaching \\ the\ lens}} = \delta\theta_2|_{\substack{receding \\ the\ lens}}$ still holds even though the Earth based observer is relatively close to the sun. [14] Remarkably, as it may seem, however, historically the solar light bending effect has been observed primarily at the solar limb, namely, the solar plasma atmosphere through which the light rays are directed along a *minimum energy* or *least time* path. [15] *Dowdye (2011)* The thickness of the plasma atmosphere of the sun, frequently referred to as the solar rim or the solar limb, is very negligible in comparison to the solar radius $R$. Table II summarizes nearly a century of observations of gravitational light bending as a function of the distance above the solar plasma limb. The bulk of the observed solar light bending events were recorded during solar eclipses. The moon has provided a near perfect masking of the solar disk, allowing only the thin plasma limb of the sun to be exposed for the astrophysical observations.

Assuming the validity of the light bending rule of General Relative, the current technical means of the astronomical techniques should have easily allowed observations of solar light bending of stellar light rays at different solar

**TABLE 2.** The Observed and Predicted Gravitational Lensing at Distances h (in units of $R_{SUN}$) above the Solar Plasma Rim

|     | Distance h above Rim ($R_{SUN}$) | Gravity $1/r^2$ Effect ($g_{SUN}$) | Observed Lensing (arcsec) | Predicted by Relativity (arcsec) |
|-----|-----------|-----------|-----------|-----------|
| [h] | 1.0 | 0.25 | none | 0.88 |
|     | 0.5 | 0.44 | none | 1.17 |
|     | 0.2 | 0.69 | none | 1.45 |
|     | 0.1 | 0.83 | negligible | 1.59 |
|     | 0 | 1.00 | 1.752 | 1.752 |

radii of analytical Gaussian surfaces, namely at the radius of 2R, 3R and even beyond 4R, where R is one solar radius, as illustrated in Figure 4. For instance, at the analytical Gaussian surface of radius 2R, the predicted light bending effect of General Relativity would have been an easily detectable effect of one half the effect of 1.752 arcsec noted at the solar limb; at the surface of radius 3R, an effect of one third the effect at the solar limb, etc., etc. The equatorial radius $R_{SUN}$ is approximately 695,000 km. The thickness of the solar limb has been recorded to be less than 20,000 km; less than 3 percent of the solar radius R. From this, we can easily see that a gravitational lensing effect in vacuum space several solar radii above the solar plasm rim should be a very noticeable effect to the modern astronomical means. Schmeidler [16], showed that for optical wavelengths a modified corrective term that varies directly proportional to $\frac{1}{r^2}$ had to be added to the theoretical light bending effect predicted by General Relativity. The results of several observations suggested the empirical formula for the deflection of light near the sun as: $\delta r = \frac{1".75}{r} + \frac{0".3}{r^2}$. Schmeidler [16] convincingly show that the solar plasma atmosphere has very different gravitational bending effect on the rays of optical wavelengths and the rays of much longer wavelengths of microwaves. Also, at the time of the publication of their findings in 1985 the solar bending effects at or near the solar limb was not very well understood.

### 3.2. The Fundamentals applied to the Orbit of S2 about Sagittarius A*

The past decades of intense observations using modern astronomical techniques in Astrophysics alone reveal an obvious lack of evidence for lensing effects on collected emissions from the stars orbiting about Sagittarius A*, believed to be a super massive black hole located at the galactic center of our Milky Way. This is most obviously revealed in the time resolved images collected since 1992 on the rapidly moving stars orbiting about Sagittarius A* [8] [9] [10] [5] [11] [12]. The space in the immediate vicinity of a black hole is by definition an extremely good vacuum. The evidence for this is clearly seen in the highly elliptical orbital paths of the stars orbiting about the Sagittarius A*. The presence of material media near the galactic core mass would conceivably perturb the motion of the stellar object s16 which has been observed to move with a good fraction of the velocity of light. The presence of any media

other than a good vacuum would have caused the fast moving stellar object s16 to rapidly disintegrate. Astrophysical observations reveal that s16 has a velocity approaching 3 percent of the velocity of light when passing to within a periastron distance corresponding to 60 astronomical units from Sagittarius A*, perceived to be a massive black hole. This gives solid evidence that the space in this region has to be, without a doubt, an extremely good vacuum. Any gravitating matter in this space would be consumed and completely gobbled up due to the intense gravitational field of the black hole. The collected emissions from the orbiting stars are in the form of ultra violent electromagnetic radiation, which are all theoretically subjected to the very same light bending rule of General Relativity. The very same rule is applied to the rapidly moving star S2 orbiting about the super massive object of approximately 4 million solar masses at the site of Sagittarius A* *as Dowdye (2007) has shown.* It is argued whether the star S2 should appear to have entirely different orbital configuration other than that of the currently observed elliptical path. A theoretical fit to the observed orbit of S2 orbiting about Sagittarius *A and the predicted lensing of the images thereof, based on the predictions of General Relativity, was compared in this Reference. *Dowdye (2007)* Some selected positions of S2 along its orbital path and the corresponding predicted lensing of the images of those positions along the orbit of S2, based on the light bending rule of General Relativity, were tabulated in the Reference *Dowdye (2007)*. The magnitude of the predicted lensing effect, as would be predicted by General Relativity, should be a very noticeable effect using current technical means. To date, clear evidence of a gravitational lensing effect based on the light bending rules of General Relativity is yet to be revealed in the time resolved images of the stellar objects orbiting about Sagittarius A*. The unlikely presence of gravitating matter in the form of a light interacting media or an *indirectly interacting* light bending media at the vicinity of a black hole appears to be confirmed by the lack of evidence for gravitational lensing, as is revealed in the images of the stellar objects orbiting about Sagittarius A*.

## 4. Discussion & Conclusions

Historically, the light bending effect has been observed primarily at the thin plasma limb of the sun. A detail calculation obtains the very same light bending equation (1) as that obtained by the light bending rule of General Relativity, [15] (Dowdye 2011) only this time equation (1) applies directly to the bending of light rays in a plasma atmosphere exposed to the gravitational gradient field of the sun. The calculated results of this research is confirmed by Lebach [6] who used VLBI techniques on extra galactic radio sources to determine the gravitational deflection of microwaves at the solar plasma limb. Findings convincingly show that a *direct interaction* between the sun's gravity and the rays of starlight in the empty vacuum space at distances significantly above the solar plasma limb is yet to be observed. The celestial skies present vast opportunities to modern Astronomy and Astrophysics to allow for the detection of gravitational lensing effects, as predicted by General Relativity, due to the large numbers of stellar objects that just happen to be co-linearly aligned with the earth based observers. This, of course, assumes that the light bending rule of General Relativity applies to the plasma-free space as well as to the plasma atmosphere of the sun and the stars. Because of the vast astronomical distances between the stars, the gravitational lensing effect would have to take place in deep space, at impact parameters such that the light rays pass clearly above the plasma limb of the lensing star. If this were indeed the case and the light bending rule of General Relativity applied to a *direct interaction* between the gravitational field of the stars and the more distant rays of light in deep space, then the entire celestial sky would be filled with images of the Einstein ring. With application of the important fundamentals, the observations reveal an *indirect interaction*, **not** a *direct interaction* between the gravitational field of the lensing stars and the rays of starlight propagating in the plasma limbs of the stars. The very same fundamentals apply directly to all celestial skies and to the events taking place at Sagittarius A*. The evidence is clearly in the everyday cosmological appearance.

## 5. Gratitude

At this point, I express my gratitude to Professor Dr. Edgar Kaucher who was til 2010 at the Institut für Angewandte Mathematik of the Elite Institute of Technology in Karlsruhe, Germany and director of the Scientific Advisory Council of the "Endowment for the Organization of Scientists", "Stiftung Vereinigende Wissenschaften", for his helpful cooperation, stimulating discussions and valuable advice.

## REFERENCES

1. Arfken, G., Hans Weber, "Mathematical Methods for Physicist", Academic Press, 1995, pp. 77-79
2. Born, M., Wolf, E., Principles of Optics, Pergamon Press, London - New York, 1975, 71, 100 - 104
3. Potton, R. J., "Reciprocity in Optics", Institute of Physics Publishing, Rep. Prog. Phys. 2004, 67, pp. 717-754
4. Jackson, J. D., Classical Electrodynamics, 3rd. ed., John Wiley & Sons, Inc., 1999, pp. 27-29
5. Blandford, R., Narayan, R., "Cosmological applications of gravitational lensing", Annual Review of Astronomy and Astrophysics, 1992, 30, 331
6. Lebach, D. E., Corey, B. E., Shapiro, I. I., Ratner, M. I., Webber, J. C., Rogers, A. E. E., Davis, J. L., Herring, T. A., Phys. Rev. Lett., 1992, 75, pp. 1439-1442
7. Carroll, B. W., Ostlie, D. A., "An Introduction to Modern Astrophysics". Addison-Wesley Publishing Co., 1996
8. Genzel, R., Schödel, R., Ott, T., Eckart, A, Alexander, T., Lacombe, F., Rouan, D., Aschenbach, B., Nature, Vol. 425, 2003, pp. 934-937
9. Melia, F., Falcke, H., "The supermassive black hole at the Galactic center". Anny. Rev. Astrophys, 2001, 39:309-52
10. Melia, F., "The Black Hole at the center of Our Galaxy", Princeton University Press, Princeton, 2003
11. Narayan, R., "Black holes: Sparks of interest", Nature, Vol. 425, 6961,2003, pp. 908-909
12. Schödel R. et al., "A star in a 15.2-year orbit around the supermassive black hole at the centre of the Milky Way." Nature, 2002, 419, pp. 694 - 696
13. Dowdye, E. H., "Time resolved images from the center of the Galaxy appear to counter General Relativity", AN, Vol. 328, 2,2007, pp. 186-191; also published on line at: http://www3.interscience.wiley.com/:DOI: 10.1002/asna.200510715
14. Dowdye, E. H., "Extinction Shift Principle: A Pure Classical Alternative to General and Special Relativity", Physics Essays,2007, Vol. 20, 56, pp. 13A - 14A
15. Dowdye, E. H., "Gauss's Law for gravity and observational evidence reveal no solar lensing in empty vacuum space", Proceedings of the SPIE, Nature of Light: What are Photons? IV. Edited by Roychoudhuri, C., Khrennikov, A., Kracklauer, A., Vol. 8121, 2011, pp. 812106-1 - 812106-10
16. Schmeidler, F., "Zur Interpretation der Messungen der Lichtablenkung am Sonnenrand, Interpretation of Solar-Limb Light-Deflection Measurements", Astronomische Nachrichten, Vol. 306, Issue 2,1985, pp. 77-80

## 6. APPENDICES

## 7. Bending of Light Rays in the Solar Plasma Rim as function of Gravitational Potential; a Minimum Energy Path Calculation

A calculation for the bending of light rays in the thin plasma limb of the sun is carried out in detail by *Dowdye2 (2007)* and *Dowdye3 (2011)*. The calculation is based entirely on a conservation of energy concept considering the gradient of the gravitational field of the sun acting directly on the rapidly moving ionized material particles of the thin plasma atmosphere of the sun. The calculation considers a minimum energy path for rays of light. The results is found to be totally independent of frequency. The rapidly moving ionized particles of the solar plasma is assumed to be bounded by the gravitational potential of the sun given by

$$\phi\left(^{r=\infty}_{r=R}\right) = \int_{r=R}^{r=\infty} \frac{GM}{r^2} dr = \frac{GM}{R}. \tag{9}$$

It may be assumed that the plasma particles of the ionized solar limb move with random velocities such that their kinetic energies are as dictated by $\frac{1}{2}mv^2 = \frac{3}{2}kT + \phi m$, where $m$ is the mean mass of the plasma particles of temperature $T(K°)$ and $v$ is the velocity of the plasma particle bounded by the gravitational potential $\phi$. The velocity $v$ of the moving ions may be assigned an upper bound of $v = \sqrt{\frac{2GM}{R}}$, the escape velocity of the solar gravity at the surface of the sun. The solar plasma particles bounded by gravity in the solar limb may be considered as a dynamic lens under the intense gravitational gradient field of the sun. It is theoretically shown here, and in detail in *Dowdye2 (2007)* and *Dowdye3 (2011)*, that a minimum energy path for light rays propagating in the solar plasma limb, subjected to the gradient of the gravitational field of the sun, yields the mathematical results of $\frac{4GM}{Rc^2}$.

It is shown that the moving ions acting as secondary sources within the plasma limb, moving with velocities not to accede the velocity $v = \sqrt{\frac{2GM}{R}}$, the frequency and wavelength of a light ray exposed to the plasma are:

$$v' = v_0(1 - \frac{v^2}{c^2}) = v_0(1 - \frac{2GM}{Rc^2}) \qquad (10)$$

$$\lambda' = \lambda_0(1 - \frac{v^2}{c^2})^{-1} = \lambda_0(1 - \frac{2GM}{Rc^2})^{-1} \qquad (11)$$

$$\lambda' \approx \lambda_0(1 + \frac{2GM}{Rc^2}). \qquad (12)$$

From this, the number of wavelengths along a minimum energy path for the light ray propagating within the plasma limb may be given as

$$n = \frac{1}{\lambda'} = \frac{1}{\lambda_0(1 - \frac{2GM}{Rc^2})^{-1}} = \frac{1}{\lambda_0}(1 - \frac{2GM}{Rc^2}). \qquad (13)$$

Thus, the energy $\varepsilon$ per unit length of the light ray along the minimum energy path is $\varepsilon = \varepsilon_0(1 - \frac{2GM}{rc^2})$. Consequently, the number of re-emitted waves per unit length along the photon path and thus the energy per unit length increases as $r$ increases. This translates to a downward, re-emitted path of the bent light ray, along a minimum energy path for the approaching segment of the light ray. If $\frac{d\varepsilon}{dr} = +\varepsilon_0\frac{2GM}{r^2c^2}$ or $\delta\varepsilon = +\varepsilon_0\frac{2GM}{r^2c^2}\delta R$, then the re-emission of the light ray in the atmosphere of ions will occur such that the total energy along the minimum energy (conservation of energy) path for a given light ray would not change. If $\varepsilon$ is the energy per unit length along the light ray and $\delta\varepsilon$ is the change in energy in the direction of the gradient potential $\phi(r)$, then the angle of change during the approach segment of the light ray is

$$\delta\theta_{app} = \frac{\delta\varepsilon_{app}}{\varepsilon} = +\int_{r=\infty}^{r=R} \frac{2GM}{r^2c^2}dr = -\frac{2GM}{Rc^2} \qquad (14)$$

and the path change for the receding segment of the light ray is

$$\delta\theta_{rec} = \frac{\delta\varepsilon_{rec}}{\varepsilon} = +\int_{r=R}^{r=\infty} \frac{2GM}{r^2c^2}dr = +\frac{2GM}{Rc^2}. \qquad (15)$$

The net change in the path of the light ray is

$$\delta\theta = \delta\theta_{rec} - \delta\theta_{app} = \frac{4GM}{Rc^2}. \qquad (16)$$

## 8. The Einstein Ring Equation; the General Case ($D_L \neq D_{SL}$)

The general case for the Einstein ring equation involves all values for the distances, whereby $D_L$ is the distance between the observer and the lens and $D_{SL}$ is the distance between the lens and the source. These are cases where $D_L$ is not necessarily equal to $D_{SL}$. The general case for the radius of the Einstein ring in units of radians is

$$\delta\theta(rad) = \sqrt{\frac{D_{SL}}{D_L + D_{SL}}\frac{4GM}{D_Lc^2}} \qquad (17)$$

The radius of the Einstein ring at the image location the distance of $(D_L + D_{SL})$ expressed in meters is

$$R(meters) = (D_L + D_{SL})\delta\theta(rad) \qquad (18)$$

where $D_L$ and $D_{SL}$ are also expressed in meters. The impact parameter ($\xi$) corresponding to the image of the Einstein ring is the nearest point of approach of the light rays to the point-like lensing mass, when observed at a distance of $D_L$ meters away from the observer, for the rays of light coming from the light source to the observer. Since this is a 3 dimensional problem, the impact parameter of the light rays that would produce an image of an Einstein ring is in itself a ring (two dimensions). The impact parameter is a *virtual ring* for purpose of the analysis of the problem. This is illustrated in Figure 3. The impact parameter $\xi$(meters) is

$$\xi = R(meters) = (D_L)\delta\theta(rad) \qquad (19)$$

where $\xi = R(meters)$ is the nearest point of approach of the gravitationally lensed light rays passing over the lensing star. It is that distance the lensed light rays will pass over the plasma limb of the lensing star, moving through the empty vacuum space well above the plasma limb of the lensing stars, moving along astronomical distances from the source to the observer. The radius of the predicted Einstein ring, according Equation (17) and the light bending rule of General Relativity, will be nearly 15 times the radius of a sun-like lensing star, the same mass and radius as that of the sun, when both are observed at the distance $D_L = D_{SL}$ = 4 light years away, where $D_L$ is the distance between us, the observer, and the lensing star. Adjusting the parameter $D_{SL}$ would cause the radius of the Einstein ring to change. The means astronomical distances between in our space dictates **impact parameters**, in the order of light-years, for potentials bent light rays, assuming the validity of the light bending rule of General Relativity. Increasing the parameter $D_{SL}$ proportionally increases the image of the Einstein ring's apparent radius (an increase in magnification), again assuming the validity *direct interaction* between gravity and starlight of General Relativity. Setting $D_L = D_{SL}$, Equation (17) becomes Equation (5), the special case.

# Growing Earth / Expanding Universe (Ge/Eu)

## Eugene Ellis

*38178 Yacht Basin Rd. Ocean View, DE 19970 United States, geneaellis@msn.com*

The energy of the universe (as contained within the elements) is declining as it ages, some of which is being stored as potential energy by converting to mass within the existing elements and the rest to an entropy that heats the elemental mass:

E (energy) <—-> m (mass) or E —-> ÉŻ (entropy - heat and temperature).

Energy and mass can neither be created nor destroyed but are interconvertible. The flow of heat is from warmer to cooler and irreversible. In a closed system, heat flows toward the empty space of the colder universe. Heat, unable to reverse flow, indicates it is not reverting to energy but causing the entropy of the universe to increase. The temperature of the universe ( 2.7 Kelvin) appears low because space is expanding much faster than the heat produced by the stars and elsewhere. Space is the container of entropy. Time is non-linear when space is expanding.

On Earth, the declining energy of eight elements (O, Fe, Si, Mg, S, Al, Ni and Ca) as exemplified by their ionization properties, is responsible for accumulating sufficient mass to double Earth's radius at least twice in the past billion years. Before that time, the energy converting to entropy from the same elements internally heated a near absolute zero planet for several billion years, cooling to a core, mantle, and crust. Afterwards, it provided sufficient heat to maintain a temperate environment to support life while exponentially growing to its present size. Ionization is responsible for oxygen becoming water and doubling in volume several times to incrementally fill the expanding ocean beds shown on the NOAA map, Age of the Ocean Floors.

Ionization is presented as a feasible mechanism for expanding and heating Earth and the other planets in the universe.

**Keywords:** expansion tectonics, growing earth, expanding universe

## 1. Introduction

Question all certainties by questioning the assumptions. Einstein's theories rest upon a primary assumption that the speed of light is constant and unchanging [linear time with atomic clocks].

The Standard Model of Particle Physics describes a universe consisting of space, matter and time yet relies on Friar Thomas' (Aquinas - 1225 to 1274 AD) premise that the essence of matter is unchanging [atoms cannot change in size or numbers]. The above assumptions led to many discoveries but neither one can answer...why the universe is expanding?...or why the Earth is expanding? Ionization can provide an answer.

Suppose another theory assumes that atoms consist of energetic elemental masses that upon ageing grow larger by converting inherent energy to mass and along with gravity, causes a time anomaly [orbital clocks]. Below are an ionic flow chart, an ionic timetable, and an explanation of two-timing clocks for such systems:

## 2. Two Timing Earth Clocks

The effect of mass growth upon the acceleration due to gravity and the force due to gravity are contained in two equations as follows:

$$F = \frac{GM_sM_e}{R^2} = \frac{CM_sM_e}{R^2} \qquad (1)$$

F = force R = Earth-sun orbital radius G = constant r = Earth radius

$$g = \frac{GM_e}{r^2} = \frac{GM_e}{r^2} \qquad (2)$$

Ms = mass of sun g = surface gravityMe = mass of Earth r = both R and r

The mass of the sun is so large and the percent change is so small, it is treated as a constant. By cancelling the constants, Ms and G, Equation 1 equals Equation (2). An 8 fold increase in mass will double the radius in each equation and an 8 fold increase of the previous mass will double the previous radius. Both equations show exponential doubling of the mass in the upper portion and of the radius in the lower portion straddling an exponential series:

The first doubling (I) of the radius (both R and r) occurs when the mass doubles three times (23) for an 8-fold increase. The second radius doubling (II) occurs when the mass doubles six times (26) for a 64-fold increase and the third radius doubling (III) occurs at nine times (29) for a 512 fold increase.

Consequently, when the radius of Earth (r) doubles, the distance between the Sun and the Earth (R) also doubles as indicated below:

Figure graphing Table of the 8-element supplement indicates the percent of radial growth equals the ref of increased gravity (% r = % g). The spin of the planet was proportionally slower during past times and increased as the gravity, the orbital radius, and the Earth's radius simultaneously increased. Constantly adding mass constantly in-

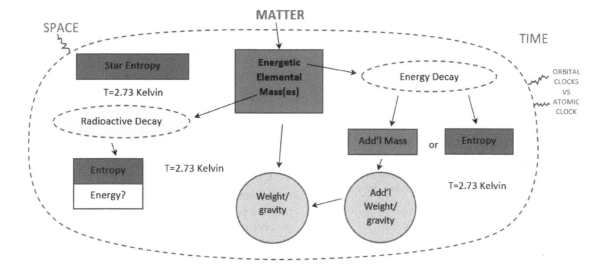

**Figure 1.**    Iconic Flowchart

| First time elemental energy converts to mass | Calcium | 8800 MYA |
|---|---|---|
| First time elemental energy converts to entropy (heat) | Calcium | 8300 MYA |
| First free electron | Cl + H = HCl | 6400 MYA |
| First water molecule | O + 2H = H2O | 1400 MYA |
| First hydrocarbon molecule | C + 4H = CH4 | 800 MYA |
| First hydrogen molecule | H + H = H2 | 22 MYA |

**Figure 2.**    Ionic Table of Firsts

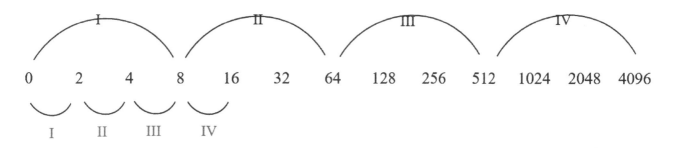

**Figure 3.**    exponential series

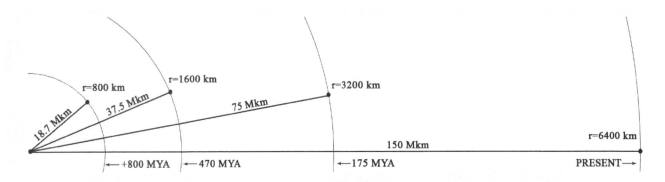

**Figure 4.**   Earth radii

creases torque such that angular momentum does not remain constant as a conserved quantity. The changes when the Earth was 1/2, 1/4, and 1/8th of its present size are:

| R kilometers | 18,750,000 | 37,500,000 | 75,000,000 | 150,000,000 |
|---|---|---|---|---|
| r kilometers | ≈ 800 | ≈ 1600 | ≈ 3200 | ≈ 6400 |
| g Nm2/kg2 ; m/s2 | 1.225 | 2.45 | 4.9 | 9.8 |
| Year in days | 2922 | 1461 | 730.5 | 365.25 |
| LOD in hours | 192 | 96 | 48 | 24 |
| LOH | 8 | 4 | 2 | 1 |
| LOM in seconds | 480 | 240 | 120 | 60 |

- R = Earth - Sun orbital radius (c-c distance).
- r = Earth radius.
- g = surface gravity.
- Year = length of orbital year in days of linear time.
- LOD = length of day (spin) in linear time.
- LOH = length of an hour in linear time.
- LOM = number of linear seconds to orbital seconds.

## 3.  Discussion

The lesser gravity of past times permitting larger life sizes that could not survive today is factual and indicates geology follows orbital time. Constantly increasing Earth's mass generates an orbital clock that is always slower than a linear atomic clock. A second on an atomic clock has the same time length it had a billion or 10 billion years ago. The time on Earth's orbital clock is governed by rates of mass accretion. The spin, the radius, and the distance from the sun all increase in unison as the energy of the planet's elemental masses ages and converts to additional mass. Past orbital time is proportional to the present linear time.

Likewise, every planet in the universe has a different non-linear clock reflecting the changes as energy converts to additional mass on those planets. The totality of expanding orbits expands the universe. Orbits expanding exponentially accelerate the expansion.

Albert Einstein spent the last 30 years of his life essentially trying to connect or explain a universe running on non-linear (orbital) clocks by using a linear (atomic) clock. Perhaps the "leap second" is such a connection. The above data indicates that leap second by leap second, the Earth leaped 75 million kilometers (46.6 million miles) in 175 million years. Theoretically, 31,557,600 leap seconds ago, the Earth was half its radial orbit and half its radial size.

## 4.  Conclusion

The same elements coalescing to start a planet grow and heat the planet as the elements age. Ionization involves a process permitting certain elemental atoms to join other elemental atoms at certain energy levels. Without assumptions of unchanging matter and time, ionization becomes the fundamental mechanism whereby energy converts to additional elemental mass or to entropy (heat). Establishing the rate of energy decay, among other things, identifies the geological time when water arrived to cool and solidify the crust of a molten planet.

Subscribing to a theory of "everything changes" does not negate or denigrate theories based on "unchanging matter" or theories based on "unchanging time" or quantum mechanics, which is consistent with the Standard Model and special relativity. The merits of each can co-exist like mathematical trains running on different gauge tracks.

## REFERENCES

1. Eugene Ellis, *onic Expanding Earth A Mass and Entropy Theory for an Expanding Earth in an Expanding Universe*, http://ionic-expanding-earth.weebly.com, 2016.

# Maxwellian Electrodynamics of Moving Bodies

## Viraj Fernando, Independent Researcher

*100, Mornelle Court, #1100 Toronto, Ontario M1E 4X2, Canada*

This paper argues that the "Trouble with Physics" we confront today originates partly from errors in the Newtonian Foundation of Physics, and partly from the disjointed and ad hoc approach that has been adopted since the beginning of the 20th century, instead of adopting the new paradigm Maxwell proposed "All phenomena depend on variations of energy" , and following the path outlined by him in his book, "Matter and Motion" [1] (see the Appendix). Unfortunately, he left just the outline of his future program, due to his untimely death within two years of writing this book. Had he lived another 25 years, we would have been spared of the unintelligible theory of relativity, and consequently spared of one whole century of groping in the dark. In its place, there would have been a theory where every single phenomenon is explained in terms of changes of states and quantities of energy in the course of their interactions, just the same way chemical changes are explained in terms of the interactions of chemical substances. This paper is an initial step in that direction.

**Keywords:** Maxwell, electric force, magnetic force, Biot-Savart, field energy, fractional charges, open systems, attraction, repulsion, special relativity, time dilation

## 1. Introduction

Hitherto, the so-called "relativistic phenomena" have not been properly accounted for in dynamical (i.e. mass, force, energy) terms, but have merely been "explained" by attributing unprovable kinematic propositions. This short paper demonstrates how the so-called "relativistic phenomena" that arise when a particle is in motion find an easy, coherent, and a natural explanation when the appropriate holistic approach is taken. When we consider the motion of a charged particle, the explanation can be done without involving the Newtonian Foundation, so we begin this quest with the motion of an electron.

We would address the errors in the Newtonian Foundation elsewhere, applying the same holistic approach to the motions of (uncharged) bodies, and thereby unify electromagnetism, mechanics and gravitation.

The punch line about how the "relativistic phenomena" involved in this example occurs is this: "relativistic phenomena" occur as "by-products" or as a consequence of generating the electric and the magnetic forces when an electron is in motion. Although nobody casts doubt on the fact that an electric force (Lorentz force) emerges when a free electron is set in motion, there has hitherto been no attempt to account for, from where the energy is drawn to generate this force. Account, as we have done, for the sources of the energy of this force and everything becomes as clear as daylight.

This force is generated (see Fig. 1 - **The figures are at the end of this paper.**) by usurping the fraction of energy $EB = mc^2(1 - 1/\Gamma)$ from the intrinsic energy of the electron. So the intrinsic energy left in the electron when in motion is $AE = mc^2/\Gamma$. Consequently, frequency of the energy drops from $f$ to $f/\Gamma$, and this manifests as the slowing down of internal processes (of the twin paradox fame). Similarly, for the generation of the magnetic force

("Biot-Savart"), the fraction $EF = pc(1 - 1/\Gamma)$ is usurped, leaving $DE = pc/\Gamma$. This is what manifests as the "relativistic momentum" being required, in order to set a particle in motion with momentum $p/\Gamma = mv$. See Fig. 2. The usurped fractions are then synthesized with field energy $CB = mc^2(sec\theta - 1)$ and $FG = pc(sec\theta - 1)$ to form the quanta $EC$ and $EG$ respectively which are the sources of the two forces as we have proved further below.

(Note: from Fig. 1, $AC = mc^2(sec\theta)$, hence, since $AC = \Gamma mc^2$ according to energy-momentum equation, $\Gamma = sec\theta$ and $1/\Gamma = cos\theta$).)

## 2. Maxwellian Electrodynamics of Moving Bodies

Let us consider an electron in the ionized state being set in motion in accordance with the energy-momentum equation. Experience tells us that in this interaction "relativistic momentum" $\Gamma mv$ will get scaled down to $mv$ (the classical level), and the internal processes will slow down corresponding to a decrease of its frequency from $f$ to $f/\Gamma$, (such that its time unit would "dilate" from $t$ to $\Gamma t$). It is these that have been given the name "relativistic phenomena" . However, they have not been explained for what they are, as **mere by-products** of the interaction of energy, governed by the energy-momentum equation, but have been left at an enigmatic and a bizarre level, attributing them as arising from the "principle of relativity" , as kinematic illusions of an observer located in a different frame of reference. On the other hand, the electron moving at velocity $v$, is known to generate an electric field $E$ and a magnetic field $H$ (Biot-Savart force), such that $H = Ev/c$, and these are presently considered to have no connection to those "relativistic phenomena" This disconnect is the crux of the matter, as regards no one having been able to comprehend how these "relativistic phenomena" really occur.

The whole enigmatic nature of the so-called "relativistic phenomena" has arisen from the failure of physicists to put the first two (relativistic phenomena) and the other two (the forces) together, and to view **all four within a single perspective** under the framework of the energy-momentum equation as shown in Figs. 1 and 2.

Further, we observe that the present day physics has considered the energy-momentum equation at the level of its outward appearance only, and limited itself only to recognize that in the interaction, kinetic energy $CB = mc^2(\Gamma - 1)$ is added to the intrinsic energy $AB = mc^2$ to form total energy $AC = \Gamma mc^2$ (and has also incorrectly inferred that the mass of the particle increases from m to $\Gamma m$, naming it yet another "relativistic phenomenon" ). Our contention is however, that this interaction is much deeper and complex, as we discuss below. We also need to take one hard look at Fig. 1. We find that $pc = \Gamma mvc = mc^2 \tan \theta$, and from this at once we recognize that $\Gamma = \sec \theta$, and $sin\theta = v/c$. Thus instead of using the cumbersome gamma-factor $\Gamma = 1/(1 - v^2/c^2)^{1/2}$, we find that we can conveniently use the above trigonometric relations in our analyses and discussions.

## 3. Other Hitherto Unforeseen Aspects of the Energy-Momentum Interaction

Firstly, (see Fig. 1) along with the fusion of kinetic energy $CB = mc^2(sec\theta - 1)$ with the intrinsic energy $mc^2$ of the electron, we contend that there occurs a parallel process, where "kinetic momentum" ("Weyl - Space-Time-Matter", p. 168), equal to $p(sec\theta - 1)$ is drawn from the field such that $FG = pc(sec\theta - 1)$. $FG$ gets added to $DF = pc$ and the $DG$ (i.e., the product of total momentum and velocity c) becomes, $DG = pcsec\theta$.

Secondly, an electron in motion is not a point particle, or a unitary piece of "brute matter" moving in space. In Fig. 2, it is a complex organism or a propulsion system consisting of four distinct quantities of energy forming into one complex whole, consisting of

$$AE = mc^2 \cos \theta, DE = mc^2 \sin \theta \qquad (1)$$

$$EC = mc^2 \sin \theta \tan \theta \text{ and } EG = mc^2 \sin^2 \theta \tan \theta \qquad (2)$$

Where all these are conjoined at $E$. In order to form the system, the part $EC$ detaches from $AC$; and the part $EG$ detaches from $DG$. These form two quanta of energy that generate the electric force and the magnetic force respectively. The propulsion system consists of the motive energy (i.e., the product of momentum and velocity c) thrusting on the electron which is equipped with the two mutually perpendicular forces.

Thirdly, what remains of the two original interactants ($mc^2$ and $pc$), as by-products, after this formation of the above quanta, are the parts $AE = mc^2 \cos \theta$ and $DE = pc \cos \theta = mvc$. It will be seen that the so-called "relativistic phenomena" of the "relativistic momentum" scaling down from $pc = \Gamma mvc$ to $mvc$ is a direct consequence of the formation of the quantum of energy $EG = pc \sin \theta tan\theta$ for the generation of the magnetic force. And similarly, the

"relativistic phenomena" of slowing down of internal processes of the electron occurs due to the scaling down of the intrinsic energy $AB = mc^2$ to $AE = mc^2 \cos \theta$ leading to the reduction of the frequency from $f$ to $f \cos \theta$, as a direct consequence of the formation of the quantum of energy $EC = mc^2 \sin \theta tan\theta$, for the generation of the electric force.

What is now required is proof that it is the energy of these two quanta (i.e., $EC$ and $EG$) that generate the electric and the magnetic forces when the electron is in motion. **This will demonstrate beyond doubt** that these "relativistic phenomena" are not mere kinematic illusions, but real occurrences due to changes of energy taking place in one part of the system, in the process of generating and equipping the system with forces to create the other part of the system, as shown in Fig. 2.

We need to challenge the paradigm that charges can exist only as integral multiples of a unit charge, by contending that fractions of a unit charge are possible under different circumstances. From the charge to mass ratio of an electron, let the charge of the electron be $q$ (unit charge) when its intrinsic energy is $mc^2$.

We contend that the same ratio of mass to charge holds for fractions of energy $mc^2$ as well. Thus when the charge that represents the energy $AB = mc^2$ is $q$ (unit charge), the charge that is representative of the energy $AE = mc^2 \cos \theta$ is $q_1 = qcos\theta$. The charge that represents the energy of the quantum $EC = mc^2 \sin \theta tan\theta$ is $q_2 = q \sin \theta tan\theta$. And the charge that represents the energy of the quantum $EG = pc \sin \theta \tan \theta$ is $q_3 = q \sin \theta tan^2\theta$, (since $pc = mc^2 \tan \theta$).

### 3.1. Proof the Quantum of Energy represented by $EC$ is instrumental in generating the Electric Force

The electric force $F_E$ is generated by the interaction of the charge $q_1$ of $AE$ and the charge $q_2$ of $EC$.

$$F_E = \frac{q_1 q_2}{2\pi r \varepsilon_0} = \frac{qcos\theta(q \sin \theta \tan \theta)}{2\pi r \varepsilon_0} \qquad (3)$$

$$= \frac{\left(\frac{q^2 v^2}{c^2}\right)}{2\pi \gamma \varepsilon_0} \qquad (4)$$

(since $\sin \theta = v/c$) **QED**.

### 3.2. Proof the Quantum of Energy represented by $EC$ is instrumental in generating the Magnetic Force

The magnetic force $F_M$ is generated by the interaction of the charge $q_1$ of $AE$ and the charge $q_3$ of $EG$.

$$F_M = \frac{q_1 q_3}{2\pi r \varepsilon_0} = \frac{(qcos\theta)(q \sin \theta \tan^2 \theta)}{2\pi r \varepsilon_0} \qquad (5)$$

$$= \frac{q^2 \sin^2 \theta \tan \theta}{2\pi r \varepsilon_0} = \frac{q^2 \sin^3 \theta \sec \theta}{2\pi r \varepsilon_0} \qquad (6)$$

$$= \frac{q^2 (\frac{v^3}{c^3}) \sec \theta}{2\pi r \varepsilon_0} \qquad (7)$$

and, since $\varepsilon_0 = 1/\mu_0 c^2$,

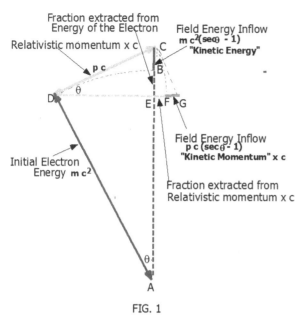

**FIG. 1**
**ALGORITHM OF RELATIVITY OF ENERGY**
(Geometric Representation of Energy-Momentum Equation)

$$F_M = \frac{(q^2 v^2)(\frac{v}{c}) \sec \theta \, \mu}{2 \pi r} \qquad (8)$$

For low values of $v$, $\sec \theta \approx 1$ and $F_M \approx (q^2 v^2)(v/c)(\mu/2\pi r)$.

Hence, $F_M = F_E v/c$ (Or $H = Ev/c$) **QED**.

## 4. Conclusion

We have shown conclusively that the electric force and the magnetic force emerge out of the interaction between the charges of parts of the system. The charges of these parts are determined precisely in proportion to the energy content of those parts. This fact establishes that the two "relativistic phenomena" that appear when a particle is in motion, **are consequences of creating the two quanta of energy to generate the above two forces**, (in the process of the energy-momentum interaction), by extracting fractions of energy from the electron as well as from the motive energy (momentum x $c$) and by augmenting these by adding field energy to them. This gives an insight as to how a repulsive force is created in general.

However, in order to understand how a repulsive force is created we need to get an idea of how its opposite - an attractive force - is created. Consider an electron in the ionized state being pushed towards a nucleus, and attaining the ground state within a Hydrogen atom. We notice that a photon is **emitted** in this process. That is, a fraction of the electron's energy is removed, thereby it **creates a deficiency** of energy within itself. This deficiency drives the electron to seek to **share the energy of the nucleus**. Such a deficiency of energy driving a body to **share the energy of another through the field** is what **attraction** is. In the case of repulsion, it would be the opposite process, where the presence of an excess quantity of energy, tending to reduce the existing level of attraction, and thereby this tending the body to distance itself away from the other. Upon distancing away, the body absorbs the excess energy, and increases its own intrinsic energy (that is, what happens here is the opposite of emitting energy, reducing intrinsic energy and getting closer).

In the case of a free electron in motion (as in the example we discussed above), we saw, both the electron setting apart the fraction $mc^2(1 - cos\theta)$ and the motive energy ($pc$) setting apart the fraction $pc(1 - cos\theta)$. This **alienation of the fractions** of energy causes deficiencies in the remnants $mc^2 cos\theta$ and $pc\, cos\theta$ of the original interactants ($mc^2$ and $pc$). The remnants are therefore mutually attracted towards one another to merge and form a system. Thereby their deficiencies become satiated. However, the above **alienated fractions** of energy are **not emitted**, but they are **retained within the system**. These retained fractions EB and EF (see Fig. 1) upon being augmented by field energy, turn into two quanta of energy which generate the electric and the magnetic force.

We have demonstrated elsewhere that in gravitation the same story also applies. If this is the case, have we not stumbled upon **Quantum Gravity**? And, if it is the case, have we not stumbled upon the **Unified Theory** as well?

## 5. Appendix: Maxwellian Approach to Relativistic Phenomena

"All phenomena depend on variations of energy" - James Clerk Maxwell (p. 72) [1]

It goes without saying that the meaning of Maxwell's above statement is that in "RWOT" (real world out there), every conceivable event without exception occurs by virtue of **interactions of energy**, (and we may add) .... in **open systems**. In an open system, there is an ingress and egress of energy from the field. In this regard, Maxwell also had the following intuition towards the development of physics, ".... when we have to deal with real bodies, we must define their state not only to the configuration and motion of their visible parts, but if we have reason to suspect that the configuration and motion of their **invisible** particles influence the visible phenomenon, we **must devise some method of estimating the energy** thence arising" (p. 71) [1]. This prompts the question whether anyone has taken this cue from Maxwell and attempted to develop a method that enables the measurement of inflow and outflow of energy from the field?

For Maxwell, development of such a method appears to have been of utmost importance to the extent that he has summarized his future program in the following statement. "In fact the **special work** which lies before the physical inquirer in the **present state of science** is the determination of **the quantity of energy which enters and leaves** a material system during the passage of the system from its standard state to any other definite state" (p. 74) [1]. Unfortunately, before he could devise the method for the above determination, he died soon after writing those words. Although, nearly 150 years have elapsed since then,

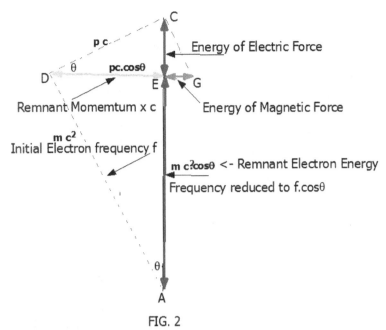

FIG. 2
INTERCONNECTION OF 2 FORCES AND 2 PHENOMENA
System in Motion Consisting of Four Energy Components

his successors have disregarded the necessity of devising of such a **method based on interactions of energy** in open systems, but instead have been satisfied with the modification of space-time physics.

In this paper, it will be found that we have "devised" this method that Maxwell called for. Further, the simple philosophical outlook "All phenomena depend on variations of energy ...." has been adapted as the working paradigm. In actual fact, as for the "method" it is not that we have devised it as such or to use Einstein's word "invented" a method based on a set of propositions along with a mathematical apparatus and then imposed it on nature. But rather, we have by diligent contemplation, **discerned** the **algorithms** that **nature uses** to govern the interactions of energy inclusive of egress and ingress of field energy. This has been achieved by way of deciphering the geometric structure that underlies the energy-momentum equation. Or in the sense of Galileo, we have discovered the very "geometric characters" that the "**Book of Nature**" of interactions of energy has been written in. Thereby we have been able to account for all the so-called "relativistic phenomena" in terms of effects of interactions of energy, without recourse to the "relativity principle", "space time relationships", *etc.*

# REFERENCES

1. J. C. Maxwell, *"Matter and Motion"*, Dover, 1991.

# The Speed of Light: Constant and Non-Constant

Raymond HV Gallucci, PhD, PE

*8956 Amelung St., Frederick, Maryland, 21704, gallucci@localnet.com, r_gallucci@verizon.net*

This article examines the relativistic assumption of a constant speed of light without Einstein's postulates, building on two dissident physicists' unique theories as a possible explanation for the phenomena by which light can travel with the speed of its source and, therefore, at variable speeds.

**Keywords:** light, relativity, Radiation Continuum Model, self-propagation

## 1. Introduction

Renshaw and Calkins have proposed rather unique theories regarding the propagation of light, which are examined in Section 4 [2], [1]. First I consider two similar situations for non-light phenomena to extrapolate to a subsequent analogy for light to contend that the speed of light need not be constant.

## 2. A Special Car Ride

Riding in a car moving at constant speed v, you hold a bocce ball (hard surface) in each hand. You place the ball from your left hand on the car floor while reaching out from the car and placing the ball from your right hand on the icy shoulder of the road. Assuming negligible air resistance and friction (rolling or sliding, at least along the icy shoulder), relative to you, both balls maintain the same position, i.e., stationary. Relative to the roadway or a stationary observer on the roadway, both balls move forward (the one on the roadway sliding forward at speed v if there is negligible friction), parallel to each other and you (also moving forward at v).

If your car's floor is glass, you see the same thing relative to the roadway, i.e., both balls moving forward at v parallel to each other, but stationary relative to you. Equivalently, you could perceive the roadway as moving backward at v relative to both balls (and you). If you picked both balls up after 10 sec on you watch, Einstein would say that you would see that the observer's watch registered < 10 sec. The observer would see you picking up the balls at > 10 sec on his Einstein watch.

Relative to you, both balls traveled the same distance - zero. The observer sees the same, relative to you. Relative to the road, since you placed the balls at the same time and place and picked them up at the same time and place (forward from their release point and time), also seen by the observer, both you and the observer conclude both balls traveled the same distance - your (the car's, or the balls') speed v (relative to the roadway and observer) x observed time (10 sec on your watch, > or < 10 sec on his Einstein watch, depending upon whose perspective).

If all seconds are created equal, then for the observer to explain how you were able to pick up both balls at the same instant and location, you must have traveled faster than v [since only (> v) x 10 sec can equal v x (> 10 sec)]. But if you had traveled faster than v, you would not have been able to pick up the ball on the roadway after 10 sec on your watch, for it would have fallen behind, unless it, too, traveled faster than v. But then we are back to both balls traveling at the same speed relative to the roadway, albeit now > v.

There is no doubt that you traveled at v, either by you or the observer. Since you obviously retrieved both balls and the observer saw this, then someone's watch is wrong. According to the observer, either yours ran slow or his ran fast (or both). But you saw his watch run slower than yours, at least in Einstein's world.

Let's start again, this time you are holding a pair of tennis balls. You simultaneously bounce one vertically from your left hand in the car and one vertically from your right hand on the roadway, catching both at your hands' release points at the same time (and position, relative to you). Relative to you, both travel down and up along the same line - there is no horizontal displacement. The observer sees the same, relative to you. Relative to the roadway, both follow diagonally symmetric paths, which both you (remember your glass floor) and the observer see equally. Relative to you, the distance traveled is purely vertical and shorter than that relative to the roadway, which has horizontal displacement as well. Your watch registered 1 sec from toss to catch for each ball. The observer's Einstein watch registered something else, < 1 sec from your perspective, > 1 sec from his. Relative to you, as seen by you and the observer, both balls traveled the same vertical-only distance at the same speed. Relative to the roadway, both balls traveled the same diagonal distance (horizontal and vertical) at the same speed, again as seen by you and the observer. How can the times differ?

In this example, we examined the same action but concurrently in two reference frames. One ball was either placed or bounced vertically in the moving car, such there there was no horizontal displacement relative to that frame. The equivalent ball was either placed or bounced vertically from the moving car onto the stationary roadway, where there had to be horizontal displacement relative to

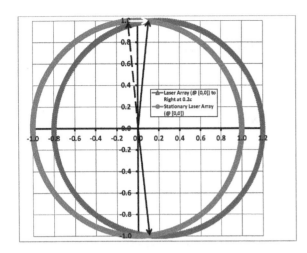

**Figure 1.** $360^o$ Laser Array: Stationary vs. Moving at 0.2c to Right

that from for you to retrieve it. Could the times for and and the two balls to accomplish the same action at the same speed over the same distance differ?

## 3. Now with Light

Replace the tennis balls with a pair of identical laser pens, both pointing vertically downward. Release a light pulse from each onto the mirrored floor of the car and a very reflective icy roadway. Would not the paths traced by both laser beams be analogous to those by the tennis balls? And would not the same question arise - how can the times differ? If the times are the same, then the explanation is simple. In the car, the laser beam traveled at c vertically downward then upward. On the roadway, it traveled at $\sqrt{(c^2 + v^2)} > c$ along symmetrical diagonals - no difference in times, only difference in distances due to difference in speeds.

Generalize to an array of laser pens at an origin (0,0) of a stationary reference frame such that each laser pen points at each integer of 360 degrees in a circle. It is a 'no-brainer' that, if the laser array is stationary, 360 pulses emitted simultaneously will travel like an omni-directional circular light wave (spherical in three dimensions, but we will stick with two for geometrical simplicity) from a point source. This is shown by the large grey circle comprised of the small circles in Figure 1.

All observers equidistant from (0,0) will see the same light beam at the same time [e.g., at 1.0 sec if located 1.0 light-sec from (0,0) in the Figure]. Now, assume the array of lasers moves to the right (positive x direction) at 0.2c. For each of the 360 lasers, the light beam will travel at the angle $\theta$ at which the laser points (relative to the positive x axis) at a speed of $c\sqrt{[0.2 + cos\theta]^2 + (sin\theta)^2} = c\sqrt{1.04 + 0.4(cos\theta)^2}$. As shown by the red circle comprised of red triangles in Figure 1, we no longer have symmetry relative to (0,0), although we still have a circle, now

centered at (0.2,0). However, since the light pulses were emitted from (0,0), they no longer reach observers equidistant from that point at the same time. Instead, they now reach observers equidistant from the sifted point (0.2,0) at the same time.

In the Figure, the solid line(s) represents the vector sum(s) of the black dashed and solid white lines, such that this vector sum(s) = c. (The near-vertical dashed line is the light beam from the laser at speed c; the horizontal white line is the array's velocity at 0.2c.) These occur only at the following angles: $\pm[arccos(-0.1) - arccos(0.98)] = \pm 84.26^o$. (Recognizing that the triangle is isosceles, the law of cosines yields the following equation to be solved for $\alpha$, the angle between the y axis and solid black line(s): $(0.2c)^2 = c^2 + c^2 - 2(c)(c)cos[arccos(\theta - \pi/2 + \alpha)]$, where $\theta - \pi/2$, the angle between the y axis and the dashed line, comes from the Pythagorean relation $c^2 = c^2[0.2 + cos\theta)^2 + (sin\theta)^2]$.) Therefore, any light beam issued from a laser pen pointing to the right of the solid black lines travels at speed > c, with the maximum (1.2c) at $\theta = 0^o$. any light beam issued from a laser pen pointing to the left of these lines travels at speed < c, with the minimum (0.8c) at $\theta = 180^o$. Thus, only observers at $\theta = \pm 84.26^o$ and 1 light-sec from (0,0) see their respective light beams at 1.0 sec as before (when the array was stationary). an observer at x = (1,0) now sees his light beam sooner than before, at $(1.0 - 0.2)/1.0 = 0.8sec$. An observer at x = (-1,0) now has to wait $1.0/0.8 = 1.25sec$ before seeing his light beam. These differences have nothing to do with variation in time, only variation in light speed due to the moving laser array. Note that the light beams themselves are still released relative to their lasers at constant speed c.

How could light, unlike sound or water waves, travel at different speeds in the same 'medium' (e.g., vacuum, if we can consider such as a medium) when, at least for sound or water waves, the medium itself determines the wave speed regardless of motion of the source? I speculate this is possible because is not a 'wave' like sound or water waves, i.e., one which is actually the movement of the medium itself (either longitudinal [sound]or transverse [water]). If it has a medium (e.g., an aether, whatever that may be since it appears undetectable), then it is not the movement of the medium itself, but some other phenomenon. Since light obviously interacts with different material media (its speed slows as it passes through denser media, such as water), it cannot be the movement of the medium through which it passes. Can it even have a medium in the traditional sense?

## 4. Two Unique Theories for Light Propagation

I now examine two very interesting postulates about the nature of light and its propagation which, when combined, appear to offer a reasonable explanation for the nature of light and its observed properties.

### 4.1. Renshaw's Radiation Continuum Model

Renshaw postulates a new model of light, the Radiation

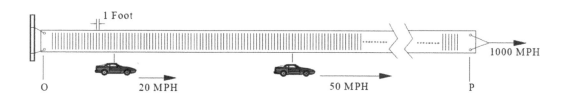

*Figure 1-1 Each automobile will remain adjacent to a specific, mark on a piece of elastic stretching alongside them as long as they maintain a constant velocity*

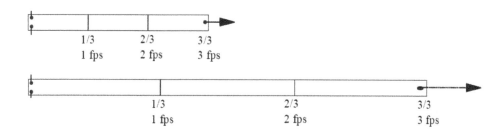

*Figure 1-2 As a piece of elastic is stretched, all points maintain their same velocities and relative separations.*

**Figure 2.**   Renshaw's Figures 1-1 and 1-2

Continuum Model (RCM), which I colloquially will call 'spring theory,' as it reminds me of the uncoiling of a spring fixed at one end. His detailed description follows [2].

"Suppose we take a piece of clear elastic, very resilient and pliable, and one foot in length. We fasten one end of this elastic to a pole, and stretch the other end to a distance of one thousand miles. While it is stretched to this length, we place a faint white line every foot from the pole to the thousand-mile point. The elastic then looks like that in figure 1-1. Once we have completed marking the elastic, we allow it to return to its original one-foot length, still anchored at point $O$ on the pole.

"An important point about the way that an elastic material stretches is that any two points on the elastic always maintain the same relative separation. For example, if we place marks dividing the elastic into thirds, then as it is stretched these marks will continue to delineate three equal sections, as in figure 1-2. An implication of this is that each point on the elastic has a unique, unchanging speed as the elastic is being stretched ... These ratios of velocity and spatial separation hold for any combination of points on the elastic. In addition, for whatever speed the end of the elastic is moving forward, a unique point can be found somewhere on the elastic that is traveling at any speed we choose between zero and the speed of that end ...

"Referring again to figure 1-1, suppose we take the loose end of the marked elastic and begin pulling it forward at a velocity of one-thousand mile per hour. at the same instant, two automobiles driven by Alice and Bob pass the starting pole, traveling in the same direction as the stretching elastic. Alice, in the first auto, is traveling at twenty miles per hour, while Bob, in the second, is traveling at fifty miles per hour. Further, each automobile is carrying a camera and pointing it directly at the elastic stretching alongside. We assume a very low light level, such that a long time exposure is required to obtain any detail in a photograph taken by either camera ... Each automobile begins a time lapsed photo thirty minutes after passing the starting pole, and allows the exposure to continue for thirty minutes.

"After the experiment is complete and the photos are developed, Alice and Bob each have a photo containing one distinct white line and nothing else. The reason for this is as follows: Given an elastic with one end stationary and one end moving forward at one-thousand miles per hour, a unique point can be found on the elastic whose velocity corresponds to any given value between zero and one-thousand mile per hour. Further, an automobile traveling at twenty miles per hour and passing the pole at the same instant the elastic commences being stretched will remain adjacent to the very point on the elastic that is also traveling at twenty miles per hour for the duration of the trip. Since there is a white line on the elastic at this point, this line will appear to be stationary with respect to the camera in the car, and will therefor appear as a distinct white line on the photographic plate ...

"When the experiment is over, Alice will conclude that the event she photographed was the release of an object with a faint white line at rest from her frame of reference (traveling at twenty miles per hour). Bob will conclude the event was the release of an object with a faint white line at rest from his frame of reference (traveling at a velocity of fifty miles per hour). If the experiment is repeated with many automobiles, all traveling at different velocities, the drivers will, after a time, conclude that the event was the release of an object with a faint white line exhibiting the unique property of appearing to be at rest from all frames of reference. In reality, the event was the release of, for all intents and purposes, an infinite stream of faint white lines, traveling at all velocities from zero to one-thousand mile per hour. The problem is that, due to the nature of the observer, only that aspect of the event remaining at rest with respect to the observer can be detected ...

"A Constant Velocity for All Frames of Reference

"Suppose we now repeat the above experiment with the following changes. The light requires only one second to expose the plate. Each automobile is a train, fifty feet in length. The camera is propelled from the back of the train towards the front at a velocity of ten miles per hour (Alice and Bob's trains are still assumed to be traveling at velocities of twenty and fifty miles per hour, respectively). The plate is exposed for the first second of the camera's trip down the length of the train ... This time, since the camera is moving at ten miles per hour with respect to the train, we have created a device that will record only objects that are moving at ten miles per hour with respect to the train ... In this manner, each train rider knows that the apparatus will record only objects that are traveling at ten miles per hour with respect to the velocity of the moving train. Clearly, from the above arguments, Alice will conclude the event produced a glowing object traveling at ten miles per hour as observed from her frame of reference (traveling at twenty miles per hour). Bob will conclude that the event produced a glowing object traveling at ten miles per hour with respect to his frame of reference (traveling at fifty miles per hour). If the experiment is repeated with many automobiles, the common conclusion will be that the event was the release of an object exhibiting the unique property of an invariant velocity of ten miles per hour for all frames of reference.

"Next imagine that we replace the camera in the above examples with a device that can only detect motion at the speed of light, c, relative to itself. The fast moving end of the elastic will need to move forward at a speed not less than c plus the velocity of any potential observer. For the time being, let us agree with Einstein and state that no observer will be traveling faster than c. This being the case, the elastic must be pulled forward with a velocity of at least two times c in order for all possible experimenters to record the white-line phenomena. When the experiment is performed by many people, all traveling at different speeds, they will undoubtedly come to a common conclusion - the event appears to be the release of an object that travel at the speed of light, c, form all frames of reference ...

"The Radiation Continuum Model of Light

"... Based on the analysis of the previous sections, we are ready to propose what we will call the radiation continuum model (RCM) of light. In this model, light does not radiate from its source at a constant velocity of c. Rather it emanates in the same manner as a piece of elastic, anchored at the source, with one end pulled forward at a constant velocity C, with the upper case C denoting a velocity that is much greater than c, and is very probably infinite. This being the case, there will be a component of the light that is traveling at any speed we pick in the range from zero to C. As important a characteristic of this model of light, and of living and electro-mechanical observers, is that only that component of light striking the observer at a relative velocity of c in the observer's frame of reference will be detected ... That is to say that regardless of our velocity, any light we perceive will appear to be striking us at approximately 300,000 kilometers per second (km/sec).

"One of the more significant implications of the radiation continuum model of light is that it allows a more intuitive 'Galilean' structure of space and time. By Galilean, we mean that the laws of electromagnetic radiation would conform to Galilean transformations, just as Newton's laws of motion do. Under such a transformation the concepts of space and time are absolute ... Now, without specifying an upper limit on the speed of light C, we have developed a model of light as a rubber band anchored at its source and moving forward through space at all speeds from zero to C [hence my term 'spring theory']. There is no obvious reason to set a bound on C at any value short of infinity. [Renshaw does not postulate an infinite speed, but rater a limiting speed C » c.]"

## 4.2. Calkins' *Relativity Revisited*

Calkins examines the nature of light from first principles, starting with the behavior of waves with which we are quite familiar - sound and water waves [1]. He postulates that the electromagnetic 'field' of light itself comprises the propagating 'medium,' analogous to what at least is partially occurring with the more familiar, tangible media like air or water for sound and water wave propagation. To me, this suggests an interesting analogy with one of McLuhan's observation, namely that "the medium is the message" [3]. Calkins' detailed description follows.

"The segue through Maxwell's equations was made to develop an understanding of how the determinants of the speed of light compare with those of the speed of sound. But before we do that, it's worth noting some of the implications and interpretations about electromagnetism that have resulted from the structure of Maxwell's equations ... When the electric current is removed [from Maxwell's fourth equation], the electric field is reduced to the same dependency on the magnetic field as the magnetic field always has on the electric field. Once an electromagnetic wave leaves its source, the only electric field it contains is the kind created by a moving magnetic field. This codependency between the two fields in an electromagnetic wave

is why it can be said that when a photon stops moving, it ceases to exist ...

"[T]he values of $\varepsilon_0$ and $\mu_0$ are not coincidental. There are underlying physical phenomena that cause them to have the values that they do. By treating them as mere constants, we end up with an equation for the speed of light [$c = \sqrt{\varepsilon_0 \mu_0}$] that depends on no identifiable physical phenomenon ... To see how this compares with the speed of sound, let's look at what is going on inside the equation for the speed of sound: $v = \sqrt{B_a/\rho_a}$ ... [where] $B_a$ is the bulk modulus of air. It describes air's resistance to compression: $B_a = -\Delta p/(\Delta v/v_0)$ ... [T]he value of $B_a$ is determined by the change in pressure ($\Delta p$) that is required to reduce the volume by a given amount ($\Delta v$) relative to the initial volume ($v_0$). (The minus sign just means that the pressure and volume change in opposite directions. When pressure is increased, volume is reduced ...). The more pressure that is required to produce a given reduction in volume (i.e., the harder it is to compress the medium), the greater the value of $B_a$ and ... the faster the wave will move. $\rho_a$ is the density of air. The greater the density, the slower the wave will move. These two characteristics of air are what determine the speed of sound. This is pretty straightforward when dealing with a stationary physical medium such as air. It is less clear when we are dealing with light propagating through what is presumed to be the vacuum of space ...

"What determines the speed of sound is the amount of resistance its longitudinal wave encounters when pushing atoms of air more closely together, thereby forcing an increase in the electric and magnetic field density of their charged particles ... An electric field that changes in time does not directly create an electric field that moves in space. What it does is create a magnetic field which, in turn, creates the next electric field. Ditto for the magnetic field's change in time which produces an electric field that is the source of the subsequent magnetic field ... The medium of propagation of the moving electric field is the magnetic field it must push into existence as an unavoidable consequence of its movement. The magnetic field starts with zero density and moves to greater density as the moving electric field pushes it into existence. It is in the nature of the field to resist having its density increased. This is the same physical phenomenon that largely determines the bulk modulus of air [plus molecules of air bouncing off each other]. The magnetic field being pushed into existence has a field density and a bulk modulus (i.e., an innate resistance to being compressed). It is inarguable that the magnetic field is a medium of propagation since it is actively created by the moving electric field; the next electric field in the wave cannot be created without it and it is the active element in that field's creation. The same happens when the magnetic field returns the favor by pushing the next electric field into existence. The same phenomena are at work in a similar manner for the propagation of light as for the propagation of sound. They are the bulk modulus and density of their mediums of propagation. In the case of sound, the medium (air) is physical and stationary. Light, on the other hand, takes its mediums along with it. But in both cases the waves' propagation through their medium(s) is governed by the physics of electric and magnetic field compression.

"What we failed to realize when we accepted $\varepsilon_0$ and $\mu_0$ as simple constants... is their underlying physical significance. $\varepsilon_0$ is not the 'permittivity of free space;' it is the ratio of the electric field's density to its bulk modulus: $\varepsilon_0 = \rho_E/B_E$ ... Likewise, $\mu_0 = \rho_B/B_B$ is the ratio of the magnetic field's density to its bulk ... Substituting these ratios into the equation for the speed of light gives us: $c = \frac{1}{\sqrt{\varepsilon_0\mu_0}} = \sqrt{\frac{(B_E B_B)}{(\rho_e\rho_B)}}$. [Through personal conversation with Calkins, he agrees that a more dimensionally consistent representation for these would be as follows: $\varepsilon_0\mu_0 = \frac{\rho_E M}{B_E M}$, such that $c = \frac{1}{\sqrt{\varepsilon_0\mu_0}} = \sqrt{\frac{B_E M}{\rho_E M}}$, where 'EM' represents the 'combined' electric and magnetic (electromagnetic) fields, which work in unison as light's propagation 'medium.' The ensuing analogy with sound and all subsequent conclusions remain the same with this slight modification.] This compares with the speed of sound: $v = \sqrt{B_a/\rho_a}$ ... the only difference in the structure of the two equations is that the parameters for the electric and magnetic fields are separately stated in the equation for the speed of light whereas their effects are combined in the pressure, volume and density parameters of air for the speed of sound."

### 4.3. Assimilation

Having provided rather lengthy (albeit somewhat compressed) discussions of these two very interesting postulates, I believe they can be combined into a reasonable description of the 'observed' constancy of the speed of light from a stationary source in any particular 'medium,' while allowing this speed to vary within the same medium with a moving source. To me, Renshaw's 'spring theory' for light is analogous to the following simple example. Consider a cannon in space (no friction, essentially no gravity), sealed at one end, open at the other, containing five cannon balls of exactly the same size and mass 'm,' each with a fixed type and amount of explosive charge between them (including one between the first ball and the sealed end of the cannon) such that, when any charge is detonated, it applies the same force 'F' linearly along the cannon tube.

If all five charges are detonated simultaneously (perhaps via some electrical means, whereby the signal to each essentially arrives simultaneously), the total force exerted on each cannon ball will be the sum of the forces from each charge lying between it and the sealed end of the cannon, i.e., 5F for the ball at the open end, 4F for the next, etc., down to F on the ball next to the sealed end. And each force will act on a total mass equal to the number of balls between it and the open end of the cannon, i.e., m for the charge between the two balls nearest the open end, 2m for the next, etc., up to 5m for the charge between the ball and the sealed end. Implicit here is an assumption that the inertia of the balls results in all forces 'pushing' off against the sealed end (via 'action-reaction' through the

various balls, depending on location [which are initially stationary due to inertia when the charges detonate], before any motion takes place). Therefore, the forces as well as the masses can be combined based on the various positions of the balls and charges, with all force and any resulting motion directly solely in the direction of the open end.

Numbering the balls from n = 1 to 5, with 1 being at the sealed end and 5 at the open, the respective acceleration 'a' imparted on each is as follows: $a_n = \frac{nF}{[5-(n-1)]m} = \frac{n/(6-n)}{(F/m)}$. In units of $\frac{F}{m}$, the ration of accelerations from the ball at the sealed end to that at the open end are $\frac{1}{5} : \frac{1}{2} : 1 : 2 : 5$. As the cannon is in space with essentially no gravity, once ejected, the balls will attain constant speeds 'v' determined by the time interval '$\Delta t$' over which the explosive charges detonated via the equation $v = a\Delta t$. Since $\Delta t$ was the same for all five detonations, the ratios of the five balls' velocities will be the same as those for their accelerations. The three ratios of the four distance '$\Delta x$' between them walso remain the same even as these distance increase over time 't,' since $\Delta x = vt$, i.e., $[\frac{1-1/2}{1/2-1/5} = \frac{5}{3}] : [\frac{2-1}{1-\frac{1}{2}} = 2] : [\frac{5-2}{2-1} = 3]$.

Now we take advantage of Calkins' 'medium is the message' approach, which provides us with a medium for light, other than the traditional aether or the non-existent medium of a vacuum, i.e., the electromagnetic field itself. As with other media (albeit non-material), it still provides a means by which to limit the light wave to a constant speed, namely c when in a vacuum from a stationary source. In summary, combining the two postulates of Renshaw and Calkins, one seemingly reasonable model for light is Renshaw's RCM that allows light to travel over a wide range of speeds, but due to Calkins' electromagnetic medium (which provides 'resistance'), limited to being observed at constant speed in a particular medium when emitted from a stationary source.

## 5. Conclusion

If light travels at a constant speed in a given medium when emitted from a stationary source, and if it is analogous to sound or water waves, then it would not exhibit different speeds when emitted from a moving source within the same medium, only the traditional Doppler Shift, i.e., change in frequency and wavelength, but not speed. However, I have already postulated that light behaves 'Galileanly' by acquiring the velocity vector of a moving source, allowing for speeds different from c. [9] Renshaw supports this by assuming the source motion 'moves' the observer to a different point on the elastic, or light beam where, while a constant speed is still observed, the 'true' speed differs from c. But this does not align with Calkins' analogy of light with sound and water waves, where the wave speed is invariant due to the resistance of the medium, regardless of the source's motion. However, if one considers light to be a different type of wave from sound or water, at least partially, perhaps these can be rectified.

In air or water, or any other material medium, Calkins acknowledges the role of the medium itself to providing resistance to the wave in addition to that inherently provided by the compression of any electromagnetic fields already present due to the atoms comprising the medium. Thus, a moving source in such a medium has its speed limited by the resistance from that medium itself. However, if the material medium itself were also moving in its entirety, say along with the source, then the net result would be a wave propagating at the constant speed in the medium PLUS that speed of the moving medium (summed vectorially), at least to an outside observer (i.e., one not moving with the moving medium). Light has no material medium in the sense of that for sound or water waves - only the electromagnetic field itself. Therefore, when the source (of light) moves, the electromagnetic field (the medium) moves along with it, since the medium is generated from the source. Could this not be the analogy that allows for Galilean addition of the $\underline{c}$ and $\underline{v}$ vectors for a moving source of light? And from Renshaw's RCM approach, could not this speed of light different from c correspond to being able to observe the true speed from a different point along the elastic beam?

# REFERENCES

1. R. Calkins, *Relativity Revisited*, http://www.calkinspublishing.com, 2011
2. C. Renshaw, *The Restoration of Space and Time: Galilean-Newtonian Relativity in the 21st Century*, http://renshaw.teleinc.com/Book/Chapter%201%20-20A%20-Model%20of%20Light.pdf, 2008
3. M. McLuhan, *Understanding Media: The Extensions of Man*, https://en.wikipedia.org/wiki/The_medium_is_the_message, 1964
4. R. Gallucci, *Questioning the Cosmological Doppler Redshift*, www.naturalphilosopy.org, Proceedings of the 1st Annual CNPS Conference (2015)

# Tidal Asymmetry

## Raymond HV Gallucci, PhD, PE

*8956 Amelung St., Frederick, Maryland, 21704, gallucci@localnet.com, r_gallucci@verizon.net*

The Earth's diametrically opposed, presumably symmetric, tides are due to the Moon's differential gravitational force varying across the Earth. This is not intuitively obvious, but becomes clear when the physics is examined mathematically. The presumed symmetry is due to an approximation that holds when the radius of the affected body (e.g., The Earth) is much less than its center-to-center distance from the affecting body (e.g., the Moon). The exact solution indicates an asymmetry, which becomes more pronounced as the assumption loses its applicability.

**Keywords:** Earth-Moon, tides, differential gravity, barycentric rotation, ring-spring

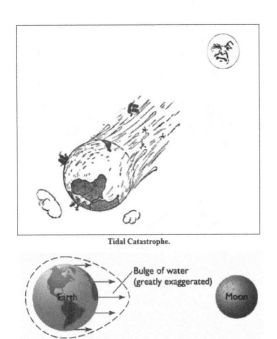

**Tidal Catastrophe.**

**Figure 1.** Tidal Misconceptions [1]

## 1. Introduction

Explaining why the Earth experiences height tides (or low tides) simultaneously on opposite hemispheres is not intuitively obvious. If due to the gravitational force of the Moon (and, to a lesser extent, that of the Sun),[1] one might expect there to be a tidal bulge solely on the 'near' hemisphere (i.e., the one closer to the Moon), as illustrated in Figure 1 [1].

This is clearly not observed. Most websites that explain the tides follow the following logic or something similar [2].

"The tidal force is a secondary effect of the force of gravity and is responsible for the tides. It arises because the gravitational force exerted by one body on another is not constant across it; the nearest side is attracted more strongly than the farther side. Thus, the tidal force is differential ... For a given (externally generated) gravitational field, the tidal acceleration at a point with respect to a body is obtained by vectorially subtracting the gravitational acceleration at the center of the body (due to the given externally generated field) from the gravitational acceleration (due to the same field) at the given point. Correspondingly, the term tidal force is used to describe the forces due to tidal acceleration. Note that for these purposes the only gravitational field considered is the external one; the gravitational field of the body is not relevant ...

"By Newton's law of universal gravitation and laws of motion, a body of mass M [i.e., the Earth] at a distance D from the center of a sphere of mass m [i.e., the Moon] feels a force $F = \frac{-GMm}{D^2}$ equivalent to an acceleration $A = \frac{-Gm}{D^2}$ [along] a unit vector pointing from the body m to the body M ... Consider now the acceleration due to the sphere of mass m experienced by a particle in the vicinity of the body of mass M. With D as the distance from the center of m to the center of M, let R be the (relatively small) distance of the particle from the center of the body of mass M. For simplicity, distance are ... considered only in the direction pointing towards or away from the sphere of mass m.

"If the body of mass M is itself a sphere of radius R, then the new particle considered may be located on its surface, at a distance $D\pm R$ from the center of the sphere of mass m, and R may be taken as positive where the particle's distance from m is greater than R. Leaving aside whatever gravitational acceleration may be experienced by the particle towards M on account of M's own mass, we have the acceleration on the particle due to gravitational force towards m as $A = -\frac{Gm}{(D\pm R)^2}$. Pulling out the $D^2$ term from the denominator gives $A = -\frac{GmD^2}{(1\pm R/D)^2}$, ... [which expands, via

---

[1] Only the Moon's effect is examined in this paper. It has been estimated to be approximately twice that of the Sun [2].

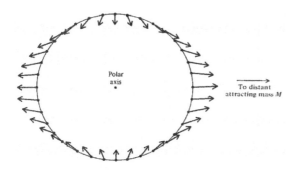

**Figure 2.** Effect of Differential (Tidal) Forces [4]

the Maclaurin series, into] ... $A = GmD^2 \pm (\frac{2GM}{D^2})(\frac{R}{D}) + ....$

"The first term is the gravitational acceleration due to m at the center of the reference body M, i.e., at the point where R is zero [i.e., Earth's center]. This term does not affect the observed acceleration of particles on the surface of M because with respect to m, M (and everything on its surface) is in free fall. When the force on the far particle is subtracted from the force on the near particle, this first term cancels, as do all other even-order terms. The remaining (residual) terms represent the difference mentioned above and are tidal force (acceleration) terms. When R is small compared to D, the terms after the first residual term are very small and can be neglected, giving the approximate tidal acceleration (axial) for the distances R considered, along the axis joining the centers of M and m [as] $A \approx \pm 2GMR/D^3$."

We see equal magnitude accelerations for the maximum tides, implying symmetry. Additional websites that explain the ocean tides often cite the hemispherical opposites as symmetric based on polynomial expansions and neglecting higher-order terms beyond the second power, e.g., "The tide generating force can be decomposed into components perpendicular and parallel to the sea surface. The tides are produced by the horizontal components ... The tidal potential is symmetric about the Earth-moon line, and it produces symmetric bulges [3]." This conclusion implicitly assumes that the ratio between the radius of the affected body and its center-to-center distance from the affecting body is « 1. A common illustration is shown in Figure 2.

## 2. Tidal Asymmetry?

The goal here is to show that, using the exact, vs. the asymptotic, solution to the differential force between the Moon's gravitational pull at the Earth's surface vs. at its center, an asymmetry between the tides will result for equal angles $\theta$ on the Earth's far and near hemispheres. This asymmetry will exist for both the magnitude of the differential force ($\Delta g$) and the angle ($\beta$). Figure 3 provides the geometry for the comparison. Note that, for the near hemisphere, the Moon's gravitational force at the surface

is almost always greater than that at the Earth's center,[2] as indicated by the first forces triangle for the near hemisphere. The opposite holds exclusively for the far hemisphere, where the Moon's gravitational force at the Earth's center is always greater than at the surface, as indicated by the second forces triangle for the far hemisphere. Calculations for the various parameters are as follows:

$$d_n = \sqrt{(D - R\cos\theta_n)^2 + (R\sin\theta_n)^2} = \sqrt{D^2 - 2DR\cos\theta_n + R^2}$$

$$d_f = \sqrt{(D + R\cos\theta_f)^2 + (R\sin\theta_f)^2} = \sqrt{D^2 + 2DR\cos\theta_f + R^2}$$

Assuming, for convenience, that G (gravitational constant) and m (Moon's mass) are both unity, $g_m n = 1/d_n^2$, $g_m f = 1/d_f^2$, $g_c = 1/D^2$. In addition, the Moon's gravitational force is assumed to act on a unit mass of $1kg$ of ocean water on the Earth's surface, so that the force equations developed below can be viewed as characterizing the force per unit of affected mass, essentially an acceleration. therefore, the differential forces between the Moon's gravitational pull at the Earth's surface and at the Earth's center are as follows:

$$\Delta g_n = \sqrt{g_{m,n}^2 + g_c^2 - 2g_{m,n}g_c \cos(\phi_n)}$$

$$\Delta g_f = \sqrt{g_{m,f}^2 + g_c^2 - 2g_{m,f}g_c \cos(\phi_f)}$$

$$\cos(\phi_n) = (D - \frac{R\cos(\theta_n)}{d_n}$$

$$\cos(\phi_f) = (D + \frac{R\cos(\theta_f)}{d_f}$$

$$\frac{g_{m,n}}{\sin(\beta_n)} = \Delta\frac{g_n}{\sin(\phi_n)}, \text{ yielding}$$

$$\beta_n = \arcsin\left(g_{m,n}\frac{\sin(\phi_n)}{\Delta g_n}\right)$$

$$\frac{g_{m,f}}{\sin(\pi - \beta_f)} = \Delta g_f / \sin(\phi_f), \text{ yielding}$$

$$g_{m,f}/sin\beta_f = \Delta g_f/sin\phi_f, \text{ yielding}$$

$$\beta_f = arcsin(g_{m,f}\sin(\phi_f)/\Delta g_f).$$

To compare corresponding angles $\theta$ on the near and far hemispheres in terms of the differences between the differential forces in terms of magnitude ($\Delta g$) and direction ($\beta$), we calculate the following pair of differences for $0 \leq \theta \leq \pi/2$: (1) $\Delta g_n - \Delta g_f$ and (2) $\Delta\beta_n - \Delta\beta_f$. For convenience, we assume D = 1 and express R as a fraction of D ranging from 0.001 to 0.5 and including the ratio for the Earth-Moon system, i.e., $R/D =$

---

[2] As $\theta_n$ approaches $90^o$, $\beta_n$ reaches a maximum then starts to decrease, with the angle at which the maximum occurs being closer to $90^o$ as R/D decreases. This will be shown later via plots of the differences between the $\Delta g$ forces for corresponding angles $\theta$ on the near and far hemispheres.

Moon is distance D from Earth (center-to-center). Earth radius is R. Define $\theta_f$ and $\theta_n$ as equal angles on f(ar) and n(ear) hemispheres when looking down from the North Pole (or up from the South), forming distances $d_f$ and $d_n$ between Moon's center and points on Earth's surface at which Moon's gravitational effect on the tides is calculated. These create two triangles with corresponding angles $\phi_f$ and $\phi_n$ between the Moon's gravitational force at the surface points and the Earth's center.

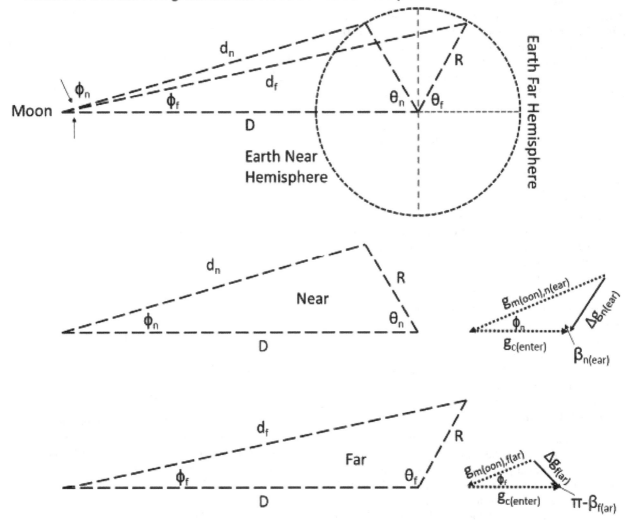

**Figure 3.** Geometry for Analysis

$(6,371km)/(384,400km) = 0.0166$. Figures 4 and 5 plot both pairs of differences over the complete range. Figures 6 and 7 are analogous plots in terms of the percent differences (relative to the average of the corresponding values for the far and near hemispheres). All four include the results for the Earth-Moon system, with g and m set to unity.

The expected trend is that the Moon's gravitational force on the near hemisphere, albeit decreasing from $\theta = 0 \ to \ 90^o$, vs. the Moon's gravitational force on the far hemisphere, always increasing, is always greater for corresponding values of $\theta$, with equality achieved only when $\theta = 90^o$. As a result, the differential force on the near hemisphere, albeit decreasing from $\theta = 0 \ to \ 90^o$, always exceeds the differential force on the far hemisphere, also always decreasing, as evidenced by the values remaining positive, albeit decreasing, from $\theta = 0 \ to \ 90^o$. This trend is evident in Figures 4 and 6, increasing as R/D increases.[3]

The trend for the direction (angle $\beta$) of the differential force on the near hemisphere vs. far hemisphere is also evident from Figures 5 and 7. On the far hemisphere, this angle always increases from $\theta = 0 \ to \ 90^o$. On the near hemisphere, it also increases over nearly the entire range, only showing a slight decrease from $\theta = 89^o \ to \ 90^o$. The result is that the difference between the angles of the differential forces is always positive (i.e., $\beta_n > \beta_f$). However, as shown in Figures 5 and 7, this difference reaches a maximum as $\beta$ approaches $90^o$, with the maximum occurring at a lesser angle with increasing R/D.[4] This maximum value occurs where $d_n = D$ ($d_f$ is always > D), i.e.,

$d_n = D$, yielding $\sqrt{D^2 - 2DRcos\theta_n + R^2} = D$

$\theta_n = \arccos(R/2D)$

Table 1 lists where these maxima occur.

## 3. Ring-Spring Analogy

Figure 8 illustrates the assumed tidal effect for the asymptotic case where $R/D \ll 1$, such that the tides are symmetric on both hemispheres. A force pulling at one end of the ring-spring (with the other end fixed), such as the Moon, translates into a differential force as if pulling at both ends (neither end fixed). An observer in the middle of the ring-spring before any force is applied sees both ends of the spring as equidistant, and the ring as circular. After the force is applied, the observer still sees both ends equidistant, albeit now equally farther away, and the ring stretched to form a symmetrical ellipse. This is the assumed behavior of the tides when R ≪ D.

Figure 9 assumes the ring-spring starts in 'deep space'

---

[3] Also shown in this figure is the trend for the Earth-Moon system with the actual values of the gravitational constant ($6.674x10^{-11} \frac{m^3}{kg-s}$) and Moon's mass ($7.348x10^{22}kg$) included. The actual center-to-center distance between the Earth and Moon and the Earth's actual radius are already accounted for by $R/D = 0.0166$.

[4] The inflection point is impossible to see until R/D reaches 0.1 due to the scale of the axes.

where there is no gravity. There, no deformation will occur. If the bottom is pulled, uniform deformation will occur, analogous to the deformation in Figure 8 since there is still no gravity. However, as the ring-spring enters a gravitational field, it acquires weight, with the weight being proportional to the length of the spring such that, towards the top, the coils feel a greater pull (more coils) than near the bottom (less coils). Now the deformation is not uniform and an observer originally at the middle of the spring when the ends were equidistant now will see the upper end farther away than the lower. The ring also deforms into more of an egg-shape than a symmetric ellipse. This is the analogy for the case where R is not ≪ D. This parallels the results from the analysis as shown in Figures 4 through 7, i.e., there is an asymmetry between the two hemispheres, more pronounced as R approaches D.

## 4. Conclusion

The explanation for the Earth's tides is not intuitively obvious, but appears to suggest an expectation of symmetry on the two hemispheres, i.e., equally-high high tides and equally-low low tides, diametrically opposite. The analysis performed here suggests that this symmetry is the result of an approximation, usually quite good when the radius of the affected body is much less than the distance between its center and that of the affecting body (e.g., Earth-Moon). However, exact solution of the differential tidal force equations demonstrates that there always is an asymmetry, more pronounced as the affected body radius approaches the center-to-center distance from the affecting body. This peaks at approximately 10 percent in terms of magnitude and direction for $R/D = 0.0166$ for the Earth-Moon system (Figures 6 and 7).

## 5. Addendum I: Effect of Earth's Rotation about the Earth-Moon Barycenter

The Earth's monthly rotation about the Earth-Moon barycenter can affect the tides. Referring to Figure 2, the Earth-Moon barycenter (B) is located $4671km$ ($4.671x10^6 m$) from the Earth's center, within the Earth itself. With a rotational period (p) about this point of 27.32 d (sidereal month [?]), the tangential speed at $\theta_f = 0^o$ (along Earth-Moon axis on the 'far' side) is $\frac{2\pi(R+B)}{p} = 29.4m/s$ for R (earth) = $6371km$ ($6.371x10^6 m$). Compared to the daily rotational speed at the equator, $2\pi R(86400s) = 463m/s$, this is small (approximately 6 percent) but not negligible. The centrifugal force on $1kg$ of ocean due to this barycentric rotation is $(1kg)(29.4m/s)^2/(R+B) = 7.82x10^{-5}N$. The differential gravitational force on $1kg$ of ocean from the Moon at this point is $\frac{Gm(1kg)}{1/D^2 - 1/(R+D)^2} = 1.07x10^{-6}N$ where m (moon) = $7.348x10^{22}kg$ and D = $384400km$ ($3.844x10^8 m$). Therefore the centrifugal force from the barycentric rotation is approximately 70 times that from the differential gravitational force at this point.

Even at the 'near' side ($\theta_n = 0^o$), the barycentric centrifugal force dominates that from the differen-

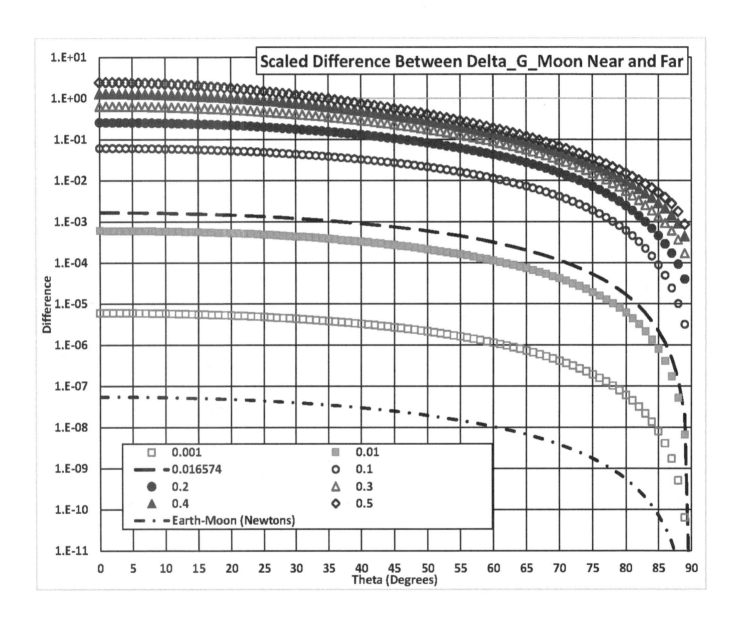

**Figure 4.** Differences between Moon's Differential Force for Corresponding Position on Near and Far Hemisphere

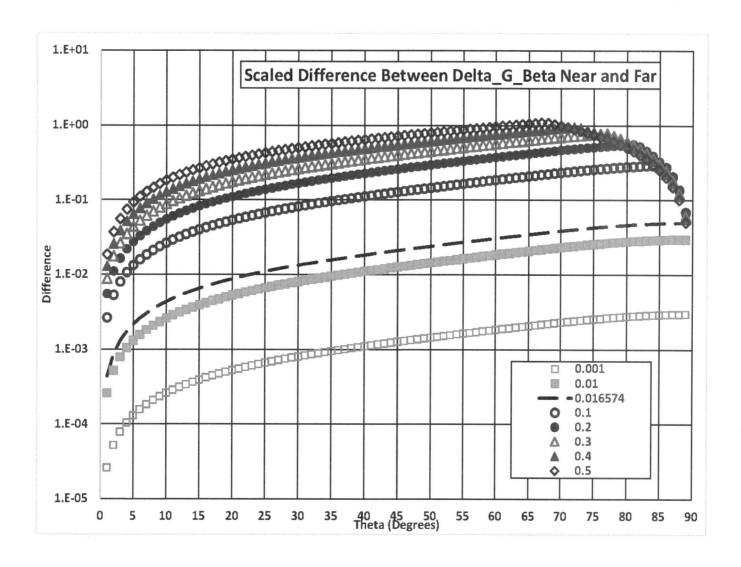

**Figure 5.**   Differences between Angles of Moon's Differential Force for Corresponding Position on Near and Far Hemisphere

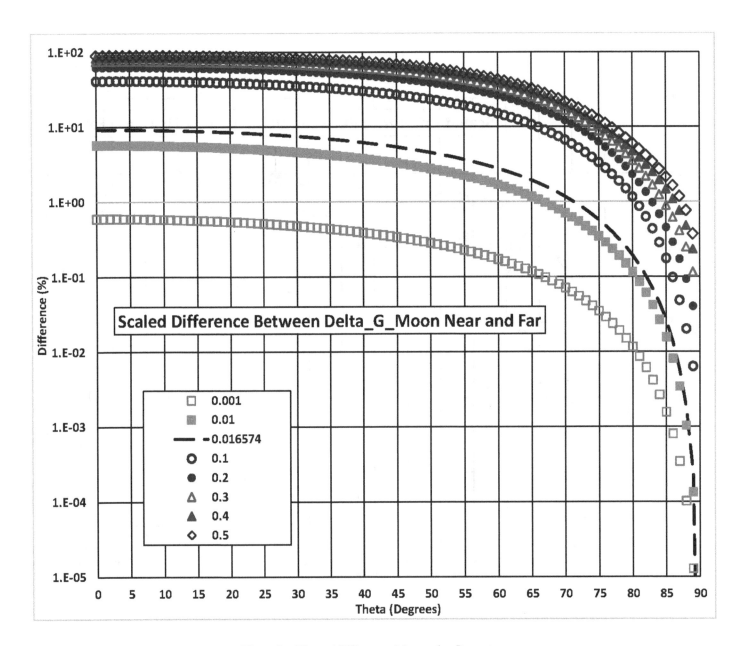

**Figure 6.**   Figure 4 Differences Measured as Percents

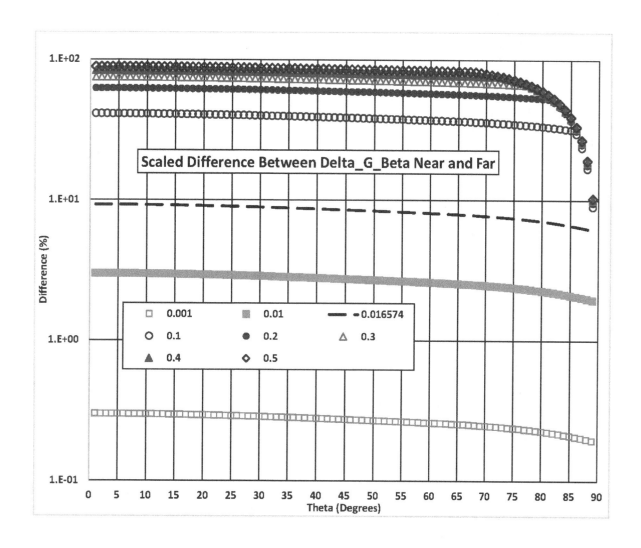

**Figure 7.** Figure 5 Differences Measured as Percents

| $\theta_n$ (degrees) for $\beta_n - \beta_f$ maximum → | R/D | | | | | | | |
|---|---|---|---|---|---|---|---|---|
| | 0.001 | 0.01 | 0.0166 | 0.1 | 0.2 | 0.3 | 0.4 | 0.5 |
| | 89.97 | 89.71 | 89.53 | 87.13 | 84.26 | 81.37 | 78.46 | 75.52 |

**TABLE 1.** Angle where Difference between Near and Far Hemisphere Tidal Forces is Maximum

tial gravitational force. At this point (along Earth-Moon axis on the 'near' side), the tangential speed is $2\pi(R - B)/([27.32d][86400s/d]) = 4.52m/s$. The centrifugal force on $1kg$ of ocean due to this barycentric rotation is $(1kg)(4.52m/s)^2/(R - B) = 1.20x10^{-5}N$. The differential gravitational force on $1kg$ of ocean from the Moon at this point is $\frac{Gm(1kg)}{1/(D-R)^2 - 1/D^2} = 1.07x10^{-6}N$. Therefore the centrifugal force from the barycentric rotation is still approximately 10 times that from the differential gravitational force at this point. Clearly, the dynamic effects from the rotation of the Earth-Moon system about its barycenter dominates over the static effect from the differential gravitational force from the Moon.

If one examines the variation of the radial (outward from center of Earth) component of the barycentric centrifugal force over each hemisphere ($C_{f,r}$ and $C_{n,r}$), one finds the difference between these forces ($C_{f,r} - C_{n,r}$) decreasing from a maximum of $6.62x10^{-5}N$ at $\theta_f = 0^o$ vs. $\theta_n = 0^o$ to $1.15x10^{-6}N$ at $\theta_f = 89^o$ vs. $\theta_n = 89^o$ (the difference is naturally zero when both $\theta_f$ and $\theta_n = 90^o$). Therefore, there is a strong asymmetry between the two hemispheres, as one would expect given $R + B \approx 7(R - B)$. Scaled to $1x10^{-5}N$, this asymmetry is shown in Figure 11. Note from the plot also the ratios of the radial component of the barycentric centrifugal force to the magnitude of the differential gravitational force on the two hemispheres. It remains between approximately 70 and 90 for the far hemisphere, peaking around $\theta_f = 75^o$, while rising from approximately 10 to 82 from $\theta_n = 0^o$ to $\theta_n = 90^o$. Clearly there is strong asymmetry predicted due to the barycentric centrifugal force, with the tides on the far hemisphere exceeding those on the near, opposite to the trend for the differential gravitational force. However, due to the dominance of the former, the latter does not come close to an offset, so asymmetric tides are predicted.

## 6. Addendum II: An Intriguing 'Coincidence?'

Neither the exact solution to the differential gravitational force approach nor incorporating the effect of the Earth's barycentric centrifugal force was able to establish the alleged symmetry of the tides across the Earth's hemispheres. However, an interesting anomaly that might bear further examination is revealed if one combines the barycentric effect with the Moon's gravitational force directly, i.e., without the differential effect. In Addendum I, the barycentric centrifugal on $1kg$ of ocean at $\theta_f = 0^o$ (along Earth-Moon axis on the 'far' side) was calculated as $7.82x10^{-5}N$. At $\theta_n = 0^o$ (along Earth-Moon axis on the

'near' side), the corresponding force is $1.20x10^{-5}N$. What are the gravitational forces (direct, not differential) of the Moon on the same $1kg$ of ocean water at these points?

At the 'far' side ($\theta_f = 0^o$), this is $Gm/(R + D)^2 = \frac{(6.674x10^{-11}m^3/kg-s)(7.348x10^{22}kg)}{(6.371x10^6m + 3.844x10^8m)^2} = 3.21x10^{-5}N$. At the 'near' side ($\theta_n = 0^o$), it is $Gm/(D - R)^2 = \frac{(6.674x10^{-11}m^3/kg-s)(7.348x10^{22}kg)}{(3.844x10^8m - 6.371x10^6m)^2} = 3.43x10^{-5}N$. At the 'far' side ($\theta_f = 0^o$), the barycentric centrifugal and Moon's gravitational forces act in opposite directions, yielding a net force radially outward of $7.82x10^{-5}N - 3.21x10^{-5}N = 4.61x10^{-5}N$. At the 'near' side ($\theta_n = 0^o$), these two forces act in the same directions, yielding a net force radially outward of $1.20x10^{-5}N + 3.43x10^{-5}N = 4.63x10^{-5}N$. These are essentially equal, both radially outward, inferring symmetry of the tides at these highest points. Is this just a coincidence, or might an explanation for tidal symmetry rely on this combination of forces, i.e., including the Moon's direct gravitational rather than its differential gravitational effect? To examine this conjecture over the entire pair of hemispheres, we employ the geometry as shown in Figure 12.

The barycentric centrifugal and Moon's gravitational (direct) forces are calculated over both hemispheres from the preceding formulas. These are then combined vectorially to yield the net forces along with the directions relative to the x-axis, also as shown in the figures. The differences between the net forces on the 'far' and 'near' sides and the differences between the angles of these forces are shown in Figure 13. Also shown are the ratio of these differences to their average values for the corresponding locations in each hemisphere.

The results are as follows. For the net forces themselves, the differences between corresponding locations in each hemisphere are quite small, on the order of $1x10^{-7}N$ or less, or < 1 percent of their average value. Similarly, the differences between the angles for these net forces at corresponding locations is quite small, on the order of 0.01 radians or less, again < 1 percent of their average value. What this suggests is that combining the barycentric centrifugal force and the Moon's gravitational (direct, not differential) forces vectorially produces the alleged symmetry between the tides on the opposite hemispheres. Might this, and not just the one differential gravitational force, be the reason for the symmetry of the alleged tides?

However, now that we are considering the direct gravitational effect of the Moon, what about that of the Sun, which is $(M/m)(D/S)^2 = 180$ times stronger, where M =

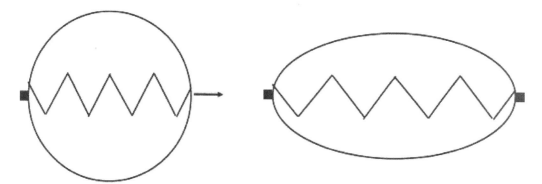

An elastic ring with a spring across its diameter is <u>fixed at one end</u> then pulled from the other. The ring expands in the direction of the force linearly, such that what was the center point of the spring remains so, still equidistant from its two ends. The ring is deformed symmetrically to form an ellipse.

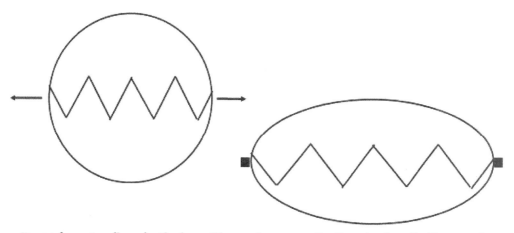

Now a <u>free-standing</u> elastic ring with a spring across its diameter is pulled by equal forces at both sides. The ring expands as before, symmetrically to form an ellipse, and what was the center point of the spring remains so, still equidistant from both ends.

**Figure 8.**    Ring-Spring Analogy for Asymptotic Deformation $R << D$

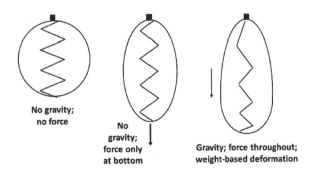

**No gravity; no force**

**No gravity; force only at bottom**

**Gravity; force throughout; weight-based deformation**

**Figure 9.**   Ring-Spring without and with Gravity

mass of the Sun ($1.989x10^{30}kg$) and S = distance from Sun's center to Earth's ($1.496x10^{8}km$)? The Moon's direct gravitational force on the near vs. far side differs by $3.43x10^{-5}N - 3.21x10^{-5}N = 2.20x10^{-6}N$, approximately 7 percent relative to the force at the Earth's center. For the Sun, this difference is $\frac{GM}{1/[S-R]^2 - 1/[S+R]^2} = 1.01x10^{-6}N$, approximately 0.02 percent relative to the force at the Earth's center ($GM/S^2 = 0.00593N$). When considering the effect of the differential gravitational forces, this is an important contributor, nearly half the value of the Moon's. However, for direct gravitational force, the variation across the Earth due to the Sun's gravity is negligible, i.e., it affects the Earth gravitationally on essentially an equal basis everywhere (0.00593 N). Therefore, as with the Earth's own daily rotational centrifugal and direct gravitational forces, the Sun's direct gravitational force is essentially uniform over the entire planet, thereby introducing no asymmetry.

We are left to ponder whether there is an alternative explanation for the alleged symmetry of the tides other than accepting the approximation employed when deriving the differential gravitational effect as in [2]. If the essentially uniform effects from the Sun's and Earth's own direct gravitational forces, as well as that from the Earth's daily rotational centrifugal force, introduce no asymmetry, might the combination of the barycentric centrifugal and Moon's direct gravitational forces explain what has so far been attributed to an approximation in the differential gravitational force derivation?

## REFERENCES

1.  D. Simanek, *Tidal Misconceptions*, https://lhup.edu/ dsi-manek/scenario/tides.htm, 2015
2.  Wikipedia, *Tidal Force*, https://en.wikipedia.org/wiki/Tidal_force, 2016
3.  R. Stewart, *Coastal Processes and Tides*, http://oceanworld.tamu.edu/resources/ocng_textbook/chapter17/ chapter17_04.htm, Dept. of Oceanography, Texas A&M University (2008)
4.  D. Simanek, *A Descriptive Explanation of Ocean Tides*, https://lhup.edu/d̃simanek/sceanrio/tides101.htm, 2014

$b_f = \{B^2 + R^2 - 2BR\cos[\pi\text{-}\theta_f]\}^{0.5} = \{B^2 + R^2 + 2BR[\cos\theta_f]\}^{0.5}$

$b_n = \{B^2 + R^2 - 2BR[\cos\theta_n]\}^{0.5}$

**Centrifugal Force:**

    $C_f$ (on 1 kg of ocean) $= v_f^2/b_f = (2\pi b_f/p)^2/b_f = b_f(2\pi/p)^2$

    p = sidereal period (27.32 d x 86400 s/d)

    $C_n$ (on 1 kg of ocean) $= v_n^2/b_n = (2\pi b_n/p)^2/b_n = b_n(2\pi/p)^2$

**Radially:**

    $C_{f,r} = C_f(\cos\gamma_f)$, where $\gamma_f = \sin^{-1}([B/b_f][\sin\theta_f])$

    $C_{n,r} = C_f(\cos\gamma_n)$, where $\gamma_n = \sin^{-1}([B/b_n][\sin\theta_n])$

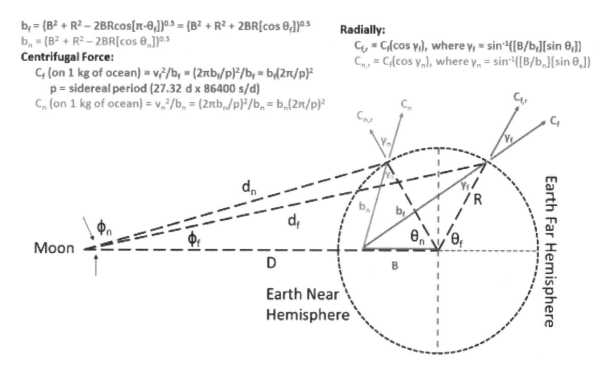

**Figure 10.**    Earth-Moon System Showing Barycenter

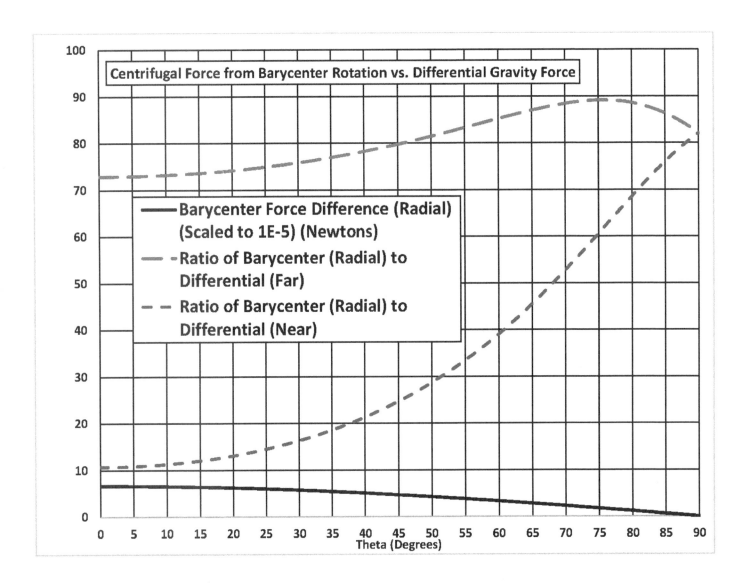

**Figure 11.**   Centrifugal Force from Barycenter Rotation vs. Differential Gravity Force

$\theta_{n,c}$ is the angle ('near side') at which the barycentric centrifugal force is exactly aligned with the y axis, i.e., $\theta_{n,c} = \cos^{-1}(B/R) = 0.748 = 42.85°$.

Far side:
Using the symbols from the previous figures, the angle relative to the x-axis at which the barycentric centrifugal force ($C_f$) occurs is $\pi - (\pi - \theta_f) - \gamma_f = \theta_f - \gamma_f$. The Moon's gravitational (direct) force ($g_{m,f}$) occurs at the angle $\phi_f$ relative to the x-axis. The net force ($N_f$) is the vector sum of these, as shown. Its components in the x and y directions are as follows:

$N_{f,x} = C_{f,x} - g_{m,f,x}$ where $C_{f,x} = C_f(\cos[\theta_f - \gamma_f])$ and $g_{m,f,x} = g_{m,f}(\cos\phi_f)$
$N_{f,y} = C_{f,y} - g_{m,f,y}$ where $C_{f,y} = C_f(\sin[\theta_f - \gamma_f])$ and $g_{m,f,y} = g_{m,f}(\sin\phi_f)$

The total force $N_f = (N_{f,x}^2 + N_{f,y}^2)^{0.5}$; relative to the x-axis, it occurs at an angle = $\cos^{-1}(N_{f,x}/N_f)$.

Near Side ($\theta_{n,c} \le \theta_n \le \pi/2$):
Although not shown, lest the diagram become too crowded, analogous formulas as above also apply here, now using the 'n(ear)' subscript, as follows:

$N_{n,x} = C_{n,x} - g_{m,n,x}$ where $C_{n,x} = C_n(\cos[\pi - \theta_n - \gamma_n])$ and $g_{m,n,x} = g_{m,n}(\cos\phi_n)$
$N_{n,y} = C_{n,y} - g_{m,n,y}$ where $C_{n,y} = C_f(\sin[\pi - \theta_n - \gamma_n])$ and $g_{m,n,y} = g_{m,n}(\sin\phi_n)$

The total force $N_n = (N_{n,x}^2 + N_{n,y}^2)^{0.5}$; relative to the x-axis (in the negative direction), it occurs at an angle = $\cos^{-1}(N_{n,x}/N_n)$.

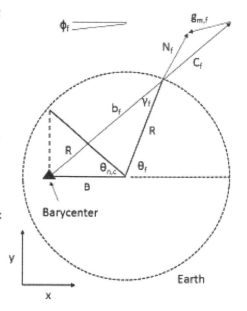

Near Side ($0 \le \theta_n \le \theta_{n,c}$):
Once $\theta_n \le \theta_{n,c}$, both the barycentric centrifugal and Moon's gravitational (direct) forces reinforce each other in the negative x direction. This leads to the following set of equations:

$N_{n,x} = C_{n,x} + g_{m,n,x}$
    where $C_{n,x} = C_n(\cos[\theta_n + \gamma_n])$ and $g_{m,n,x} = g_{m,n}(\cos\phi_n)$
$N_{n,y} = C_{n,y} - g_{m,n,y}$
    where $C_{n,y} = C_f(\sin[\theta_n + \gamma_n])$ and $g_{m,n,y} = g_{m,n}(\sin\phi_n)$

The total force $N_n = (N_{n,x}^2 + N_{n,y}^2)^{0.5}$; relative to the x-axis (in the negative direction), it occurs at an angle = $\cos^{-1}(N_{n,x}/N_n)$.

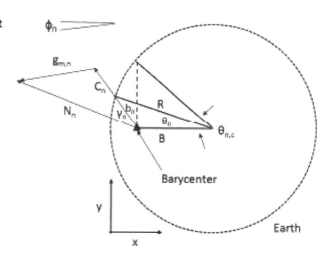

**Figure 12.** Moon's Direct Gravitational and Barycentric Centrifugal Forces

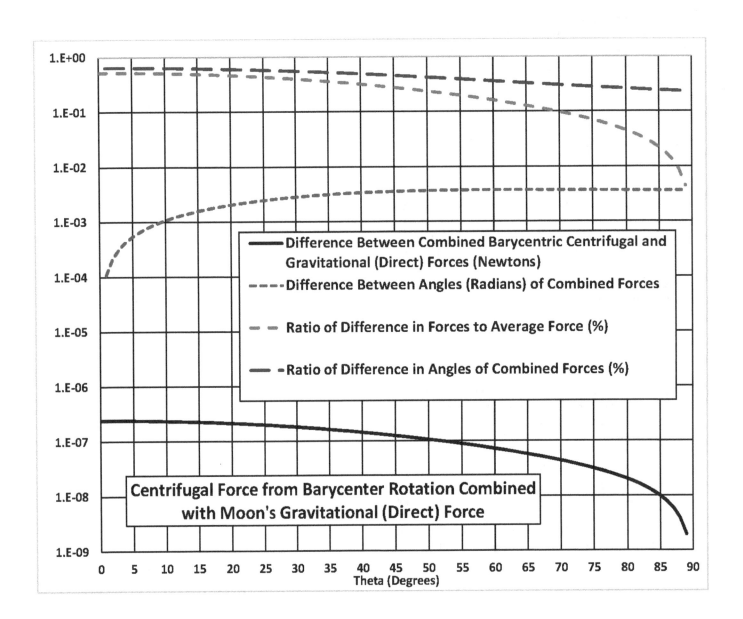

**Figure 13.** Centrifugal Force from Barycenter Rotation Combined with Moon's Gravitational (Direct) Force

# Experiments to Test Whether or Not Light Acquires the Velocity of Its Source, Using Current Technology

Richard O. Calkins and Raymond HV Gallucci, PhD, PE

*2125 Sahalee Drive E., Sammamish, Washington, rocalkins@msn.com; 8956 Amelung St., Frederick, Maryland, 21704, gallucci@localnet.com, r_gallucci@verizon.net*

A friendly debate between the authors characterizes one that is prevalent among the community of 'dissident' physicists who do not accept Einstein's relativity as the final explanation for the behavior of light. They wonder whether or not light acquires the velocity of its source. Maxwell's equations strongly suggest a fixed speed for light upon its emission from a source. Is the emission point fixed in space? Would motion of the emitter alter the trajectory (and speed?) of the emitted light? Light's immense speed makes determining this extremely difficult to answer on a scale less than astronomical. For example, despite supposed 'definitive' proof that there is no aether and light speed is universally constant alleged by proponents of a 'null' result from the 1887 Michelson-Morley Interferometer Experiment, debate continues over both of these subjects. The authors propose experiments using current technology that might be able to offer a definitive resolution to this debate, or possible open up even more speculation.

**Keywords:** light, relativity, experiments, airplane, optical laser, rocket sled

## 1. Introduction

Author Richard Calkins (<u>The Problem with</u> Relativity) and his editor, Raymond Gallucci, have continued a friendly debate as to whether or not light acquires the velocity of its source. [1] Their contentions characterize a debate prevalent throughout the community of 'dissident' physicists, i.e., those who do not worship at the altar of Einstein's relativity, the Big Bang, black holes, dark matter, dark energy, etc.

Calkins believes in the primacy of Maxwell's equations and contends that light will always be released in a straight-line vector if uni-directional, e.g., from a laser, or spherical array or straight-line vectors if omni-directional, e.g., a light bulb, at constant speed c from a fixed point regardless of whether or not the source (e.g., laser or light bulb) is in motion. Besides Calkins' <u>The Problem with</u> Relativity, *Relativity Revisited* and *A Report on How the Optical Laser Disproves the Special Theory of Relativity* [1]; other proponents of this viewpoint include Justin Jacobs in *The Relativity of Light* [2], and Carel van der Togt in *Unbelievable: From Paradox to Paradigm* [3].

Gallucci believes that, while Maxwell's equations are valid relative to light's emission from its source, light can acquire the source's velocity as well, as in classical mechanics, such that it travels from its fixed release point as the vector sum of $\underline{c}$ and $\underline{v}$ (source velocity). [6], [9], [7] Similar proponents include Stephen Bryant in his website www.RelativityChallenge.com, Bernard Burchill in *Alternative Physics: Where Science Makes Sense* and the late Paul Marmet in *Stellar Aberration and Einstein's Relativity*. [4], [5], [6]

Figure 1 illustrates the competing theories. If light does

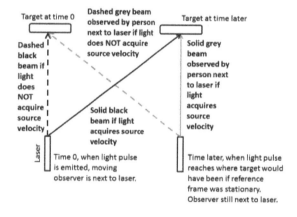

**Figure 1.** Competing Perspectives Depending upon whether or not Light Acquires the Velocity of its Source

not acquire its source's velocity, it travels the dashed paths. A stationary observer would see the dashed black path, while a moving observer would next to the laser would see the dashed grey path. If light acquires its source's velocity, it travels the solid paths, the black seen by the stationary observer while the moving observer sees the grey path.

This paper asks if current technology can resolve this debate experimentally? Both Calkins and Gallucci propose experiments that can be performed here on Earth using current technology that might be able to do so, without having to resort to astronomical observations over vast distances where independent verification of the distances and times is difficult, if not for all practical purposes impossible, to achieve definitively.

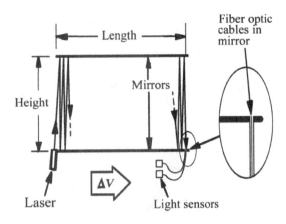

**Figure 2.** Calkins' Generic Experimental Apparatus

## 2. Calkins' Airplane Experiment

A complete description of Calkins' proposed experiment and the theory behind it are provided in The Problem with Relativity [1] They are too extensive to reproduce here; therefore, only the experiment itself is described.

To keep the physical dimensions of the experimental apparatus tractable and increase the accuracy of measuring distance, a design similar to the one illustrated in Figure 2 is proposed. The test apparatus consists of a horizontal assembly of two mirrors facing each other vertically. A laser is mounted at one end of the bottom mirror and two fiber optic cables are terminated at the other end of the bottom mirror. The fiber cables are placed one behind the other in terms of the vector direction of travel (i.e., the laser, optical fiber and the test platform's velocity vector all are on the same straight line).

The laser is oriented vertically except for the miniscule angle required to reflect through the mirror array. The optical fibers route the light to the light intensity sensors. The mirror assembly allows a much longer optical path between the laser and the targets than would be manageable using a long, straight vertical pole. The fiber optic cables can be mounted either on the top mirror or the bottom mirror depending on whether an even number or an odd number of reflections best matches the expected test conditions.

The experiment consists of aligning the laser so that its beam of light strikes the open end of the farthest optical fiber (the alignment detector) while the test platform is in an inertial state of motion. The test platform then is accelerated to a new inertial reference frame which is moving horizontally at $\Delta v$ relative to the first reference frame. The specific value for $\Delta v$ will be determined by the total length of the path through the mirror assembly and the distance $d_{\Delta v}$ between the centers of the optical fiber detec-

tors. The multiple reflections through the mirror assembly and the short distance between the optical fibers allow one to measure a change in the light beam's trajectory with a physically small test assembly at an achievable platform velocity.

### 2.1. Example Test Assembly

The design objective is to make it possible to perform the experiment using available optical technologies and an existing physical reference frame while maintaining the integrity of the empirical results. The following assumptions are used for illustration based on a cursory review of available technologies.

1. The optical laser can be focused to have a beam width of $100\mu m$ at a distance of up to $135m$.

2. Fiber optic cables can be used to detect the laser's light beam and direct it to the light intensity sensors.

3. Fiber optic cables which are suitably shielded and clad can be obtained with a total diameter no greater than $100\mu m$.

4. Existing light intensity sensors can determine within acceptable limits of accuracy when the light intensities received from two fiber optic cables are equal to each other and when the respective light intensities have been reversed from what they were in the first reference frame.

5. Mirrors up to $1.5m$ in length facing each other at a distance of up to $0.5m$ can be made with tolerances which will not significantly alter the total length of their reflections or interfere with the ability to deliver the laser's beam to the distant end.

The following terms, symbols and conversions are used in the example design.

1. $d_{\Delta v}$ is the distance between the alignment detector and the test detector (i.e., the fiber optic cables mounted in the bottom mirror at the far end from the laser). This is the distance the laser's vertical light beam will shift when the laser's horizontal velocity is changed by $\Delta v$.

2. $d_c$ is the total length of the reflected laser beam between the laser and the alignment detector.

3. $d_h$ is the vertical distance between the faces of the mirrors.

4. $d_m$ is the distance between the center line of the laser's output window at one end of the bottom mirror and the center line of the alignment detector at the other end.

5. $d_r$ is the distance between adjacent reflections on the surface of the mirrors.

6. $d_{RT}$ is the distance the laser beam travels on one round trip (RT) between the mirrors. It includes the effect of the vertical distance between the mirrors and the horizontal distance between reflections.

7. $d_v$ is the vertical component of the laser beam's total reflected path through the mirror assembly. This is what the length of the reflected path would be if it

were not necessary to put space between reflections to avoid interference.

8. $\Delta v$ is the change in the laser's horizontal velocity which is required to shift the laser's beam from the alignment detector to the test detector.

9. $1km = 0.62317mi$.

10. $c = (299,792.5km/s)(0.62317km/mi)(3600s/hr)$, i.e., $6.7062x10^8 mph$.

## 2.2. Example Design Procedure

The design begins with the selection of a practicable size for the experimental assembly and a practicable speed for the mobile test platform. It also must be large enough to assure accurate alignment with the mobile test platform's in-motion velocity vector and to allow enough distance between adjacent reflections on the mirror surfaces to avoid interference. The two countervailing objectives must be appropriately balanced.

It appears that a practicable size for the experimental assembly would be horizontal mirrors not longer than $1.5m$ and spaced not more than about $0.5m$ apart. The laser must be rotated slightly from vertical to reflect through the mirror assembly to the fiber optic detectors. The test velocity $\Delta v$ should be such that it can be achieved by virtually any readily available business jet. After several trial attempts, the example design was developed by selecting the following starting objectives:

1. The objective speed $\Delta v$ to conduct the experiment was set at $500mph$.

2. The vertical distance between the facing mirrors $d_h$ was set at $0.5m$.

3. The distance $d_{\Delta v}$ between the center line of the alignment detector and the center line of the test detector was set at $100\mu m$.

4. he distance between adjacent reflections on the mirrors $d_r$ was set at $10mm$.

Given the above design selections, the objective value of $d_c$ would be $cd_{\Delta v}/\Delta v = (6.7062x10^8 mph)(100x10^{-6}m)(500mph) = 134.124m$. That is the total length of reflected beam required for a horizontally moving laser's beam to shift $100\mu m$ from the alignment detector tot he test detector at a velocity of $500mph$. With a vertical distance between the mirrors $d_h$ of $0.5m$ and a horizontal distance between reflections $d_r$ of $10mm$, the distance $d_{RT}$ traveled by the light beam in one RT between the mirrors is $2\sqrt{d_{h^2} + (0.5d_r)^2} = 1.00005m$. The number of RTs required to produce the beam length of $134.124m$ would be equal to the beam length $d_c$ divided by the distance traveled in each RT between the mirrors $d_{RT}$, i.e., $(134.124m)/(1.00005m) = 134.117RTs$. Because the number of RTs must be an integer number, this is set at $134RTs$.

With $134RTs$ required between the mirrors and a distance between reflection of $10mm$, the physical distance between the laser and the alignment detector on the bottom mirror will be $(134RTs)d_{\Delta v} =$

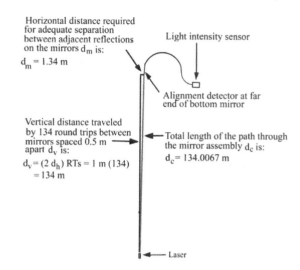

**Figure 3.** How the Optical Path through the Test Assembly Compares with a Vertical Path

$(134RTs)(10x10^{-3}m/RT) = 1.34m$. $d_m$ is the horizontal component of the light beam's travel through the mirror assembly. The vertical component of its drip $d_v$ is $2d_h(134RTs) = 2(0.5m)(134) = 134m$. The resulting length of the trip through the mirror assembly $d_c$ is the hypoteneuse of a right triangle whose horizontal side is $d_m$ and whose vertical side is $d_v$, i.e., $\sqrt{d_v^2 + d_m^2} = \sqrt{134m^2 + 1.34m^2} = \sqrt{17957.7956m^2} = 134.0067m$.

As shown in Figure 3, this produces an essentially vertical path between the laser and the alignment detector. Also, the effect of the mirrored design's limitation to an integer number of RTs and for an adequate distance between reflections has very little effect on the velocity required to perform the experiment. The effect of all of these limitations imposed by the architecture of the mirror assembly is simply to change the required value of $\Delta v$ from $500mph$ to $500.44mph$, i.e., $cd_{\Delta v}/d_c = (6.7062x10^8 mph)(100x10^{-6}m)(134.0067m) = 500.44mph$.

The resulting experimental design is shown in Figure 4. It is intended to create an effectively vertical path from the laser to the alignment detector within a readily transportable test assembly which can ride in a jet aircraft. The dimensions of the mirror assembly can be modified tosuit a wide variety of available test platforms, of which this design is only one example.

## 2.3. Conducting the Experiment

The experiment consists of the following stages:

1. Install the experimental assembly in the mobile test platform (e.g., jet aircraft). Align the laser and optical fibers (mounted at opposite ends of the bottom mirror) so that they will be in line with the aircraft's velocity vector when in flight. Secure the assembly to maintain that orientation. The alignment between the laser and the detectors must be on the same straight

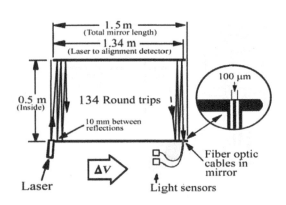

**Figure 4.**    Example Experimental Design

line as the aircraft's velocity vector when the aircraft is in level flight in a constant direction.

2. Pre-align the laser so that the center of its beam is aligned at the center of the alignment detector when the number of RTs is equal to 134.

3. with the aircraft on the runway for take-off, fine tune the laser to assure that the light's maximum intensity is directly centered on the alignment detector. Record the light intensity on both detectors.

4. Place the aircraft in flight and establish a straight, level flight path which is in the same vertical and horizontal orientation as when the laser was aligned.

5. Increase the velocity of the aircraft to $240mph$. Then, very slowly, increase its velocity until the alignment detector and the test detector have identically the same level of light intensity. Record the aircraft's velocity and the light intensity at the detectors either continuously or at short intervals of time to assure detecting the specific velocity at which equal intensity occurs. If light responds to the momentum of its source ()i.e., acquires its source's velocity), as required by the first postulate of Einstein's relativity, the intensity measured at the alignment detector and the test detector will be unchanged from what it was at alignment and the test detector will remain essentially non-illuminated. If light does not respond to momentum (i.e., does not acqire its source's velocity), the light intensity measured at the alignment detector and the test detector should be equal when the aircraft is at a velocity of approximately $250.2mph$.

6. Increase the aircraft's velocity to $490mph$. Then, very slowly, increase its velocity until the light intensities of the alignment detector and the test detector are precisely reversed from what they were at alignment. If light responds to momentum (i.e., acquires its source's velocity), the light intensity measured at the

**Figure 5.** Rocket Sled Accelerates to Constant Speed at $O$, where Laser Beam is Emitted Simultaneously toward Equidistant Detectors at A and B

alignment detector during alignment will remain unchanged and the test detector will remain essentially dark. However, if light does not respond to momentum (i.e., does not acquire its source's velocity), the intensity readings at the alignment detector and the test detector should be fully reversed when the aircraft reaches a velocity of approximately $500.44mph$.

## 3. Gallucci's Rocket Sled Experiment

As illustrated in Figure 5, a rocket sled (star) accelerates from Points A to $O$, reaching a speed of $(10,000km/h)(2.8km/s)$, then decelerates to Point B. This distance between A and B is $50,000ft(15km)$. (Speed and distance taken from Hollomon High Speed Test Track, Hollomon Air Force Base, Alamogordo, New Mexico [8]). At $O$, the rocket sled shoots a pair of laser rays (perhaps a beam split from one laser to ensure uniformity) in opposite directions such that each travels $15/2 = 7.5km$ to reach detectors at A and B. To account for the curvature of the Earth (radius $6,400km$), each is raised by $\sqrt{6400^2 + 7.5^2} - 6400 = 0.0044km(4.4m)$ relative to the track along which the rocket sled travels. This ensures the pair of laser rays traveling in straight lines reach each detector.

When stationary, the laser rays each take $(7.5km)/(300,000km/s) = 2.5x10^{-5}s(25\mu s)$ to reach each detector when released at $O$. If light does not acquire the velocity of a moving source, both rays will reach the detectors at this same time when the rocket sled is speeding at $2.8km/s$ when it shoots the laser rays at $O$ (as per Special Relativity with time dilation/length contraction). If light acquires the velocity of a moving source (contrary to Special Relativity), the ray traveling from $O$ to B will speed at $300,000 + 2.8km/s$, reaching B in $7.5/300,002.8s$, while the ray traveling from $O$ to A will speed at $300,000 - 2.8 = 299,997.2km/s$, reaching A in $7.5/299,997.2s$. The difference in arrival times will be $7.5(\frac{1}{299,997.2} - \frac{1}{300,002.8}) = 4.7x10^{-10}s$ $(0.47ns)$. This is measureable with today's technology (e.g., [10]).

### 3.1. A Stationary Counterpart?

As per Calkins, et al., assume light does not acquire the velocity of its source, i.e., it is released from a fixed point in some sort of absolute space in a straight-line vector at constant speed c. Since the Earth rotates about its axis, the Earth orbits the Sun, and the Sun (solar system) orbits the galactic center, there is no such thing as a stationary point in absolute space anywhere within our galaxy except at its absolute center (ignoring possible movement of the galaxy itself relative to other galaxies). So, by definition, any light emitted from a laser on Earth, if not acquiring this velocity relative to our galactic center, should always veer off any vertical path - the laser need not be "moving" relative to the Earth's surface in any way.

Since the Earth orbits the Sun at $30km/s$, and the solar system orbits the galactic center at $220km/s$, then any object on the Earth's surface would be moving from 190 to $250km/s$ relative to this "absolute space" (ignoring the Earth's equatorial rotational speed of $0.5km/s$). As discussed below, light that does not acquire source velocity (in this case the Earth relative to the galactic center) should exhibit a rather profound shift from the vertical without its source moving at all relative to the Earth's surface.

If light does not acquire the velocity of its source (and note that Einstein appears to assume it acquires the direction but not the speed of its source, with the latter being held constant at $c = 300,000km/s$ via time dilation), then light from a laser pointing vertically upward at the equator to a target $1km$ immediately above it at midnight when the Earth and Sun lie directly in line with the galactic center would have to veer away from the target as a result of both the laser and target moving together somewhere between 190 and $250km/s$ away from the initial emission point of the laser light.

Independent of the source velocity, the light beam will travel at speed $c = 300,000km/s$ over a distance of $(1km)/\cos(\arcsin(\frac{190\ to\ 250km/s}{300,000km/s})) = 1.00000020\ to\ 1.00000035km$. For all practical purposes, this is still $1km$, so the time for light to travel this distance is $(1km)/(300,000km/s) = 3.33\mu s$. Over this time, the target and laser, in perfect vertical alignment, will have moved $(3.33x10^{-6}s)(190\ to\ 250km/s) = 0.00063\ to\ 0.00083km$, or 0.63 to $0.83m$ away from the point from which the laser initially emitted its light.

Therefore, if we could find (or construct) a vertically clear span at the equator (or actually anywhere on Earth, since the Earth's rotational speed is negligible compared to the speed about the galactic center) 1-km high (e.g., a sheer cliff?), we may be able to settle the issue as to whether or not light acquires the velocity of its source since $0.63 - 0.83m$ would be an indisputable shift off the vertical. A cliff such as El Capitan, 900-m high, would suffice, since the shift would still be a quite observable and indisputable $(0.63\ to\ 0.83m)(0.9km/1km) = 0.57\ to\ 0.75m$.

## 4. Summary

Calkins and Gallucci continue to engage in a friendly debate over whether or not light acquires the velocity of its source, characteristic of a difference of opinion among many 'dissident' physicists. Both have proposed experiments using current technology which might be able to come to a definitive conclusion, or else open up even more speculation if the results favor neither.

## REFERENCES

1. R. Calkins, *The Problem with Relativity; Relativity Revisited; A Report on How the Optical Laser Disproves the Special Theory of Relativity*, www.calkinspublishing.com, 2011-2015

2. J. Jacobs, *The Relativity of Light*, www.RelativityOfLight.com, 2009-2011

3. C. van der Togt, *Unbelievable: From Paradox to Paradigm*, www.paradox-paradigm.nl, 2009

4. S. Bryant, *The Relativity Challenge*, www.RelativityChallenge.com, 2016

5. B. Burchill, *Alternative Physics: Where Science Makes Sense*, http://alternativephysics.org/index.htm, 2016

6. R. Gallucci, *Does Light Acquire the Velocity of a Moving Source?*, www.naturalphilosophy.org, Proceedings of the 2nd Annual CNPS Conference (2016)

7. R. Gallucci, *Michelson-Morley Interferometer Experiment of 1887: 'Null' Result*, www.naturalphilosophy.org, Proceedings of the 1st Annual CNPS Conference (2015)

8. Hollomon-Air-Force-Base, *Hollomon High Speed Test Track*, http://en.wikipedia.org/wiki/Rocket_sled, Alamogordo, New Mexico (2015)

9. R. Gallucci, *Questioning the Cosmological Doppler Redshift*, www.naturalphilosopy.org, Proceedings of the 1st Annual CNPS Conference (2015)

10. Surface-Concept, *Time Measurement: Electronics Devices for Time Measurement down to the Picosecond Range: Compact, Fast and User-Friendly*, www.surface-concept.com/products_time.html, 2011

# Does Light Travel with the Velocity of a Moving Source?

## Raymond HV Gallucci, PhD, PE

*8956 Amelung St., Frederick, Maryland, 21704, gallucci@localnet.com, r_gallucci@verizon.net*

Einstein resolves the issue of whether or not light travels with the velocity of a moving source by assuming time dilates (and length contracts) in a moving inertial reference frame. Based more on belief than empirical evidence, this resolution enables the theory of special relativity to claim validity, even though there are other explanations and interpretations that are simpler and more consistent with Occam's Razor. Some dissident physicists counter Einstein both by assuming the constant velocity of light is preserved, albeit without time dilation, as well as assuming light travels with the velocity of its source. While I am in the latter camp, I attempt to examine both sides of the argument from a non-relativistic perspective.

**Keywords:** light, relativity, stellar aberration, pulsar, de Sitter

## 1. Introduction

Is the speed of light constant as proposed by Einstein in his Theory of Special Relativity? By manipulating time (dilation) and length (contraction), Einstein manages to render moot the question as to what effect motion of the light source has on light speed. Only the relative velocity between source and observer is relevant, and regardless of which is moving (undeterminable in his theory), the speed of light seen by the observer is always c. However, many dissident physicists, as well as myself (though not a physicist, but a nuclear engineer with a keen interest in physics), question relativity, and a key point of contention appears to be whether or not light travels with the velocity of its source, thereby enabling it to propagate faster or slower than c. While there appears to be general agreement that a moving observer will see light from a stationary source traveling faster or slower than c depending upon whether or not the observer approaches or recedes from the source, there clearly is not general agreement for the stationary observer and the moving source. Unlike Einstein, here I speak of moving against the vacuum medium of space, not relative speed between source and observer, although that is there regardless of which one moves.

## 2. Two Camps

Among the camp of dissidents favoring the position that light does not travel with its source velocity, a key point appears to be that Maxwell's equations define light speed as always c in a vacuum. Among these authors, I have come across the following: Richard Calkins, Justin Jacobs and Carel van der Togt [1], [2], [3]. They contend that to be immutable such that the light always emanates from its point of emission against the background of the vacuum medium and travels in spherical waves outward from this point at c (or in a straight line at c if emitted from, e.g., a laser) even if the source is moving. It is the point of emission that is critical.

Among the camp favoring the position that light does travel with its source velocity, the key is that, while light is emitted at c in the vacuum, it travels spherically outward at speeds ranging from c - v to c + v relative to a stationary observer, where v is the source velocity. Among these authors, I have come across the following: Stephen Bryant [4], Bernard Burchill [5] and the late Paul Marmet [6]. What both camps agree upon is that, for a stationary source and moving observer (at v), the light speed seen by the observer will range from $c - v$ to $c + v$. It should be apparent that, for the first camp (light not traveling with source velocity), there is an asymmetry in perceived light velocity depending upon whether it is the source or observer that is moving against the background of the vacuum medium. For the second camp, the two cases are symmetric.

## 3. Illustrative Examples

In this article, I examine three examples that show the (a)symmetry and then propose an experimental observation that, at least at some hopefully not too far future date, might solve the debate.

### 3.1. Moving vs. Stationary Spaceship

Figures 1, 2, and 3, show a fairly simple example where a red spaceship flashes a light at time zero toward a green spaceship. In Figure 1, the red ship is stationary and the green ship approaches at 0.5c, starting from 450,000 km away at time 0. After 1 s, light has traveled 300,000 km and green ship 150,000 km closer, such that it sees the flash. In Figure 2, the green ship is now stationary, and the red ship approaches at 0.5c, having flashed its light at time 0 when 450,000 km away. If light travels with the velocity of a moving source, the flash from the red ship at time 0 reaches the green ship as before, at 1 s. This is symmetric with the first case where the observer, not the source, moves.

Figure 3 is analogous to Figure 2, but where we assume that light does not travel with the velocity of the source. In this case, the green ship does not see the light flash until 1.5 s have elapsed, 0.5 s longer than when it was moving toward the stationary source at 0.5c. This case is not symmetric with the first case where the observer, not

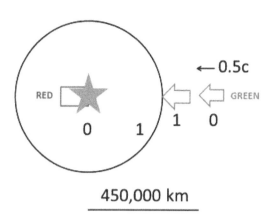

**Figure 1.** Stationary red spaceship with green spaceship approaching at 0.5c from 450,000 km away. After 1 second, green spaceship sees the flash.

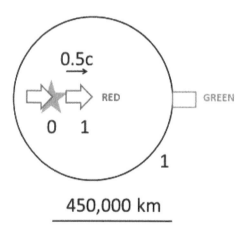

**Figure 2.** If light travels with the velocity of a moving source, the flash from the red spaceship reaches the green spaceship as before, at 1 sec.

the source, moves. Which is correct?

### 3.2. Two Moving/Stationary Spaceships and a Stationary/Moving Pulsar

Figures 4 and 5 add a pulsar to the two spaceships, now either both moving or stationary. In Figure 4, the two ships, one red and one green, each start at a distance d at time 0 on radially opposite sides of a pulsar with the same velocity, such that the red one approaches the pulsar at speed $0.5c$ while the green one recedes at $0.5c$. The pulsar emits a light burst at time 0, known to travel spherically outward at c. At time 1, $t_1$, the light burst reaches the red ship, which measures the effective light speed as the initial distance $d = 0.5ct_1 + ct_1$ divided by the time $t_1$, i.e., $1.5c$.

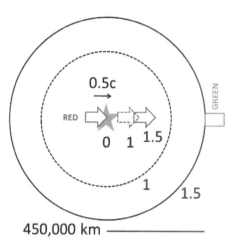

**Figure 3.** If light from moving source does NOT travel with the velocity of the source, green spaceship does not see the light flash until 1.5 seconds have elapsed.

At time 2, $t_2$, the light burst finally reaches the green ship, which measures the effective light speed as the same initial distance d divided by the time $t_2$, i.e., $1.5ct_1/t_2$. However, knowing that it traveled an additional $d = 0.5ct_2$ farther away from the pulsar, which was originally $d = 1.5ct_1$ away, the green ship calculates the elapsed time as $t_2 = 3t_1$ from $d = 1.5ct_1 = 0.5ct_2$ yielding $t_2 = 3t_1$. Therefore, for the green ship, the effective light speed is $0.5c$.

### 3.3. Two Moving/Stationary Spaceships and a Stationary/Moving Pulsar

Figures 4 and 5 add a pulsar to the two spaceships, now either both moving or stationary. In Figure 4, the two ships, one red and one green, each start at a distance d at time 0 on radially opposite sides of a pulsar with the same velocity, such that the red one approaches the pulsar at speed $0.5c$ while the green one recedes at $0.5c$. The pulsar emits a light burst at time 0, known to travel spherically outward at c. At time 1, $t_1$, the light burst reaches the red ship, which measures the effective light speed as the initial distance $d = 0.5ct_1 + ct_1$ divided by the time $t_1$, i.e., $1.5c$. At time 2, $t_2$, the light burst finally reaches the green ship, which measures the effective light speed as the same initial distance d divided by the time $t_2$, i.e., $1.5ct_1/t_2$. However, knowing that it traveled an additional $d = 0.5ct_2$ farther away from the pulsar, which was originally $d = 1.5ct_1$ away, the green ship calculates the elapsed time as $t_2 = 3t_1$ from $d = 1.5ct_1 = 0.5ct_2$ yielding $t_2 = 3t_1$. Therefore, for the green ship, the effective light speed is $0.5c$.

Now, in Figure 5, the spaceships are stationary, but the pulsar approaches toward the red one and recedes from the green one along the same radial path at speed $0.5c$, with both ships originally (time 0) equidistant (d) from the pulsar. A light burst emitted at time 0 reaches the red ship at time 1 after the pulsar has approached $0.5ct_1$ closer. It measures the effective light speed as the initial distance

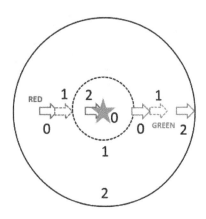

**Figure 4.** Two spaceships one red and one green equidistant from a pulsar traveling with the same velocity at 0.5c

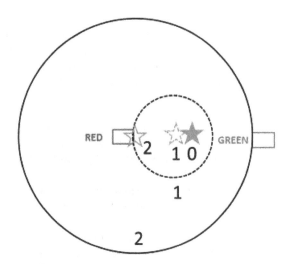

**Figure 5.** Now, the spaceships are stationary but the pulsar approaches toward the red one and recedes from the green one along the same radial path at speed 0.5c

d, consisting of the pulsar's approach and the distance traveled by the light burst from time 0, i.e., $d = 0.5ct_1 + ct_1$, divided by the time $t_1$, i.e., $1.5c$. As the pulsar continues to recede from the green ship, the initial light burst finally reaches it at time 2, at which the green ship measures the effective light speed as the same initial distance d divided by the time $t_2$, i.e., $1.5ct_1/t_2$. However, knowing that the pulsar moved an additional $d = 0.5ct_2$ farther away, the green ship calculates the elapsed time as $t_2 = 3t_1$ from $d = 1.5ct_1 = 0.5ct_2$ yielding $t_2 = 3t_1$. Therefore, for the green ship, the effective light speed is $0.5c$.

It should be clear that assuming the light burst travels with the velocity of the moving source (Figure 5) yields symmetrically equivalent results with Figure 4, where the

spaceships but not the pulsar are moving (parallel pair of different effective light speeds depending upon the relative movement between the ships and the pulsar, regardless of which is moving). If this symmetry is broken by assuming the light burst does NOT travel with the speed of the moving source, then Figure 5 (stationary ships, moving pulsar) will always yield effective light speeds of c for both ships, while the results from Figure 4 with the moving ships remain as before (different effective light speeds).

This asymmetry indicates that an observer (ship) could distinguish between a moving ship and a moving source based on the measured effective light speed (always c if the source is moving; never c if the observer is moving [except for the unique case of perfectly circular motion]). If light always emanates from a source at c relative to the source (traveling with the source velocity if moving), we have symmetry. If light always emanates from the source at c regardless of whether the source is moving (i.e., dependent only upon the source's position at the time of emanation), we have asymmetry depending upon whether the observer is moving. Which is correct?

### 3.4. Stellar Aberration

Figures 6, 7, 8 examine the phenomenon of stellar aberration, comparing the classic case of moving Earth (observer) and stationary star with one where the star moves and the Earth is stationary. In Figure 6, light from a stationary star (dotted vector) and fixed, infinitely-distant background point A (dashed vector) emanates from the star's position at time zero and travels 10 light-years (L-y) at 300,000 km/s to position 1 (combined light shown as a black dot) at the front end of a 30+-m long telescope moving with the Earth's velocity of 30 km/s to the left (30+ indicates that the telescope is ever so slightly longer than 30 m because it is ever so slightly tilted off the perpendicular). After $0.05\mu s$, the combined light travels 15 m (300,000 km/s x 5E-8 s = 0.015 km) halfway down the telescope to position 2 (the telescope has moved 1.5 mm to the left [30 km/s x 5E-8 s]). After $0.1\mu s$, the combined light travels an additional 15 m (now a total of 30 m) to the end of telescope at position 3 where the observer's eye sees the star against background position A (the telescope has now moved an additional 1.5 mm, or a total of 3 mm, to the left).

Now, in Figure 5, assume the star is moving at 60 km/s to the right which, when compared to the Earth's 30 km/s velocity to the left, can be viewed as the star now moving 30 km/s, i.e., $0.0001c$ to the right relative to a stationary Earth. If light travels with the velocity of its source, then light emanated from the star at time 0 will travel $\sqrt{[10Ly^2 + [10x0.0001Ly]^2} = 10.00000005Ly$ diagonally (mixed vector) in 10 years to position 1 at the front end of the 30+-m long telescope. However, now that the Earth is stationary, the light from background position A (dashed vector) that had reached the star at time 0 lags 0.001 Ly to the left (at position 1') when the star light reaches position 1. It is now light from background position B (dotted vector) which arrives with the star light

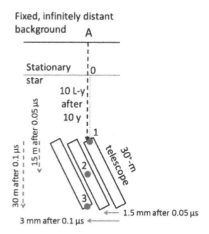

**Figure 6.** Stellar aberration for stationary star + moving earth at 30 km/s to left

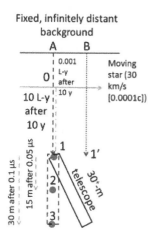

**Figure 8.** Stellar aberration for stationary earth + moving star at net speed of 10 km/s (0.0001c) top the right (light does not travel with source speed)

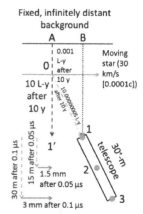

**Figure 7.** Stellar aberration for stationary earth + moving star at net speed of 30 km/s (0.0001c) top the right (light travels with source speed)

at position 1 after 10 y, having reached the future position of the star (now its current position) 10 y ago. However, unlike the star light traveling along the diagonal, the ever so slight tilt of the telescope will prevent that dashed vector from traveling down the telescope to the observer's eye. Therefore, in this case (stationary Earth and moving star), the observer sees the star (black dot) against some sort of ever so slightly (possibly undetectable) muddled background, similar to, but not exactly, the same as in Figure 6.

In Figure 8, again assume the star is moving at 60 km/s to the right which, when compared to the Earth's 30 km/s velocity to the left, can be viewed as the star now moving 30 km/s, i.e., 0.0001c, to the right relative to a

stationary Earth. However, if light does not travel with the velocity of its source, then light emanated from the star at time 0 will again travel in tandem with the light from background position A that had reached the star 10 y ago, reaching position 1 at the front end of the telescope after traveling 10 Ly in 10 y (black dot). However, now neither the light from the star nor that from background position A can travel down the ever so slightly tilted telescope to reach the observers eye. He will see neither. In this case, the telescope would have to be aligned perfectly with the perpendicular for the observer (dashed telescope) to see the star against background position A as in the first case.

Again, as in the previous two examples, we see symmetry when light is assumed to travel with the velocity of a moving source (except for some possible muddling of the background, which may be undetectable), but asymmetry when it is assumed not. Which is correct?

## 4. Observing a Pulsar

Having presented three examples illustrating the difference between observations when light travels with the velocity of its source vs. always traveling from the source at c (in a vacuum), namely symmetry vs. asymmetry between analogous situations where the observer moves but the source is stationary vs. moving source and stationary observer, the following is a potential experimental observation that could answer the question I posed after each - which is correct?

As shown in Figure 9, a millisecond pulsar is detected from Earth. Assume it has a typical pulsar radius of 10 km [7], such that its rotational speed is approximately $2\pi(10km)(1000/s) = 60,000km/s$, or 0.2c. If light velocity is independent of source motion, the pulse must be emitted at A and travel along the dashed vector at speed c to be detected. If light velocity travels with the velocity of the source, the pulse must be emitted earlier at B and travel along the vector sum of the solid (c) and dotted (0.2c) vectors, i.e., along the mixed vector at speed approximately $1.02c = \sqrt{(c^2 + [0.2c]^2)}$ which, though shown askew for clarity, is just the same vector as the dashed but with a higher speed.

If the exact distance between the pulsar and Earth were known (and the extremely rapid spin of the pulsar [0.2c] greatly exceeded any relative translational motion between the pulsar and Earth, such that they could be considered stationary relative to each other), the travel time from A (along the dashed vector) would be slightly longer than that from B (along the mixed vector), in the ratio of 1.02:1.00, or approximately 2 percent. While knowing the exact spin and radius of the pulsar, and its exact distance from Earth, is beyond present technology, at least theoretically a 2 percent time difference would be readily detectable even by today's technology and settle once and for all the question as to whether or not light travels with the velocity of its source.

## 5. Conclusion

I am unfortunately unable to make a conclusion regarding whether or not light travels with the velocity of its source. I believe it does, but philosophically there are convincing arguments for both pairs of views such as those that I have presented. However, until we can definitively travel at speeds that are not negligible fractions of the speed of light, or can precisely measure distances to pulsars along with their radii and rotational speeds (as required to carry out my proposed experimental observation), this debate will continue. The enormous speed of light compared to anything humans have ever experienced renders experimental observations from interstellar or intergalactic space speculative at best and completely dependent upon assumptions regarding virtually unmeasurable distances, speeds, sizes, etc. Given the negligible fractions of light speed usually involved, the precision needed to verify minuscule differences between phenomena renders experimental observations speculative, at best. Nonetheless, as food for thought, the problem remains most intriguing and likely will continue to occupy the human psyche until the necessary technological progress is achieved, well beyond our lifetimes and probably those of many future generations.

## 6. Appendix

In his treatise *The Relativity of Light*, Jacobs examines the question "Does the transmission velocity of a light ray at velocity c relative to the medium of empty space vary depending upon the speed and direction of motion of the source body from which such light ray is emitted?" [2] For his answer, Jacobs "... defer[s] to Willem de Sitter's empirical binary star theory which asserts that the orbital velocity (v) of a light emitting binary star must not be added to (c + v) or subtracted from (c - v) the velocity c of the light which the star emits, because this would necessarily result in 'ghost star' images in a binary star

system, which images have never been observed. Based on De Sitter's binary star observations and his resulting empirical theory, Einstein postulated 'that light is always propagated in empty space with a definite velocity c which is independent of the state of motion of the emitting body.'"

Jacobs concludes that "De Sitter's theory and the underlined part of Einstein's postulate are compatible with Maxwell's equations based on the wave theory of light, with the 1851 interference experiment of Fizeau ..., with the null result of the Michelson [and] Morley experiment ..., and with empirical measurements of the speed of sound waves. Measurements of the velocity of starlight received on Earth from stars with different relative speeds also appear to confirm these conclusions. Therefore, let us accept De Sitter's theory and the (underlined) second part of Einstein's above postulate as valid."

I was intrigued by this explanation for light not traveling with its source velocity and the claim that no ghost star images having ever been seen and measurements of light velocity from stars with different relative speeds have confirmed Jacobs' (and certainly others') conclusions. I performed the following illustrative calculation.

Assume a binary star system rotating counterclockwise of diameter $0.001\pi Ly$ rotates at $0.001\pi Ly/y$. At $t_0$, both a green star (approaching Earth, from the left) and red star (receding from Earth, from the right) are 10 Ly from earth (with both stars aligned along an axis perpendicular to the line of sight from the Earth, i.e., a typical horizontal x axis). What would we observe over the next 12 months?

Assuming observations made at monthly intervals n/12 y, where n = number of months since $t_0$, the vector component of each star's speed (in units of $Ly/y$) would be $v = +0.001\pi cos(2\pi \frac{n}{12}) = +0.001\pi cos(n\pi/6)$, with the + sign depending upon whether the star was approaching (+) or receding from (-) the Earth at month n. The corresponding light speed of each star (in Ly/y), if acquiring the velocity of the source, would just be $1 + v$. For each star, the time for the light to traverse the 10 Ly distance to Earth would be $10/v$ y, while the time at which the light reached the earth would be $(n/12 + 10/v)$ y.

If we assume the red star's position (receding from the right) at $t_0$ to be 0 radian (and, thus, that of the green star approaching from the left to be $\pi$ radians), the position of each star relative to its angular position when its light is seen on Earth would be $n\pi/6$ radians for the red star and the following for the green star: (1) At time $t_n$ for n = 0, $\pi$ x (1 + twice the difference between times when light from red and green stars reaches Earth); (2) At time $t_n$ for n > 0, position at time n = 0 + $\pi$ x (twice the difference between time when light from red star reaches Earth at n and time when light from green star reached Earth at $t_0$).

Of interest are the horizontal (x-axis) displacements (in Ly) relative to each other that an Earth observer would see for each star at his monthly viewing. For the red star, that displacement would be $0.001\pi cos(n\pi/6)$ occurring either slightly before or after the monthly time as measured by each star in its rotation, depending upon whether the red

| Binary star system of diameter 0.001π L-y rotates at 0.001π L-y/y. At time 0, both green star (approaching) and red star (receding) are 10 L-y from Earth. | | Vector Component - Star Speed [L-y/y] | | Vector Component - Light Speed [L-y/y] | | Time for Light to Travel 10 ly to Earth (y) | | Time When Light Reaches Earth (y) | | Red Star Position "Seen" When Light Reaches Earth | | Green Star Position "Seen" When Red Light Reaches Earth | | Perceived Midpoint "Seen" When Red Light Reaches Earth |
|---|---|---|---|---|---|---|---|---|---|---|---|---|---|---|
| Month | Year | Green Star | Red Star | Green Star | Red Star | Green Star | Red Star | Green Star | Red Star | π rads | x disp (L-y) | π rads | x disp (L-y) | x disp (L-y) |
| 0 | 0.000000 | 0.003142 | -0.003142 | 1.003142 | 0.996858 | 9.968682 | 10.031515 | 9.968682 | 10.031515 | 0.000000 | 0.003142 | 1.125665 | -0.002900 | 0.000121 |
| 1 | 0.083333 | 0.002721 | -0.002721 | 1.002721 | 0.997279 | 9.972867 | 10.027281 | 10.056200 | 10.110615 | 0.166667 | 0.002721 | 1.409529 | -0.000881 | 0.000920 |
| 2 | 0.166667 | 0.001571 | -0.001571 | 1.001571 | 0.998429 | 9.984317 | 10.015733 | 10.150983 | 10.182399 | 0.333333 | 0.001571 | 1.553099 | 0.000522 | 0.001046 |
| 3 | 0.250000 | 0.000000 | 0.000000 | 1.000000 | 1.000000 | 10.000000 | 10.000000 | 10.250000 | 10.250000 | 0.500000 | 0.000000 | 1.688300 | 0.001752 | 0.000876 |
| 4 | 0.333333 | -0.001571 | 0.001571 | 0.998429 | 1.001571 | 10.015733 | 9.984317 | 10.349066 | 10.317650 | 0.666667 | -0.001571 | 1.823600 | 0.002671 | 0.000550 |
| 5 | 0.416667 | -0.002721 | 0.002721 | 0.997279 | 1.002721 | 10.027281 | 9.972867 | 10.443948 | 10.389533 | 0.833333 | -0.002721 | 1.967367 | 0.003125 | 0.000202 |
| 6 | 0.500000 | -0.003142 | 0.003142 | 0.996858 | 1.003142 | 10.031515 | 9.968682 | 10.531515 | 10.468682 | 1.000000 | -0.003142 | 2.125665 | 0.002900 | -0.000121 |
| 7 | 0.583333 | -0.002721 | 0.002721 | 0.997279 | 1.002721 | 10.027281 | 9.972867 | 10.610615 | 10.556200 | 1.166667 | -0.002721 | 2.300700 | 0.001841 | -0.000440 |
| 8 | 0.666667 | -0.001571 | 0.001571 | 0.998429 | 1.001571 | 10.015733 | 9.984317 | 10.682399 | 10.650983 | 1.333333 | -0.001571 | 2.490267 | 0.000096 | -0.000737 |
| 9 | 0.750000 | 0.000000 | 0.000000 | 1.000000 | 1.000000 | 10.000000 | 10.000000 | 10.750000 | 10.750000 | 1.500000 | 0.000000 | 2.888300 | -0.001752 | -0.000876 |
| 10 | 0.833333 | 0.001571 | -0.001571 | 1.001571 | 0.998429 | 9.984317 | 10.015733 | 10.817650 | 10.849066 | 1.666667 | 0.001571 | 2.886432 | -0.002944 | -0.000686 |
| 11 | 0.916667 | 0.002721 | -0.002721 | 1.002721 | 0.997279 | 9.972867 | 10.027281 | 10.889533 | 10.943948 | 1.833333 | 0.002721 | 3.076196 | -0.003052 | -0.000166 |
| 12 | 1.000000 | 0.003142 | -0.003142 | 1.003142 | 0.996858 | 9.968682 | 10.031515 | 10.968682 | 11.031515 | 2.000000 | 0.003142 | 3.251330 | -0.002212 | 0.000465 |

__TABLE 1__.    Positions of Red and Green Stars as Seen from Earth when Viewed at the Time the Light from the Red Star Reached Earth Based on the Stars' Monthly Intervals of Rotation

**Figure 9.** Positions of red and green stars as seen from earth when viewed at the time the light from the red star reached earth based on the star's monthly intervals of rotation

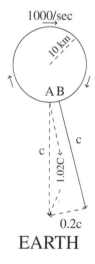

**Figure 10.** A millisecond pulsar is detected from Earth with a typical radius of approximately 10 km, such that its approximate rotational speed is $2\pi(10km)(1000/s) = 60,000km/s$ or 0.2c

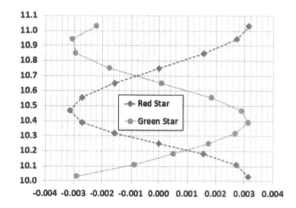

**Figure 11.** Star positions as seen

star is approaching or receding from Earth. For the green star, assuming the viewing took place when the light from each monthly interval from the red star reached Earth, this would be $0.001\pi cos(\pi)$ x angular position calculated above).

Table 1 and Figure 2 show the positions for the 'dance" of the red (diamonds and dashed line) and green stars (circles and solid line) as seen from Earth when viewed at the time the light from the red star reached Earth based on the stars' monthly intervals of rotation. Month n = 0 corresponds to 10 y after time 0 when the stars 'began' their rotation cycle.

## REFERENCES

1. R. Calkins, *The Problem with Relativity; Relativity Revisited; A Report on How the Optical Laser Disproves the Special Theory of Relativity.*, textttwww.calkinspublishing.com, 2011-2015.

2. J. Jacobs, *The Relativity of Light.*, textttwww.RelativityOfLight.com, 2009-2011.

3. C. van der Togt, *Unbelievable: From Paradox to Paradigm.*, textttwww.paradox-paradigm.nl, 2009.

4. S. Bryant, *The Relativity Challenge.*, textttwww.RelativityChallenge.com, 2016.

5. B. Burchill, *Alternative Physics: Where Science Makes Sense.*, texttthttp://alternativephysics.org/index.htm, 2016.

6. P. Marmet, *Stellar Aberration; Einstein's Relativity.*, textttwww.newtonphysics.on.ca/aberration/index.html, 1996.

7. NASA, *Pulsars.*, texttthttp://imagine.gsfc.nasa.gov/docs/science /know_11/pulsars.html, 2006.

# Explanation of How the Speed of Light May be Exceeded without Violating the Requirement of Infinite Energy

## J. O. Jonson

*Stockholm University, SE-10691 Stockholm, Sweden (Alumnus) and KTH Royal Institute of Technology, SE-10044 Stockholm, Sweden (Alumnus), mailing address: Oestmarksgatan 50 n.b., SE-123 42 Farsta, Sweden. E-mail address: jajo8088@bahnhof.se*

The paper proposes an explanation to the problem of exceeding the speed of light, discussed in a paper by Hill and Cox, who have made an extensive calculation of how the Lorentz transformation might be applicable to velocities larger than the speed of light, provided it would be possible. The solution focuses on the fact that when a moving body, due to the Lorentz transformation, becomes increasingly smaller, the Uncertainiy Principle may be applicable, causing thus velocities larger than speed of light to appear.

**Keywords:** Special Relativity Theory, Lorentz transformation for velocities larger than speed of light, exceeding the speed of light possible, Uncertainty Relation

## 1. Theory

J. M. Hill and B. J. Cox propose an extension of Special Relativity theory beyond the speed of light, without being able to explain how particles might be able to develop velocities greater than speed of light, c [1]. They focus on describing how the Lorentz transformation might be applicable for particles exhibiting velocities greater than the speed of light c. Thus far, the opinion has been that surpassing the speed of light requires that the energy of the particle exceeds infinity, which is, of course, impossible, since infinity is a concept for something that is by definition impossible to exceed. However, it may be observed that in the process of increasing the velocity, the Lorentz transformation describes how the moving object becomes increasingly smaller. At some point the extension in the direction of movement becomes so small that the Uncertainty Relation becomes relevant, as otherwise treated [2], [3]:

$$\Delta x \times \Delta p \geq h \tag{1}$$

For some $\Delta x$ then,

$$\Delta p \geq mc \tag{2}$$

Since Eq. 2 is regarded to be a natural law, it follows that due to the smallness of $\Delta x$, the momentum may jump so much between two measurements that the speed of light is exceeded, but without touching the speed of light. One may describe the event by saying that the object is tunneling between the below speed of light region and the above speed of light region.

From Quantum Mechanics it is already well-known that the usual deterministic laws cease to exist. Hence, there will be no problem in connection with the process of surpassing the speed of light. It will just happen with some non-vanishing probability.

## REFERENCES

1. James M. Hill, Barry J. Cox, *Einstein's special relativity beyond the speed of light*, Proc. R. Soc. A, doi:10.1098/rspa.2012.0340
2. D. Park, *Introduction to the Quantum Theory*, Mc Graw-Hill, 197, p. 49
3. R. T. Weidner, R. L. Sells, *Elementary Modern Physics*, Allyn and Bacon, 1974, p. 165

# Why the free Electron mass plus free Proton mass Exceeds the Bohr Hydrogen mass

## Carl R. Littmann

*25 Washington Lane, Wyncote PA 19095, clittmann@verizon.net*

The National Institute of Standards and Technology (NIST) gives the mass of the simple Bohr Hydrogen atom (H-1) as less than the sum of NIST values for a free electron rest mass plus a free proton rest mass. NIST is likely correct, but that contradicts a few writings by this author and some other scientists too. When a distant electron travels very fast toward its orbit around a proton, one might think that causes a "relativistic" mass increase. While there are externally forced ways to increase mass with increased velocity, yet for isolated systems, their internal potential energies may act to increase the velocity of their parts without the systems mass increasing. We discuss that and a few of the many related and profound issues in this paper.

**Keywords:** Bohr, hydrogen, velocity, mass, decrease

## 1. Introduction

Despite statements in some of author's previous papers about the Bohr atom having more mass than the greatly separated electron and proton rest mass, the 'NIST" data now indicates the opposite. And the author now tries to explain why NIST is likely right. The issue has profound implications and raises many additional questions, but only a few can and will be addressed in this limited space paper. (Hereafter, this author will often refer to himself as I, me, or he.)

Important: Almost all physics oriented scientists realize and accept that there are very powerful cyclotrons and other accelerators that accelerate basic particles to nearly the velocity of light. And thus the particle mass can be greatly increased! For example, using rather recent scientific advances, the proton may be accelerated enough to incur a mass increase of about 100 times its rest mass. Yet, when a simple "free" electron is naturally attracted toward a proton, moves closer to it and commences to orbits it speedily, that orbiting electron has lost mass! (The proton, although mutually orbiting much more slowly, has likely lost some mass too.) Even if one adds the emitted photon mass to the mass of the Hydrogen-1 atom – that total mass might equal, but still will not exceed – the total mass of the greatly separated proton plus electron mass before the atom was formed.

So the above seems somewhat paradoxical – a mass gain for one moving particle, and a mass loss for the same particle under seemingly not very different circumstances?

I find this and many related issues difficult to explain in all their details, but I think this paper makes some progress toward that goal. But readers are encouraged to note any possible pitfalls, because, for example, I may sometimes draw nearly obvious inferences, but not fully justified, or even harbor misunderstandings about experiments and evidence.

The subject of the mass of the free electron plus free proton vs. the mass of the Bohr atom – has been rather well introduced by at least one "chat-group" [1]. Most got their conclusions right by arguing roughly as follows: ""It takes the input of 13.6 eV of energy, or work, to push the electron of the Bohr atom to a most outer orbit or slightly further. That is also known as the "ionization energy" for the hydrogen atom. Thus, the energy of the Bohr atom in its ground state is less than the sum of the free proton and free electron energies. Thus, it follows, presumably, that the sum of masses of the latter exceeds the ground state mass of the Hydrogen atom, by the mass equivalent of that much ionization energy, also!""

And for a second Bohr atom in its ground state, the reverse could occur. After, say, the electron of the first atom jumped to its inner-most orbit and emitted a photon – that photon could fly to the far away second Bohr atom which would absorb that photon energy and mass. And that would cause the ejection of its inner-most orbital electron to a far away ("ionized") location. And then the mass of the free electron plus proton rest masses would exceed the mass of the Bohr atom, which previously hosted the orbital system.

((Introductory college physics textbooks generally have the potential energy of attraction imparting kinetic energy to the electron so it will obit the proton. And also so that it makes a photon and send it fast away from the scene. But, alternatively, maybe we should imagine that that potential energy has merely, in a catalytic way, interacted with, triggered, and converted the already existing rest masses and their $mc^2$ energies in such a way as to achieve the final outcomes! (The so-called "lost potential" energy may still exist, but is hidden inside or outside the particle systems).))

Einstein published two papers on Special Relativity Theory in 1905, the first, on June 30, which was rather long, which we will call his "6-30-1905 paper" [2]. But on Sept. 27, 1905, Einstein published his second paper, this time very short and on "$E/c^2 = m$ ", which we will call his

"9-27-1905 paper"[3].

The first paper seems to discuss the mass vs. velocity relations for an electron travelling parallel vs. normal to a potential field, and I found it confusing, misleading, irrelevant or wrong when I tried to apply it to the Bohr model and action. (A few years after 1905, others adapted certain aspects of its equations to describe velocity vs. mass changes for other masses such as protons, neutral particles and bodies in the way we recognize today. And as occurs in many important kinds of physical behaviors.)

But the later paper by Einstein, his 9-27-1905 paper, seemed more relevant and helpful, regarding the Bohr atom and its actions. In effect, it simply stated that if radiation energy, i.e., a photon with energy "E", is emitted by a body, then the mass of the emitting body is decreased by the mass of that radiation, (the mass of photon emitted). And the mass,"m", of the radiation emitted (the photon) is equal to the Energy "E" of that photon, divided by $c^2$, the speed of light squared: I.e., $(E/c^2) = m$.

Let us now apply that by supposing that an initial proton and a far away electron constitute a system. Then, regardless of subsequent events and motions purely internal to that system, let us suppose that system emits radiation, a photon with energy "E". (And that "E" is received, measured and verified by a very special photo detector external to the system.) Since that photon was traveling at speed "c", the 9-27-1905 paper of Einstein says that the emitting body (or atom) incurred a mass decrease of $(E/c^2)$. And that now seems experimentally correct for that class of actions, and that seems supported by NIST data!

(Because the electrostatic force between a proton and electron is about $10^{36}$ times stronger than the gravitational force, the Bohr atom can likely reveal to us some important concepts easier and less expensively than some other means. Easier than difficult astronomical tests likely associated with the General or Special Theories of Relativity. And the Bohr atom is, so-to-speak, right under our noses and like a microcosm of the universe.)

Returning to that 9-27-1005 paper, I think Einstein broke new ground which was previously foggy at best, and he presented a very helpful overview. But somewhat related to all that was a paper by Niels Bohr about eight years later [4]. There, by tackling many of those internal and external dynamics of the hydrogen atom in detail, Bohr also broke new ground and discovered new, important, and valuable relationships.

## 2. Overview of Solution to Paradox

Now back to the main question. Why does a particle in some cases incur an increased mass after its velocity is increased – and yet, in a seemingly pretty similar case, it incurs no increase in mass after its absolute velocity is increased?

I believe that powerful accelerators, like the Van de Graaff generator and cyclotron, and probably the Betatron – externally bully the accelerated charged particles forward against an aether near the front face of the particle. It

is sort of like being hit in the back by many powerful gamma rays (high energy photons) – one immediately after another. And that the aether near that front face during much of that forward acceleration is at least as pressurized and dense as that of average ethereal space. That leads to a different response regarding the increased speed of the particle and the resulting change of its mass – compared to that which results from a natural electrostatic attraction between an electron and proton. The latter accelerates and increases the velocities of the electron and proton toward each other in a "natural" way and in a natural, but special, environment. On the other hand, cyclotrons are like being in an airplane on an aircraft carrier and being quickly accelerated by a catapult to a high takeoff speed, and you feel the great discomfort of a very high "G" force!

So in contrast to that – a far away electron, being gently attracted to a proton, accelerates in a natural voltage gradient (a pressure gradient) toward the proton – with a naturally lower ethereal pressure and density in the region between them. I.e., on the faces of each that face each other. And, at most, just normal ethereal pressure and density are applied to their back faces, and even that pressure decreases as the electron gets nearer and nearer to the proton. So that, contrary to the case in the previous paragraph, no mass increase of the electron or proton need occur. And none seems to empirically occur, then. It is like gravitational free-fall, acceleration but the astronaut does not feel it.

I believe that long-lasting particles have spin that can also plays a key role regarding mass increase vs. travel velocity. Try to imagine yourself carrying a clock with a thin clock-hand having a very massive pointer at the end of its hand. Imagine the clock-hand and pointer rotating fast, say, even as fast as the speed of light. But, say, when your forward speed and that of the clock you are carrying reaches nearly the speed of light, the rotational speed of the clock-hand must nearly stop. I.e., otherwise the vector velocity of the clock pointer would exceed the velocity of light, "c". So, unless something special happens, the rotational angular momentum of the clock-hand must decrease to nearly zero. So unless something else happens to compensate for the slowing rotational velocity (which would normally be expected to decrease the angular momentum) – the law of "conservation of angular momentum" will be violated.

So, roughly speaking, we'll just say that the violation of the law, here, is prevented by the following: The more slowly rotating clock-hand receives more mass from the mass of the aether or from the mass of hitting photons, and thus the clock-hand incurs a mass increase! And thus the clock-hand can now rotate slower, but its added mass will tend to support its former appreciable angular momentum. And thus conform to the conservation of angular momentum law. Now that description may not be perfect, but it may help us visualize why the accelerated particle or clock-hand gains mass, under the conditions somewhat like presented. (And thus the slower rotation of the clock-hand seems to cause time to slow down when the forward travel velocity of the clock is increased.)

Now, back to the case of the simple electron being attracted to the proton and moving toward it or beginning to orbit it. As it does so, the ethereal region from its far face to its near face (the gradient encountered) is going from slightly less than a normal pressure and density – to even less than that! Under those conditions, perhaps the electron's spin can slightly exceed the speed of light or its radius may increase. Thus, the electron can LOSE a tiny percent of its mass and still maintain the same angular momentum as a free electron at rest. (More on that later.)

That situation, in a major way, is opposite the situation of "the high G catapult" test described earlier. The case of "electrostatic attraction" is likely much like "gravitational attraction". That is – when you are dropped in a gravitational field and thus are accelerated downward, faster and faster, you experience a DRIFTING weightlessness. I.e., that is like "free-fall", instead of feeling great pressure against your back like the "catapult"!

But even in the earlier described, lower pressure and lower density aether cases, say, if you suddenly hit high density water, your mass might increase until you assumed a slower rotational spin and better hydrodynamic shape. After that, per this attempted analogy, your mass need no longer increase.

We will discuss later the behavior of a photon, an entity that responds differently than a typical particle described above. And for that and related reasons – I think the photon should be considered a "pseudo-particle".

## 3. Miscellaneous Holistic Comments

There seems to me to be about four major classes of phenomena occurring – that relate possible velocity variation with possible mass variation. But those uniquely challenge most of us to understand them because of their simplistic description. We will only tackle a few of them in some detail in this limited space paper:

Class 1: The mass and energy of the photon changes as it is going into (or out of) a gravitational field, even though its speed does not change!

I think we learn, at least in that case, that those photons (pseudo-particles) change in mass, even though their speed holds constant. And that in each such event, even the directly measurable ($mc^2$) energy and (m) mass do not likely hold constant. That is because the photon, and also the body that is gravitationally attracting it, likely both gain a "small tad" of mass and energy. And we should likely accept that these challenging events occur because a hidden aether has mass, and can transfer real mass, as well as energy, to a pseudo-particle, i.e., a photon. (And aether can also receive mass from the photon – after the photon finishes its pass close to the attracting body and leaves that region.) I believe those actions happen and are contrary to the limited notion of a "superfluous aether", the term Einstein used in his 6-30-1905 paper.

So I think that aether has potential energy and useful

mass. ((Even before the very helpful $E = mc^2$ by Einstein (instead of $E - 0.5mc^2$), and before the concept of particle spin – Hertz, in his last work, cautioned the following: "If we try to understand the motions of bodies around us, and to refer them to simple and clear rules, paying attention only to what can be directly observed, our attempt will in general fail" [5].))

A sometimes overlooked implication of the two paragraphs above is this: Suppose a photon likely gains and then loses a tiny part of its total mass when it passes near a gravitational body, on its way to a more distant absorbing target. Thus, even though the same total amount of mass of the photon – that left the emitter – may finally arrive near its target, some of that arriving photon mass is NOT its original. And that is a major aspect of "what makes a wave a real wave" instead of a pure traveling particle, an aspect or paradigm that is seldom mentioned or well-discussed in textbooks. And perhaps for some very long, special routes traveled by photons – maybe almost all of its mass that it delivers to the target, is "newly substituted mass" in place of the old lost mass. If we wisely accept that aether does have mass and various sorts of capabilities (such as changing the photon's mass) – then that will greatly enhance our understanding of some other mysterious physical events, too.

Class 2: Free Neutron decay, which results in production of a proton and electron, and the electron flies away from the scene. But in one somewhat extreme case, the electron flies away at nearly the velocity of light, with its mass increased (and thus equal to about 2.5 times that of a rest mass electron). That is nearly the mass difference between a free, at-rest, neutron and the proton left behind in such free neutron decay. But in another contrasting and pretty extreme case of free neutron decay, the electron barely gets away and only at a slow speed and without a significant increase in its mass. And many physicists try to maintain the wished-for conservation of mass and energy, despite the different case behaviors, by supposing that a strange, hard-to-find anti-neutrino is also emitted in the decay. In one case they postulate a low-mass anti-neutrino, and in the other case a much higher mass anti-neutrino. Regretfully, we cannot address this interesting and challenging dichotomy in detail in this limited paper.

Class 3: Electron-Positron Annihilation – where an electron and positron, orbiting each other, converts to a pair of photons and each photon flies away from the scene. Each departing photon has a neutral mass equal to each mass of the original mutually orbiting particles before they "annihilated". Again, we cannot address this interesting event in detail in this limited paper.

Class 4: The Bohr atom and its actions have already been previously described to some extent. And in some ways that applies to other atoms with many protons in their nucleus, but stripped of all orbiting electrons except for just one electron. And that one electron might be "pulled" toward such a nucleus, say, a nucleus containing 83 protons – to orbit it at well over half the speed of light and also in a very near orbit! (The latter paradigm has too deep of indirect implications to fully discuss in this paper, especially if its nucleus consists of 83 or more protons.)

One problem with the Bohr atom is that a very "small chip" of mass seems to have been stolen from its orbiting electron and proton – for building that photon that flew away from the scene. That is the logical conclusion based on NIST data and other considerations. But it is the full original mass of the electron that is envisioned as orbiting – in the textbook Bohr model presentations. And if that full electron is not used, an extremely small error will seemingly arise, even if too small to measure. Of course, one might envision a small electromagnetic action between the very slowly orbiting proton and much faster orbiting electron – as neutralizing some or all of that possible error. Or that in combination with other factors – maybe the proton lost the small chip of mass. But we will let that discrepancy to be pursued by some talented specialist, if interested.

Other Remarks: Now, think of the large number of atoms and molecules in the universe with orbiting electrons due to "natural" charge-related attractions! And the nucleons that lose a small percent of their mass during nuclear fusions and may have fast orbits or other special motions in the nucleus. (And maybe neutral or charged particles or bodies orbiting a large body due to gravity. However, their angular momentum would then drastically exceed that of the Bohr hydrogen atom's electron. And thus the mass loss paradigm may not apply to the gravity case involving greatly separated orbiting, i.e., great distances compared to the hydrogen atom's "small quantum world".) But still, the percent of particles that have experienced a mass decrease, despite their increase in speed – may be appreciable compared to those incurring a mass increase with increase in their speed. Perhaps an important balancing principle maintaining and driving our universe as we know it.

I think a lot of special phenomena arise in the universe because it is not totally occupied by an "ultra low density aether" alone, but instead a small percent of space is occupied by rather compact, high density mass particles. And that the aether flow increases in velocity and decreases in pressure as aether flow tries to squeeze between those particles. And that slight "Venturi" pressure reduction, the Venturi effect, is the source of, at least, attractive nuclear forces. (And other types of ethereal flows might occur, perhaps cyclone-like and anticyclone-like.)

In a sense, Chemistry, with its formation of atoms with orbiting electrons and their ionization energies – may be just a microcosm version of nuclear physics phenomena, with its drastically larger nuclear fusion energies. But both actions arise from a similar cause, I think. There is a very slight occupancy–related congestion of ethereal space that arises, even between a proton and a small electron in the ground state of the Bohr orbital model. And that arises even though they have about a $0.53x10^{-10}$ meter separation. But there is a much greater occupancy congestion be-

tween nucleons in a nucleus, say with only small grooves between nucleons. I.e., about $1x10^{-15}$ meter between nucleons. Thus, a much greater Venuri-flow attraction or the like – with the much lower ethereal pressure developed between nucleons, in the case of nuclear forces.

Optional remark: A very rough description of the Einstein General Theory of Relativity is sometimes given by picturing a knitting or fabric of "space–time" as becoming deformed or curved near two bodies that are close together. But I prefer, instead, to picture the flow of aether as curved or deformed between those bodies. And perhaps something like a Venturi effect (relative pressure reduction) or attraction thus arises between those bodies.

To avoid excess length, we will skip roughly modeling a fragile photon vs. a sturdier electron or proton. And just discuss the following basic difference between the photon and the basically more sturdy electron or proton:

First, based on the work of A. H. Compton on x-ray or photon deflection, we can surmise the following: Imagine that a photon travels in an overall pretty straight line, except for being deflected, first, somewhat to the left and then back an equal amount to the right, and that that shuffling occurs, say, fifty times. And that those deflections were caused by encountering electrons at rest, or moving slowly – close to its path. After that, the photon could likely have almost no mass and energy remaining. But that outcome cannot happen with a STURDY proton or electron traveling that path. Regardless of the deflections along the way, and regardless, after that, of whether it is traveling at its original speed or zero speed, the outcome is different from the photon case. The final elementary particle will still have, roughly speaking, its standard "rest-mass" or perhaps an even greater "relativistic" mass. That sturdiness differentiates a conventional real particle from a photon pseudo-particle.

Back to the photon. If the photon must maintain a constant speed, c, while moving toward the source of the gravity pressure gradient; it is not free to undergo the natural adjustment of "speed change under acceleration forces". And thus maybe avoid a change in mass – an option available for a conventional particle. So that, more than otherwise – the photon may experience a greater pressure against its back as it gets closer to the source of the attracting potential gradient. In other words, we can likely expect it to behave differently from a conventional particle.

One crucial last important point: The proposition of a very energized and thus high-pressurized, low-density aether – leads to the following expectation regarding a high-density compact, stable particle mass in the aether: Imagine a small volume region that is somehow temporarily devoid of mass, aether, and its pressure. And, say, that vacuum amounts to $10^{-45}$ cu. meters, about the volume of a compact proton. Then there is a modest limit as to the velocity, energy, and angular momentum that a proton can acquire by being sucked into such small, limited volume. Or likely even a smaller volume. But contrast that with what can happen over the vast ethereal space outside of that small volume. Since energy can equal the product of roughly "pressure times volume", there is almost no limit as to how much energy a high-density conventional particle can acquire when accelerated to high velocity through vast space! I.e., especially if the high-density particle faces a normal density aether in front of it and some of that aether sticks to it. And that is the ultimate reason why, even in powerful nuclear fusions, the nucleons lose only about 1 percent of their original, free particle masses. But with cyclotrons and the like, then formerly "at-rest" particles can see their mass increased by about 100 times.

That is the greatly important reality that we witness in the experimental world. And I do not think that that outcome can be rationalized, instead, by trying to model a universe where all or most of space is devoid of any aether! (And like a fish adapted to water, or gravity that we are so accustomed to, what would be the strongest evidence for a certain conclusion – is evidence often overlooked. I.e., because we are so adapted to what would otherwise seem strange.)

## 4. The NIST data – likely accurate enough

I found it difficult to surf through the NIST website efficiently to find the various data below, including trying to choose effective words to put into their search window. But I finally found it there [6]. Below is the relevant data I found. And how I works with it is shown adjacent an asterisk:

Free electron mass: 0.00054857990946(22) u

Free proton mass..: 1.007276466812(90) u

*Total of above free (separate) masses. ..................................:1.007825046721 u

But note the following: (H-1), or "Hydrogen-1", has the mass.....................:1.00782503223(9) u

(That is the "Bohr atom" in its ground state as author found by surfing the NIST website 9-7-2015.)

*Note the SUM of the masses of the Individual (independent) "free" parts EXCEEDS the Mass of (H-1), or "Hydrogen-1" atom by the following difference between the above...................: 0.0000000145 u

Even without a lengthy discussion regarding the accuracy, the parentheses, and statistics associated with the above, I think we can fairly say this: Regarding the amount by which the the mass of Hydrogen-1 empirically seems to differ from the very greatly separated free, at rest proton plus electron, 0.0000000145 u, we conclude this: It is unlikely that the '4' in that sequence, '145', will change. But even if it would change from 4 to 5, or from 4 to 3, we would still have the seemingly reliable empirical fact that Hydrogen-1, the Bohr atom, decreased in mass when formed!

In the Bohr electron model and theory, the ground state orbital electron velocity is calculated as $0.022x10^8$ meter/sec. That is a little less than a hundredth of the speed of light, 'c'. If a free, at rest electron were speeded up to $0.022x10^8$ meter/sec. in 'free space' (not by attraction to the proton) its then theoretical 'relativistic mass gain'

would approximately equal the mass lost by the Bohr Hydrogen atom (H 1) when formed. I.e., formed from its formerly at rest, unbound parts. That seems indicated by the NIST data above, even though it may seem a little surprising. That much mass lost is also approximately equal to the 'equivalent mass' of the photon which (H-1) emitted when formed, and is equivalent to the energy that that emitted photon has when it flew away from the scene at velocity 'c'. (We skip displaying the 'conventional relativistic calculations' here to shorten and simplify the paper).

Now remember this: The kinetic energy of the high velocity orbiting electron plus the total "$mc^2$" energy of the emitted photon was prompted or provided by "the potential electrostatic energy lost" when the orbital system was formed. I.e., the electron and proton orbital system was formed when the electron "jumped" into the "ground state orbit" – after the electron had been previously drifting slowly a great distance from the proton.

((The above outcomes support rather well the groundbreaking discoveries arising from the Bohr atomic theory, model and treatment (at least with regards to the magnitude of the equalities that Bohr calculated). And as also presented in many long-standing respected textbooks. That is very good, despite at least one drawback in that Bohr atomic model, as follows: It is likely that not quite all of the full rest mass of the electron, that was originally a long distance from the proton, was carried with it when it became the orbiting electron in the Bohr atom. So there may be a very slight theoretical problem with the standard textbook treatment of the Bohr atom. So imagine that a very small chip off the orbiting Bohr electron or proton was donated to make the photon mass. Then, roughly, if we multiply that donated mass by $c^2$, we obtain the total energy that the photon has when created and emitted.))

## 5. Conclusion and Summary

A reasonable interpretation of "NIST" data and other considerations have now led this author to change some of his opinions that he expressed earlier in a few papers. He now regards it as thus very likely that the Bohr hydrogen atom, especially in its ground state, has less mass than the sum of the rest masses of a proton plus a slowly drifting, far away "free" electron. This may seem surprising since it implies that the speedily orbiting electron has not only failed to incur a "speed-related relativistic mass increase". That electron, and perhaps the proton, have also lost mass by donated it to make the photon that flies away from the scene! (That may mean that there is a very slight unexplained discrepancy in many textbook presentation of the Bohr atomic model.)

Since that photon has received a total energy "E" from the orbital system it left, then according to the Einstein 9-27-1905 paper, the emitting body or system suffers an ($E/c^2$) worth of mass reduction. (So the mass of the Bohr atom was decreased by that, and apparently the photon flew away with that donated mass. And thus – the shortest of two papers by Einstein in 1905 is likely applicable and suitable here.)

So the two above paragraphs prompt this question: How can a particle, accelerated to a high velocity, say by a cyclotron, incur a great mass increase – and yet an electron, attracted to a proton and thus accelerated to a high velocity, not incur a mass increase? In fact a mass decrease after providing the mass for the deporting photon!

We propose this: Very stable, very compact protons and somewhat less compact electrons occupy at least some space in the otherwise very low-density, highly energized ethereal space of the universe. So naturally, ethereal flows develop, and its flow speeds up while trying to squeeze between particles – like the electron and somewhat close proton. Thus, a natural Venturi flow effect arises, i.e., an "attraction-like" force between particles or bodies, a natural potential energy gradient.

That special "voltage pressure gradient" has less than normal ethereal pressure between the attracting particles, but a closer to normal pressure on the far faces of the particles. That contrasts with being unnaturally hit hard in the back by many gamma rays and thus knocked forward even against average or higher-than-average pressure against the front face of a particle or body.

And the feeling of a catapulted aircraft carrier pilot vs. the different feeling of a space astronaut in-training – illustrates the different feelings, experiences and realities above: First, the very uncomfortable high G force of a powerful "catapult forward", as an airplane is launched from an aircraft carrier. But, in contrast, when under gravitational "free–fall", the astronaut is drawn faster and faster toward, say, Jupiter – but he then feels no force, i.e., like just drifting "weightlessly".

Roughly, that is why some stable bodies, (those that maintain at least a substantial minimum mass at all times – like the proton and electron) gain great mass when "bullied" forward by the cyclotron against a normal pressure ethereal region. Or when they enter such normal pressure ethereal region after the cyclotron push.

There are many other questions and propositions that might be prompted by the major subject of this paper, and ideas for testing of them, too. But we could only touch on a few in this paper. For example, a photon under gravity may likely gain or lose some mass without incurring a speed change. But the photon is sort of a 'pseudo-particle' and not in the same class of particles as the sturdy proton and electron. For example, if a photon bounces gently off a thousand separated electrons at rest, as is imaginable in Compton-like experiments, the photon has no significant minimum mass left after that. But even in nucleon fusions, the nucleons and nucleus retain about 99 percent of the rest mass of the particles from which they ultimately originated. And if, in exothermic chemical reactions, there is still much less mass lost – maybe chemical reactions are just small microcosms of nucleon fusions.

## REFERENCES

1. Members,
   texttthttps://www.physicsforums.com, 2001->.

2. Albert Einstein, *On the Electrodynamics of Moving Bodies.*, Ann. Phys., Physical Review D, Vol 17, 891, 1905.
3. Albert Einstein, *Does the Inertia of a Body Depend Upon its Energy Content?.*, Ann. Phys., Physical Review D, Vol 18, 639ff, 1905.
4. N. Bohr, *On the Constitution of Atoms and Molecules.*, Phil. Mag, 1913.
5. Heinrich Hertz, *The Principles of Mechanics Presented in a New Form, (English Translation).*, MacMillan and Co., Ltd, Introduction, Part III, pg.25, 1899.
6. NIST,
   texttthttp://www.nist.gov., 2016.

# The Trouble with Modern Physics and the Solution Based on Logic and Metatheory

Charles W Lucas Jr, PhD, Theoretical Physics

*29045 Livingston Drive, Mechanicsville, Maryland, 20659-3271, bill.lucas001@gmail.com,*

Modern physics has many problems with infinities, dark matter, dark energy, black holes, too many adjustable parameters, and logical inconsistencies. Since modern science poses as an authority more sure than the world's major religions, it seems appropriate to evaluate the truth of modern physics from the perspective of logic and metatheory. Logic reveals that the postulates or axioms of modern physics are based on assumptions known by experiment to be false. These assumptions lead to conclusions that are in disagreement with common sense. Metatheory (the theory of theories based on logic) gives logical arguments that all the current major theories of modern physics are incomplete and incompatible with each other. From metatheory the simplest solution that completes modern science and removes the incompatibilities in modern science is to properly complete electrodynamics such that the theories of Maxwell's electrodynamics, the Copenhagen version of quantum mechanics, Einstein's special and general relativity theories, and the standard model of elementary particles are replaced by a single more comprehensive version of electrodynamics.

**Keywords:** relativity theory, modern physics, logic, metatheory, electrodynamics, universal force

## 1. Introduction

The development of science from ancient times was based on some intuitively obvious assumptions about the universe. These are as follows:

1. **Determinism** - There are natural causes for everything that happens in the universe.
2. **Objective Truth** - Observations of the universe can be made independent of the observer.
3. **Consistency** - The same causes produce the same effects everywhere in the universe.

These assumptions have been challenged by the theories of modern science. For instance the Copenhagen version of quantum mechanics claims that the universe is governed 100 per cent by random statistical processes and that there is no Law of Cause and Effect thereby denying Determinism and Consistency. Also this version of quantum mechanics, according to Heisenberg, claims that reality is in the "observation process" and so is not independent of the observer, and thus there is no Objective Truth.

The purpose of this paper is to uncover the fallacies of the main pillars of modern science, i.e. Maxwell's electrodynamics, Einstein's special and general relativity theories, the Copenhagen version of quantum mechanics, and the standard model of elementary particles, and to show from logic and metatheory the path back to true science.

## 2. The Axiomatic Method

The axiomatic method was invented by the ancient Greeks as the proper way to organize and demonstrate inductive and deductive logical reasoning in the pursuit of natural philosophy. The axiomatic method is a logical procedure by which an entire system of natural philosophy (e.g. a branch of science or mathematics) is generated in accordance with specified rules of logical deduction from certain basic propositions (axioms or postulates), which in turn are constructed from a few terms (charge, mass, length, velocity, acceleration) taken as primitives. These axioms are to be defined and constructed by inductive logic from observed patterns in nature or intuition by which some warrant for their truth is felt to exist. One of the oldest examples of the axiomatic method is the ancient Greek Euclidean geometry.

Euclid, in the process of developing geometry, defined the axiomatic method of proof to be used in logically establishing theorems in geometry. To the extent that the axioms or postulates he chose to start with were valid, his logically developed theorems would be valid.

The ancient Greeks were so impressed by the work of Euclid that they put the slogan "Let No One Ignorant of Geometry Enter Here" over the door of their academies of natural philosophy. The modern world has also been impressed by Euclid to the extent that his book **Elements (of Geometry)** [1] has been published in more languages and editions than any other natural philosophy or scientific book in the history of the world. [2]

Euclid's approach worked well in geometry where the propositions could be imagined or justified by simple geometrical constructions using a straight edge and compass, but in physics and other areas of natural philosophy, the ancient Greek natural philosophers were not able to discover the appropriate axioms or postulates so easily. This is due to the fact that the axiomatic method was primarily a method of logical organization of abstract proofs of theorems or theories, but not a general method for postulate or axiom discovery of objective reality.

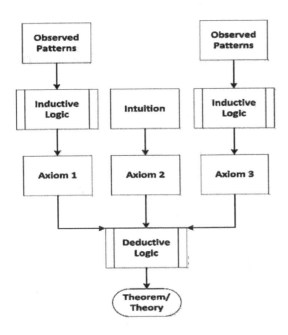

**Figure 1.** Axiomatic Scientific Method

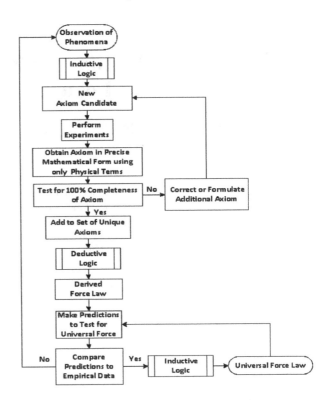

**Figure 2.** Newton's Empirical Scientific Method

## 3. Empirical Method of Axiom Discovery

When Isaac Newton published his **Principia** [3] or **Mathematical Principles of Natural Philosophy**, he stated that he intended to illustrate a new way of doing natural philosophy that overcomes some of the limitations of the axiomatic method. This method is now called the empirical scientific method. The goal of Newton's method was to find empirically the axioms and appropriate terms from which the forces of nature could be derived by logic.

Newton claimed that in the past natural philosophers tried to understand nature in vain, because they did not use an empirical approach for finding the axioms leading to the fundamental forces of nature based upon experimentation. The empirical approach is more effective and efficient in discovering the causes and effects of nature. As a result he argued that the empirical approach combined with the logic of the axiomatic method was a more secure path toward truth in natural philosophy. The problem faced by the ancient Greek philosophers was that they could not guess or discover by observation the relevant propositions and appropriate primitive terms for natural philosophy upon which to apply logic to derive the theorems or theories of natural philosophy outside of geometry and mathematics. These needed to be discovered by experiment.

Before Newton, Kepler discovered three empirical laws for the motions of the planets about the sun.

1. The planets orbit the Sun in ellipses with the sun at one focus.

2. The line joining the sun and a planet sweeps through equal areas in an equal amount of time.

3. The square of the period of a planet's orbit P is directly proportional to the cube of the semi-major axis A of its elliptical path, i.e. $P^2 = kA^3$.

Although these empirical laws were practical and useful, the fundamental cause of the motions of the planets was not revealed by them. Newton's emphasis on empirical forces turned out to be much more useful than Kepler's Laws and to give a better and simpler understanding of the mechanics of the solar system that could be applied even to processes on the Earth. From his empirical force laws of equations (1) and (2) below Newton was able to deduce Kepler's Laws. However, in 1766, Titius Bode revealed his empirical law showing the quantum periodicity of the orbits of the planets. This indicated that Newton's empirical force laws were incomplete.

Newton's empirical approach emphasizing forces does not lead to all truth at once, as Newton himself recognized with regard to his study of inertia and gravity. He never claimed to understand the causes and nature of inertia and gravity, even though he could define the empirical force of inertia and the empirical force of gravity as shown below.

$$\text{Force of Inertia} \quad F_I = m_I A \qquad (1)$$

$$\text{Force of Gravity} \quad F_G = \frac{G m_{G1} m_{G2}}{R_{12}^2} \qquad (2)$$

When Newton was asked what inertial mass $m_I$ was, he replied that inertial mass was a measure of some characteristic of matter that caused the force of inertia and that increased as the amount of matter increased. When Newton was asked what gravitational mass $m_G$ was, he replied that gravitational mass was a measure of some characteristic of matter that caused the force of gravity between bodies of matter and increased as the amount of matter increased. When the ratio of the experimental inertial and gravitational masses were found to be equal in magnitude for the same two bodies, Newton realized that instead of the force of inertia and the force of gravity being different fundamental forces, they might have a common cause. Newton believed that scientists needed to continue doing additional experiments to discover more of the fundamental axioms of nature until one day, following his empirical scientific method of deriving more complete force laws using more complete sets of empirically discovered axioms, the universal force law would be discovered.

# 4. Existential and Post-Modern Scientific Method

The scientific community was greatly impressed with the progress that Newton had made in science. He had expressed scientific laws in precise mathematical terms and equations that described many things not previously described or understood. Even though they knew that Newton claimed his work was incomplete, they established a new approach to science based on his experimental empirical approach and his use of precise mathematical equations to express scientific theories.

They modified the scientific method to de-emphasize the role of logic as shown in their diagram of the scientific method in Figure 3 and substituted the much weaker criterion of falsifiability of hypotheses. The reason that they de-emphasized the strict role of deductive logic and truth in science is that they did not believe in ultimate truth and purpose in the universe, but they were greatly impressed with what Newton had accomplished in science by describing nature in precise mathematical terms without knowing (1) what inertial and gravitational mass was, (2) what was the cause of the inertial and gravitational forces, and (3) how the gravitational and inertial forces were transmitted between bodies.

This weaker version of the scientific method became known as the existential scientific method. It allowed idealizations to be freely used in scientific theories just as Newton had temporarily used the concepts of inertial and gravitational mass and action-at-a-distance forces. As modern science was developed, the Maxwellian version of electrodynamics, the Copenhagen version of quantum mechanics, Einstein's relativity theory and the standard model of elementary particles were based on many similar idealizations including the point particle idealization. In 1957 Robert Hofstadter received the Nobel Prize for his electron scattering experiments in which he measured the finite size and three interior substructures of the proton and neutron. Since logic was no longer the criterion for falsification, the theories above, which are the pillars of modern science, were not falsified for the incorporation of the false point-particle idealization.

# 5. Logical Arguments from Metatheory

Metatheory, the theory of theories, is a branch of metamathematics. It is the study of principles such as consistency, coherence, stability, continuity, superposition and other aspects of logical systems. From the days of the earliest natural philosophers science or natural philosophy has been developed as a logical system derived from postulates or axioms. Such scientific theories are subject to various logical principles based upon inductive and deductive logic and consistency.

Henri Poincare is generally credited as founding the field of metatheory or metamathematics. Being one of the last of the true natural philosophers, he was concerned about the logical structure of scientific theories and the logical basis of truth. Poincare was the co-discoverer of relativity theory with Einstein, and he actually published one year before Einstein. However, neither he nor Einstein ever received the Nobel Prize for this work, because of Poincare's own arguments from metatheory below discrediting relativity theory.

Poincare made logical arguments from metatheory [4] that no two fundamental theories in nature could employ the same fundamental constants, such as c the velocity of light. This was then combined with another logical argument that only fundamental theories could be true theories.

**Electrodynamics uses c in its wave equation**

$$\nabla^2 \Phi - \frac{1}{c^2}\frac{\partial^2 \phi}{\partial t^2} = \frac{-\rho}{\varepsilon_0} \tag{3}$$

$$\nabla^2 \vec{A} - \frac{1}{c^2}\frac{\partial^2 \vec{A}}{\partial t^2} = \frac{-\mu_0}{\vec{J}} \tag{4}$$

$$\lambda f = c \tag{5}$$

**Special Relativity uses c in its space-time interval**

$$ds^2 = dx^2 + dy^2 + dz^2 - c^2 dt^2 \tag{6}$$

**Quantum Mechanics uses c in its energy quantum**

$$E = hv = h\left(\frac{2pic}{\lambda}\right) \tag{7}$$

**General Relativity uses c in its field equation**

$$G_{uv} + \Lambda g_{uv} = \frac{8\pi G}{c^4 T_{uv}} \tag{8}$$

Poincare noticed that four "so-called" fundamental theories of modern science used the same fundamental constant c for the velocity of light, i.e. electrodynamics, special relativity, quantum mechanics, and general relativity. According to his logical criterion only one of these four theories could be fundamental or true. Poincare suggested that the fundamental theory was electrodynamics and that a more complete version of electrodynamics would eventually explain all of the data explained by these other theories.

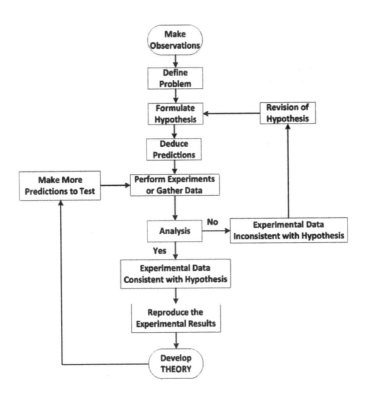

**Figure 3.** Existential and Post-Modern Scientific Method

Poincare also published the interesting logical argument from metatheory that no two fundamental force laws could have the same mathematical form such as $\frac{1}{R^2}$. [5] Now the electrostatic Coulomb force law and Newton's gravitational force law both have a $\frac{1}{R^2}$ form. Since Einstein's General Theory of Relativity which describes gravity also involves the fundamental constant c, Poincare reasoned that gravity must be of electrodynamic origin.

$$F_G = \frac{-Gm_1m_2}{R^2} \text{ and } F_{EM} = \frac{q_1q_2}{(4\pi\varepsilon_0 R^2)} \qquad (9)$$

The Superposition Principle [6] of metatheory describes the properties of linear systems needed for coherence and stability. Systems may be elementary particles composed of quarks, leptons, etc., or an atom composed of electrons, protons, and neutrons, or a molecule composed of a collection of atoms that are described by a combination of theories to describe these systems such as electrodynamics, relativity theory, and quantum mechanics.

A linear system is one that satisfies the homogeneity and additivity properties required by the Superposition Principle for coherence and stability shown below.

$$F(x1 + x_2 + ...) = F(x_1) + F(x_2) + ... \text{ Additivity}$$
$$F(ax) = aF(x) \text{ for scalar a Homogeneity} \quad (10)$$

If one wants to describe matter in the form of an elementary particle, an atom or a molecule by combining electrodynamics, relativity theory, quantum mechanics and the

standard model of elementary particles, each of these theories must satisfy the Superposition Principle.

$$F(x) = F_{EM}(x) + F_{SR}(x) + F_{QM}(x) + F_{SM}(x) \qquad (11)$$

Maxwell's electrodynamics cannot be combined with Special Relativity, because the electrodynamic field and force is nonlinear in r.

$$\vec{E}(\vec{r}) = \frac{q\hat{r}}{4\pi\varepsilon_0 r^2} \qquad (12)$$

Special Relativity is not a proper theory to add to electrodynamics, since it modifies electrodynamics further making it more nonlinear by giving rise to the expression for the electric field that is nonlinear in v due to the $\beta^2 = (v/c)^2$ terms.

$$\vec{E}(\vec{r},\vec{v}) = q(1 - v^2/c^2)\hat{r}/[4\pi\varepsilon_0 r^2(1 - (v/c)^2 sin^2\phi)^{3/2}] \qquad (13)$$
$$where sin\phi = \hat{r}x\hat{v} \qquad (14)$$

In quantum mechanics the principal task is to compute how a certain type of wave propagates. The wave is called the wave function. The equation governing the behavior of the wave is the non-relativistic Schroedinger wave equation or the relativistic Dirac wave equation. The primary approach to computing the behavior of a wave function is to write the wave function as a quantum superposition of special wave functions known as stationary states.

Since the non-relativistic time-dependent Schroedinger wave equation and the relativistic Dirac wave equation are linear in the wave function $\Psi$ where $\Psi$ is a linear superposition of the probability states of the system, the non-relativistic and relativistic wave equations of quantum mechanics are linear.

**Schroedinger Equation**

$$i\hbar\frac{\partial\Psi(\vec{r},t)}{\partial t} = \left[\frac{-\hbar^2}{2m}\bigtriangledown^2 + V(\vec{r},t)\right]\Psi(\vec{r},t) \qquad (15)$$

**Dirac Equation**

$$i\hbar\frac{\partial\Psi(\vec{r},t)}{\partial t} = \left[Bmc^2 + c\left(\sum_{n=1}^{n=3}\alpha_n p_n\right)\right]\Psi(\vec{r},t) \qquad (16)$$

In the Standard Model of Elementary Particles, the short range strong interaction and weak interaction forces governing beta decay are a function of $1/r^3$ to $1/r^5$ indicating that they are highly non-linear.

Another argument from metatheory is based on the experimental fact that all electromagnetically charged particles such as electrons and protons give off radiation continuously when accelerated in cyclotrons and other accelerators. Furthermore electromagnetically charged particles recoil when absorbing or emitting radiation. From metatheory the argument is made that any theory in modern science involving electromagnetic charges or the movement of light are incomplete if they do not include terms that are a function of r relative separation, v relative velocity, a relative acceleration, and da/dt relative recoil or radiation reaction. Since the earth is accelerated due to rotation on its axis, its orbit around the sun, the orbit of our solar system about the center of the Milky Way galaxy, and the orbit of the Milky Way galaxy about the center of the universe, there are no known phenomena in the universe where the acceleration a and radiation reaction $\frac{da}{dt}$ do not play a role.

## 6. Conclusions from Metatheory

From the perspective of metatheory we see that Electrodynamics is a nonlinear theory, Special Relativity is a nonlinear theory, the Standard Model of Elementary Particles is a nonlinear theory and quantum mechanics is a linear theory. According to the Superposition Principle no two of these theories may be combined to describe matter in the form of an elementary particle, atom or molecule, because a nonlinear theory cannot be combined with another nonlinear or linear theory. Only linear theories can be combined. Only one nonlinear theory is possible. If a nonlinear theory is valid, it has to be the one and only theory, i.e. the universal theory. Of the pillars of modern science, i.e. electrodynamics, quantum mechanics, special relativity, general relativity, and the standard model of elementary particles the only one capable of becoming the universal force according to metatheory is electrodynamics. However since none of these theories contain all the r, v, a, $da/dt$ terms, none are complete.

The recently published book **The Universal Force volume 1 - Derived from a More Perfect Union of the Axiomatic and Empirical Scientific Methods version 6** [7] confirms all of these arguments from metatheory. It derives in a logically proper manner an improved version of the electrodynamic force from a complete set of the empirical equations of electrodynamics as axioms. This version of electrodynamics explains radiation and radiation reaction better than the relativistic version of Maxwell's equations and it conserves energy and satisfies Newton's 3rd law which Maxwell's equations do not. Then it derives an improved version of the force of gravity and the force of inertia from the improved version of the electrodynamic force obtaining a new second term for each. These new terms explain all the phenomena for which dark matter and dark energy were invented in order to rescue general relativity theory from falsification plus they explain the quantization of gravity as discovered by Bode and the unusual inertial gyroscope experiments of Eric Laithwaite. The book shows how to derive the universal gravitation constant G from electrodynamics and to properly define gravitational and inertial mass. It also shows how to derive the value of quantum mechanics Planck's constant h from electrodynamics alone.

Subsequent volumes in the series present improved electrodynamic models of elementary particles, atoms, nuclei, and molecules. Furthermore they explain the electrodynamic basis of life and the operation of the living cell. However the most significant contribution of the first book in the series is in showing how to correct the scientific method to properly include logic and to make progress in the direction of truth.

## REFERENCES

1. Euclid, *Elements.*, 300 BC.
2. Lucas Nicolas Hendrik Bunt, Phillip S. Jones, Jack D. Bedient, *The Historical Roots of Elementary Mathematics (Dover Publications Inc., New York, page 142 1988)..*
3. Isaac Newton, *The Principia, Mathematical Principles of Natural Philosophy: A New Translation (University of California Press, Berkeley, 1999)..*
4. Henri Poincare, *Oeuvres, Vol 9, p 497 1954..*
5. Henri Poincare, *Oeuvres, vol 9, pp 489-93 1954.*, textthttp://alternativephysics.org/index.htm, 2016.
6. Wikipedia, textthttp://en.wikipedia.org/wiki/superposition principle.
7. Charles W Lucas Jr, *The Universal Force Volume 1 - Derived From A More Perfect Union of the Axiomatic and Empirical Scientific Methods, (Create Space, version 6 July 2014)..*

# The Tron Theory
# A novel concept for the Ether and Matter

Richard Marsen, EE* and James Marsen, MSME†

*Deceased (1910-1974)
†63 Park St., Ridgefield Park, NJ 07660, james.marsen@caa.columbia.edu

The Tron Theory is proposed for unifying physical science. It presents a new fundamental particle called the tron. Trons are much smaller than electrons. Trons are simple spherical-like structures. They are composed of a variable number of smaller particles called rons. Rons have the same structure as trons. Rons are composed of even smaller particles called Ons. The average diameter of a tron depends on the number of rons it contains. Adjacent trons are premised to attract each other with an elemental force that is neutral of charge. This force is inversely proportional to the distance between tron centers. The composition and dynamic properties of the tron and ron are set forth in seven axioms forming the Tron Postulate. The Tron Theory is derived from the Tron Postulate. The Tron Theory claims: There is an ether (herein to be referred to as the tronos). It is composed of tenuous arrays of contiguous trons. The tronos has a variable density that depends on the local electric or gravitational potential. Highly compressed arrays of trons cohere to form the fundamental particles. The phenomena of Quantum Mechanics arise from interaction of the fundamental particles with the tronos in a completely deterministic and causal manner.

**Keywords:** Ether, Electricity, Magnetism, Gravity, Matter, Quantum Mechanics

## 1. Introduction

Despite its comprehensive scope the Tron Theory requires relatively few theorems; it is not highly mathematical; it is essentially mechanistic. It presents a physical basis for matter, for gravitation, for electromagnetic fields, for nuclear binding, and chemical bonding. The phenomena of Special and General Theory of Relativity are shown to have alternative explanations. The concept that the universe has three dimensions and absolute universal time is restored.

The tron theory presents a new basis for the physical fields as rarified mediums that are orderly tron assemblies. There is a distinctive tron-array for each respective type of field, including gravitational space. All radiant energy is shown to be wave trains propagated through the tenuous medium.

The Tron theory presents a way of describing the physical world that is comprehensive and consistent. It enables one to visualize particles and fields and their interactions. The electric, electromagnetic, and the gravitational fields of space are interrelated through their common tron basis. The properties of the ether derived from the Tron Theory are very different from other ether concepts. We assert that this new ether concept overcomes the objections that led to its banishment. We give it a new name: tronos.

The unification of the macro and micro worlds is also achieved. Duality between waves and particles is dispelled. The wave nature of micro-particles is revealed to be a harmonic perturbation of the average velocity of a free micro-particle or the size of a bound micro-particle. The particle-like properties of electromagnetic radiation are shown to arise from pulses of electromagnetic radiation. This insight is derived from the Tron Postulate and is the basis for explaining and deriving the phenomena of Quantum Mechanics. It provides a view of micro-particle behavior that is mechanistic, causal, and deterministic.

## 2. The Tron Postulate

The tron is presented as the as a universal dynamic particle. Myriads of them are shown to construct the atoms, bind them into observable matter, and also form the imponderable physical fields. Trons are premised as inherently contiguous, filling up the cosmos. The tron concept could possibly present the primordial material that underlies physical Nature. The Tron Theory provides significant correlations of known physical phenomena and data. Elemental physical processes can now be visualized through the dynamic tron constructs. The tron theory views physical Nature as a completely causal and deterministic. It will be shown to evolve from the fundamentals in common sense ways.

The Tron Theory of the physical world is constructed from the following Seven Axioms forming the Tron Postulate for the unseeable trons and rons. It is developed therefrom in congruence with established phenomena and data:

Axiom-1. Trons are particles that are very tiny, far tinier than electrons. Each tron is constructed in the same manner, with a miniscule mass-core that is embedded in a pliant cloud. Trons have minute mass and are neutral of charge.

Axiom-2. The tron's cloud is an array of numerous rons. Rons are particles similar to trons, but much minuter in size. The tron's core is formed of compressed rons. Rons thus underlie and support the trons. The rons in turn are similarly supported by even tinier ons.

Axiom-3. Rons are arranged around a tron core as a cloud of successive shells generally spherical in shape. The size of each ron is proportional to its distance from the tron's center. Each full ron-layer about a tron is made up of the same number of rons regardless of radial position. A tron's size or diameter is determined by the number of its ron-layers.

Axiom-4. An intrinsic characteristic of each tron is its continual potential to attract rons onto itself, and make its ron cloud bigger. Such ron attraction potential by each tron is inversely proportional to the radial position of its outer rons. Rons attract ons onto themselves in a similar manner.

Axiom-5. The size and shape of a tron stabilizes when its peripheral rons are the same size as the boundary rons of trons that surround it; and similarly for a ron as to contiguous ons.

Axiom-6. Tron displacements are communicated swiftly by corresponding displacements of the rons that are thereby peeled off the trons. The ron displacements are along paths of contiguous trons. The ron displacements are similarly telegraphed ahead by displacements ons along ron paths. In the density of tron space adjacent to the earth's surface the speed of ron transmission is the electro-magnetic $c$. This speed is lower through regions of higher tron density, and vice versa.

Axiom-7. The Universe is filled with myriads of trons. All trons are contiguous with other trons, throughout. Rons fill the interstices between contiguous trons. Ons fill the interstices between contiguous rons.

## 3. Discussion

Trons are represented in tron diagrams as small circles with a dot in the center. Their diameters indicate their relative "size". A larger tron has more ron layers and is thereby "softer" at its peripheral region than a smaller diameter tron. The ron is composed of successive on-layers, in similar relation. Fig 1 shows a cross section of a spherical tron. Its ron diameters increase with their radial position. There are innumerable ron-layers. The same number of rons are in each ron shell. The actual tron is tiny, with a most minute tron core (tc). The core (tc) is formed of compressed rons. The cloud (rc) of successive ron-layers is of generally spherical shape, as is the tron. See Axioms 1, 2, and 3.

Note, the concentric circles are only meant to represent ron layers and are not really part of a tron's structure. Also note that the outer boundary of a tron is not fixed. It is effectively the radius where the rons in a ron layer reach a maximum diameter. Beyond that point the rons begin to decrease in diameter as they are associated with the core of adjacent trons.

Trons will be seen to be very adaptable. The Tron Postulate sets each tron as attracting rons onto itself, onto its ron cloud (rc). This force of ron attraction increases as the diameter of the tron's cloud (rc) decreases, and vice versa.

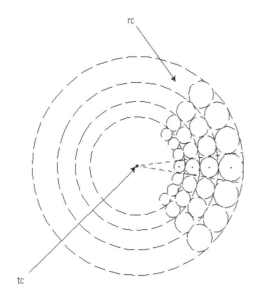

## Fig 1.

**Figure 1.** Cross Section of a Tron

It is a mechanical force, neutral of charge (Axiom-4). The tron attraction of rons is a characteristic of fundamental importance. It is the elemental force that trons exert to cohere with adjacent trons. Figure 2 is a plane view of cohering trons (ta). Figure 3 is a denser tron group (tb); its trons are smaller and have fewer of ron layers. A tron array is formable into a physical field. The electromagnetic and gravitational fields of space are diverse tron arrays, termed tronos.

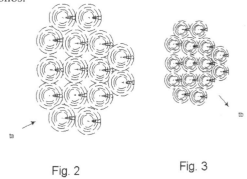

Fig. 2　　　　　　Fig. 3

When a group of trons are pressed together more compactly as from (ta) of Figure 2 to smaller trons in Figure 3, rons are released. The diameters of the ron-clouds (rc) of the trons (ta) reduce and rons flow out as ron-flux (rf) as indicated in Figure 4. The released rons are directly acquired by the adjacent outer trons (tb). Such ron absorption reduces the tron density of the outer tronos (tb), as the density of inner trons (ta) increases. Such displacement process or ron-flux (rf) and tron density change is signifi-

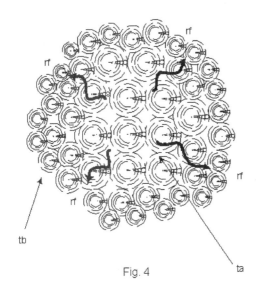

Figure 2.    Ron flux from central trons to outer trons

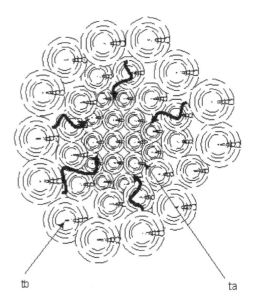

**Figure 3.**    Ron flux from outer trons to central trons

cant. It results in the generation and propagation of radiant waves through the tronos.

The ron-flux slows and then reverses when the inner tron group (ta) reaches its maximum density (minimum tron diameter) and the outer group (tb) reaches its minimum density (maximum tron diameter). The result is Figure 5. The inner trons of group (ta) exert their increased ron attraction potential on the surrounding larger diameter tron group (tb). Rons flow from the outer layers of the larger diameter trons (tb) to the outer layers of the smaller diameter trons (ta) in the center. The trons of inner tron group ta become larger in diameter and less dense while the trons of outer tron group tb become smaller in diameter and more dense until we return to the configuration of Figure 4. This dynamic cyclic interaction continues: the array of Fig 4 alternates with Fig 5. The amplitude of this exchange slowly decreases over time. Eventually an equilibrium is reached where the effective tron density is substantially uniform within the region; see Axiom-5. It is to be understood that these two dimensional tron diagrams actually represent three-dimensional entities and tron actions. The circles and lines of the diagrams are illustrative purposes and are not real.

In the Tron Theory basic phenomena are interrelated through their common tron heritage. Atoms have compressed trons as their cores and individual tron-surrounds about the cores. Matter is immersed in ambient tron-fields, termed tronos. Micro-particles are shown to interact continually with tronos in causal activity. Electric and gravitational fields are gradients of the density of trons in the tronos. Magnetic force arises from the displacement of trons. Radiant energy is generated by surging particles that create corresponding waves in their tronos, and propagate with transverse components. Physical processes and phenomena of the universe are presented as arising from the

Tron Postulate that applies in common from the nucleus to the galaxies; and applies to the electric, magnetic, and gravitational tronos. The tron-universe is the sum of its tron-constructed parts; see Axiom-7.

## 4. New insights into Relativistic and Quantum Phenomena

The Tron Theory reintroduces the concept of an ether. Electromagnetic fields have a material basis. It is asserted that the Tron Theory can account for the phenomena of classical as well as contemporary physics.

The diameter of a tron is that of its surrounding ron cloud, and is readily physically changeable. The size of a tron is influenced by the number of trons in its immediate region; namely by the tron density thereat. Nuclear binding energy is the enhanced force among tron groups that are highly compressed together at the core.

The interface of a parfield with its tronos field is shown to continually fluctuate, resulting in the incessant harmonic oscillation of the particle as a whole in the tronos. The causal continuous surges of microparticles can be analytically tracked. Such cyclic movements of micro-particles generate corresponding electromagnetic waves in their ambient tronos field, at the particle frequencies. Spectral radiation involves photons that are interrupted continuous wave trains, such as 10 million waves long, and even longer. Such trains result from shifts of electrons in orbit about their nuclei. Continuous spectra result from the superposition of the EM radiation generated by a group of particles with a distribution of kinetic energies like a black body. Each particle emits EM radiation at a frequency proportional to its kinetic energy ($E = hf$).

The Tron Theory provides fresh insights into atomic and sub-atomic processes: atoms in closer focus; micro-particles in causal movement; the generation, propagation and transfer of radiant energy in determinate display. The versatility of the Tron Theory unfolds as it is applied to physical disciplines.

The forces of nature, including nuclear binding force, emerge from the simple postulated characteristics of the trons and the rons. Matter does not appear or disappear from the universe. In a fusion reaction trons belonging to the nucleons are squeezed out from where the nucleons join. They become disassociated from the nucleons and become part of the local tronos. A part of the potential energy of the released trons is transferred to the tronos - the local tron density (which is proportional to its potential energy) is increased. The other part of the potential energy is converted into kinetic energy - the motion of trons in the tronos (including electromagnetic waves) and the motion of the micro-particles involved in the fusion reaction.

1. The fundamental particles (electrons and nucleons) are derived elementally out of a tronos by the concentration of trons from the tronos into structured cores for the particles. Trons thereupon directly surround each core in successive tron layers, forming a relatively less dense parfield to complete each particle.

2. The radius of the parfield inherently oscillates harmonically in its ambient tronos. This causes the velocity (and therefore instantaneous kinetic energy) of a free micro-particle to vary harmonically about its average observed velocity. The wavelength of these oscillations is the De Broglie wavelength. We can now calculate a particle's exact position and momentum simultaneously all times.

5. The particle oscillations generate radiant waves in the tronos, ahead of their movement. The frequencies of these waves are the same as the concurrent frequencies of their associated particles ($f = E/h$).

6. Radiant phenomena are shown to be a mechanistic process involving the generation of continuous waves as well as truncated trains (i.e. pulses) of continuous waves. Such waves propagate through the tronos at electromagnetic speed. They are equivalent to what are today called photons.

The density of the tronos is proportional to its potential energy. It is inversely proportional to its distance from a center of mass and is proportional to the magnitude of the mass:

$d = kM/r$

d = tronos density (trons/cm3), M is the magnitude of the mass center, r is the distance, and k is a constant (to be determined).

It is asserted that the minute mass of individual trons in the interstellar tronos is the explanation of the nature dark matter. The reason why experiments haven't been able to detect dark matter particles or observe radiation from dark matter is that dark matter is actually the mass of the tronos; it is the medium that transmits EM radiation. Note that the distribution of dark matter calculated from

measuring the orbital velocity of the stars in a galaxy is approximately $1/r$. This corresponds to the gravitational potential function ($U = km/r$) and therefore to the mass density of the tronos.

Also note, the velocity of electromagnetic waves is inversely proportional to the density of the tronos. This accounts for the bending of light by a star.

One also finds a calmer cosmology: The red shift is seen to result from an imperceptible but nonetheless continual energy loss occurring in stellar radiant waves as they propagate through the intergalactic tronos. It does not arise from the expansion of the universe or Doppler shift of receding galaxies.

The energetic cauldron found at the cores of galaxies provides the extreme conditions where trons are condensed into electrons and nucleons.

## 5. Conclusion

Is it not reasonable to surmise that matter, fields, and the basic forces of Nature all derive from a common underlying tiny entity? And that multitudes of such entities would be involved in the formation of electrons and nucleons. Each such entity would be much smaller than the electron and have a very minute mass. Myriads of such particles would form into arrays as the respective physical fields. These particles would possess a generic form of attraction that would constitute electric, nuclear and gravitational force. Such an underlying entity is shown to be the tron; its involvement in Nature is the Tron Theory.

The Tron Theory is built from the Tron Postulate. It asserts that everything physical is made up of trons and that Nature's fields, forces, and interactions involve trons. The tiny tron could well be the primordial material. The tron theory reveals insights that expand one's knowledge and perspective of physical Nature.

One may ask: why should we consider a radical new approach to the structure and operation of Nature? One cannot alter the facts and factors of physical phenomena. However, let us consider: A new theory may better penetrate the micro-world, or view the cosmos with more meaning. The tron theory does both, and much more. With the seven-axiom Tron Postulate, a unified approach for matter, the fields, and the forces and energies of Nature is developed. It provides a firm basis for radiant energy generation and its propagation; for electrical, magnetic and chemical phenomena, and atom formation.

It will be shown that the fountainhead of the basic energies, as well as the ultimate source of the basic forces including nuclear binding energy, derive from trons and their physical characteristics. Its elemental phenomena and matter are developed in three-dimension form, and in causal relationship.

It does not require the doctrines of Special or General Relativity, Indeterminacy, Complementarity, or Duality. It proposes a Universe that is fundamentally rational and causal.

The Tron Theory accomplishes these physical insights and correlations:

(a) It provides a consistent basis that unifies matter, the fields, and the fundamental forces of Nature, with a common underlying substanceâĄętrons. (b) It resolves the duality of radiant waves versus photons and particle mass versus particle waves. (c) It formulates quantum phenomena in causal format with continuous parameters for the dynamic actions of particles. Micro-particle action can be analyzed deterministically. (d) It presents the essence of Nature's phenomena and processes in a way that can be clearly visualized. It is congruent with real observations and determinations.

With the Tron Theory one may view the universe with its physical parts interrelated on a tron basis. The theory starts with trons and proceeds from the infinitesimal to the galactic cluster. When one formulates Nature's basic entities and processes in their tron settings, a three-dimensional universe is realized.

## 6. Appendix

This paper has presented the fundamental description of the tron, and the Tron Postulate. Future papers will explore the topics presented here in detail.

It should be noted that the author conceived the concept of the wave nature of particles being a harmonic oscillation in the velocity of the particle in the early 1960's. He called it the Vibra Theory. An almost identical concept was derived independently by Petr Beckmann's in his book, "Einstein Plus Two" [1]. He deserves credit for the concept; he derives it directly from E/M theory with the of a local entrained ether.

## REFERENCES

1. Petr Beckmann, *Einstein Plus Two, 1987*, Golem Press, New York, ISBN: 0-911762-39-61987.

# The Theory of Reality

## Steven C Mulford

*750 Franklin Rd APT 29-H, Marietta, Georgia, 30067, yobeht@gmail.com*

Standing on the shoulders of giants; Galileo, Newton, Maxwell, Hubble, and Arp. This paper not only rejects the Big Bang and Einstein's Relativity, but also creates a logical replacement, which is easier to compute and non-metaphysical. Using a new energy-mass equivalence formula to demonstrate examples with muons, at CERN, and more. Time Dilation is only a visual effect. This paper also solves the Theory of Everything, as gravity is simply an illusion. Expansion and electro-magnetism create these effects that feel like gravity. All matter expands, when their nuclei spin. Heat is this enlargement of an atom. A new way to synchronize up GPS satellites. Plasma currents flow through the entire universe. New black holes that have no singularities, as they are a phenomena of extreme charge, and weaken over time. The Black Hole is renamed to Galaxian Magnitizer or Gmag for short. Analyzing gamma ray bursts of the types of Long-Soft and Short-Hard. The 1919 Gravitational Lensing experiment was a hoax. Red shifting is due to Recessional Velocity, the Youth Factor, and the age of light. Thus, the universe does not need to expand and Dark Energy is unnecessary. Quantum Effects are due to electrostatics. Experiments that can prove it all.

**Keywords:** Energy-Mass Formula, Time Dilation, Theory of Everything, Expansion, Electro-Magnetism , Heat, GPS, Plasma Currents, Gmag, GRB, Gravitational Lensing, Red Shift, Dark Energy, Quantum, Experiments

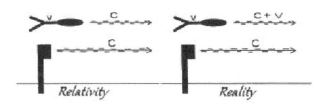

**Figure 1.** Einstein is restricted by his Invariance of Light.

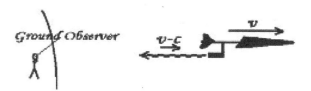

**Figure 2.** Craft turns invisible as the photons do not reach.

## 1. Introduction

It is vital for mankind to adopt this theory, for the survival and prosperity of all of humanity. All the resources humans could ever need are out in the vastness of the universe, just waiting for us, but Relativity blinds our mentality to dramatically underestimate these resources. This is because, the Twin Paradox suggests when a person travels at very high speeds to the nearest star and back, all of the traveler's friends and family will have aged a century more than oneself. No one would want to travel in such conditions. Also, being limited to a velocity of c, it would take lifetimes to get to the nearest star anyway. Instead, if we simply allow ourselves to surpass c, then we can travel to the nearest star in just a decade, if we travel at a constant acceleration of 4g.

## 2. Assumptions

### 2.1. Invariance of light

Because Einstein was wrong in his belief of the Invariance of Light, to make his data accurate, he had to alter the constants of physics; mass, space, and time. This theory strives to keep physics intuition based, simply by keeping these constants of physics, constant. The universe is only three-dimensional, as we can only move forward and back, up and down, and side to side. Man cannot move through time. Light travels at c, greater than the velocity of its source. There is no limit to velocity of any object, mass never increases due to acceleration, and time is just a tool to schedule events.

### 2.2. Time Dilation

Time Dilation is nothing more than a visual effect. An observer will see an object traveling away from oneself in slow motion, due to each light beam of the next instant having to travel a further distance.

[1] "At a constant distance from the observer the revolution of the sails appears to be just as quick as it actually is. If, however, the observer moves very quickly away, the revolution must appear slower, because the light from each successive position reaches him later."

An object accelerating faster than c, in respect to the observer, would visually disappear, since light emitted from the object back to the observer will have a velocity away from the observer.

### 2.3. Energy-Mass Equivalence

Einstein would state mass and energy are interchangeable always. This theory claims energy and mass are interchangeable only while particles are being formed, to allow one to sustain the constancy of mass. This theory does not have to use the Lorentz Transformations to alter one's data before using Einstein's equation. Just use the Galilean raw data instead.

## 3. Energy-Mass Formula

### 3.1. Formula

$$E = \frac{mc}{sqrt v^2 + c^2} \qquad (1)$$

### 3.2. Muons

Muons are created when protons traveling at high velocities from the universe strike the Earth's atmosphere, breaking apart into muons and other bits. Due to their half life, they exist for only 2.2 microseconds, thus Relativity limited to a velocity of c, suggest these muons can only pass through a small portion of the atmosphere before decaying, however these muons are commonly recorded to strike the surface of the Earth. Relativists suggest the length of the atmosphere itself reduces by a factor of (gamma), via Length Contraction. However, by allowing velocities to surpass c, Length Contraction is not necessary. Simply travelling at a velocity of $\gamma * c$, for those 2.2 microseconds, the muons travel the entire atmospheric length to the surface of the Earth.

### 3.3. Proof

$$E = \frac{mc^2}{\sqrt{1 - \frac{u^2}{c^2}}} \qquad (2)$$

Relativity's velocity is u and is capped at c.

$$p = mv = \frac{mu}{\sqrt{1 - \frac{u^2}{c^2}}} \qquad (3)$$

Setting the momentum equal to each other

$$v = \frac{u}{\sqrt{1 - \frac{u^2}{c^2}}} \qquad (4)$$

Ratio of velocity between theories, Solve for u:

$$v^2 = \frac{u^2}{1 - \frac{u^2}{c^2}} \qquad (5)$$

$$u^2 = v^2 - \frac{V^2 u^2}{c^2} \qquad (6)$$

$$v^2 c^2 - v^2 u^2 = u^2 c^2 \qquad (7)$$

$$v^2 c^2 = u^2 c^2 + u^2 v^2 = u^2(c^2 + v^2) \qquad (8)$$

$$u^2 = \frac{v^2 c^2}{c^2 + v^2} \qquad (9)$$

$$u = \frac{vc}{\sqrt{v^2 + c^2}} \qquad (10)$$

Plug u into Einstein's energy equation

$$E = \frac{mc^2}{\sqrt{1 - \frac{\frac{vc}{\sqrt{v^2+c^2}}^2}{c^2}}} \qquad (11)$$

$$E = \frac{mc^2}{\sqrt{1 - \frac{\frac{v^2 c^2}{v^2+c^2}}{c^2}}} \qquad (12)$$

$$E = \frac{mc^2}{\sqrt{1 - \frac{v^2}{v^2+c^2}}} \qquad (13)$$

$$E^2 = \frac{m^2 c^4}{1 - \frac{v^2}{v^2+c^2}} \qquad (14)$$

$$E^2 - \frac{E^2 v^2}{v^2 + c^2} = m^2 c^4 \qquad (15)$$

$$E^2 v^2 + E^2 c^2 - E^2 v^2 = m^2 c^4 v^2 + m^2 c^6 \qquad (16)$$

$$E^2 = m^2 c^2 v^2 + m^2 c^4 = m^2 c^2(v^2 + c^2) \qquad (17)$$

$$E = mc\sqrt{v^2 + c^2} \qquad (18)$$

### 3.4. CERN

Scientists at CERN do not realize what the speeds of the protons are. Billions of them make up two beams traveling anti-parallel. These beams are brought closer together via a magnetic force until collision. They have no idea the actual positions of individual protons inside these beams. They simply push the limits of their machinery up to 7TeV. Relativity states protons traveling at .99999999c contain a mass 7450 times their rest mass. However, using this theory, one can show these protons are actually traveling at 7463c with normal mass.

### 3.5. Math

$$E = mc\sqrt{v^2 + c^2} \qquad (19)$$

$$7TeV = \sqrt{v^2 + c^2} \frac{938 MeV}{c} \qquad (20)$$

$$7TeV^2 = \left(\frac{938 MeV}{c}\right)^2 (v^2 + c^2) \qquad (21)$$

$$7TeV^2 = 938 MeV^2 + 938 MeV^2 \left(\frac{v}{c}\right)^2 \qquad (22)$$

$$7TeV^2 - 938 MeV^2 = 938 MeV^2 \left(\frac{v}{c}\right)^2 \qquad (23)$$

$$v = c\sqrt{\frac{7TeV^2}{938 MeV^2} - \frac{938 MeV^2}{938 MeV^2}} \qquad (24)$$

$$v = c\sqrt{\frac{4.9E25eV}{8.7985E17eV} - 1} \qquad (25)$$

$$v = c\sqrt{5.5691E7 - 1} \qquad (26)$$

$$v = 7462.64c \qquad (27)$$

$$Accurate Velocity = c\sqrt{\frac{Total Energy^2}{Rest Energy^2} - 1} \qquad (28)$$

$$E = mc\sqrt{v^2 + c^2}$$

**Figure 3.** Mass is constant. Velocity is unlimited. Does anything Einstein could but with increased accuracy and simplicity.

A simple computation that is mostly accurate, it gets more accurate as velocity increases:

$$v = c\frac{TotalEnergy}{RestEnergy} \tag{29}$$

$$v = c\frac{7TeV}{938MeV} \tag{30}$$

$$v = 7462.687c \tag{31}$$

### 3.6. Adding Frequency

$$E = mc\sqrt{v^2 + c^2}\frac{f}{Hz} \tag{32}$$

### 3.7. Photons
Photons are particles with frequency and little mass.
### 3.8. Deducing Mass of a Photon

$$When\, v = c : E = hf = mc\sqrt{c^2 + c^2}\frac{f}{Hz} \tag{33}$$

$$When\, v = c : E = hf = mc^2\sqrt{2}\frac{f}{Hz} \tag{34}$$

$$hf = mc^2\sqrt{2}\frac{f}{Hz} \tag{35}$$

$$h = 4.13567E - 15(eV)(s) \tag{36}$$

$$mc^2\sqrt{2}\frac{1}{Hz} = 4.13567E - 15(eV)(s) \tag{37}$$

$$m = 4.13567E - 15\frac{eV}{\sqrt{2}c^2} \tag{38}$$

$$m = 2.92436E - 15\frac{eV}{c^2} \tag{39}$$

### 3.9. Examples
Say we need to activate an electron to be released from a material which requires 10 eV activation energy. This can be done with increased frequency, velocity, or a combination of both of the striking photon. With a velocity of 6.8c, what is the frequency?

$$E = \frac{mc}{sqrt v^2 + c^2}\frac{f}{Hz} \tag{40}$$

$$10eV = 2.92436E - 15\frac{eVf\sqrt{(7.8c)^2}}{cHz} \tag{41}$$

$$10Hz = 2.92436E - 15f\sqrt{7.8^2} \tag{42}$$

$$f = \frac{10Hz}{22.81E - 15} \tag{43}$$

$$f = 4.384E14Hz \tag{44}$$

Einstein is incapable of relating these.
To test against Relativity, set velocity to c:

$$E = mc\sqrt{c^2 + c^2}\frac{f}{Hz} \tag{45}$$

$$10eV = \sqrt{2}\frac{2.92436E - 15eV f}{Hz} \tag{46}$$

$$10Hz = \sqrt{2}2.92436E - 15f \tag{47}$$

$$f = \frac{10Hz}{4.1357E - 15} \tag{48}$$

$$f = 2.41797E15Hz \tag{49}$$

Einstein would do it like this:

$$E = (h)(f) \tag{50}$$

$$h = 4.13567E - 15(eV)(s) \tag{51}$$

$$E = 10eV = (4.13567E - 15eV(s)(f) \tag{52}$$

$$10Hz = 4.13567E - 15(f) \tag{53}$$

$$f = \frac{10Hz}{4.13567E - 15} \tag{54}$$

$$f = 2.41799E15Hz \tag{55}$$

## 4. Expansion

### 4.1. Gravity
[2] "When we measure gravity the only thing that can be positively verified is that, here on the surface of the earth, gravity is an extremely constant upward acceleration. All of the Famous Gravity Theories began by completely ignoring gravity's only experiment fact and then crafting magical assumptions such as fields, infinite attractions, curved space-times, moving aethers, impinging virtual particles etc. All of these assumptions are metaphysical in nature and thus not subject to any positive experimental verification. All of this just to refuse to step back and look at what gravity is actually doing.

Gravity can only be measured as a constant upward acceleration. Therefore, we must conclude that gravity is just an upward acceleration. This acceleration can only result from the linear expansion of the matter comprising the earth. It is this universal expansion of matter that is the simple and local cause of gravity."

The g-forces felt clinging one to the Earth, thought to be gravity, is actually the expansion of all atoms of the Earth taking up more space. Atoms expand because their galactic magnetic field causes their nuclei to spin, creating their own magnetic field that accelerates their electrons. This enlarges the electron-shell, which denotes the electrostatic border between atoms.

Quantised energy levels still exist and stay proportional to the expansion. As matter gets larger, so too does the measuring instruments, thus the expansion of all matter is visually unnoticeable, due to everything expanding in proportion. An accelerometer free falling toward Earth will register an acceleration of zero, but once it comes to rest on the Earth, the accelerometer will register g.

When an apple appears to fall from a tree to the ground, the apple actually remains at its constant initial velocity equal to the branch at the moment of disconnection. Then, as the atoms of the Earth expand, this forces the branch, which is physically connected to the Earth, to accelerate away. Also the surface of the Earth accelerates up and crashes into the apple.

When a skydiver jumps out of a plane, the skydiver no longer gets lift from the plane, and stays with its initial constant velocity equal to the plane at the moment of disconnection. The plane accelerates upward away from the skydiver due to its lift. The atoms of the Earth expand, causing the surface of the Earth to accelerate upward at g toward the skydiver. And the atmosphere is pressed up and around the skydiver creating the air resistance.

### 4.2. GPS

Acceleration causes atomic clocks to mechanically slow down, like pendulum clocks mechanically speed up. Once in free fall, all atomic clocks tick at its rest state 43,700 ns per day faster than the clocks on Earth, as the clocks avoid the acceleration of the Earth's expansion.

Also, the centripetal acceleration slows down these clocks. As the orbital radius of the atomic clocks increase, they run faster due to less centripetal acceleration.

Atomic clocks slow down this much when accelerating, 10,053 ns per day : 1 meter per $s^2$

$0.568$ meter per $s^2 = \frac{(3,900m)^2}{26,752,000ms^2}$

$0.568 * 10,053$ ns per day $= 5,700$ ns per day.

$43,700 - 5,700$ ns per day $= 38,000$ ns per day

Relativity sync up atomic clocks aboard orbiting GPS satellites using velocity and elevation. These clocks are sped up 45,000 ns per day due to less gravity at an orbit of 4.18 Earth radii. Also the clocks are slowed by 7,000 ns per day due to time-dilation from their high velocity of 3.9 kilometer per second.

$45,000 - 7,000$ ns per day $= 38,000$ ns per day

### 4.3. Heat

Heat is not due to vibrations in solids and liquids, nor particles randomly bouncing back and forth in gasses. An atom is hotter than another if the electron shell is proportionally larger. Heat will transfer from the larger atom to the smaller until both atoms are of the proportionally the same size. This trend is obvious as solids are the smallest and coldest, then liquids, then gasses are the hottest and largest of atoms. In the even hotter, plasma state, the electron shell is so large it escapes the nucleus. Undisturbed gasses do not move about at all, as air can become stale in caves or tunnels. A hot air balloon rises as the hot gas molecules are proportionally larger and less dense than the surrounding molecules, simply creating pressure.

## 5. Electro-Magnetism

### 5.1. Galaxian Magnetizer or Gmag

A Gmag is created when a star explodes, when it is

**Figure 4.** Molecules of equal size randomly bouncing off walls of balloon and one another.

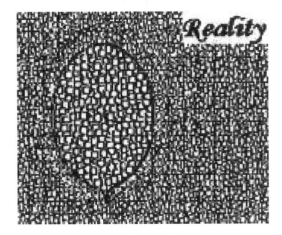

**Figure 5.** Size variable molecules stagnant while undisturbed

too old and hot. The nuclei can no longer electrostatically attract inward their electron shell, as the electrons are too far from the nuclei. All the electrons are thrown outward at very high velocities, bombarding objects, making them more (-), and joining the currents of the plasma universe. The nuclei are left behind to implode via the strong force, creating a (+) giant nucleus.

The stars, planets, and other (-) matter in the universe are attracted toward the (+) Gmag. Neutral matter drifts

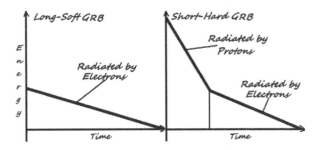

**Figure 6.** Gamma Ray Bursts

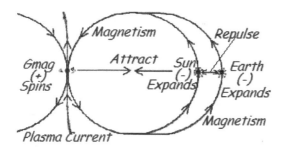

**Figure 7.** The universal plasma current flows up through the Gmag causing it to spin.

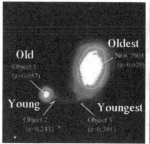 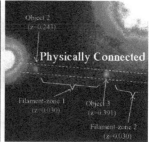

**Figure 8.** [6]"There are many cases of low-redshift galaxies that are physically associated with high-redshift galaxies and quasars"

into a Gmag via induced electrostatic attraction. The event horizon is a function of the massive electrostatic potential. The molecules are stretched and ripped apart, as the (+) nuclei are flung outward, and the (-) electrons are pulled in to collide with the Gmag.

The Gmag creates a neutron with every collision with an electron and neutralizes its charge slightly. Eventually this process will turn the Gmag into a neutron star. These neutrons stars are detected as pulsars, because in the past the Gmag was spun very fast from the Universal Plasma Jets passing through them.

### 5.2. Long-Soft Gamma Ray Bursts

Created when a star explodes, causing massive amount of electrons to accelerate radiating high energy photons. The afterglow of this burst exists for months to even years afterward, as the great quantity of electrons strike the surroundings in their pathways. When these impacts occur, the electrons are decelerated, radiating photons for a second time. This afterglow contains a mix of lower energy photons, as the electrons strike surrounding objects of different locations to radiate. These speedy electrons can travel much distance away before striking an object, which radiation will be redshifted and take some extra time to reach Earth.

### 5.3. Short-Hard Gamma Ray Bursts

Occur when matter enters a Gmag. These massive electrostatic forces tear apart the molecules, the electrons accelerated inward, and the nuclei accelerated outward. The initial mega spike of highest energy photons are the ones radiated from the acceleration of the protons, as they are heavier than electrons. The following lesser energy photons are due to being radiated from the accelerating electrons. The proton radiated photons arrive just before the electron radiated photons, as most of the protons have already been thrusted a little bit away from the Gmag, while they are still accelerating, and most of the electrons have been pulled in a little bit by the Gmag. The afterglow occurs only briefly as the quantity of particles thrown outward is much less.

### 5.4. Universal Plasma Flow

Matter expands taking up more space, and repulsion keeping these objects proportionally at distance via magnetism and electrostatics. Universal plasma currents flow

through the (+) Galaxian Magnetizer, causing it to spin very fast, creating a powerful magnetic field that expands across the entire galaxy. The Sun, Earth, and all galactic objects are (-) and share this magnetic field created from the Gmag in the center of their galaxy. Orbiting satellites receive a (-) charge when passing through the ionosphere of the Earth on takeoff. Allowing them to stay in orbit via repulsion, with a minimum tangential velocity.

## 6. Red Shift

[3]"The evidence that many objects previously believed to be at great distances are actually much closer confronts us with the most drastic possible revision of current concepts."

### 6.1. Gravitational Lensing

[4]"Initially, stars did 'appear' to bend as they should as required by Einstein, but then, the unexpected happened; several stars were then observed to bend in a direction transverse to the expected direction and still others bent in a direction opposite to that predicted by relativity."

Even though the machinery failed due to heat waves, Eddington was overly determined to prove Einstein's theory correct. Eddington discarded 85 percent of the data, being afraid people would figure out the truth. In the end, he submitted only two photos to be published. At the time, the scientific community found this outrageous, and did not except this expedition as any proof.

[5]"That's what the astronomer Arthur Eddington did in 1919 when he cherry-picked among his observations of an eclipse. The idea was to prove Einstein's general theory of relativity. However, Eddington's analysis of the data was questionable enough for the Nobel Prize committee to exclude relativity from Einstein's 1921 Nobel Prize for physics. Assessing the merits of relativity was impossible until it was 'confirmed in the future,' the committee said."

### 6.2. Einstein Cross

[7]"Fritz Zwicky started looking for an extragalactic object which might be directly behind another, and thus have its outer light rays bent inward by the gravitational field of the foreground object so that it formed a ring or halo. Some 'ring galaxies' were found, but they all seemed to be physical rings around the galaxy and not magnified background objects. The more common situation to be

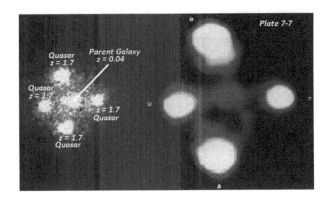

**Figure 9.**   The Eistein Cross

expected was when the background object was not exactly centered and the gravitational ring collapsed into an one sided arc. But no striking examples of that were found either, so the subject had gone dormant. The sudden revival of gravitational lensing to the huge industry it is today is simply due to the quasars.

Color Plate 7-7 shows the breathtaking result: the western quasar (D) is connected directly into the elongated galaxy nucleus! There is absolutely no way to escape the overall result that the quasars are connected and generally elongated toward the low redshift nucleus... There is a putative Lyman alpha filament connecting quasar D to the galaxy nucleus. What is the spectrum had confirmed was that this indeed was a low density, excited hydrogen filament connecting the two objects of vastly different redshift. We are again seeing trails of material resulting from ejection and tendencies for orthogonal ejection from the parent galaxy."

Modern physicists believe there is just one quasar far away in the background, lensed into four. However, this forces them to assume the quasar is ultra luminous, as its radiation must travel across the 'entire universe.' Instead, the Einstein Cross is simply four new quasars that have been ejected from their older parent galaxy. This means the quasars are really only moderately luminous, because they are actually much closer. Also these Einstein Arcs are ejections from central parent galaxies as well, combined with gasses and plasmas.

### 6.3. Doppler Shift

[8]"'If the redshifts are a Doppler shift ... the observations as they stand lead to the anomaly of a closed universe, curiously small and dense, and, it may be added, suspiciously young. On the other hand, if redshifts are not Doppler effects, these anomalies disappear and the region observed appears as a small, homogeneous, but insignificant portion of a universe extended indefinitely both in space and time.' But the analogy between the Doppler effect in sound waves and the observed redshift in light was so compelling to astronomers that they quickly dropped Hubble's cautionary 'if.' "

### 6.4. Static Universe

[? ]"The false dawn of universal expansion came from faulty data. Edwin Hubble was the first to realize it. '...it seems likely that red-shifts may not be due to an expanding Universe, and much of the speculation of the structure of the universe may require re-examination.'"

Because modern physicists assumed Hubble's Redshift was only recessional velocity, this demands that the universe to expand at an accelerating rate. If instead Hubble's Redshift was also do to the Youth Factor and the age of light. The universe does not need to expand at all.

### 6.5. Red Shift Triality

The Youth Factor occurs when a new galaxy or atom is created, they are at their highest redshift and smallest size in proportion. As they get older, the electron shell increases causes more energetic photons. Losing redshift as they age.

Photons use up energy to exist and create light. For every second a photon exists the redshift increases by a certain amount.

A Gmag's redshift is opposite of that of matter, as the Gmag does not contain atoms. It is blue-shifted when it is created due to the Gmag being of strongest positivity. The first electron accelerates faster than any other electron that will be accelerated into that Gmag. This highest acceleration of a charged particle cause photons to radiate at their highest energies, creating the most blue-shift during the infancy of a Gmag.

### 6.6. Fading Redshift

Arp's reason why red shift fades over time was due to electrons getting more massive over time. This would cause the acceleration of these heavier electrons to radiate more energetic photons over time.

[? ]"If the mass of an electron jumping from an excited atomic orbit to a lower level is smaller, then the energy of the photon of light emitted is smaller. If the photon is weaker it is redshifted. Lower-mass electrons will give higher redshifts and that younger electrons would be expected to have lower mass."

However, one can not alter this constant, mass. Reality can explain what is really going on. When matter ages, the atom's electron energy levels get further apart, due to expansion accelerating these electrons. So now, the electron has to jump a further distance to change energy level. This requires more voltage potential to be built up to send the electron, thus the electron is accelerated at a higher rate. This greater acceleration of a charged particle causes more energetic photons to be radiated. Due to this increase in the energy of radiation, the redshift diminishes as matter ages.

## 7. Quantum Mechanics

The effects of Quantum Mechanics during any slit experiment are created due to the electrostatics of passing by very closely to the negative edge of all matter. Electrons repulse away from the edge of matter because it is a negative particle. Protons attract inward from because it is a positive particle. Molecules repulse away from the edge of matter because of the negative electron shell. Photons too repulse away because of its negative shell of some type. Photons must behave like a tiny atoms.

## 8. Experiments

### 8.1. Atomic Clocks

Time Dilation suggests atomic clocks slow down due to cruising at high velocities, however using the Theory of Reality, these clocks mechanically slow down due to the smashing effect of g-forces via accelerating, decelerating, and turbulence. To test this, one could place an atomic clock on board of a plane, fly it at a certain elevation for a short flight. Then fly another atomic clock on a flight at the same elevation and cruise velocity for a much longer flight. Relativists would state the longer flight would be slowed down more, due to cruising at higher velocities longer. With this theory, the atomic clocks ought to be the same, as they experience equal accelerations. Keep in mind turbulence has a slowing effect also and needs to be accounted for.

### 8.2. Surpassing the Speed of Light

Going beyond c will appear to disappear. Send an unmanned craft with enough acceleration to watch it break the invariance of light. Einstein would state it is impossible as the mass goes to infinity. Without this restriction, it is very simple. Or one could have a source travel at high velocities and measure the speed of its light. It should be faster than c, but need to keep in mind most modern devices cannot detect faster than c.

## 9. Conclusion

New technology will only take us in circles if we do not have the proper mindset to fully embrace it. Luckily we have the internet at our fingertips nowadays, opening our eyes to what is truly going on in the universe. Mankind must move to another planet before the Earth is no long livable. We are going to need to travel at least to the next solar system, but more likely have to travel to the next galaxy to find a livable planet. If we just let ourselves surpass c, all of these problems are solved. Technology needs to advance in the direction of applying g force to the human body and gear to travel faster.

## REFERENCES

1. Harry H. Mark, *C the Speed of Light: A Tale of Scientific Blunder.*, iUniverse, New York Bloomington, p. 912010.
2. James Carter, *The Other Theory of Physics.*, Absolute Motion Institute, p. 972010.
3. H. Arp, *Catalogue of Discordant Redshift Associations.*, Apeiron, Montreal, p. 462003.
4. G. Burniston Brown, *What is Wrong With Relativity?.*, texttthttp://homepage.ntlworld.com/academ/ whatswrongwithrelativity.html, 1927.
5. Michael Brooks, *Scientists Behaving Badly.*, texttthttp://www.huffingtonpost.com/michael-brooks/scientists-behaving-badly_b_1448729.html, 2012.
6. David Pratt, *Trends in Cosmology: Beyond the Big Bang, Redshift Controversies.*, texttthttp://davidpratt.info/cosmo.htm#c3, 2012.
7. H. Arp, *Seeing Red.*, Apeiron, Montreal, p. 169-1751998.
8. Hilton Ratcliffe, *The Static Universe: Exploding the Myth of Cosmic Expansion.*, Apeiron, Montreal, p. 252010.
9. I. Newton, *Mathematical Principles of Natural Philosophy.*, 2000.

# Non-Conservativeness of Natural Orbital Systems

## Slobodan Nedić

*University of Novi Sad, Faculty of Technical Sciences, DEET*
*Trg Dostieja Obradovića 6, 21000 Novi Sad, Serbia, nedics@uns.ac.rs; nedic.slbdn@gmail.com*

The Newtonian mechanic and contemporary physics model the non-circular orbital systems on all scales as essentially conservative, closed-path zero-work systems and circumvent the obvious contradictions (rotor-free 'field' of 'force', in spite of its inverse proportionality to squared time-varying distance) by exploiting both energy and momentum conservation, along specific initial conditions, to be arriving at technically more or less satisfactory solutions, but leaving many of unexplained puzzles. In sharp difference to it, in recently developed thermo-gravitational oscillator approach movement of a body in planetary orbital systems is modeled in such a way that it results as consequence of two counteracting mechanisms represented by respective central forces, that is gravitational and anti-gravitational accelerations, in that the actual orbital trajectory comes out through direct application of the Least Action Principle taken as minimization of work (to be) done or, equivalently, a closed-path integral of increments (or time-rate of change) of kinetic energy. Based on the insights gained, a critique of the conventional methodology and practices reveals shortcomings that can be the cause of the numerous difficulties the modern physics has been facing: anomalies (as gravitational and Pioneer 10/11), three or more bodies problem, postulations in modern cosmology of dark matter and dark energy, the quite problematic foundation of quantum mechanics, etc. Furthermore, for their overcoming, indispensability of the Aether as an energy-substrate for all physical phenomena is gaining a very strong support, and based on recent developments in Aetherodynamics the Descartes' Vortex Physics may become largely reaffirmed in the near future.

**Keywords:** gravity, anti-gravity, orbital motion, open systems, aether physics, vortex physics

## 1. Introduction

Following the Newton's fitting of elliptical planetary orbits to the single central force inversely proportional to the square of its distance to the Sun, all natural systems - from atomic to galactic scales - have been treated as non-conservative (work over closed loop in the field of potential force equaling to zero). The exclusive reliance on gravitation as the only central force does not allow for the formally exact prediction of the planet's trajectories in accordance with the Kepler's First law [1], and furthermore orbit fitting to an elliptical shape is contingent on the initial conditions [2]. The basic shortcoming of Newton's theory of orbital motion is the presumed absence of the tangential acceleration component, quite contrary to well established observational results, which is deduced either from the 'naive' interpretation of the Kepler's Third law, which actually is related to the average values of the orbital radius and elapsed time, or from the improper interpretation of Kepler's Second law as angular momentum, its presumed constancy implying only the circular motion.

For theoretical foundations and practical calculations the factual time-dependence of the force (thus non-zero rotor field) is neglected and one proceeds from the constancy of the sum of kinetic and potential energies, on one side, and the constancy of the angular momentum, on the other, although in actuality neither of the two is the case. Only recently, within explorations of biological molecular systems, as well as in certain domains of particle physics, the need starts arising for looking at such systems as non-conservative, the so-called "open systems", which within the classical formalisms turn out to become the "non-integrable" orbital systems (inability to be reduced to "circular coordinates" by even applying the time-varying transformations of the coordinate systems). This has led to modifications and specializations of the formalisms of the classical axiomatic mechanics having been developed by Euler, Lagrange, Hamilton, Noether and others for essentially conservative systems to be applicable to the non-conservative ones. However, a critical analysis of the matters suggests that all the natural orbital systems are open, that is non-conservative (including the planetary, atomic and galactic ones), and that neither the energy nor the (angular) impulse is constant over the time, so that the very basic foundations turn out to be erroneous.

Although epistemologically quite appealing, the Le Sage's theory of gravitation as an effect of the objects'mutual shadowing from a postulated isotropically acting energy-agent could hardly pass the test of producing the well-entrenched Newton gravitational law, and the fairly successful reproductions of its mass-depended form [3] may only have hindered wider appreciation of its intrinsically dynamical nature. As the matter of fact, the Newton's gravitational law was derived in a rather tautological (circular) manner, relying on the 'larger' object's mass also in the definition of the gravitational constant. The incorporation of his third law of action and reaction, which even Newton himself had been reluctant to rely on explicitly (and despite many objections — notably Leibniz's statement that they cannot be simulateneously applied to the same body) into the theory of orbital motion, has been another misdeed, both with detrimental impact on the further development of physics, and the almost insurmountable difficulties it has been facing, including the forces' unification. On the other side, in the concept of Thermo-Gravitational Oscillator (TGO) [4] developed by combining Le Sageian gravitational and thermal as anti-gravitational changing of permittivity to the mutual shadowing 'pushing' effect, the central acceleration results in the form of two-components $(-a/r^2 + b/r^3)$ that Leibniz had proposed within his critique of the Newton's orbital dynamics, and without any reliance on the Newton's third law, by using M. Milanković's (one over r-squared) law of planets'warming. Besides an overview of the TGO concept, here are provided results of simulation which produce the non-zero minimal work for the nominal Keplerian ellipse, serving as a clear indication of invalidity of the traditional assumptions of the energy and angular momentum (erroneously related/identified to/by the Second Kepler's Law) time-constancy, that is 'conservation'.

The orbital trajectory is produced by direct minimization of the Work needed to be done over the 'closed' path, without any reliance on initial conditions (commonly considered as even a part of natural laws in the context of traditional minimization of variation of the Action - time-integral of difference of the kinetic and potential energies of an orbital body). While the gravitational constant (a, above) is considered as not the "universal" one (introduced as ratio of Kepler's constant and mass of the Sun, and measured on Earth by two metal balls!?) and basically dependable on actual configurations, the mass get entirely dropped-off from the considerations, and in place of it (in b, above) comes the body's thermal capacity (or its specific heat). As further support for righteousness of this approach can be offered that the same form of the central accelerations, i.e. the 'attractive' and 'repulsive' forces are manifested within the thoroidal vortex atomic-level structures, respectively for the ring (electric field related) and thoral (magnetic field related) streaming of the (gaseous Aether with viscosity nd compressibility) particles [5]. For the TGO-apprach it comes as a true 'miracle' that the vortexes related attractive and repulsive forces, in the context of the Aether as gaseous substance with viscosity and compressibility, along the lines of the pressure/velocity/temperature gradients and their impacts decrease and increase, respectively have exactly the same $(-a/r^2 + b/r^3)$ forms. Based on this is established groundlessness of the postulation of "dark" both matter and energy at the cosmological level as pursued by the conventional astrophysics, and the road is opened toward understanding the omnipresence of the Golden Mean relationship in nature at all scales. (While the formula for gravitational attraction derived by Atsukovsky in [5] supports gravitational constant's non-universality and involves thermal coefficients therein, its first approximation for relatively small distance reveals similarity with the Milgrom's

MOND theory conjecture on attraction force proportional to inverse of the relatively large distance. It might be quite interesting to note that the first approximation of the GTR, as well as of its counterpart proposed as an enhanced form in [6] turn out to formally have the same form as the two component central force in TGO (when taking out the inverse distance squared part), but in both parts then figures the same "universal gravitation constant" only, along the velocity of light in the anti-gravitational counterpart of b.)

In the following, firstly a related historical and philosophical account has been provided, followed by direct critical remarks to the Newtonian theory of orbital motion. Subsequently, the overview of derivation and conceiving of orbital motion as a dynamical equilibrium is provided, along the utilization of the formulation of the planetary temperature dependence in line with the Milutin Milanković's one-over-distance-squared-law, which leads to the two-component radial acceleration of the form proposed by Leibniz. Finally, along the conclusions, relevance to the outstanding problems and anomalies are provided, with a certain outlook to all natural systems.

## 2. A historical and philosophical perspective

By conceiving gravitation as Le Sageian effect of mutual shadowing, the room opens for both Aristotle's Unmoved Mover realm (which may have an analogon in the Aether substrate with both spontaneous and inducible structuring) and for his concept of 'virtual-' or 'hidden-forces', a form of (conditionally) contactless dynamic, for which the equality of Action and Reaction in terms of the Newton's Third Law may by far not hold. The reliance on this principle as applied in the Newton's non-circular orbital motion Leibniz had criticized on the ground of untenability of its object be the same body, as the'equilibrium' between the centrifugal and centripetal forces/accelerations imply, the stance he had supported by the two-component central acceleration, derivable (in case of the presumed constancy of the angular momentum) from the consistent vector calculus based dynamics of curvilinear motion.

To (it turns out virtually, due to still present central position of mass notion in modern physics, and in particular the postulated equivalence between its "gravitational" and "inertial" 'forms') refute the Aristotle's doctrine on falling bodies (the heavier ones fall 'quicker' than the lighter) it has needed a very long time-span - from Lucretius (cc. 99 - 55 BC, De Rerum Natura: " - wherefore all things carry on through the calm void, moving at equal rate with unequal weights", over quite numerous experimenters in 16-th century (Djuzepe Moletti, 1576 in Padova; Jakopo Maconi, 1579 in Pisa; Simon Stevin 1583 with Jan Koret Glot, in Delft), to Glileo Galilei's (in 1586) confirmation of those findings by inclined plain experiments, which have led to $s = 0.5 \cdot g \cdot t^2$.

In light of the subsequent TGO concept development overview, the same way the Aristotle's falling-body assertion was the "progress hampering" hypothesis, such was the Newton's concept of Gravity as the result of bodies's "mutual attraction". The Nikolas Fatio de Duillier's (1690) and Georges-Luois Le Sage's (1748) gravitation as effect of bodies mutual 'screening' (shadowing) from isotropic and homogeneous energy substance (ultra-mundane corpuscles) - a hypothesis which Newton (1642-1726) could have had an opportunity to (still) consider (vs. "Hypotheses non fingo"), kind of served to 'open' the particular orbital motion system towards its environment.

For the path that has led to the current unsatisfactory situation in physics of most importance seems to be the Newton's, and in particular of his followers, derailing of its development from the Descartes'Vortex Physics tracks. In that context the most symptomatic is the Newton's notebook, by him explicitly banned to be published [7], with his comments and apparent frustrations during the reading of Descartes' "Principles of Philosophy". Another resurfacing of the work not intended for publication is Feynman's scrutinizing and attempting to overcome the noticed week point in Newton's geometrical fitting of elliptical orbits to the central force inversely proportional to the squared distance is the above first cited [1], where Feynman had attempted to correct the inconsistency of Newton's geometrical fitting of the elliptic path to the squared distance inverse central force. It is deplorable indeed, that Feynman did not persevere and was not able to apply his favorite Least Action Principle to that problem, instead of stepping into the further support the otherwise unsoundingly set-up quantum mechanics by calculation of the (notably non-zero!?) works on all possible paths of an electron and assigning their reciprocal values to the probabilities, and further going into quite controversial development of the "Qauntum Gravity".

## 3. Critique of the conventional approach in solving the Kepler's/Newton's problems

When it comes to determining the intrinsic feature of an orbital system, that is whether is it conservative or non-conservative, by all means of prime importance is the topic of a system energy balancing — evaluation of difference between the de-facto performed work and the (knowingly) available applied energy (re)sources. If the former exceeds the latter, or if the traditionally conceived and established law of sum of kinetic and potential energy conservation does not 'hold', we must be missing the awareness of the true nature mechanisms and the availability of the unaccounted for 'environmental' effective energy input(s).

As the historically firstly considered, the Sun's planetary orbital system should indeed be the right one for these considerations, in particular that the established theory and its further developments have detrimentally affected all other physics' and in general science domains — form the atom- to galactic-levels, and from chemistry to biology. In direct relation to the orbital energy balancing stands the concept of energy conservation with the related work over a closed-path being equaled to zero, as intrinsic feature of the so-called potential fields (the 'central' force vector field having form of gradient of a scalar potential field).

Since the time-dependent central forces (or better, accelerations) for non-circular orbits evidently (due to the non-zero curl of the related force field vector) cannot basically belong to this category, for the commonly conducted analysis and the contradictions involved it is symptomatic that every effort has been made to avoid explication of the essential time-dependence of the orbital central force(s). In the following, in form of a 'dialog' with the critique (by Gerhard Bruhn) of the most famous critic (G. Bourbaki, alias of Goerges von Brauning) of the established practices of simultaneous use of both the energy and the momentum conservation principles [8] (with the translation from German by the author of this paper), evidence and comments will be provided towards debunking of this misleading approach, relying indeed on two erroneous and untenable premises — the (sum of kinetic and potential) energy conservation in the sense of its time-independence, on one, and the conservation of the angular momentum in spite of its factual non-constancy, that is the identification of the distance-squared-times-phase-first-derivative, $r^2\dot{\varphi}$, with the surface of area swept by the radius vector, on the other side. The very notion of potential energy as a negative 'quantity', while formally acceptable in static situations, has been largely 'misused' in the dynamical context with the mere (apparently, up-front intended) effect to trade it for the kinetic part over a closed path (or, rather, only the radial direction) to produce balance proclaimed for the feature of conservativeness, without any intentional (besides Feynman's purposeful) back-checking for the validity of such assumption by the evaluation of actual closed-loop work need/done on the same closed path.

"Central forces $\mathbf{F}(\mathbf{x},t)$ are always directed to a fixed point $\mathbf{x}_0$, wherein we place the origin $\mathbf{O}$ of the coordinate system:

$$\mathbf{F}(\mathbf{x},t) = \frac{\mathbf{x}}{r} f(\mathbf{x},t) \qquad (1)$$

Newton's movement equation for a solid punctual mass m then is:

$$m\ddot{\mathbf{x}} = \frac{\mathbf{x}}{r} f(\mathbf{x},t) \qquad (2)$$

with $r = |\mathbf{x}|$. Vector multiplication with $\mathbf{x}$ gets

$$\frac{d}{dt}(m\mathbf{x} \times \dot{\mathbf{x}}) = m\mathbf{x} \times \ddot{\mathbf{x}} = 0, \qquad (3)$$

so that

$$m\mathbf{x} \times \dot{\mathbf{x}} = \mathbf{C} \qquad (4)$$

with a constant vector $\mathbf{C}$. Therewith one has Angular momentum conservation:

The angular momentum of a punctual mass m stays exactly then constant, when on it acting force $m\ddot{\mathbf{x}} = \mathbf{F}$ is a central force."

sn — This very first step predetermines (strict) co-linearity of the overall acceleration with the direction of (central) force, although in general (non-zero curling and/or time varying force fields) that has not to be the case.

Here (4) already forces the trajectory to be circular, by suppressing 'freedom' of having acceleration components not collinear with the radius vector.

"Central force movements always happen in one plane through **O** perpendicular to the (constant) angular momentum vector **C**. Then from (4) follows

$$\mathbf{C} \cdot \mathbf{x} = m(\mathbf{x} \times \ddot{\mathbf{x}}) \cdot \mathbf{x} = 0.$$

We give to the z-axis of a Cartesian coordinate system the direction of the angular momentum. In x,y-plane normal to it, the plane of movement, let $(r, \varphi)$ be the polar coordinates. Then it follows for the points **x** in the plane of movement the representation

$$\mathbf{x} = r \cdot \mathbf{e} \tag{5}$$

with $\mathbf{e} = (\cos\varphi, \sin\varphi)$. Differentiating **e** on $\varphi$ produces the to **e** perpendicular unit-vector

$$\dot{\mathbf{e}} = (-\sin\varphi, \cos\varphi). \tag{6}$$

Therewith, for the velocity of a central movement one gets

$$\dot{\mathbf{x}} = \dot{r} \cdot \mathbf{e} + r \cdot \dot{\varphi} \cdot \mathbf{e}$$

and

$$\dot{\mathbf{x}}^2 = \dot{r}^2 + r^2 \cdot \dot{\varphi}^2.'' \tag{7}$$

sn — For the subsequent discussion it will be necessary to state the general (planar) form of the material point's acceleration as time-derivative in he upper part of (7), with C defined as in (9)

$$\ddot{\mathbf{x}} = a_r\mathbf{e} + a_t\mathbf{e}'$$

$$a_r = \ddot{r} - r\dot{\varphi}^2$$

$$a_t = r\ddot{\varphi} + 2\dot{r}\dot{\varphi} = \frac{1}{r}\frac{d}{dt}(r^2\dot{\varphi}) = \frac{1}{r}\dot{C}. \tag{8}$$

"That produces

$$\mathbf{x} \times \dot{\mathbf{x}} = r^2 \cdot \dot{\varphi} \cdot \mathbf{e} \times \dot{\mathbf{e}} = r^2 \cdot \varphi \cdot \mathbf{k}.$$

Therewith the law of conservation of the angular momentum goes over into the known surface-law

$$r^2 \cdot \dot{\varphi} = C = |\mathbf{C}|, \tag{9}$$

since $r^2 \cdot \dot{\varphi}$ is the surface swept per unit-time by the trajectory vector, which therefore is constant"

sn – As expected based on (8), constant C implies $a_t \equiv 0$, thus absence of non-zero transverse, that is (by its projection on the tangential line) the tangential acceleration, which means the (pre-assumed) zero work on any path's segment, as well as the trajectory in the whole. On the other hand, evidently (by evaluation on the parametrized ellipse, or the subsequent solution this derivation results in) this quantity C is differing from constant (as seen in Figure 1 bellow), and it at all does not correspond to the 2-nd Kepler's sectoral surface-law.

"For the kinetic energy

$$K = \frac{m}{2}\dot{\mathbf{x}}^2 = \frac{m}{2}\left(\dot{r}^2 + r^2 \cdot \dot{\varphi}^2\right). \tag{10}$$

applies as following from the Newton's movement equation $m \cdot \ddot{\mathbf{x}} = \mathbf{F}$ the general Energy law: The change in kinetic energy is equal to the work done by the force **F**

$$\frac{dK}{dt} = \mathbf{F} \cdot \dot{\mathbf{x}}. \tag{11}$$

In integrated form that means that between two arbitrary time-instants $t_o$, $t_1$ along a path $\mathbf{x}(t)$ applies the relationship

$$K_1 - K_0 = \left(\frac{m}{2}\dot{\mathbf{x}}^2\right)_{|t=t_1} - \left(\frac{m}{2}\dot{\mathbf{x}}^2\right)_{|t=t_0} = \int_{t_0}^{t_1} \mathbf{F} \cdot \dot{\mathbf{x}} \cdot dt.'' \tag{12}$$

sn - The expression on the right-most side of (12) is figuring as definitional form of the work done over a path, which here becomes related to the change of kinetic energy by (implicit) avoidance of explicitly accounting for the time-dependent central force, that is the related acceleration

$$m \cdot \ddot{\mathbf{x}}(t) = \mathbf{F}(\mathbf{x}, t),$$

in that the sub-integral expression

$$m \cdot \ddot{\mathbf{x}}(t) \cdot \dot{\mathbf{x}} \cdot dt$$

is replaced, by using the chain rule

$$\frac{d}{dt}\left[\dot{\mathbf{x}}^2(t)\right] = \frac{d}{d\dot{\mathbf{x}}}\left[\dot{\mathbf{x}}^2(t)\right] \cdot \frac{d\dot{\mathbf{x}}}{dt} = 2\dot{\mathbf{x}}(t)\ddot{\mathbf{x}}(t),$$

by

$$\frac{1}{2}\frac{d}{dt}\left[\dot{\mathbf{x}}^2\right] dt = \frac{1}{2}d\left[\dot{\mathbf{x}}^2\right].$$

While this seems to be correct, except that the time-variable/ility is entirely hidden, it should be noted that the scalar product in the sub-integral function implies only the work over the radial direction.

"Consequence: By taking of a mass m with the angular momentum **C** from the orbital path $r = r_0$ into the orbital path $r = r_1$ by means of a central force (1), the central force does the work

$$K_1 - K_0 = \frac{m}{2}C^2\left(\frac{1}{r_1^2} - \frac{1}{r_0^2}\right). \tag{13}$$

Since along the path applies the angular momentum conservation, that is in accordance with (9) $r_0^2\dot{\varphi}_0 = C = r_1^2\dot{\varphi}_1$, and besides that for the orbital paths $r = r_0$ and $r = r_1$ are $\dot{r}_0 = \dot{r}_1 = 0$, due to (10)

$$K_1 - K_0 = \left(\frac{m}{2}\dot{\mathbf{x}}^2\right)_{|t=t_1} - \left(\frac{m}{2}\dot{\mathbf{x}}^2\right)_{|t=t_0} =$$

$$\left(r^2 \cdot \dot{\varphi}\right)_{|t=t_1} - \left(r^2 \cdot \dot{\varphi}\right)_{|t=t_0} = \frac{m}{2}C^2\left(\frac{1}{r_1^2} - \frac{1}{r_0^2}\right).''$$

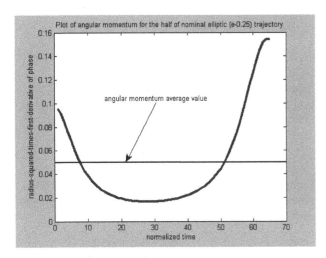

**Figure 1.** Dependence of the angular momentum on (normalized) time (for the first half, starting from the perihelion) for Keplerian ellipse with excentricity factor of e=0.25, along its average value.

sn - For those two particular instants, since (also in general) $C_o = r_o^2 \dot{\varphi}_o \neq C_1 = r_1^2 \dot{\varphi}_1$, one gets $K_1 - K_o = \frac{m}{2}\left(\frac{C_1}{r_1^2} - \frac{C_o}{r_o^2}\right)$. It should be noted that (usually) these energy terms are associated with the so called virtual potential (related) energy parts. To the extent to which it 'de-balances' the sum of total (kinetic and potential energy) in the sense of the "conservation of their sums", that is their independence on the position of the orbit, it should possibly be attributed to essentially "anti-gravitational" central force.

In Figure 1 is shown the variation of the angular momentum on the Keplerian ellipse as function of time, along its average value. It can clearly be seen that the assumption on its constancy is not tenable.

(By 'allowing' for the $C = r^2(d\varphi/dt)$, incorrectly taken for the (constant) sectorial speed, to be time-variable, it is possible to arrive at the radial velocity needed in the astrophysics to determine presence of planets in the distant stars, as shown in [11]), the result that on its practical merits can be considered as an indirect refutation of the angular momentum conservation law validity.)

"Example 1; Central force with time-independent potential: This example is treated in detail in [Friedhelm Kuypers: Klassische Mechanik, 4. Auflage, VCH 1993, S. 85 ff.]. Required and sufficient condition for the existence of a potential V of the central force (1) is the condition

$$rot\, \mathbf{F} = rot\left(\frac{\mathbf{x}}{r}f(\mathbf{x})\right) = \mathbf{0}. \qquad (14)$$

After differentiation that produces

$$rot\left(\frac{\mathbf{x}}{r}f(\mathbf{x})\right) = -\frac{\mathbf{x}}{r} \times grad\,(f(\mathbf{x})) = \mathbf{0},$$

that is $f(\mathbf{x})$ can only be dependent on $r = |\mathbf{x}|$. Therewith we have

$$\mathbf{F} = -grad\,(V(r)). \qquad (15)$$

This condition gives for the work-integral in (12)

$$\int_{t_0}^{t_1} \mathbf{F} \cdot \dot{\mathbf{x}} \cdot dt = -\int_{\mathbf{x}_0}^{\mathbf{x}_1} grad\,(V(r)) \cdot d\mathbf{x} =$$

$$-\int_{r_0}^{r_1} \dot{V}(r) \cdot dr = V(r_0) - V(r_1).$$

The energy-law (12) thus takes the form of a/the law of energy conservation:

$$\frac{m}{2}\dot{\mathbf{x}}^2 + V(r) = E, \qquad (16)$$

with a constant $E$, or due to (7) and with accounting for the angular momentum conservation law

$$\frac{m}{2}\left(\dot{r}^2 + \frac{C^2}{r^2}\right) + V(r) = E. \qquad (17)$$

The radial movement $r = r(t)$ thus takes part under influence of the "effective potential" $V_{eff}(r) = V(r) + \frac{m}{2}\frac{C^2}{r^2}$. One should consider that the effective potential depends on the constant of the angular momentum $C$. The energy conservation law now becomes

$$\frac{m}{2}\dot{r}^2 + V_{eff} = E.'' \qquad (18)$$

sn — While under the presumption of the angular momentum conservation $r^2\dot{\varphi} = constant$, the energy conservation may hold (?!?), that is not the case in actual situations, so that

$$\frac{m}{2}\left(\dot{r}^2_{|r=r_1^2}\right) + \frac{m}{2}\cdot C_1^2 \cdot \frac{1}{r_1^2} + V(r_1) \neq$$

$$\frac{m}{2}\left(\dot{r}^2_{|r=r_0^2}\right) + \frac{m}{2}\cdot C_0^2 \cdot \frac{1}{r_0^2} + V(r_0),$$

and $m/2r + Veff(r) = E(t)$ !?!

Direct refutation of the validity of the law of energy conservation in terms of its constancy over time, that is time-independence, can be made based on evaluations on the nominal Keplerian ellipse. As the results shown in Figure 2 and Figure 3 suggest, where respectively the E(t) is respectively plotted (for the first half of the trajectory, starting from the perihelion) in the considered case with excentricity e=0.25, for the factually time-varying angular momentum and its average value, as per Figure 1. This undoubtedly means that the assumption on the time-independent orbital energy is not tenable either. The plot of the effective potential itself is shown in Figure 4.

"Points of the path with $\dot{r} = 0$ are named reversal points. They satisfy the condition

$$V_{eff}(r) = E, \qquad (19)$$

A movement is possible only in the r-ranges in which

$$V_{eff}(r) \leq E, \qquad (20)$$

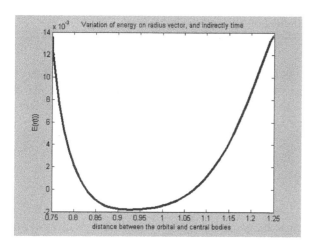

**Figure 2.** Total classically evaluated energy of the Keplerian elliptic trajectory with e=0,25 with the factually time-varying angular momentum.

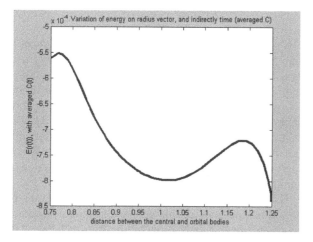

**Figure 3.** Total classically evaluated energy of the Keplerian elliptic trajectory with e=0,25 with the factually time-varying angular momentum replaced by its average value, as per Figure 1.

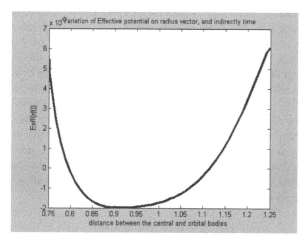

**Figure 4.** Plot of the effective potential with the factual angular momentum shown in Figure 1.

In general, these get limited from bellow and up."

sn — In the light of the above observations, at these points (perihelion and aphelion positions) besides of the radius(es) also derivatives of the angle(s) are zero, meaning $C_1 = C_2 = 0$, so that only potential energy terms ($m/r_1$ and $m/r_0$ ) remain, invalidating (19) and the essentially time- (i.e. position-) invariant total energy $E(t)$ undermines the importance of the condition (20), and leaves it only as relevant for ensuring non-negative values of the argument of the square-root part in (21) bellow.

"The differential equation (18) can be solved on $dt/dr$ and (subsequently) integrated. For the initial condition $r(0) = r_0$ one gets

$$t(r) = \frac{2}{m} \int_{r_0}^{r} [E - Veff(\rho)]^{-1/2} d\rho, \qquad (21)$$

what determines the trajectory $r(t)$. Note: There are laypersons who hold that the angular momentum and energy conservation are not commensurate with each other, see for example [12]; (this link is unfortunately replaced by another content, comment by sn), [13]. Based on the above example one though can see, that the movement under central force is determined by the potential's part of the energy-law (21), whereas the angular momentum law in form of the area-law (9) with known $r(t)$ through differential equation

$$\dot{\varphi} = \frac{C}{r^2(t)}, \qquad (22)$$

determines the angular velocity of the closed path movement. Here, both of the two conservation laws are responsible for one of the two degrees of freedom (respectively, radial and azimuthal). Therefore, about a contradiction cannot be a question at all."

sn — It rather turns out that the 'conciliation' of the angular momentum and the energy conservations has (implicitly) been forced due to the inconsistencies related to the essentially time-varying nature of the central acceleration/force and its adoption to represent potential fields. In that way, the incorrect presumption allows for the rather awkward evaluation firstly of the time as function of distance in (21) by solving (18) with subsequently inversing $t(r)$ into $r(t)$, and then to use the alleged angular momentum conservation in (22), which, along (9), actually represents nothing else but $\dot{\varphi}(t) \equiv \dot{\varphi}(t)$ !?! Also, reversing the functional relationship in (21) is not straight forward, and generally should not allow for the closed form expression for the $r(t)$.

There are various methods for overcoming of the intrinsically deficient foundations of the Newtonian gravitation and orbital motion theories towards solution of the so-called Kepler's/Newton's problem (for example, [9]) which, if (again, erroneously) rely on the angular momentum conservation, they do not explicitly involve the energy conservation 'law'. All of them, however, are less or more sensitive to the properly selected initial conditions, and the resulting quite miraculous reconstruction of elliptical trajectories with manifested (contrary to the presumed only radial) presence of non-zero tangential accelerations must be the result of essentially redundant elliptical geometry?! By all means the separate use of the two conservation laws as respectively "responsible" for the radial and azimuthal degrees of freedom appears to be quite artificial, and in light of the offered empirical proofs for essential invalidity of these laws, they should be deemed as inappropriate and largely misleading.

An at least more proper way to approach the orbital motion problem should be to consider two counteracting central acceleration (gravitational and thermal) components [4], and the conventional methods have been scrutinized in retrospect, after setting up of the TGO concept. It turns out that the $1/r^2$ proportional dependence of the planets temperature with distance goes over into $-1/r^3$ (or with reversed signs, as anti-gravitational terms) to account for to it proportional component which (with alleged constancy of angular momentum) corresponds to the "virtual potential", or (scaled by a constant) to the Leibniz's second central acceleration term. Besides a (non-Newtonian) gravitational constant, role plays also the body's thermal coefficient.

## 4. Orbital motion as a dynamical equilibrium — Thermo-Gravitational Oscillator

The following considerations are based (in the phenomenological sense) on dynamical equilibrium between the Le Sage-like gravitational and the postulated thermal components of the effective 'force' driving the planet around the Sun over certain path (by co-author of [4], Vujo Gordić www.tdo.rs). In essence, the gravitational component itself could be viewed at as essentially thermal, and what is exposed here is more like an outline of an ultimately thermo-dynamical theory of orbital motion. Here it goes about the extension and specialisation of the Gordić's quasi-dynamical, differential formulation.

With the reference to Figure 5, starting from the radial components of the Lesage's and the postulated co-linear thermal 'force' components, their projections on the tangential line to a non-predefined orbital trajectory path bear the same ratios (as those very components) due to the sameness of the opposite angles made by crossing of two straight lines. Starting from the elementary work done on the elementary segment $dr$ of a trajectory, the work done is the result of two components - a work component from the gravitational ('field') force, that is the corresponding acceleration towards the Sun ($\gamma$ representing the gravitational, not necessary "universally valid" Newtonian constant)

$$dE = m \cdot \frac{\gamma}{r^2} \cdot dr, \qquad (23)$$

and the component (energy) of the 'thermal field', which actually acts as a kind of counter-force to the former one (the centrifugal force, generally differing from the centripetal one), that is (with $\delta$ representing the thermal coefficient of a planet's body)

$$dQ = m \cdot \delta \cdot dT. \qquad (24)$$

In order to represent the two field force components by the same variable, the actual dependence of the planet's global temperature ($T$) on its distance from the Sun is needed. What is required is the related function

$$T = f(r), \qquad (25)$$

so that (24) goes over to

$$dQ = m \cdot \delta \cdot f'(r) \cdot dr, \qquad (26)$$

where the prime mark denotes the first derivative over the argument $r$.

Based on (23) and (24), the dependence of the effective force (per unit mass) of the composite thermo-gravitational field on the planet-Sun distance can be represented as

$$F(r)/m = \frac{\gamma}{r^2} + \delta \cdot f'(r). \qquad (27)$$

It will be interesting and possibly insightful to mention here two things: first, the term 'force' — differently from its use by Newton - has been used in only a descriptive, and not the causative sense; second, although the (Earth) body mass is figuring in such a formal elementary works definition, it falls-out from considerations due to equating the total work over the trajectory to zero (for conservative system premise), or in the alternative, and possibly more appropriate application of the Principle of Least Action (as minimization of work done over a closed path).

This is how the mass becomes totally irrelevant for the orbital motion consideration/explanation, in quite a good agreement with the observations from well before the Galilean time, which support full independence of the acceleration caused by the Earth and other planets on the objects's mass. Actually, even in conventional determination of the orbital path the mass appears on the both sides of the differential equations and it essentially becomes irrelevant. For the energy balance evaluation within the TGO approach, the mass is to be used in product with acceleration to determine the classically defined work over the path, and the total thermal energy received from the Sun can then determine the efficiency factor, that is the extent to which there is a 'surplus' of energy! When the function $f(r)$ is not known, in particular the one that characterizes the effective radial component that is counteracting the Le Sageian gravitational push, one possibility is to arrive at it by starting from the known trajectory's elliptical equation and some sort of combined numerical/analytical determination of it, based on evaluation, that is minimization of expression

$$\oint \left\{ \left[ \frac{\gamma}{r^2} + \delta \cdot f'(r) \right] \cdot \cos(\alpha) \right\} \cdot dr, \qquad (28)$$

where the integration is done on the given (known) ellipse equation. (The value of this closed-path line integral is

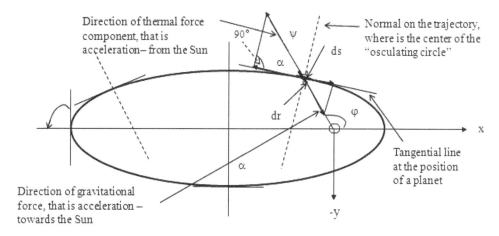

**Figure 5.** Illustration of thermo-gravitational equilibrium in the motion of a planet around the Sun.

given by the area of the vertical wall 'erected' on the two-dimensional trajectory as its basis, with the height defined by the sub-integral function.)

Considering that radial acceleration $\ddot{r} = -\gamma/r^2 + C^2/r^3$ (which results from the conventional derivations, being exclusively the one with assumption of constant $C$) is same one (given by $\ddot{r} = -a/r^2 + b/r^3$) proposed by Leibniz [4] ([16] and [17] therein) in place of just the first one that figures in Newtonian set-up, the fact that might be telling a lot regarding the historical contoversy over priorities in founding the differential calculus. On the other side, the planetary temperature dependence on the separation from Sun, found in Milanković's "Solar Cannon" book (reference 9 in [4]) being proportional to $1/r^2$, inserted into (5) casts the right-most term into $-\xi/r^3$, so that (with looking at the accelleration towards center) one gets $\ddot{r} = -\gamma/r^2 + \xi/r^3$, which very well matches the two expressions referred to immediately above. (The evident non-constancy of C would hint to somewhat position-dependent $\xi$. However, non-constant $C$ essentially retains the transverse acceleration as a utmost important part, and its very presence might have largely accounted for the observed - for example, Mercury-perihelion 'anomalous' precession phenomenon.)

In order to corroborate the validity of the TGO approach as a way towards arriving at the general orbital motion theory, evaluation of the work over the closed elliptical path has been evaluated with variation of the nominal Keplerian ellipse with excentricity e=0.25 over its vertical axis. With the definition of thermal dependence as per the Milanković's planetary warming 'law', the work over the varied quasi-elliptical paths is numerically calculated by using the following two expressions (the second one, angle between the radius vector and tangential line, is taken from [14]).

$$\oint \left| \left\{ \left[ -\frac{\gamma}{r^2(t)} + \frac{\xi}{r^3(t)} \right] \cdot \cos[\alpha(t)] \right\} \frac{dr(t)}{dt} \cdot dt \right|, \quad (29)$$

$$\pi/2 - \alpha(t) = \psi(t) = arctng(\frac{dr(\varphi(t))/d\varphi(t)}{r(\varphi(t))}). \quad (30)$$

(Of general interest might be the fact that the minimization of work - in this evaluation, hopefully justifyingly not making difference between the positive and negative tangential accelerations/de-accelerations - turns out to be the same as minimization of the closed-path integral of differentials of the kinetic energy or, equivalently, the closed-path integral over time of the time-derivative of the kinetic energy ($K = \frac{1}{2}v^2(t)$), as shown by the steps bellow.

$$\oint \frac{d}{dt} \left\{ \frac{1}{2} v^2(t) \right\} dt = \oint v \cdot \frac{dv}{dt} \cdot dt = \oint v \cdot dv =$$

$$= \oint \frac{dv}{dt} \cdot v \cdot dt = \oint \mathbf{a}(t) \cdot d\mathbf{s}(t).$$

While the conventional Lagrangian formalism makes use of time integral of difference between the kinetic and the potential energies, with the actual path being supposed to minimize its variations, it should be noted that no explicit involvement of time variable is needed when the work over the closed path is evaluated. The importance of this can be in the again long time ago 'closed' issue over the relevance of the Newton's momentum or the kinetic energy itself, i.e. Leibniz's "vis-viva" (product of mass and velocity squared). In the sequel are also given some comparative evaluations of Lagrangean approach in the same nominal Keplerian ellipse 'variations'.)

The four figures (Figure 9, Figure 2, Figure 11 and Figure 12) present the work over the half of the vertically scaled elliptic trajectories, the scaling factors indicated on the horizontal axes.

In the Figure 13 is evaluated time-vise integral of time derivative of the kinetic energy, as per last (non-numerated equation).

For comparison, conventional variational approach of time-vise integral of the randomly varied/perturbed Lagrangian L=K-E is illustrated in Figure 14.

From the above results it can be seen that the paths corresponding to the nominal Keplerian ellipse correspond to the minimal work needed to be done for its traversing or the minimal integral of the time-variations of the orbital

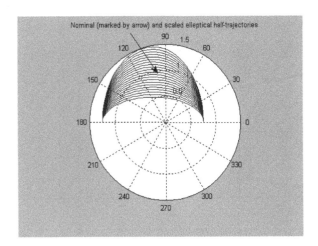

**Figure 6.** The first half of the paths used for the evaluations: shapes of scaled nominal (marked by the arrow) ellipse (with e=0.25).

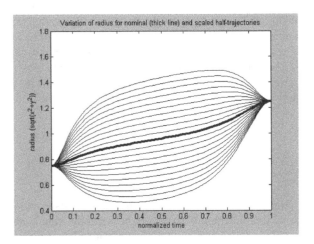

**Figure 7.** The first half of the paths used for the evaluations: variation of corresponding radiuses.

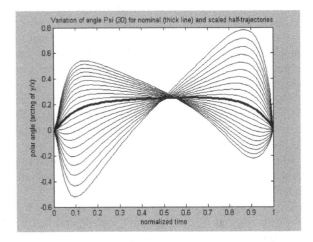

**Figure 8.** The first half of the paths used for the evaluations: variation of the related angles between the radius-vector and the tangential line at the position of the orbital body (angle $\psi$ in Figure 5) and the equation 30.

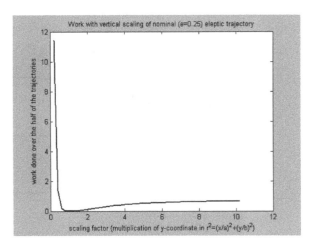

**Figure 9.** Evaluation of work done over the vertically scaled nominal Keplerian ellipse: the overall shape of the work resembles the conventionally evaluated potential energy "well".

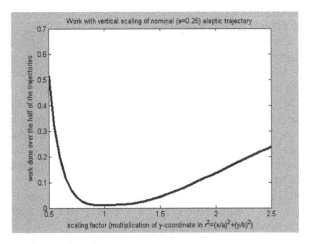

**Figure 10.** Evaluation of work done over the vertically scaled nominal Keplerian ellipse: hile the overall shape of the work resembles the conventionally evaluated potential energy "well", the minimum of work is of a positive value and correspond to the nominal ellipse - scale factor equaling 1.

body kinetic energy. (It should be noted that in the latter case there is no involvement of calculation of the angle between the radius vector and the normal to the tangential line, with exhibited rather peculiar variations related to the method of its calculations in polar coordinates of (30), highlighted in Figure 12). Through the calculations of integrals of Lagragians, it has been to some extent indicated soundness of the conducted evaluation (although the minimal variance of the random values in Figure 8 falls at the scale 3 rather than (visually) expected value of 1. (Only with Vujicić's [10] modified Lagrangian L=2K-E it comes closer to 2; it might be worthwhile noting that the doubled kinetic energy corresponds to the Leibnizt's "vis-viva" related squared velocity).

Based on these evaluations, it is to be expected that inherently stable orbital paths can be produced just by min-

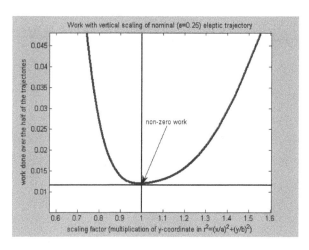

**Figure 11.** Evaluation of work done over the vertically scaled nominal Keplerian ellipse: the minimum of work is of a positive value and correspond to the nominal ellipse - scale factor equaling 1.

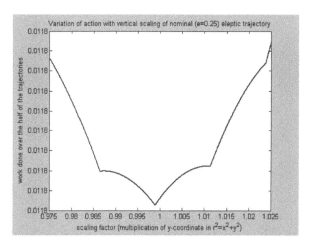

**Figure 12.** Evaluation of work done over the vertically scaled nominal Keplerian ellipse: the deep zoom-in in this drawing reveals peculiarity in using the polar coordinates in calculating the angle $\psi$ based on (30).

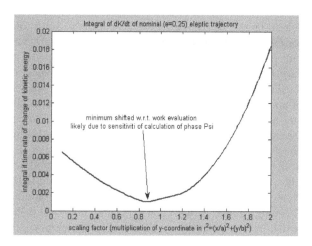

**Figure 13.** Evaluation of integral of rate of change of kinetic energy: minimum near the nominal ellipse.

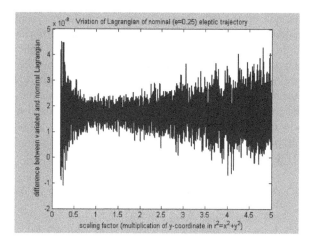

**Figure 14.** Indication of optimal path by calculation integral of the Lagrangian, L=K-E.

imization of the work integral, instead of minimization of its variation, and that may bring profound changes regarding the abandoning or greatly modifying the traditional methodologies.

## 5. Concluding remarks and wider implications and the relevance of Aether for physics

From the above developments and evaluations it follows that it is not true that the concurrent use of the two separately and unjustifyingly established laws of energy and angular momentum conservations are indispensable for the determination of stable orbital paths. Direct minimization of work done over the closed path can determine the path which is likely to be inherently stable since its derivation was not tied to any initial conditions. By virtue of this, and

the demonstrated essential untenability of the traditionally obeyed 'laws', it can be concluded that all natural orbital systems are essentially non-conservative, and that the quest for the non-accounted (outside) forces/effect should be directed towards revealing the hidden resources and structuring potential features of the very Aether substrate. The commonality of the two constituent central forces $-a/r^2$ and $b/r^3$ with the attracting and repulsive forces related to electric and magnetic phenomena respectively, suggests that by taking all the possible four combinations of the signs and appropriate constants delimitations of different nature forces ("the four forces of nature") shall be abandoned along the traditional efforts to their "unification", and all the systems - from chemical to biological ones be treated by relying on such two force/acceleration dependencies.

The way the TGO is formulated, along the critic of the shortcoming of the very Newton's law of gravity (Appendix I in [4]), besides established irrelevance of mass hinting to wrongly postulated so-called "Dark Matter", the actual (large) cosmological objects heat can be substituted for the missing "Dark Energy". The non-conservative nature of orbital systems put under big question-mark the very foundation of the modern Quantum Mechanics, related to explanation why electron does not fall into nucleus of an atom that emits energy. Since the basic electrostatic and magnetostatic laws have been formulated following the essentially circularly derived and largely miss-leading Newton's Gravity law, the very electromagnetism and electrodynamics would need certain extensions and modifications, as already to an astounding extent conducted in [5]. Numerous gravitational anomalies, geostationary satellites "dancing", Lunar paradox and in general three- and many-bodies'problems appear to be solvable by adopting the principle formulation of TGO and the implied reliance on the Aether. As an example, the so-called Pioneer 10/11 (reference 14 and Appendix III in [4]) anomaly is solvable by considering the heat generated by the nuclear reactor situated on the side turned towards the Solar barycenter actually de-balancing the purely gravitational equilibrium, in that the effect of the Ether push in-between the vehicle and the Solar system is reduced, thus the anomalous acceleration "towards the Sun" (having been) taking place. (The currently accepted solution is based on direct violation of the conservation of the linear momentum of the closed system, in that the heat is 'hitting' the co-located dish-antenna and pushes the vehicle in the 'anomalous' direction.)

# REFERENCES

1. D.L. Goodstein, J.R. Goodstein, *Feynman's Lost Lecture, the motion of the planets around the Sun.*, Vintage Books, 1997.

2. P. Enders, *Equat causa effectum and central forces, Symmetry breaking by initial condition.*, available by request sent to enders@dekasges.de , or the author of this paper.

3. M. R. Edwards, *Pushing Gravity : New Perspectives on Le Sage's Theory of Gravitation.*, Aperion Montreal, 2002.

4. S. Nedić and V. Gordić, *Towards general theory of orbital motion - Thermo-gravitational oscillator.*, submitted to GED Journal in 2014; available at https://www.researchgate.net/publication/285587999 _Towards_a_General_Theory_of_Orbital_Motion_the _Thermo-Gravitational_Oscillator .

5. V.A. Atsukovsky, *Obshaya Ephirodinamika.*, IP Radio Soft, 2016.

6. R. Hatch, *A new theory of gravity, overcoming problems with general relativity.*, Physics Essays Vol. 20 2009.

7. I. Newton, *Ueber die Gravitation.*, Vittorio Klostermann GmBH, Frankfurt am Mein, 1998.

8. G.H. Bruhn, *Energie- und Drehimpulssatz bei Bewegungen von Massenpunkten um ein Zentrum.*, http://www.mathematik.tu-darmstadt.de/ bruhn/Zentralbewegungen.htm

9. various authors https://en.wikipedia.org/wiki/Kepler_problem

10. V. Vujicić, *Dynamics of Rheonomic Systems.*, Mathematical Institute of the Serbian Accademy of Science, Editions Speciales, Belgrade, 1990.

11. K. Clubb, *The radial velocity equation, a detailed derivation of.*, http://astro.berkeley.edu/ kclubb/ pdf/RV_Derivation.pdf

12. G. Bourbaki, *Ueber Wirklichkeit und Wahrheit in der Physik.*, http://www.bourbaki.de/a01.htm

13. G. Bruhn, *Bourbaki contra Newton.*, http://www.mathematik.tu-darmstadt.de/ bruhn/BCONTRAN.HTM,

14. various authors http://math.stackexchange.com/questions/175191/ normal-to-ellipse-and-angle-at-major-axis

# Analyzing Special Relativity's Time Dilation Within The Context of Lorentz Relativity

## Nick Percival

*79 Haviland Rd, Ridgefield, CT 06877, NPercival@SNET.net*

Einstein's Special Relativity dramatically changes Lorentz Relativity by adding a false claim, namely, the Constant Velocity of Light Principle and declaring that all inertial frames are equal and all those inertial frames simulate the properties of Lorentz Relativity's single, preferred frame. This transformed a valid physics theory, Lorentz Relativity, into an inherently flawed physics theory, Special Relativity, that "fortuitously" served as a useful math tool during the period when the identity of the correct preferred frame was unknown. Focusing on "time dilation", it will be seen how GPS data makes this view clear in two dramatic ways.

**Keywords:** Special Relativity, Lorentz Relativity, GPS, time dilation, clock retardation, Twin Paradox, particle accelerator, muon decay

## 1. Introduction

This paper will first give a summary of Lorentz Relativity (LR) and then discuss Special Relativity (SR) within the context of that theory with a special focus on SR's time dilation versus LR's clock retardation. Then a brief look at the empirical data for those two theories will be examined with a special focus on GPS.

## 2. Lorentz Relativity (LR)

Prior to Einstein's 1905 paper [1] that laid the basis for Special Relativity (SR), Lorentz had developed Lorentz Aether Theory (LAT). A subset of LAT is Lorentz Relativity (LR) which is a preferred frame theory that is independent of whether there is or is not an aether and which covers the same domain as SR's time dilation and length contraction and, by extension, much of kinematics.

In LR, there is a single preferred frame which is the only frame where the speed of light is c in vacuo in all directions.

The key construct of LR is absolute velocity as measured from the single, preferred frame. In LR, clock retardation is the phenomenon of clock slowing as the absolute velocity of that clock increases whether that clock is in an inertial frame or not (e.g., it's accelerating). This effect is a physical, asymmetric effect. In other words, if clock A has increasing absolute velocity with respect to the preferred frame, then clock A's clock rate, or proper time accumulation rate, will physically slow with respect to clocks at rest in the single, preferred frame.

Similarly, in LR, the length of objects shrink as a function of absolute velocity along the direction of that absolute velocity.

Following from the above, LR deals with absolute kinetic energy which is a function of absolute velocity.

As part of LAT and LR, Lorentz developed the Lorentz Transformation equations (LTs). The LTs are used in transformations from the single preferred frame to any other frame. The velocity parameter in the LTs is absolute velocity as discussed above.

Leaving aside for now whether LR is "correct", LR is a straightforward physics theory which describes what's happening physically without any hint of internal contradictions or paradoxes.

## 3. Special Relativity (SR) In The Context of Lorentz Relativity (LR)

The author assumes the reader is familiar with the basic tenets of SR. Einstein at different times claimed that there was no preferred frame or alternatively, if there was a preferred frame, it could not be identified. From the above, it can be seen that Einstein addressed this dilemma, in SR, by having every inertial frame simulate the single, preferred frame of LR (e.g., the constancy of the speed of light in each and every inertial frame, time dilation (decreased proper time accumulation rate) and length contraction as a function of velocity with respect to each and every inertial frame, the use of the LTs with v being velocity with respect to each and every inertial frame.) This is why, in SR, many paradoxes and contradictions appear when one analyzes a physics scenario from two frames.

Understanding this distorted simulation reveals how SR achieved limited success, why SR was erroneously awarded additional success and what the severe limitations of SR are.

## 4. Interpreting The Physics Meaning of SR's Time Dilation

What is the meaning of the time dilation equation in SR? Sometimes relativists explicitly or implicitly interpret ""time dilation"" as meaning that each clock is observed or measured to be running slow with respect to the other clock as a function of their relative velocity. Hence, in this case, "time dilation" would be a "just observed" effect without any physical effect as having two clocks both running slow with respect to each other is not only counter intuitive but counter logical. This interpretation is analogous to twins who separate and, as their relative separation increases, both twins observe the other twin as shrinking in size whereas no physical shrinking occurs for either twin. This interpretation would seems to be required as SR's time dilation is symmetric between clock A and clock B so whatever the "time dilation" effect for clock A versus clock B, the exact same "time dilation" effect must occur for clock B versus clock A.

However, sometimes relativists explicitly or implicitly interpret time dilation as meaning that one (or both) clock is running slow (i.e. is accumulating proper time at a slower rate) with respect to the other clock. Hence, in this case, "time dilation" would be an asymmetric, physical effect. Einstein seemed to explicitly give this interpretation in his 1905 paper when, directly after deriving the time dilation equation, he wrote, "From this ..." and went on to claim that for two clocks starting in the same frame with one clock then making a round trip a net proper time difference (NPTD) would result indicating that the "traveling" clock would have accumulated less proper time during the round trip. Much of the physics community objected to this claim, by, in essence, asking, *"How can an asymmetric result come from an inherently symmetric phenomenon?"* . This controversy was dubbed the Clock Paradox and in 1911 was renamed the Twin Paradox.

Einstein was clearly affected by criticism of his "Clock Paradox/Twin Paradox" claim [2] and two years after he developed General Relativity (GR), in 1918, Einstein explained the Twin Paradox claim entirely in terms of GR and totally abandoned his prior claim about SR's time dilation causing an NPTD [3]. As C. S. Unnikrishnan summarizes Einstein's 1918 position, *"Curiously, the discussion starts with a complaint by the critic that none of the relativists had adequately responded to the criticisms of relativity by many in journals. In fact, the critic accuses relativists of 'shirking' the issue. This certainly suggests that Einstein considered that none of the earlier discussions adequately addressed the problem and that it was necessary to respond. Ironically, Einstein's resolution goes against the standard resolutions discussed in textbooks and in most other writings! As the physical cause of the asymmetry he uses the pseudo-gravitational field and the gravitational time dilation of general relativity, after admitting that special relativity is not suitable for resolving the issue due to the fact that one of the twins undergoes accelerations during his trip"* . Many other physicists such as Max Born [4], followed Einstein's rejection of using SR's time dilation for asymmetric physical effects. As Herbert Dingle pointed out, if one interprets SR time dilation as describing a physical effect, then one is saying that SR *"requires that A works more slowly than B and B more slowly than A – which it requires no super-intelligence to see is impossible. Now, clearly, a theory that requires an impossibility cannot be true"* [5].

In contrast, LR's clock retardation equation is inherently

asymmetric and requires being interpreted as describing an asymmetric, physical effect. Hence, we need to see if the empirical data supports SR's symmetric, "just observed" time dilation or LR's asymmetric, physical clock retardation.

## 5. Empirical Data

### 5.1. Particle Accelerators

Particle accelerator (e.g., CERN) data showed that time dilation/clock retardation was consistent with SR's time dilation equation. However, the data would also be consistent with LR clock retardation if the velocity parameter was velocity with respect to LR's preferred frame. The velocity parameter used was velocity with respect to the Earth Centered Inertial (ECI) frame which GPS data later showed is, in fact, the local LR preferred frame. Hence, the particle accelerator (e.g., CERN) data showed that time dilation/clock retardation was also consistent with LR's clock retardation equation. This was ignored by the mainstream physics community as they assumed SR was correct and either didn't consider LR or assumed LR was incorrect.

For particle accelerator data, there was no way to differentiate SR's time dilation from LR's clock retardation. Such a determination required that one get data from both the ECI frame and a particle frame. Different types of empirical data, as discussed below, were able to so differentiate.

Note that particle accelerators showed that the time dilation/clock retardation phenomenon is a function of instantaneous velocity and further it is NOT a function of acceleration per se [6].

### 5.2. Atmospheric Muon Decay

Muons are created in the upper atmosphere as byproducts of high energy cosmic ray proton impacts with atomic nuclei. Due to the thickness of the atmosphere and the very short half-life of the muon, very few such muons would be expected to reach the earth's surface. However, a great quantity of muons do reach the earth and even penetrate 100s of meters into the earth. This experimental result is interpreted as proof of Special Relativity's (symmetric) time dilation, but this is not a logically consistent interpretation. We note that the atmosphere is approximately 20km thick and since the maximum speed for the muon is at most c (299,792,458 meters per second), that means it would take approximately 0.00007 seconds for the fastest muon to traverse the entire thickness of the atmosphere. However, the mean lifetime of a muon at rest in the earth frame is approximately 300 times smaller than that. To match the empirical data on muons reaching the surface of the earth, even a set of "highest speed" muon clocks must be physically slowed by a large factor [7] .

Since this phenomenon involves a threshold event, namely, the decay or non-decay of the muon, the phenomenon cannot be explained by relative simultaneity or in terms of Special Relativity - this is true of any velocity dependent effect that involves a threshold. In the current case, either the muons are traveling at greater than the speed of light in the earth frame, which is not consistent with Special Relativity, or their half-life has been physically and asymmetrically extended between the event of being created in the upper atmosphere and the event of reaching the earth. The asymmetric, physical slowing of the atmospheric muons is based on two absolute facts, namely, the upper limit speed of c (according to Special Relativity) and the fact that the muon successfully survived its trip from the upper atmosphere to the surface of the earth and perhaps beyond. (For additional analysis, see http://twinparadox.net/ section 2.4.)

Hence, the empirical data from muons created in earth's atmosphere supports LR clock retardation as opposed to SR's ""just observed"" time dilation!

### 5.3. Hafele-Keating Experiment

The Hafele-Keating experiment has been criticized as not having reliable data. Yet, it is often cited as proof of SR's time dilation. However, if one judged the Hafele-Keating paper [8] as being accurate, it would be strong evidence for LR clock retardation as opposed to SR's ""just observed"" time dilation. The Hafele-Keating results allege that atomic clock rate is a function of velocity relative to the ECI frame and is not a function of relative velocity between the clocks being compared [8]. This would mean that the phenomenon is not consistent with SR's symmetric, "just observed" time dilation, but rather is consistent only with LR's asymmetric, physical clock retardation. Since the Hafele-Keating experiment is conceptually very similar to the highly credible and very precise GPS, detailed analysis is left to the next section.

### 5.4. The GPS Data

The designers of GPS thought they were using SR and some GPS engineers continue to assume that GPS is built on SR. However, some of the top GPS engineers/consultants such as Tom Van Flandern [9] and Ron Hatch [10] (holder of 30+ GPS patents and internationally recognized expert on navigation systems) realized and published that GPS did not use the SR physics model, but rather used the LR physics model. In addition, other physicists such as Tom Phipps [11] independently realized and published that GPS used the LR physics model.

Note that much of the discussion that follows applies not only to GPS but also to the Hafele-Keating experiment. SR time dilation uses relative velocity between A and B to compute how much clock A will "measure" clock B as running slow and how much clock B will "measure" clock A as running slow. It was NOT derived to be used by a 3rd party (inertial or non-inertial) to compare clock A and B, as the results, in SR, will vary widely depending on the state of the chosen 3rd party frame. For example, if one has observer C at rest in the ECI (Earth Centered Inertial) frame at the origin of some arbitrarily selected axes and one has A going along the positive x-axis at velocity u with respect to C (and the ECI) and B going in the opposite direction along the x-axis at velocity -u with respect to C, then, using Special Relativity, C will compute that A and B have slowed equally with respect to C's own clock and,

hence, will compute that they are running at the same rate. In contrast, when either A or B, using Special Relativity, compute time dilation using their relative velocity, each computes the other as having the slower clock and, hence, both are in sharp disagreement with the preferred frame clock retardation methodology and with computation done by a 3rd party at rest in a 3rd frame. However, GPS uses the single, 3rd party frame methodology that is consistent with the LR physics model, but which, as shown above, is NOT consistent with the SR model.

In addition, both the satellite clocks and instrumentation and earthbound clocks and instrumentation measure and agree that (absolute) velocity with respect to the (single) ECI frame causes the satellite clock to slow with respect to the earthbound clocks. In other words, the effect is an asymmetric, physical effect, namely, a relative slowing of proper time accumulation. (Other effects cause other relative rate changes.)

Furthermore, this effect is cumulative; the difference in proper time accumulation increases for each orbit revolution and within each revolution.

Furthermore, since the orbits of the satellite clocks are not perfect circles, their velocities change during an orbit and those changes must be accounted for due to the high precision requirements of GPS. Hence, the GPS data is very robust on the exact nature of clock retardation not only per orbit but also for variations during any orbit. In addition, even if one interprets SR's symmetric time dilation equation as describing "just observed" views by clock A and separately by clock B, that interpretation also fails as both A and B will agree on which clock is slower and which clock is faster. The effect is an asymmetric physical effect and observed to be so by both observers. The GPS data is very credible because GPS works and works to a high degree of precision no matter where the GPS satellites are in their orbit. If one looks at the GPS data honestly and objectively, one cannot claim that the GPS data is consistent with the SR physics model as time will confirm!

Other prominent physicists, such as the aforementioned Tom Van Flandern [9], Ron Hatch [10], and Tom Phipps [11], have independently published concerning the disparity between the special relativity model and GPS data.

## 6. Why Has The Above Not Been Recognized?

The academic physics community assumes that SR is correct and has been validated by experiment to 9 decimal places and is part of the foundation of modern physics and conversely, it has written off LR as obsolete. Furthermore, when looked at as pure math equations, SR's time dilation equation and LR's clock retardation equation look EXACTLY the same. Hence, academia often uses LR's clock retardation equation which looks like SR's time dilation equation and, if the results match, assumes that SR has been confirmed.

Further, for particle accelerators, for example, because

the base frame was fortuitously chosen to be the Lorentz preferred frame, the empirical data matched both SR's time dilation equation and LR's clock retardation equation and the latter match was ignored.

Further, for atmospheric muon decay, the Hafele-Keating experiment and GPS, the data was consistent with the LR clock retardation equation which looks like the SR time dilation equation and the mismatch between how the equation was used and SR's physics model was ignored.

It's human nature to adhere to one's strongly held belief system especially if that belief system is also held in high esteem by all one's peers so the physics community's erroneous interpretations of the data are predictable, readily understandable and readily explained.

## 7. Other Examples Of Simulation

Other examples of where SR implies a model of what is happening that has little to do with what's actually happening physically are discussed below. but only briefly as they are handled in detail elsewhere.

### 7.1. The Relativistic Doppler Effect

Prof. D. R. Frankl [12] starts out, *"We consider the propagation of a periodic signal at speed s through a medium from a source to a receiver both in motion, at velocity v and u, respectively, relative to the medium. ... Using the three inertial reference frames S for the medium, S' for the source, and S" for the receiver, ... our objective is to calculate the period ratio."*

Frankl does some algebraic manipulation employing *"u' as the speed of the receiver relative to the source using the usual relativistic addition of velocities formula"* and concludes, *"When the signal travels at speed c, an essential difference sets in. Motion relative to the medium becomes meaningless, and only the relative velocity between source and receiver has any meaning"* .

Thus, Frankl is able to replace the source's and receiver's velocity relative to the medium with their mutual relative velocity. Frankl characterizes this transition as making velocity relative to the medium "meaningless" as the phenomenon *can* now be explained solely in terms of relative velocity. However, it can also be said to make velocity relative to the medium be "hidden" . Just because relativistic formulae may be expressed in terms of relative velocity does not mean that the physics underlying those formulae does not involve velocities with respect to a specific frame.

The SR equations describe how observers observe Doppler phenomena whereas the classical equations describe the physical model that gives rise to those phenomena. Since the Doppler effect is a symmetric, "just observed" effect, SR *can* address this effect. However, since proper time accumulation is an absolute physical effect and NPTD is about an asymmetric **accumulation** of that physical effect, SR is very limited in correctly describing the physics of proper time effects.

### 7.2. Kinetic Energy, Collisions and Particle Creation

SR and a straight forward extension LR using absolute velocity (call it ELR) have very different concepts of kinetic energy. In ELR, kinetic energy is described as in SR except that the v always refers to velocity with respect to the preferred frame. Hence, I've dubbed the ELR concept of kinetic energy as "absolute kinetic energy" and the SR concept of kinetic energy as "relative kinetic energy" .

In SR, it's not clear how much kinetic energy a particle has as it depends on what frame of reference the observer is in. In addition, when one examines collisions between particles, the total amount of kinetic energy associated with the particles involved can vary depending upon what frame of reference the observer is in. However, the predicted results are invariant with respect to all inertial frames including ELR's preferred frame. Hence, SR predictions about collisions for all inertial frames must be consistent with ELR predictions, using velocities as measured in the preferred frame.

Furthermore, when a collision converts kinetic energy into mass and produces a new particle, all SR observers will predict the same results even though their observations about the total amount of kinetic energy (and momentum) involved may differ from the total absolute kinetic energy as determined using ELR preferred frame. That invariance is due to the laws of conservation of energy and momentum which constrains the amount of kinetic energy that is *available* to be converted into a new particle to be the same amount for all inertial frames, including the preferred frame.

Hence, ELR gives a single, very specific, observer independent, physical description of the collision by defining absolute kinetic energy in terms of velocity with respect to the preferred frame. In contrast, SR's construct of relative kinetic energy is a math or bookkeeping construct as it is observer dependent with many different possible values. Hence, it's clear that while SR may be a valid math tool for giving the right answers for collisions, it's not directly describing what's happening physically.

## 8. Limitations of SR

Whether SR is claimed to be built on the assumption that there is no preferred frame or alternatively on the assumption that the preferred frame is unknowable, SR is missing the construct of a preferred frame. Unfortunately for SR, the physical processes of most phenomena are dependent on the construct of a preferred frame.

Reference frames are math constructs and they serve as a useful shorthand. However, in [E]LR the key construct is not so much the preferred frame but rather the key construct is a physical medium through which light and objects move. The physical effects are due to the interactions caused by moving through the medium. So it gives more physics insight to say that in LR, absolute velocity is velocity with respect to that medium.

In contrast, a key SR construct is the set of all inertial frames, but no physical role is given to that set of frames. They just play a math role. Relative velocity in every inertial frame is alleged to have equal meaning. However,

SR's relative velocity is not tied to velocity with respect to any physical entity nor is it tied to interaction with a physical entity that might cause the effects we've discussed above.

SR equations are symmetric between the observer and the observed so they can't be directly describing asymmetric physical effects.

Einstein chose to limit the domain of SR to the set of inertial frames. This by itself is incredibly limiting and is usually only invoked to get around cases where SR seems to lead to a contradiction or is at odds with the data. However, I'd suggest that limiting SR to the set of inertial frames is a misunderstanding. What Einstein's choice really does is eliminate the need to deal with external forces.so that one can more easily theorize about the effect of velocity per se, whether or not it's constant velocity. In fact, the data from accelerators confirms this is the correct view as the data shows that the effects are due to the instantaneous velocity of a particle and occur whether or not the particle is at rest in an inertial frame [6].

## 9. Summary

Because the SR model for what happens is inherently observer dependent including the key constructs of relative velocity, relative simultaneity and relative kinetic energy, it's clear that SR is not describing what's happening physically, but, at best, it's simulating what's happening. Since LR's equations and constructs are inherently asymmetric, it can be interpreted as directly describing what's happening physically.

Since for kinematics, the two theories' equations are the same except for SR using relative velocity and [E]LR using absolute velocity, SR can correctly predict results as long as physical reality doesn't peak through. [E]LR gives the correct physical model for what's happening physically. Maintaining that SR describes what's happening physically is most misleading.

## REFERENCES

1.  A. Einstein, *On the Electrodynamics of Moving Bodies.*, 1905.
2.  C. S. Unnikrishnan, *On Einstein's resolution of the twin clock paradox.*, 2005.
3.  A. Einstein, *Dialog about objections against the theory of relativity.*, 1918.
4.  M. Born, *Einstein's Theory of Relativity.*, Dover, 1965.
5.  H. Dingle, *Science at the Crossroads.*, Martin Brian and O'Keefe, 1973.
6.  C.W. Misner and K.S. Thorne and J.A. Wheeler, *Gravitation.*, W.H. Freeman and Co., 1973.
7.  J. H. Field, *Muon decays in the Earth's atmosphere, time dilatation and relativity of simultaneity.*, http://arxiv.org/abs/physics/0606188, 2009.
8.  J.C. Hafele and R.E. Keating, *Around-the-World Atomic Clocks: Observed Relativistic Time Gains.*, 1972.
9.  T. Van Flandern, *Global Positioning System and the Twins Paradox.*, 2003.
10. R. Hatch, *Those Scandalous Clocks.*, 2004.
11. T. E. Phipps, Jr., *Old Physics For New.*, Aperion, 2006.
12. D.R. Frankl, *General treatment of the Doppler effect in special relativity.*, 1984.

# Cause of Gravity - Disruption of Intermolecular Bonds

## Rajendra S. Prajapati, PhD, PE

*Tel: +91 9726132100 Mail: raju2180@gmail.com*

Gravity is considered as one of the four fundamental forces, but it is not been unified with the other fundamental forces. Scientists are clueless about the weakness of gravity. There are number of scientists who feel that there must be a physical mechanism for gravity which causes only attraction. Below hypothesis uses surface energy that quantifies the disruption of intermolecular bonds that occurs when a surface is created . Consider the Earth floating in the universe and full vacuum on outside. Here, average molecule in side it is saturated by the bonding. The molecules on the surface cannot be fully saturated by bonding. So, they pulled inward. This creates positive absolute internal pressure like any ordinary object. Here, this thermodynamic phenomenon leads to Young-Laplace theory that is "If no force acts normal to a tensioned surface, the surface remains flat". Same logic may be predicted by Einstein in general relativity. Here, absolute internal pressure differs from outside full vacuum, this pressure difference times projected area results in a normal force [1]. Here, Earth atmospheric pressure tends to balance it. That means variation in atmospheric pressure influences gravity value [2]. The remained absolute internal pressure still to be balanced which causes inward vacuum drag that attracts objects towards the Earth that is known as gravity. This hypothesis answers why Einstein's theory confirms most of tests and why it significantly changes at distances smaller than an atom. That is because surface energy concept in the limit of a single molecule not works. The root cause for intermolecular bonds is electromagnetic forces that by validating unification with other fundamental forces.

**Keywords:** Surface Energy, Intermolecular Bonds, Absolute internal Pressure, Vacuum Drag, Half Sphere, Conservation of Energy

## 1. Introduction

The notion of doing experiments to find out how nature works was an unknown concept until Galileo demonstrated classic experiments on gravity [3]. Newton explained gravity as how it works but not why it works. Attempts by physicists to identify the relationship between the gravitational interaction and other known fundamental interactions are not yet resolved. Still it is an open question how quantum theory can be related with the general relativity. Einstein's general relativity assumes that gravity is a property of the universe rather than of individual objects, which does not postulate a physical force as the cause of gravity; rather, it provides a geometric explanation for gravity (figure 1).

The new theory uses concept of surface energy which is defined as the excess energy at the surface of a material compared to the bulk. Consider half sphere of the Earth. It should be noted that for solids the inside pressure cannot be balanced by elastic membrane as occurs in liquid. So, pressure difference occurs on the Earth surface. To conserve law of energy, It drags molecules which finally forms atmosphere which tends to reduce inside absolute pressure by reducing its surface area to have spherical shape. Note that, all instruments measuring atmospheric pressure actually works on the principle that the fluid is sucked by full vacuum. So, atmosphere has no energy to do work except balancing inside absolute pressure. That is why we don't experience tremendous pressure on our head. The remained absolute pressure still need to be balanced which causes all objects to attract towards the surface at same rate

that is known as free fall.

### 1.1. Material and Methods

Let us assume surface energy of Earth half sphere (figure 2). Here, The gravity force and inertia force both are same. So, it will be the multiplication of Earth radius r in meter and gravity force (vacuum drag) g in Newton. Note that, this energy is not an absolute but resultant after deduction due to Earth atmospheric pressure.

For Earth, Half sphere surface energy $S.E/2$ is equal to,

$$\frac{S.E}{2} = gr \tag{1}$$

Where, Mean Radius of Earth $r = 6371000$ m and Gravity Force $g = 9.806$ N

$$\frac{S.E}{2} = 9.806 x 6371000 Nm \tag{2}$$

$$\frac{S.E}{2} = 6.25E + 07 Nm \tag{3}$$

Here, surface tension introduced to find absolute inside pressure indirectly. Note that, there is no role of surface tension except to find absolute internal pressure.

Now, Surface Tension ($\gamma$) of Earth = Surface energy of Earth half sphere /Earth half sphere area.

$$\gamma = \frac{S.E}{A} \text{(2 removed from both sides)} \tag{4}$$

Where, A is Half Surface area of Earth

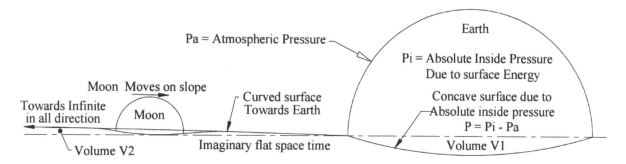

**Figure 1.** Einstein's space time concept in real physics: Earth and Moon as a bubble floating on a liquid surface (as a flat spacetime). Inside absolute pressure(P) causes concave surface inside bubble. That is balanced by infinite convex surface outside bubble. Volume (V1) displaced inside bubble balanced by Volume (V2) displaced up outside bubble. The outside curved surface causes Moon to follow the slop towards Earth that is known as space time curvature.

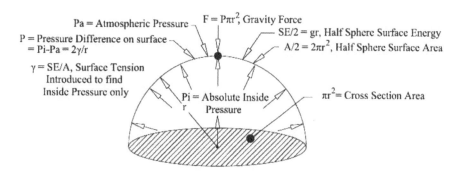

**Figure 2.** Schematic Illustration of Gravity Force (F), Absolute internal Pressure (P), Radius (r), Surface Area (A), Surface Energy (SE) and Surface Tension($\gamma$) of Half Spherical Earth

$$\gamma = \frac{6.25E + 07}{2\pi 6371000^2} \tag{5}$$

$$\gamma = 2.45E - 07 Nm^{-1} \tag{6}$$

Now, Consider spherical Earth of radius r floating in a gravity-free universe and in full vacuum. The absolute inside pressure can be calculated by using thermodynamic approach. Here, for Earth, The Interfacial energy equation can be written by $Ei = 4\pi\gamma r^2$, in a thermodynamic sense, work has been done to give it a spherical shape and keep it that way. From the definition of work, $dW = pdV$. And from the conservation of energy term, work done should be equal to the interfacial energy, therefore $dW = dE$. Taking the surface tension as constant, $dEi = 8\pi rdr\gamma$. Also, a volume element in spherical coordinates is $dV = 4\pi r^2 dr$. Now, work done,

$$dW = pdV \tag{7}$$

$$p = \frac{dW}{dV} = \frac{dE}{dV} = \frac{8\pi rdr\gamma}{4\pi r^2 dr} = \frac{2\gamma}{r} \tag{8}$$

The above definition can be used for solid surface energy to find absolute internal pressure. Here, For Earth, absolute internal Pressure cannot be balanced by elastic membrane as occurs in liquid. So, pressure difference occurs on Earth surface. From the conservation of energy term, the generated absolute inside pressure must be balanced by same magnitude inward pressure. From the above equation pressure difference on Earth surface will be,

$$p = \frac{2\gamma}{r} = \frac{2 x 2.45E - 07}{6371000} \tag{9}$$

$$p = 7.69E - 14 Nm^{-2} \tag{10}$$

It is the absolute inside pressure remains after deduction of opposing Earth atmospheric pressure. So, It must be balanced at outside which causes vacuum drag towards Earth surface. This can be calculated by multiplying remained absolute pressure and projected cross section area. This is normal Force (F) towards Earth's cross section.

Force,

$$F = \pi r^2 p = \pi x 6371000^2 x 7.69E - 14 \tag{11}$$

$$F = 9.806N \tag{12}$$

Now, calculate the vacuum drag at $r_o$ distance from Earth center. Here, vacuum drag inversely proportional to radial distance.

$$\pi r^2 p = \pi r_o^2 p_o \tag{13}$$

Where, $p_o$ is vacuum drag on object at $r_o$ radius $r_o = 2r$
Dist. of an object from Earth center = 12742000 m

$$r^2 p = r_o^2 p_o \qquad (14)$$

$$p_o = \frac{r^2 p}{r_o^2} \qquad (15)$$

$$p_o = 7.69E - 14x \frac{6371000^2}{12742000^2} \qquad (16)$$

$$p_o = 1.92E - 14 Nm^{-2} \qquad (17)$$

This is the vacuum drag pressure on object at $r_o$ distance. This value cannot be measured directly as it represents effectiveness of vacuum drag in space. Now, Find vacuum drag force towards Earth at radius $r_o$,

Here, Earth radius (r) considered in equation. As the normal cross section area of Earth is only facing area.

Force, $F = \pi r^2 p_o$

$$F = \pi x 6371000^2 x 1.92E - 14 \qquad (18)$$

$$F = 2.45N \qquad (19)$$

It is equal to gravity Force (vacuum drag) towards Earth at radius $r_o$. The Universal gravitational constant G in Newton's theory and in Einstein's General relativity can be derived as below.

Compare equation 12, $F = \pi r^2 p$ and Newton gravitation equation, $g = \frac{GM}{r^2}$

$$\pi r^2 p = \frac{GM}{r^2} \qquad (20)$$

$$\pi r^2 p = \frac{4}{3} r \rho \frac{G}{r} \qquad (21)$$

Where, Earth density $\rho = 5513 kg/m^3$

$$G = \frac{3rp}{4\rho} \qquad (22)$$

$$= \frac{3x6371000x7.69E - 14}{4x5513} \qquad (23)$$

$$= 6.67E - 11 Nm^2/kg \qquad (24)$$

Note that, Variation in value of G is due to changes in surface conditions of Moons/Planets/stars etc in a too long time span so the changes will be very Little.

## 1.2. Discussion and Conclusions

Compare the figure 3 of gravity anomaly with topography of the Earth's terrestrial land surface, ocean basins and erupting volcano sites figure 4 From that, it should be concluded that gravity depends on surface conditions (topography) like shape, roughness, exposed surface, elements, volcano eruption, atmospheric pressure, temperature [4], composition, purity, elevation, etc [5]. For example ring of

fire of Pacific Ocean has more gravity because of high elevation, low opposing atmospheric pressure , more exposed surfaces due to mountains and heavy elements exposed due to volcano eruptions whereas, Hudson Bay, Indian Ocean etc. have lower gravity due to concave surfaces, high opposing atmospheric pressure, no volcanoes and light sediments dragged due to rivers. Venus has heavy elements exposed on surface due to volcano eruptions So, it has very high surface energy which is to be balanced by atmospheric pressure whereas, Mars had erupting volcanoes earlier, so it had higher pressure compared to today's none erupting volcanoes. It is noted that planets/moons which have volcanoes have higher gravity compared to none volcanic (Table 1). Here, Einstein GR not able to explain the difference in atmospheric pressure for Earth and Venus which have nearly same gravity. Due to dependence of so many parameters, it is difficult to find the surface energy of objects like planet directly. This hypothesis of gravity (vacuum drag) can give all unknown answers like, why universe objects seem spherical in shape, why 1/2 multiplied in kinetic energy equation; Why Dinosaurs mass extinction occurs, that is because surface gravity was lower during the era of dinosaurs [6]. An asteroid struck the Earth that triggered huge volcano eruption followed by sudden increase of gravity. This had not allowed all heavy and tall life to bear their own weight except life floating on water who adjusted them self in shallow water to overcome increased static head [7]. It should be noted that astronauts can jump higher on Moon due to their muscles evolved to work in stronger gravity of Earth. Tidal bulge can be explained as the Moon attraction causes ocean of the Earth to bulge symmetrically that is because the moon decreases Earth surface energy on facing half sphere that decreases absolute internal pressure and it must be same for whole Earth. In other words Earth is suspended in vacuum drag of Moon like spherical elastic ball fixed in pressure difference. The pioneer anomaly can be explained as it increases its own gravity due to increase of distance from the Sun. Here, Einstein's GR is not considering gravity addition/subtraction in moving away/towards object. Precession of Mercury perihelion advancement discrepancy can be explained by cumulative asteroids striking force exerted at perihelion is higher than aphelion (Table 2). Gravity works in closed system due to its summation/abstraction property like pressure/vacuum do. In Newton's gravity equation, two object attracting each other. But as per above theory one object attract the other. So, here, inverse square law is applicable to falling object only. Clock time run faster on Earth surface than clock in satellite that is because the clock itself has lower surface energy on earth compared to above in satellite.

It is known that Gravity has a property that only directly interacts with pressure and not to other types of energy. Gravity and vacuum drag both have infinite range in universe. Gravity and vacuum drag both only attractive. Inverse square law is applicable to both gravity and pressure difference. Free fall experience in gravity and in pressure difference is same. Gravity of two objects on third object is summation/abstraction. Pressure difference also follows the same. Here, it means to say gravity force and inertia force both are same that is called principle of equivalence.

As mentioned in introduction, The General Theory of Relativity which uses only units kg, length and time gives a geometric explanation of how gravity works. That's why it has so far passed many unambiguous observational and experimental tests. However, there are strong indications the theory is incomplete. The problem of quantum gravity and the question of the reality of space time singularities remain open. Observational data that is taken as evidence for dark energy and dark matter indicates the need for new physics. In my view, till date cause of gravity was a mystery. Development of a simple physical concept for the cause of gravity is needed that is hypothesised above. It is concluded that gravity is a thermodynamic property of an object and not a fundamental force, and there is no any mediating element which causes this phenomena. It is the surface energy of an object that causes gravity (vacuum drag).

### 1.3. Possible Experiments

Testing can be done by observations and experiments both. Observing the free fall of objects from outside the atmosphere of the Earth it will fall towards normal to the Earth cross section area. Vacuum drag can be demonstrated for low mass particle starts moving first towards vacuum compared to heavy mass with same acceleration. Also, one kg mass with different density must start move simultaneously towards vacuum drag. Another potential site is the gravity midpoint between the Earth and Moon that by validating gravity depends on objects diameter and surface conditions. Red shift can be demonstrated in vacuum drag system. As gravity depends on so many parameters, Earth local surface conditions can be compared for variation in gravity value. The most difficult test for gravity to work is to demonstrate an object in closed (shielded) suspended chamber. Here, it should be noted that vacuum drag of Earth causes closed suspended chamber facing surface to have reduced surface energy (that should be measured) which is to be balanced. The easy experiment is to measure Mercury elements gravity. it takes spherical shape. Also, it has higher density and surface tension. So, it will defy Newton's gravity equation.

### 1.4. Acknowledgements

I am thankful to journals/scientists who have posted their data for freely accessible on internet. The paper is developed by author own as an individual and not taken any financial or technical support from Organization/Institution/Govt. body. I am also thankful to David de Hilster who has compiled the paper in ShareLatex.

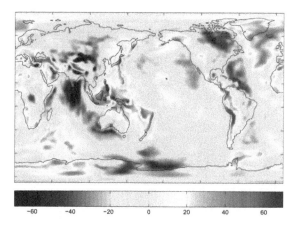

**Figure 3.** A gravity anomaly is the difference between the observed gravity and a value predicted from a model. Source: http://photojournal.jpl.nasa.gov/jpeg/PIA04652.jpg

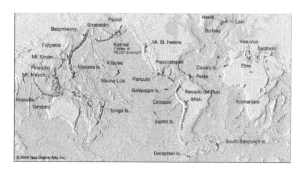

**Figure 4.** World map Volcano and Topography. Source: http://jeremyrenners.blogspot.in

| Table 1: Gravity Vs Volcanic Activity | | | | |
|---|---|---|---|---|
| Planets / moons | Rad ius r m | Den sity $g/cm^3$ | Grav ity g N | Volcanic Activity |
| Earth | 6371 | 5.513 | 9.81 | Volcano |
| Mercury | 2440 | 5.427 | 3.7 | Volcano |
| Venus | 6052 | 5.243 | 8.87 | Volcano |
| Mars | 3389 | 3.934 | 3.7 | Volcano |
| Io | 1822 | 3.528 | 1.8 | Volcano |
| Moon | 1737 | 3.346 | 1.63 | Volcano |
| Europa | 1561 | 3.013 | 1.32 | Volcano |
| Haum-R | 620 | 2.55 | 0.44 | Volcano |
| ErisR | 1163 | 2.52 | 0.66 | Volcano |
| Ceres | 481.5 | 2.17 | 0.29 | Volcano |
| Triton | 1353 | 2.061 | 0.78 | Volcano |
| PlutoR | 1184 | 2.03 | 0.61 | Volcano |
| Ganym. | 2634 | 1.936 | 1.43 | Volcano |
| Titan | 2576 | 1.88 | 1.35 | Volcano |
| Callisto | 2410 | 1.834 | 1.24 | No data |
| Titania | 788.4 | 1.711 | 0.38 | No data |
| Ariel | 578.9 | 1.66 | 0.27 | NoVolcano |
| Charon | 603.5 | 1.65 | 0.28 | NoVolcano |
| Neptune | 24622 | 1.638 | 11.1 | NoVolcano |
| Oberon | 761.4 | 1.63 | 0.35 | NoVolcano |
| Dione | 561.4 | 1.478 | 0.23 | NoVolcano |
| Umbriel | 584.7 | 1.39 | 0.23 | NoVolcano |
| Jupiter | 69911 | 1.326 | 24.8 | NoVolcano |
| Uranus | 25362 | 1.27 | 8.87 | NoVolcano |
| Rhea | 763.8 | 1.236 | 0.26 | NoVolcano |
| Iapetus | 734.5 | 1.088 | 0.22 | NoVolcano |
| Tethys | 531.1 | 0.984 | 0.15 | NoVolcano |
| Saturn | 58232 | 0.687 | 10.4 | NoVolcano |

| Table2: Asteroid Striking rate and Velocity | | | |
|---|---|---|---|
| Planets / Moon | Local Plan- etesimals in Heliocen- tric Circular Orbits | Asteroids and Short Period Comets | Long Period Comets |
| Mercury | 4.7 | 20 | 64 |
| Venus | 11.5 | 18 | 49 |
| Earth | 12.5 | 18 | 42 |
| Moon | 6.1 | 14 | 40 |
| Mars | 5.6 | 10 | 33 |

## 2. Bending Of Light By Sun's Vacuum Drag

As per Newton's law of gravity the mass of an object falling under the influence of Earth's gravity has no effect on its acceleration, i.e., all objects must accelerate equally toward Earth regardless of their mass. Therefore he assumed light would follow the same rule. Newton concluded that light from distant stars grazing the Sun's limb would fall towards the Sun as they passed by, resulting in a slightly curved trajectory. But the observation is double than predicted. Einstein came with exact solution and he had calculated the angle based on his general theory of relativity, that the deflection of a sun-grazing light beam would be 1.75 arc sec instead of 0.87 arc sec. Here, it is argued that the phenomenon responsible for double deflection is light takes longer time to move through a gravitational field. But this argument doesn't give fundamental reason. Below theory uses escape energy which is required for an object with molecules in it to escape vs. light which has no molecules that means it has no surface energy. Any object escaping from the Sun's surface has lower surface energy because it counters vacuum drag. As the object is given an external energy against vacuum drag to escape, it recovers the loss at infinite distance (here, it has higher gravity). Note that, surface energy depends on molecular bonds. Light has no molecules so, it doesn't recover energy loss. Instead it loses its energy initially highest then gradually decreases by red shifting. Consider Schwarzschild gravitational radius for light not to escape.

$$r = \frac{2GM}{c^2} \qquad (25)$$

$$c^2 = \frac{2GM}{r} = \frac{2GMr}{r^2} \qquad (26)$$

$$c^2 = 2gr \qquad (27)$$

In above equation, escape velocity required is speed of light. And the energy required to escape for light is $mc^2$. Now, consider any object with molecules in it for above radius which can accelerate/decelerate. It will require energy equal to $\frac{1}{2}mc^2$. So, it should be concluded that the energy required for light will be double. That means it suffers more energy loss to escape than any object with molecules. That is why it makes double deflection angle. On surface object has some initial surface energy due to vacuum drag from gravitating body which reduces internal absolute pressure of the object. But light has no molecules and doesn't have initial surface energy. So, to escape it has to spent more energy than any object with molecules. Same is applicable to sub atomic particles like electrons, protons, neutrons etc.

For light escaping from the Sun's surface tangentially, The deflection tangent angle of light can be calculated by comparing ratio between required escape energy vs. actual total energy.

Required to escape energy $V_e$ / Initial Energy posses by Light.

$$Ratio = \frac{mV_e^2}{mc^2}$$

$$\delta = \frac{617028.54^2}{2997924582^2} = 4.236x10^{-6} \qquad (28)$$

Convert to second unit $4.236x10^{-6} x 3600 = 0.01525$ second (")

Convert to arc second.

$$= \frac{0.01525x180}{\pi} = 0.8738 \text{arc second} \qquad (29)$$

This is a half angle for light just generating from limb. Same deflection angle on opposite side can be measured when light coming out from distance star. So, total deflection made by light when it passing just sun's tangent line will be double.

total $= 2x0.8738$ arc second $= 1.7475$ arc second

For an object escaping in parabola trajectory ($e = 1$) from the Sun's surface. The deflection tangent angle can be calculated by comparing ratio between required escape energy vs. actual total energy.

Required to escape energy $V_e$ / Initial Energy posses by an object.

$$Ratio = \frac{\frac{1}{2}mV_e^2}{(\frac{1}{2}mV_a^2 + mgr)} \qquad (30)$$

Here, mass of an object removed from both side.

$$Ratio = \frac{0.5x617028.5^2}{(0.5x617028.5^2 + 273.6x695800000)} = 0.5 \qquad (31)$$

Convert to arc deg.

$$\delta = \frac{0.50x180}{\pi} = 28.648 \text{ arc deg.} \qquad (32)$$

This is a half angle for an object escaping tangent from the Sun at radius r. Same deflection angle on opposite side can be measured when object coming out from infinite distance. So, total deflection made by object when it passing just sun's tangent line will be double.

## 3. Gravitational Red Shift Of Light By Vacuum Drag

As per the general relativity equivalence principle, gravity influences all the physical objects and same is also applicable to light. It is experimentally proved that light travels towards gravitating object are blue shifted. Whereas light travels opposite direction is redshirted; Means it gains and loss energy respectively. It is known as the gravitational frequency shift. It has been measured in the laboratory and using astronomical observations. Same can be explained by new vacuum drag theory which depends on surface energy and same is depends on molecular bonds. Light has no molecules and hence, it cannot make bonds, so, it doesn't experience surface energy loss, Instead it loses its energy initially highest on surface then gradually losses it by red shifting.

Let us consider Photon travelling straight from Sun surface to Earth surface in the line of centers. Its Initial energy is 14400eV (rays used in Pound-Rebka experiment in 1959). On reaching Earth, it will loss energy due to gravitational force. This loss of energy can be calculated as per fundamental theory of cause of gravity.

Now, T = Time taken by Photon to reach Earth, 499 sec, C = Speed of Light per second, 299792458 m/sec d = Distance traveled by photon to reach Earth,

$$d = 499 * 299792458 = 1.496E + 11m \qquad (33)$$

Now, Consider Surface Energy of half sphere Sun, $S.E = 1.9042E + 11$ Nm

Now, Surface Tension ($\gamma$) of Sun = Surface energy of Sun half sphere/Sun half sphere area.

$$\gamma = S.E/A(2 \text{ removed from both side}) \qquad (34)$$

Where, r is Radius of Sun, 696000000 m and A is Half Surface area of Sun.

$$\gamma = \frac{1.9042E + 11}{2\pi x696000000^2} \qquad (35)$$

$$\gamma = 6.26E - 08Nm^{-1} \qquad (36)$$

$$p = \frac{2\gamma}{r} = \frac{2x6.26E - 08}{696000000} \qquad (37)$$

$$p = 1.798E - 16Nm^{-2} \qquad (38)$$

It is the absolute pressure remains after deduction of Sun atmospheric pressure.

Now, Normal Force on Sun surface,

$$F = \pi r^2 p = \pi x696000000^2 x1.798E - 16 \qquad (39)$$

$$= 273.587 \text{ N}$$

Now, calculate the inward pressure at Sun $r_o$ distance. Here, Pressure inversely proportional to radial distance.

$$\pi r^2 p = \pi r_o^2 p_o \qquad (40)$$

Where, p = Vacuum drag on object c/s area with r radius, $N/m^2$
$r_o$ = Dist. of the Sun to Earth Surface = 1.496E+11 m

$$r^2 p = r_o^2 p_o \qquad (41)$$

$$p_o = \frac{r^2 p}{r_o^2} \qquad (42)$$

$$p_o = \frac{696000000^2 x1.798E - 16}{1.496E + 11^2} \qquad (43)$$

$$p_o = 3.892E - 21Nm^{-2} \qquad (44)$$

This is vacuum drag at Earth surface due to Sun. Here, Photon travels from higher vacuum drag to lower vacuum drag.

Now, Find Gravity Force towards the Sun at radius 1.496E+11 m, (Earth to Sun distance) Here, Sun radius (r) considered in equation. As the normal cross section area of the Sun is only facing area.

Force, $F = \pi r^2 p_o$

$$F = \pi x 696000000^2 x 3.892E - 21 \quad (45)$$

$F_o = 0.005922N$ Which is equal to gravity Force towards the Sun at the Earth surface

Equivalent Mass of Photon $m_p = \frac{E_p}{C^2}$

$$m = \frac{14400}{299792458^2} kg \quad (46)$$

Where, E Energy of Photon, $eV = 14400eV$

$$m_p = 1.6026E - 13 kg \quad (47)$$

Energy gain/(-)loss by Photon, Ep = mass of photon x (cross s/c area of Sun x inward pressure at Earth surface x distance traveled by photon from center)- (cross s/c area of Sun x inward pressure at Sun surface x distance traveled by photon from center)

Energy loss by Photon,
$$\Delta E_p = m_p(\pi r^2 p_o r_o - \pi r^2 pr)$$

$$\Delta E_p = 1.6026E - 13(3.14159x696000000^2 x$$
$$3.892E - 21x1.496E + 11 - 3.14159x696000000^2$$
$$x1.798E - 16x696000000) \quad (48)$$

$$E_p = -3.0366945E - 02 \quad (49)$$

This is the energy loss by Photon. Earth and other objects Gravitational force and other effects are not considered for ease of calculation.

With same procedure, pound-Rebka experiment for gamma photon(14400 eV) energy gain can be calculated for 22.56m which will be +3.55E-11 eV.

## 4. Precession of the Perihelion of Mercury: Cumulative Force of Asteroids Strike

The French Astronomer Le Verriere had tried to explain the strange advance of Mercury's orbit by proposing additional planet Vulcan with Newtonian laws of gravity. Which need to be existing in an orbit between Mercury and the Sun. However, no one found its existence.

By Newton's equations, taking into account all the effects from the other planets a precession of 5557 seconds of arc per century predicted. But the actual precession of Mercury's orbit was measured 5600 seconds of arc per century. There is a discrepancy of 43 seconds of arc per century. Einstein's theory of relativity solved the problem by introducing wrapping of space time due to Sun. But predicted magnitude of other planets have differences from observation as one gets farther away from the Sun. Below theory provides a fundamental physics behind the discrepancy of Precession of the perihelion of all orbiting objects. The new theory considers the extra force required for precession of Mercury is due to periodically asteroids strikes at perihelion is higher than aphelion. As Sun's gravity is too much compare to all orbiting planets, Objects are

attracted radially towards it. So, the probability of asteroid strike is higher when the object is near the Sun compared to further away. That is why Mercury experiences very high rate of asteroid strikes compared to Pluto even though later is highly eccentric compared to former one. Also, Einstein's calculations predict a shift for Venus and Earth is far away than observations. That is because they both experiences asteroid strike but due to nearly circular orbit they experience same striking force in all locations in orbit. Also, their atmosphere, soft surface and Water absorbs the striking force and produce dampening effect whereas Mercury, Mars and Moon have hard surface and nearly no atmosphere to counter the force. To falsify Einstein concept of space time, satellite need to be sent in orbit of Sun same as Mercury but in opposite direction. It will not precess as mentioned in general relativity. The effect of impact velocity and planetary focusing on the diameter of impact craters on different planetary bodies provided in (Table 2). Source: "The Surface of Mars", by Mike Carr.

## 5. Gravitational Tidal Bulge

Gravitational tidal bulge can be calculated in a physical fundamental way by considering Earth floating in a vacuum drag produced be the Moon and The Sun. Here, the Moon and the Sun decreases surface energy of Earth facing half sphere that decreases absolute internal pressure and it must be same for whole Earth. Here, it is known that object in the pressure difference always tries to reduce its facing cross section area (normal) towards source of force due to its inertia. Here, Earth inertia tends to oppose it. Resulting in reduction in cross section area by allowing it bulge symmetrically.

Let find the Earth tidal bulge caused by Sun gravitational pull.

Now, Consider Surface Energy of half sphere Sun, S.E/2

$$\frac{S.E}{2} = 1.9042E + 11Nm \quad (50)$$

Here, surface tension introduced to find absolute inside pressure. Note that, there is no role of surface tension except to find absolute inside pressure.

Now, Surface Tension ($\gamma$) of Sun = Surface energy of Sun half sphere /Sun half sphere area.

$$\gamma = S.E/A(2 \text{ removed from both sides}) \quad (51)$$

Where, r is Radius, 696000000 m and A is Surface area of Sun.

$$\gamma = \frac{1.9042E + 11}{2\pi 696000000^2} \quad (52)$$

$$\gamma = 6.26E - 08Nm^{-1} \quad (53)$$

$$p = \frac{2\gamma}{r} = \frac{2x6.26E - 08}{696000000} \quad (54)$$

$$p = 1.798E - 16Nm^{-2} \quad (55)$$

It is the absolute pressure remains after deduction of Sun's atmospheric pressure.

Now, Normal Force (F) on Sun surface,

Force, $F = \pi r^2 p$

$$F = \pi x 696000000^2 x 1.798E - 16 \qquad (56)$$

$$F = 273.59N \qquad (57)$$

Now, calculate the vacuum drag pressure at $r_c$ distance from the Sun.

Here, Vacuum drag inversely proportional to radial distance.

$$\pi r^2 p = \pi r_c^2 p_c \qquad (58)$$

Where, $p_c$ = Pressure on object $c/s$ area with $r_c$ radius, $N/m^2$, and r = Distance of between Sun to Earth Center = $1.496E + 11m$

$$r^2 p = r_c^2 p_c \qquad (59)$$

$$p_c = \frac{r^2 p}{r_c} \qquad (60)$$

$$p_c = \frac{696000000^2 x 1.798E - 16}{1.496E + 11^2} \qquad (61)$$

$$p_c = 3.8912E - 21Nm^{-2} \qquad (62)$$

this is inward absolute pressure at Earth center due to Sun.

Similarly, $p_n = 3.8915E - 21Nm^{-2}$, this is inward absolute pressure at Earth nearside by Sun.

Now, Find Gravity Force towards Sun at radius $1.4959E + 11m$, Here, Sun radius (r) considered in equation. As the normal cross section area of Sun is only facing area. Force,

$$F_c = \pi r^2 p_c \qquad (63)$$

$$F_c = \pi x 696000000^2 x 3.8912E - 21 \qquad (64)$$

$$F_c = 0.0059184N \qquad (65)$$

Force towards Sun at a distance Earth center. Similarly, Find Gravity Force towards Sun at radius $1.4959E + 11m$, Earth nearside due to Sun. Force,

$$F_n = \pi r^2 p_n \qquad (66)$$

$$F_n = \pi x 696000000^2 x 3.8915E - 21 \qquad (67)$$

$$F_n = 0.0059189N \qquad (68)$$

Force towards Sun at the Earth near side surface.

Now, find the Tidal force experienced by The Earth due to pressure difference.

$$Ft = F_n - F_c \qquad (69)$$

$$Ft = 0.0059189 - 0.0059184N \qquad (70)$$

$$Ft = 5.0412E - 7N \qquad (71)$$

By Same procedure, Tidal force on Earth far side can be calculated 5.0405E-7 N. Similarly, Moon tidal force acting on Earth can be calculated. Near side 1.128E-6 N and far side 1.074E-6 N Here, above calculation answers why Moon tidal force is higher than Sun by 2.238 times at near side and 2.130 times at far side.

Note that, no force is acting on perpendicular to line of action of gravity force. But internal pressure reduced due to reduction in surface energy. This is balanced by increase in cross section area in perpendicular direction.

# REFERENCES

1. Lozano. P., *Notes on surface tension phenomena.* Lecture notes MIT edu.
2. J. B. Merriam, *Atmospheric pressure and gravity,*Geophys. J. int. (1992) 109, 488-500.
3. Jacob N. Israelachvili, *Historical perspective, Intermolecular and Surface Forces*, Third Edition, 2010, P. 3-9, P. 60.
4. Dmitriev, A., *Temperature dependence of gravitational force: experiments, Astrophysics,Perspectives*, St-Petersburg University of Information Technologies, Mechanics and Optics, Russia.
5. Truman, O.H., *Variation of gravity at one place*, Astrophysical journal, Vol. 89, p. 445-462.
6. Stephen W. Hurrell, *A new method to calculate palaeogravity using fossil feathers*, NCGT Journal, v. 2, no. 3, September, 2014.
7. Emily R. Morey-Holton, *Chap 9 The impact of gravity on life, Evolution on Planet Earth*; ISBN 0-12-598655-6, p. 143-159.

# Relativity Is Self-Defeated(1 of 3)
## —In Terms of Mathematics

### 2016 © Cameron Rebigsol

*P.O. Box 872282, Vancouver, WA 98687, crebigsol@gmail.com*

If $c = 0$ is what a physics theory leads itself to conclude for the speed of light, anyone would reject this theory without question. However, $c = 0$ is exactly what relativity "impeccably" leads itself to, with its own mathematical derivation. Not only this conclusion must violate a well-known fact $c = 3 \times 10^5 km/sec$, which relativity takes as an indispensable assumption for the development of its calculation, but $c = 0$ thus also directly destroys the Lorentz factor: $1/\sqrt{1 - (v/c)^2}$.

How much tolerance can the Lorentz factor have if $c = 0$ is forced in its denominator? If the Lorentz factor's validity must be removed, all concepts found in relativity, such as length contraction and time dilation and speed limit brought up by relativity, will no longer find any space to survive in the science world. However, $c = 0$ is a result that relativity's derivation inescapably leads itself to.

The Lorentz factor is an inevitable and solid mathematical outcome of the phenomena called aberration. Invalidating the Lorentz factor by putting up $c=0$, relativity must ruin its own validity. To see how the Lorentz factor is inevitably brought up by the aberration of a light source, which is typified by the so called stellar aberration, a reader is cordially invited to visit the other two articles of the same series by this author: ***Relativity Is Self-Defeated** (2 of 3) —in terms of physics*, and ***Relativity Is Self-Defeated** (3 of 3)—Lorentz Factor, Aberration, and Ether.*

**Keywords:** Lorentz factor, speed of light, diameter of the Milky Way, length contraction.

## 1. The mathematical work leading to $c=0$

The most renowned mathematical work laying the foundation for the debut of relativity is the so called Lorentz transformation. The Lorentz transformation begins its work with an equation set that can be summarized, but with more direct wording, as shown in the textbooks introducing special relativity to students:

$$x' = a_{11}x + a_{12}y + a_{13}z + a_{14}t \tag{1}$$

$$y' = a_{21}x + a_{22}y + a_{23}z + a_{24}t \tag{2}$$

$$z' = a_{31}x + a_{32}y + a_{33}z + a_{34}t \tag{3}$$

$$t' = a_{41}x + a_{42}y + a_{43}z + a_{44}t \tag{4}$$

The task of (Eq. 1-4) is to find all a's as unknowns while all x's, y's, z's, t's are given the status as if they had been constants. With many supplemental conditions, (Eq. 1-4) finally boils down to the following set:

$$x' = a_{11}(x - vt) \tag{5}$$

$$y' = y \tag{6}$$

$$y' = y \tag{7}$$

$$t' = a_{41}x + a_{44}t \tag{8}$$

If all a's remain as unknowns, (Eq. 5-8) is a set with three unknowns but only two relevant equations, which

are (Eq. 5 , 8), and is then unsolvable. To overcome the difficulties, both the derivation of Lorentz transformation and Einstein's work introduce new information with

$$x^2 + y^2 + z^2 = c^2t^2 \tag{9}$$

$$x'^2 + y'^2 + z'^2 = c^2t'^2 \tag{10}$$

Given that $y'=y$ and $z'=z$ are redundant and they eventually reduce to zero, the useful information in (Eq. 9, 10) actually only contains

$$x^2 = c^2t^2 \tag{11}$$

$$x'^2 = c^2t'^2 \tag{12}$$

Putting everything together, all the above information can lead to an equation set that reads

$$x' = a_{11}(x - vt) \tag{13}$$

$$t' = a_{41}x + a_{44}t \tag{14}$$

$$x^2 = c^2t^2 \tag{15}$$

$$x'^2 = c^2t'^2 \tag{16}$$

The introduction of (Eq. 9, 10), or equivalently, the introduction of (Eq. 11, 12), makes it indisputable that the set of (Eq. 13, 14, 15, and 16 ) is conditioned to be solved in the following way: No matter how time develops, each observer must see that the origin of one's own axis and the center of the light sphere coincide forever in each observer's inspection. (Eq. 13, 14, 15, and 16 ) obviously mandates that the three unknowns must simultaneously satisfy four equations.

Mathematically, the introduction of (Eq. 9, 10) is to say that the spherical space occupied by the light starts its expansion at $t=t'=0$. As far as each of the $\mathbf{X}$ axis and $\mathbf{X'}$ axis is concerned, light must propagate along them in both the positive and negative directions with speed of equal absolute value, which is $c$. Therefore, in the inspection of the $\mathbf{X}$ observer, he must say that the $\mathbf{X'}$ axis and the light front both move in the same direction pointing toward the positive end of his $\mathbf{X}$ axis. While looking toward the negative end, the same observer must say that the light front and the $\mathbf{X'}$ axis move in opposite direction between each other (Fig. 1).

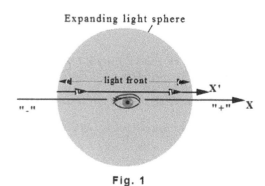

**Fig. 1**

**Figure 1.** With respect to the eye, light moving to the right of the page has speed $c$ but $-c$ moving toward the left of the page, while both ends of the $\mathbf{X'}$ axis indifferently move at speed $+v$ toward the right.

The distance between the light front and a certain point on the $\mathbf{X'}$ axis, such as the origin, must continuously changes in his inspection. It is at this point that Einstein's relativity steps in to guide how the observer should calculate the distance change in identical situation. The guidance can be found in a paragraph from §2 of the very first paper of relativity published in 1905:

*Let a ray of light depart from A at the time $t_A$, let it be reflected at B at the time $t_B$, and reach A again at the time $t'_A$. Taking into consideration the principle of the constancy of the velocity of light we find that*

$$t_B - t_A = \frac{\mathbf{r}_{AB}}{c-v}, for-same-direction \qquad (17)$$

and

$$t'_A - t_B = \frac{\mathbf{r}_{AB}}{c+v}, for-opposite-direction \qquad (18)$$

[Both (Eq. 17) and (18) are numerically labeled by this author, and the direction comments are notes from this author as well]

In this quoted paragraph, right at the very moment of emission of the ray, the location on the stationary system where point $A$ matches must be seen by relativity as where the light source of the ray is, or equivalently, as the center of a light sphere is. Among all the rays forming this sphere, the ray in the concern of the above quoted paragraph is only one of them. Please note: the light source as a physical entity may be attached to $r_{AB}$, or be attached to the $\mathbf{X}$ axis, but may not be both. Regardless of how the source is attached, however, in the observation of the $\mathbf{X}$ observer, the center of the expanding light sphere must, as mandated by (Eq. 9), be stationary to the $\mathbf{X}$ observer once the light ray emits.

The quoted paragraph further tells us that, for the light and the axis that an observer sees moving in the same direction, the relationship between distance, time, and speed should be established according to (Eq. 17). If the light and the axis are moving in opposite direction, the relationship between distance, time, and speed should be established according to (Eq. 18). In both situations, time is quoted from a clock next to the stationary observer.

Therefore, with the principle found in the above quoted paragraph, when seeing the light ray and the $\mathbf{X'}$ axis moving in the same direction, the $\mathbf{X}$ observer will obtain a distance $r'_+$ on the $\mathbf{X'}$ axis such that

$$\frac{\mathbf{r'}_+}{c-v} = t \qquad (19)$$

where $t$ is the amount of time that the ray requires to cover $r_+$, starting from $t=0$, of course, and registered by the clock next to the $\mathbf{X}$ observer.

For the movement in the opposite direction, this observer will obtain a distance $r'_-$ covered by the light traveling on the $\mathbf{X'}$ axis with the same amount of time $t$ such that

$$\frac{\mathbf{r'}_-}{c+v} = t \qquad (20)$$

(Eq. 19) and (Eq. 20) must lead this X observer to have

$$\frac{\mathbf{r'}_+}{c-v} = t = \frac{\mathbf{r'}_-}{c+v} \qquad (21)$$

or further

$$\frac{\mathbf{r'}_+}{\mathbf{r'}_-} = \frac{c-v}{c+v} \qquad (22)$$

To the observer on the $\mathbf{X'}$ axis, with $v=0$ for his own frame with respect to himself, and with the center of the light sphere to be seen at a point equivalent to point A (of $r_{AB}$) and to be motionless to him, (Eq. 12), (Eq. 17) and (Eq.18) all together require that he must see

$$r_+ = r_- = ct' \qquad (23)$$

where $t'$ is quoted from a clock in his $\mathbf{X'}$ axis, $r_+$ and $r_-$ are the rest lengths seen on his own $\mathbf{X'}$ axis.

(Eq. 10) thus leads to

$$\frac{r_+}{r_-} = 1 \qquad (24)$$

Then, (Eq. 11) and (Eq. 9) lead to the following development:

$$1 = \frac{r_+}{r_-} = \frac{r_+\sqrt{1-(v/c)^2}}{r_-\sqrt{1-(v/c)^2}} = \frac{r'_+}{r'_-} = \frac{c-v}{c+v} \qquad (25)$$

where $r'_+ (= r_+\sqrt{1-(v/c)^2})$ is the moving length seen by the $\mathbf{X}$ observer corresponding to the stationary length $r_+$ seen by the observer on the $\mathbf{X'}$ axis, and so is $r'_-$ to $r_-$.

(Eq. 12) can be satisfied only if $v=0$; no other value besides $v=0$ can satisfy it. This $v=0$ is a plain statement that the introduction of a sphere of light to make (Eq. 1-4) solvable implicitly forces the set to be solved with a predetermined speed value $v=0$.

Since (Eq. 13) is supposed to enable us to study the movement of the origin of the $\mathbf{X}$ axis, where $x=0$, with respect to the $\mathbf{X'}$ axis, it naturally leads us to have

$$x' = a_{11}(0 - vt) \qquad (26)$$

However, in the same set of equations, (Eq. 16) gives $x'=ct'$. Then, (Eq. 13), with the implicit condition $v=0$, inevitably becomes

$$ct' = a_{11}(0 - 0t) = 0 \qquad (27)$$

Through (Eq. 14), relativity declares that **the speed of light must be *zero*** whenever and wherever $t' \neq 0$ is found.

**With $c=0$, relativity's derivation must force a zero value of $c$ to be planted in the denominator of the Lorentz factor that reads** $1/\sqrt{1-(v/c)^2}$.

Clearly, so leading to $c=0$, relativity has made Lorentz factor an illegitimate expression in terms of mathematics. Without this factor, there is no relativity. With this factor carrying $c=0$ at its denominator, where is the validity of relativity? Because of the mathematical illegitimacy forced on the Lorentz factor by relativity, this author believes that the science world must pay serious attention to review the acceptance of some concept in physics, such as $ct$ or $ct'$ as the fourth dimension of the universe and the so-called light-cone fantasy that is built on this fourth dimension.

## 2. Paradoxes

For a theory that must rely on $c=0$ in the denominator of its mathematical expression to earn credibility, one should not wonder that paradoxes can be endlessly generated from this theory. Besides the famous twin paradox, relativity should also lead us to believe that we can zap across the Milky Way in just one second. Here is how:

A captain of an extremely long space vessel, with a clock next to him, adjusts the speed of his vessel so that the Milky Way is passing the vessel at speed of

$$v = \frac{10^5 \times (3600 \times 24 \times 365)c}{\sqrt{1 + [10^5 \times (3600 \times 24 \times 365)]^2}} \qquad (28)$$

where $c = 3 \times 10^5 km/sec$.

With this speed, the length contraction equation from relativity will make the captain see the otherwise stationary diameter of the Milky Way as one light-second long, of course, with a clock next to him. With this speed, if relativity is right, how will the captain not pass the Milky Way diameter from end to end in ***one*** second?

## REFERENCES

1. A. Einstein, *§2. On the Relativity of Lengths and Times, I. Kinematical Part, ON THE ELECTRODYNAMICS OF MOVING BODIES, 1905.*
2. Robert Resnick, *INTRODUCTION TO SPECIAL RELATIVITY, 1968* ,
3. Wikipedia, the free encyclopedia, *LORENTZ TRANSFORMATION, 2016*

# Relativity Is Self-Defeated(2 of 3)
## —In Terms of Mathematics

### 2016 © Cameron Rebigsol

*P.O. Box 872282, Vancouver, WA 98687, crebigsol@gmail.com*

The velocity addition theorem that witnesses the "impeccability" of relativity is actually an exact declaration rejecting the existence of the physical world fantasized by special relativity. The physical reality brought up by frequency shift related to movement, or the so called Doppler effect, must also ruin the concept of time dilation advocated by relativity. As relativity can only end up invalidating the physical world it promotes, human beings should have good reason to revive the concept of ether that relativity asserts not existing

The Michelson-Morley experiment, devised to verify the existence or nonexistence of ether, turns out that it has just placed itself in a wrong environment for its performance. Therefore, this experiment has actually never done anything to confirm or reject the existence of ether. Of course, then, it has never offered any physical evidence that relativity can use as a support. Possibly it is to many people's surprise that the Ives-Stilwell experiment and stellar aberration are actually physical evidence demolishing the credibility of relativity while they are still thought supporting.

**Keywords:** medium, ether, projectile, frequency shift, aberration, Michelson-Morley experiment, Ives-Stilwell experiment

## 1. Relativity Declares Its Own Invalidity via The Theorem of Velocity Addition

In Fig. 1, we assume water existing everywhere, inside and outside of the blue chamber and up to infinity, but the chamber is so tight that water inside and outside of the chamber have no connection to each other. Rod **EDM** locating at the midpoint of the chamber is so designed that when it generates sound, sound beams simultaneously emit in every direction. Let's assume that the sound's natural speed in water is $c$, and that $V_+$ is the speed of the chamber moving with respect to the ground. Water outside of the chamber as an entire bulk has zero speed with respect to the ground.

Now, when **EDM** is turned on, sound beams inside the chamber will reach the end wall KL and GH at the same time regardless of the value of V+, and regardless of the measurement is made by an observer inside the chamber or by an observer staying on the ground. However, both of their measurement would show that the time for the sound beams outside the chamber reaching the end walls will be different. Let's assume that at time instant $t_1^m = 0$ (Letter $m$ here denotes only location, the midpoint, carrying no mathematical significance) a beam from **MD** is sent. It reaches JK at $t_1^+$. If $V_+ \neq 0$, the observer should have $ct_1^+ = R + V_+ t_1^+$ and therefore

$$t_1^+ = \frac{R}{c - v_+} \qquad (1)$$

If **EDM** is turned off at $t_2^m = t_1^m + \Delta t$, the last instant $t_2^+$ for JK to receive the beam is

$$t_2^+ = \Delta t + \frac{R}{c - v_+} \qquad (2)$$

Then,

$$t_2^+ - t_1^+ = \Delta t \qquad (3)$$

Equation (3) means that the time duration $\Delta t$ of the beam is faithfully duplicated at JK, regardless of the value of V+. We can also have

$$t_2^+ - t_2^m = \frac{R}{c - v_+} \qquad (4)$$

Equation (4) means that the time duplication at JK happens with a time delay compared to the happening of $\Delta t$ at **EDM**.

With the same reasoning leading to equation (4), the time duration of the beam is duplicated at FG with a time delay as shown below:

$$t_2^- - t_2^m = \frac{R}{c + v_+} \qquad (5)$$

At the first instant that the inside sound beam reaches KL, this sound beam viewed by a ground observer would have covered a distance on the ground as $L+ = R + V_+(R/c)$, where $(R/c)$ is the time needed for the inside beam to complete the distance $R$. Therefore the speed of the sound beam $(V_{+,s})$ with respect to the ground should be

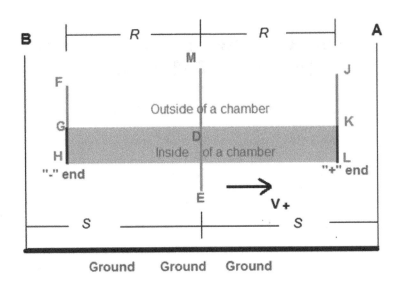

**Figure 1.**

$$V_{+,s} = \frac{R + V_+(R/c)}{R/c} \qquad (6)$$

$$= c + v_+$$

Looking toward the GH direction, the same reasoning would lead the speed of the sound beam $(V_{-,s})$ with respect to the ground as

$$V_{-,s} = \frac{R - V_+(R/c)}{R/c} \qquad (7)$$

$$= c - v_+$$

The above calculation for speed addition viewed by the ground observer is plain and rigid in arithmetic. However, equation (6) and equation (7) are offensive to special relativity if $c$ has the value of $3 \times 10^5$ km/sec. With this value and with its own reasoning, special relativity must lead itself to have speed addition, parallel to equation (6), to be calculated as

$$V_{+,s} = \frac{c + V_+}{1 + \frac{cV_+}{c^2}} \qquad (8)$$

$$= c$$

or, parallel to equation (7),

$$V_{-,s} = \frac{c + (-V_+)}{1 + \frac{c(-V_+)}{c^2}} \qquad (9)$$

$$= c$$

Regardless of the form of equation for speed addition, if $c$ is to represent the speed of sound in water, $c$ is physically explained as a natural characteristic of water, which is a medium enabling energy to be conveyed without any mass to be permanently relocated. However, if $c$ is to represent the speed of light as stipulated by relativity, $c$ is explained as a natural characteristic of some projectile, whose movement means the permanent relocation of both energy and mass. With a property so characterized for projectiles, any equation describing the movement of such a projectile should be expected being in some form that is completely independent of a medium. Surprisingly, relativity fails to do so in presenting corresponding equations. Instead, equations put up by it must show reliance of a medium. Evidence can be found in the following paragraph quoted from relativity:

*Let a ray of light depart from A at the time\* $t_A$, let it be reflected at B at the time $t_B$, and reach A again at the time $t'_A$. Taking into consideration the principle of the constancy of the velocity of light we find that*

$$t_B - t_A = \frac{R_{AB}}{c - v} \qquad \text{(Eq. Rela-A)}$$

*and*

$$t'_A - t_B = \frac{R_{AB}}{c + v} \qquad \text{(Eq. Rela-B)}$$

*where $R_{AB}$ denotes the length of the moving rod ——measured in the stationary system.*

*\*"Time" here denotes "time of the stationary system" and also "position of hands of the moving clock situated at the place under discussion".*

[Notes from this author: (1) The above "*" note is from the original paper; (2) both (Eq. Rela-A) and (Eq. Rela-B) are numbered by this author. ]

Comparison between equation (4) and equation (Rela-A), as well as between equation (5) and equation (Rela-B), equation (Rela-A) and equation (Rela-B) show that relativity has obviously established its equations based on the reliance of the presence of some medium, which stays motionlessly with the clock that shows "time of the stationary system". If light has been consisted of projectiles that have constant speed with respect to its source, at the absence of any medium, equation (Rela-A) and (Rela-B) should have been rewritten as

$$t_B - t_A = \frac{R_{AB}}{c} \qquad \text{(Eq. Rela-A, corrected)}$$

and

$$t'_A - t_B = \frac{R_{AB}}{c} \qquad \text{(Eq. Rela-B, corrected)}$$

Then, $c$ in the above two equations should take some other values, such as, $c'$ or $c''$, with respect to the stationary clock and lead to the establishment of the following equations

$$c'(t_B - t_A) = c(t_B - t_A) + v(t_B - t_A), \text{ ( for the initial ray)}$$

and

$$c''(t'_A - t_B) = c(t'_A - t_B) - v(t'_A - t_B), \text{ ( for the reflected ray)}$$

If relativity must force $c' = c$ and $c'' = c$, it can have only $v = 0$ for the above two equations to hold.

If relativity has fidelity to itself, since the ray is chasing $R_{AB}$ on the frame of $R_{AB}$ from A to B at speed $c$, it is only fair for relativity to adhere to what it advocates. Then, from the view of the stationary clock and with the consideration of the Theorem of Velocity Addition, relativity should have equation (Rela-A) to be given as

$$t_B - t_A = \frac{R_{AB}(moving)}{(c+v)/[1+\frac{cv}{c^2}]}$$
$$= \frac{R_{AB}(rest)\sqrt{1-(\frac{v}{c})^2}}{c} \qquad (10)$$
$$= (\frac{R_{AB}}{c})\sqrt{1-(\frac{v}{c})^2}$$

where $R_{AB}(rest) = R_{AB}$

Unfortunately to relativity, however, the above equation hereby declares one "principle": *moving clock is seen running faster*. It costs less time from the stationary clock , shown as $t_B - t_A$ on this equation, to see light completing the journey from A to B on $R_{AB}$ with time shown as ($R_{AB}$

/$c$) , the time recorded by a clock running together with $R_{AB}$ .

Let's imagine that in a physical system an observer riding on object A detects object B moving away from him at speed $V$. He further sees a projectile moving away from B at speed $c_1$ with respect to B and on the same line defined by A and B. Naturally, he can conclude that the projectile moves away from him with another speed called $c_2$, which is resulted by $V$ and $c_1$ working together. According to relativity, $c_2$ must obey the following mathematical relationship

$$c_2 = \frac{c_1 + V}{1 + \frac{c_1 V}{c^2}} \qquad (11)$$

Equation (11) inescapably leads us to have

$$V = \frac{c_2 - c_1}{1 - \frac{c_1 c_2}{c^2}} \qquad (12)$$

If the projectile is a packet of light, we must have $c_1 = c$ , as well as $c_2 = c$ according to relativity's assumption and conclusion forced by equation (11). Then equation (12) can only lead to $V = 0 \div 0$, witnessing a *disastrous result to relativity* in mathematics. Relativity then just plainly declares:

**No speed value can ever be found in the real world to materialize a physical system fantasized by special relativity**.

## 2. Results from the Ives-Stilwell Experiment Rejects Special Relativity

Special relativity holds that light, without the presence of a medium, is consisted of photons that act like projectiles thrown out by a source. Once disengaged from the source, each photon must be a moving entity carrying its own clock, which, while moving at speed $c$ in any observer's inspection, no longer receives any influence from the source's clock. Here is the relativity's claim about the behavior of a moving clock:

*...the time marked by the clock (viewed in the stationary system) is slow by* $1 - \sqrt{(1-(\frac{v}{c})^2}$ *seconds per second...* [§4. Physical Meaning of the Equations Obtained in Respect to Moving Rigid Bodies and Moving Clocks. **ON THE ELECTRODYNAMICS OF MOVING BODIES**, By A. Einstein, 1905]

In the stationary observer's inspection, before a photon is separated from the source, he deals with only one running clock, which is attached to the moving source. This clock forever runs at speed less than $c$ in relativity's stipulation. Once a photon is separated from the source, the observer must deal with one more clock, which is attached to the photon. Since photon must run at speed $c$, the mathematical result about time from the above quoted statement must be so written: "...the time marked by the clock (of photon) is slow by $[1-(0)]$ seconds per second..." This literally says that the time lapse shown by the photon clock is seen frozen by the observer, because any oscillator is seen to stay at the same invariant state forever by the observer, i.e., no frequency of any kind is found by him. How frequency shift detection is made possible by an observer when he sees no frequency?

Therefore, **if relativity is ever genuine to itself, the above quotation should have been enough to make it reject any idea of frequency shift of light caused by motion.**

Nevertheless, relativity has the following equation connecting the pace of time lapse between a running clock and an observer's stationary clock:

$$t = \frac{t' + (v/c^2)x'}{\sqrt{1-(v/c)^2}} \tag{13}$$

where all primed coordinates belong to the light source, or the moving clock, and the non-primed coordinates belong to the stationary clock of the observer.

If the running clock starts with $t' = 0$, then

$$t = \frac{(v/c^2)x'}{\sqrt{1-(v/c)^2}} \tag{14}$$

If the running clock is approaching the observer, $v$ takes negative value. With the time advancement of one period $p'$ in the moving clock, the observer's clock should have advanced to an instant $t_1$ such that

$$t_1 = \frac{p' + (-v/c^2)x'}{\sqrt{1-(v/c)^2}} \tag{15}$$

Now, we have

$$
\begin{aligned}
t_1 - t &= \frac{p' + (-v/c^2)x'}{\sqrt{1-(v/c)^2}} - \frac{(-v/c^2)x'}{\sqrt{1-(v/c)^2}} \\
&= \frac{p'}{\sqrt{1-(v/c)^2}} > p'
\end{aligned}
\tag{16}
$$

Obviously, $t_1 - t > p'$, or $[1/(t_1-t)] < (1/p')$, is a result disregarding the direction of $v$ of the moving light source, whether approaching an observer or moving away. Equation (16) thus must fail to describe how frequency read from a running clock is affected by the corresponding moving direction. For example, no blue-shift can be presented by equation (16) to an observer who sees a clock approaching him, but instead, ironically, equation (16) must inform him of red-shift. Indeed, equatin (16) even shows that the higher the $v$ becomes, the more shifting toward the red could have been shown. The outcome so concluded

from equation (16) completely violates common knowledge and thus inevitably destroys relativity's credibility in explaining frequency shift caused by movement.

If we compare between equation (10) and equation (16), we do find this "truth" from relativity: **Liberally unbounded inconsistency is displayed in relativity.** With equation (10), relativity advocates *moving clock runs faster* via the theorem of velocity addition; with equation (16), relativity advocates *moving clock runs slower* but at the cost of the complete failure of presenting the relationship between moving direction and frequency shift.

We all know that there is one famous experiment claiming to have confirmed the frequency shift predicted by relativity. It is the Ives-Stilwell experiment done in 1938. That experiment shows that, for a light source approaching an observer, frequency shift is shown as

$$f = f'\sqrt{\frac{c+v}{c-v}} \tag{17}$$

where $f'$ is the actual frequency of the light source and $f$ is the corresponding observed value. Equivalently, with the notation we have been using, we can have

$$\frac{1}{t_1 - t} = \frac{1}{p'}\sqrt{\frac{c+v}{c-v}} \tag{18}$$

If $(t_1 - t)$ represents the same time duration in both equation (16) and (18), and if relativity is to make itself meaningful, these two equations must lead to

$$\frac{p'}{\sqrt{1-(v/c)^2}} = p'\sqrt{\frac{c-v}{c+v}} \tag{19}$$

Then, $v = 0$ must be concluded from equation (19).

If the source is moving away from the observer, the Ives-Stilwell experiment gives

$$f = f'\sqrt{\frac{c-v}{c+v}} \tag{20}$$

Similar reasoning leading to equation (19) would give

$$\frac{p'}{\sqrt{1-(v/c)^2}} = p'\sqrt{\frac{c+v}{c-v}} \tag{21}$$

Once again, $v = 0$ must be concluded.

Data obtained by the Ives-Stilwell experiment is from a real world, and it is these data that enable equation (17) and (20) to be empirically summarized. That $v = 0$ is so inevitably demonstrated in equation (19) and (21) in "witnessing" Doppler effect can only mean that the world fantasized by relativity cannot fit itself in the real world whenever $v \neq 0$ must be dealt with. Therefore, **Doppler effect**

**recorded from the real world can only serve as exclusive physical evidence demolishing the validity of relativity**. What should happen as revealed by equation (17) and (20) in the real world cannot happen in the world of relativity, or vice versa. Although relativity's derivative work coincidentally leads to some mathematical expressions that look like equation (17) and (20), ending up with $v = 0$ must violate the moving status that relativity has assumed for the moving source.

Besides the Doppler effect caused by movement between the light source and the observer, the real world has another piece of solid evidence against relativity. It is called **stellar aberration**. Stellar aberration has been conventionally regarded as one of many pieces of physical evidence encouraging the debut of relativity. However, analysis more in details finds that the conventional study has troubled itself with a speed higher than $c$ for the propagation of light but is unaware of this error. We all know that, so far, speed higher than $c$ for the light propagation is unacceptable by any school. To remove this error and restore the true nature of the light propagation, it needs quite lengthy preparation. So this author would like to present corresponding discussion in another paper. For this, a reader is cordially invited to visit *Relativity Is Self-Defeated (3 of 3) —Lorentz Factor, aberration, and ether*, presented in the **CNPS** Conference of July 20-23, 2016.

## 3. Reviving the Concept of Ether

We cannot imagine a third manner for the propagation of light besides these two: Light by itself is some kind of projectile, or light is something whose relocation must rely on the conveyance of something else, or the so called medium, at the expense of its own energy. Due to the failure we have seen with relativity, which assumes light as possessing the property of some kind of projectiles, we are left with only one choice, which is to view that light's relocation is involving only with energy relocation, and such relocation must therefore rely on some medium.

The science world did once introduce the concept of some conveyor, or medium, which is called ether, for the propagation of light; relativity misleads us to have it abandoned. For or against ether, however, the science world has one view in common: once disengaging from the light source, any packet of light in space will have its own moving status. This is possible only if the light packet has been completely disassociated with the source; no influence of any kind from the source can be received by this packet after the disengagement. If not projectiles, then, after the moment of disengagement, the packet of light must be completely arrested by a substance and subsequently governed by the characteristics of this substance whose existence is independent of the light source. If a light source can generate light wherever it goes through, such substance must offer itself to be readily available at anywhere the source

shows up. Therefore, that light has been detected in every corner of the universe must force us to accept that such substance serving as a light conveyor exists everywhere in the universe.

One of the "facts" that is used as "indisputable" evidence forcing the science world to abandon the belief of the existence of a medium for light conveyance is the Michelson-Morley experiment. Unfortunately, if this experiment is ever devised to study "ether wind", it can be said that it has been placed in an environment more suitable to study "air wind". Essentially, it is a set up similar in principle to what Fizeau experiment of 1851 shows. The difference between them is that (1) the medium in the Michelson experiment is the atmosphere while the medium in the Fizeau experiment is water and (2) the speed of the medium in the Michelson experiment is zero while that in the Fizeau experiment is 7 meter/sec. If the Fizeau experiment requires a speed of 7 meter/sec for its medium, what should be the speed of the medium in the M-M experiments that is supposed to present the velocities of all "upstream", "downstream" and "cross-stream" with respect to the apparatus, given that the atmosphere has a refractive index of 1.0003? Of course, extremely high speed should be expected; but sadly, zero speed is what has actually always been applied in history whenever the M-M experiment is repeated. Although 1.0003 is extremely close to 1, the M-M experiment cannot ignore the fact that its performance is not done directly through ether but through the atmosphere, which has only zero speed with respect to the earth, and subsequently to the experimental equipment.

What is said in the above paragraph is not to devalue the brilliance of the idea leading to the Michelson-Morley experiment. However, this experiment does conceive a wrong medium to have pervaded through its apparatus. It expects ether, but actually it is the atmosphere. Suppose we all were marine animals and had performed the experiment in water, the concept of a wrong agent pervading the apparatus in the M-M experiment may have been easier to be aware of.

By the way, in today's physical study, we have been made get used to a term "the constant speed of light in vacuum space". How is the "vacuum space" defined? Will such a vacuum space be made free of "dark matter", neutrinos, as well as many other exotic materials? If the absolute absence of such materials cannot be guaranteed, it may be more proper for the scientific world to establish a speed value in a medium other than in a vacuum space. It is an irreplaceable principle that if there is no medium, there would be no sound. This principle should also be true for the propagation of light.

As to ether, we can consider it as a fluid, which, as an entire bulk, can serve as an absolute inertial reference for movement to be measured in the entire universe. A metaphor is like this: the water body of the earth would never go anywhere with respect to the earth; so the entire bulk of ether will not go anywhere with respect to the universe. We always say something like "the sound speed in water is 1,500 m/s" but without any frame reference attached to this statement, such as "with respect to the earth". However, any local collection of water may never be absolutely still with respect to any chosen point of the earth. Such local collection, although moving, never presents a problem for us to understand the speed of sound in water. So in the similar manner, ether, soaking entirely with the universe everywhere, should be able to offer us an absolute inertial reference frame, regardless of whether some local collection out of its entire bulk may or may not move. In other words, for example, a collection of ether may be mechanically hurled to move with the Milky Way at comparatively low speed, but the vortex thus agitated may not affect the propagation of light, which is of electromagnetism in nature.

To study how light really propagates in ether, only large distance of its traveling can present us a more complete picture. Then, stellar aberration should be ideal for the study. For this, please continue to *Relativity Is Self-Defeated (3 of 3) —Lorentz Factor, Aberration, and Ether*, which is presented in the CNPS Conference of 2016 (July 20-23).

## REFERENCES

1. A. Einstein, *ON THE ELECTRODYNAMICS OF MOVING BODIES, 1905.*

2. Robert Resnick, *INTRODUCTION TO SPECIAL RELATIVITY, 1968* ,

3. Wikipedia, the Free Encycloedia, *MICHELSON-MORLEY EXPERIMENT*, 2016.

4. Wikipedia, the Free Encycloedia, *FIZEAU EXPERIMENT*, 2016.

5. Wikipedia, the Free Encycloedia, *IVES-STILWELL EXPERIMENT*, 2016.

6. Wikipedia, the Free Encycloedia, *RELATIVISTIC DOPPLER EFFECT*, 2016.

7. Cameron Rebigsol, *RELATIVITY IS SELF-DEFEATED (1 of 3) —In terms of Mathematics*, Presented in the CNPS Conference of 2016

# Relativity Is Self-Defeated(3 of 3)
# —Lorentz Factor, Aberration, and Ether

2016 ©  Cameron Rebigsol

*P.O. Box 872282, Vancouver, WA 98687, crebigsol@gmail.com*

The Lorentz factor is an inseparable mathematical outcome of the so called aberration phenomenon. This article will show that the aberration phenomenon, an illusion, potentially appears in all observations in which an observer has movement in relation to the light source that he examines.

Detailed analysis on the true nature of aberration ends up giving us confidence on the existence of ether. Without ether, no aberration of anything is possible. Unfortunately, the conventional explanation of this illusion has been misled even long before the debut of relativity, but relativity, with its miss in calculation, just "legitimizes" the misleading, which then in turn gives relativity physical "evidence" galvanizing the "indisputable" look of relativity.

The conventional explanation about stellar aberration relies heavily on one equation, which is $tan\beta = v/c$, where $v$ is the orbital speed of the earth and $c$ is the speed of light. Simple trigonometry mandates that this equation requires the existence of a right triangle that has a hypotenuse of value of $\sqrt{c^2+v^2} > c$ . During the observation of stellar aberration, on the inertial frame attached to the corresponding telescopes, it is exactly along such a hypotenuse that the light leading to the discovery of the apparent position of the star is found. As such, an observer directly facing the oncoming light traveling inside the telescope cylinder must determine whether the light hitting his eye is traveling at speed $c$ or $\sqrt{c^2+v^2}$ . If the observer has doubt, he can just simply asks himself what if this light is the only light that he ever sees in the world during the time he finds this star. No known reason can support him if he chooses to claim that the light he sees is traveling at speed $\sqrt{c^2+v^2}$.

A more thorough study on stellar aberration helps us to prove that time as one physical element is absolute; **time advancement has nothing to do with any clock movement**. The **Ives-Stilwell** experiment, thought to have helped confirming the nonexistence of ether, turns out to be solid evidence confirming the existence of ether.

With the invalidity of relativity displayed in the articles *Relativity Is Self-Defeated* (1 of 3) and (2 of 3) by this author, all the upcoming consideration in this article has no need to make separate argument to exclude the interference from relativity.

**Keywords:** frequency shift, ether, stellar aberration, light bulb aberration, Lorentz factor, mirage, mirage section, time dilation, Michelson-Morley experiment, Ives-Stilwell experiment

## 1. Frequency Shift Caused by Movement —A Hint for the Existence of Ether.

Let's suppose the light beams from **EDM** in Fig. 1 reach all the way to wall A and wall B via the protruding portion DE. For the beam moving toward wall A, let it start at time $t_1^m = 0$ (letter $m$ just denotes location, the midpoint, and has no mathematical significance) and reach wall A at $t_1^A$ (like letter $m$, letter $A$ just denotes location). Regardless of the value of $V_+$, we have

$$t_1^A = \frac{S}{c} \qquad (1)$$

where $c$ is the speed of light.

If **EDM** is turned off at $t_2^m = t_1^m + \Delta t$ , the last instant for wall A to receive the beam is

$$t_2^A = \Delta t + \frac{(S - \Delta t V_+)}{c} \qquad (2)$$

Subsequently,

$$t_2^A - t_1^A = \Delta t + \frac{(S - \Delta t V_+)}{c} - \frac{S}{c}$$
$$= \Delta t \times \frac{c - V_+}{c} \qquad (3)$$

or,

$$\frac{t_2^A - t_1^A}{\Delta t} = \frac{c - V_+}{c} < 1 \qquad (4)$$

If $\Delta t$ represents a period of event happening at **EDM**, $(t_2^A - t_1^A)$ means that a shortened period, or equivalently a higher frequency, or blue shift, of the beam is detected on wall A.

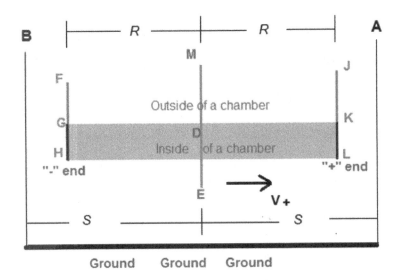

**Figure 1.**

For a beam from DE reaching wall B at $t_1^B$, also starting at $t_1^m = 0$, we can have

$$t_1^B = \frac{s}{c} \qquad (5)$$

The same reasoning leading to equation (4) leads us to have

$$\frac{t_2^B - t_1^B}{\Delta t} = \frac{c + V_+}{c} > 1 \qquad (6)$$

Equation (6) indicates a red-shift of the same beam detected on wall B.

The blue shift and red shift shown by equation (4) and (6) are rigid mathematical duplication of some frequency cast by a moving source. However, the frequency shifting for light are not duplicated with the same value in the Ives-Stilwell experiment, which is supposedly devised to verify relativity —we shall soon find that the equations from this experiment actually confirm the existence of the so called ether. The experiment leads to the observed values to be indicated by the following equation for blue shift:

$$f = f' \sqrt{\frac{c + v}{c - v}} \qquad (7)$$

where $f'$ is the actual frequency of the light source and $f$ is the corresponding observed value, or equivalently,

$$\frac{1}{p} = \frac{1}{\Delta t} \sqrt{\frac{c + v}{c - v}} \qquad (8)$$

where $p$ is the observed period in the experiment.

For red-shift, the Ives-Stilwell experiment gives

$$f = f' \sqrt{\frac{c - v}{c + v}} \qquad (9)$$

or equivalently,

$$\frac{1}{p} = \frac{1}{\Delta t} \sqrt{\frac{c - v}{c + v}} \qquad (10)$$

In its original paper of 1905, relativity presents one equation shown as $t_B - t_A = r_{AB}/(c - v)$** to lead its work to refute the existence of ether. However, comparing this equation with equation (3), we find that the term $(c - v)$ in the denominator of this relativity's equation strongly suggests that its formulation has implicitly accepted the role of a medium in its development. [** $t_B - t_A = r_{AB}/(c - v)$ is marked as (Eq Re-A) and quoted in *Relativity Is Self-Defeated (2 of 3) —in Terms of Physics* by this author.]

If we let $f^A = 1/(t_2^A - t_1^A)$, $f' = 1/\Delta t$ and $V_+ = v$ in equation (3), and also let $f^{emp} = f$ be the frequency empirically observed on the same wall as shown in equation (7), we can have

$$\begin{aligned}
\frac{f^A}{f^{emp}} &= \frac{f' \cdot [c/(c-v)]}{f' \cdot \sqrt{(c+v)/(c-v)}} \\
&= \frac{c}{\sqrt{c^2 - v^2}} \\
&= \frac{1}{\sqrt{1 - (v/c)^2}}
\end{aligned} \qquad (11)$$

If we let $f^B = 1/(t_2^B - t_1^B)$, similar reasoning leading to equation (11) will lead to

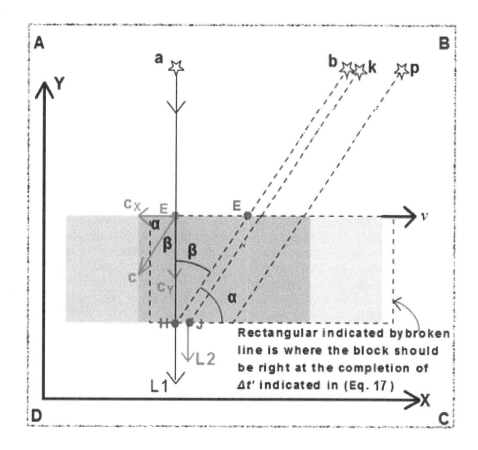

**Figure 2.**

$$\frac{f^B}{f^{emp}} = \frac{c/(c+v)}{\sqrt{(c-v)/(c+v)}}$$

$$= \frac{c}{\sqrt{c^2 - v^2}}$$

$$= \frac{1}{\sqrt{1-(v/c)^2}} \qquad (12)$$

That equation (11) and (12) end up with the same value equal to the so called Lorentz factor is certainly an interesting outcome to us. We will come back to it after we give an exploration more in detail than what is conventionally done on the topic **stellar aberration**.

## 2. Stellar Aberration

In Fig. 2, space ABCD is assumed to be fully filled with some medium that enables light propagation and this medium is called ether as traditionally so called. A coordinate system called X-Y and a motionless star are embedded with ABCD. A colored rectangular block is also fully filled with ether but is moving at speed $v$ with respect to X-Y. With the nature of both areas so described, light must transmit through both areas with the same transparency. At time $t_1$, the block is shown in pink. At a later time $t_2$, the block is at a new location and shown in blue. The grey portion shown in the picture is where the two blocks overlapping.

A light beam L1 from the star at position $a$ shines down and hits the block at point E (in red) at time $t_1$. L1 is perpendicular to the ceiling of the block. If the block is not moving, or $v = 0$, nothing will alter the progress of L1. Its loci "printed" on ABCD or on the pink block are identical. However, if the block is moving, upon the entrance of the beam at E, the block must detect a component $c_X$ of the beam's movement in parallel to the X axis, and a component $c_Y$ in parallel to the Y axis.

Conventionally, in studying stellar aberration, an angle $\beta$ is recognized as being formed by the axis of a telescope cylinder and a line perpendicular to the earth's orbital plane. When the image of the star appears at the eye piece of the telescope, the value of angle $\beta$ is considered to be determined by $\tan\beta = v/c$, where $c$ is the speed of light and $v$ is the orbital speed of the earth. Simple trigonometry mandates that a right triangle that warrants $\tan\beta = v/c$ would have to have a hypotenuse of a value of $\sqrt{c^2 + v^2}$.

In the observation of stellar observation, we must allow an inertial frame attached to the telescope, and this frame can be equivalently represented by the colored block in Fig. 2. Now, how ready are we going to accept that the light has a speed of $\sqrt{c^2 + v^2} > c$ on the path prescribed by the light in the telescope frame, doubtlessly a slanted line pointing at the star's apparent position?

As the result of the movement of the telescope, loci caused by the light's propagation and printed on the block is displayed by line E(in blue)H in Fig. 2, where H is the exit point of the light leaving the block. Star aberration tells us that along line E(blue)H only the apparent position of the star is found, not the star. If we happen to be an ant living inside this telescope, E(blue)H, but nothing else, is the only light path enabling us to discover the existence of this star. So it is only reasonable for us to accept that light is moving at speed $c$ on E(blue)H, the only light path in our observation. Subsequently, as shown in Fig. 2, we have $c_Y = c\cos\beta$, and unable to have $c_Y = c$ as what is conventionally believed. Following this we have

$$c_x = c\sin\beta = -v \qquad (13)$$

and

$$\begin{aligned} c_Y &= c\cos\beta \\ &= c\sqrt{1 - \sin^2\beta} \\ &= c\sqrt{1 - (\frac{-v}{c})^2} \\ &= \sqrt{c^2 - v^2} \end{aligned} \qquad (14)$$

Let $h$ be the height of the block. With $v = 0$, the time that the light beam needs to penetrate $h$ is $\Delta t = h/c$. If $v \neq 0$, the time $\Delta t'$ that the light needs to penetrate $h$ is

$$\Delta t' = \frac{h}{c_y} = \frac{\Delta t}{\sqrt{1 - (v/c)^2}} \qquad (15)$$

(Point to watch: *Missing this time relationship begins relativity's improper confidence on length contraction and time dilation, but we are not going to dwell in this discussion.*)

Equation (15) tells us that, when the star light completes the penetration, it actually cannot exit at H as L1 but, due to the movement of the block, exits at some other point as L2 with a time delay. Let's call this exit point J. Upon the light's exiting, the block would have moved a distance of

$$d = v\Delta t' = \frac{v\Delta t}{\sqrt{1 - (v/c)^2}} \qquad (16)$$

Therefore the distance $\Delta L$ between H and J should be

$$\Delta L = \frac{v\Delta t}{\sqrt{1 - (v/c)^2}} - v\Delta t \qquad (17)$$

Equation (17) would thus tell the observer that the star's apparent position is at location k other than b in Fig. 2.

Upon entering the ether that is at rest with ABCD, $c_X$ is canceled out by $v$, and $c_Y$ takes the full magnitude of $c$. This results in a new path L2, which would continue at the direction parallel to L1 with speed $c$ that is characterized by ether. However, L2 so resulted must suffer a time delay behind L1, which is a path that has experienced no movement of the block.

If $h = 0$, meaning the floor and the ceiling of the block being the same, then $\Delta t = 0$, and then L2 exits at H, suffering no time delay and becomes identical to L1. However, this result also leads us to accept that aberration exists regardless of the thickness of the block. This equivalently tells us that for any observer moving in a direction that forms a nonzero angle with the light propagation, aberration is an inevitable phenomenon, regardless of his observation facility, either a piece of sophisticated equipment or directly his naked eyes. As such, for analysis genuine to the true nature, **the component $c_X$ and $c_Y$ have to be resolved at a point that is part of the moving detector.** This may even mean that this point could have been found at the cornea of the observer's naked eye.

The above paragraph presents to us the following picture: A light beam is on a direction perpendicular to the direction of the movement of a light detector. As soon as the light strikes at the detector, either the objective lens of a telescope or the cornea of a naked eye, the light must change the direction of its path to continue its propagation, and only on this new path does it keep its constant speed $c$ (for simplicity, let's ignore any consideration brought up by refractive index of the material on the new path for now). As to how much change the new direction would end up depends on the detector's speed and the tilting angle of the intercepting surface of the detector. It is on the opposite extension of this light's new course that the apparent position of the light source is found. However, the image of the light source at the apparent position is merely a mirage. The physically real light does not exist on the section of the course between the apparent position and the point where the detector actually intercepts the light. To distinguish, for example, no photochemical reaction can be made happen within this section, but photochemical reaction can be made happen on the new course of the light propagation. We will call the section unable to cause photochemical reaction the mirage section for the rest of this article, while the section where true light exists the genuine section.

As a matter of fact, aberration can happen in any angle besides a perpendicular angle as illustrated in the stellar aberration. Because of aberration, the image in the apparent position would lose certain fidelity of the true appearance of the light source.

Now, let's study a situation that can be considered to

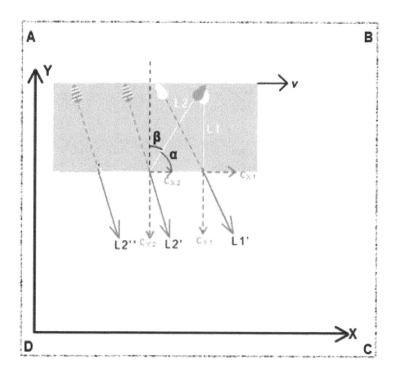

**Figure 3.**

be reciprocal to stellar aberration. In Fig. 3, both the orange and yellow light bulbs are moving together with the block at speed $v$ with respect to space ABCD. L1 shining down from the yellow bulb is perpendicular to the floor of the block. Upon L1 exiting the block and entering ABCD, an observer stationary to ABCD, led by similar reasoning shown above for the stellar aberration, will see a light path that can be regarded as being composed of two components, $c_{X1}$ and $c_{Y1}$. Since $c_{X1} \neq 0$, this light path, named as L1', will not form a right angle with the floor of the block. However, it is on this L1' that speed of the light possesses the value of $c$. L1' will make this observer see the yellow bulb on the opposite extension of L1'. Of course, the bulb so appearing in his observation is only a mirage. We can call this phenomenon the light bulb aberration. A reader can imagine himself seeing the light bulb as a star hanging extremely high over in the "sky" of the block, and, because movement is relative, he can now further imagine himself moving to the left of the picture with respect to the sky that is part of the block. Then, we can all accept that stellar aberration in the previous explanation and the light bulb aberration are identical in nature.

Similar analysis regarding the yellow bulb will make the observer of ABCD also see the orange light bulb at a location on the opposite extension of L2'. However, L2' forms an angle that is different from what L1' forms with the floor. Upon entering ABCD, the horizontal component $c_{X2}$ of the light path is determined by

$$c_{X2} = v - c\cos\alpha \qquad (18)$$

L2' will be perpendicular to the floor only if $c_{X2} = v - c\cos\alpha = 0$. Regardless of what angle L2' forms with the floor, only on this path L2' does light progress with the exact speed of $c$ after it leaves the block. If the block has a nonzero thickness, according to equation (17), L2' would not have been what the observer sees but L2". If the thickness is zero, then L2' and L2" are identical.

In all this analysis, the image appearing as a mirage must disappear once the light path delivering this phenomenon moves out of the vision of the observer. If the light source and the observer are moving on two different straight lines with respect to each other, the observer must constantly adjust the angle of the telescope to arrest the mirage. The reason that we on earth can continuously see aberration of the same star is because of the earth's movement on a close orbit, which is centered about the sun.

What we are doing in the stellar aberration study is like this: a telescope is lying on the surface of a huge cone and pointing straight up toward the apex (well, nearly) of the cone. This apex is where the star is, and is also the center of the bottom of a small cone, which is pointing upside down in relation to the telescope's huge cone of movement. The bottom of the small cone is a circle traced out by the apparent position of the star. If the star happens to be on the earth's orbital plane, the huge cone is flattened out. Then, the telescope would always have to point at the center of the circle that is defined by the earth's orbit. If the circle is big enough, certain angle of constant value between the telescope axis and the radius of the circle must be formed for the star to have a chance to appear forever at the lenses of the telescope. Then the apparent position of the star would trace out a small circle surrounding the star on the plane. If the earth's orbit is an open orbit, this angle will not be a constant one but must be adjusted constantly. Otherwise this star must sooner or later disappear from the sight of the observer.

Now, after all this discussion on aberration, let's review one critically important scenario with which relativity supporters promote the legitimacy of the idea of time dilation. After the true nature of this scenario hid by aberration is unveiled, we will find no difficulty to return the absoluteness back to the physical element that is called time.

## 3. Time Is Absolute to Both the Observers on the Train And on the Ground

Relativity has made us all familiar with this scene applied in the analysis supporting relativity's concept of time dilation: A flashlight bulb in a moving train sends a light pulse at instant $t_1'$ straight up toward the ceiling, and after reflection, this pulse comes back at $t_2'$ to the point where it was emitted. Both instants $t_1'$ and $t_2'$ are registered by a clock moving with the train. The path of the pulse so seen by the train observer is represented in red lines in Fig. 4. Seeing the propagation of the same pulse, an observer on the ground, according to relativity's conjecture, would describe that the pulse starts its journey at instant $t_1$ from point E(in red) toward G, the point of reflection, then reaches and ends at H at instant $t_2$ . Both instant $t_1$ and $t_2$ are registered by a clock on the ground. Then, for the ground observer, relativity leads itself to a conclusion shown as

$$\frac{t_2' - t_1'}{t_2 - t_1} = \sqrt{1 - (v/c)^2} \qquad (19)$$

Right away, with all the preparation we have had about aberration, we can confidently claim that the ground observer is never able to see how the pulse propagates except at some restricted locations: To see the light pulse, he must locate himself directly on the course of the light's propagation so that he can either intercept the true image of the bulb like the observer on the train or the mirage of the light bulb like the observer viewing the stellar aberration. All this is based on some very simple facts like the following: An observer can see light coming from star A or star B, but he can never see any light traveling between star A and B. To see the light traveling between star A and B, he must have his light detecting facilities placed between A and B, either his naked eyes or some kind of instrument. Likewise, for two light beams from the same star but forming a nonzero angle between them, he can only see either one of them at a time, but unable to see both of them at the same time. These basic facts must bring out skepticism about the legitimacy of equation (19), which is based on a fallacious assumption that an observer can see the light

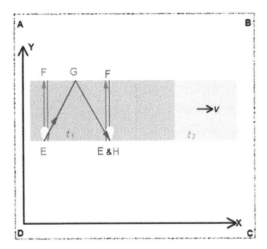

The same block is shown in pink at time $t_1$ and blue at $t_2$. The grey area is where the two blocks overlapped.

**Figure 4.**

beam without placing himself on the course of the light's propagation. Genuinely, the ABCD observer in Fig 4, or equivalently the ground observer, cannot stay anywhere in ABCD and still be able to detect the light. For simplicity, let's begin with only the examination of the light path E(red)G in Fig. 4 , which is repeated in Fig. 5.

(Before we go any further, though, we must clarify one thing. On earth, we do always see some light beams without directly locating ourselves facing the on coming light beams, just like we can see a light beam from certain spotlight in the night sky but standing at a distance on earth from the spotlight. That this is possible is only because of the light scattering action of many tiny particles such as dusts. In such situation, all tiny particles on the path of the light beam just reflect the light beam at all possible angles, and some of the reflected light at certain angle is able to invade our vision. Now, the light coming to our vision is from innumerable sources other than just one, i.e., the spotlight.)

In Fig. 5, point G belongs to ABCD and F(in blue) belongs to the blue block but they share each other at the instant the light pulse hits F, the point of reflection. Comparing the light path so presented with the analysis given to L1 and L1' in Fig. 3, we would easily conclude that the actual light path, by which the naked eye stationary to ABCD discovers the existence of the bulb, is along the broken line (or equivalently the solid L1' in Fig. 3). He would not see the light at anywhere else. At the instant the observer conceives seeing the bulb at E(red), what he sees is only the apparent position of the bulb, a mirage.

Since point E(red) is also a point shared by the train and ABCD at instant $t_1'$, Line E(red)G can be regarded as a real

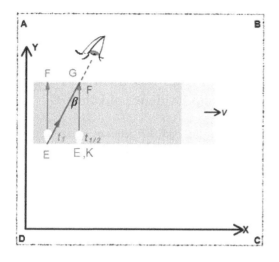

**Figure 5.**

graphic printed on ABCD due to the traveling of the light. To the observer at rest with the bulb, the bulb's position is never a mirage but forever real to him. So he can simultaneously see (1) the progress of the creation of this graphic as a real physical entity on ABCD and also (2) the progress of time advancement from instants $t_1'$ to $t_2'$ that is recorded by his clock. While the time advancement mentioned in (2) is determined by the true speed c of the light and the height of the ceiling, the progress of the simultaneous creation of the graphic mentioned in (1) is determined by the same amount of time and the length of the real graphic. During the creation of the graphic, E(red)G expands with some linear speed $v_{EG}$ along line EG, which is a hypotenuse of a right triangle whose vertical catheti is EF(both points in red) and the horizontal catheti is E(red)K. Therefore, $v_{EG}$ is found as

$$v_{EG} = \frac{\sqrt{|EF|^2 + |E(red)K|^2}}{t_2' - t_1'}$$
$$= \frac{\sqrt{[c(t_2' - t_1')]^2 + [v(t_2' - t_1')]^2}}{t_2' - t_1'} \quad (20)$$
$$= \sqrt{c^2 + v^2}$$

Equation (20) shows that $v_{EG}$ is determined by only two elements, c and v , which are commonly shared by both frames. Therefore, $v_{EG}$ is good to the observers of both frames.

Since only along E(red)F(red) does the observer moving with the block see the light propagating, therefore, to him, c is only found on EF, and he thus has

$$c = v_{EG} \cos \beta \quad (21)$$

as well as

$$|E(red)F(red)| = c(t_2' - t_1')$$
$$= v_{EG} \cos \beta (t_2' - t_1') \quad (22)$$

To the observer staying with ABCD, E(red)G is a line of real graphic on his frame and the creation of E(red)G must have taken some time interval between certain instants $t_1$ and $t_2$ that are recorded by his clock. However, he must be aware of one fact: By the time he sees the mirage of the light bulb, the creation of E(red)G would have completed. Depending on the distance between the block and his light detecting facility, he may find E(red)G right at the instant of $t_2$ or later, but can never find it before $t_2$. While the observer in the train can instantaneously watch the entire process of the creation of E(red)G, the observer of ABCD cannot. He can only find how E(red)G has expanded in his frame ABCD in history. Needless to say, to him, the expansion must start from E at $t_1 = t_1'$. When the expansion reaches G, from history, this observer of ABCD can have

$$|E(red)G| = v_{EG}(t_2 - t_1) \quad (23)$$

As mentioned above, $v_{EG}$ is a speed true to both observers, because it contains only the elements but nothing else that is commonly shared by them.

Since

$$|E(red)G| = \frac{|E(red)F(red)|}{\cos \beta}$$
$$= \frac{c(t_2' - t_1')}{\cos \beta} \quad (24)$$
$$= v_{EG}(t_2' - t_1')$$

Comparison between equation (23) and (24) immediately gives

$$(t_2 - t_1) = (t_2' - t_1') \quad (25)$$

Equation (25) just simply tells us that time advancement has nothing to do with the movement of any clock. With $t_1 = t_1'$, the consequence of $t_2 = t_2'$ is natural and inevitable—**Time as a physical element is therefore absolute!**

After the light pulse being reflected by the ceiling, the ABCD observer must lose the sight of the light. To see the same pulse again, he needs to go to the other side of the block to meet the course of the reflected pulse (Fig. 6). There, the spot of the reflection, point G, would be a mirage to him when he conceives seeing it. At this instant, the actual location of the reflection spot marked on the block but printed as a history record on ABCD should have been at F(blue). Following the reasoning done for the path of E(red)G, he will come to another exact relationship shown in equation (25) concerning time advancement, although now he, as well as we, may have used $t_2$ and $t_2'$ to denote

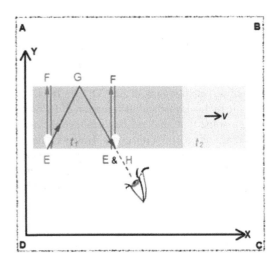

**Figure 6.**

the instant when the pulse hits the floor at E(blue) and H; E(blue) and H share each other at this instant, and this instant only, which is indifferently the instant of $t_2$ or $t_2'$ .

So contrary to what is portrayed by the analysis supporting relativity, in the scenario of a moving train and a ground observer, in order to see the light pulse moving along E(red)F(red), the ground observer must fly in the air above the train. Again, when he discovers the bulb, what he sees is a mirage. The "path" E(red)G is a section of mirage distance to him. By the same principle, the same observer cannot see the actual light path represented by the broken line in Fig. 6 by just standing on the ground. He must go under the floor of the train. Oh, well, the job is too dangerous to anyone, but he can use some equipment. Liberally bestowing the ground observer with ability to see the light from a moving source regardless of his position, such conventional analysis has really violated many principles in physics. To summarize these principles briefly: (1) a light detector must be on the course of the light in order to verify the existence of the light; (2) a light path that a detector claims to have detected may be a mirage one and should not be confused with the one on which light does physically propagate; (3) only on the genuine path, but not the mirage path, can the detector find the true speed of the light.

With equation (25), that time is absolute is affirmed. Immediately following this affirmation is that length as a physical element must also be absolute. This is simply because length is one of the only two physical elements in the speed expression. If time is absolute and speed is unique, length cannot escape from being absolute.

Since this article has presented detailed analysis on aberration that leads to the confirmation that time is absolute, this author feels no need to go into a redundant job to

affirm length being absolute by applying aberration again. The readers' time must be fully respected.

## 4. The True Nature of Frequency-Shift Shown in the Ives-Stilwell Experiment —The Solid Evidence of Ether

In Fig. 2, on the path Hb leading to the discovery of the apparent position of the light source, there is only one section, the HE section, on which light is physically propagating, while the other section, Eb, is a mirage section, on which, as mentioned before, no photochemical reaction can be made happen. If the height of the block $h$ shrinks to zero toward point H, the entire line Hb would become a mirage section, and the light as a physical entity will propagate at speed $c$ only after it leave point H. With $h = 0$, and if the distance of the vertical line aH=s, the length of Hb is then

$$|Hb| = \frac{s}{\cos \beta}$$
$$= \frac{sc}{\sqrt{c^2 - v^2}} \quad (26)$$

Equation (26) simply tells us that, because of aberration, a light detector would always conceive an instantaneous image of the moving light source existing at a distance larger than the actual distance. As we have always emphasized, this image is a mirage.

In Fig. 7, the star light beam enters the moving block at an angle $\delta$, and results in a new course represented by the yellow line on the blue block. It is on this yellow line that the true light beam travels at speed $c$. From $\Delta EKH$, we have

$$c^2 = c_x^2 + m^2 - 2mc_x \cos \phi \quad (27)$$

Because of $\delta + \phi = 180^o$, and $c_x = v$ , equation (27) leads to

$$m = -v \cos \delta \pm \sqrt{c^2 - v^2 \sin^2 \delta} \quad (28)$$

For obvious reason, only the "+" sign is kept, so we actually have

$$m = -v \cos \delta + \sqrt{c^2 - v^2 \sin^2 \delta} \quad (29)$$

The proportional relationship between the two similar triangles $\Delta EKH$ and $\Delta Eab$ leads to

$$\frac{D}{d} = \frac{c}{m}$$
$$= \frac{c}{-v \cos \delta + \sqrt{c^2 - v^2 \sin^2 \delta}} \quad (30)$$

where D is the length of the mirage section of the light path "seen" by an observer moving with the blue block.

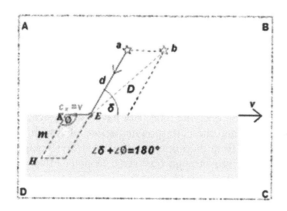

**Figure 7.**

If $\delta = 90^o$ , equation (30) leads to $D = d(c/\sqrt{c^2-v^2})$ , which is an identical result shown by equation (26). If $\delta = 0^o$, we have

$$D = d(\frac{c}{c-v}) > d \qquad (31)$$

At this point we must be aware of one fact that, for any value of angle of $\delta$ other than $\delta = 0^o$, after striking at point E in Fig. 7 and entering the block, the true light path must separate from the path that is an extension of line aE, the original light path. Indeed, it is because of this separation that enables the discovery of transverse Doppler effect. However, the separation will not happen for $\delta = 0^o$; the true light path and the extension line that is equivalent to the aforementioned aE must forever merge in the same direction. As such, for $\delta = 0^o$, we must also expect to see transverse Doppler effect when the light source, the mirage, and the detector are on the same line. While the mirage can stay in the detector's interception for only a limited time for all $\delta > 0^o$, the mirage can stay in the detector's interception forever for $\delta = 0^o$ —well, for as long as the light source having not yet collided with the detector.

For a source emitting light of frequency $f'$ and moving through a medium toward the detector, equation (3) and (4), which are in some form depicting Doppler effect, tell us that wall A in Fig. 1 would show the frequency received as

$$f^A = f' \times (\frac{c}{c-v}) \qquad (32)$$

where, referring to all equations directly derived with Fig. 1, $f^A = 1/(t_2^A - t_1^A)$, $f' = 1/\Delta t$, $v = V_+$.

While $f^A$ is so far a theoretical figure, it can also be regarded as an empirical figure if it can also be collected through experiment. When it is collected as an empirical figure, we replace $f^A$ with $f_1^{emp}$; and if the data match what equation (32) shows, we can assume to have legitimacy to write an equation shown as

$$f_1^{emp} = f' \times (\frac{c}{c-v}) \qquad (33)$$

Equation (33) is typically a Doppler effect equation showing how a receiver would have read the frequency-shift corresponding to the frequency sent by a source that is moving through a medium and approaching the receiver.

However, besides this Doppler effect that seems so straightforward in our experience, wall A must also have detected aberration effect and duplicate it accordingly if the distance between the wall and the source constantly shortens with speed $v$. We have had plenty preparation knowing that it is the aberration effect that would necessarily and sufficiently enable the detector to sense a section of light path on which light is moving with its invariably characterized speed $c$. So when the distance between the source and the detector, i.e., our wall A, persistently diminishes, the frequency received by the detector cannot be the original frequency of the source but would have changed to some other value. Let's use $f_{abrt}$ to denote this new value, where the subscript $abrt$ means aberration. This change is conditioned as if the detector was receiving the $f_{abrt}$ through a stationary medium with respect to which the source was also stationary. It is the stationary status of the medium and the source conceived by the detector that makes it (the wall) sensing the genuine path of the light for the light beam. A stationary medium and a stationary source can only mean that the distance's diminishing is realized by the movement of the detector. So, for the $f_{abrt}$ so resulted, we would have the Doppler equation shown as

$$f_{abrt} = f' \times (\frac{c+v}{c}) \qquad (34)$$

If both $f_1^{emp}$ and $f_{abrt}$ are frequencies from two genuine light sources, when both frequencies cast at the same location, wave interference would occur. We can consider the interference is either resulted by $f_1^{emp}$ modulating $f_{abrt}$ or $f_{abrt}$ modulating $f_1^{emp}$ . For $f_1^{emp}$ modulating $f_{abrt}$ , we will have a new frequency corresponding to an amplitude modulation function

$$(1 + f_1^{emp}) \cdot f_{abrt} = f_{abrt} + f_1^{emp} \cdot f_{abrt}$$

For $f_{abrt}$ modulating $f_1^{emp}$, we will have a new frequency corresponding to another amplitude modulation function

$$(1 + f_{abrt}) \cdot f_1^{emp} = f_1^{emp} + f_1^{emp} \cdot f_{abrt}$$

However, there is actually only one genuine light source and no reason can support an argument that the amplitude of one of the frequencies is bigger than the other. Therefore, 100 % modulation is expected in either case. All this makes it natural that, after the modulation, only what is commonly shared by the two new frequency expressions can be left to be detected. What we can find commonly shared by the two new expressions is $f_1^{emp} \cdot f_{abrt}$. Thus we have

$$f_1^{emp} \times f_{abrt} = (f' \times \frac{c}{c-v})(f' \times \frac{c+v}{c}) \quad (35)$$

The frequency $f_{abrt}$ as we know is actually from a mirage, carrying zero energy to have made any physical interference possible, but the presence of $f_{abrt}$ must still cost energy. This energy can only come from the only energy component that is otherwise maintaining $f_1^{emp}$. Let's use $f^{emp}$ to denote the frequency produced by the modulation. This should be the new and ultimate only frequency feature discovered in the observation. Since lower energy of a wave train usually means a lower frequency for the wave train of the same amplitude, we thus expect $f^{emp} < f_1^{emp}$. Now, to the detector, what it receives from a wave train that carries the genuine speed of light is $f^{emp}$ instead of $f_{abrt}$. This means that the true light with a genuine wave length that is sourced from a mirage wave length should have a shorter wave length than the mirage wave length. The mathematical relationship between the genuine wave length and the mirage wave length can be established through equation (31), in which $d$ can be regarded as the genuine wave length, and $D$ can be regarded as the mirage wave length. A shorter wave length would lead to a higher frequency. So we can expect $f^{emp} > f_{abrt}$. The uniqueness of $f^{emp}$ but with a value that fits the relationship $f_1^{emp} > f^{emp} > f_{abrt}$ allows us to have the following equivalency:

$$(f^{emp})^2 = f_1^{emp} \times f_{abrt} \quad (36)$$

Combining equation (35) and (36), we have

$$(f^{emp})^2 = (f' \times \frac{c}{c-v})(f' \times \frac{c+v}{c})$$
$$= f'^2 \frac{c+v}{c-v} \quad (37)$$

or

$$f^{emp} = f'\sqrt{\frac{c+v}{c-v}} \quad (38)$$

The frequency $f^{emp}$ matches what is observed in the Ives-Stilwell experiment for blue-shift. The same reasoning can lead us to have similar equation for the red-shift, which is

$$f^{emp} = f'\sqrt{\frac{c-v}{c+v}} \quad (39)$$

Interestingly, the comparison between $f_1^{emp}$ and $f^{emp}$ shows to us the following ratio

$$\frac{f_1^{emp}}{f^{emp}} = \frac{1}{\sqrt{1-(v/c)^2}} \quad (40)$$

Equation (40) matches equation (11), leading us to a value of Lorentz factor. This means that to synchronize

into the ultimate frequency, $f_1^{emp}$ has to moderate itself to a lower value. The moderating should have been governed by $f^{emp} = f' \times c/(c-v)$. However, since the source and the mirage are on the same line, the mirage section therefore occupies the entire distance all the way up to the intercepting point, which is part of the detector. Only from this point on does the light path have the physically genuine light and the corresponding speed of $c$ with it. The frequency from the mirage section is always regarded as being received through transverse Doppler effect by the detector and lowered by a factor of $\sqrt{1-(v/c)^2}$. Therefore, we now again have

$$f^{emp} = f' \times \frac{c}{c-v}\sqrt{1-(\frac{v}{c})^2}$$
$$= f'\sqrt{\frac{c+v}{c-v}} \quad (41)$$

Equation(38) and (41) are identical to each other. We can use the similar reasoning to obtain an equation for redshift that would display as

$$f^{emp} = f'\sqrt{\frac{c-v}{c+v}} \quad (42)$$

Equeation (42) is identical to equeation (39).

Since relativity as a theory shows so self-defeated, it has no credit to offer valid verification to anything. Indeed, as shown by equation (18) and (20) in the article *Relativity Is Self-Defeated (2 of 3) —In Terms of Physics* by this author, relativity even disastrously ends up forcing $v = 0$ in the equations summarized by the Ives-Stilwell experiment. Therefore, because of relativity's failure, data shown in the Ives-Stilwell experiment can inevitably be said to have stayed as empirical data and equation (7) and (9) stayed as empirical equations the entire time ever since this experiment is performed in 1938. Now, with the modulation explanation, we can say that they are theoretically confirmed.

As what we have shown in this article, the key for the Ives-Stilwell equations to be theoretically confirmed is the 100% reliance on the existence of a medium serving as the energy conveyor for light. Such reliance allows us to come back to common sense and use "classic treatment" in exploring the puzzles regarding light propagation. The so called common sense has been accompanying with human beings all their generations, and the classic treatment has been so laid for us ever since all those great minds such as Euclid, Archimedes, Copernicus, Galileo, Kepler, Newton, Faraday, Maxwell and many more pioneered the research in mathematics and physics. Has human beings found any reason why such classic treatment must be given up only because new discovery seems keeping a distance from the comprehension of a certain group of people?

Through all our derivation we find that the Lorentz factor is nearly omnipresent. In some cases, its appearance is because of the need of geometry in the deduction, such as in the stellar aberration analysis. In some cases, its appearance nearly has nothing to do with geometry, such as in the process of confirming the Ives-Stilwell equations. In some cases, the need for its appearance is in between, such as in the study of light bulb aberration. Nevertheless, its appearance is so unshakable. Now, we may have seen enough how aberration necessarily and sufficiently evidences the physical existence of a medium for light conveying and how the Lorentz factor must potentially accompany with the aberration analysis. The Lorentz Factor thus in turn serves as an ironclad manifesto to galvanize in theory the existence of a medium for light propagation. Without this medium, light cannot propagate, but with this medium, the light's propagation must be invariably characterized with a constant speed and potentially presents the phenomenon of aberration for the light source in our observation.

**The medium so mentioned here has been traditionally called ETHER or AETHER by scientists of many generations!**

## 5. Simultaneity

Now, we would like to wade into another topic, simultaneity, that relativity has made popularly believed with the scenario presented in Fig. 8. In the "thought experiment" shown in Fig. 8, at time $t_1$ , lightning bolts simultaneously strike at two different locations, A and C, that have equal distance from observer B on the stationary frame F. Since frame F' is moving, according to relativity, observer B' should have seen the lightning bolts striking at F' at different instances. Even before any quantitative consideration is given, we should already see the discrepancy of this thought "experiment". If the observer on frame F sees the same color from both lightning bolts, the observer on frame F' must see two bolts of different color. The bolt he is approaching should appear bluer than the other, which should appear redder to him. How do they judge things being the same if the bolts they see appear differently to each of them? What makes the validity of the thought experiment more skeptical is relativity standardizing the timing with an observer's subjective view (which bolt he sees first) in place of the objective recording of the clocks.

Now, let's see how the clocks work out in confirming relativity's thought experiment. Suppose an observer on frame F next to clock B is at the origin of his frame with equal distance $|a|$ from each striking locations where clock A and C are respectively found. If clock B and B' face each other on the same line at instant $t_1$, relativity would predict that a clock called A' on frame F' can be found matching $t_1$ with $t_1^{(A')}$ , which shall be shown as

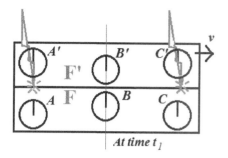

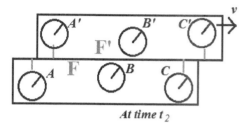

Picture is drawn according to relativity's ideas but clock advancement is displayed according to "classic" understanding——space and time are independent from each other and absolute.

**Figure 8.**

$$t_1^{(A')} = \frac{t_1 - [v(-a)/c^2]}{\sqrt{1-(v/c)^2}} \tag{43}$$

and equivalently, a clock C' on F' should be found showing an instant as

$$t_1^{(C')} = \frac{t_1 - [v(+a)/c^2]}{\sqrt{1-(v/c)^2}} \tag{44}$$

For an instant of $t_2$ shown by clock B, we can have the following equations for clock A' and C' correspondingly

$$t_2^{(A')} = \frac{t_2 - [v(-a)/c^2]}{\sqrt{1-(v/c)^2}} \tag{45}$$

and

$$t_2^{(C')} = \frac{t_2 - [v(+a)/c^2]}{\sqrt{1-(v/c)^2}} \tag{46}$$

As far as clock A' is concerned, we could have

$$t_2^{(A')} - t_1^{(A')} = \frac{t_2 - t_1}{\sqrt{1-(v/c)^2}} \tag{47}$$

Since clock A, B, and C are all stationary to the observer of frame F, one reading of time from any one clock must mean the same to the rest of all others and to the observer himself as well. So regardless of which reading between $t_2$ and $t_1$ is quoted from which clock, so long as they are quoted together to mean simultaneous, it must mean $t_2 - t_1 = 0$ . Now, conditioned by equation (47), relativity must accept $t_2^{(A')} - t_1^{(A')} = 0$, and subsequently $t_2^{(A')} = t_1^{(A')}$. Plainly, relativity would have at least one clock, i.e., clock A', in the moving frame fail from recognizing a nonzero time gap to match the zero time advancement recorded by clocks in a stationary frame.

For clock C', with the same reasoning, we can have

$$t_2^{(C')} - t_1^{(C')} = \frac{t_2 - t_1}{\sqrt{1 - (v/c)^2}} \tag{48}$$

Equation (48) means that more than one clock besides clock A' on the F' frame can be found failing relativity's understanding on simultaneity. The relationship $t_2^{(C')} - t_1^{(C')} = 0 = t_2^{(A')} - t_1^{(A')}$ must make all these four time elements equal to each other, unless relativity is to relinquish its stipulation that all clocks in the same frame are well synchronized; clock synchronization requires that the reading from any one clock means the same reading to all clocks. Since clock A' and clock C' can be randomly found in frame F', relativity's thought experiment is found being put up without valid argument.

Therefore, intuitively from the point of view of frequency shifting caused by movement, or logically with calculation more in details, relativity's concept about simultaneity is unable to convince us for a reasonable acceptance.

There are many versions about how to understand the significance of simultaneity elaborated with relativity's guidance. This article only chooses one to reveal the nature of such understanding. For a theory that must lead a zero value to end up at the denominator of an equation (where the Lorentz factor is involved) that this theory derives, it will not serve too much purpose to pick out all of these versions to explain why they fail. As we know, zero in a denominator means no certainty—one can thus have as many versions as he likes to think of, just like all those paradoxes built based on relativity.

Interestingly, since our argument against relativity is based on the existence of ether, when simultaneity is found, we can find from the color of the lightning bolts to judge which frame between F and F' is the one moving through the ether and which is stationary. Easily, we can claim that the observer seeing the same color from two bolts of the same nature is stationary to the ether; otherwise, the one seeing different colors is moving through the ether.

## 6. Conclusions

(1) That ether exists is undeniable.

(2) Aberration effect would potentially show up to an observer if the light source he observes has movement

in relation to him. So the only reliable speed of light, together with the natural frequency of the same light, is obtained only if the observer, the source of light, and the medium through which light propagates are all absolutely stationary to each other.

(3) Time and space as two physical dimensions are **absolute** and independent from each other.

(4) Relativity is an invalid theory, and its validity falsely assumed existing is brought up historically by the misunderstanding shown in the following practices:

(a) Michelson-Morley experiment. So far, the performance of this experiment has always been done with a zero speed through a light carrying medium, which is the atmosphere, but is thought to have been in traveling through the ether, in case its existence is evidenced, with the earth's orbital speed.

(b) An assumption that falsely visualizes an unrestricted freedom of location for a ground observer in viewing the propagation of a light beam, which emits from a source moving with a train but also returns to the same moving source after reflection.

(c) In applying $\tan \beta = v/c$ in the calculation of stellar aberration, a negligence has escaped from the common attention. For more than two centuries, this negligence has allowed a falsified speed $\sqrt{c^2 + v^2}$ to be taken for granted but without awareness for the genuine light traveling in the inertial frame defined by an astronomical telescope.

(d) There always exists a prejudice that has everlastingly veiled relativity from serious mathematical scrutiny. If this prejudice had not been there, the mistaken result of $c = 0$ being forced into the Lorentz factor in solving Relativity's most fundamental equation set would have long been exposed. This $c = 0$ outcome is so inevitably led to by an implicit condition of $v = 0$ that the said equation set must have for it to get a chance to be "solved".

(e) The prejudice mentioned above is so overwhelming that it has even enabled the glamorization on a violation of the most ancient mathematical concept, which is *zero $\neq$ nonzero*, by enforcing the acceptance of that a zero value (the time advancement represented by simultaneity) in one frame can mathematically produce a nonzero value (of time advancement) in another frame.

Finally, in the study of physics, there is no "classic" nor "non-classic" (or a fancier term: relativistic) treatment, but only correct or incorrect treatment. Let's not deviate even lightly from the method and thinking system that all those great minds have laid for us before the debut of relativity.

## REFERENCES

1. A. Einstein, *§2. On the Relativity of Lengths and Times, I. Kinematical Part, ON THE ELECTRODYNAMICS OF MOVING BODIES*, 1905.

2. Robert Resnick, *INTRODUCTION TO SPECIAL RELATIVITY, 1968* ,

3. *MICHELSON-MORLEY EXPERIMENT*, Wikipedia, the Free Encyclopedia, 2016.

4. *FIZEAU EXPERIMENT*, Wikipedia, the Free Encyclopedia, 2016.

5. *IVES-STILWELL EXPERIMENT*, Wikipedia, the Free Encyclopedia, 2016.

6. *RELATIVISTIC DOPPLER EFFECT*, Wikipedia, the Free Encyclopedia, 2016.

7. Cameron Rebigsol, *RELATIVITY IS SELF-DEFEATED (1 of 3) —In terms of Mathematics*, Presented in the CNPS Conference of 2016

8. Cameron Rebigsol, *RELATIVITY IS SELF-DEFEATED (2 of 3) —In terms of Physics*, Presented in the CNPS Conference of 2016

# A Test of Relativistic Simultaneity

## Curt Renshaw

*680 America's Cup Cove, Alpharetta, GA 30005, crenshaw@teleinc.com, www.renshawphysics.com*

This paper proposes a clear test of the relativistic assumption of the relativity of simultaneity. Special relativity assumes that two relatively moving observers instantaneously collocated will both see light from a distant event at the same place and time. This assumption is embedded in Einstein's original train embankment thought experiment. It is reconciling this assumption with the presumed constancy of the speed of light that led to relativistic length contraction and time dilation for the moving observer. An uncomfortable by product is the fact that these two observers can now no longer agree on where and when an event occurred. If they are viewing two separated events, and one observer concludes the events occurred simultaneously, the other observer will conclude that the two events were not simultaneous; thus the relativity of simultaneity. Two events that are simultaneous in one reference frame are not simultaneous in a different reference frame.

Until recent years, a test of the relativity of simultaneity would not have been possible. A direct test has never been attempted due to the great distances, high speeds and extremely small variances in time to be observed. Even if these could all be overcome, the ability to perform one part of the experiment in the moving frame and obtain results that do not require converting back to the stationary frame are extremely problematical.

But currently, we have many satellites at distances of 20K km and greater, routinely transmitting with carrier signals in the GHz range. We are able to accurately model the ephemerides of these satellites, and even account for atmospheric disturbances. We have very stable oscillators in the same range in lab environments, with the ability to phase-lock their outputs to another signal, and phase detectors able to provide voltage outputs proportional to the difference in phase of signals with wavelengths in the 20 cm and smaller range. Similarly, clock and code signals can be compared in the same manner as phase shifts by combing signals. Phase detection is a much simpler and preferred method for determining subtle differences in light travel times. The most notable example in recent times is the LIGO gravitational wave detector, which uses an interferometer with 2.5-mile arms to detect an extremely subtle phase shift due to the varying gravitational field caused by rapidly orbiting black holes. As will be shown, the proper use of phase measurements eliminates any reliance on clock synchronization between the moving and stationary frames, or between either of these frames and the source itself, and allows for a realistic test of relativistic simultaneity.

**Keywords:** light, relativity, simultaneity

## 1. A Brief Theoretical Introduction

Maxwell showed electromagnetic (EM) radiation travels at a speed of $c$ given by (1).

$$c = \frac{1}{\sqrt{\varepsilon_0 \mu_0}} \qquad (1)$$

Maxwell's equations give no reference frame against which to measure $c$. All experimenters obtain the same values for $\varepsilon_0$ and $\mu_0$, so $c$ is the same in any observer's own reference frame. Since the speed of the moving observer can assume any value, the EM energy leaving the source must have speed components in a continuous range, including $c$ as measured in any arbitrary frame. This frame independent nature of Maxwell's equations does not prohibit a range of velocities, but rather dictates this to be so, thus there are physically detectable components of any EM energy that reach an observer faster or slower than a component traveling at $c$ measured by that observer. This peculiar nature of light led to the development of special relativity, but it is easily shown that the Lorentz transformations are nothing more than an elegant manipulation of the Galilean transformations with no physical basis of support. Historically it was an attempt to develop a frame invariant

form of Maxwell's equations that initially led Lorentz to propose length contraction, but Einstein, assuming a constant value of c that itself was frame invariant developed the length contraction and time dilation inherent in the special theory. Maxwell's equations have been shown to be frame invariant in a Galilean framework as well (Renshaw [2]).

We will derive the relation between two inertial reference frames in the absence of special relativity, using an example similar to the train embankment thought experiment invoked by Einstein. We will then work our way into the special relativistic Lorentz transforms, demonstrating an inherent lack of underlying meaning behind them.

Consider the case of the $K$ and $K'$ frame (Bob and Alice respectively at the origin of each frame), both stationary in the lab frame, but not collocated. A flash occurs a distance $d$ from the origin of $K$ and a distance $d'$ from the origin of $K'$. Clearly, the light will reach the observer in frame $K$ at time $t = d/c$, and will reach the observer in $K'$ at time $t' = d'/c$. Both these observations are independent of any motion of the source.

In figure 2 below, Alice, moving to the right at $v$, and Bob stationary, each again see the flash from an event some

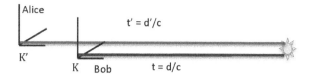

**Figure 1.**   Two Stationary Frames

distance to the right. Each ascribes the same velocity, $c$, to light from the flash, independent of the source's motion, and therefore each sees the light at $t'$ and $t$ respectively as in figure 1, where we have replaced $d$ with $x$ to develop some equations later on.

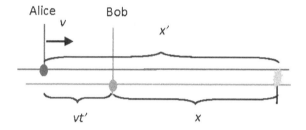

**Figure 2.**   Relatively Moving Frames

Light moves from source to Bob at $c$ measured in his frame, traveling $\Delta x$ in time $\Delta t = \Delta x/c$, and from source to Alice at $c$ measured in her frame, traveling $\Delta x'$ in time $\Delta t' = \Delta x'/c$.

We establish things so that at $t = t' = 0$, the frames coincide and $x = x'$ for any $x$. At any other time, the Galilean relation (2) holds as in the figure.

$$x = x' + vt' \qquad (2)$$

For $t < 0$, Alice is to Bob's left ($vt'$ is negative). For $t > 0$, Alice is to Bob's right. Relation (2) holds for any value of $x'$ or $t'$, but the specific case of the time it takes light from an event to reach an observer is the important observable.

Establish Alice momentarily next to Bob at the instant she sees the flash, at time $t' = t = 0$ as established above. Each carries a rod on which the flash leaves a mark measuring the distance to the event as $x'$ for Alice and $x$ for Bob. Alice determines the flash occurred at $t'$, given by (3), where $t'$ is negative since the flash occurred before being seen by Alice at $t' = 0$. Inserting (3) into (2) gives (4), the distance to the flash measured in Bob's reference frame.

$$t' = -\frac{x}{c} \qquad (3)$$

$$x = x' + vt' = x'\left(1 - \frac{v}{c}\right) \qquad (4)$$

Unremarkably, (4) reflects the Galilean transformations for one reference frame moving at a constant velocity with respect to another at a particular time $t'$ and given $x'$.

Recognizing the time it takes light to reach Bob in his reference frame as $t = -x/c$, and that the times of observation in the two frames are not simultaneous, rearranging the terms in (4) provides interesting results for $x'$ in terms of $t$ and $x$ produces (5), where $\gamma$ is defined in (7). Recalling that $t = -x/c$ and dividing through by $-c$ in (5) provides $t'$ in terms of $t$ and $x$ (6). Note that this is still the Galilean transform of events seen by Alice and Bob.

$$x' = \frac{x}{\left(1 - \dfrac{v}{c}\right)} = \frac{x\left(1 + \dfrac{v}{c}\right)}{\left(1 - \dfrac{v^2}{c^2}\right)} = \gamma^2 x\left(1 + \frac{v}{c}\right) = \gamma^2(x - vt) \qquad (5)$$

$$t' = -\frac{x'}{c} = \gamma^2\left(\frac{-x}{c} + \frac{vt}{c}\right) = \gamma^2\left(t - \frac{vx}{c^2}\right) \qquad (6)$$

$$\gamma \equiv \frac{1}{\sqrt{1 - \dfrac{v^2}{c^2}}} \qquad (7)$$

Multiplying both sides of (5) and (6) by $\gamma^{-1}$ doesn't change the validity of the equations, but allows the arbitrary definition a contracted length of Alice's rod as $\overline{x'}$, and a dilated time in Alice's frame as $\overline{t'}$ in equations (8) and (9).

$$\overline{x'} \equiv \frac{x'}{\gamma} = \gamma(x - vt) \qquad (8)$$

$$\overline{t'} \equiv \frac{t'}{\gamma} = \gamma\left(t - \frac{tx}{c^2}\right) \qquad (9)$$

Note that since we said nothing about motion with respect to the source, we could as easily have assumed that Bob was moving left at $v$ and Alice was stationary, or even invoked an arbitrary reference frame in which both Alice and Bob are moving, but with relative velocity of $v$, and we would obtain the same results. There is no preferred reference frame in this derivation.

Beginning with the Galilean transform (2), the terms have simply been rearranged to derive the special relativistic Lorentz transformations for motion along the x-axis, (8) and (9). *There is no physics here; this is simply mathematical manipulation.*

The Lorentz transforms of special relativity are thus simply a rearrangement of the observations of light propagation in a strictly Galilean framework with no additional meaning, despite the convoluted way and assumptions under which they were initially derived. They are a way to derive elapsed time and distance travelled from emission to detection by one observer from elapsed time and distance travelled from emission to detection by a relatively moving observer. The simplest and most useful form is seen in Maxwell's light speed equation (1) combined with the Galilean transform (2), but casting them in the odd form of (8) and (9) provides insight into the special theory of relativity.

In the Galilean framework presented, relatively moving observers instantaneously collocated will not both see the flash from a distant event at that time of collocation. In developing SRT, Einstein assumed that instantaneously collocated observers will both see the flash from an event at that time if either sees the flash at that time, concluding that events simultaneous in one reference frame are not simultaneous in another. SRT takes the manipulated equations (8) and (9), and ascribes real meaning to the relations established and the value of $\gamma$ derived. The values $\overline{x'}$ and $\overline{t'}$ become the distance to and time since the event seen by the moving observer as measured in the lab frame. In the moving frame, lengths are contracted by (8), and time is dilated by (9). In order to force these manipulated values to take on physical meaning, special relativity derives a non-linear velocity transform in which the maximum attainable velocity for anything (matter, energy or information) is $c$. Additionally, Alice and Bob cannot agree on where and when the event occurred from their momentarily collocated position. Special relativity produces a mathematically equivalent set of transforms between frames, but they lack any underlying physical basis, and worse, destroy the notion of simultaneous events, distance and time when taken to the extreme.

This untested and unverified difference in interpretation of simultaneous events in Galilean and special relativistic frameworks forms the basis of this paper. If the signals from the satellite and lab frame are received simultaneously in both frames, as predicted by special relativity, then this will represent the first conclusive confirmation of the relativity of simultaneity, and provide support for the theory in a new and important area. If, however, as expected, the signals are not received simultaneously in both frames, the most basic assumption of special relativity will be invalidated, along with length contraction and time dilation, and the existence of superluminal signals will also be verified.

## 2. Conceptual Basis

The basic form of the experiment is deceptively simple. This test will use signals from a satellite and from across a lab. A phase detector in the lab frame confirms a specific output from mixing the two signals. A similar detector on the moving frame will compare the arrival of the lab and space signals in the moving frame. The phase shift between the two signals is proportional to the difference in arrival time (if any) due to motion. A velocity on the order of 5 m/s will produce a measureable phase shift between the two (depending on satellite angle and other variable factors), and exceed the error bars of various systemic factors. Varying the speed of the moving detector will change the phase shift proportionally.

If the relativistic assumption of relative simultaneity is correct, there will be no phase shift in the moving detector, and the output will match that seen in the lab frame.

But, should the two detectors record different phase shifts proportional to velocity as expected, the assumption of relativistic simultaneity will be invalidated. A test that until recently was impossible is now achievable.

Other experiments have used the phase shift from various GPS satellites as a "test" of special relativity (e.g. Wolf and Petit [1]). However, all such tests to date involve measurement in one frame only, though the source signals are in various frames. Generally such tests take the form of a test of the one-way speed of light, but only as measured in a specific frame. As such, none of these tests is an actual test of the relativity of simultaneity, and confirm only that the speed of light in a given frame is equal to the distance from the receiver at time of detection to the source at time of emission divided by the time of flight. This is ultimately not really a test of anything, but is simply a confirmation of the definition of $c$ espoused by Maxwell.

## 3. Expected Results from Theory

### 3.1. Special Relativity Theory

The situation from the special-relativistic point of view can easily be worked out mathematically as is done below for the Galileo-Newtonian paradigm in the next section, but it can be explained easier in just a few words within the basic tenants of SRT. Due to the relativistic assumption of the simultaneous arrival of light in both the moving and lab frame at any given collocated point and time, it is a simple matter to show that no phase difference will be expected in the moving frame if there is none in the stationary frame. Imagine, as a visual thought experiment, a single point at the peak of a wave of the satellite emitted carrier signal, as in figure 3. That point will travel at a speed of $c$ and will remain at the peak of that wave for the entire trip to the lab in any reference frame. Thus a moving observer instantaneously collocated with the lab-frame observer at the instant that point strikes the lab detector will also detect that point at that time.

**Figure 3.**   Carrier and a Point

As a result, the moving observer will also detect the peak of the wave at that time. As we can establish lab frame observers at any point in the lab, then whichever part of the incoming wave strikes them when the moving observer is collocated with them will be the same part of the wave that strikes the moving observer by simple extension. We can also imagine a source in the lab emitting a signal and a point as in figure 3. If there is no phase shift in the lab frame between the lab signal and the satellite signal, then, under special relativity, there will be no phase shift between the lab signal and the satellite signal in the moving detector either (there is still a Doppler shift due to the motion, and it is for this reason that radial Doppler arises in SRT, but the Doppler shift is the same for both the lab and satellite generated signals, and has no effect on the measured phase difference, which is identical for the lab and satellite based signals in the moving frame).

To be perfectly clear, it is the assumption that collocated relatively moving observers will see light from a distant source at the same place and time that supports this argument. Under special relativity, if two wave peaks from two sources arrive in-phase for the stationary observer, they will also be in-phase for the moving observer. The two observers will disagree on where and when the peaks were transmitted, as reflected in the relativistic length contraction and time dilation as applied to the "moving" observer, but that does not alter the necessary requirement that the two peaks arrive in-phase for both.

### 3.2. Galileo-Newtonian Relativity

In the Galilean-Newtonian view, as in the theoretical introduction, in the frame of either observer, light travels from the source to the observer in a time given by the distance to the source at the time of emission in the frame of that observer divided by $c$. Distance is measured the same in the lab frame or the moving frame (arbitrarily defined as moving with respect to the lab frame), as length contraction is not invoked in either frame.

In the moving frame, both the lab and the satellite signal experience the same Doppler shift, so, as in the relativistic case, if the waves are in phase in the lab frame, they will be in phase in the moving frame as well, though at a different frequency. Considering the instant when the lab detector and moving detector are collocated, the time from the satellite to the lab frame is given as $d_S/c$, while in the moving frame it is $d_S'/c$, where

$$d_S' = d_S + vt_S. \qquad (10)$$

The time from the lab generator to the detectors is $d_L/c$ and $d_L'/c$ respectively. As this distance ($d_L$ is on the order of meters), the time is on the order of 3E-9 sec, and the time difference for moving and lab detectors is on the order of 1E-17 sec, and may be safely ignored for this discussion. So we are concerned only with the difference in arrival time of the satellite signal at a given point. In the moving frame, the time from satellite emission to reception is:

$$t_S' = \frac{d_S'}{c} = \frac{(d_S + vt_S)}{c} = t_S\left(1 + \frac{v}{c}\right) \qquad (11)$$

Thus the time difference between the moving and lab frames is given by:

$$t_S' - t_S = t_S\left(\frac{v}{c}\right) \qquad (12)$$

This time difference will manifest itself as a phase shift in the moving frame between the received satellite signal and the lab-based signal that has been locked to the satellite signal in the lab frame. As we can imagine virtual "lab-based" detectors all along the path, the phase shift is clearly constant for any given speed of the moving detector, and proportional to that speed.

If we consider a satellite in geosynchronous orbit (36,000 km) for example, $t_S$ is roughly 0.12 sec. For a 1 m/s moving frame velocity, the time difference is roughly 4E-10 sec. In the case of a 1 GHz signal, this small time difference will manifest itself as a phase shift of about 40% of a wavelength compared with the lab generated signal. This phase shift will adjust linearly with velocity of the moving frame. (Simplifying assumptions for discussion had the motion of the moving frame along the line of sight to the satellite, which will generally not strictly be the case in the actual realization). Different carrier frequencies and different velocities will produce different, predictable phase-shifts, allowing for elimination of error sources.

## 4. Technical Approach

### 4.1. Top Level Conceptual Approach

A top-level block diagram of the experiment is shown in figure 4. The blocks labeled $K$ and $K'$ represent phase detectors in the lab frame and moving frame respectively. The $K'$ detector is able to move at a controlled and measured speed on a track. This speed is on the order of 1 to 20 m/s. The detector blocks consist of S band antennas and carrier detectors, low noise amplifiers, band pass filters and other components required to detect and isolate the L1 signal from one or more GPS satellites, as well as the locally generated generate signal from the lab. This signal is shown as being created from a phase-locked-loop (PLL) feedback from the lab-based phase detectors, but, as discussed above, it is not required that the lab-generated signal be locked to the received satellite signal. The advantage of a phase-locked signal is to minimize variances and drift between the lab-based and satellite signals that arise due to satellite and earth motions, atmospheric effects, etc. However, these differences will also be detected and measured by the K frame phase detector.

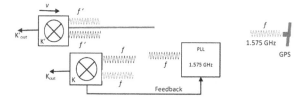

**Figure 4.** Top Level Block Diagram

The output of the $K$ and $K'$ phase detectors is a voltage proportional to the phase shift (figure 5) between the satellite and lab-generated signals. This output will be recorded over time and stored for data reduction and analysis. The GPS L1 carrier is optimum for this test due to the timing signals embedded in the signal that can be used for phase identification, as will be described later. The phase shift will be proportional to the velocity of the moving detector. Using a variety of speeds for the moving frame will confirm the proportionality to velocity and allow any fixed offsets due to experimental error or systemic errors to be factored out.

The absence of an offset in phase between the moving and stationary detectors will confirm for the first time

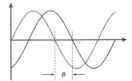

**Figure 5.** Phase Shift

Einstein's assumption of the relativity of simultaneity.

## 4.2. Detailed Approach

In a practical implementation of this experiment, one cannot actually use the L1 carrier as the phase reference, as it is spread away from the center frequency with a combination of codes and a 50 Hz clock. However, the presence of the C/A code provides the same information required to perform the test.

Any transition in the C/A code is equivalent to the point above the carrier identified in figure 3. Thus, if such a transition arrives at a specific point and time in the lab frame, according to special relativity it will arrive at the same point and time in the moving frame. The C/A code can be readily extracted from any incoming GPS signal, either by a lab-frame or moving receiver. For our choice of the lab based signal we are not restricted to a replica of the GPS carrier, and are free to choose any signal, as long as we can identify arrival of a specific point on the signal in both the lab and moving frames. A simple choice is a 1000 MHz or greater carrier modulated with a 1.023 MHz reference pseudo random square wave, to allow identification of specific pulses.

Instead of comparing the phase of two carrier signals, we XOR the recovered C/A code with the reference code and record the output. The width and arrangement of the outputs pulses provides extremely accurate information about the arrival time of the transitions in the C/A code compared with the locally generated code. For the moving frame, the overall length of each code will be factored by the Doppler (decreased for motion toward, increased for motion away), but under special relativity, the phase of the two signals will not change, and the modulo 2 output transitions will match those from the lab frame but for the appropriate Doppler scaling.

In the Galilean framework, as discussed, the moving frame signals will not be received simultaneously with collocated lab frames. For motion toward the satellite, at any given lab frame point, the moving frame will receive the signal at a later time given roughly by (12). The locally generated signal, however, will essentially arrive at the moving observer's frame at the same time as a collocated lab frame observer, due to the relatively short (compared to GPS orbit) distance travelled. This difference in arrival times of the GPS and lab based signals as compared with a lab based detector will appear as a phase difference between the C/A code and the reference random code. This difference will be manifested in the modulo 2 output of the two signals, and can then be measured and compared to

the lab signal after all data are recorded. An exaggerated example is provided in Figure 6.

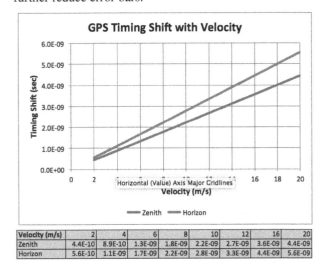

**Figure 6.** Sample Phase Shift Result for Lab and Moving Frames

The phase difference is directly proportional to the velocity of the moving frame. Figure 7 illustrates and tabulates the difference in phase of the C/A and reference random codes in seconds for velocities ranging from 2 to 16 m/s, for a satellite at zenith and on the horizon. A satellite on the horizon is a better acquisition target for several reasons. Being further away, the time offset is up to 20% greater. Also, the moving frame velocity can be along the ground, while for a satellite at zenith it would need to be vertical. Even so, a satellite at zenith is useful for comparing the moving and lab stationary equipment and verifying the absence of a shift due to equipment concerns. The absence of a shift for a satellite at zenith under otherwise identical conditions as for the satellite on the horizon will indicate that the equipment is performing as planned in both frames. By acquiring two satellites on each run, one near the horizon and one near zenith (especially two in the same orbit), the integrity of the equipment can be checked against results during the run, and the information used to further reduce error bars.

### GPS Timing Shift with Velocity

| Velocity (m/s) | 2 | 4 | 6 | 8 | 10 | 12 | 16 | 20 |
|---|---|---|---|---|---|---|---|---|
| Zenith | 4.4E-10 | 8.9E-10 | 1.3E-09 | 1.8E-09 | 2.2E-09 | 2.7E-09 | 3.6E-09 | 4.4E-09 |
| Horizon | 5.6E-10 | 1.1E-09 | 1.7E-09 | 2.2E-09 | 2.8E-09 | 3.3E-09 | 4.4E-09 | 5.6E-09 |

**Figure 7.** GPS Timing Shift with Velocity for Satellites at Zenith and Horizon

The expected phase offsets are quite small for the velocities indicated. Increasing the velocity raises its own concerns, however, so a moving frame in the 8 - 20 m/s range is preferable. At these speeds, the expected induced code phase shift is on the order of many sources of error within the GPS system. It is shown that most of these sources of error are identical in both frames, and need not be considered. Clock jitter (on the order of $10^{-9}$) is of particular concern, and must be minimized. Use of the P code in place of the C/A code would cut the clock jitter error by as much as a factor of ten, placing it well below the expected results.

While most error sources (especially clock jitter) are RMS type effects, the phase offsets proportional to velocity are decidedly one sided. Multiple runs in multiple directions at multiple velocities will aid in the accuracy of the results. Additionally, as the lab-based frame can be defined arbitrarily, the entire "lab" setup can be placed in motion in a direction opposite the "moving" frame, effectively doubling the expected timing shifts. It is also possible to arrange to sample more than one satellite on each run, with different results expected for each due to orientation and direction differences.

The experimental block diagram is shown in figure 8. The GPS Satellite sends out a 1.023 MHz C/A code on the L1 1.575 GHz carrier. The Reference Code Generator is in the lab frame but some distance (on the order of 1,000 m or less) from the receive antennas. The Reference Code Generator modulates a 1.023 MHz pseudo random reference code onto a 1000 MHz carrier.

The setup in the $K$ (Lab Frame) and $K'$ (Moving Frame) equipment is the same. A GPS receiver detects the signal from the satellite, and provides the C/A code as an output. The Reference Code Processor receives the 1000 MHz modulated carrier and extracts the reference code. The C/A code and reference code are XOR'd together to produce a sum code. The sum code can be used to accurately determine any time (phase) shift in the received C/A and reference codes. The C/A code, reference code and sum code are fed to a processor. The receiver also provides satellite time and range data to the processor for future data reduction. All signals and data are stored in RAM for retrieval and data reduction. The equipment can also be used to process multiple GPS signals for improved error reduction and calibration, and comparison between motion along the line of sight to a satellite or perpendicular to it.

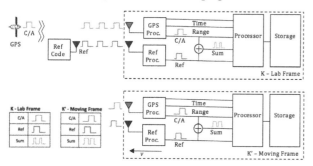

**Figure 8.** Block Diagram of Experiment

### 4.3. Final Implementation

The setup in the detailed approach section uses a lab

based pseudo C/A carrier generated locally to eliminate the time delay in reception between the moving and lab frames to something on the order of $10^{-17}$ seconds, several orders of magnitude below the $10^{-9}$ test results. However, we can accomplish the same sensitivity using two GPS satellites in the same orbit, with one near the horizon and one near zenith. The satellite on the horizon will be the C/A test signal, and the C/A code from the satellite at zenith will be the reference signal. The reason this works is illustrated in figure 9.

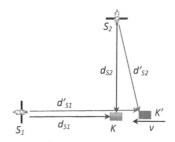

**Figure 9.** Two Satellite Configuration

GPS $S_1$ is on the horizon, while GPS $S_2$ is essentially overhead. Recalling (10), (11) and (12) for $d'_s$, $t'_s$ and $t'_s - t_s$, we will apply these formulas to the situation in figure 9 for each satellite. We take the liberty of using an equal sign for any value that is within 10E-14 of the actual value, 5 orders of magnitude smaller than the result we are testing. We first need an estimate of $(vt_{s_1})^2 / d_{s_2}^2$. The satellite distance is roughly 2E7 meters. The time from the satellite is on the order of $d/c$ or 6E-2 seconds. The velocity of the moving frame is 10 m/s or less. Thus, $(vt_{s_1})^2 / d_{s_2}^2$ is on the order of 9E-16, and may be safely ignored where it appears in the equality.

$$d'_{S_1} = d_{S_1} + vt_{S_1}. \tag{13}$$

$$d'_{S_2} = \sqrt{d_{S_2}^2 + vt_{S_1}^2} = d_{S_2}\sqrt{\left(1 + \frac{vt_{S_1}^2}{d_{S_2}}\right)} = d_{S_2}. \tag{14}$$

$$t'_{S_1} = \frac{d'_{S_1}}{c} = \frac{(d_{S_1} + vt_{S_1})}{c} = t_{S_1}\left(1 + \frac{v}{c}\right) \tag{15}$$

$$t'_{S_2} = \frac{d'_{S_2}}{c} = \frac{d_{S_2}}{c} = t_{S_2} \tag{16}$$

Thus the time difference between the moving and lab frames is given by:

$$t'_{S_1} - t_{S_1} = t_{S_1}\left(\frac{v}{c}\right) \tag{17}$$

$$t'_{S_2} - t_{S_2} = 0 \tag{18}$$

Equations (17) and (18) show that an overhead satellite can be used in place of the lab generated signal. It serves the same function of providing a reference code for comparison purposes that arrives essentially in phase at the moving $K'$ and stationary $K$ frames.

With this enhancement, the reference code generator can be replaced with a second GPS satellite, we eliminate the psuedo code, and the reference processors can be replaced with GPS processors identical to the ones already being used. The final block diagram is in figure 10, where the test signal is from $GPS_{Hor}$ on the horizon, while the reference signal is from $GPS_{Zen}$ near zenith. Satellite ephemeris data is also passed to the processor for inclusion in data reduction calculations from the satellites not being actually horizontal and vertical from the test lab.

### 4.4. Technical Risk Areas

The statistic of interest is primarily a fixed timing phase offset between the two GPS C/A codes in the moving $K'$ system compared with any seen in the lab-frame $K$ system. This allows for elimination of many sources of error as described below. In the end, best-fit phase vs. velocity plots with error bars will verify the presence or absence of a Galilean simultaneity phase shift. Capture and isolation of error sources will allow for better modeling and data reduction, reducing the uncertainty in the final results. Accurate control and disposition of such errors will ensure a valid determination of the presence or absence of the Galilean simultaneity phase shift for various speeds and satellites.

**Clock synchronization.** The use of a local phase detector will determine the phase between the two GPS C/A signals in each system ($K$ and $K'$) with no clock synchronization between the two required. Since we are interested only in the difference of arrival times of the codes in the lab and moving frames as measured by the equipment in those frames, no synchronization between the frames is required.

**Relativistic time dilation.** For the velocity of the moving frame, relativistic time dilation effects are on the order of $10^{-15}$, well below the expected phase shifts of $10^{-9}$. As such, relativistic time dilation and length contraction cannot be invoked to explain away any time shifts as great as those expected in a Galilean framework. In fact, it is the relativistic time dilation and length contraction in the first place that allows special relativity to assert that the moving and stationary frames each "sees" a distant event at the same time, causing the resultant disagreement as to the simultaneity of the events themselves.

**Doppler due to moving frame.** The speed of the moving frame should be known with respect to the lab as precisely as possible to allow a determination of the predicted Galilean simultaneity phase shift. In the first experimental configuration, since the signal from the lab-based generator experiences the same Doppler as does the GPS received signal, errors due to less precise velocity measurements of the moving frame are not of concern in phase measurements. There will be an overall change in the size of the recorded modulo 2 output string proportional to the Doppler, but this will have no effect on the shape and structure of that output. In the two GPS signal approach, Doppler must be taken into account in the moving system

since only the $GPS_{Hor}$ signal will experience the shift.

There is an error introduced due to the motion of the GPS satellite, and its elevation angle with respect to the lab not being 0 degrees. However, this phase error is measured independently by the lab-based system, and we are interested in the differences between the moving frame system and the lab-based system. The phase errors due to satellite motion and elevation are the same for both systems, and can be accurately modeled and filtered out of the results to leave only the Galilean simultaneity phase shift. In the two GPS signal approach, the ephemeris data will be used in the calculation of elevation and motion effects for both satellites.

**Position measurement of moving system.** The location of the moving system with time needs to be known as accurately as possible for reducing systemic errors. However, as has been shown, the moving system can be compared at any time to a "hypothetical" lab-based system that is instantaneously collocated with the moving system. The phase error in each of the hypothetical lab-based systems will be identical to the actual lab-based system, except for minor variations due to elevation angle and relative satellite speed along the path, which have been shown to be on the order of $10^{-19}$. For an entire experimental footprint of hundreds of meters, these effects are negligible, especially for satellites near the horizon. The more precisely the location with time is known, the smaller these errors become. However, these errors are substantially below the Galilean simultaneity phase shift expected, and the use of multiple satellites again allows these errors to be factored out.

**Internal delays of receiver systems (antenna, coax, LNA, etc.).** These delays can all be calculated explicitly by having both the moving frame and lab frame systems stationary in the lab frame. The delays can be accurately measured and removed initially in software or later during data reduction. Systemic or theoretical delays introduced by placing the moving frame in motion will be experienced on both the $GPS_{Hor}$ and $GPS_{Ver}$ signals to equal degree, and these are also on the order of $10^{-15}$. The main concern is the difference in "path length" or phase between the GPS receiver short antenna-coax and the lab signal receiver short antenna coax. But once modeled and accounted for, there is no additional variation or concern. Absence of unmodeled internal delays can be verified by reversing the roles of the moving and lab frame equipment.

**Acquisition of L1 carrier.** Both the $K$ and $K'$ systems can lock onto the appropriate signal prior to placing the $K'$ system in motion. The problem is then one of tracking an already acquired signal (GPS and lab-based) as the motion begins. This is an on-going process that the electronics manage on their own, and eliminates the need for a (relatively) long acquisition cycle for a platform moving at 2 - 16 m/s in the lab.

**Low SNR.** Acquiring and tracking the GPS L1 carrier in a low SNR environment, while difficult, has been overcome in all modern GPS receiver systems. The use of a higher-gain antenna and LNA in close proximity reduces

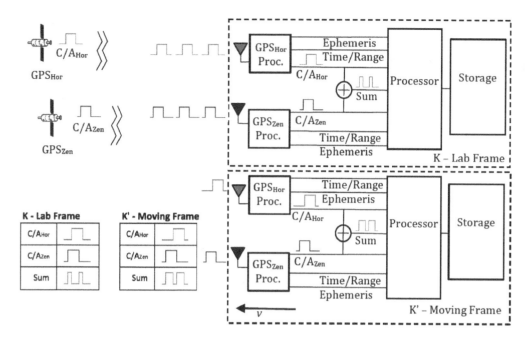

**Figure 10.** Final Experiment Block Diagram

this source of error. In an experimental setup such as this, where size and weight is not of paramount importance, a higher gain antenna is easily accommodated.

**Ionospheric and other disturbances to the carrier phase**. These types of effects are modeled as noise, and do not represent a fixed offset in either the $K$ or $K'$ system. Any such effects will be nearly identical in the $K$ and $K'$ frame, allowing for elimination of consideration of phase variations due to such disturbances.

**Ephemeris Errors**. Since the GPS signal is not being used to provide actual precise location or range data, ephemeris errors are relatively unimportant. Ephemerides are accurate to within meters. Additionally, any ephemeris-induced anomalies will be experienced equally by the lab-based and moving platforms. Relativistic variances on interpretation of the ephemeris data in the moving system are on the order of $10^{-15}$.

**Clock Jitter**. There is no concern of clock jitter on the space segment, as we are not actually using the GPS signal to recover precise location information. Whatever variance exists in the transmitted signal will be received equally by the moving and lab frames. It is therefore important to extract the C/A random codes as precisely as possible on the receive side. This will be a particularly important design consideration on the receive side, as any variance from the actual signal time must be below $10^{-9}$. Several approaches already exist in various implementations to get below this value (Ward [3]). Even if the uncertainty remains on the order of $10^{-9}$, data accumulation over many runs, directions and orientations will allow an actual phase shift in the signals to rise above the noise.

## REFERENCES

1. Peter Wolf, *Satellite test of special relativity using the global positioning system*, Physical Review A, V 56 No 6 Dec 1997.
2. Curt Renshaw, *The Radiation Continuum Model of Light and the Galilean Invariance of Maxwell's Equations*, IEEE Aerospace and Electrodynamic Systems Magazine, V 13 No 10 Oct 1998.
3. Phillip Ward, *Satellite Signal Acquisition, Tracking, and Data Demodulation*, Understanding GPS Principal and Applications, 2nd Ed.

# Infinity and Reality The Universe is Otherwise - Part 2a.

## Paul Schroeder

*8244 Anna Ave. Wind Lake, Wi. 53185 pshrodr8@aol.com*

Infinity Contradicts Current Cosmologies Overall understanding of cosmology would be altered, improved, and simplified by redefining the universe as being infinite in space and time!

**Keywords:** universe, pushing gravity, light, aberration, EM radiation, big bang

## 1. Introduction

The issue for discussion here is changing the overall nature of the universe. There are 2 options. The universe is either infinite in time and space or it has boundaries. Accepting an infinite universe is more than looking forward to its future. Will it end in space or time? If you decide it won't end you chose an infinite future. But infinity also implies no beginning in space or time. Choosing complete infinity leads to a revised view of reality. The universe is all space, ie a container for everything else. You either picture the universe as endless without a beginning or you picture it as bounded. The idea of a boundary means there is a beyond, whether in space or time. Bounded theory requires edges where the universe ends. An infinite boundary of infinite edges provides an infinite number of explanations for events at edges. The big bang is a prime example.

There are other mystic and disconnected physical models that have flourished without sufficient concern about what the universe itself is. Space and time lost their reality and multiple dimensions were introduced as somehow being logical. This document is a redefinition of the nature of the universe. The process of redefining physics with a new paradigm requires rethinking and repackaging of all existing knowledge. New experiments and mathematical equations are not the key to a Holy Grail – new perspective of physics.

There are many revelations associated with the infinite view. Acceptance may take significant time. A cosmology based on the infinite and the current one based on the finite universe are incompatible with each other. Comparing them provides a mental exercise. The infinite assigns to gravity a physical nature and the logical physical interaction of pushing. An infinite universe stimulates incentives to restudy rotations, mass, the nature of space, orbiting, gravity, light and EM radiation, and transferring of images. Relativity made headway in those directions. This system further connects space and mass, energy and light, in ways that will clarify physics. Space affects mass and mass affects space similarly as in Einstein's formula that led to the standard model. Numerous looks at Newtonian systems and at Relativity help bring the thinking together. Consider what follows to emulate an introductory course/overview of a new science.

## 2. Beginnings and Endings – Boundaries

Our local environment is logical and ordinary. Why are our cosmological views about distant space and the universe so mystic? Why should things be so different far away or long ago? We will examine the reasons and build a path that reexamines the beliefs upon which our science stands today.

The overriding factor affecting how one views the universe depends upon their view of the concept of "infinity".

Our local environment is logical and ordinary. Why are our cosmological views about distant space and the universe so mystic? Why should things be so different far away or long ago? We will examine the reasons and build a path that reexamines the beliefs upon which our science stands today. How do we deal with the extremes for our measures of distance, size, time, etc.? The big and small sizes, the close and far distances, and the short and long time frames are either infinite or bounded. We must reveal that the infinite boundaries provide more places to analyze and thus employ many more researchers. However there will be many new perspectives to pursue with universal infinity as suggested within.

In the bounded view there are end markers and the beyond to deal with. There are beginnings and ends to account for. And then, whatever is beyond the end lines must be defined. Today's theories accept boundaries. For the big bang beginning religion has contributed support in order to retain the Genesis statement "in the beginning". Continued development of the big bang and expansion has dominated cosmology. Within this view continuous new concepts and terminology are encouraged as speculation about new concepts for theoretical physics theory. We all want to understand and address the end lines.

Our alternative perspective based on infinity leads to much simpler views of our cosmos. We simply need to understand why space and time can exist and function eternally. The following analysis of motions and gravity springs forth from an infinite view of the universe.

Infinity cannot be assigned to most things. There is no specific "infinite motion" for example. The infinite is specifically for the universe. What is the universe? It contains all matter and anything else that has form. It is the volume of space as defined by the whole of the X Y Z coordinate system. How far do the coordinates extend? That is the measure separating an infinite or a bounded universe. Is it bounded at one end with a beginning, bounded at the back end with an end, or bounded in both directions? Does it end somewhere beyond our imagination? Accepting infinity is a hard choice. The choice has been debated over the centuries. The concept of infinity has varied between acceptance and rejection.

Today the big bang theory is the creation of the universe followed by the ongoing extension of existence. As the bounded universe expands an edge exists between that which is the space contained within the universe and what is not space. That boundary must also expand. Likewise, there is also the concept of time. The big bang also assigns time a beginning boundary. Although full of contents, the universe and time are both just concepts, not real physical things. Einstein merged time with space within Relativity theory. He created their virtual form by encasing them in 4 dimensional space time. In that form they lose their ability to serve as measures as well as losing their form.

The dominant boundary is "in the beginning". Where did the existence of things start? Space, as we understand it, is obviously real. Thus it has to contain something that gives reality to its measure. A void in space, cannot exist as it cannot extend any measure of that space. Space provides a place for the transfer of things, and thus assists motion. Motion begins as an action of gravity, an effect that reaches far across space. The identifiable contents, including the force of gravity become bounded in current theory. In the big bang theory, gravity didn't even exist until well into the big bang expansion time and it grew from there. The concept of boundaries establishes a platform for the exercise of mind bending contemplations. There have become very many edges to evaluate in infinite ways. All this exercise inhibits finding an ultimate understanding. Why did a cosmology with limits take hold? Science seeks beyond limits. We keep tracing mankind further back, and we trace more distant components of space. We were expanding imagined limits. Religion also played a part by accepting the big bang as a replacement for its creation. "In the beginning"summarized God's revelations to mankind. The Bible is a presumed history of us and everything leading forward from beginnings. The universe, night and day, and mankind all were given beginnings. Admittedly everything material exists and had a beginning and end, both in time and in space. All real physical phenomena do have beginnings within the overall, the universe. Man and the earth and the sky can have beginnings. It is the universe itself, where measurement resides, that shouldn't be assigned a beginning. Religion doesn't assign a beginning or an end to God! So God is apparently infinite. He is the universe within which all things exist and are contained. Thus biblical ideas are more in tune with an infinite universe than with a big bang universe.

Our universe is infinite in space and time. Infinity also extends to the size measure so things can be infinitely large or small. In a sense infinity makes you give up on defin-

ing things beyond the region of common interest. But the payoff is that it allows the assumption that everything beyond the local arena is similar to what we know locally. We can remain in our local neighborhood and still understand the universe by simply extending current and local understanding of matter and effects, ie. matter and motion. Motion is a relationship of the time and distance factors. Unfortunately, time and distance are currently merged into Space time and lose their identity. Someday physics logic and cosmology will revert to and accept a simple infinite universe and extend our measurements and understandings. As a sidelight it is interesting that mathematics has created procedures for eliminating infinities to support boundary investigations.

Acceptance of infinite space will disrupt physics. Today new cosmological ideas consist of ever more extreme and excessive concepts created to describe some region of a boundary. The list is extensive. We will also find little ongoing use for some of our current research and investigation. Most experiments and math formula are used to attach new ideas to existing theory. When that theory is gone the relationship dies. Just as an example, output from the Hadron Collider will always be useful on the detail scale, as we remain interested in finding smaller things. Its findings however diminish for understanding the universe. The Higgs boson wont be a universal particle. Physicists downplay theorizing, but theory reveals understandings while experimentation tests it. We will discuss many concepts of boundaries later on. An example is the fantasy of extra dimensions which lead to the"standard model". Many accepted theories don't hold water if space and time are infinite.

## 3. Absolutes

Theories are built upon some logic base. That base redefines the ideas that separate one model from other models. We all think differently, some people view the world as black and white while others see things as grey. All physical models have needed to have some type of fixed concept, value or idea to build upon. Relativity demands a fixed basis when it identifies a fixed and limiting velocity for light. That choice has of course led to many debates over the years. Light itself had been assigned a fixed structure of being massless. With the photo-electron Einstein then converted light into a dual behaving flow with fixed structure and fixed photons of mass.

The big bang theory implies an absolute beginning. Mathematics depends upon constants that are fixed and absolute. Boundaries themselves are absolutes. Newton's model contains the assumption that space is empty. While his 3 laws of motion refute any beginning, within an infinite universe, all contents must have beginnings. It is only the base that extends indefinitely. Newton's motion of orbitals also imply "forever"as an absolute for the motion. But maybe he preferred the weird ideas of some beginning gas clouds condensing into orbitals? Anyway, motion cannot be an absolute.

Relativity accepts Maxwell's views of light velocity c as fixed, dependent upon its medium. No gravity or other causes are allowed to affect light velocity. Thus c fixes the geometry of space for relativity. The theory is then established and sold as if all distance can be measured by the time travel of light. Can a model exist without fixed laws and limits? We do some of this every day in our assumptions about life.

## 4. Is Space Empty?

Space itself has to be real. As mentioned, it can't be an empty vacuum or it wouldn't exist. From early times, from Aristotle to Copernicus, to Galileo, to Tycho Brahe, mankind studied space but had little interaction with space. Everything contemplated, such as gravity, was centered to the earth. Galileo provided tests of gravity force and his telescope by which he revealed planet detail. Copernicus identified the orbiting motions within our solar system. Tycho Brahe diagrammed the orbits with relation to the earth. Kepler gave a partial explanation of the orbital motions which finally implied a motion source related to the sun. There has been no understanding of why orbits existed or why the motion within orbits continued unchanged. Why don't the bodies fall away or why aren't they slowed by friction? Motion continuing unchanged implies empty space.

That brings us to the arrival of Isaac Newton. Much of subsequent knowledge and of the science of Physics revolved (pun) around his work. He applied explanations of gravity at work on earth to events in space. His theories lead to interactions of spatial bodies and of all masses. In order to propose an ongoing centripetal gravity force that supported orbital motions, he had to overcome friction. He did so with his 3 laws of motion. A body at rest remains at rest unless externally affected. Motion of a body continues unchanged, (and thus the body is in a form of rest) unless interfered with. And finally, interference (by other moving bodies) imparts a new velocity and direction of motion to the body. Building a theory based upon an absence of influence by something (friction in his case) was necessary for Newton to build a world system and an absolute space theory. But in today's world of technical and detail knowledge, the absence idea needs to be discarded in favor of an ongoing impetus.

Newton's views competed with and overcame the whirlpool theories of Descartes as a source of orbital motion. A whirlpool representation of motions of space itself didn't match central spin experiments such as controlling fluids in a bucket or rotating within a fluid medium that extends to infinity. In neither example do the velocities or actions of the fluids simulate velocities as calculated using the formula of Kepler's third law. These examples probably led to disinterest in Descartes's model. What is needed and provided later in paper 3 is a more extensive examination of the environments in which planets revolved and the variation in effects contributed by the sun as central source. There are different sources of rotations resulting in a different measure of central controlled whirling motions.

Since friction is interference, it was defined away by designation of space as a vacuum. We know today that space is not empty. Therefore space must cause frictional interference. That led science to claim that light radiation has no mass and thus can't cause a pressure of interference nor vary its velocity. But then there are meteorites, solar wind, etc. And actually light does cause pressure upon earth and upon eyes,

Newton could only propose no friction in space in order to propose his super equality in which gravity maintains original motions by attracting planets with a perpendicular offset accorded to the original motion. Somehow everything exactly offset. Without a motive force, imagine the scary thoughts of collapse if the equality is broken.

The history of cosmology over thousands of years has knowledge sourced from a central perspective. Mankind lived on earth so spatial reality has been a function of the relationship with earth. Theory was that matter dominates space. Tom Van Flandern extolled that view by suggestion we imagine the creation of the universe from one universal sphere and gradually add space and more masses. But space is everywhere serving as the container of masses. So in reality space dominates matter. Thus the collected knowledge is oriented incorrectly. It is time for the 180 degree reorientation of perspective. In a later chapter we will analyze a motive force that creates the motion that is required to offset the centripetal inward gravity effects. That motive force is actually supplied by the same gravity that pulls the bodies together and so stability is guaranteed. Given that space is real, what is it made of? Gravity is a component. We don't view force as a thing that can serve as contents. Beyond gravity, there is light passing through space. What is light and what makes it travel?

## 5. EM radiation

Light became known as a form of radiation from the work of Faraday and Maxwell. Faraday discovered that magnets could distort the flow of electricity. Ultimately he proposed magnetism and electricity as being joined as radiation. Faraday also recognized that space was full of radiation which included the flow of electricity and magnetism. Since light flowed thru space it must be radiated waves. Light became the foundation of the Electromagnetic scale, and the spectrum was formed.

Maxwell believed in Faraday and created some related mathematics. His findings included the idea that radiation has a fixed and maximal velocity from which we get the constant c. Maxwell also proposed that gravity is not instant but has a velocity of its own. Maxwell failed in his attempt to connect EM radiation with gravity but he had some thoughts, ultimately rejected, about pushing gravity.

Faraday and Maxwell had focused on the flows of electricity and magnetism and Faraday found a commonality in their flow. The two forces were joined radiation flows whose waves are differently directed. In the linear view waves are a distortion of flow and jut off line in the XY direction or the YZ direction. The choice of offset plane determines magnetism vs electricity. Three dimensions have a third coordinate direction which happens to be the XZ direction of the flow. They didn't include Gravity. It shouldn't have been hard since gravity effects and magnetism effects are similarly seen as attractions. Gravity must flow.

## 6. Light

Matter and the flow of light/EM radiation is a prime focus of cosmology. Mankind has made important discoveries throughout the ages related to light.

The whole EM radiation structure started with the study of light. Clearly light travels through space. The sun and stars prove that. We restate here that light itself had been assigned a fixed structure by being considered to be massless. That feature failed in certain situations including an apparent pressure by light beams when they hit the eye or when beams arrive from the sun. This pressure concept led Einstein to propose a dual structure for light in which light was wave like as well as mass like. Einstein assigned light wave beam structure to include the photon particle.

Prior to that light was massless by definition. But light waves have a nature and move or flow forward. Shouldn't everything that has a nature be subjected to gravity? Letting only massive items be affected is the making of a boundary and leads to a constant speed for light. But let's say that light beams/photons are launched by the source star. A related visual model is a rocket being fired upward. The rocket will probably slow and possible fall back to the surface. Light moves so fast that for efficiency sake the gravitational effect has always been ignored. That allows the velocity base c and limit for Relativity. But it cant be absolute! Light should be affected and no matter how little the gravity effect can muster, the source body remains directly behind the flow of the light for many light years. At some point science must consider the trivial (due to distance) continuing gravitational "attraction"on a photon against the extensive time continuation of the flow. Isn't red shift a logical sign of some minor slowing of the flow of light? Stretching a wave into a longer beam gives fewer arrivals and thus a slower flow. This is not just a terminology answer. That slowing would be simulate the expansion of space between the source and the destination if light velocity were constant. Expanding this logic, isn't that source gravitational causing slowing of the beam and thus causing a redshift? That redshift is gradually overcome by the gravitational attraction of the destination star. That star pulls the light so it goes faster. The overall speed and appearance of the light beam becomes blue shifter relative to earlier in its flow and recovers its emitted form upon its subsequent arrival. The Pound - Rebka test supports this gravity model. That test is done with light in space near earth which is sent down to earth. The test suggested and proved that the destination pull is occurring for incoming light and is causing a blue shift. If you accept the gravitational red-shift, which would occur during the first half of the light transfer from source to destination, then it serves as an alternate to the Doppler idea of bodies moving apart and thereby causing the red shift. Expansion is no longer a logical model of space and the universe. We have mentioned that beams of light are continually red shifted throughout their passage across the universe so that, at some distance, the shift exceeds the visible red range. The waves become infrared, microwaves, or radio waves. Appropriately, an isotropic microwave background is observed signifying an approximate distance from which all light from very distant sources is shifted beyond the visible. This background has been given a whole existence of its own and is called black body radiation. Due to science's backward perspectives about the source, this background radiation gives the false impression of a boundary to the universe.

Light is formed when spatial beams initiate interactions with mass particles. Spatial beams gain increased frequency. Heavenly bodies such as our sun convert penetrating flowing beams and create and release light and heat. Nothing is really burned up or used up even by particle conversion within a sun. Its output is simply a converted form of the penetrating paep beams entering it on the opposite side.

In 1826, Olber proposed a paradox in which the night sky should be solid light from an infinite number of stars. He was in fact correct, however the light has continually been red shifted. As the waves extend in length they become infrared, microwaves, radio waves and beyond. The current concept is that space contains a microwave background that is isotropic. All directions reveal a similar amount of starlight shifted into the microwave range. Olber claimed that the night sky should be fully lighted because of the infinite number of stars providing light. The cosmic background radiation is Olber's starlight ablaze allover. Science never convincingly solved the diminishing of light across space. Obviously gravity causes it.

Light beams have properties and thus act in a manner similar to matter. Light is subject to forces such as gravity. There is no need for a dual nature or for the photon. All actions of light such as its impact and penetration can be viewed as controlled by its wave/coil nature. Since the model we are building removes the fixed value of c, we continue the making of a new model without any absolutes of measure.

## 7. Motion

The elementary activity in the universe is motion of celestial bodies relative to each other. Once infinity is addressed, an all-inclusive physical theory should focus next upon spatial motions. The second level of interest becomes the tools for measurement of the motion. A fundamental oversight in relativity theory is the transmission of light dictating the nature of space.

What we have is an entanglement between the motions of bodies and their signals to others. Light/radiation and our goal of external pushing gravity are the two transmissions which convey the nature of celestial bodies. If we assume that what we see is what is, then the light signal dominates. But Einstein pointed out an issue with light where significant motion of bodies relative to light signals distorts their location and time measures. Light signals likewise can be influenced by motion of the observer, which action is specified as aberration. Our conundrum is that light conveys the picture of motion while the motion influences the transmission of the light beam.

## 8. The Nature of Space

After Newton's gravity work and in his in depth analysis of light, the finding of a transmission system for light and radiation gained importance. The concept of Aether came into use. The Aether was to be the body of space whether it was a solid or more like gaseous. Questions arrived such as Is the Aether the same away from vs near masses? How about within masses? Does it carry radiation as well as matter bodies? Extensive debate continued until Einstein refuted the concept of Aether using the Michelson & Morley findings about the lack of interference with light from the sun by Earth's motion.

Accepting MM as a correct interpretation is an example of improper specification of the base for an analysis. The test was of light relative to us. Our examination of "attraction"gravity tends to be relative to a base mass. For pushing gravity we will seek an improved orientation and view it from the base of space itself. For studying light frequency is affected by equilibrium. Earth exists because of equilibrium of impacting forces. While light will switch frequencies crossing space, it can retain its frequency upon earth. We should recognize that its absence of interference is an output function of its flow through space. In reality, earth and other mass bodies in space are in equilibrium. Equilibrium on cosmic body surfaces is a lateral situation. Gravity removes equilibrium in the vertical direction but that was not what was tested. No net of forces offset local activity parallel to the ground such as running and driving motions. Ultimately the MM test only proves an absence of aberration of the sun's light as it arrives on earth. See the aberration chapter.

The Aether continues to be proposed today as scientists need something to exist as space. Here we decline the Aether in a major revelation! What travels thru the cosmos? Light and thus all radiation emitted from stars and other bodies everywhere. The emissions are all radiation (rays). Given the nearly infinite number of stars all destination points are receiving beams from "in the beginning"directions all the time. The radiation travels rapidly and together the beams join to create a blanket of existence that is simulates a solid. There is no void area. You may object that in the extremely small points there are empty spaces between the beams of radiation. Such voids would refute continuity. But here we use a similar perspective that Heisenberg used for his uncertainty principal. Recognize that the beams travel at the near the infinite velocity of c. Likewise the beam sources are in constant

motion. Although very minimal, displacement continually occurs within any remote point flowing beams can shift perpendicularly relative to all receiving points. In the time it would take to isolate an empty point in space it would be reformed by a further beam angling in at some slightly different direction. Therefore it is radiation alone that defines our space and no Aether is needed. Space is radiation and all space is real and similar throughout. No concocted concepts are needed. The farther radiation travels from its source the greater the distance between rays. That gap is filled by rays from other sources. With all these rays from every direction defining space there is no need for additional mediums. Space is filled by EM radiation which becomes both the action and the medium. We call this the fabric of space. Essentially the light waves are examples of the movement of the medium just as sound comes from the movement of air. Science has observed that light moving in one direction does not affect light moving in other directions when they intersect. The same non-interference could then apply to all EM radiation. While the radiation is moving the interaction of waves from all directions gives the impression of stasis, or no detectible motions. Space can appear void while moving internally in all directions, even at speed c.

**See references in paper "Building Theories Upon Theories Hinders Science".**

# Structure and Gravity The Universe is Otherwise - Part 2b.

## Paul Schroeder

*8244 Anna Ave. Wind Lake, WI. 53185*
*pshrodr8@aol.com*

Once you have read Infinity and Reality you can apply the logic there to gain a finer understanding of gravity. The structure of the universe leads logically to a pushing type of gravity which leads to an understanding of orbiting.

**Keywords:** light, relativity, orbiting, aberration, pushing gravity, EM radiation, rotation, revolution

## 1. Introduction

The details of working with space are well analyzed and understood by astrophysics study but big parts are overlooked within most cosmological views. Particle physics is the breaking down of matter into components such as atomic particles. The purpose is to gain understanding of all matter and its place in the universe. Radiation is separated from particle views and simply viewed as in motion serving as lines of flow. Overall views using field and vortex analysis is insufficient. A detailed analysis of radiation reveals a connection with and a new nature for gravity.

## 2. Attraction Gravity is a Metaphysical Concept

When mankind's base of reality is the solid earth, then all actions can be related to local masses. Thus gravity, which pulls objects downward toward Earth is called an attraction. Gravity pulling is denoted as an "action at a distance". It is this awkard term that stimulated a need for correction by future gravity theories such as Relativity. "Action at a distance" is the concept that an object can be moved, changed, or otherwise affected without being physically touched (as in mechanical contact) by another object. That is, it is the nonlocal interaction of objects that are separated in space. The term attraction was used most often in the context of early theories of gravity and electromagnetism to describe how an object responds to the influence of distant objects. For example, Coulomb's law and the law of universal gravitation are such early theories.

Attraction is a mystic term that is not treated as a physical action in the study of physics as no motive can cause a pull without some background of pushing being involved. Although it is metaphysical, attraction also found believers as a mystical answer to the Copenhagen EPR paradox. This accepts magic known as "quantum entanglement" to explain how separated atoms can seem to react simultaneously to an action. This would negate the limiting speed of light and all other limits to simultaneous responses. The acceptance of "action at a distance" led science in questionable directions long ago by claiming the failure of early

atomistic and mechanistic theories which sought to reduce all physical interaction to collision. That is the same issue we face today. The quantum mechanics of Physics logically wants all actions to be caused by contact and has had to work around gravity to get there. The exploration and resolution of this problematic phenomenon led to all the concepts of the Standard Model physics, from the concept of a field, to descriptions of quantum entanglement and the mediator particles .]

## 3. Pushing Gravity

God created the universe in seven days. Mankind was then left to make sense in some detail, of the universe, its motions, and interactions. We accumulate detailed theories and solutions until the complexity is overwhelming. Then a change of perspective is useful. An example was the change from the geocentric to the heliocentric view of the universe. So many epicycles were needed to determine celestial motions that Copernicus's simpler perspective took hold in the face of a seeming impossible challenge as our senses denied the newfound motion of earth. Understanding of spatial motions today must focus on gravity and related concepts. Current theories tend to be piecemeal, not addressing complete facets of human knowledge. The perspective presented here is all encompassing and simple. What follows uses redefined gravity to restore perspective to our universe. Some building blocks are:

1. Gravity is an external event.
2. Gravity is a "net effect" force resulting from interacting beams of radiation particles.
3. Gravity is multi-directional, not simply a down force.
4. Gravity particle beams penetrate and exit from masses. The beams are bent by the rotation as they depart the rotating body.
5. Kepler's 3rd law relates planet times to orbital distances. The sun causes Kepler's formula to work. So the center must somehow provide impetus for orbitals.

### 3.1. Introduction

The structure of the universe is a simple concept though

mankind continually complicates it. The universe is essentially isotropic within a 3 dimensional framework, allows for motion and structure, and contains a force that holds macro bodies together. That force is of course gravity. In the hierarchy of theories, the view of the universe proposed here is the most basic. It is simpler in its concepts and terminology than is current theory. A complete overall perspective starts via a rationalist view before succumbing to the experimentation - proof requirements of empiricists.

Since gravity dominants action in the universe, a proper focus on gravity as the prime mover provides an optimum perspective of our universe. We have not logically defined gravity. Most concepts and definitions lead to misrepresenting gravity as a metaphysical force. Scientists begin their theorizing with mass and define motions using concepts of fields, forces, charge, and energy rather than begin by relating to gravity.

Scientific investigation within physics and astrophysics produce experimental results that lead to new concepts, ad infinitum. But they rarely lead to understanding. Many analyses are designed to alter exiting theories such as relativity. Instead there are advantages to considering a perspective that eliminates many current concepts. We start with gravity.

### 3.2. New Perspective

The concept of attraction is not a physical event. It is a perception resulting from the "net" effect of beams arriving at masses. Physics should have dealt with this issue eons ago. Physical events demand interaction via contact so gravity must be a push upon things. We perceive the pressure as gravitational 'attraction' and will see that gravity keeps masses together. As we begin seeking interaction we will relate actions to linear beams which are easier to understand and work with than are fields.

Understanding gravity as an external event is the key to understanding. Consider gravity pushing rather than attracting. Doing so addresses a logical requirement for Physics, the requirement for contact. Push contact occurs between two or more particles. The push is continuous suggesting gravity travels as a beam. The part of the beam associated with the contact is the wave. The varying altitude within a wave gives it impact potential. I had named the wave as a particle called a Paep for ease of discussion. Gravity (however defined) must move in order to create pressure. By default it must move in all directions. Thus, in the void of space, all gravitational push is in balance. To get "gravitation pressure" there must be an imbalance. One way that occurs is by more gravity beams moving in one direction and overwhelming the offsetting gravity from the opposite direction. Understanding that gravity acts as a result of a "net" force is important. Gravitation at a point can be variable depending on the force contained within opposing beams. The common spherical curvature of spheres such as earth hid the variability of gravity throughout the ages. Gravity varies due to modification by masses or by radiation.

Treating gravity as a pressure alters a myriad of concepts. Start with a physical gravity which pushes upon things. A simple corollary defines its opposite, what we call anti-gravity. If gravity is a push, then anti-gravity must be a push in the opposite direction. It is not some mystic situation in which everything disintegrates, born of those who thought of gravity as an attraction and cant reconcile an anti attraction which lacks physical attributes. Anti gravity causes the repelling of 2 bodies from each other, as opposed to attraction. Imagine a mass levitating on earth. In fact we may cause such anti-gravity by interfering with gravity from one direction. We will explain magnetism, the other "attraction force". Magnetism is directional, both attracting and repelling. It occurs only in limited situations. We may someday expand the situations.

To do away with the occult nature of gravity in existing systems we have to have a push source that provides gravity. That observable push is the "net" of all pushes upon any object from all 3 dimensional directions. This statement removes the dependence upon earth itself as the reference point and resets space as the reference for ongoing cosmology. The "Universe is Otherwise" and all gravity exists as pushing forces throughout space. What is it that pushes? The pushing must be done by the radiation beams throughout space as there is nothing else that fills space. In most places, such as remote space, the pushes net out to full equilibrium and no motion happens. The finding of a net pressure and therefore motion within any place in space indicates an imbalance of gravity push upon that place from the various directions. Without gravity providing the basic push there would not be any basic source for motions.

Radiation flows in all directions everywhere. We usually don't recognize that flow in any measure because all motion nets out. We recognize that light beams do not interfere with light from any other direction. So within a point of space, radiation is flowing everywhere at speed c and is undetected.

We can make use of the term attraction only if we recognize we are discussing the apparent motion relative to us. We do measure the downward falling motions in measures such as meters/sec. Extending the time beyond the fixed measure of one second, we create the concept of acceleration as a way to reference the change of the apparent motion over time.

1. Our pushing gravity is the source or cause of the pressure that produces detectable effects. This source is currently undefined and has been since the time of Newton.

2. The term gravity is often used to denote the detectable effects of actions which are caused by the source of gravity. The effects of gravity upon matter bodies results in detectable motions or pressure. The effect is the "attraction" of matter toward mass bodies. The attraction effect is expanded by Newtonian dynamics to include the potential motion of 2 or more spatial bodies toward each other

The concept of attraction is not a physical event. It is a perception resulting from the "net" effect of beams arriving at masses. Physics should have dealt with this issue eons ago. Physical events demand interaction via contact so gravity must be a push upon things. We perceive the pressure as gravitational 'attraction'and will see that gravity keeps masses together. As we begin seeking interaction we will relate actions to linear beams which are easier to understand and work with than are fields.

Understanding gravity as an external event is the key to understanding. Consider gravity pushing rather than attracting. Doing so addresses a logical requirement for Physics, the requirement for contact. Push contact occurs between two or more particles. The push is continuous suggesting gravity travels as a beam. The part of the beam associated with the contact is the wave. The varying altitude within a wave gives it impact potential. I had named the wave as a particle called a Paep for ease of discussion. Gravity (however defined) must move in order to create pressure. By default it must move in all directions. Thus, in the void of space, all gravitational push is in balance. To get "gravitation pressure" there must be an imbalance. One way that occurs is by more gravity beams moving in one direction and overwhelming the offsetting gravity from the opposite direction. Understanding that gravity acts as a result of a "net" force is important. Gravitation at a point can be variable depending on the force contained within opposing beams. The common spherical curvature of spheres such as earth hid the variability of gravity throughout the ages. Gravity varies due to modification by masses or by radiation.

Treating gravity as a pressure alters a myriad of concepts. Start with a physical gravity which pushes upon things. A simple corollary defines its opposite, what we call anti-gravity. If gravity is a push, then anti-gravity must be a push in the opposite direction. It is not some mystic situation in which everything disintegrates, born of those who thought of gravity as an attraction and cant reconcile an anti attraction which lacks physical attributes. Anti gravity causes the repelling of 2 bodies from each other, as opposed to attraction. Imagine a mass levitating on earth. In fact we may cause such anti-gravity by interfering with gravity from one direction. We will explain magnetism, the other "attraction force". Magnetism is directional, both attracting and repelling. It occurs only in limited situations. We may someday expand the situations.

To do away with the occult nature of gravity in existing systems we have to have a push source that provides gravity. That observable push is the "net" of all pushes upon any object from all 3 dimensional directions. This statement removes the dependence upon earth itself as the reference point and resets space as the reference for ongoing cosmology. The "Universe is Otherwise" and all gravity exists as pushing forces throughout space. What is it that pushes? The pushing must be done by the radiation beams throughout space as there is nothing else that fills space. In most places, such as remote space, the pushes net out

to full equilibrium and no motion happens. The finding of a net pressure and therefore motion within any place in space indicates an imbalance of gravity push upon that place from the various directions. Without gravity providing the basic push there would not be any basic source for motions.

Radiation flows in all directions everywhere. We usually don't recognize that flow in any measure because all motion nets out. We recognize that light beams do not interfere with light from any other direction. So within a point of space, radiation is flowing everywhere at speed c and is undetected.

We can make use of the term attraction only if we recognize we are discussing the apparent motion relative to us. We do measure the downward falling motions in measures such as meters/sec. Extending the time beyond the fixed measure of one second, we create the concept of acceleration as a way to reference the change of the apparent motion over time.

## 4. The concepts and components of external pushing gravity.

### 4.1. Radiation

Radiation has provided the advancements of science in the last 100 years. But it has not been properly assigned its place within our universe structure. Radiation arrives everywhere from all directions. Likewise it comes from all 3 dimensional directions throughout the universe. A point in remote space exists because radiation continuously passes through from all directions. There is no void in the universe. Though one might imagine that nothing exists between lines or between particles, our reality stems from continuous motions changing all the time. Should one seek void space within a point, that void would vanish to the ongoing radiation flow coming from continuously shifting angles. The structure of the universe is defined by flowing lines of radiation. There is no need for an Aether to carry light and EM radiation.

Radiation is called rays as it departs a source and beams as it travels and arrives. What we called a source, such as a lamp or a gravitational body, is but a modifier changing the characteristics of existing radiation. All radiation travels at velocity c depending on its medium as defined within physics. The prominent characteristic of radiation is wave length and frequency. The wave altitude is also important. Light is the predominant radiation and serves as a central focus of a scale of all possible radiation. The EM spectrum, detailed by wave length, describes the various radiation effects which depend on the wave frequency.

EM waves in space are known to be transverse in form. They are pictured as sin waves on a document which is a 2 dimensional representation. Unlike water waves, radiation waves are 3 dimensional. We would see the sin wave by inspecting the flow from the side from all directions, be it side, top, or bottom. Being three dimensional we must picture a wave as a coil. A sequence of coils emulates the spring in a pen. The whole spring is moving rapidly at speed c suggesting its forward flow of the waves/coils. We may use the terms coil and wave interchangeably.

Radiation has the ability to push matter. This violated early physics laws and led to the duality of wave/particle nature of light. Light is known to push in order to cause vision and X-rays are known to push from the Compton Effect studies. Pushing is a transfer of motion and does not depend on light having photon particles. Comptons x ray charts support radiation push but science has missed the proof of pushing gravity within.

## 4.2. Penetration

The whole EM spectrum of radiation is available for us consider as gravity beams. The gravity waves are coils whose frequency determines whether a wave impacts matter mostly at the surface or within the mass. A beam with low frequency waves arrives more like an arrow and penetrates the mass. High frequency impacting waves may apply greater surface pressure. However, the total of surface pressure is minor relative to the penetration pressure of long waves which continues contact throughout the mass. Penetration contact applies throughout the internal field of mass. Matter is considered as mostly empty except for the nucleus. Gravity beams that exit the mass must be less potent than unblocked incoming gravity beams that did not penetrate any mass yet. The "net" pressure then becomes a downward push on and near the body's surface. It is that simple to create the "attraction". Remember the word "NET"'.

Since matter modifies the push intensity of gravity, mankind should also ultimately be able to modify it. A simple case suggests inserting sufficient gravity beam blocking material above some something in order to cause a reduction of earth's gravity downward. If the reduction were extensive it may overcome the total push in the original direction. The result would be anti-gravity, a net push in the opposite direction. If spinning causes blockage, maybe spinning by propellers or rotators is actually a blocking of gravity?

Long wave radiation has more potential to penetrate matter than does higher frequency short waves. Long straight beams are like arrows and lack the wave that impacts and stops the flow. The penetrating long wave beams both push masses and are modified by the masses.

## 4.3. Gravity Modification

The modifying action within masses has atomic particles interfering with the beams. Two parallel beams may wrap together into one wave without quite doubling the frequency. Wave merging continues throughout any penetration of masses and results in fewer beams of higher individual frequency. But what remains is less total frequency, and thus less energy. The longer the path of merging, the fewer beams remain to exit. Thus the exiting beams cannot offset the incoming downward beams and a 'net'downward pressure occurs. The mass center is the average pressure/force point causing the reduction process rather than creating attraction. The diameter determines the path length. By time of exit the remaining penetrating

beams have higher frequencies and exit on average as radio beams for example from earth and as light beams from the sun. The new frequencies upon exiting depend on the celestial body size.

The reduction process outlined here is unique. The net pressure idea replaces Newton's model in which motion in space continues without change unless impacted by other matter. The concept of prior unchanging motion in space solved the friction issue with space defined as void. We know today that space is not empty. A driving force is needed to explain continuation of orbital motions. For orbital motion that driving force must relate to the center body in some way. Orbiting is revolution relative to the center, actually the relative rotation of the center.

That center, which rotates relative to an orbital body, is ejecting the diminished gravity beams while pushing them in its rotation circle. Solar beams arrive at an orbiting planet from the right causing pressure toward the left. We accept that planets are pushed toward the sun by a net amount of the inward gravity. Now we recognize that the orbital is also pushed counterclockwise around the sun. The two "net" force directions, inward and leftward, achieve balance. Both light and gravity beams from the sun curve in toward earth avoiding any appearance of earth overtaking the beams. Rotation is the highly overlooked source motion maintaining the universe.

Physics could never work with their gravity source as it is a linear pull to an unattainable center. Switching to an external incoming source opens a whole new chapter for modifying the gravitational effects of gravity beams. We can work with it. We can try to block it. The common 'attraction'force of magnetism can be seen as a redirecting of gravity beams by the spinning of matter, ie electrons. There is no reason this can't be done on larger scales. We spin propellers such as helicopter blades. They raise up a big carriage/cockpit attached below. Propeller The theory is that the spinning air pushes downward, but isn't it easier to view the motion as being caused by the blades pushing aside the incoming gravity beams. Then the push from below can equal or exceed the push from above. By extension, how did the ancients move the huge blocks forming pyramids and stones such as those at Stonehenge and Easter island? Clearly the blocking of gravity would be a logical method?

## 4.4. Non Linear Force

Pushing gravity can act upon a body from all directions. Current "attraction gravity" is simply a linear effect. The force acts in only one direction, straight downward toward the center of mass. Now consider all the beams arriving at a spherical body, planet. They create a net downward push in all directions. They become the force that gives bodies structure. In sum they are the "nuclear" force. That force is claimed to be much stronger than gravity, but that is because attraction gravity is linear while a nuclear force as well as any pushing gravity is spherical. Pushing has a nearly infinite number of additional lines of force. That same nuclear force extends to masses of any size and in the atomic region it provides the nuclear force that causes the structure of atomic particles such as nuclei. All spheres receive a similar surface pushing force of downward gravity on their surface. A difference in the attraction is the "net" force which includes the force caused by exiting beams from the opposite direction. The smaller a spherical particle is, the less penetrating gravity beams will be diminished.

A side issue is that the binding upon nuclear to cosmic particles can be broken by interfering with or redirecting incoming gravity beams. Such event leads even to nuclear bombs.

### 4.5. Pushing and Bending

As external gravity particle beams penetrate and exit masses their beams are slightly bent as they depart the rotating body. They absorb the rotational motion. There never can be a concept of straight up in our universe due to rotating sources and revolving observers. Absolutely all radiating beams in the universe curve and the universe itself is curved throughout for all relationships. Upon arriving at orbital distances some pressure is parallel to the central body surface. Bent gravity beams essentially push orbitals in their orbits. Gravity thus provides both the centripetal force and the perpendicular motion offset called centrifugal force. The common source provides unprecedented stability and rejection of any doomsday collision concerns.

## 5. Orbiting

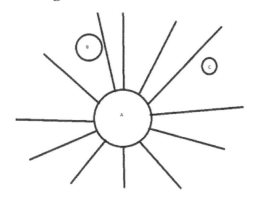

**Figure 1.**   radiation exiting the sun

Our goal here is to emphasize rotation controlled orbiting with a diagram showing how a rotating body can cause motion for a second body. Consider first a two-dimensional picture of two equatorial circles A and B. Circle A is larger. It spins counterclockwise and has lines radiating out from it. The lines are attached to and rotate with the circle. The key question is what will the lines do when encountering matter in their path? They may:

1. not interact with the matter
2. push and carry the matter along with them.
3. partially push on the matter

If they don't interact with matter we have no orbiting. Assume the lines to be massive so that they can push upon and carry with them anything they encounter in their path.

A line encounters and pushes circle B to the left, somewhat like the force we call centrifugal. This push will also cause motion by B angularly away from A as B rolls out further along the line. There is no retaining wall.

We can't have circle B moving away from A in our analogy. Our example produces a linear motion, and we need an attraction toward center as a partial offset. We need something to attract/push B toward A with exactly the right force to balance the leftward motion caused by the central body spin. This attraction is a centripetal force, the attraction of gravitation. The source for this is the net amount of push along the lines where the outward push is diminished by body A. The result is an inward pressure from pushing radiation beams.

We have developed the beginnings of an external gravity system. Netting the sideways pushes with the attraction pushes in concert results in orbiting. But in the example given, the left pushing radiation beams will push any object around the center in the same time frame. If a second body such as circle C is located further than B is from A, it will travel faster but its rotational velocity will be the same. That assumes the pushing beams likewise dominate motion at all distances, that the original radiation lines retain the same leftward carry ability at all distances. The model needs to be modified so a partial push occurs due to a weakness of the lines.

At this point we have orbital angular motion for B which corresponds with the surface spin of A. But this is not how orbiting works as we know that spatial objects usually do not retain their position in space over the same surface point permanently. In this example the period of revolution would be independent of the distance R. There does happen to be an example to this unusual relationship as the earth nearly retains its position over a point on the moon's surface. This can only occur due to the moon being a minimal source of earth's motions.

Orbiting has remained somewhat mysterious and its function is often related to particle spinning. What Kepler sought and we here are seeking is a relationship between orbital motions that varies somehow depending on the distance from a central body - sun. This relationship has been quantified in a complex formula for the closest 6 planets by Kepler's third law.

- **T** is the period of a full orbit cycle,
- **R** is the distance of the center of the planet (B) from the surface of the (A) sun, (for elliptical orbits, R is the major axis.)
- **K** is constant for every planet connecting their periods to a central body action.

We called the lines coming out of the sun (A) radiation beams. With current logic they would be unable to push sideways if we assume they are like light moving rapidly outward at the speed of C. Theoretically light beam has no mass. But we do know light creates some pressure upon impact. Light has waves that emulate a particle upon impact. Light is only considered massless if at rest. For our radiating lines to push, they must have some sideways motion toward the mass being pressured. Radiation traveling at speed C is usually considered linear motion. If the waves bend a bit sideways a miniscule amount of their push can be in the lateral direction. One might call the sideways impact glancing blows. So any bending of the radiation line toward the impacted mass should provide motion to the mass. Bending of the beam relative to circle B must occur given our definition that A is spinning relative to B. For a radiation line to move up against B it has traveled to our left. That leftward motion L occurs while the beam moves outward at speed C. So L/C is the amount of sideways push delivered to B. This is a very small portion of the speed of light.

Figure 2. Bent transmission beams from the sun that push earth

What happens as beams exit rotating massive bodies?

We have pictured orbiting. Here we analyze in more detail the issues involved in orbiting. Exiting solar beams apply less outward pressure upon planets than do incoming beams from outer space. Gravity thus nets out to form "attraction" of planets toward the sun. Then we are interested in planetary direction of travel.

Picture a straight line through the center of the sun. A gravity beam will not quite remain straight as it approaches center. The sun is rotating (spinning). The beam is being pushed in one direction by the atomic particle contents of the sun into a slightly curved path. It passes very near center, after which the pushes impact the beam from its opposite side. By the time it exits the entry point and exit point may connect directly through the center as a straight line. It is upon exit that the beam is maximally shifted to the left. Describe the bend. Is the shift of the wave found by dividing the surface rotation velocity by the speed of light or 2/ 300,000 for the sun? But this is the linear offset. In fact it is the angular lateral push due to the circular motion of the sun that is carried along. It is awkward to relate angular motion to linear motion. The angular offset varies with distance of departure as the circumference increases. It requires a flow of continuous recalculation.

The beam continues on in its most recent direction which appears to observers as bent from the straight up direction. The bend is at a maximum at the surface. As the beam rises it mixes with ever more perpendicular nonpenetrating beams. An intersecting motions and the mixing of irregular beams are greatest at the surface. We see this activity at the sun as solar flares. The lateral impact upon exiting beams suggests we first view them as two dimensional transverse waves since two directions, up and left, of force were applied to them. They become coils with interactions in space over time.

Beams flow thru the sun in all directions and exit with various distortions. Most as they aren't directed toward earth. Some beams that exit very near the equator we do see. We receive fewer beams from off the orbital plane. Beams penetrating at higher latitudes and passing by the polar axis will have traveled less distance thru the sun and

encountered a slower moving surface. Waves passing thru but not near the axis acquire irregular wave lengths relative to observer. The waves creating our rotation are primarily two dimensional as we might view them on a piece of paper.

Any motion of matter causes exiting radiation beams to bend. The micro world has EM waves traveling at speed c being impacted laterally by matter particles traveling much slower at the rotation rate of the spatial body. The particles are discreet and the beam is essentially continuous. Therefore the beam will not be cut when impacted by atomic particles, but part of the flow will be pushed to the side by each particle impact. The impacts are repetitive and cause the wave nature of the beam. At the same time the overall flow has been redirected.

**Figure 2.**   Bent transmission beams from the sun that push earth

## 6. Aberration

Light/radiation and external pushing gravity are the two transmissions which convey the nature of celestial bodies. While the linear motion of sources is insignificant the transmission of that light signal is subject to the orbital revolution motion of the observer body

In order to understand the aberration for light etc. one inspects the relative motions of the bodies involved in the transmission of the EM waves. The motions of relevant bodies are especially important within the solar system such as sun to earth transmission.

There are four relative motions between two bodies. The first motion of interest is the motion of earth around the sun. Analyzing this we first imagine two circles and a straight line connecting the two circles and serving as a beam of light. The paper we draw on is static space and ignores the revolution motion. Given the beam takes 8 minutes to transmit, and earth moves to the left, counterclockwise, during that time, the beam will pass behind earth. To correct for this we select a beam aimed ahead on earth's path which we intend will hit exactly the center of earth in 8 minutes. That straight line beam will appear to bend slightly backward to earthly observers upon arrival pitting earth's motion of 29.8 KM/sec against the outward velocity C of the beam. The bending is called aberration.

The next, and most important motion, is the rotation of the sun. Consider an observer on the sun and the launch of the light beam. Say a beam is launched straight up like an arrow toward a chosen point. After 8 minutes is the beam still straight up from the solar observer? Since the sun has rotated a bit (its period of rotation is 24 days), it is above and somewhat behind the observer and the point of origin. The beam has not gone straight up! What does straight up mean? What is static space? The motion should be represented by a curve drawn to compensate for the rotation of the solar surface. Then the arrow can be pictured as straight up at some future times. In fact this representation does occur in some form as the launch site was moving sideways while the beam headed upward. The first assumption about the form of the sideways motion is that the beam will move toward the left at the sun's rotation rate, which is 2 km/sec pitted against the upward velocity of C. But this offset, at 2km/sec vs 29.8km/sec. of earth's revolution velocity, is insufficient to explain earth's revolution; it bends the beam only1/15th as much as needed. Note that we are considering only the lateral effect of the perpendicular push in a static space. The other offset perspective is that of angular velocity, a much more significant factor. The sun rotates in 24 days, which is 15 times faster than earth's revolution. Applying this rotation to an EM transmission throughout would have the beam arriving at earth from behind. This would suggest a large reverse aberration.

Essentially there is gradually fading lateral equilibrium at the surface of both earth and the sun. Space is not a static medium. The angular velocity is the initial offset to C at the surface of the sun. But the angular velocity applied to radiation beams diminishes as the beam departs the source. To understand source to receiver (sun to earth) transmissions vs the motions of earth we must consider the real condition of space.

External gravity is long wave radiation beams traveling at velocity C. These beams are the fabric of space. Gravity beams behave as does other EM radiation. The exiting beams acquire the rotation of the sun. If we assumed the solar rotation angularly pushed these beams throughout they might push earth 15 times as fast its actual revolution rate. The sun rotates in 1/15th of our year. But intensity diminishes with distance. The density of the original beams and of space itself diminishes with distance. Think of master beams as continually modifying themselves by absorbing beams angling inward.

The solar atmosphere which rotates with the sun's surface gradually loses its connection with increasing altitude and its rotation contribution slows to that of the planets orbit speed. That happens because the sum of the master beam representing our gravity beam absorbs increasing portions of beams that did not originate at the sun but angled in. In any case, there is no aberration in gravity as it is the motive force of the planet's motion. The whole explanation to Kepler's third law comes from netting together the beams that have gained bending by exiting from the sun.

External gravity and light are both EM radiation beams. The absence of gravity aberration applies similarly to light. Gravity is also the cause of the whirling space in which light beams follow the flow and arrive without aberration.

## 7. Mass and Radiation

### 7.1. Looping Intersections

A family connection between gravity radiation and mass is the spectrum of existence. Everything is waves from very long to so dense they become mass. The wave length variation across the whole spectrum dictates the penetration ability. The shorter the wave, the less it penetrates and the more it mimics mass. Short wave radiation such as gamma or X rays usually perform mass creation adjustments upon approaching the unbalanced gravitation near spatial masses.

Short wave coils are most prone to intersecting with adjacent waves in their beams when the beam is bent. The bending and wave nature cause beam line intersects or crossings. The interactions become electrons. The interior of the coils becomes protons and/or neutrons similarly as magnetic beams are created within electrified coiled wires. While motion continues within the beam lines, the overlap location remains in place as unmoving mass. Matter occurs when beams bend sufficiently to create a loop within itself or when intersecting other beams.

So, a mass is the action of coils which constantly repeats and remains in place. Mass is composed of intersecting and looping beams. The amount of mass within a volume of space is the density of the beam crossings which are also spins in physics terms. Mass is the existence of spin relative to a local equilibrium of space. The spin of internal components of a body and of the body as a whole, taken together, defines the density of mass and ultimately the existence of mass.

Mass is created by unbalanced intersections of Paep gravity beams at points in space and creation continues very gradually in accord with the equation . This inverts Einstein's energy release equation.

Masses exist as rotation relative to the local equilibrium. The rotations can be of the components such as protons and electrons, and/or of the whole mass. Non-spinning mass doesn't exist.

Since the particles of matter spin their surface becomes somewhat perpendicular to arriving or penetrating waves thus creating interaction. The interaction becomes a push relative to the matter particle. It can create a wave or shorten and bend the gravity wave.

### 7.2. The Universe

Since gravity is only variable upon interaction with mass it must be infinite in range. The gravity beams define all infinite space. The universe is space fully defined as beams like radiation and can exist without mass. It is the actions of radiation beams that build matter over time creating hydrogen on up to the largest suns.

Interacting bent radiation beams that bend enough to loop back such as gravity or EM radiation are what creates mass and matter. We can discard concepts that have planets created by condensing of gasses, which gas could never mimic all the various orbital revolutions.

Mass as a build up over time can occur in space where

we identify the simplest existence of hydrogen every-where. Repetitious intersecting of waves in space occurs primarily when beams bent by different sources interact. An optimum location is where streams from the sun and from Jupiter interact and build masses called Trojan aster-oids in the Lagrangian L4 and L5 points of Jupiter's or-bit. Mass buildup also occurs within masses where gravity beams bend and interact with existing mass particles. The output of such interactions in the sun provides light and heat. These are radiation because gravity, the source, is es-sentially radiation.

The same events occur within earth where minor heat and light originates. Likewise earth's mass gradually grows. Continental drift with shifting tectonic plates over time is a current scientific theory. But we expect a slow expansion of earth. The plates, separations, earthquakes and volcanism are products of interior expansion pressur-ing the surface. Analysis should extend back to the plan-etary beginning. Early features of the surface are replaced by newer ones as the earth grows. As gravity beams pene-trate, such things as water and oil are continually recreated below the surface. Unbalanced gravitation forces pushing down vs up collide and form matter. The penetration is what leads to earthquakes, volcanism and rifts separating sections of land. All the elements and types of mass that we identify are created and constantly rebuilt over long time periods.

### 7.3. Charge

There is a concept called charge, a defining concept of electricity and current. Charge is labeled positive or negative and assigned to nuclear particles. But to me, charge is simply a magnetic effect that emphasizes the "direction" of gravitational push. Charge has one constant value, and the amount of charge depends on the number of gravity beams that aren't offset by opposites. Science however classifies charge as attraction and repulsion of oppositely charged particles. Simplicity suggests dropping the charge concept, replacing it with a sum of effects of interacting push motions arriving from various directions.

### 7.4. Curvature

The universe exists and all fits together based on the curvature of a single force. Even with vector analysis, extra dimensions, or calculus as tools we can't numerically outline curvature within the universe. Curvature varies with place distance and time. In a view to be included, the motions of space are counterclockwise for all bodies relative to the center of their space. It also depends on the local Z axis.

Since we reside in the solar system where the motive for orbiting is controlled by the sun, it is not often we consider the effects of similar masses on each other. But now that we understand that the motive force for orbiting is con-tained within the rotations of a central body, we can con-

## Mutual Revolution

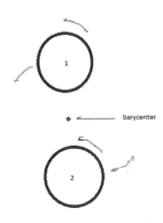

**Figure 3.**

sider the dual centers situation. In the picture of mutual revolution, the rotation of body 1 causes body 2 to move and ultimately attempt to orbit body 1. That pusher body 2 initially backward in the picture. Simultaneously body 2 is rotating and pushes body 1 toward our left to ultimately or-bit body 2. The center of the orbiting becomes a barycenter external to both masses. The picture shows counterclock-wise rotation and that is the norm for the universe. With all rotation being counterclockwise the universe retains sta-bility. If one of the masses in the picture were orbiting the opposite way the pushes would bring them together and a crash would occur.

## 8. Planetary Rotation and Atmospheres

Besides pushing orbitals in their orbits, solar originated bent gravity beams cause the counterclockwise rotation of the orbital by penetrating, in average, to the right of center as they approach from the right. For Venus's clockwise rotation, the majority of bent streams pass just left of center.

The effect pictured above shows solar beams that pass through earth's atmosphere. This is the source of winds. The beams don't penetrate, but do cause atmospheric ro-tation. These upper beams surround the earth and push the atmosphere from West to East, causing our flow of jet streams and clouds. The top of the picture shows the west-erly pressure at the equator at midnight directly opposite the sun. The bent gravity beams here pictured in exagger-ation to arrive bent 45 degrees thus tangent to the surface at 1:30 per clock diagram. The atmosphere - 1300 miles up is pushed by solar bent gravity and earth's bent gravity and travels faster than earth does.

Note also that external gravity beams together come as a blanket of beams approaching all latitudes of earth. Toward the poles the flowing velocity will be greater as the bent beams have less distance to travel around while still providing the same worldly velocity of push as at the

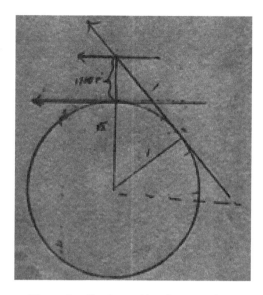

**Figure 4.**  Gravity pushing the atmosphere

equator

Drawing pictures of the upward exiting gravity beams helps relate to the overall concept of external gravity. A picture below shows beams exiting earth and those exiting the sun interacting near earth. The magnetosphere consists of solar and earthly bent beams. Beams exit the sun and bend left due to solar rotation. Some of those beams bending across the face of the earth rather than striking earth are seen from the back by earthlings and are labeled as solar wind. That term apparently came from the observation of variable and directional pushing by solar gravity beams. The earth also bends exiting paep beams to its left. Picture a region between the sun and earth where the beams from the sun and earth interact, each bent counterclockwise relative to their origin body. There will be turbulence surrounding a small region of equilibrium which is the focus of the magnetosphere. Such an effect has I believe been detected for Jupiter. The solar wind concept somewhat misrepresents the motion. Diagrams showing the disturbed atmosphere occurring near earth such as the one below miss much of the bending activity.

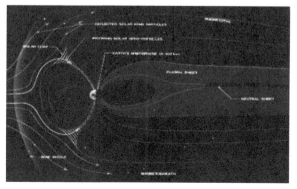

**Figure 5.**  Magnetosphere

## 9. Now Mass Rotation Controls Orbiting

### 9.1. Background

Prior to the development of physics as a science it was sufficient to have motion that offsets a perpendicular gravitational force and continues forever. A total absence of any friction was attributed to the "void" of space. But perpetual motion and empty space are now seen as fallacies. Continuous motion needs a driving force for impetus.

An elementary activity in the universe is motion of celestial bodies relative to each other. An all inclusive physical gravity theory must address spatial motions. We provide the reason that Kepler's third law worked for the first 6 planets.

A function of physics is to want to understand fields and matter better by searching for their components in the atomic universe. Particle theory is the search within three dimensional space for one dimensional pieces such as molecules, atoms, protons, electrons, photons, etc. Similarly the view of a whole field can be broken into linear pieces much like physicists break it into particles. Consider string theory which is the search for two dimensional linear connections or flows. This model introduces Paeps as one-dimensional particles, which serve as individual waves when in motion. That motion is the linear two-dimensional piece called a beam. This External Gravity model implies joining particle theory and string theory with emphasis on longer strings, i.e. spatial beams moving throughout space. "External Gravity" says:

1. The universe is infinite and isotropic.
2. Actions are the motions of matter. There is no perpetual motion of matter without a perpetual source causing the motion. Gravity is the perpetual source.

### 9.2. Newton

Our ideas of space develop from Newton's system of celestial mechanics. Essentially Newton applied gravity to Kepler's third law and realized that the mass of each body would then be a factor. Newton's orbital control infers that orbiting occurs because nothing interferes with the linear forward component of motion. So, to him, the linear component of motion is perpetual, devoid of outside influences such as friction. By extension the rotation of bodies themselves, like the orbital motion of revolution, lack outside influence and would also be perpetual. We now understand that space is not a void.

Physical science today depends on cause and effect and must come forward and correct these ideas. The cornerstone of attractive forces and of frictionless space comes from application of Newton's laws. But: A discussion of gravitational force by Newton follows:

"For here I design only to give a mathematical notion of those forces, without considering their physical causes. – Wherefore the reader is not to imagine that by those words, I say where take upon me to define the kind, or the manner of any action, the causes or the physical reason thereof, or that I attribute forces, in a true and physical sense, to certain centers (which are only mathematical points); when at any time I happen to speak of centers as attracting, or as endued with attractive powers". "You sometimes speak of gravity as essential and inherent to matter. Pray do not ascribe that notion to me; for the cause of gravity is what I do not pretend to know.

In addition, Newton had said "I would not refute gravity as a motive particle if it didn't hinder the motion of orbitals."

Building a theory on an absence of influence by anything was necessary to build a world system and an absolute space theory. But in today's world of technical detail knowledge, the absence needs to be discarded in favor of an ongoing impetus.

Newton's views competed with and overcame Descartes' whirlpool theories as the source of orbital motion. A whirlpool representation of motions of space itself didn't. match central spin experiments such as controlling fluids in a bucket or rotating within a fluid medium that extends to infinity. In neither example do the velocities or actions of the fluids simulate expected planetary velocities as calculated using the formula of Kepler's third law. These examples probably led to disinterest in Descartes' model. What is needed and I provide elsewhere is a different source of rotations resulting in a different measure of central controlled whirling motions.

### 9.3. Pushing Gravity Theories

Previous pushing gravity theories suffer from concern about particles inhibiting the flow of orbitals. One recent alternative pushing gravity theory suggests an ultra high speed of pushing gravity particles. This was probably not part of LeSage's original pushing gravity theory, but comes from LaPlace, Van Flandern, and others as incorrect solutions to pushing gravity theories, all of which ignore curvature. The proper solution using bending/curvature of space is entirely new here.

## 10. The Cycle of Gravity

As we stress infinity, we see that gravity itself is also an infinite force. It is infinite because it is continually transported across space as radiation. All radiation is continually sourced as rays originated as light and other EM transmissions. As we reject the absolute speed c for light, we can say that the time of transmission along with the mass of the source determine how the radiation will gradually expand its wave length. What starts as light becomes red shifted into microwaves, sound waves, and ultimately long wave gravity beams. As mentioned all waves provide some gravitation but the greater force is from the longer wave. As they lengthen, the total gravitation increases. But, while this paragraph focused on discussing the increase of gravitation across the universe, there is an offset.

The whole offset is what we have examined here as the "netting" out of gravity forces when beams penetrate masses. We lose total local gravitation as weaker beams exit earth and fill the surface and nearby space with weaker force.

Pushing gravity beams recycle. Light from distant

stars gradually fades out as the wave lengths get longer. The lengthening is caused by the retention pull of the source and the forward pull of the destination body. Light stretches into infrared, microwaves, sound waves and finally gravity waves. This gravity rebuilding is needed as the beams that penetrate matter locally lose some of their energy. That energy loss is the gravity we recognize here on earth and for other planets.

So gravity force diminishes as beams pass through matter and increase as beams flow across space! The situations offset and the total gravity force in the universe remains constant!

Physics theories mistakenly view gravity forces as different in galaxies. Theoretically the cause is missing mass. To compensate for the "needed" mass they invented dark matter and dark energy. Nobody promoting that understands our solar system. The orbiting is a function of the central body sun, which is almost all of the mass. The central body is the motive for orbiting.

The galaxies, as we examine them, are regions of similar mass stars throughout. Therefore no star is the central body and all stars affect others depending on their distance of separation. There is no missing gravity in galaxies. The section on galaxies details that issue. There is no dark matter due to galaxies and no dark energy for a bounded universe.

**References, see paper Building Theories Upon Theories Hinders Science**

# Infinity and Pushing Gravity Lead to Revelations The Universe is Otherwise - Part 2c.

Paul Schroeder

*8244 Anna Ave. Wind Lake, WI. 53185*
*pshrodr8@aol.com*

The two preceding papers set the stage of the new perspective for science and a book: "Infinity Contradicts Current Cosmologies". Continuing forward here we investigate how the changes in perspective apply to numerous situations and provide value to these new perspectives. The revelations are detailed in a number of papers that provide views of what is really happening in space and cosmology. This document provides summaries of many of my key papers that reveal better perspectives. Details of the whole system follow. Finally new laws of motion are provided.

**Keywords:** cosmology, gravity, Kepler, Galaxies, eclipse bumps, light, relativity, red shift, matter creation, motion, magnetism rotation, black holes, atmosphere

## 1. Summaries

1. Magnetism. Magnetism is the other attraction action. It is also a pushing action. Free electrons can serve as a cause. When the electrons are flowing they redirect gravity beams by up to 90 degrees so the direct flow of gravity is lessened. The redirected gravity flow simulates and becomes a flowing magnetic field created perpendicular to the original direct gravity flow. The example is the electromagnet. The field is outside while the flow is within. The increased push is at one end, the diminished push at the other end. Reading my magnitism is suggested.

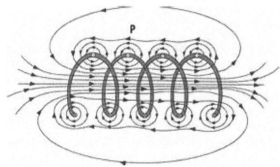

**Figure 1.**

2. Creating Matter. Creation is partly addressed on in these papers. The details within the nuclear structure are involved. Matter is built by intersecting bent beams. The number of coils within the beams and the degree of bending influence the creation and the number of electrons.Matter remains in place while beams flow onward. Reading is suggested.

3. Earth's rotation – local effects When beams penetrate a rotating sphere and exit, their direction is changed, bent. The maximum bending occurs at the equator. Further from the equator, at higher latitudes, the weaker the rotation effects become. Planets around the sun and moons around

planets lose containment. The energy to drive orbitals decreases with the shrinking bending. The decrease continues by latitude to the poles. The beam exiting in Antarctica will mostly wrap around itself and not cause any lateral beam flow. The polar beams do not offset the incoming beams well and holes are created. Perhaps the net speed of radiation varies there. Is space travel differently affected by gravity above or below the solar system?

4. The Sun. The sun is simply larger mass which diminishes penetrating gravity beams more than planets do. When penetrating gravity beams exit, the difference in force between exiting and incoming beams is so great that intense heat and light are the result along with the intense net downward pressure. Scientists have been surprised upon recently finding that the maximum heat of the sun is at the surface rather than being internal. Pushing gravity requires that it be that way.

5. Continental Drift. The creation of matter begins in the nuclear environment and increases over very long time. Earth and other bodies are growing such that the history of any ERA can be investigated if the surfaces that cover it can be removed. Rather than drift explanations, the surface changes are functions of expansion. Growth is gradual and all matter, by size, nuclear structures and types, that are created increase in complexity. Oil and water began to accumulate at some size and continue to form today.

6. Gravity bumps during eclipses. Solar gravity force is expected to diminish during an eclipse of the moon. Instead it diminishes just before and just after an eclipse of the moon. Why didn't the decline occur at the exact time of eclipse? As explained, gravity beams from the sun arrive at earth from behind as they push us in orbit. Thus they are blocked by the moon just before it arrives at eclipse line. Then when the moon has passed total eclipse it blocks those other gravity beams that earth is about to experience by overtaking them. Gravity's pressure is not

simply straight down.

7. Galaxies. The mistaken idea that gravity is different within galaxies ignores the fact that the solar system is central body dominated and galaxies have no such central body. We have shown that space structure is under the control of rotation. The apparent flow of star positions over time is a function of the rotation of all nearby stars. The picture here shows a series of rotations affecting a series of suns and creating the curves that causes arms. The paper addressing this is somewhat involved but the simple ideas can be seen in the laws of motion section that follows here.

## Galaxial Arms

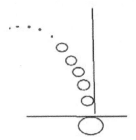

**Figure 2.**

8. Kepler's laws. No issue was ever raised that the rotating surface of the sun did not fit with Kepler's formula for planetary time and distances in which the first 6 planets are coordinated. Note that although clouds and the atmosphere circle earth faster than earth rotates; celestial bodies revolve earth slower than earth's rotation. The revolution reversal applies to all planets and extends to a geosynchronous point for earth at which the orbital motion matches our rotation. The sun has such a synchronous point also, maybe at 11R, which serves as the focal point of orbital drive. Then calculating the 2 dimensional push to reveal the diminishing push for the motion of the 6 planets by solar radiation as radial distance grows gives an approximate but insufficient total. There is additional solar push from the suns rotation sourced from greater solar latitudes. Gravity beams exiting the sun just above or below its equator may influence a nearby planet orbit but angle above or below further orbits and have no effect there. The analysis is complex.

9. Einstein and Compton. a. Regarding general relativity, there is a lack of simplicity in the space time: four dimensional base of relativity theory. The elimination of time as a factor fogs any understanding of motion. At some level mysticism did fade away with a formula leading to a unified field theory. . It states that space causes matter to move and matter causes space to curve. The unified field theory was to unify the general theory of relativity with electromagnetism, A "theory of everything" is closely related to unified field theory, but differs by not requiring the basis of nature to be fields, and also attempts to explain all physical constants of nature.

The formula is Gn + Agw = 8piG/c4xTm

For my similar statement: I say: Space is a flow (caused by its radiation contents interacting with matter bodies which transfer their revolution and rotation motion), so given space is flowing it moves matter. Matter allows space to flow through during which the penetrating space beams become modified and redirected so that its overall flow becomes curved.

Space causes matter to move and matter causes space to curve.

b. Einstein proposed photon particles within light waves and an x-ray test by Compton where the waves are deflected supposedly confirmed the photon as a bundle of energy. The thought was that the energy of photoelectrons should increase with intensity. The frequency shouldn't matter. Red and Blue signals were compared and surprisingly intensity didn't matter but frequency did. Supposedly that confirmed the photon. But it doesn't. The different penetrating and rebound action by different frequencies confirms that the variable coil separations of our pushing EM radiation beams are the source. The graphs, where Compton deflected X-ray beams, show dual waves of different frequencies and variable heights. No reason is known. Using wave coils the bending results in 2 arrivals at different angles and perfectly explains the graphs.

10. Electricity-lightening. We mentioned earlier that bent gravity beams from the sun form the winds upon earth beginning at points of arrival mostly near evening time. The amount of wind varies due to fluctuations in earth's revolution motion and in solar sunspots etc. Similar fluctuations occur for vertical incoming beams that intersect each other as they focus inward. If the intersecting is unusual, the fabric of the downward push of incoming beams is exposed as lightning or as centers of rotation such as tornadoes.

11. Ancient Aliens. When searching through the history of mankind we find the ancients have left us scrolls, cave pictures, pyramids, upright monoliths and circular and linear landscapes. It seems what was really happening was a system of documenting their capabilities to show to other tribes or civilizations and to us in their future. We haven't understood the messages! They are telling how they could deal with gravity! Just the huge blocks forming the pyramids could never have been created and moved, even by armies of millions. Even more difficult to understand are the upright stones of Stonehenge where hundreds more upright monoliths have been found somewhat buried. How were they raised? The "simple" way to move such mass is by blocking the downward push of gravity! Once gravity is blocked you can even move the mass elsewhere. Also there is a pattern of 2 miles of 8 across stones in Thailand. It matches the pattern of 2 miles of holes in Peru. Possibly the stones were transported half way across the world. Then there are the Easter Island stone figures. They are all similar. A monolith is created by slowly detaching and raising sections of granite. If the rising were not straight up at Easter Island but was rotated a few degrees off center back and forth a few times during the lift. That would

leave indentations within the granite. If done by design they could create the face design on the rocks. Something is needed to help separate the monolith from its laterally attached ground while lifting. The finding of liquid Mercury in significant places suggests Mercury could serve the blocking gravity role that electrons do for magnetism.

12. Black Holes and Other Fantasies Since much of Astrophysics focuses on light, many bad theories abound. The idea that there are things with mass and things without mass led to the massless nature of light and EM radiation. That led to photons which caused the wave particle duality which becomes an impediment to physics. We choose the rate of travel of light to map the universe. That led to establishing a constant velocity for light, at least within a given medium. Then came the red shifts which gained the Doppler function assuming stars move away and cause expansion. Given that model even some red shifts exceeded theory and we gained white and neutron stars which held back light via gravitation. Expanding that model led to black holes as the ultimate retention of light. Such stars/holes had to have nearly infinite mass and thus density. Thus anything became possible such as time tunnels and worm holes. All of this would not have happened if light was allowed a variable velocity, no matter how small the deviations might be. The basic ignored argument is that if black hole gravity could stop light then what about a mass that almost could stop light. We would get gravitational redshifts rather than Doppler red shift from stars depending on density etc. This reveals the idea that both the mass of the source and the distance of the source work together to determine the red shift. Since External Gravitation removes fixed light speed it opens up the universe to logical interpretations. We are seeing some relevant interpretations about Quasars for example. Other fantasies include dark matter due to misunderstanding galaxies. Also dark energy was needed for universe boundaries. Extra dimensions are illogical as are worm holes.

I will send copies of referenced papers or discuss ideas with anyone interested.

## 1.1. Summary of Theory Components

By resolving my gravity concepts with relevant physics issues I have developed different views about numerous concepts including how rotating centers cause orbiting as measured by Kepler's third law of planetary motions. Fundamental concepts include:

a. The term gravity can refer to the source or to the detectable effect of the action of the source. The effects are motion and the existence of matter.

b. Gravity is a push rather than an attraction. As such it solves 'action at a distance'.

c. The push implies the source is external from matter. The source is beams with velocity. Motion of beams is confirmed by waves within the beams.

d. Gravitation pushes as if it contained moving particles - Paeps âĂŞ 'particles applying external pressure'. But gravity particles can't be matter. They would cause too much heat upon impact and would interfere with orbiting.

So paep is a generic term for gravity source.

e. Gravitation is best pictured as lines rather than fields. Beam lines help analyze and contemplate a linear push. Pressure gradients that summarize the situation inhibit analysis.

f. Gravitation functions as beams pushing from all directions upon every point of space. Thus matter takes on spherical shapes. Attraction gravity is linear and is insufficient to understand the universe. We need transverse radiation wave/particles that strike matter with impact. The amount of impact depends on the wave amplitude/energy. Light and EM radiation are composed of waves/coils which can apply pressure like particles can. This removes the separate concept of photons solves science's wave/matter conflict.

g. EM radiation such as light slightly penetrates masses due to its wave structure. But longer wave gravity radiation theoretically penetrates more and extends its push throughout masses. Thus gravity beams replicate long wave EM radiation.

h. Gravity beams, like radiation rays, move at velocity 'C'.

i. The universe is infinite and isotropic. Space primarily contains EM waves. Gravity beams are the structure of space simulating the aether others refer to. Like-wise gravity is the undetectable background . j. Gravity interacts with matter. Matter exists as rotation/spins relative to the local equilibrium. The spin may be of the atomic particles such as protons and electrons as well as spin of the entire mass. The amount of spin determines the density of masses. The lack of relative spin signifies the absence of matter.

k. Equilibrium is the net balance of horizontal pushes, yet with an imbalance of vertical pushes -gravity. Structural equilibrium causes equivalent light speed in both directions. A better answer than Einstein's time dilation.

l. Gravity beams mostly penetrate matter. Atoms are mostly empty space. Paep waves interacting with atomic particles both modify each other.

l2. Penetrating gravity beams exit the mass and are modified. Beam amplitude is diminished, beam wavelength modified into shorter waves as heat and light radiation, and the beam's motion is redirected.

l3. The gravitational push at a mass surface offsets diminished exiting beams with undiminished incoming beams resulting in a 'NET' downward push often called attraction gravity.

m. $R^2$ laws apply for attraction gravity because it is centered at a central point of matter. Pushing gravity also requires a mass to centralize the modification of the beam. This leads to the same central point of reference needed for equations.

n. During gravity penetration impacted matter particles are modified into radiation or different matter. The sun's eternal power is caused by continuous penetration and exiting of modified gravity beams.

o. Paeps can be redirected by spin of atomic particles or

by the spin of the whole mass. As noted in point 10, spin defines matter because the moving mass particles intersect incoming gravity beams.

p. Redirected paep beams exit in a bent path relative to both the source and the observer. They curve throughout their travels. We draw as lines and curves but can view as a mean average line. These curves have 3 components, the long up line - C, the minor sideways value and a diminishing component value of the line vs local space as it travels.

q. Space is 3 dimensional but its contents flow and distort linear analyses.

r. Undiminished gravity beams flow in all directions across earth's surface, not just downward. They mostly net out. A minor extra counterclockwise flow of exiting beams bent by the rotation of the mass occurs. The flow matches the mass's rotation yielding local equilibrium.

s. Counterclockwise motion relative to our Z axis north and to orbital centers dominates the spins and orbital motions of the universe. Antigravity would result from clockwise flow.

t. Newton said orbital motion continues absent external forces, thus no friction. The implied void of space can't exist given radiation, meteors, and solar winds. A motive force is needed.

u. Newton's "motive" external force was centrifugal force, subsequently inertia, a force with no source. Newton's inertia is more properly defined as 'adhering to the local flow of gravity'. The application of inertia saved Newton from explaining the source of motions.

v. Planets incur lateral pushes of gravity caused by the bent beams from the rotating sun, and moons incur pushes from the sun and their rotating planet. This is the motive force causing orbiting. The revolution push by spinning bodies upon their orbitals is maximum at their equator and decreases with altitude. So Bode's law finds planets to exist at the extension of the solar equator and not at significant altitudes

w. Orbital revolution rates must be less than their central body rotation rate. Multiple centers complicate the analysis. Rotation of the master (sun) adds to the local central body (planet) push upon moons.

x. The lateral pushes on orbitals causes the rotation of the orbital as well as the revolution. The rotation rate is dependent on how far to the right of the 12 o'clock/6 o'clock axis the push is centered.

1. Rotating bodies usually rotate counterclockwise relative to their central body. Central body bent gravity beams add to atmospheric rotation as well as the masses 'rotation' for orbitals. The sum of bent gravity beams from earth's rotation and from the sun causes winds on earth.

2. Solar gravity beams are the solar wind when passing by earth. Magnetosphere pictures are attempts to represent bent gravity beams. At a point between planet and the sun, bent beams from each source will collide, creating a small void.

3. Sufficient bending of radiation beams and interaction with other beams creates mass. Electrons are beam crossings.

4. The nuclear – strong force is simply the sum of gravitation beams pushing from all directions.

5. Magnetism is the 'net' push of gravity beams when beams from one direction are redirected.

6. Charge is simply the direction of flow. As noted in point 21, anti-gravity is pushing in the opposite direction.

7. A spectrum of existence associates waves from the longest Paep gravity beams, thru EM radiation, and extending to mass itself. All relates to the wave structure in the spectrum of EM radiation.

8. Three dimensional waves are best pictured as coils. Consider a flowing beam wrapping around inside a straw like a counterclockwise screw.

9. Diminished gravitation occurring locally within the sun or stars is replenished by the gravitational stretching of light beams into microwaves, then radio waves, and further into paep gravity beams as they travel from very distant stars. The gravity source is continuously recycled.

10. Rotating bodies cause orbitals to encircle them. Kepler detected this and determined orbital times for our solar system with a large central body. More nearly equal rotating bodies are not similarly studied. Given their joint revolution action forcing each to orbit the other significantly changes/decreases the orbital times calculations. Proper calculations would override Kepler's third law. In galaxies.

11. Kepler's third law is that the inner planets revolution period is a constant times the 3/2 power of the solar distance R for each planet. Thus the central body sun has to be the source of their orbital times. It is the push by bent solar gravity beams that forms this relationship as the orbits increase by $R^2$. The factor R is the 2 dimensional component and $R^{1/2}$ is the Z axis contribution.

12. The bent flow of gravity defeats any exact linear calculations of gravity effects in large geometric analyses. The difficulty increases when multiple rotating masses contribute to the flow.

13. Actions within our solar system contend simultaneously with the linear flow of gravity at speed C (300,000 Km/sec) and the perpendicular flow from the solar rotation of 2 Km/sec.

14. Gravity beams condense together approaching mass bodies and the beams interact such that crossings are electrons, regions are protons and neutrons. Thus the higher frequency waves can create matter. 15. Regions of matter creation occur when beams from 120 degree angles interact. The Trojan asteroids are such a place where solar and Jupiter EM radiation beams interact.

16. A proper picture of gravity beams diminished by the sun and traveling toward earth shows them bent inward from the right. The motion of earth causes unbent beams to arrive from our left as if bent by earth's motion. Thus beams from both sides show the bending flow of the magnetosphere.

17. The mentioned bending of gravity beams produces

both sides of the bumps of gravity detected during a lunar eclipse. The causes are different for each bump. Refer to discussions of the Wang eclipse.

## 1.2. The Laws of Motion

Rotations, Revolutions and Apparent Motions of Heavenly Bodies:

Summarizing my views of galaxies suggests outlining a preliminary set of motion laws, and corollaries. We first step back to the Copernican revolution ending the Ptolemaic, Earth centered sun revolving, view. Earth centric worked with sub orbitals, but sun centered requires less adjustments. Are revolution vs rotation in two body systems interchangeable? Impressions are that it is the outside issues from which one decides what is right. Revolution vs Rotation That the planets most logically orbit the sun is what led Copernicus to propose the sun centric system. But given enough subsystems, could we go back to earth centric system? There is even a third workable two body system in which earth circles the sun daily. It takes the Paep pushing gravity systems to lock in the sun centric system. Paeps become the outside component, like planets, that define the center.

A. The relativity of rotation:

Law 1. Rotation and revolution are interchangeable concepts between two bodies,in a vacuum, which are in relative motion while retaining the same distance. Neither is a privileged non-rotating or stationary body.

Corollary 1. Specifying rotation vs revolution motion depends upon our determination of apparent motions of other relevant bodies

Rotation 2 Corollary 2. Specifying rotation vs revolution may alter if a determination of other relative motions is changed. For example, ignoring other motions allows converting the Copernican revolution, in which earth revolves counterclockwise around the sun, back to the sun circling the earth.

Rotation 3

Law 2. Paep gravity is the "other relevant motion" negating law 1.

Law 3. Specifying the nature of spatial motion is deeded to an outside observer stationed, or imagined to be, north of the defined platform/plane containing the motions. A participating observer makes assumptions by becoming a virtual outside observers in order to theorize the nature of motions.

Law 4. Orbital directions in space may be labeled clockwise or counterclockwise relative to an outside observer. That corresponds to our usual view of earth's activities from the north Z axis. All larger planes such as the ecliptic and galaxy planes have a Z axis whose north is 'by definition' within 90 degrees of earth's north. So revolutions are counterclockwise.

B. "Otherwise" Laws of Space.

Law 1 Space serves as the container for substance and provides the forces which create motion among the substances. Space provides the gravitational mechanism we call attraction. Space, distorted by rotating mass, provides the "drive motive" which offsets the attraction force by providing the rotational impetus for motion.

Corollary 1 Rotations within space insure continual separation of bodies. Corollary 2. There is no absolute vacuum region, as suggested by Newton, where motion continues for lack of potential interference such as friction. Such a void would not exist as space nor have dimension.

Corollary 3. Two bodies in space neither collide nor separate permanently because of the way their relative rotations modify space locally.

law 2 of Space Any body, such as the sun, serving as the center, and as the cause of revolution for other bodies/orbitals, is likewise influenced by each orbital and attempts to revolve around the orbital. The small quantity of force generated, along with the motion of the orbital results in the suns motion approximating rotation rather than revolution. The related force calculations upon the sun and upon the planets are separate and result in a baryc enter of gravity around which each body revolves.

Corollary 1. Most centers of gravity lie within the sun for our solar system because of the extreme differences in size. The multiple centers each form a rotation center for the sun.

Law 3 of Space The more equal in size two masses are, the more central is their theoretical revolution point. Given two equal masses, each mass serves as origin to a revolving coordinate system of which the other body is a part. The revolution periods are $\hat{A}ij$ or less of that determined by Kepler's formula. Choosing which mass to consider as the center of revolution is optional.

Corollary 1. Two bodies revolving around a central point provide optional views of relative revolution. One body may be thought of as stationary in which case the center of mass and the other body revolve around it, both in the same time period. Equivalently one body may be stationary and rotate such that the other body and the center of mass are stationary relative to it. The relative action of outside bodies determines which motions are assumed.

Law 4 of Space When equal sized adjacent bodies are rotating in similar directions, their rotations drive each other into orbital motions. corollary 1. A body #2, orbiting another and approaching others may be driven and passed from one orbital center to the next rather than completing its original orbit. The more bodies supplying the drive, the more linear becomes the appearance of body 2s line of passage.

Law 5 of space Were there 2 adjacent bodies rotating oppositely (clockwise vs counterclockwise) along a common plane, they would push each other in the same linear direction and create swirls that violate the continuation of separation. Picture them occupying 2 ends of a figure U, moving down together, and eventually colliding at the bottom center.

Corollary 1. Opposite rotation can occur in a plane only when radial separation of the orbitals is immense. Overlapping push causes turbulence that leads to inclined orbits. Collisions are avoided throughout space

Law 6 of Space If body 1, originally driven by body 2, passes between body 2 and a body 3, the body 1 orbital must follow an inclined path to avoid the center of revolution vortex and to avoid body 3.

Law 7 of Space Assume all equal sized bodies in a group are rotating counterclockwise. An outside or a participating observer will determine that all bodies are revolving relative to their adjacent bodies. The relative revolutions along a line of bodies are cumulative so that the farther the observer looks in any direction; the more rapid the orbital motions measure spherically relative to him.

Corollary 1. Apparent linear motion velocity depends on the angular motion of the line of sight. Apparent velocity of distant bodies increases up to 90 degrees of cumulative angles of revolution. Higher angles curve motion back toward the observer, limiting the apparent speed and ultimately the distance of separation between observer and target.

Law 8 of Space It is the spin of a central body that determines the action and existence of its orbitals. The quantity of effect varies with the tilt of the orbital plane. The maximum rate of spin occurs at the equator and diminishes as you approach its poles.

Corollary 1. In the solar system, most orbital bodies exist near the ecliptic, on the spin line of the sun, because that is where the sun supports them by its maximum rotation velocity.

Law 9 Orbits are elliptical rather than circular because there is a secondary force of attraction centered at a second focus which represents the summary influence of all outside forces.

Corollary 1. The real body being orbited supplies the revolution impetus. The secondary/imaginary focus provides no revolution impetus and interferes with the ongoing revolution. That causes an orbital to redirect toward perigee, incur less swirling and lose some of its forward motion pressure.

C. Laws of motions within galaxies

Galaxy Law 1. A series of equally spaced stars in a line, rotating counterclockwise, will each swirl their adjacent star into orbit so that the line may gradually bend to the left. The bending establishes the apparent speed of rotational motion. Observers will view a nearby rotating body as revolving and will calculate that more distant bodies in linear sequence move faster. The relative revolutions add up. The maximum linear speed occurs when the revolution angles sum to 90 degrees.

Galaxy Law 2 Bent lines of stars form arms and stars far from a galaxy center form arm ends. As the angle of bending approaches or exceeds 90 degrees at arms end, the distant stars apparent motion will either: 1. Appear about to escape. 2. Achieve the exact velocity to continue orbiting the galaxy center. 3. Further increase the angle thus falling back toward the galaxy center. The actual motion depends on the length of the arm, the distance of adjacent stars and the stellar concentration within the center and within the arm.

Galaxy Law 2 Corollary 1. Fall back/returning stars, in arms which bend 180 degree, will probably not complete orbiting their neighbor nor pass between two stars. They will be passed from one mainline star's control to another and 'slide' along the bottom of the arm. Corollary 2. A dense bunch of stars will bend an arm more than a sparse region does. Stars sufficiently departed from dense regions have a linear motion which reduces the bending relative to the center.

Galaxy Law 3 The gravitational retention and the velocity of an orbital depend on the rotation speed of a dense galaxy center. Rotation speed is maximum at the equator and lesser at higher latitudes. The greater the angle above or below the galaxy disk, the less the center will retain lines of orbitals. The shortened lines will suggest a dome above and below the center.

Galaxy Law 4 Orbits of stars near the galaxy center or a cluster center are tilted relative to the disk of the galaxy. The highest declinations occur nearest the galaxy center. They display polar regions to the galaxy plane presenting a different look. Thus they appear different, giving us the impression of being older stars. Galaxy Law 4 Cont.

Corollary 1. Stars along the galaxy disk rotate approximately in our plane so their makeup appears similar to our sun. We see their brightness and call them younger.

### References

[1] The Free Dictionary, The American HeritageÂő Dictionary of the English Language, Fourth Edition copyright (c)2000 by Houghton Mifflin Company. Updated in 2009. Published by Houghton Mifflin Company.

[2] Paul Schroeder, The Universe is Otherwise (Booksurge/Createa- space, 2006).

[3] Paul Schroeder, "Paeps: External Gravity Particles (The Universe is Otherwise: Part 1)", (2008), http://www.worldsci.org/php/index.php?tab0=Abstracts &tab1=Display&id=3224&tab=2.

[4] Paul Schroeder, "The Spectrum of Existence (The Universe is Otherwise: Part 2)", (2008), http://www.worldsci.org/php/index.php?tab0=Abstracts &tab1=Display&id=4152&tab=2.

[5] Paul Schroeder, "Motions, Rotations and Revolutions (The Universe is Otherwise: Part 3)", (2008), http://www.worldsci.org/php/index.php?tab0=Abstracts &tab1=Display&id=3229&tab=2.

[6] Paul Schroeder, "Gravity from the Ground Up", Proceedings of the NPA 7: 498-503 (2010).

[7] Paul Schroeder, "Get 'Real' About Gravity' ", Proceedings of the NPA 8: 521-529 (2011).

[8] Paul Schroeder, "Ignoring Newton's Hints Brought Scientific Chaos" ", Proceedings of the NPA 8: 521-529 (2011).

[9] Isaac Newton, Principia; in James Newman, The World of Mathematics, Vol. 1, p. 261 (Dover, 2003).

[10] Greg Volk, "A Matter of Definition", Proceedings of the Space, Propulsion & Energy Sciences International Forum (College Park, 2011); "The Meaning of Maxwell's

Equations", unpublished.

[11] Leonardo Motta, "1905 and all that", on internet quoted in Eric Weissteins world of physics under Michelson Morley experiment - ether. 1996-2007 Scienceworld - wolfram.com vol,pg,yr unidentified.

[12] Xin-She Yang and Qian-Shen Wang, " Gravity Anomaly During the Mohe Total Solar Eclipse .." Astrophysics and Space Science 282: p245-253 2002.

[13] Paul Schroeder, "Gravity and Revolution Rates Within Galaxies" ", Proceedings of the NPA 9 (2012).

[14] Paul Schroeder, "Creating Matter From EM Radiation" ", Proceedings of the NPA 9 (2012). pp. 510-513

[15] Paul Schroeder, "Mass Rotation Controls Orbiting" ", Proceedings of the NPA10 (2013).

[16] Paul Schroeder, "Creating Matter From EM Radiation" ", Proceedings of the NPA 10 (2013).

[17] Paul Schroeder, Arthur Ramthum, Robert De Hilster, "Gravity is a Pushing Force.", Proceedings CNPS (2016).

# Maxwell's Aether: A Solution to Entanglement

## Duncan W. Shaw

*1517 Angus Drive, Vancouver, BC, Canada, V6J 4H2,*
*duncanshaw@shaw.ca*

This paper argues that the solution to the problem of entanglement lies in viewing entanglement in the context of the medium of aether as conceived by James Clerk Maxwell, rather than as a phenomenon of quantum mechanics. It is argued that the apparent correlation of 'spin up' and 'spin down' photons that is said to constitute entanglement, is in fact a phenomenon caused by polarization of the medium of aether, not by travelling photons as envisaged by quantum mechanics.

**Keywords:** Entanglement, Aether, Maxwell's Aether, Quantum Mechanics

## 1. Introduction

Entanglement is said to occur where there is correlation between spin-up photons and spin-down photons that are propelled from a common source in opposite directions. The correlation is that if the photons travelling in one direction from the source are spin up, the photons travelling in the opposite direction from the source will be spin down, or visa-versa. Many experiments have been carried out to prove correlation and to establish a rational explanation for the correlation. The correlation has been well proven, but the experiments have not provided an explanation that makes sense. This has led to speculation that there must be instantaneous communication between the receptors of the photons that triggers the correlation. This explanation does not sit well with most scientists because they believe that communication between separated points must take some measurable time.

From the writer's reading on this subject, it has become apparent that all the experiments and investigations into this phenomenon are based upon the quantum mechanics theory. It is a fundamental cornerstone of quantum mechanics that photons physically travel from source to destination. This proposition is in conflict with the aether theory, which says that space and matter are permeated with a sub-atomic substance called aether, and that electromagnetic radiation occurs by way of waves through the medium of aether, like sound waves through the medium of our atmosphere.

This paper argues that basing the entanglement experiments on the quantum mechanics theory is a fundamental error. This error has inevitably led to the incorrect speculation of instantaneous action-at-a-distance between the receptors. This paper further argues that, if entanglement is considered in the setting of Maxwell's aether theory, it leads to a rational explanation and eliminates the need of communication between the receptors (instantaneous or otherwise).

## 2. Aether Versus Quantum Mechanics

In 1865, James Clerk Maxwell published his seminal treatise, The Dynamical Theory of the Electromagnetic Field [1]. In his treatise, Maxwell rejected the concept of instantaneous action-at-a-distance. [2] He posited that there must be a substance through which electromagnetic phenomena occur. [2] He called this substance 'ether'. He described it as consisting of 'parts and connections' that have the property of elasticity and the capacity to propagate waves. [3] Further, he described polarization as a 'forced' state of aether that is placed under stress by electromotive force. [5]

Maxwell's aether theory has since fallen into disuse, largely as a result of the Michelson-Morley experiments that many scientists say disprove the existence of aether, and partially because Einstein, in his Special Relativity paper, On The electrodynamics of Moving Bodies, opined that if his theory is accepted, there would be no need for aether.

The present author, in an article entitled Reconsidering Maxwell's Aether, published in 2014 [7], argues that Maxwell was on the right track with his aether theory, and that it should be reconsidered. The article sets out fundamental problems with quantum mechanics as raised by various prominent physicists, including David Griffiths, J. D. Jackson, Richard Feynman, Alastair Rae, Bryan Cox and Jeff Forshaw, George Greenstein and Arthur Zajonc, and Patrick Cornille.[8]

In 1935, Albert Einstein, D. Podolsky and N. Rosen, in their 'EPR' paper, Can Quantum-Mechanical Description of Physical Reality be Considered Complete? [10], concluded that the description of physical reality posed by quantum mechanics is incomplete.

The Reconsidering Maxwell's Aether article points out that acceptance of Maxwell's aether opens up potential explanations of numerous problem areas of electromagnetism. [9] One of those areas is entanglement. The present paper considers how entanglement may be explained in the context of Maxwell's aether.

## 3. Entanglement Experiments

In The Quantum Challenge: Modern Research on the

Foundations of Quantum Mechanics, Second Edition [11], George Greenstein and Arthur Zajonc describe numerous experiments that have investigated entanglement. The experiments range from those of Clauser, Horne, Shimony and Holt in the 1960s, Freedman and Clauser, Kasday, Ulman and Wu, and Lamehi-rachti and Mittig in the 1970s, Aspect, Grangier and Roger, Aspect, Dalibard and Roger, and Ghosh and Mandel in the 1980s, Greenberger, Horne and Zeilinger, and Greenberger, Horne, Shimony and Zeilinger in the 1990s, and Bouwmeester, Pan, Daniell, Weinfurter and Zeilinger in the year 2000. [12]

One common element of all the experiments stands out. They were all based on the assumption that the particles that were being tested (generally photons) were considered as having travelled from the source of the transmissions to the receptors. None of the experiments were analyzed on the assumption that the emissions were waves through the medium of aether. The experiments assumed the correctness of quantum mechanics and ignored the possibility of the so-called 'arriving' particles being in fact aether cells located at the receptors and being activated by waves travelling through the medium of aether. None of the experiments considered the possibility that Maxwell's aether might provide an explanation for the correlation of the data recorded by the receptors and a solution to the evident absurdity of the action-at-a-distance concern.

This paper questions the premise of applying quantum mechanics to entanglement and suggests that what is in fact occurring is the transmission of waves through a medium, that medium being Maxwell's Aether.

## 4. The Aether Approach

Maxwell considered aether as being made up of individual parts. He said: [4]

'Thus, then, we are led to the conception of a complicated mechanism capable of a vast variety of motion, but at the same time so connected that the motion of one part depends, according to definite relations, on the motion of other parts, these motions being communicated by forces arising from the relative displacement of the connected parts, in virtue of their elasticity.'

Maxwell's parts (the present author calls them aether cells) do not travel from source to destination. Rather, they form a medium through which vibrations of electromotive force are transmitted as waves. When the waves arrive at the destination, they activate the aether cells in the medium at that location. The activation of these aether cells gives the impression (albeit a false impression) of the arrival of 'photons'.

The distinction between photons and aether cells is important in regard to the phenomenon of polarization. As noted earlier, Maxwell considered polarization as the forced state of a medium caused by the application of electromotive force.

In contrast, in the quantum mechanics approach to entanglement, polarization is viewed as the state of photons that are travelling from source to destination, such as spin-up and spin-down.

With this distinction in mind, visualize space as being permeated by the medium of aether. Make the assumption that aether can be polarized by electromotive force. Picture polarization forcing aether to collectively form into three-dimensional patterns, with these patterns providing planes of polarization through which electromagnetic waves travel. The planes of polarization can rotate [13], and when they do, this causes rotation of the electromagnetic waves. [13] [14]

The next step is critical. Visualize a central source sending out electromotive energy in opposite directions. If the aether theory is applicable, the electromotive force will polarize the aether medium in both directions. Assuming that this in fact occurs, it stands to reason that the patterns of polarization in both directions will be correlated. The correlation is caused by the polarization resulting from the common source of electromotive force being applied to the common surrounding medium.

Because the electromotive force that causes the polarization emanates from a central source and is directed outwards in opposite directions, it follows that the pattern of the polarized aether in one direction will be the mirror image of the pattern of the polarized aether in the opposite direction. Thus, the recording of the nature of the waves arriving at the receptors should give opposite readings. Further, while the readings at the receptors may be characterized as spin-up and spin-down, but the receptors are actually receiving rotating waves, then it seems reasonable to assume that the readings are being mischaracterized and are in fact of rotations of the electromagnetic waves.

In this picture of events, no instant communication between the receptors is needed. Indeed, no communication at all is necessary. This is because entanglement is the result of polarization of the aether medium, and the polarization is set by the electromotive force that emanates from a common source. Thus, apart from the receptors being recording devices, they play no role in entanglement.

## 5. Conclusion

Maxwell's aether provides a rational explanation of entanglement.

Quantum mechanics does not.

## REFERENCES

1. J. C. Maxwell, *The Dynamical Theory of the Electromagnetic Field.*, Wipf and Stock Publishers, 1996.
2. J. C. Maxwell, *The Dynamical Theory of the Electromagnetic Field.*, Wipf and Stock Publishers, page 34, 1996.
3. J. C. Maxwell, *The Dynamical Theory of the Electromagnetic Field.*, Wipf and Stock Publishers, page 35, 1996.
4. J. C. Maxwell, *The Dynamical Theory of the Electromagnetic Field.*, Wipf and Stock Publishers, page 39, 1996.
5. J. C. Maxwell, *The Dynamical Theory of the Electromagnetic Field.*, Wipf and Stock Publishers, page 70, 1996.

6.  J. C. Maxwell, *A Treatise on Electricity and Magnetism.*, Dover Publications, Inc., New York, pages 65-70, 1954.
7.  Duncan W. Shaw, *Reconsidering Maxwells Aether.*, Vol. 27 Phys. Essays 601, 2014.
8.  Duncan W. Shaw, *Reconsidering Maxwells Aether.*, Vol. 27 Phys. Essays 601-602, 2014.
9.  Duncan W. Shaw, *Reconsidering Maxwells Aether.*, Vol. 27 Phys. Essays, at pp 604-606, 2014.
10. "A. Einstein, B. Podolsky, and N. Rosen", *Can Quantum-Mechanical Description of Physical Reality Be Considered Complete?.*, Vol. 47 Phys. Rev. 777, 1935.
11. "G. Greenstein and A. G. Zajonc", *The Quantum Challenge: Modern Research on the Foundations of Quantum Mechanics.*, Jones and Bartlett Publishers, 2nd ed., 2005.
12. "G. Greenstein and A. G. Zajonc", *The Quantum Challenge: Modern Research on the Foundations of Quantum Mechanics.*, Jones and Bartlett Publishers, 2nd ed., pp. 149-184, 2005.
13. E. U. Condon, *Molecular Optics.*, Handbook of Physics, 2nd ed., McGraw-Hill Book Company, at pp. 6-113 to 6-130, 1967.
14. R. Feynman, *The Feynman Lectures on Physics, Definitive Edition.*, Pearson Addison Wesley, pp. 33-1 to 33-7, 2006.

# Call for a Repel of Physical Theories of the 20th Century

## Peter Sujak, RNDr

*Hradesinska 60, 10100 Prague, Czech Republic, peter.sujak@email.cz*

In this paper, the substance of gravity and inertial forces is debunked. The substance of mass is recovered. The nature of time in physics is revealed. The reality of the double-slit experiment is revealed. This paper shows that Quarks and Higgs boson hardly exist. This paper documents that, for past four hundred years, there is no distinguished physicist who would not have recognized the existence of the ether. It shows that filling the space of the Universe with swirling ether is all that is needed for the self-evolution of the Universe. It further provides an overview of the opposition of the physicists against the mainstream physical image of the world for the past hundred years. And finally, it documents the basic historical, philosophical and physical reasons for denial of the main physical theories of the 20th century.

**Keywords:** Gravity, Inertia, Mass, Ether, Double slit experiment,

## 1. Introduction

Since the appearance of thinking man on Earth, he has tried to find an answer to the question of the meaning of the existence of his own life. The answer to this question is connected with the answer to the question of what is the meaning of life itself and of the universe, as well as what is the image and order of the surrounding physical world and what is man's position in it.

The ruling power structures reduced the misery of man with the answer to this question and mainly brought him answers that ensured his loyalty. Physics and other sciences have always been the tools for gaining ascendancy and domination of one group of people over others. Physical knowledge of the physical picture of the world has always been a special tool used by the ruling power structures of nations and states to maintain control over their own nations.

Therefore, from ancient times up to today, the officially established order of the universe has been the single untouchable truth and that the opposition or questioning this truth is perceived as an attack on the establishment of governmental power structures. The veracity of this order of the universe is a minor issue for the ruling powers as is also the case with those physical theories of the 20th century.

The purpose of these physical theories (by theoretical physicists) produced during the 20th century (special and general relativity, quantum mechanics, force fields theories using force-mediating particles, the standard model of quark theory, the Big Bang and the Higgs boson theories) was to conceal the existence of physical fields as an actual material media. Force action of these media is replaced in these theories by the mathematics of kinematical non-material quantities.

In fact, these kinematical quantities describe the physical material world, which works on the principle of balance and changes of pressure of the densities of the ma-terial bodies and of the material force fields surrounding these bodies. Without the recognition of the existence of physical fields as actual physical substance, all mathematical descriptions of physical reality are merely the kinematical numbers of the ratios of the lengths and times on paper.

Even the easiest physical processes, such as the collision of two bodies, cannot be reasonably explained by a thinking person without the existence of the force fields associated with these bodies. Newton - *"without the Mediation of anything else, by and through which their Action and Force may be conveyed from one to another, is to me so great an Absurdity that I believe no Man who has in philosophical Matters a competent Faculty of thinking can ever fall into it"* . Maxwell - *"In fact, whenever energy is transmitted from one body to another, there must be a medium or substance in which the energy exists. All theories lead to the conception of a medium in which the propagation takes place"*.

Under the supervision of the ruling power structures and the mass information media, these physically deformed theories of the 20th century are untouchable truths of the order of the universe, as was the case in the past in Ptolemy's geocentric mathematical description of the universe - an untouchable truth for 1500 years.

Special relativity (STR) removed from the physics of the ether as a real physical media discovered by many generations of physicists at hundred year interval, exploring the phenomena of electricity and magnetism during the 19th century. General relativity (GTR) eliminated the ether from physics as a real physical media of the gravitational field discovered by many generations of physicists surrounding Newton. Although Riemann, whose differential geometry of curved space became the basic language of the GTR, asserts to us that space without material content filling it is nothing more than a three-dimensional manifold devoid of all form, this basic fundamental of Riemann is concealed in GTR.

Big Bang removed the media from the Intergalactic Space (ether, dark energy) about which Hubble (until the end of his life) assumed that it may be the main cause of the observed red shift in the spectra of galaxies. Quantum mechanics (QM) and the theory of Higgs boson removes the ether from the physics, in quantum physics known as initial medium at creation and the annihilation of matter particles from and into electromagnetic waves.

Although astronomers bring daily evidence concerning the births and deaths of stars and galaxies from and into interstellar gas and dark energy, the Big Bang theory is forced upon the public as the only possible explanation for the creation of the universe. Although the observed redshift of spectra of galaxies can be physically explained in at least five possible ways, only this one, as the sole and irrefutable evidence of the expansion of the universe, is forced upon the public. Although from the measurements of observed redshift of spectra of a Galaxy it cannot be distinguished from the kinematic point of view, if the Galaxy is moving in a straight line away from us or is moving in any various direction up to right angle from this straight line or moves along a circular path around us, this fact is fully ignored in the Big Bang theory.

Today we know that by annihilation of protons with anti-protons we produce electromagnetic radiation and vice verse, that by waving a magnet around a wire we produce electro-magnetic waves that are able to produce protons. This experimental fact is the full evidence of the existence of the ether as a real physical substance. Yet current physics says that all matter was solely created from the Higgs boson.

## 2. Historical facts in the development of the view of a man concerning his surrounding physical world

Philosophers and astronomers of the culminant era (around 500-300 BC) during the development of the Greek philosophy of nature (Pythagoras, Democritus, and many others) were convinced [1, p. 511] that the Sun is in the center of the known universe, that under the stars drifting in the sky through the ether on a rotating sphere, six planets orbit around the Sun, that the Earth also as one of these planets also orbits around the Sun in an annual cycle and that the Earth daily rotates around its own axis. They had numbered five comets and were convinced that comets circulate like planets around the Sun on a very eccentric orbit. They were convinced that the Milky Way was made up of individual stars and had named the center of the Milky Way Nebula. They were convinced that matter is composed of the smallest indivisible particles of atoms. (N.B. For Greek atom today would be called our today's further indivisible proton).

From continuing recognition [2] of artifact Antikythera clockwork mechanism unearthed in 1900–1901 and dated to 200–100 BC, we know that ancient Greeks mastered the computing of eclipses of the Sun and the Moon, the positions of stars in the sky and the position of the five planets in their orbit. They were even able to include in this computing a different velocity along the elliptical motion of the Moon around the Earth and obviously also a different velocity along the elliptical motion of the Earth around the Sun. Included in the longest period during this computing was the Callippic cycle (proposed by Callippus in 330 BC) of 72 years that was represented by Hipparchus later as he fully discovered (127 BC) the precession of the Earth's axis in period of 26,000 years or 1 ° every 72 years.

Greek theoretical astronomy was based on the experimental observations of their predecessors in the previous thousands of years (the Sumerians, Egyptians, Babylonians, Chaldeans and Babylonian star catalogues appearing from about the 12th century BC). To consider the ancient mechanic who designed the Antikythera clockwork mechanism, performed on papyrus complex calculations of the size and number of required teeth on more than fifty wheels of the mechanism, manufactured them and thereby realized in the previous thousands of years of celestial observations with the precision of one ten thousandth (carried out reconstruction of mechanism was hard task even in our laser and computer technology era) strike us dumb with astonishment.

From the beginning of the exploration of the surrounding physical world, in addition to the physical motion of objects originating in their mutual mechanical action (which men could see with their own eyes) a man also meets with the existence of the phenomena of electricity and magnetism (which are to his own eyes invisible) that fields operate by motion on the physical objects in their vicinity. In the 6th century BC there are written records of ancient Greeks (Thales of Miletus–loadstone attracts iron because it has a soul) that mention the magnetic properties of loadstone and electrical properties of amber (called an electron).

In Greek mythology, ether represented a pure substance that the gods breathed. Aristotle claimed that only the natural motion of the ether as the fifth element (quintessence), which is located in the area of the sky, is its circulation in the circle and therefore stars also circulate along their celestial orbits. (Likeliest the correct explanation for the observed compact rotation of galaxies in 20th century).

The new power-political structure after its accession in the first centuries of the new era claimed the Ptolemy (Claudius Ptolemy 90–168 AD, outstanding scholar of Alexandria) geocentric image of the universe as the official and the only tolerable image of the universe (in 1600, Giordano Bruno was burned to death when, in lectures at Oxford, he claimed that the stars are remote Suns also surrounded by exoplanets and that the universe is infinite. The condemnation of Galileo in 1633 to life imprisonment was only thanks to the fact that the then Pope was a former friend of Galileo from their youth). This image of the Universe persisted until several decades after Kepler (1609 Astronomia nova).

The reason for the provisions of the Ptolemy geocentric image of universe as the official and the only tolerable image of the universe (though there existed the heliocentric view of the ancient Greeks), was its consistency with the idea of the principles of creation. The main proof of the correctness of the Ptolemy geocentric image of universe was found in the mathematics (the complex geometry of the cycloids) of the calculation of the motion of other planets around the Earth. The complex and complicated math of cycloids, for which no one could give reasons from the physical point of view, was declared the finding of the order of the universe and the confirmation of the accuracy of the physical condition that the Earth is the center of the universe.

Ptolemy's mathematical description of the motion of the planets, even though based on an incorrect physical assumption, calculated the position of the planets on their orbits with even better precision than the physically roughly right Copernicus (De Revolutionibus 1533) heliocentric model of planetary motion along circular orbits around the Sun. This was one of the reasons why the Copernicus model was not accepted.

Kepler (Astronomia Nova 1609) after ten years of hard work finding the mystical mathematical formulas to explain the data of the movement of the planets from Tycho Brahe's precise astronomical observation finally came to the simple mathematical rule of three that describes the movement of the planets along their elliptic orbits around the Sun.

Based on the heliocentric model, Kepler described the kinematics of movement of the planets by a simple mathematics and with better accuracy than Ptolemy. But he had not discovered the physical causes, I mean the physical order by which the movement of the planets is governed in the solar system.

Kepler's simplification of the mathematical description of the motion of the planets to the mathematically trivial relationships allowed Newton to discover the physical cause and order, which is governed by the mathematics of kinematic description of the orbital system of the solar system. Newton discovered that the physical cause determining the order of movement of celestial bodies is the existence of a gravitational field as a real physical substance, existing in the surroundings of each mass body. This gravitational field around the mass body is inseparable from any mass body and Newton came to the general validity of the law of mutual gravitational interaction of all matter.

Newton explains the circulation of the planets around the Sun so that any two celestial bodies through their own gravitational fields attract each other (just as a falling apple from the tree also gravitate the Earth, although by negligible power). The forces of gravitational fields are well-balanced for a stable system of celestial constellations by centrifugal inertial forces on their mutual orbits and thus always circulate around a common center of gravity. In the case of negligible mass of the planet to the mass of the Sun, this center of gravity is located inside the Sun, as a result

of which the movement seems as if only the planet circulates around the Sun along the elliptical orbit. The planet actually orbits around the Sun, though not exactly around its center.

Newton attributed the gravitational forces, without any doubt, as so many of his contemporaries, to the existence of a force field as a real physical substance in the surrounding of each body.

"Gravity so that one body may act upon another at a distance thro' a Vacuum, without the Mediation of anything else, by and through which their Action and Force may be conveyed from one to another, is to me so great an Absurdity that I believe no Man who has in philosophical Matters a competent Faculty of thinking can ever fall into it. Gravity must be caused by an Agent acting constantly and according to certain laws" [3].

Evidently Newton was so strong a believer in the medium that we call the ether, though he could not work out its mode of action, that he was ready to discount the intelligence of any man who doubted it.

This Newton belief is formulated in his main work, where it states that gravity is "as a certain power or energy diffused from the center to all places around to move the bodies that are in them" [1, p. 76]. Or also as formulated in Newton's Letter to Robert Boyle [4] in 1678-9 "I suppose, that there is diffused through all places an etherial substance, capable of contraction and dilatation, strongly elastic, and, in a word, much like air in all respects, but far more subtle".

This Newton's concept of subtle we can quantify, if we take into account his physical procedure for calculating velocity of sound in the air. Then first estimation is ratio of sound velocity in the air and light velocity in a vacuum so $10^{-6}$ of an air molecule. Second more likely estimation is their quadratic ratio $10^{-12}$ what corresponds to mass of neutrino. So the proton consist at least $10^5$ particles of ether or more likely $10^{11}$ neutrinos.

In 1708 Newton wrote thus: "Perhaps the whole frame of nature may be nothing but various contextures of some certain ethereal spirits or vapors, condensed, as it were, by precipitation; and after condensation wrought into various forms, at first by the immediate hand of the Creator, and ever after by the power of nature".

Newton instead of this supposition and guess could have talked about surety if he had known that the Maxwell's electrodynamics has brought us knowledge of generation of electromagnetic waves of ether and that particle physics has brought us the knowledge of generations of a solid mass particles from these electromagnetic waves (as is substantiate later in paper).

Newton's laws ( gravity law as gradient of force of medium, force law as resistance against acceleration in medium, law of action and reaction, law of resistance of a body moving in a fluid proportional to the square of the speed of movement, the calculation of the speed of sound in the air and an estimate of the size of the elementary particles of air) were for Newton the particular steps in his effort to confirm the existence of this ethereal substance as it will be also referred further in this paper.

Newton already knew the existence of the invisible phenomena of electricity and magnetism, which through force fields causes motion among bodies and adds the phenomenon of gravitational forces, which is a much weaker phenomenon compared to electricity and magnetism in regards to the bigness of their source. At the same time, with the discovery of the gravitational field around any mass body, Newton (together with Galileo and other physicists) discovered the existence of the inertial forces that were also inseparable from any mass body.

Contemporary Physics, during one hundred years since the inception of relativity, publicly repeats countless times the false claims about Newton's notion of mutual gravitational forces as the force between two mass bodies acting immediately and remotely through the void space of a vacuum with infinite speed. Newton, however, holds gravitational forces as the power through the medium and apparently assumes the final speed of gravitational forces in this medium, which may be the reason Newton interested himself and calculated the speed of sound in the air.

General relativity, on the basis of plagiarism, claims Newton's idea of gravitational force as the forces acting at a distance through a vacuum and also conceals Riemann's necessary condition that curvature of space unavoidably requires material content filling it. GTR then finally brings to our civilization the allegedly greatest achievement of all history of the human spirit in understanding gravity as the curvature of non-material notions of space and time.

The mathematics of Riemann's differential geometry of curved space became the basic language of the GTR, but Riemann himself, although a mathematician, *"asserts, on the contrary, that space in itself is nothing more than a three-dimensional manifold devoid of all form; it acquires a definite form only through the advent of the material content filling it and determining its metric relations"* [5, p. 98].

GTR is based on the same concept of the description of gravity, as a description of electromagnetism with perspective of their integration so the phenomena of electromagnetism (the electric field, magnetic field, electromagnetic fields) in parallel to GTR would also be assigned to the curvature of space and time. For nearly thirty years, from 1926 until his death in 1955, these were the central focus of Einstein's research, but his unified theory was an unmitigated disaster. No physicist was willing to admit that the electric, magnetic or electromagnetic fields are a curvature of non - material space and time.

Most of the physicists involved from 1800 to 1900 in intensive exploration of electric and magnetic phenomena (Coulomb, Volta, Ampere, Orsted, Faraday, Ohm, Maxwell, Hertz, Edison, Weber, Tesla) came to a full belief in the existence of the electric and magnetic force fields as a real physical substance, called ether and they confirmed this substance in their experiments. This substance can spread the waves of this substance caused by oscilla-

tions of the sources of gradient of fields in this substance. This waves can even spread independently of these sources and transmit with these source inserted power (energy) into this substance.

Let us recall for all these physicists the statement of Maxwell who, in very last clause of his Treaties [6] (1873), declared *"In fact, whenever energy is transmitted from one body to another, there must be a medium or substance in which the energy exists. . . . all theories lead to the conception of a medium in which that propagation takes place. . . and this has been my constant aim in this treatise "*.

The conviction of physicists to the end of the 19th century of the full existence of ether can best be seen in the search work of H.A. Lorentz - Ether theories and eather models (1901-1902), examining the work of many distinguished physicists of the 19th century on ether (Stokes, Planck, Fresnel, Maxwell, Kelvin, Neumann).

In 1925, Edwin Hubble announced his evidence confirming that the bright fog formations in the night sky (in the meantime called nebulas) are separate groupings of stars and galaxies and that all the other stars we observe in the night sky, free and with our own eyes, belong to our Galaxy, the Milky Way.

For proof of the theory of the Big Bang, current physics considers increasing the red shift with the distance of galaxies, measured in the spectra of galaxies firstly by Hubble (1929). Hubble himself, even when he was pressured (mainly by Lemaitre at the IAU meeting, 1928), however, disapproved with this unilateral interpretation until the end of his life. The Nobel Prize for astronomy till the 1950s was not granted, and so Hubble did not have to succumb to this pressure (Unlike Millikan in 1921).

Hubble for a more likely explanation than explaining the red shift spectra by mutual receding of galaxies, considered the explanation of this shift by the loss of light energy passing through the medium of interstellar space.

We can cite from the work of Hubble [7, p. 1] (1937), The observational approach to cosmology, *"The features, however, include the phenomena of red-shifts whose significance is still uncertain. Alternative interpretations are possible, and, while they introduce only minor differences in the picture of the observable region, they lead to totally different conceptions of the universe itself"*. *"The cautious observer naturally examines other possibilities before accepting the proposition, even as a working hypothesis. He (Hubble) recalls the alternative formulation of the law of red-shifts - light loses energy in proportion to the distance it travels through space. The law, in this form, sounds quite plausible. Interior nebular space, we believe, cannot be entirely empty"*.

Also cited from A. K. T. Assis at. all [8] -Hubble's Cosmology: From a Finite Expanding Universe to a Static Endless Universe - *"We show, by quoting his works, that Hubble remained cautiously against the big bang until the end of his life, contrary to the statements of many modern authors " .*

Even today, the hundreds of non-fiction documentary films of the most respected television or most respected Web sources of information dedicated to the description of the evolution of opinion of mankind on the physical image of the universe state that Hubble's observations are evidence of the expanding universe.

See Wikipedia:

-Big bang (en.wikipedia.org/ wiki/BigBang) "In 1929, from analysis of galactic redshifts, Edwin Hubble concluded that galaxies are drifting apart, important observational evidence consistent with the hypothesis of an expanding universe".

-Edwin Hubble (en.wikipedia.org/wiki/EdwinHubble) "Hubble is known for showing that the recessional velocity of a galaxy increases with its distance from the earth, implying the universe is expanding ".

Physics, in 1932 (Anderson) and in 1955 (Laboratories in Berkeley), with the discovery of the production of pairs of particles and antiparticles of electrons and protons from electromagnetic (etherial) radiation, brought full proof of the existence of the ether. With the mechanical waving of a magnet nearby copper wire we produce electromagnetic radiation with a frequency equal to the frequency of the waving magnet. At the sufficient frequencies, the mass of pairs of electrons or protons can be produced from electromagnetic radiation. For an arbitrarily long time we can do this waving with a magnet and produce any amount of photons, electrons or protons, but from the magnet or wire wane not even a piece of mass.

This physical fact in no way be explained by force fields theories using force-mediating particles. On the contrary, at the annihilation of these particles with antiparticle arise two photons of electromagnetic radiation. These two photons in subsequent scattering on atoms, e.g. steel ball in void space, transfer its energy to this ball and completely dissipate into nothingness. This steel ball, after a short warm up from the photons, cools down again at the temperature of the universe around -270 °C. I mean we have under current physics, right before our eyes, an experiment concerning the invalidity of the law conservation of mass and energy.

The body of an astronaut when leaving the rocket into the void space without a space suit would freeze immediately to a temperature close to absolute zero. His or her thermal energy disappears although according today physics no air as well as any material substance is situated nearby. Their loss of thermal energy must be related to thermal radiation, as all matter with a temperature greater than absolute zero emits thermal electromagnetic radiation. But what substance are astronaut bodies balanced to in thermodynamic equilibrium (balance between two ambient) at a temperature around -270 °C? No doubt this temperature is different in separate areas of space so the reverse process must also exist when bodies translocate from one temperature to another.

The energy of the electromagnetic field, and subsequent mass of the electron or the proton we have created under current physics from nothingness -waving a magnet around a wire. This matter by annihilation into electromagnetic radiation energy afterwards disappeared before our eyes into nothingness by scattering.

The creation of pairs of particles and antiparticles is not a limited phenomenon of physicists in laboratories, but is a common and well examined phenomenon of the interaction of electromagnetic radiation with matter. Electromagnetic radiation up to energy of 1.02 MeV interacts with matter in photoelectric effect or scattering processes (Compton, Rayleigh scattering). For interactions over 1.02 MeV and up to 1.9 GeV, electron positron pair creation predominates and over 1.9 GeV out-weighs the creation of proton antiproton pairs.

In the universe and nature all around us on Earth this phenomenon is continuously going on in a great quantity from the gamma radiation of radionuclides present to a greater or lesser extent in every substance on the ground (up to 20 MeV), from storm lightning (100 MeV) and the high energy gamma radiation (80 GeV to millions TeV) incidents on our Earth in great quantity from the universe.

So, the annihilation of protons and anti-protons was confirmed experimentally, which is the conversion of mass into an electromagnetic curl of the ether and vice verse. But current physics claims in of the Higgs field theory that the Higgs boson is the only method by which all particles of matter in the universe acquired its mass.

Perhaps current physics does not want us to claim that in creation of the proton from the electromagnetic radiation at energy 1.9 GeV or vice versa in the process of conversion of a proton into the 0.94 GeV electromagnetic radiation between the proton (0.94 GeV) and electromagnetic radiation stands energetically more than a hundred times greater than Higgs boson 125 GeV.

Perhaps current physics in the Standard model does not wants us to claim that before process of creation of proton-antiproton pairs (or all other particles-antiparticles pairs) from electromagnetic waves, some of the three free quarks or of three free antiquarks (later synthetized) exist in photons of these electromagnetic waves. Or perhaps also does not wants us to claim that after the annihilation of proton-antiproton pairs these quarks are separated and somewhere exist or vanish in two photon of electromagnetic waves. But for separation, so also for synthesis of quarks infinite amount of energy is necessary according to the Standard model.

In 1964, Gell-Mann introduced the purported existence of quarks as particles of which the hadrons as parts of an ordering scheme for hadrons are composed, even if there was little evidence for their physical existence. Gell-Mann conceived of a mysterious physically inconsistent principle that quarks can never be directly observed or found in isolation, because an infinitely huge power is necessary for their possible separation. This (proofless) speculation includes in itself the impossibility to uproot it.

Later in 1968 it was declared that accelerator experiments at Stanford Linear Accelerator Center allegedly provided evidence for the existence of quarks.

The main work referred-to for this allegedly provided evidence for existence of quarks is the outstanding researcher at Stanford Linear Accelerator Center, J. D. Bjorken. However, Bjorken in 1969 declared on page 4 in his paper [9] that *"There are various theoretical models which try to explain or at least describe these features of data but none work really well, or are totally satisfying. We will discuss three of these theoretical descriptions of the data; these are: 1) incoherent scattering from pointlike constituents within the proton - the parton model, or Thomson nucleon, 2) vector dominance, or Rutherford electron, 3) current commutators"*.

In Bjorken's paper, no clear advantage for any model is provided. Last but not least, it should be noted that in all models the electron is taken as an approximately dimensionless point-like probe which is opposed in our previous paper [30] [11]. The robust fantastic theory of the so called Standard Model enabled mysterious physical properties (as fractions of unit electrical charge and their different ratios to mass, infinitely huge power for separation) was generated in the mid-1970s to accommodate the results. Later and whenever necessary, go-as-you-please other mysterious physical properties were fabricated into this model.

T. Ferbel in his text book [12] states that the Standard Model has many parameters, e.g., masses of the leptons, quarks, gauge bosons, and of the Higgs, various coupling strengths and elements of the CKM matrix, with all values seemingly perplexing and ad hoc.

T. Ferbel, in his presentation [13] in 2012- Belief and Observation: The Top Quark and Other Tales of 'Discovery', describes his personal adventures with keen physicists at SLAC experiments searching for top quarks which verbalized their approach to experimental work- I'll find top, even if it's not there!

The so called Standard Model contains quite a large number of theories [14]. Physicists complain about these theories because the simplest one has 19 adjustable constants and the more elaborate version has 29 adjustable constants. But constants in physics represent a calibration point of physical law, so each of these 19 up to 29 constants represent unknown physics. Yet the physicist claims that the Standard Model is the best theory in science of particle physics.

Physicists at CERN announced to world in 2012 that their experimental results of one hazy hump (increase amount of events) on smooth curve through these 29 adjustable constants without doubt clearly points at their single one primordially picked physical model and that so Higgs boson was discovered and that thus even the existence of Higgs boson was confirmed.

This detected one hump through these 29 adjustable constants can point at to at least another 29 primordially picked physical models explaining the measured data. On top of that the mass of Higgs boson, which the physicist

at CERN allegedly discovered, does not fit to any one of these theories based on 19 up to 29 adjustable constants contained in the Standard Model.

The claim that the standard Higgs boson model is a single correct model, without considering the correctness of other physical models, has nothing to do with the scientific methods in physics. It is pure tautology, obscuring the lack of evidence or valid reasoning supporting the stated conclusion. It also was not distinguished whether this is a resonance or particle by the following collision or decay experiments with this allegedly discovered particle as is usual for confirming the discovery of a particle in particles physics. On top of that physicist at CERN simply declared discovery of the Higgs boson and the Nobel Prize was immediately awarded for it but they do not know its lifetime! which is just predicted to $10^{-22}s$ !

It is hearsay that the physicists at CERN in fact formed a division with the different opinion to CREN official opinions kept among themselves because they are afraid of losing their jobs. Concerning the veracity of the allegedly discovered Higgs boson from the 17 principle investigators at CERN, 15 of the 17 said that they do not think they had found the Higgs boson and two said they did.

Within the mainstream scientific community half of physicists judge that Higgs was not discovered and particles such as Higgs do does not even exist. How is it possible that without any defence before the scientific community the discovery of the Higgs boson is simply declared and the Nobel Prize is immediately awarded for it. But for the CERN budget of 1 billion euro per year (equals around to the Gross Domestic Product of Liberia with 4 million citizens) it is unthinkable not to return the breakthrough results, no matter if they are true or not.

In 1971 Kuti and Waisskopf, in a nucleon model in addition to the three quarks, requested a sea of quark-antiquark pairs and neutral gluons for the composition of a nucleon.

In the last decade and based on experimental results, physics came to the conclusion that the mass of particles (till then asserted as a static composition of quarks with gluon fields in elementary particles) lies in the spinning quark-gluon field and the actual mass of the quarks has but a minimal contribution to the mass of the particles.

In 2015 team of physicists at CERN announced another brake trough discovery of a pentaquark !

In 2015 another international team of physicists at CERN had produced quark-gluon plasma at the Large Hadron Collider by colliding protons with lead nuclei at high energy. They contrarily reported [15] that this state of matter doesn't (as was initially expected) behave like a gas of quarks and gluons, but rather like a continuous liquid (no quarks or any particles).

This report on the absence of quarks (which stand in the hierarchy of the Standard Model on the bottom level) means as well the absence to quarks conjoined the Higgs boson (which stands in the hierarchy of the Standard

Model on the supreme level).

The lifetime existence of all (around a hundred) so called elementary particles, except stable protons, electrons, photon or neutrinos (or neutron max 15min) is one-millionth of a second to a billionth of a billionth of second (hyperons from $10^{-10}s$ to $10^{-20}s$, mesons from $10^{-8}s$ to $10^{-20}s$, leptons - muon $10^{-6}s$, tauon $10^{-13}s$). All decays of hyperons from the largest energy through less energy terminate at protons (as do neutrons) and energy is washed away by neutrinos, photons or electrons.

All decays of mesons (composed allegedly of two quarks) from largest energy through less energy terminate at electrons (containing no quark) and energy is washed away by neutrinos or photons (whereas quarks at these decays simply vanish without any physical reasoning of how and where, though infinite energy is allegedly necessary for their separation). Lepton decays (muon and tauon) - terminate at electrons and energy is washed away by neutrinos.

Thus vice versa, we can say that all leptons and mesons are a series of excited energy states (more stable) or resonance (less stable) of electrons (or positrons). Hyperons are a series of excited energy states or resonance of protons (or antiproton). We can say that this is the most natural and physically simple first approach to the primordial model and classification of so called elementary particles.

No quarks exist. No Higgs boson exists, because there is no reason why other excited states or the resonances of proton energy series in higher energy ranges above energy detected in 2012 at CERN hereafter could not be found.

## 3. Main philosophical and physical flaws of GTR and STR from an overall view

### 3.1. The identity instead of equivalency of the inertial and gravitational forces

Newton found that the physical cause of the order of movement of celestial bodies is the existence of a gravitational field as a real physical substance, existing in the surrounding of each mass body. This gravitational field around mass bodies is in-separable from any single mass body. At the same time, with the discovery of the gravitational field around each of the existing masses, Newton (along with Galilei and other physicists) discovered the existence of inertia as also inseparably linked with every mass body. The inertia force of a 1 kg spherical body is measured in its mass center (in the middle), but its own gravitational force is measured at a distance of 1 m from this center.

Newton says that physical origin of inertial forces, which emerge when bodies are accelerated is unknown to him. He will not find its physical cause, but relies upon the mathematical description of the inertial forces, using the quantity of acceleration of these bodies. Logically, the simplest physical conclusion which applies would lead Newton to determine the cause of inertial forces as forces of the resistance of the body against its own medium of the gravitational field.

Inertial force of one kilogram of mass, however, is the enormous power $10^{12}$ times stronger compared to the gravitational force measured at a distance of 1 m from its center. Newton, in addition, did not know the size of his own gravitational constant $G \approx 10^{-12}N$ (Cavendish's 1798). He also did not know the size of the depth of the structure of matter into atoms, $10^{-10}$ (Perin 1913) and protons $10^{-15}$ (Rutherford in 1920) that are the source and origin of the manifestation of all forces of mass bodies. We can show [11] that the sum of the gravitational forces on the surface of atoms of the 1kg mass body is equal to its inertial force.

In this is a remarkable view of Newton that appears right in the first paragraph, when he defines mass states and says *"I have no regard in this place ( place of definition of quantity of matter) to a medium, if any such there is, that freely pervades the interstices between the parts of bodies"* [1].

His 'Principia' closes thus: *"And now we might add something concerning a most subtle spirit which pervades and lies hid in all gross bodies; by the force and action of which spirit the particles of bodies mutually attract one another at near distances and cohere if contiguous; and electric bodies operate to greater distances repelling as well as attracting the neighboring corpuscles, and light is emitted, reflected, inflected, and heats bodies"*.

Today we know, that photons (electromagnetic radio waves, X- rays, gamma rays), neutrinos, protons, electrons, alfa particles (and others) pervade freely through bodies and matters in an amount corresponding to penetrant attenuation coefficients of their mass densities.

We can prove [11] that more than 99 percent of the forces of the gravitational field are located within the mass bodies and that these forces are, in fact, magnetic and electrical forces that keep the mass body as a compact object together.

Likewise, assignment of great inertial forces to the resistance of mediums (ether), however, would lead to decelerating of bodies moving at a constant speed in this environment (the initial principle of physics since the time of Galileo and Newton, where without the influence of forces bodies remain in the rest or uniform rectilinear motion).

For the past hundred years it has been omitted that the absence of the resistance of ether in uniform linear motion was the main argument even at the condemnation of the ether at the time of interpretation of the M-M experiment. This irrefutable contradiction concerning the mechanical resistance of the ether in a uniform motion of bodies in free environments can, however, be removed after the discovery of the depth of the structuring of the mass and spin properties of all the particles of matter in the last hundred years. Since the 1930s, we found that all elementary particles are rotating spherical objects.

From results of fluid dynamics and continuum mechanics, we learned that, on the spherical symmetric rotating body moving at constant speed in an ideal fluid, only the same force exists from all directions perpendicular to the surface of a spherical body. The drag force on a rotating body, moving with constant velocity relative to the fluid, is zero. I mean the rotating spherical object is not decelerated in uniform motion in an ideal fluid environment against the direction of its movement (already the evidence of d'Alembert in 1752 that *square* = 0, at d'Alembert's paradox ).

The power of the resistance of the environment on a rotating body in a fluid environment in the direction of its movement is only manifested in the accelerating or decelerating of the body between the two speeds. The subsequent perpendicular pressure on the surface of the rotating spherical body moving at various constant velocity in a fluid environment is proportional to its speed of motion in that environment. As a result of the pressure changes of the surrounding environment on the spherical surface of the compressible rotational body, the change in the radius of its volume occurs.

This physical concept fills the conviction of Lorenz and Fitzgerald about contraction of dimensions of solid bodies as a consequence of different pressure of ether at different speeds of bodies within that ether.

H. A. Lorentz, in his 1904 paper [16] mentioned: *"The first example of this kind is Michelson's well known interference experiment, the negative result of which has led FitzGerald and myself to the conclusion that the dimensions of solid bodies are slightly altered by their motion through the ether "*.

The actual physical reality of relationship of inertial and gravitational forces is disguised in current physics by the damaging principle of the equivalence of inertial and gravitational forces in the GTR, in which the force of inertia of one body (the test body) is given equality with the gravitational force of another body (the central body). The gravitational force of the central body must be searched in relation to the inertial forces of the central body.

For Newton, the use of the law of action and reaction make no different in what kind of a force on the body (test) acts; for example the force of the impact of another body, dragging the body (e.g. lift) by a rope or the force of gravity [1, p. 84]. *"This law (action and reaction) also takes place in attractions, as will be done in the next scholium "*.

The forces in law of action and reaction are the same, but the motion of bodies is not. The motion of bodies is only inversely proportional to the mass of bodies in the moving center of their mutual inertia frame. The independence of the nature of the forces acting on the body (the test) is Newton's statement about the equality gravitational and inertial mass of the body. The reaction of mass of the body when exposed to the same gravitational or mechanical forces is the same Fa/Fg = ma/mg, so that gravity mass equals acceleration mass. As was shown above, there is also no contradiction in it.

But, from this statement, Einstein concluded that consequently, in gravity field gravitational forces on bodies are opposite and equal to inertial forces. So, as the sum of forces acting on bodies is zero and despite of that bodies move with g acceleration, so a curved non-material space and time is caused which creates motion of bodies in gravitational fields.

Einstein GTR begins with Galileo's law that all bodies, independent of their mass, fall to the earth with the same g acceleration. But Galileo's law is valid only within the limit case when the mass of the falling body as well as the gravity of the falling body can be neglected by the mass of the earth. If the mass of the falling body equals the mass of the earth, then they fall mutually on each other with 2g acceleration. In this case, according to Einstein from the equivalency principle of gravitational and inertial mass, also arises that gravitational and inertial forces of earth as well as the falling body are balanced and so it is proven that no forces between them exist. So, according Einstein, in this case when on earth a body falls with a mass that equals the mass of earth, their mutual action is caused by their two curvatures of non-material space and time.

The invalidity of this Einstein's basic postulate of GTR can be demonstrated in a simple experiment in the interaction of two small disk loadstone magnets facing each other with the same polarity. By the action of first magnet that we have in hand, we can remotely (at a distance) push the second not fixed magnet in motion. The second magnet moves, despite according to the law of action and reaction, its inertial force equals and is opposite to the pushing force of magnetic field of the first magnet. Forces (contact pressure) equal, but the movement of the magnets will depend on the ratio of their acting mass. In other words, on a path, along which the force acts (path integral).

But according to Einstein's equivalence principle, based on a thought experiment, the second magnet should remain in the same place, since the inertial force of second magnet has the same and opposite magnitude as the pushing magnetic force of the first magnet. According to GTR, curved space time is then cause, which creates the motion of the second magnet.

In this experiment we can also place and let hover a second magnet, above the first magnet that we have in hand. With regard to GTR by magnet in our hand we canceled the space time curvature of earth. But we will feel in our hand the distance gravitational force of the weight of the second magnet!

In both cases, the existing reality of the mediating material substance is so evident that it can be replaced in our mind by solid bar.

The experiments confirming the equality of gravity and inertia mass (e.g. Eotvo's experiment) are subsequently deceivingly considered as full evidence of the correctness of the basic principle of GTR concerning the equivalency of gravitational and inertial forces, meaning that zero forces act on falling bodies in gravitational fields.

The equality of the gravitational and inertial mass of one body and the movement of bodies in their mutual action are two entirely different items. The physical reality is that although the forces are the same in earth gravity, each body falls to earth by neglecting the mass of body to the mass of earth.

The principle of equivalence in the GTR confuses and mixes Newton's statement concerning the equality of gravitational and inertial mass with a false embracement of the law of action and reaction. Law of action and reaction is hold in the GTR as the same time and same place equality and reverse orientation of the forces exerted by actions and reactions.

Unfortunately, while occurring countless times in the current physics (although never mentioned by Newton) leads to a standstill of the entire universe. The crash or any force of action between any two bodies would have had to stop the movement of these bodies. The body in the gravitational field would not have moved, since the force of gravity and inertia are opposite and balanced. Therefore it is necessary that the move of the body in the gravity field be attributed to the non-material curvature of space and time.

In the basic physical thought experiment of GTR on equality gravity and inertia, the man standing in a stationary elevator in a gravity field is pressed to the floor of the elevator by the same force as the man standing in an elevator pulled by rope, with acceleration equal to the acceleration of the gravity field.

This thought experiment is, however, a misleading asymmetric description of physical reality. The situation in the stationary elevator cannot be made equal to the non-stationary elevator pulled by a rope. The force of gravity pulls the elevator, but for all parts of the atoms of the lift and all parts of the man standing in it.

I submit that the situation of the stationary elevator, in shaft at a floor, blocked in the gravity field is symmetrical with the elevator pulled in the free space of the universe by pulling rope with the thousands of invisible glass fibers, that pull at the same time for all the atoms of the elevator and all parts of man, and the free movement of the elevator is prevented by block against the rope mounting.

A man standing in the stationary elevator in the gravity field would feel pressure on the soles of his feet as the pressure of his own body and no pressure on the top of his head. In the stationary elevator in the free space pulled by a rope with thousands of invisible fibers, the man standing on his head, would feel the pressure on the top of his head and no pressure on the soles of his feet.

In the case of deletion blocks in both cases, the person would feel no pressure and would feel free fall or free acceleration. The biggest blunder of the GTR is the claim that at the free fall of a body in gravity (equivalent case to 'free acceleration') no forces exist and so the movement in gravity (just as at case of 'free acceleration') has to be assigned to the curvature of the space and time.

Finally, today we now know that to change the height of the orbit of a satellite circulating around the Earth we must turn on the reactive engines acting on the satellite by force in the direction or in the opposite direction to the gravitational forces (not against non-material space-time) and add or subtract energy to the satellite (as cumulative force) according to the desired size of the orbit height changes of the satellite.

Inertial forces as the first and direct evidence of ether are abolished from physics in 20th century. Inertial forces are named as fictitious or pseudo forces which does not arise from any physical interaction between two objects, but just from the acceleration of the non-inertial reference frame itself. Also gravity is named the fictitious force as distortion of space time due to mass of objects. Even in Wikipedia the section named Inertial forces was abolished and returns redirection to fictitious force.

## 3.2. GTR

Since 1925 (Hubble's discovery of galaxies, 1926 Lindblad's discovery of rotation of galaxies), we understand that all the stars and constellations that we see in the night sky with the naked eye or binoculars (numbering about 2000 stars) are just a small part of our nearest surrounding universe in a sphere with a diameter of 2 to 10 thousand light years in our Milky Way Galaxy, which has a diameter around 100 to 500 thousand light years. These naked eye visible stars in this sphere rotate along with the Earth and the Sun around the center of our galaxy. The ancient Greeks, Newton and Einstein (at the time of 1905, 1915) considered these with naked eye visible stars within this sphere with radius from 2 to 10 thousand light years in the sky (together with a few nebulas and the belt of the Milky Way nebula), as the entire universe.

Newton, after the formulation of the general principle of gravity of all masses, could not avoid the question of why the universe had not gravitationally collapsed. Newton's reply to this question is based on the knowledge of his predecessors, that for the previous 3000 years the universe appears to have been stable and, secondly, on the knowledge of his own discovery that in the solar system the gravitational force of the Sun acting on the planet is compensated by the centrifugal inertial force of planets orbiting the Sun.

Therefore, Newton was convinced [1, p. 514] that the gravitational forces acting on the stars in the sky do not route to the Earth or Sun, but to their own force center on the particular orbits of these stars.

Since 1925, we understood that Einstein's description of the image of the universe in general relativity theory for the universe known to Einstein (a sphere within a radius of 2 to 10 thousand light years) is mistaken. This is because the universe known to Einstein as a whole rotates around the center of the Milky Way Galaxy and the mutual gravitational interaction of stars within this sphere is not the determining factor of the physical image of our universe.

The discovery of whirling galaxies meant the end of GTR. Newton's far-sighted belief has proven correct with the minor change that all the stars of the universe known to Newton (so as to Einstein) rotate around the common power Center of the Milky Way Galaxy.

After this proof of the blunder to use GTR for stars in our Galaxy (a universe known in 1915) it was claimed that GTR is but valid for newly discovered universe of galaxies. It is very alarming that these allegations of current physics, supporting this theory as applicable continue to be put forward. However, again the Big Bang theory of physicist and priest Lemaitre (1927) is put forward as truth.

Physics during the last 100 years has shown that the basic manifestation of the mass of the observable universe around us is its rotary and curl movements. Fields of alleged quark-gluon particles curl inside the proton and neutron. The proton and neutron most probably rotate as fields at shells in atomic nuclei, electrons rotate as fields at shells around atomic nuclei. The Sun and planets rotate individually, the planets around the Sun, the Solar System and other stars rotate around the center of the Milky Way Galaxy. With full physical conviction we must then assume rotary movements, even for galaxies and their higher grouping. However, from the measurements of the observed redshift of spectra of a Galaxy we are unable to determine the Galaxy's direction of possible movement in space.

Even with the evidence of the last twenty years that Galaxies form filaments in web-like super cluster complexes and move at curved paths along these filaments, we are not yet able to get the academic community to a clear rejection of the Big bang theory forced daily upon them under the supervision of power structures and public mass media.

The initial natural idea by non-physicists, would have seen the curvature of light in the gravitational fields of the celestial mass body would consider that, in the surroundings of this mas body is something that curves the trajectory of light, rather than the idea that there is nothing that causes this curvature (proven by the ordinary experience of curved glass or on the passage between two various matter densities or within gradient of fluids). There is no logical reason why from a physical point of view held by all physicists in the late 19th century on this matter ( the gravity as a gradient of the real physical ethereal substance), the light path should not be curved in the gradient of this substance of the gravitational field.

It was not necessary to carry out large expeditions type of that Edington's in 1919 for the purpose of observation a light bend near the Sun at the eclipse of the Sun. According to the fundamental experimental knowledge of optics since Newton, we know that light curves when it passes closely around the edge of any object that we have at hand.

To consider, however, the phenomenon of the curvature of light in gravitational fields as evidence of the validity of a physical claim that gravity is the curvature of the non-material space and time is clear Dadaism. It can best be captured by the words of Nikola Tesla (1856-1943) in the New York Herald Tribune, 11. Sept 1932[17],

*"I hold that space cannot be curved, for the simple reason that it can have no properties. Of properties we can only speak when dealing with matter filling the space. To say that in the presence of large bodies space becomes curved is equivalent to stating that something can act upon nothing. I, for one, refuse to subscribe to such a view "*.

Tesla in his works claimed that Einstein's relativity, which discards the ether, is entirely wrong and he proved that no vacuum (void space) exists. He asserts that all attempts to explain the workings of the universe without recognizing the existence of ether and the indispensable function it plays in phenomena are futile. He asserts that there is no energy in matter other than that received from the environment.

Special relativity as a mathematical construction is without any physical contemplation firmly rooted in purported zero result of the experimental investigation of the speed of light, carried out by Michelson-Morley. General relativity emerged from Einstein's purely theoretical and somewhat misguided speculations about a possible relativity of acceleration.

Gravity, electricity and magnetism were explored independently in physics and are also currently presented in physics in independent parts of the science. Gravity in physics is referred to as (and often as the only) universal power and universal attribute of matter. However, after the last hundred years of exploring molecules, atoms, protons, electrons, and other elementary particles, we know that each atom or molecule, each proton or electron, and other elementary particles of matter exhibit a magnetic field in its vicinity and in their inside or around the electric field.

If we see into tables and catalogues (CODATA, Wikipedia or others) showing the basic properties of elementary particles and atoms, we find that for every particle or atom is given one or both values of the force of the electric or the magnetic field. Even the neutron has a magnetic field equal circa to the magnetic field of a proton!

However, for these elementary particles in these tables we find that no value of the size of the gravitational forces fall to the size of the mass of these particles, even when the size of these gravitational forces on the surface of the particles or atoms equals at least their magnetic force [11].

We can prove [11] that more than 99 percent of the forces of the gravitational field are located within the mass bodies and that these forces are in fact magnetic and electrical forces that keep the mass body together as a compact object. These same forces hold together electrons, protons and neutrons inside atoms as well as hold fictitious gluons and quarks inside protons and neutrons. The gravitational field surrounding the mass bodies is much smaller than a one percent remnant of these forces.

The explanation of gravitational fields lies in the extension of Van der Waals experimental study (1910 Nobel Prize) on the existence of mutual attractive forces between the molecules and atoms of substances emerging as an averaging remnant (magnetic field) at their random thermal rotating (spinning) movement of their thus rotating dipole and multipole electrostatic fields.

We can consider, with great conviction, that the gravitational force is not a universal fundamental attribute of matter, and that the force of gravity as the individual fundamental power of atoms and particles does not exist. We can consider that gravitational fields and gravitational forces surrounding great mass objects represent the sum of a huge number (1kg steel ball $10^{26}$ atoms) of disordered magnetic fields of the atoms and elementary particles from which these mass objects are composed.

We can consider that the gravitational field of the Earth is the dominant vertical component of the sum of a huge number of the disordered magnetic fields of atoms and elementary particles of the Earth. The magnetic field of the Earth is a manifestation of the asymmetry of the layout of the dominant vertical component of the magnetic fields of atoms of the earth caused by the spherically asymmetric ellipsoidal shape of the Earth. For the measurement of the magnetic field of the Earth, e.g. by a compass, we have to eliminate this main dominant component of the field and spar the needle of the compass in the middle (in its center of gravity).

Subsequently, under the so-called gravitational waves of large gravity mass bodies established in GTR, it is necessary to consider the broad spectrum of the disorderly flow of so-called thermal electromagnetic radiation of the individual atoms and elementary particles from which these large gravity mass objects are composed. Maybe relic radiation (cosmic microwave background) is just a manifestation of this way in which the existence of so-called gravitational waves are presented. They can be seen as the broad spectrum of the disorderly flow of very low electromagnetic radiation frequencies of the individual atoms of large mass bodies rotating in solar system, the Milky Way and other Galaxies. Analogous to cyclotron radiation, they are exposed to acceleration components along an orbital path.

GTR at introducing the magic object called the Black Hole, claims that no escape (light or any bodies) is possible beyond the boundary of the region called the 'event horizon' and that Black holes can be identified upon the basis of their gravitational interaction in otherwise boundless distances. The Black Holes are allegedly placed in the centre of galaxies. Black Hole by massive gravity field keep the rest of galaxy together.

The first simple and logical question then is how the gravity forces itself or the gravity field of the Black Hole escapes within boundless distance beyond event horizon? This was never raised in GTR and so much the more never answered. GTR, on the other hand, at the same time also claims that Black Holes can produce gravitational waves that transport energy to boundless distances as gravitational radiation, a form of radiant energy similar to electromagnetic radiation. But electromagnetic radiation and light are the same.

Later the fantasy about particle of gravity called a graviton was added to GTR. Substance of a graviton has to be the curvature of space and time as it is particle of curvature of space-time field. May be if to a graviton is added another fantastic feature, that it can move with velocity higher than light or infinite velocity, it can solve the trouble with range of gravity beyond the event horizon.

Riemann's assertion, that the space acquires a definite form only through the advent of the material content filling it and determining its metric relations, Einstein in GTR transformed into a demagogic physical and philosophical phantasm of the mystery of the curvature of non-material notion of space and time. This was a continuation of the mystery of time dilation in STR, where the mutual velocity of body and light is always constant, regardless of the direction of movement of the body to-wards the light in equation $v + c = v - c = c$. The difference in velocities is the difference in the traveled paths. Path divided by time is velocity. So for come true the validity of this equation, the mystery of time dilation is introduced. But from time dilation follows the deceleration of velocities. In this equation the reference frame is also not defined.

In relativity, using the multiple of speed and time, we are not able to measure the traveled paths because from an increase in velocity follows dilation of time and length contraction and so also follows the deceleration of velocity itself. We find ourselves in a typical mysterious Einstein pathological circle, where no basic unit of quantity and no basic reference frame is definitively defined.

In relativity, all basic units of quantities and their relevant reference frames (so all physical law) is changing according to their ratio to the velocity of light. But no reference frame exists for the velocity of light.

But physics is a fully comparative science. No single absolute numerical value exists in physics. Physical constants (the basic physical unit of quantities) are firm calibration values of physical law for comparing the development of observed phenomena. Without fixed calibration values of basic physical units of quantities and fixed reference frames to which these calibration value are related, we can't discuss physics.

Albert Einstein, on his 70th birthday, in a letter to Maurice Solovine, 28 March 1949 [18, p. 328]- *"You imagine that I look back on my life's work with calm satisfaction. But from nearby it looks quite different. There is not a single concept of which I am convinced that it will stand firm, and I feel uncertain whether I am in general on the right track "*.

B. Riemann in his work [19, p. 11] says *"in a discrete manifoldness (existence of particles in all neighborhoods), the ground of its metric relations is given in the notion of it, while in a continuous manifoldness, this ground must come from outside. Either therefore the reality which underlies space must form a discrete manifoldness, or we must seek the ground of its metric relations outside it, in binding forces which act upon it "*.

The conclusions of Riemann imply that, we can get rid of infinite space just in case the metric space is filled with discrete particles and it must be added that these discrete particles must be at rest.

Riemann's conclusion should today be competed with the physical reality of the production of discrete particles as curl compression of the continuous ether, so we must seek the ground of metric relation of space filled with such discrete particles also outside of it.

Since today we know that particles move at huge speeds within the expected continuous manifoldness of space, consequently Riemann's idea of construction of metric of space grounded on the property of discrete particles inhered in mutual neighborhoods are also rather illusory. Again, it would be necessary to construct a metric space based on the pressure of the media at a given point and the total pressure of the space with opposite pressure outside of this space.

In the deprivation of infinity we also seek a reason why the power structures in physics support the theory riding off the continuous ether (special and general relativity, quantum mechanics, force fields theories using force-mediating particles, the standard model of quark theory, the Big Bang and the Higgs boson theories). These theories are merely based on the existence of rigid particles what together with the theory of curved space-time provide requested finiteness of the dreamed of universe in which when we move in any direction, we will always move on curved path within this space.

This unproven speculation has a basis in the discovery of the roundness of the Earth, while till then some assumed that the Earth was flat and a sea cruise ended on the horizon with a subsequent fall to hell. They were even afraid of many sailors on the Santa Maria during Christopher Columbus revelatory voyage in 1492 that discovered America.

Frank, intelligent, honest and fair physicists must clearly tell the public and physical community that an understanding of infinity is beyond the current ability of the human spirit and of today's civilization. An experimental possibility for the inspection of the infinity of the macro world is always as inaccessible as infinity itself. It is not in our hands, because the ratio of any range of telescope to infinity is always zero.

In contrast to the inspection of the infinity of the macro world, the situation for the inspection of infinity or finiteness of physical zero (existence or non-existence of smallest particles or fluid quanta of the physical world) of the micro world is not so gloomy and is in our hands. Understanding the essence of the micro world of physical fields (ether) here, directly under our hands, can support our understanding of infinity and of the macro world of the universe.

## 3.3. STR

An entire generation of hundreds of physicists of classical mechanics and electricity and magnetism, at least from Newton until 1905, when most of them after decades with their own hands personally carried out direct experimental observation of the physical world around us, came to the claim of the existence of force fields as real physical substances around the physical body. This claim did not appear after two years of speculation about a single Michelson-Morley's (M-M) experiment behind the table in an office.

Moreover, concerning Michelson-Morley's experiment, we now know (the discovery of composite rotary motion of the earth in a surrounding space, around the Sun as (30 km/s), around the center of the Galaxy (220km/s), to the Group of galaxies 700-1000 km/s) that the basic physical assumptions of the explanation of this experiment were wrong.

The assumption of the Earth's rotation around the sun at the rate of 30km/s, as the only motion of the Earth in space, is not valid. Also invalid, is the assumption of the rectilinear of the motion of one arm and the rectilinear of motion of the second arm of an interferometer toward the surrounding space, that is, the ether. So it is invalid that relation represents time difference of flight through light in perpendicular arms of M-M interferometer.

It is necessary to mention that all the experiments similar to the M-M experiment (yet since time of Fizeau, 1848) in which medium of transmission of light propagation was under the "control" (interferometers embedded or filled with gaseous or liquid medium (e.g. Mach - Zehnder interferometer) confirmed the expected result of time difference of flight through light in two perpendicular directions. In addition, the Sagnac (1913) experiment with a rotating Interferometer in a vacuum also provided the expected results.

In all physics textbooks, the illustrative explanation of the M-M experiment is presented by situations when one boat or swimmer swims a distance across the river perpendicular to the constant stream of flow from one bank of the river to the other, and at the same time a second swimmer swims from the same starting point the same distance along the banks of the river downstream and upstream of the river.

In the case of mutual rotation of the interferometer and the fluid in its surrounding environment, we can present this situation as only the rotation of a fluid. For the illustrative explanation, we can present a situation with a swimmer swimming at a constant speed in a circular pool, rectilinearly from the center of the pool to the edge of the pool and back while the stream of water in this pool, rotates at a constant speed around the center. A swimmer can swim rectilinearly from the center to the edge of the pool and back in two perpendicular directions or in any two directions and his swimming times will always be the same. That means, in the case of mutual rotation of the interferometer and the ether the time of passage of light in perpendicular arms of the interferometer will be the same in any rotation.

It is evident that the M-M experiment was based on false

assumptions and expected the wrong conclusions. We can be convinced that the pertinent null result of the M-M experiment represents proof of the rotating mutual movement of the Interferometer and ether in its surroundings.

Another fundamental consideration about the outcome of the M-M experiment is the view of Fressnel (1818) or Stokes (1844) that the ether is partially or completely dragged by Earth and thus shares its motion at Earth's surface which gets a factual physical image on the basis of the results of this work.

These results show that all smallest elementary particles are spin products of curl compression of ether and their existence inevitably brings existence of force fields (electric, magnetic, gravity) in its surrounding (as well as for their gathering in great mass bodies) as the gradient of ether otherwise uniformly filling space in other parts of the universe. This gradient, firmly fixed with any bodies, is moving through space together with great mass objects as well as the smallest elementary particles. As a result, photons of light as spin products of the electromagnetic curl compression of the ether are slowing down or speeding when moving in this moving gradient.

A hundred years after the inception of the special theory of relativity, we lived to see the speed of material objects of protons equal to almost the speed of light. Protons accelerated in the LHC tunnel at CERN reach 99.9999991% of light speed almost 1c. Two direct beams of protons flying against each other with each at 99.9999991% of the speed of light with mutual speed $1c + 1c = 2c$ collide in a tunnel.

But STR in the equation for composition of velocities $u = (u' + v)/(1 + u'v/c^2) = (c + c)/(1 + cc/c^2) = c$ claims that this mutual speed is in fact $1c + 1c = 1c$.

This is a clear evidence of a distortion of the physical reality in STR but in spite of that it is taught as the reality for hundred years even at secondary schools all over the world.

In the STR beam of protons from which we do measurement stands or better said its own velocity is in STR eliminated, because of his own time dilated to infinity (exactly 55555556 times ) and its own length contracted to zero (55555556 times).

Time dilatation is the most serious forgery of STR. Basic physical relations established by Einstein are already in full contradiction in the issue of time dilation. In relation for the energy of the photon $h\nu = mc^2$ (Planck's idea), the frequency with increasing energy increases

$$\nu = m_o c^2 / h \sqrt{1 - v^2/c^2}$$

so time unit (one tick) shortens, but in STR relation for time dilation $t = t_o / \sqrt{1 - v^2/c^2}$ time unit dilate with increasing energy.

Similarly, in GTR with increasing gravity towards the central source of gravity, so with increasing energy, time unit dilate. Clock moved near a source of gravitational field run more slowly, as its frequency is lower. But in GTR, according to gravitational redshift, the frequency of photons as moved near a source of gravitational field is higher and as moves away is lower.

Relativity introduced the claim that the mutual velocity of bodies moving at any speed and any direction relative to the movement of the light always equals to the speed of light. However, this claim completely excludes any consideration of the possibility of the existence of waves in medium.

This claim completely excludes any construction of Maxwell equations or Lorentz force, cause this construction requires ratio of velocity of the source or of the receiver to the velocity of light v/c. The waves in a medium originate as changes of density of the medium caused by ratio of velocity of the source of this changes against the constant propagation velocity in this medium which is also the carrying medium of this waves.

This claim completely excludes also the phenomenon known as the Doppler shift, as well as the Lienard - Wiechert retarded and advanced potentials. The essence of the Doppler shift is in the varying number of waves of media impact on the receiver, depending on the varying speed and direction of motion of the receiver relative to these waves.

In relativity, albeit from its first principle of the same mutual velocity of receiver and light waves, for an explanation of the Doppler effect the receiver can suddenly move between the two fronts of waves (moving against the receiver always with constant speed) with various speed v + c or v - c. Since, however, must pay c + v = c - v = c this perverse code reincarnates into the mystery of time dilation. As is shown below, time dilation is identical with the change of speed and so for time considerations sick code $1/t_c + 1/t_v = 1/t_c - 1/t_v = 1/t_c$ also is valid.

Moreover, relativity brings various declarations associated with the phenomenon of Doppler shift, which mainly includes a debate on the relativity of the red shift in conjunction with the expansion of the universe.

### 3.4. Essence of time in physics

The physicist who seeks to seriously ponder what represents a quantity of time in physics, may spend any time figuring this, but in the end the man must come up with only a single answer. This answer is the same as Aristotle's that time is the measure of the speed of movement. The same answer attributes to physicist Julian Harbour who, after a 50 year inquiry into what is time in physics, came to the conclusion that *"Time is nothing but a measure of change and time itself does not exist "*.

If there is no movement of objects, no time or velocity exists. It is the only existing change we are unable to assign any time any velocity or any acceleration. For two mutually moving objects we are unable to assign any speed and we need a third comparative calibration of speed in order to do so. Time, velocity and acceleration represent the comparison of the count of speed of one change to another.

Time in contemporary physics is not an arbitrarily chosen variable, which could by itself span, lapse and vary independently of objects. The basic concept of modern physics for the last four hundred years lies in the fact that, by establishing basic units of length and time, at the same time, the basic unit of uniform velocity is defined as the ratio of this unit length and unit time. The calibration values of all fundamental physical constants are based and firmly linked to this basic definition. By this definition the concept of unit time in physics is established as speed of movement on a defined distance in the space, whereas at once the basic calibration comparative value of velocity is defined.

So the unit time and unit velocity are firmly fixed and represent the same in inverse proportionality- basic comparative speed of movement. If a body moves ten times faster than the unit velocity, it then travels ten times more unit length in one unit time or travels one unit length in one-tenth of the unit time. The change of the time unit is the change of the basic comparative unit of velocity.

We can express the velocity identically as the ratio of travelled unit length to the unit time, or the inverse ratio of elapsed unit times to length unit. We do so also in many practical situations. The speed of the runners, e.g. at a distance of hundred meters we express by the ratio of ran-off times. The acceleration of cars we express by the ratio of elapsed times at the fixed distance.

In 1983 (17th CGPM) a length of 1m was defined as length of the path travelled by light in a vacuum in $t_c = 1/299792458$ second. By this definition the ratio of unit velocity, unit length and unit time compared to velocity of light in vacuum was inseparably fixed. The unit of time ,1 second, is the speed of the movement measured on unit length, which in comparison with the speed of light is 299 792 458 times slower.

Basic relation of STR $v/c$ for ratio of velocities can be identically expressed as an inverse relation of times $v/c = t_c/t_v$ where ratio of two velocities or inverse time is compared by third- basic unit velocity or unit time. The unit of time of one second then does not represent the ticking of the clock but the basic comparative speed of movement of the body for comparing other speeds on the length of one meter.

In STR for the comparative speed the speed of light is selected, which is constant in all inertial frames. Light moves on one meter in the system of the observer or on the contracted meter in the moving frames at the same speed and thus a unit of time per 1 second is also established and fixed in all STR inertial frames.

If, by changing the speed of the inertial system, the unit of length contacts in STR as $l = l_o/\sqrt{1-v^2/c^2}$ then to ensure the validity of international SI definition of 1 meter from 1983 and ensure a constant velocity of light in all inertial frames as well as ensure validity of the calibration value of all basic physical constants we must also contract unit time as $t = t_o/\sqrt{1-v^2/c^2}$.

Time dilation $t = t_o\sqrt{1-v^2/c^2}$ fixed firmly with length contraction $l = l_o/\sqrt{1-v^2/c^2}$ in accordance with STR leads to the disintegration of the calibration value of all basic physical constants.

So if unit time in STR changes as $\sqrt{1-v^2/c^2} = t_o/t_c$ than basic comparative unit of velocity change as $\sqrt{1-v^2/c^2} = t_o/t_c = v_c/v_o$. So if STR claims that in STR time dilates then also the basic comparative unit of speed as well as speed of light in inertial frames with increasing speed is slowing down ( for speed of light is also valid 1c+1c=1c) so also dilates.

So for keeping constant speed of light in any inertial frames any ratio of changed lengths and changed times must be always constant in any inertial frames. If length 1m contracts to half meter so in order the speed of light remains constant the ratio of unit length and unit time must remain the same and 1 second has also be contracted to half second. If STR claims that when length 1m contracts to half meter then 1 second dilate to 2 second then the speed of light falls to one quarter. In fact, but in STR basic comparative speed unit has four times changed.

## 4. The main historical and physical flaws of Quantum mechanics and quantum physics from an overall view

The principle of least-action is the central principle of QM. In least-action, the variational principle introduced by Maupertuis in 1747 is used to find the shortest path or 'least time' to obtain the equations of motion for that system. In the principle of least-action, the physical cause or any material physical phenomena responsible for movement of bodies are suspended. This principle becomes more and more a central principle of today's physics to derive the QM and Relativity equations (and even the equations of classical physics).

In 1746 Maupertuis wrote the work - Derivation of the laws of motion and equilibrium from a metaphysical principle - with two head chapters - I. Assessment of the Proofs of God's Existence that are Based on the Marvels of Nature, II. Need to Identify Proofs of God's Existence in the General Laws of Nature.

Let we recall the E. Mach judgment on this principle [31] in 1919. *"Maupertuis, in 1747, announced a principle that he called the principle of least-action. He declared this principle to be the one that eminently accorded with the wisdom of the Creator. He took as the measure of the "action" the product of the mass, velocity, and space described, or mvs. Why, it must be confessed, is not clear. By mass and velocity definite quantities may be understood; not so, however, by space, when the time is not stated in which the space is described. If, however, a unit of time be meant, the distinction of space and velocity in the examples treated by Maupertuis are, to say the least, peculiar. It appears that Maupertuis reached this obscure expression by an unclear mingling of his ideas of vis viva and the principle of virtual velocities.It will thus be seen that*

*Maupertuis really had no principle, properly speaking, but only a vague formula that was forced to do duty as the expression of different familiar phenomena and not really brought under one conception It would seem almost as if something of the pious faith of the church had crept into mechanics".*

(Since this paper is written not only for physicists, active in the topic of QM but also for the wider physical community or non-physicists, the equations in this section are written not in their full rigorous mathematical form but rather as equations in their most simplified form manifesting their physical concepts to the general public.)

If we seek to evaluate a chapter of physics called quantum mechanics (QM), we must indicate what QM is. Quantum mechanics is a procedure that attempts to describe the motion or motion-states of fundamental particles of matter (primary electrons) in mainly two situations - a central force field in the vicinity of different atoms and in free movement without the action of external forces.

In the case of the motion of the electron in the central field of the protons for the hydrogen atom (two-body problem), physics (now called classical physics) satisfactorily provided (in the presented relationship of Bohr and in the first presented relationship of Schrödinger) an explanation for the amount of energy needed to be added or removed from electrons (the spectral lines of hydrogen) for the occurrence of electron at different distances from the center of the proton.

Today we can treat electron in atoms as the spin of sphere shell field with corresponding thickness where quantization means that two shells cannot naturally concur or 'occupy' the same space of a shared shell.

Subsequently, in other cases than the hydrogen atom, it would necessarily have been stated that the force fields around the nuclei of atoms composed of a large number of nucleons have a complex character (and so also their spectra as the energy states of electrons). Also, in classical physics, we can't even satisfactorily solve the three-body problem analytically. Moreover, as was learned later (after 1930), nucleons in nuclei at least spin, if not spin at shells and, in addition, the composition of the atomic nuclei from protons and neutrons was not known by 1932.

From a global perspective, quantum mechanics can be characterized by two fundamental distortions.

The first is the deformation resulting from the impermissibility of refusal or even opposition to Einstein's linear relationship for energy, with frequency of the photon after which energy matches photon momentum. The impermissibility of this refusal is overcome in QM by introducing a mysterious de Broglie's wave-length of matter and Schrödinger's wave function.

Secondly, it is a deformation resulting from the impermissibility of refusal of Einstein's claim about the absence of ether and the inevitability of its repeated introduction in quantum mechanics in the concept of the energy of vacuum by providing it the physical properties equivalent to ether in electrodynamics.

Schrödinger started [20] from a basic physical supposition - *"The wave-function physically means and determines a continuous distribution of electricity in space, the fluctuation of which determines the radiation by the laws of ordinary electrodynamics. In the case of the hydrogen atom, it has been possible to compute fairly correct values for the intensities e.g. of the Stark effect components by the following hypothesis: the charge of the electron is not concentrated in a point, but is spread out through the entire space proportional to the quantity $\psi\bar{\psi}$. The fluctuation of the charge will be governed by $(\psi\bar{\psi})$ applied to the special case of the hydrogen. To find the radiation, that by ordinary electrodynamics will originate from these fluctuating charges, we have simply to calculate the rectangular components of the total electrical moment integrating $(\psi\bar{\psi})$ over the space".*

For the Atomic Spectra of elements other than the hydrogen atom with the larger number of nucleons in the nucleus of an atom, Schrödinger's procedure failed to provide a satisfactory value. Instead of considering that the electromagnetic field around atomic nuclei other than hydrogen atoms are complex and hitherto unknown (eke unknown spin 1930 and neutron 1932), during the formation of quantum mechanics 1924 -1930 continued the hunt for provisions of mathematical constructions describing the spectra of atoms.

In fact, the spectra of atoms show us how the electromagnetic fields, gradient of ether, around nuclei of these atoms look and so the most physically natural approach would have been in an effort to model this field by the laws of ordinary electrodynamics.

But ether was slain and banned by special relativity and gotten rid of by general relativity, where force fields turned into the curvature of non-material quantities of space and time. Schrödinger's good-will for mathematical structure associated with specific physical realities was dismissed (shortly also by Schrödinger). Theorists Born, Heisenberg, Jordan, Hilbert, Wiener, Pauli, Eckart, Kramers, Dirac, Sommerfield, Weyl, Neumann and Wigner bred fictive, bizarre mathematical structures which combined the physical unknown go-as you-please quantities, variables and parameters.

Conceptions such as operators, matrices, extra matrices and continuous matrices, commutators and anti-commutators, approximation, group methods and symmetries, frequencies, wave lengths, wave functions, relativistic and non- relativistic corrections, delta functions and coupling constants were incorporate in various -statistical, probabilistic, uncertainty, energetic, time, momentum- interpretations of quantum mechanics.

These go-as-you-please quantities, variables and parameters have mostly no connection to physical reality and so, to this day, no one understands quantum mechanics and nobody knows how the particle moves in a force field described by quantum mechanics.

Noteworthy is the Dirac attempt to link his theory with

physical reality, which arrived with the statement (known as the Dirac sea) that the whole universe is filled with anti-electrons.

In 1927 Ehrenfest in his theorem linked the classical and quantum pictures without approximations at declaration that the expectation of quantum mechanics is equal to the expectation value of the negative gradient of the potential function equivalent to Newton's second law of motion.

The beginning of the formation of wave and quantum mechanics mainly connects with the names of de Broglie and Schrödinger. In the case of de Broglie, although Einstein was not head of the de Broglie doctoral thesis (major work of de Broglie), Einstein led de Broglie through the steps of his work. De Broglie final version of his doctoral work was even sent to Einstein for approval. Without this approval, the defense would not have been accepted. In the case of Schrödinger, his written thanks to Einstein, which states that the formation of his equation would not be possible without the decisive contribution provided him by Einstein speaks for itself.

Einstein's equations for photon energy $E = h\nu$ and photon momentum $p = h/\lambda$ from which arise relation $E = h\nu = hc/\lambda = pc$ are primary physical relations in physics until today. These relations are the primary physical relationships that caused the degeneration of the physics of the 20 century [30], [11]. In 1900, Planck in accordance with at that time still valid scientific principles, carefully declared that photon energy can be considered proportional to frequency of a photon $E \approx h\nu$. Einstein, without any experimental evidence, in 1904 made a 'big scientific discovery' when he simply declared $E = h\nu$ and based STR on it.

For confirmation of this 'discovery', Millikan carried out the experiment in 1914. With all respect to the greatness of Millikan's physical experimental skills, he succumbed to the pressure of the power structures and agreed with their interpretations concerning the validity of the linear relationship of energy on the frequency of a photon in his experiment. This agreement by Millikan was a condition of the Nobel Committee for the award of the Nobel Prize to Einstein in 1921 for the photoelectric effect. In 1921 he became director of the laboratory at CalTech and won the Nobel Prize in 1923.

Opposition to these relationships was (and still is) not permissible. So de Broglie or Schrödinger introduced mystical physical non evincible quantity (dimensionless point particles connected with wavelength in infinity or wave function) employed through obscure operators in constructed robust mathematical theories, so that using them could accommodate experimental data and at the same time keep Einstein's relations valid. From the physical point of view these theories are, even for top specialists, beyond all understanding.

Feynman (the Nobel Prize laureate for quantum physics! 1966): *"I think I can safely say that nobody understands quantum mechanics"*. *"We have always had a great deal of difficulty understanding the world view that quantum mechanics represents (1965)"*.

Einstein's degeneration of the relation of physical quantities of momentum and energy for photons and, as was also shown in [30] for mass bodies, has become the default physical premise of the theory of special relativity and quantum mechanics, linking these physical quantities $E = pc = (h/\lambda)c = mvc$ which then differs only by the constant $c$. For relation of photon energy $E = h\nu$, (that in the form of differences of energies at photoelectric effect was awarded by the Nobel Prize), however, neither Einstein nor physics up to today has told us what physical reality represents the Planck constant itself (action of what it is ) and what is the frequency of a photon or what the physical properties of the photon we have to the frequency of the photon assignee [30], [11].

The frequency of a photon cannot in any way be measured. We can measure the wavelength of the photon and, in relation $\nu = c/\lambda$ tie the photon wavelength to its unknown physical quantity frequency. Then for Einstein's explanation of photoelectric effect the difference in momentums in fact primitively explains this effect.

De Broglie (1924) extended this deformation with the dispersion relationship of frequency and wavelength for material particles at the group velocity relation $w = \Delta\lambda\Delta\nu$ . But these fictitious mathematical construction of frequency and wavelength can't anyhow be experimentally measured. Nobody up to today knows what physical properties represent the frequency of particles and don't even know what is the wavelength (defined in infinity) of these particles.

The principle of de Broglie's construction of wave of matter for particles or macroscopic body moving at velocity v in relation $mv = h/\lambda$ is physically wrong, because the movement of one body we can consider as the movement of more parts of this body together or as several smaller bodies bound to each other. Wave function of the macroscopic body as a whole has microscopic value, but each of its divided smaller parts has wave functions growing to infinity.

In our previous paper [30], [11] it was shown that the Planck constant must be bind with basic flat density and pressure of ether in void space. Subsequently, in relation $h/\lambda = mc$ wavelength $\lambda$ constitutes the dimension of curl compression of the photon momentum, as well as a dimension of localization of spinning internal momentum of rigid elementary particles at rest.

Thus the correct de Broglie consideration about moving rigid particles at velocity v (in comparison to basic calibration 'rest' state) represents [30], [11] the relation $h/\lambda - h/\lambda_o = mc - m_oc = mcv/c = mv = p$ constituting the responding contraction of each of the primary construction particles of macroscopic bodies. This contraction is a result of a change of pressure of the force fields surrounding particles (gradient of ether freely pervading interstices in matter and inseparable joined with particles of matter which are spin products of ether) on the surface of those particles, due to the change of velocity. Its consequence is a contraction of the macroscopic body as a whole.

In the case of the classic experiment of QM, electron microscope, instead of assign to the dimensionless point electron obscure wave function $\lambda$ in fact $\lambda$ constitutes the dimension of localization of electron. The greater is the velocity of electron so much greater is its energy what equals to the shorter dimension of electron localization $\lambda$.

Although Compton up to 1923 during 20 years of his experiments on the collision of photons with matter used for photon momentum the relation $p = h\nu/c = h/\lambda$ and for photon energy the relation $E = h^2\nu^2/c^2 = h^2/\lambda^2$, Schrödinger in 1926 arrived with another of the greatest achievements in the history of mankind in his equation $\Delta E = h\Delta\nu = hc/\Delta\lambda = \psi h^2/\Delta\lambda^2$ (1933 Nobel Prize). Up to today nobody has yet told us what is the wave function $\psi$ (as well what is frequency or Planck constant) and to what physical properties it belongs.

To date there are no universally accepted derivations of Schrödinger's equation from appropriate axioms just like of Einstein's energy equation $E = mc^2$.

In 1926 the so called relativistic Schrödinger equation in a Klein-Gordon (K-G) form equation (falling short of a Nobel prize award) was presented as

$$\hbar^2\nu^2/(m_o^2c^2)c^2 - \hbar^2/(m_o^2c^2)\lambda^2 = -\psi/\psi$$

, from which follows [30], [11] that energy equals

$$E = h^2\nu^2/c^2 = h^2/\lambda^2 = m^2c^2$$

. So the correct writing of Schrödinger equation is

$$E = h^2\Delta\nu^2/c^2 = h^2/\Delta\lambda^2$$

and no wave function $\psi$ is needed. Subsequently, in 1928 Dirac (1933 Nobel prize) presented equation

$$\hbar\nu/(m_oc)c - \hbar/(m_oc)\lambda = -\psi/\psi$$

, in which nobody up today knows what physical properties represents the frequency $\nu$ of particles, what physical properties represents the wavelength $\lambda$ (defined in infinity), what is the wave function $\psi$ or to what physical properties it belongs, what represents the Planck constant itself or action of what it is. From Dirac's equation it follows [30] that momentums $p = h\nu/c = h/\lambda = mc$ equal so he at last allegedly reached (of course in advance dictated) the first quantum mechanics theory that fully accounts for special relativity. Cultish equations for energy of photons $E = h\nu = (h\nu/c) \times c = pc$ and energy of particles

$$E = mc^2 = (mc)c$$

or

$$E_k = (mc)c - (m_oc)c = mvc = pc$$

glorified not by physicist but by mass media in which Einstein simply purposefully multiplied momentums by c

together with parallel cultish Schrödinger equation $\Delta E = h\Delta\nu = hc/\Delta\lambda = \psi h^2/2m_o\Delta\lambda^2$ were not rejected from physics to this day.

In our previous paper [30], [11] it was shown that, in fact wavelength $\lambda$ represents the diameter of real dimensions of photons and particles as spin products of spherical curl compression of ether. Frequency $\nu$ represents the time of the light's flight through this diameter $\lambda$ of photons and particles. Thus consequently, since a photon is an entity in quantum mechanics as well in Maxwell's electrodynamics, we receive for photon the same physical base in both theories as

$$\partial^2\varepsilon/\partial t^2 = \frac{1}{\varepsilon_o\mu_o}\partial^2\varepsilon/\partial r^2 = c^2\partial^2\varepsilon/\partial r^2$$

so

$$\varepsilon^2/c^2dt^2 = \varepsilon^2 dv^2/c^2 = h^2 dv^2/c^2 =$$
$$\varepsilon^2/dr^2 = h^2/d\lambda^2 = dm^2c^2$$

and from the Pointing vector in electrodynamics, from Compton's works as well from the right hand side of Schrödinger equation we know that this writing represents writing for energy. So energy of photon is proportional to energy $E \approx h\nu$ but in proportionality$E \approx h^2\nu^2 \approx h^2/\lambda^2 \approx p^2$.

If we look into any experimental paper or textbooks in the field of particle physics [21] we find that relations

$$p \cdot p = m^2v^2 = E^2/c^2 = \gamma^2 m_o^2c^2$$

and

$$p = mv = E/c = mc^2/c = \gamma m_oc$$

are valid relations for the actual physical phenomena.

With respect to momentum of photon $p = h/\lambda = h\nu/c$ Einstein's relations for energy of particles $E = mc^2$ as well as for photon $E = h\nu$ do not represent energy, but momentum intentionally multiplied by c. Energy of particles for reliance on velocity equal $E = m^2c^2 = \gamma^2 m_o^2c^2$. So also energy in relativistic mechanics represents relations

$$m^2c^2 = m_o^2c^2 + m^2c^2v^2/c^2$$
$$m^2c^2 - m_o^2c^2 = m^2c^2v^2/c^2$$

as equivalent relations to Klein-Gordon (K-G) equation or to the right hand side of the Schrodinger equation. So we receive the unified physical base for unification of classical mechanics, relativistic mechanics, quantum mechanics and classical electrodynamics in kinetic (added) energy as

$$E_k[2m_0] = p^2 = m^2v^2 = \gamma^2 m_o^2c^2 \cdot v^2/c^2 =$$
$$h^2/d\lambda^2 = h^2 dv^2/c^2 = \varepsilon^2/c^2dt^2 = \varepsilon^2/dr^2$$

. This unification has to be done for kinetic energy because classical and quantum mechanics does not know the concept of rest energy for free particle. These energies represents the amount of cumulative forces embedded into particles caused by change the speed v of particles or of bodies or by change the volume dr of particles, or energy embedded into ether at creation of photon of diameter of d$\lambda$ or dr

$$p = mv = \gamma mcv/c = h/d\lambda = hdv/c = \varepsilon/cdt = \varepsilon/dr$$

We often hear the argument that the justness of application of quantum mechanics lies in the great accuracy of its math calculations. But in fact, the quantum mechanics so as was the Ptolemay epicycles is a procedure for finding of mathematical construction to the existing experimental data which this mathematics has to arrive at. We can always find the mathematical relationships that describe experimental data or, if not, we can construct a new mathematics to describe the experimental data. But finding such mathematical constructions (theories) do not confirm the veracity of the basic physical principles (models) upon which these construction are based.

### 4.1. The Double-slit experiment and Casimir effect

The double-slit experiment is another in a row of experiments for which explanation of the physics of 20th century simply selects the most miraculous explanation. In 1801 a simpler form of the double-slit experiment was originally performed by Thomas Young. The double-slit experiment has later become a classic thought experiment, allegedly for its clarity in expressing the central puzzles of quantum mechanics.

In this experiment, the experimental data is accommodated by physically obscure and mysterious wave functions based on the mathematics of quantum mechanics theory. From this theory follows the mystery that particles or bodies can split and occur at two separate places simultaneously or the mystery that two particles separated by arbitrarily large distances can mutually communicate and transfer information with infinite velocity (the so called entanglement).

These mysterious explanations have subsequently for a hundred years been accepted by the power structures and mass information media, forcing to public as well as the wider physics community to accept them as the only possible explanation, although more simple, wise and feasibly reasonable physical explanation exist.

The primary physical condition of the double-slit experiment is that the sizes of two slits are equal to, or closer in size to the light's or electron's wavelength. If the slit's width enlarges (compared to the light's or electron's wavelength), the constructive interference picture becomes more and more unnoticeable.

In basic quantum mechanics textbooks, as well as in hundreds of papers and documentary films showing the alleged difference between the behavior of the classical objects and the mysterious behavior of quantum particles of matter, it is presented using the thought experiment, in which tennis or golf balls on a plate with two parallel slits are fired. The resulting image of two lines, where these balls supposedly fall is presented and is compared with the many lines interference image that arises when the beam of light or electrons passes through plate with double-slit.

But our physical thinking concerning the double-slit experiment must begin from the experimental knowledge of optics (since Newton) that light curves when passing closely around the edge of any object that we have at hand.

And so it is with the electron beam. Physical answer, why the electron path is curved passing at close proximity to the edge and path of a golf ball not, is simple. The gravitational forces (identical with magnetic forces) at close distances (comparable to electron wave length - dimension of electron) around the material edges has sufficient power to cause the curvature of the electron's path, but have absolutely no chance to influence the path of a billion times billion heavier and greater (the most part of a golf ball is very far in this gravity field) golf balls.

We can simply say, that the forces by which are bound the surface layer of atoms of the edges to the layer of atoms underneath roughly equal to the forces in vicinity of edges at the distance approaching the size of atom so approaching the wavelength of light's or electron's dimension (wavelength).

The result of this influence of the large size of the gravitational forces on the microscopic quantum objects are curved paths in close proximity to the atoms of the surface of the material. This is then observed as the interference picture in the double-slit experiment.

In quantum mechanics, however, this natural difference between the behavior of macroscopic and microscopic objects, demonstrated by the double-slit thought experiment, becomes the basis for claims concerning the mysterious and beyond all understanding behavior of quantum particles. It allegedly is completely incompatible with the concepts of classical physics.

Johannes van der Waals (Nobel Prize in 1910) studied for decades, both experimentally and theoretically, the existence of mutual forces between the molecules and atoms of substances emerging as an averaging remnant (magnetic field) at their random thermal rotating movement of their thus rotating dipole and multipole electrostatic fields. The thermal averaging effect is much less pronounced for the attractive induction. Van der Waals also used the Greek letter $\psi$ for the free energy of a system with different phases in equilibrium at critical temperatures, describing the phenomena of condensation.

The Casimir effect is an experiment of the same nature as the double-slit experiment. The Casimir effect shows that the infinitesimal (non-measurable) forces of a small number of atoms of a material applied to macroscopic objects (golf balls) moving in the vicinity of these atoms (as is the case with double-slit experiment) may become an observable and measurable effect even for macroscopic objects if the number of interacting atoms increases many orders of magnitude, as it is in the case of the Casimir effect. A typical example is two uncharged neutral finite plates in a vacuum, placed a few nanometers apart at a distance comparable with the size of atoms.

As was shown in our previous paper, at such small distances in classical descriptions, the gravitational forces (identical with magnetic forces) manifest themselves to a non-negligible extent.

But we can simply say, that the forces by which are bound the surface layer of atoms of the plates to the layer of atoms underneath roughly equal to the forces between plates if the distance between plates is approaching the size of atom.

A distorted physical premise was the basis of H. Casimir that, in a classical description, there is no field between the plates and so no force would be measured between them.

Casimir formulated the theory in 1948 predicting a force (Casimir - Polder force) between these plates on the mysterious claim that this force has nothing common with plates and they exclusively flow from outside pressure of the vacuum, because not all wave lengths of simple harmonic oscillators of vacuums can fit between plates. According to the second quantization of quantum field theory, space is filled with zero vacuum point energy, containing an infinite quantity of oscillators of all possible energy values and wavelengths.

It is remarkable that, in quantum field theory, excitations of the field correspond to the elementary particles of particle physics. This is fully in contradiction with the Higgs boson theory that all particles in the universe have obtained their mass from Higgs bosons soon after the Big Bang.

Surprisingly, in the last decade mainstream physics came to state that Casimir effects can be formulated and Casimir forces can be computed without reference to zero-point energies. The Casimir force is simply the (relativistic, retarded) van der Waals force between the metal plates [22] *"They are relativistic, quantum forces between charges and currents. Thus it can be interpreted without any reference to the zero-point energy (vacuum energy) of quantum fields"*.

## 5. Man's ability to perceive the physical reality of his surrounding world

Exploring the rest of the world by man over the course of the last two hundred years shifts the world from what he can see with his own eyes, to the world of what cannot be seen with his own eyes. Man discovered that the functioning of the macro world of animate and inanimate nature, visible to him, is based on the functioning of an invisible micro world of cells, molecules, atoms, protons, electrons, and photons. He discovered that outside the cosmos of stars and nebulas visible to him with his own eyes there exists a space of galaxies and other structures in the universe.

If a physicist today sees a steel sphere about 1 kg in weight lying still on the table, he knows that inside, this ball is unimaginably "live". In this sphere of billions of movements and physical processes exist what physics is unable to grasp even at the level of atoms, or able to grasp only a small part of them.

Today we know that in this sphere there are a billion times billion the basic (roughly $10^{26}$) construction elements of this sphere-atoms of iron. These atoms are vibrating in their equilibrium positions, emitting thermal infrared radiation and electromagnetic fields. In its vicinity tremendous gravitational and magnetic forces act (if gravity and magnetic force are not identical powers). Even greater electric power is located in each interior of these atoms of iron, where 26 electrons as force fields swirl in all various directions in 26 shells around the nuclei of these atoms. In each interior of these nuclei 26 protons and 26 neutrons most likely swirl in all various directions in force field shells. In each interior of these 26 protons and 26 neutrons swirl force fields as unknown number alleged gluons and alleged 3 quarks.

Physicists till 1919 had not even the slightest knowledge of this structure of atoms.

Also "live" is the vicinity of this steel ball. Today we know that in every surrounding cubic meter of space surrounding us (anywhere in the universe) there are more than a billion times a billion photons of electromagnetic radiation, at least a billion neutrinos, one hundred million photons of relict radiation and hundreds of hard actual particles of matter - protons.

When looking at this steel ball from a distance of 1 meter, a physicist knows that (in line with his perspective) around 100 million atoms of air occur on this line. These atoms of air we don't see and we are not able to grab in our hands. When waving our hands in the air, we can sense the pressure of air resistance on our hands, evidencing the existence of fluid around us, in which we are plunged. This fluid air presses on the surface of our bodies with a force of around 15,000 kg and we do not feel this pressure if we find ourselves at rest in the air.

Convincing the general public of the veracity of the existence of this huge pressure required considerable effort from physicists. We recall the famous experiment of German scientist Otto von Guericke's in 1654 in which, after pumping air from the space of two half-meter hemispheres of iron, freely attached to each other via a seal, 8 pair of horses drawing ropes fixed to each hemisphere (a total of 32 horses) were unable to pull these hemispheres apart.

If the part of the air around us in a room is accidentally lit by the rays of the Sun we'll see a huge amount of dust in the air around us. We only see dust particles larger than roughly the size of 1 micrometer, so we see just particles containing more than one million times a million atoms. We can capture these aerosol particles by filters of nanometer size.

From the total amount of the entire electromagnetic spectrum of photons (wavelengths in range of more than 15 orders of magnitude from hundreds meter to $10^{-15}m$) which occur around us we can see only a tiny portion of less than one fiftieth of the whole spectrum (wavelengths in range less than one order of magnitude from 0.2 to 0.7 micrometers).

For creation of the optic perception in the eye the continuous stream of photons must last at least 1/16 of a second from one place. As the action of one photon with wavelength around 0.5 micrometers lasts $10^{-15}s$ we fail to see streams of photons of less than a million times a million. Therefore we don't see the spokes of a rotating bicycle or car wheel.

If, at a distance of 1 meter, a 1 cm thick and perfectly transparent glass sheet is placed before this steel ball, nearly 100 million atoms of glass will stand between, the existence of which our eyes provide no information. The existence of this sheet we learn only by its feel when we move our hand against it. Similarly, we hardly see living beings, such as transparent jellyfish, in the sea or stranded on the beach. We fail to see billions of viruses, bacteria and protozoa around us.

From the photons around us we see almost nothing or, we see just the photons that are important for our life.

## 6. An overview of the opposition of physicists for past hundred years against the deformed physical image of the world forced by power structures upon the public

The history of mankind traces the fact that the more centralized the power structures of human society, the more the physical picture of the world and the freedom of human thought is under the control of these structures. During that period in time (100 - 1600) when Ptolemy's geocentric mathematical description of the universe was under the supervision of the ruling power structures as an untouchable truth for 1500 years, is today described as a dark period in the history of mankind. Those were times when man was hindered in his progress in exploring the real physical picture of the surrounding world. The normal development of the physical sciences was stopped in its tracks for over 1500 years.

Next mainly the period within 16th and 18th century is a clear example of a conspiracy of the power structures against the physical reality of the image of the world. In this period physicists again discovered the discoveries of ancient Greek thinkers. The books of the most outstanding physicists (including Newton, Galilleo, Tycho Brahe, Kepler and Copernicus) of this period (till 1835) were declared heretical and banned on Index Librorum Prohibitorum which was abolished not until 1966. Bann also involved the restrictions on printing this books in Europe. Most Greek science other than Aristotle's was banned. Up to 1758 all books that supported heliocentrism were banned. Violation of this ban could lead to the death penalty. Not until 1992 was the Inquisition against Galileo repealed and was admitted that the heliocentric approach in physics was correct.

In the 20th century, a crusade of the power structures against the actual reality of the physical world around us continues.

The experimental results of the research of whole generations of hundreds and hundreds of outstanding physicists in the field of mechanics (from Galileo and Newton to Mach) celestial mechanics (from Galileo to Hubble), electricity and magnetism (from Volta to Tesla) are in substantial parts again rejected in the 20th century and replaced by mystical theories of non-material mathematical structures of several theoretical physicists in the 20th century.

There are no unequivocal physical evidences for the mathematical construction of these theories such as special and general relativity, quantum mechanics, force fields theories using force-mediating particles, the standard model of quark theory, the Big Bang and the Higgs boson theories. These theories are based on mysterious claims of light velocity, of space time curvature, of non-existing of simultaneity contra existence of simultaneous body presences everywhere in the universe, of wave functions of bodies in infinity, of the invalidity of the law of conservation of energy.

After the Edington's British expedition on Principe Island for the purpose of the observation a light bend of stars near the Sun at the Eclipse of the Sun in 1919, the greater part of mainstream physicists by intervening tried to prevent the publishing of Edington's articles. In spite of intervention bombastic subtitles upcoming in most mass journals, mainly in the UK and Germany glorified relativity heavenward.

After this unsuccessful intervention, in 1920 the most respected physics of world, including W. Vien, P. Lenard, Sommerfeld, Nernst, Weyland, Debye and the Rubens based Union of German Natural Scientists organized a putsch in the Nauhaim Conference congress in 1920. Sommerfeld was the President of the German physical society in 1919-1920 and from 1917 until his death in 1951 he was each year proposed for Nobel prize. Lenard was laureate of the Nobel Prize in 1905.

The content of the putsch was *"Einstein as a plagiarist; Anybody who supports the relativity theory is a propagandist; the theory itself was Dadaist (this word was actually uttered!)"*.

*"Einstein's relativity principle could only achieve general validity by dreaming up suitable fields. The abolition of the eather was announced in Nauheim. Nobody laughed. I do not know if it would have been otherwise if the abolition of air had been announced"* Lenard retorted at one point [23, p. 239].

Stark, in the English journal Nature declared, *"The relativistic theories of Einstein constitute an obvious example of the dogmatic spirit,"* and he announced, *"I have directed my efforts against the damaging influence of Jews in German science, because I regard them as the chief exponents and propagandists of the dogmatic spirit."*

Ernst Rutherford declared that the theory of relativity of Einstein, quite apart from its validity, cannot but be regarded as a magnificent work of art.

E. Gehrcke thought that relativity was a fraud and that its acceptance by the public was a case of mass suggestion.

P. Weyland believed that Einstein's theories had been excessively promoted in the Berlin press, which he imagined was dominated by Jews who were sympathetic to Einstein's cause for other than scientific reasons.

In a memorable confrontation at the first Solvay Conference in 1911, Poincare asked Einstein, *"What mechanics are you using in your reasoning?"* and Einstein replied, *"No mechanics,"* which left Poincare speechless. All that Einstein's formulation of relativity says by way of an explanation of length contraction and time dilation is that these phenomena are required to keep the speed of light constant. This failure of Einstein's theory to provide physical explanations for several of its basic assertions was what had led Sommerfeld to complain, with some justification, about "unvisualizable dogmatics" and "the conceptually abstract style of Semites".

Relativity, contrary to standard physics, does not explain the physical phenomena in nature but prescripts, without any explanation of how this phenomena must be.

The attention needed applies mainly to the work executed by Michelson [24] in the Michelson-Gale experiment (1925). A massive interferometer experiment, spread over fifty acres outside of Chicago, detected a fringe shift of 0.236 of one fringe due to the Earth's rotation. This was in agreement with ether theory and within the limits of observational error.

Also outstanding is Dayton Miller's 1933 paper in the Reviews of Modern Physics that details the positive results from over 20 years of experimental research into the question of ether-drift. It remains the most definitive body of work on the subject of light-beam interferometry. Miller's conclusion already in 1925 was *"The effect (of ether-drift) has persisted throughout. After considering all the possible sources of error, there always remained a positive effect."*

Einstein's reply to Millers conclusion was *"My opinion about Miller's experiments is the following. Should the positive result be confirmed, then the special theory of relativity and with it the general theory of relativity, in its current form, would be invalid. Experimentum summus judex. Only the equivalence of inertia and gravitation would remain, however, they would have to lead to a significantly different theory."* [25].

The procedure, under which Einstein first created the theory and then tried in experiment demonstrate the validity of his theory, was typical for him and is typical for all main theories of the 20th century. If theories had heretofore represented a second step for the possible explanation of the experiment carried out in the first step theories of the 20th century are produced in first step by theoretical physicists, in second step they look for experiments that explain these theories.

If the experiment was not in accordance with his theory, Einstein acted fully in accordance with the dictum which he proclaimed that if an experiment does not fit the theory, it is needed to change the experiment. This was the case in his proposed experiment (1915), gyromagnetic ratio, in which the value 1 should be measured by his theory.

Einstein himself, in carrying out the experiment measured values of 1.02 and 1.45, but in translation for the Physical society he reported 1.02 and discarded 1.45. Although experiments of other physicist during the next six years showed beyond a reasonable doubt that the correct value is 2, Einstein stubbornly insisted on his 1.02 value [26, p. 311].

Since the establishment of special and general relativity, quantum mechanics, force fields theories using force-mediating particles, the Big Bang and the Higgs boson theories to the present, hundreds of physicists and many associations of physicists around the world show fatal errors in these works and controversies concerning these theories.

A good overview of the physicists and the Association of physicists, though not complete, can be found in the publication of 10-year long project [27], completed in 2006: G.O. Mueller- 95 Years of Criticism of the Special Theory of Relativity involving 3789 publications criticizing the theory.

The message of the project to the German public is:

*Since 1922 the criticism is suppressed, the critics are calumniated, the public is told lies about the scientific value of the theory of special relativity. In 1922 the physics community, as part of the greater science community, has broken away from the tradition of search for the truth, a rupture of the tradition - as far as we know - never before committed by a whole branch of science and with the knowledge and support of the greater scientific community.*

*We are confronted with the great mystery of modern physics:*

*(1) Why has the rupture of the tradition been tolerated by the whole "scientific community"?*

*(2) Why has it not been detected by the public?*

*(3) How can the academic physicists hope to continue forever with-out one day being called to account for their acting?*

*(4) What are the motives of the academic physicists?*

*During several years of research concerning the criticism of special relativity, we found the following answers.*

*(1) The public in Germany has been cheated since 1922 and is cheated by the influential scientific community until today. Academic physics exert strong pressure on newspapers, journals, publishers and congresses not to accept any criticism of special relativity for publishing. Critical papers are suppressed, critical persons are excluded from any participation in the scientific dialogue.*

*(2) The academic physicists believe that nobody can expose the truth about their actions to the public because the public would never dare to doubt the integrity of these scientists because of the great achievements of natural science in the last centuries, and that the general public will always trust the physics establishment more than any critics.*

*(3) The motives of the physics establishment are subject of several speculations. Probably the strongest motive is that physicists are thankful for a theory that "does not*

*need the ether". This was the position expressed in Einstein's paper of 1905. But only 15 years later, in 1920 in a conference held in Leiden he discovered the need of an ether. The relativists were not amused about this conference of their master. This change of idea in 1920 should have led, as a logical consequence, to a revision of special relativity, which, however, has not taken place until today. This remarkable fact of non-revision seems to be a strong argument that the ether may be at least one fundamental motive.*

*About 1914, special relativity had already been directly refuted by several experiments and indirectly by the absence of experimental confirmation. The Michelson-Morley-Experiment and its repetitions have had positive results, in complete contrast to the relativist's propaganda until today of an alleged null-result: these experiments have found velocities of the Earth of about 6 km/sec (1887), 10 km/sec (1902), 7,5 km/sec (1904) and 8,7 km/sec (1905), In 1913 Sagnac, with his rotating interferometer, also found moving fringes, the rate of motion of the fringes depending on the rate of rotation of his instrument. On the other hand, there were no experimental confirmations for the pretended length contraction and time dilatation. This desperate experimental state of affairs before World War I has never been recognized by the relativist textbooks.*

*The apparent great success of relativity came with observations of the Sun's eclipse in 1919 which were said to have confirmed the general theory of relativity. This supposed result was immediately rejected by several important critics in different countries as misleading the public (for instance: A. Fowler, Sir Joseph Larmor, Sir Oliver J. Lodge, H. F. Newall, Ludwik Silberstein in England; T. J. J. See in the USA; Ernst Gehrcke, Philipp Lenard in Germany). - But the relativists informed the printed media of that time about the greatest achievement of mankind! The public opinion was made enthusiastic about "Relativity" and was told that now both theories, the special and the general relativity, were undisputable truths and nothing less than a revolution of our thinking about space and time and gravitation.*

*In Germany critical authors are strictly outlawed since 1922 by academic physics and therefore unite the critical arguments against both relativities in a booklet titled "Hundert Autoren gegen Einstein"[A Hundred authors against Einstein] published in 1931, protesting against the "terror of the Einsteinians";*

*The critical reader comes to the conclusion that special relativity is an unreasonable theory propagated to the public in academic and high school teaching to be the greatest achievement, together with suppression of any criticism.*

*"Relativity" as a whole and especially "Special Relativity" as the first of two theories, are hailed by academic physics and their propagandists as one of the greatest achievements of mankind in the 20th century, as announced to humanity by the "new Kepler-Galilei-*

*Newton" and the like, revolutionizing our ideas of space and time. This picture of magnificence and glory can hardly be outdone. The normally suspicious and critical reader of relativity textbooks and the original papers of Albert Einstein very soon find many points of the theory questionable and is irritated that no relativist author, not Albert Einstein himself nor his disciples, is ready or able to deal with these evident critical questions and irritations which arise from simple logical analysis.*

*An author who declares the same effect sometimes as "real" and sometimes as "apparent"(Einstein 1905) cannot escape the notion of what he is eventually going to tell. Instead, the relativists declare any criticism as incompetent and stupid and the critics to be maliciously motivated. Generally the relativists abhor common sense and advise the reader not to trust it, but they fail to show which better sense the brave relativist is using.*

*As a surprise in 1958 the Japanese Nobel laureate Hideki Yukawa is reported to have criticized Special Relativity in a conference at Geneva during the UN Conference on the Peaceful Uses of Atomic Energy: the difficulties are such that "it would probably be found necessary to have a breakdown of the special theory of relativity".*

In addition to the publications and associations listed in the extensive research G.O. Muller project after 2006 until today, we can additionally specify the association mainly as thus:

The John Chappell Natural Philosophy Society - American Association of hundreds of physicists around the World (from 2014 the main branch of former Natural Philosophy Alliance). Since 1993 they organized conferences, published Conference proceedings and currently keep a database of around 6,000 publications of dissident physicists.

The database of publications of hundreds of dissident physicists since 2007 around the web archived as vixra.org, that holds around 14000 publications.

The General science journal, a web journal that from 2011 holds around 5,000 publications.

As it was always in the past history of mankind, the physical picture of the world, mainly in the period from 1905 until the end of the Second World War continuing to the present once again became the subject of a struggle between international power structures at the highest political level. Mainly from 1920, after the Congress in Bad Neuhaim, to the 1925 German physicists disagreeing with establishing relativity as a single description of the physical world, are isolated and persecuted. After the change of political power in Germany in 1933, the roles of the persecuted and the persecutors reversed and, after 1945, reversed again until today.

During the 20th century until today, physicists whose livelihood depends upon state power structures (the vast majority) and who dare to question or disagree with those power structures' established physical theories are admonished, isolated, persecuted or fired from jobs or cut from the sources of their livelihood.

The publication is impossible of physical views other than those officially adopted in journals and the mass information media. An appraisal of physicists and other scientists (not only by principals but also for highest scientific awards) is executed on the basis of the number of papers and the rating of so called impact factors of the journals in which their papers were published. By this instrument, editors and publishers have decisive power over who will be a significant and award-winning physicist and what kind of the physical image of the world is established within society.

This power of publishers in recent decades, in order to maximize their profits, attained an unlimited dictation and the terror of the publishers reigned against dissidents as well as all even conforming scientists. Scientists, for the publication of their many years work in journals not only fail to receive remuneration, but pay the full cost of the edition of the magazine. Scientists are forced by publishers on waste considerable time to learn and write their articles in the format of complex poly-graphic publishing typesetting systems like TEX or LATEX. Otherwise the chances of acceptance of their articles for publication are slim. Any grammatical error in the text is unacceptable and authors must pay for their own linguistic proofreading.

Publishing houses and mass media corporations have decisive influence on governments of states or vice verse, because the owners (media magnates) of these corporations are often persons participating in governments. Most of the physics journals in countries of the world are owned (or are in cooperation with) just four transnational publishing houses.

We can point to Randy Schekman, a US biologist who won the Nobel Prize in medicine in 2013. He said his lab would no longer send research papers to the top-tier journals, Nature, Cell and Science. *"Leading academic journals are distorting the scientific process and represent a tyranny that must be broken. I have published in the big brands, including papers that won me a Nobel Prize. But, no longer. An impact factor was the toxic influence on science that introduced distortions. A paper can become highly cited because it is good science - or because it is eye-catching, provocative, or simply wrong."*

*"These journals aggressively curate their brands, in ways more conducive to selling subscriptions than to stimulating the most important research. In extreme cases, the lure of the luxury journal can encourage the cutting of corners, and contribute to the escalating number of papers that are retracted as flawed or fraudulent. I have now committed my lab to avoiding luxury journals, and I encourage others to do likewise."*

All fictions and fantasies that are daily forced to the public as reality are also accepted by most of current civilization as physical reality. For the alleged confirmation of these science fictions are, without hesitation, lavished by enormous amounts of money in experiments at CERN or NASA.

The argument for receiving money for building ELI, the largest laser facility in the world in the Czech Republic in 2015 was - A team is planning to build an enormously powerful laser that could rip apart the fabric of space.

A few years ago, NASA sent four satellites into space with gyroscopes to test the relativity theory, a project called Gravity Probe B. Just the fact that NASA is testing the theory speaks for itself. Why otherwise would you test something if it is right and taught for almost 100 hundred years as a reality in universities and secondary schools?

On the other hand, almost no money is granted to experiments searching for what constitutes the electromagnetic waves that we daily produce by our mobile phones (connection with operators or at Wifi or Bluetooth connection) or that we use for inductive charging of our mobiles without plugging them into an electric socket. According to GTR in this double situation the curvature of space and time flows into and out of our mobile phones.

Instead of massive support for the finest experimental methods to explore the most subtle nature of the present real physical world around us, by enormous financial resources are supported the CERN big crash experiments, allegedly demonstrate how the physical world looked over 14 billion years ago or to demonstrate the fairytale of the rip of non-material time and space.

From 1905 until today there has been an opposition group of a hundred dissident physicists which consist, outside of admirable exceptions, physicists upon whom the ruling power structure have very small influence. These are physicists shortly before their retirement or in retirement, physicists who left physics and after migrating elsewhere to earn enough money, returned as independent physicist. It includes physicists who were fired from their jobs in physics.

These physicists do not hanker after glory, fame or awards. They have no reason to speak anything other than the truth. For no financial reward, they endeavor to fill the congenital need of human beings for knowledge of the actual real world around us. In groups of the retired, or about to be retired, we found a huge number of professors, academics and scientists with remarkable scientific careers and even a few Nobel Prize winning physicists.

Of all the names of the celebrities we recall Louis Essen Ph.D., Dr.Sc., FRS, O.B.E. (1908-1997). His research led to his development of the atomic reference quartz ring clock in 1938 and in 1955. In the 1960s and later, he was among the first candidates for a Nobel Prize. In defiance of this, in 1971 he published The Special Theory of Relativity: A Critical Analysis, questioning special relativity, which apparently was not appreciated by his employers. Essen, in 1978 said, "No one has attempted to refute my arguments, but I was warned that if I persisted I was likely to spoil my career prospects". Though he could effectively work for at least the next ten years, he involuntarily retired in 1972 and died in 1997. In October of 1978 he published a paper titled Relativity and Time Signals in the Wireless world journal.

In this paper [28] he penned that *the comparison of distant clocks by radio is now a precise and well known technique. This was not the case in 1905, when Einstein published his famous paper on relativity and there is some excuse for the mistakes he made in the thought- experiments he described in order to determine the relative rates of two identical clocks in uniform relative motion. But there is no excuse for their repetition in current literature. The mistakes have been exposed in published criticisms of the theory, but the criticisms have been almost completely ignored; and the continued acceptance and teaching of relativity hinders the development of a rational extension of electromagnetic theory.*

*These criticisms were rejected by Nature [the most prestigious journal in science]. It could be argued that the truth will eventually prevail, but history teaches us that when a false view of nature has become firmly established it may persist for decades or even centuries. The general public is misled into believing that science is a mysterious subject which can be understood by only a few exceptionally gifted mathematicians. Students are told that the theory must be accepted although they cannot expect to understand it. They are encouraged right at the beginning of their careers to forsake science in favour of dogma. Since the time of Einstein and of one of his most ardent supporters, Eddington, there has been a great increase in anti-rational thought and mysticism.*

From a recent author's we can recall Hans C. Ohanian - B.S. from UC Berkeley, Ph.D. from Princeton University, has taught at Rensselaer Polytechnic Institute, Union College, the University of Rome and today is Adjunct Physics Professor at the University of Vermont. From 1976 to 2008 he published more than half a dozen textbooks and several dozen articles on physics.

In his book, Einstein's Mistakes [26], he concludes that Einstein's unified theory was indeed an original, exclusive Einstein contribution-and it proved an unmitigated disaster.

The most grandiose mistakes of Einstein's career were his several unified theories of electricity and gravitation. For nearly thirty years, from 1926 until his death in 1955, these were the central focus of his research. Guesswork (identical with works in special and general relativity) inspired by God and unsupported by fact are perhaps suitable for theology and theocracy but they are not suitable for physics.

Not surprisingly, all of Einstein's several attempts at unifying theories were trash, and it is the crowning tragedy of Einstein's scientific career that this was obvious to all his close colleagues. Out of our compassion and respect for the great old man, only a few could bring themselves to tell him so.

When the physicist Freeman Dyson arrived in 1947 at the Institute for Advanced Study in Princeton, where Einstein had spent his final years, he was eager to make contact with Einstein's *"living legacy"* and made an appointment with him. For discussion he got copies of Einstein's recent papers from a secretary. The next morning he realized that although he couldn't face Einstein and tell him that his work was junk, he couldn't not tell him either. So he skipped the appointment and spent the ensuing eight years before Einstein's death avoiding him.

Einstein's unified theories were a grand delusion. They led to papers and more papers on abstruse mathematics, but they never yielded anything of lasting interest in physics. Bern described the weak point in Einstein's work in those final years: *".. now he tried to do without any empirical facts, by pure thinking. He believed in the power of reason to guess the laws according to which God has built the world."*

In 1928, after Einstein announced another in a series of definitive solutions of his finally proven theories the hectic bombastic medial and publicity furor from 1919 was repeated and this theory was a worldwide sensation. A thousand copies of the dry-as-dust journal of the Prussian Academy containing Einstein's paper were sold out instantly and several thousand extra copies had to be printed.

Eddington wrote to Einstein, *"You may be amused to hear that one of our great department stores in London (Selfridges) has posted your paper on its windows (the six pages pasted up side by side), so that passers-by can read it all through. Large crowds gather around to read it"*. In the United States, The New York Times had anticipated Einstein's publication with the headlines *"Einstein on verge of great discovery resents intrusion,"* and *"Einstein reticent on new work; will not count unlaid eggs"* And when Einstein's paper appeared, the newspaper gushed, *"The length of this work, written at the rate of half a page a year-is considered prodigious when it is considered that the original theory of relativity filled only three pages."*

The New York Herald Tribune outdid the Times by printing a translation in its pages of Einstein's paper, including all those incomprehensible mathematical formulas. The Tribune had prearranged for the transmission of Einstein's paper from Berlin to New York via Telex, using a special code for the transmission of the mathematical formulas. Einstein contributed to the newspaper furor by offering a lengthy explanation of his new theory in the Sunday edition of the New York Times in which he called it the third stage in the development of relativity.

But the new theory was another dismal failure. Einstein had written down a set of equations that made no sense. After strong opposition from then most outstanding physicist, it took Einstein three years to recognize that his another theory was dead.

He included his final field equations for the unified theory in an appendix to the 1949 edition of one of his earlier books, The Meaning of Relativity, and The New York Times promptly reprinted the equations on its front page with the headline *"New Einstein theory gives a master key to the universe."*

This was wishful thinking, but the Times was just as stubborn as Einstein, and when the 1952 edition of the same book appeared, the Times greeted it again with the headline *"Einstein offers new theory to unify law of the cosmos."* The trouble with Einstein's *"master key to the universe"* was that it was not actually a key but only a dream about a key.

Einstein made so many mistakes in his scientific work it is hard to keep track of them. There were mistakes in each of the papers he produced in his miracle year 1905, except for the paper on Brownian motion. But there were in 1905 a few similar papers on setting the dimension of atoms from Brownian motion [e.g. M. Smoluchowski, Bull. Intern. Acad. Crac. 1903]. And there were mistakes in dozens of the papers he produced in later years.

It is apt to mention that the participants of the 2nd International Conference on Problems of Space and Time in Natural Science, 1991, from the USSR, the USA, Canada, Italy, Great Britain, Germany, Brazil, Austria, Switzerland and Finland issued the following declaration:

*"Due to prohibiting or hushing up the publications which contradict Einstein's theory, modern theoretical physics and astrophysics have come to a crisis. We propose to give up teaching relativity theory in secondary schools, which would give time for studying the origin and development of classical methods in mechanics and physics. Teaching relativity theory in higher educational institutions ought to be accompanied by discussions of alternative approaches."*

## 7. Conclusion

The claim that the cause of gravity is the curvature of non-material void space and time is the greatest degeneration of physical and philosophical thinking in all the history of mankind.

The curvature of space in fact represents a change of spatial density of real material substance ether (dark energy, polarization of vacuum, ether in electromagnetism) and the curvature of time represents the change of velocities imparted to bodies by this spatial change in density of the ether.

Time is a measure of the change of moving objects and time is not an arbitrarily chosen variable, which could by itself span, lapse and vary independently of the moving objects. Without moving objects time does not exist.

In mechanics, unit of time and unit of velocity are firmly fixed and represents the same in inverse proportionality-basic comparative speeds of movement.

Space in itself is nothing more than a three-dimensional manifold, devoid of all form, which acquires a definite form only through the advent of the material content filling it and determining its metric relations.

Gravitational force as an individual fundamental power does not exist and gravitational force is not a universal fundamental attribute of matter. Such a huge force as is the force of gravity on the surface of the atoms (which equals to at least the magnetic force) was never found.

Gravitational forces and gravitational fields surrounding great ponderable objects are made up of the superposition of a huge number of disordered magnetic fields of atoms and elementary particles, from which these mass objects are composed. Gravity is just a tiny remnant of huge electromagnetic forces placed inside these objects.

Elementary particles of mater are spin products of curl compressions of ether as a local increase in the density of the flatly distributed field of the ether in space. Thus is formed the mass of particles of matter (more likely $10^{11}$ neutrinos in proton).

As a consequence of this curl compression into spin particles, radial force fields arise circumambient to these particles as a change in density (radial gradient from particles surface to afar) of ether in particles surroundings. This force field provides opposite pressure on the surfaces of particles [11] balancing the internal pressure of spinning particles that holds mass-energy inside and keeps particles together.

Inertial forces are forces of the resistance of particles and bodies emerging at accelerating particles and bodies against the force fields of ether medium surrounding them.

Acceleration leads to changes in velocities that result in pressure changes in the surrounding force fields on the surface of the particles of bodies that returns the change in the radius of the particles and volume of bodies.

This concept allow us to explain [11] the physical mechanism between mass and sizes of the gravitational field in surrounding of ponderable objects, provides an opportunity to explain the origin of gravitational fields and the internal energy of particles of mass bodies. We can thus explain the origin of inertial forces, where the energy inside the particles of mass bodies come from, how energy gets into the particles and how is this huge energy in the particles is held.

Special and General relativity, as well as Quantum mechanics, does without these basic physical considerations and premises, which such theories should essentially be based upon.

Ether constitutes real material substances, infiling the space in each unit of its volume. Ether is the real rippling and curling material substance (maybe curling oscillating neutrinos) with a vast amount of this curl in the form of electromagnetic radiation and large amounts of this curl in the form of mass particles, mainly in the form of protons.

All the great mass objects are the concentration of these mass particles in small local parts of universal space. After the gravitational collapse of local shrinks and explosions of supernovae, this shrink of mass is spread again mainly by the electromagnetic radiation across the space of the universe.

Filling the space of the Universe with swirling ether is

all that is needed for the self-evolution of the Universe as well as for creation of our Earth, Suns, Stars and clusters of Galaxies. If Darwin's scientific theory of the evolution of species is also valid at the first beginning of living nature, then all our known universe's living and non-living nature formed itself in evolution, from the initial filling of the space of the Universe with swirling ether and without the outside need for the intervention of a supernatural creator.

It was shown in this work that relativity was not introduced into physics on the basis of a consensus of physicists. On the contrary, relativity was introduced to physics by the force of power structures through mass information media, despite the resistance and opposition of a majority of then most outstanding physicists.

It was documented in this work that from sets of existing physically based theoretical explanations of several new physical phenomena of the 20th century just those theories that are in conformity with the creation principle, but most distort the physical reality of world around us are selected, supported and promoted by power structures and mass information media. All others are suppressed and repudiated. This crusade in prevention, hindering and distorting the independent development of physics in the 20th century in fact simply maintains the same state during the previous 2000 years, without major changes.

It was documented in this work that for the last 400 years in physics, there has been no distinguished physicist (including Einstein in 1921) who would not had recognized that, without the existence of the ether, it is not possible to explain the physical world around us. Opinions of these physicists are massively distorted on a daily basis and falsified by mass information media and power structures that created the physical picture of world around us without ether.

This recognition of the existence of an actual physical media filling out the entire universe, from which all the particles of rigid bodies and force fields around these bodies in the universe are made up, is the greatest physical discovery of contemporary civilization. But this discovery is concealed from us. This discovery is an actual physical source of amazement; however it does not fit the power structures any more than the rediscovery of the circulation of the earth around the Sun.

Therefore, instead of researching ether as the first task of our civilization, the development of physics was diverted into multiple physical mysteries and mysterious mathematical constructions, introduced by the power structures through mass media.

Theories of 20th century eliminate form physics:

- Inertial forces as the first and direct evidence of ether. Inertial forces are named as fictitious or pseudo forces which does not arise from any physical interaction between two objects, but just from the acceleration of the non-inertial reference frame itself. Also gravity is named as fictitious force.

- Accelerations, gradient of fields and forces (Einstein's relativity) because they directly point at changes of density of ether.

- The existence and gradient of fields around atoms and particles (double-slit experiment, Schrodinger equation, de Broglie waves, Casimir effect) because they directly point at changes of density of ether.

Accelerations, gradient of fields or forces are in relativity replaced by mystery of space and time. Gradients of fields around atoms are in Quantum mechanics replaced by fictitious mathematical construction of frequency, wavelength or wave functions, non-measurable or unverifiable experimentally.

It can be safely said that Quarks and Higgs boson do not exist. The waves of matter, wave functions, quantum entanglements and waves of zero point energy presented by the vision of quantum mechanics do not exist.

The claims that space and time is the fabric of a space-time continuum, that space can be ripped or torn, that time itself can slow down or be ripped, that there are possible parallel universes as well as wormholes, that black holes exist by the vision of current physics, that future events could precede and affect past ones are pure fantasy. They have nothing to do with physical science describing physical reality and belong exclusively to science fiction literature.

But all these fictions and fantasies that are daily swallowed by the public as reality are also taken by most of current civilization as physical reality.

All our known universe of the animate and inanimate nature of rigid bodies and force fields (also gravity) is the result of the interaction and the superposition of the electromagnetic force fields around atoms, molecules, and elementary particles.

The existence, interaction and superposition of electromagnetic fields are the actual physical basis for the explanation of new physical phenomena in the 20th century, rather than explaining this phenomena in mysteries of relativity and quantum mechanics.

Exploration of subtle nature of ether and force fields around elementary particles is the main task of today's civilization. But instead of the massive support of the finest sensitive experimental methods to explore the most subtle nature of today physical world around us, the CERN big crash experiments persist. This allegedly demonstrates how the physical world looked over 14 billion years ago or demonstrates the fairy tale of the rip of non-material time and space and is supported by enormous financial resources.

## REFERENCES

1.  I. Newton, *Mathematical Principles of Natural Philosophy*, (Daniel Adee, New York, 1846)
2.  Carman at all, *On the pin-and-slot device of the Antikythera mechanism with a new application to the superior planets*, Journal for the History of Astronomy 43: 93-116 , 2012)
3.  Isaac Newton, *Letters to Bentley*, 1692/3

4. Newton's Letter to Robert Boyle, *On the Cosmic Ether of Space*, Isaac Newton, Cambridge, Feb. 28, 1678-9

5. Hermann Weyl, *Space Time Matter*, Methuen & co. ltd., London, 1922

6. J. C. Maxwell, *A treatise on electricity and magnetism*, (Calderon Pres, Oxford, 1881)

7. E. Hubble, *The observational approach to cosmology*, (Clarendon Press, Oxford, 1937)

8. A. K. T. Assis at. all, *Hubble's Cosmology: From a Finite Expanding Universe to a Static Endless Universe*, (arXiv:0806.4481v2, 2011)

9. J. D. Bjorken, *Theoretical ideas on high-energy inelastic electron-proton scattering*, SLAC pub. 571, march 1969

10. P. Sujak, *Big Crash of Basic Concepts of Physics of the 20th Century?*, Proceedings of the Natural Philosophy Alliance, 20th Annual Conference of the NPA, Maryland, 2013

11. P. Sujak, *On the General Reality of Gravity as Well as Other Forces in Nature and the Creation of Material Particles and Force Fields in the Universe*, Proceedings of the Natural Philosophy Alliance, 20th Annual Conference of the NPA, Maryland, 2013

12. Das & Ferbel, *Introduction To Nuclear And Particle Physics*, World Scientific, 2003

13. T. Ferbel, *The Top Quark and Other Tales of "Discovery"*, Universities of Rochester and Maryland, 2012 www.thphys.uniheidelberg.de/ plehn/ includes/badhonnef12/ferbel.pdf

14. CH. W. Lucas, *Talk at Natural Philosophy Alliance Video conference*, Open Debate on Did the Mainstream Discover the Higgs Boson, 2015

15. V. Khachatryan et al., *Evidence for Collective Multiparticle Correlations in p-Pb Collisions*, Phys. Rev. Lett. 115, 2015

16. H. A. Lorentz, *Electromagnetic phenomena in a system moving with any velocity smaller than that of light*, Proceedings of the Royal Netherlands Academy of Arts and Sciences,

17. Nikola Tesla, *New York Herald Tribune*, New York, 11. Sept 1932

18. B. Hoffman, *Albert Einstein: Creator and Rebel*, Viking Press, New York, 1972

19. B. Riemann, *On the Hypotheses which lie at the Bases of Geometry* Nature, Vol. 8, Nos. 183, 184, 1998

20. E. Schrödinger, *Physical review*, Vol.28, No.6, 1926

21. A. Das, T. Ferbel *Introduction to nuclear and particle physics*, World Scientific, London, 2003

22. R. L. Jaffe, *The Casimir Effect and the Quantum Vacuum*, arXiv: hep-th/0503158v1, 2005

23. M. Eckert, *Arnold Sommerfeld*, (Springer, New York, 2013)

24. A. A. Michelson, H. Gale and F. Pearson *The Effect of the Earth's Rotation on the Velocity of Light*, Parts I and II, Astrophysical Journal, 61, 137-145, 1925

25. Einstein, *letter to Edwin E. Slosson*, 8 July 1925

26. H.C. Ohanian, *Einstein mistakes*, W.W. Norton and company, New York, London, 2008

27. The G. O. Mueller Research Project, *95 Years of Criticism of the Special Theory of Relativity*, (http://www.ekkehard-friebe.de/, Germany, 2006)

28. L. Essen, *Relativity and Time Signals*, Wireless world, October 1978

29. P. Sujak, *On Energy and Momentum in Contemporary Physics*, American Physical Society Meeting, Denver, March 2014, Y33, 3

30. P. Sujak, *On gravity, other forces in nature and the creation of mass particles and force fields in the universe*, Bulletin of the American Physical Society Meeting, Savannah, April 2014, T1, 56

31. E. Mach, *The science of Mechanics*, The open court publishing company, London, 1919

## Author Index